INITIATION

Dearest Yauti
& Richard,

May you love
be eternal

Alex ☺

NY 9. 2011

INITIATION

Elisabeth
HAICH

AURORA PRESS

Box 573, Santa Fe, N.M. 87504

First published in 2000 by:
Aurora Press Inc.
P.O. Box 573
Santa Fe, NM 87504 USA
1-505 989-9804 Fax 505 982-8321

Library of Congress Cataloging-in-Publication Data
99-65374
Elisabeth Haich March 20, 1897-July 31, 1994
Initiation, Elisabeth Haich

ISBN: 0-943358-50-7

Cover Photo: Falcon Pendant © Araldo De Luca
Valley of the Kings, Tutankhamun's Tomb
18th Dynasty, 1333-1323 BC

Cover Design: Barbara Somerfield

Manufactured in the United States of America

FACTS ABOUT ELISABETH HAICH

Elisabeth Haich, March 20, 1897-July 31, 1994, was the second of four children born into an upper middle class family in Budapest, Hungary. Even as a young child, her unique gifts were expressed as a pianist, painter and sculptress. Her sculptures are exhibited in Hungary, as monuments and in plazas. She was married and had one son who later joined her in teaching Yoga in Switzerland. In close connection with Selvarajan Yesudian, she began giving Yoga lectures in 1939.

At the end of World War II, she was forced to leave Hungary with the assistance of Selvarajan Yesudian and resettled in Switzerland where she lived until the end of her life. In cooperation with Yesudian, she began the oldest and largest Yoga school in Europe.

In 1953 Elisabeth Haich wrote her bestselling book, *Initiation,* which has been translated into seventeen languages with millions of copies sold worldwide. Her other books include, *The Day With Yoga, Sexual Energy and Yoga, Wisdom of the Tarot* and authored with Selvarajan Yesudian, *Self Healing Yoga and Destiny.* All of these titles are published by Aurora Press in English.

Until the end of her life, Elisabeth Haich lectured and counseled seekers.

ELISABETH HAICH
AND
SELVARAJAN
YESUDIAN
With Mrs. Haich's
painting and sculpture
Zurich, Switzerland
1981
© Barbara Somerfield

AUTHOR'S NOTE

IT IS far from my intentions to want to provide a historical picture of Egypt. A person who is living in any given place has not the faintest idea of the peculiarities of his country, and he does not consider customs, language and religion from an ethnographic point of view. He takes everything as a matter of course. He is a human being and has his joys and sorrows, just like every other human being, anywhere, any place, any time; for that which is truly human is timeless and changeless. My concern here is only with the human, not with ethnography and history. That is why I have, in relating the story which follows here, intentionally used modern terms. I have avoided using Egyptian sounding words to create the illusion of an Egyptian atmosphere. The teachings of the High Priest Ptahhotep are given in *modern* language so that *modern* people may understand them. For religious symbols also, I have chosen to use modern terms so that all may understand what these symbols mean.

People of today understand us better if we say 'God' than if we were to use the Egyptian term 'Ptah' for the same concept. If we say '*Ptah*' everyone immediately thinks, 'Oh yes, *Ptah*, the Egyptian God'. No! *Ptah* was not an Egyptian God. On the contrary, the Egyptians called the same *God* whom we call *God*, by the name of *Ptah*. And to take another example, their term for *Satan* was *Seth*. The words *God* and *Satan* carry meanings for us today which we would not get from the words *Ptah* or *Seth*. For people living in our times, these latter terms, *Ptah* and *Seth*, are empty, dry and meaningless. The term *Logos* and the expression *creative principle* have a meaning for us today which we would not get from the term '*Horus Hawk*'. Electricity was just as much electricity thousands of years ago as it is today, and an atom was an atom, simply by a different name. I make these comments here so that my readers may be able to devote their attention to the content of the story which follows here, without being halted unnecessarily by what may appear to be an anachronism merely because of the terms used—as for example when the Egyptian High Priest speaks of a 'chain reaction'! I have intentionally avoided trying to reproduce or imitate the ancient terminology for phenomena we now know under names everyone is accustomed to using.

Like the falcon, symbol of Horus, the creative principle crosses space and creates worlds. Because God's law is operative in the creative principle, Horus carries on his head the double tablets representing the Ten Commandments

THE DIVINE HORUS   *Cairo Museum*

FOREWORD

THE NATIONAL rhythm of the Indian people is religion. With every heart-beat the Indian feels himself a step closer to the eternally glorious goal of the realization of God.

Whenever he hears the name of God on the lips of someone passing by, his sharp ear picks up the melody and he starts to sing a paean of praise. Even though he may have neither food nor a roof over his head—for often enough the arch of heaven is his shelter—he still has God in his heart. He knows that in this arena of life he has come uncounted times and gone again, through myriad births, that he has enjoyed all the created world has to offer, and that, as he knows the truth 'Everything here on earth passes away', nothing more can satisfy him. His wish is now to find and reach that source from which the stream of manifestations flows.

That is why, from early childhood he prays: 'I meditate on the magnificence of the being that has created this universe. May *it* illuminate my mind.'

The majesty and beauty of nature, reminding him of that being, becomes an object of his adoration. Every holy writing, of whatever religion, which breathes the breath of that being becomes an object of his respect and admira-tion. And every one who has found that being and speaks about the way to *him* becomes an object of respect and admiration. I have the great fortune to sit at the feet of an illumined soul: Elisabeth Haich is my teacher, my guru. In her presence the delicate petals of my soul began to unfold. Often a word from her opens my eyes, and sometimes an understanding glance is enough to strengthen me in my conviction. A friendly comment can sometimes drive away all my doubts. Every moment in the presence of my teacher brings me new experiences and hastens my progress. Very often when certain things have bothered me, I have found help in the words of my guru: 'Don't live for the present; don't allow transitory things to influence you. Live in eternity, above time and space, above finite things. Then nothing can influence you.'

In the presence of my teacher I enjoy absolute independence of thought, for I have learned that it is wrong to want to apply the thoughts of another person in one's own life. 'I don't want you simply to follow me on the path I am following to reach the goal,' she has told me. 'Go your own way, on the path you select for yourself, corresponding to your own innermost inclina-tions. Don't accept any statement because I made it. Even if it is true a hundred times over, it still is not *your* truth, it still is not *your* experience, and it will not belong to you. Bring truth into being, and then it will belong to you. Regard the lives of those who have achieved truth only as proof that the goal can be reached.'

At these words of my teacher's, I was seized by an irresistible drive towards absolute independence, and this urge freed me from the nefarious attitude of expecting help from outside. I don't need a teacher that influences me, but a teacher who teaches me not to allow myself to be influenced.

For many years I have had the great privilege of hearing the profoundest truths explained in the simplest words. I have yet to hear anyone else explain the revelations of the Bible as clearly as Elisabeth Haich, and in a manner as applicable to our daily living. I have travelled far, and in all my travels no priest has been able to explain the true meaning of these revelations, even though I have asked hundreds. How, after all, could he if he has not reached 'the kingdom of Heaven within'? How could it be otherwise as long as he has not experienced within himself the truth of the sentence: 'Ye are the light of the world', as long as he does not yet recognize: 'Ye are the living temple of the Holy Spirit'?

Hundreds and thousands have attended the weekly lectures and meditation groups led by Elisabeth Haich. It has been the wish of all of us to possess her teachings in book form.

Through the experience of each lecture our souls thirsting for truth were enriched to an undreamed of extent. It is a great joy for all of us to know that at last part of this knowledge will now be availal le in the concentrated form of a book. This book is an introduction to the high art of reaching and achieving the divine in us and of learning to recognize this unknown creature called man. We will discover the great truth: Self development is revealing the perfection which has been in man from the very beginning. Religion is the activation of the divine principle which awaits its manifestation in man.

SELVARAJAN YESUDIAN

Zurich, April 1962

CONTENTS

ILLUSTRATIONS

INTRODUCTION

written by a disciple of the author

I AM a seeker. I seek an explanation for life on earth. I would like to know what sense there is in the fact that a person is born, grows from a child to an adult through all kinds of difficulties, marries, brings more children into the world, who also grow up to adults through just as many difficulties, also marry, also bring more children into the world, who then with advancing age lose the skills they took so much trouble to learn, and finally die. An unending chain, without beginning, without end! Constantly children are being born. They learn, they work hard, they want fully to develop both body and mind—and after a relatively short time everything is over, and down under six feet of sod they become fodder for worms. What is the sense in all of this? Going on and on just to produce more and more generations of people?

And when certain people not only leave their descendants behind them, but also the work of the mind and spirit, why do they have the same kind of experience? Why do they grow old and take their high gifts to the grave with them? A Michelangelo, a Leonardo da Vinci, a Giordano Bruno, a Shakespeare, a Goethe, and many many others—why were these titans born, if finally they had to decay in the same way as the worm that fattened itself on their bodies?

No! It is not possible for life on earth to be so senseless! Behind this seemingly unending chain of birth and death there must be a more profound meaning, even if it seems to be inexplicable for a prejudiced mind. There must be a completely satisfactory and sensible explanation—seen from the *other side*!

How and where can I find this *other side* of all things that definitely must exist? How and where can I find a way to get acquainted with it? Whom should I ask for directions? Where do I find a person initiated into this mystery, a person who can tell me about this hidden truth?

For throughout all recorded time there have been outstanding people on earth who spoke out with unshakable assurance about the secret of life and even witnessed their conviction with their life—initiates as they have been called. But where and from whom have these 'initiates' received their initiation? And into *what* were they initiated?

Socrates for example. Consider him taking the cup of poison with divine calm, drinking it to the last drop, speaking fearlessly and objectively, quietly and pleasantly about the effect of the poison, reporting how under the influence of the poison first his feet get cold and die, how the deathly cold gradually crawls up from his feet towards his heart like a snake. He is aware that he is about to die, he takes leave of his faithful students, and closes his eyes. Such unshakable peace and calm in the face of death can only come from sure *knowledge*! Where did Socrates get this knowledge?

And where have various other titans living on earth at different times got their knowledge about the secret of life and death—their *initiation*? Even today there must be such 'initiates' living on earth, and there must be some way to obtain initiation, the really great *initiation*.

Life has taught me that the Bible is not a book of fairy tales, but has been written by initiates to transmit hidden truth to us in a secret language. And the Bible tells us: 'Seek and ye shall find; knock and it shall be opened unto you.'

I obeyed! I began to seek. Everywhere I could. In books, in old writings, among people who I thought might know something about the initiation. At all times I kept my eyes and ears open, and in my searches through books, old and new, as well as in the teachings of people both living and dead, I kept trying to discover hidden mosaic stones with which to piece together the secret of the initiation.

And I found! At first on rare occasions; here and there, with my inner ears, I heard the voice of truth speaking in a book or in the words of a living person. And I always went further in the direction indicated by this mysterious voice. Like the thread of Ariadne, this secret voice always led me on. Sometimes I found someone in my own home town who could give me valuable information for my further search, and sometimes this voice led me far away into strange lands, where I often found information that was in remarkably close agreement with the words I had heard at home.

Thus my path led me to people with ever greater knowledge who explained more and more to me about initiation and about the meaning of life. Naturally I also met many ignorant people and people with half knowledge who pretended to know. But I got so I could recognize immediately when 'the hands were Esau's, but the voice was Jacob's.' These poor charlatans, pretending to be 'initiates', gave themselves away very fast. They were not even in harmony with themselves and their own life, so how could they have taught me anything about the deepest truth of life, about initiation? In such cases I simply went on seeking someone with true knowledge, a true initiate.

Whenever I found someone who could tell me more than I already knew, I stayed there to learn as much as I possibly could learn.

In this way I once came into the presence of an old woman living in a retreat as if in a convent. She was surrounded by countless seekers, like a lump of sugar to which long rows of ants make a steady pilgrimage to get food.

She was working in very close spiritual association with two very much younger men, one from India and the other from the Occident, whom the old woman called 'son'.

The old woman was tall, of majestic stature and bearing, but extremely simple and completely natural in her movements. Her deep blue eyes were surprisingly big, and her long dark brown eye lashes gave them a remarkable expression. Her eyes were smiling, friendly, full of understanding, but so penetrating that most people were embarrassed when she looked at them.

People felt that this woman could see right through everybody, that she could clearly see their thoughts, the entire structure of their souls. Very often while listening to her lectures among a group of other persons, I felt a number of questions arising within me. She kept on talking, but she smiled and then in her next few sentences she made a point of answering my unspoken questions. A number of other listeners of hers told me they had had the same experience. I just could not cope with this woman. The more I learned from her and the more my spiritual eyes were opened, the greater she seemed to me and the more the field in which her knowledge surpassed mine seemed to expand in every direction. The longer I stayed with her, the less I felt I knew her. Every time I saw her, she appeared to me a 'different person' until I got the impression that this woman carried within her and could manifest the whole range of human personality and consequently had no personality herself at all. Because to be *everything*, simultaneously means to be *nothing*.

'Mother,' I asked her once, 'who are you really?' 'Who?' she asked in return, '*what* is that *who*? There is only one being that *is*, and every person, every animal, every plant, and even every sun, every planet and every other heavenly body is only an instrument for the manifestation of this one and only being that *is*. How many "who's" would there be? The same *self* speaks through my mouth as through yours and through all living creatures. The only difference is that not every living creature knows perfectly its own *self* and consequently is not able to manifest *all* characteristics of the *self*. But anybody who knows the *self* completely and perfectly can manifest all the characteristics that exist in the universe, because all these characteristics are the various aspects of the one and only being that *is*, the one and only *self*. The external form which you see before you, thinking that it is 'I' is only an instrument through which the *self* manifests that particular aspect of itself that is *necessary* at any given time. So don't ask any more nonsense like "who" I am.'

'Mother,' I said, 'how have you come to know the "self" so completely and perfectly as to be able to manifest all its possible characteristics? I would like to be so far advanced too! Tell me! Through what experiences have you come in order to become such a versatile instrument for the manifestations of the one and only being that *is*? Or have you always been on this level? Were you born in this condition?'

'Born?' she echoed, 'I born? When have you ever seen that an "I" was born? Have you ever seen an "I"? The "*I*" has *never* been and *never* will be born, only the body. The true, divine self is perfection itself, so a development in *it* is not possible. *Only the body must develop in order to be able to manifest higher and higher vibrations and higher and higher frequencies of the self.* Even the most highly developed instrument, the most highly developed body, must go through this process, including mine, which by the way is still far from perfection. Everything is only a phase of development. The creation of a body is always a chain reaction—as such processes are called nowadays—and whenever a chain reaction has made a beginning, it runs through various periods until it comes to an end. No material form of manifestation can escape from this law. And parallel with the development of the body, the condition of consciousness naturally changes also.'

'That means that you have had to go through a period of development too, doesn't it, Mother? Please tell me what it was like! What kind of experiences did you have that caused you to grow into your present condition of consciousness? Please tell me all about it.'

'Why should I tell you about it?' she replied. 'Everyone must achieve perfect *recognition of self in his own way*. What good would it do you for me to tell you *my* way? You could not follow *my* way. Events themselves are not important, only the experiences and the lessons that you get from them. Just take it easy. On your way you will learn the same lessons as I on mine. There are innumerable pathways, but they all lead to the same goal.'

'Mother, you are right. I see clearly that I would not be able to make progress on your path. Nevertheless it would help me very much if you would tell me how you have acquired your experience, because I and all the others who would listen to your story would be able to learn *how one can profit from experiences*. I am not curious about your story, but merely anxious to hear *how you began to seize upon and learn the lesson that is in every event*. Please tell me about the path you have followed, Mother. It would be so valuable for us to learn your attitude towards life and *how* you reacted toward your fate so as to develop your spiritual horizon to such an all-inclusively great extent. We could learn a great deal from your story.'

The old woman looked at me for a long time. Finally she said, 'So you are curious as to *how I reacted*? And you believe it will help you and others to hear about it? All right! Perhaps it really will be a good thing to tell you about the experiences that gradually opened my eyes to the *inner laws of life* and the various relationships that bound together the destinies of different people. Come back tomorrow. I will tell you and a few others whose eyes are opened to the essential things in life about the experiences that helped me find what people call illumination. I will tell you how I experienced my initiation!'

The next day found me and a number of her most advanced pupils sitting in front of the old woman. And she began to tell us the story of her initiation.

That is how this book was written.

—— I ——

AWAKENING

LIKE A flash of lightning a pain went through my body—and a moment later I landed on the floor.

Danger! Help! But not from this adult here beside me who is now so shocked and wants to examine me—No! I don't want him now! I love him, but in a moment of danger he is not the person I want.

I ran back into the room towards a strange, beautiful woman to whom we had just said good night. I knew that she would help me in a completely understanding way. At other times, too, I liked to be near her; I always liked the scent about her, and I always found I was in perfect safety in her presence. Now, in my panic, I ran to her in search of help. I whined as I showed her my plump little hand that was hanging down like a limp rag, refusing to obey me any more. The beautiful woman looked at my hand, threw aside the dress on which she was sewing and cried out:

'Robert! Robert! Come quickly!'

A door opened, and the grown-up man about whom I dimly knew that he lived with us and somehow belonged to us, came in. For the first time I looked at him with real attention. He was a tall man with a face like ivory; hair, beard and moustache as black as ebony, eyes glowing black, and he always radiated so much force and strength, that everybody around him was kept at a certain distance. He cast one glance at my limp and useless hand and said, 'A doctor! Stefi, get a doctor immediately.'

Uncle Stefi ran away and the tall dark man asked us what had happened. So we told him. After Grete and I had said good night, Uncle Stefi took me on to his back and carried me that way into the bedroom. There he let me slide off, but I slid too fast. To keep me from falling, he suddenly grabbed my hand. In the same moment I felt a violent stab of pain in my right wrist. Then when I tried to raise my hand, it just hung limp.

'Yes,' said the tall adult, 'her wrist is sprained. The worst part of it is that I am just leaving on a business trip and cannot wait until the doctor comes. All night long I will be sitting on pins and needles. Wire me as soon as the doctor is through; tell me what he has done.'

He kissed us and mother and went away. I looked up astonished to the strange beautiful woman who had always pointed to herself and said 'Mother' and whom we therefore called mother.

Up to that moment I had been crying and bawling for all I was worth. I was badly disappointed and frightened to find out that the adults could not help me. They were not able to stop the pain that was torturing me more and more; nor were they able to fix my hand the way it was before. When I heard that the tall dark adult was going to have to spend all night sitting on pins and needles, I was so astonished and so concerned for him that I suddenly forgot about crying and asked mother, 'Why is he going to have to sit on pins and needles all night long?' At first mother gave me a look of amazement and then began to laugh and said, 'Because father is all excited about your hand'.

But what kind of an answer was that! Simply nonsense! It didn't explain anything. The tall man we called 'father' was completely in earnest when he said he was going to be sitting on pins and needles—and now mother was laughing at me. Why? I had only repeated what father had said. What did she mean by saying that father was 'all excited' and why did that mean that he was going to have to sit on pins and needles? Would that mean that he was going to be dangerously pricked? Mother spent a lot of time sewing and she had shown me how dangerous a needle can be; the point of a needle can be very unpleasant. That hurts! That's why needles should *only* be used for sewing. So what kind of nonsense was this, the adults were giving me again—just because my hand was so helpless and painful that I had to hold it with the other hand? Why did that mean that father was going to spend the whole night sitting on pins and needles, when after all they are only supposed to be used for sewing? I was already pretty used to the fact that adults often talked nonsense and did senseless things, but this was too much, and I insisted on knowing more. But I did not get the chance to ask more questions about this 'sitting on pins and needles' because Uncle Stefi returned with the doctor.

The doctor was a tall, impressive, friendly man who looked at me as if we had known each other a long time. He lifted me up high and so took me out of the protective nearness of my mother. That filled my heart with terrible fear; the movement caused a new wave of torturing pain, and I began to bawl again for all I was worth. The doctor set me on the table—I saw my little feet dangling very close under my breast—and he shook his head as he laughed and said, 'Oh how ugly this little girl is when she is crying!'

I was stunned. What? He says I am ugly when I am crying? How does he know that? Up till now I always thought one could see everything except *me*. Everything and everybody else, the adults, the cook, Grete, the canary bird, my toys—in fact *everything* round about me was visible, even my hands, my little tummy, and my feet, but *I* myself could not be seen. *I* was present, but yet not present, somewhere but invisible. I had never yet seen *myself*, and I could not for the life of me imagine how it could be possible to see this something, this 'I'. So how could it be possible for this adult to see my desperation, my pain, my crying: that is 'me'? Goodness! If he sees me, my amazed and horrified condition, that must really be 'ugly'. For sheer wonder and amazement, I stopped crying and looked at the doctor quizzically.

Then all the adults began to laugh out loud, and mother said, 'See how vain this little girl is! She is even suppressing her pain in order not to appear ugly.'

There we were again. Here was another one of those senseless remarks by adults. 'Vain'—what is that? How could I be vain when I didn't even know what that was, and how could I 'appear' when I did not even know that I was visible? Up to now I had always thought that *I* was the person doing the *seeing*. I it was who saw everything round about but *I* was in some way or other *outside of the visible*. All this was going around in my head, and I just wanted to ask another question when the doctor took hold of my limp little hand and pulled it hard, so hard I wanted to scream again—it hurt so terribly! —The crazy man is going to pull my hand clean off! I thought—but then he twisted the little hand that somehow or other was fastened on to me, because it hurt 'me' terribly, and all of a sudden it was in its right place again.

'There we are,' said the doctor. 'Now the joint will swell up a little bit, so for tonight we will bed it down on a pillow, and pretty soon we can forget the whole matter.'

Then the adults went on talking about how vain I was, saying that for pure vanity I had not even cried out when the doctor was twisting my wrist back into place. Mother was particularly impressed by this and that made me sad. I could see that the strange beautiful woman whom I already loved very much just did not understand me. And even though the doctor could see me, *I was certainly invisible to mother*. Nevertheless she radiated a wonderful love, and a little later, as I lay in my bed, with my hand resting on a pillow, I was happy that her fine sweet face leaned over me from time to time and smiled down at me encouragingly. She radiated sweetness and warmth, and as long as she was near I did not feel alone or abandoned. I knew that I could count on her; to a certain extent she was in my power, and I had complete confidence in her. Gradually I fell asleep. The night passed, and my hand again became the obedient instrument, the faithful friend that, later on in life was to bring me so much joy—so very much joy—and was to help awaken me out of my unconscious state.

But the doctor was wrong! I never did forget the matter, and through the law of association he has remained permanently and indissolubly connected with my first awakening and my first becoming conscious in this life. From now on my consciousness—my memory—was constantly awake. From now on I observed everything, everything around me as well as within me, with the greatest attention and with uninterrupted concentration. From now on I knew that I lived in a home where the tall, dark, and powerful adult was unconditionally master. Mother called him 'Robert' and we had to call him 'father'. The whole household revolved around him; mother belonged to him body and soul. His power spread over all of us, and later over many thousands of people, like a tent, like a protective envelope. Everybody that belonged to father's sphere of influence enjoyed help, security and prosperity.

During the morning hours father was not at home so I could be with mother. I was permitted to accompany her in the whole apartment, even in the kitchen, and ofttimes when she sat quietly embroidering a big tablecloth with brightly coloured threads, I was permitted to sit beside her and amuse myself by 'embroidering' various patterns according to my own imagination, using the same brightly coloured threads. At midday father came home, and after lunch Grete and I had to go to the children's room, something I did not like at all. Grete was also a child of the house, like myself, only—as I was told—she was three years older than I. At the time I sprained my wrist she was four and a half and I one and a half.

The following summer we spent our vacation in a village beside a great body of water. We lived in a little farmhouse that was surrounded by a large garden and a big farm. Grete and I were allowed to run around barefoot, and we were also permitted to accompany a woman with a very brown and wrinkled face when she went to the barn where there was a cow, a calf and a number of rabbits with red eyes. That was all very thrilling. In the garden there were gigantic yellow flowers, seemingly as high as trees, that always turned in the direction of the sun. I liked them too, father came only from time to time, and when he did people said, 'Today is Sunday'. The rest of the time we were alone with mother and I could spend the whole day with her. Every day we went down to the lake and bathed and splashed happily in the water.

One day mother said, 'Tomorrow is Sunday, but today is already a big day, and we are going to have a lot of fun, because father is coming.' That definitely did not impress me as such a happy event, because I was only very slightly interested in father and I knew for sure that when he was with us mother's time was always taken up with him. At such times I had to go for a walk with Grete and with Sophie, the grown-up daughter of the wizened old farmer's wife.

During the evening while we were waiting for father, I suddenly heard our neighbours telling mother that the 'Train had run off the track' and that was the reason why father had not yet arrived. Mother was horror struck. She called Sophie, entrusted me to her care, asking her to pay close attention to me and not to leave me alone a moment. Then she hurried to the station. Grete was allowed to accompany her, as Grete was 'three years older' and could walk better than I could. I stayed alone with Sophie.

It was already dark, and for the first time I was allowed to be up and outside in the garden at this time of day. It was very thrilling, although I did feel a bit uneasy, as I was accustomed to seeing everything in daylight, and now the world around me was so unclear. I had a feeling of being near trees and flowers, rather than of seeing them. And the poplar trees whispered in such a mysterious way. But there was no more time for me to make further observations about the garden and the flowers, because suddenly something fearful happened: Sophie picked me up, crooked an arm about me and carried me to the garden fence where a horrible apparition rose up out of the darkness. It looked like a man but had a fearful kind of bush of feathers on its head, its eyes sparkled in the darkness like burning coals, on its jacket there were tiny buttons, and over its shoulder it carried something I instinctively felt to be terribly dangerous. Later I heard the name 'rifle'. I found this sinister being very repugnant and hoped that Sophie would take me away as fast as possible. But to my great amazement, Sophie again did something completely senseless —true to form, of course. Instead of running away, she went up very close to the fence and allowed the horrible apparition to whisper something to her in a terribly deep voice. Then the man—by this time I knew it was a man—put his arms around her and held her tight. Since Sophie was holding me in one arm, he was holding me tight too, much to my distaste and great displeasure. But that wasn't all! He had a gigantic moustache, and its two 'branches' stuck out from his face like sharp horns. Next he pulled Sophie quite close to himself and acted as if he wanted to bite her. I expected that Sophie, in the face of this deportment, would finally run away. But no, with her free arm she embraced the neck of the terrible apparition, and when he wanted to bite —or eat—her, she did not turn her face away but held her mouth to his, and both of them acted as if each were absolutely bent on eating up the mouth of the other. All this time they were squeezing me so hard I could scarcely breathe. I fought with all my strength to keep this horrible apparition as far away as possible, struggling to keep my nose free. His presence was unspeakably unpleasant. He smelled of all kinds of things, and a certain kind of bitter smell was particularly repugnant. But neither he nor Sophie paid the least attention to me, squeezing my head so tightly that I heard the man's heart beating, while both of them acted for all the world as if each wanted to slip into the mouth of the other. Gracious! these adults and the funny things they do! As they hugged each other, I could not for the life of me imagine what had got into the modest, quiet little Sophie. She was like a strange person who paid no attention to my struggles. And then, just as suddenly as it had appeared, the horrible apparition released us and disappeared into the darkness. A moment later I heard the comforting voices of mother and father, and soon their happy faces appeared out of the darkness. All the neighbours gathered round and asked father about the derailing of the train. Sophie acted as if nothing had happened, not even bothering to tell anybody what a horrible being had held her in its arms only a few minutes earlier. She just stood there with her calm, innocent face. That was another big surprise for me, but I had no time to think about it, for father had brought us bonbons from the city and I was extremely eager to find out whether I was going to get as many as Grete.

I was satisfied; to each of us he had brought the exact same bonbons. And now it was mother's turn to spoil my fun; for just as I wanted to stick all the bonbons into my mouth at once, she took them away and gave me just one, promising that I could have another one the next day after lunch. Oh my! Someday when I'm grown up, I'll eat as many bonbons as I want all at once!

But this time I had to give them up and go to bed. As mother was putting me to bed, I asked her just before we said our prayers (for afterwards I was not allowed to speak), 'Mother, what is it that wears a bush of feathers on its head, carries something strange on its shoulder, has buttons that shine in the dark, and smells so terribly bad—Mother, what is it?'

Mother gave me a surprised look and said, 'Why, darling, that's a soldier.'

'Mother,' I asked again, 'do soldiers eat people?' I wanted to know whether he really wanted to eat Sophie, or *what else* could he have wanted?

'No, no,' mother answered laughing, 'they take care of good people; don't be afraid, he doesn't want to eat you.'

I wanted to tell her that it was Sophie he wanted to eat, not me, but mother kissed me, covered me up and said, 'Now, just go to sleep, dear, I have to go to father.'

I lay there alone with my thoughts, and went on wondering for a long time. I just could not understand what the soldier could have wanted from Sophie, and why Sophie let him hold her so tight that I was forced into his unpleasant presence. What did this all mean? Like everything I could not understand, the matter upset me. But finally I fell asleep. Next day the sun shone brightly, and after I had received my bonbon, we all went down to the lake to bathe and splash. On the way we met the soldier. Then I saw in daylight that he was a friendly adult who spoke cheerfully with father. Only I could not understand why he acted as if he had never seen me before in his life. He certainly must have known what happened yesterday! But I was still afraid of his gigantic moustache and did not dare ask any questions. . . .

Dating from this same summer there is another memory that I have carried with me through the years, arising from an experience that made a profound impression upon me. One afternoon—father was with us and the farmers were all sitting in their good clothes in front of their houses, so I knew that it was Sunday—we heard the village bells ring. But their ringing was not at all of the usual kind. They rang as if they couldn't stop ringing. They rang and rang. Their ringing put an end to the Sunday peace and quiet for the whole village. In a few minutes everyone seemed to be running past our house, all going in the same direction. Then father and the son of the wizened old woman ran off too; everyone was carrying buckets and axes. Mother and a few other women remained behind with us children, and the woman kept repeating the same words: 'Oh, my Heavenly Father, do not desert us, Oh, my Heavenly Father, do not desert us!' Mother, too, was very serious as she said: 'We must all of us pray together that father comes back to us alive.'

I asked where he had gone and why. Mother said that a fire had broken out in the village, and father had gone to help fight it. We prayed, but I was very curious about what 'fire in the village' meant. One woman vouchsafed the information that 'the tongues of flame' could be seen from the edge of our garden. I wanted to go to look, but mother did not allow me. Grete, however, was allowed to go along with the son of the owner of the nearby grocery store, to look at the fire, something I considered bitterly unjust. Why should she be allowed, again and again, to do things I was not allowed to do, just because she was three years older? If fire is dangerous, then it's just as dangerous for her as for me, even if she is 'three years older'! Oh, these three years! How many more times will I have to hear that she is three years older, every time she is allowed to do something and I am not, and every time I refuse to recognize and tolerate her authority!

Late in the evening a few men came back past our house, then more and more, all exhausted from their efforts and talking about how father had saved several houses, how he had defied death again and again by plunging into burning houses to save children or animals, and how he had been an untiring leader whom all the rest of the men had obeyed. With a steady stream of inspired ideas and with his unshakable courage, he set an example that others followed so that everyone performed extraordinarily well and the fire was finally localized. Mother listened proudly, and when father finally came home with the son of the wrinkled, old farmer's wife, mother threw herself into father's arms. 'Oh, you dear, dear Robert, how wonderful you are! Wonderful in every way!'

Father smiled silently. He was covered with soot, and withdrew quickly to wash and get cleaned up.

To me it seemed a completely natural thing that father was such an exceptional person. The concept 'Father' was identical in my mind with that of the 'Great Master' who was above everyone and whose will everyone had to follow. His word is law, and obviously he is perfect. If it were not so, he would not be the 'Great Master'! In those days I was only very slightly interested in father. He simply meant for me an unshakable feeling of security. He was no problem for me, so I paid very little attention to him. Only when the whole family was out walking—father, mother, Grete and I—and with his powerful hand he took hold of mine to help me across a street, I noticed that his hand seemed to radiate tremendous strength and that his finger nails were always as clean as fresh snow. So for me it was obvious that father wanted to wash himself free of soot and grime immediately.

The summer passed, and we were back at home again. Once I noticed that when mother was getting me ready for a walk, she bundled me up in a heavy coat and fur cap. The air outside felt as if it were biting my skin. People told me that it was 'cold'. My nose and my feet did not like it. But there were white flakes floating down out of the sky, and everywhere in the stores there were Santa Clauses with white beards. And later there came a time when mother put a straw hat on my head and helped me slip into a light coat. The fields and gardens were alive with flowers, and we were permitted to play with our ball and our hoop in the city park.

This was a period in my life when I could have been completely happy if my mother had not made my life bitter from time to time by cutting my finger nails. I was even afraid in advance when I sensed that the day for trimming my nails was nearing. The skin under my finger nails was so sensitive that to touch anything at all after my nails were cut, even the contact with the air itself, caused me terrible suffering. After each trimming I would run around the room screaming, with my fingers spread apart, not allowing anything to touch me. I could not say that it was pain I felt. No, it was not pain, but an unbearable feeling. When mother noticed it for the first time, she did not know what was wrong with me. She thought she had perhaps cut me without noticing it and wanted to inspect my fingers. But I yelled when she merely touched me, so loud that she was frightened and called our family doctor and asked him what could be the matter with me. He explained to her that my nerves were over-sensitive to a very unusual degree. He advised my mother to bathe my hands in lukewarm water, each time she trimmed my nails, letting me splash around in the water for a while. That did help somewhat, but many years were to pass before my skin was strong enough for me to cut my nails without undergoing this unbearable sensation.

My dear, darling mother! With how much loving understanding and tenderness you tried to overcome all the difficulties caused by this over-sensitivity of mine. If you had not surrounded with your tender love my sensitive nerves, I would have died in early childhood. Only with your help was I able to grow up in health, slowly and purposefully developing resistance. The warm soft nest that you and our loving, generous father built for us children enabled me to become a useful person. You helped me learn, through consciously developed powers, to keep my sensitivity in balance. I was just a child then and had not the slightest inkling about my sensitivity. I merely observed everything and wanted to know everything, while with regard to my health I merely followed your advice. I had perfect confidence in you!

— 2 —

LION AND LIGHT

IN THIS way a few winters and a few summers went by. Once I heard that I was four years old. Grete was already going to school, and I often listened with the greatest attention to what she read out of her primer. She also had a children's newspaper and read me stories from it too. When she was not at home, I pestered my grandmother, the mother of my father, who some time before had come to live with us, and I kept on teasing her to read something to me, for I was always curious as to what was going to happen next in the story. I never tired of listening to what happened to people. I was full of curiosity about life. It was simply marvellous to think of all the things that could happen! There was just nothing I liked more than fairy tales!

My Aunt Adi, the sister of my mother, visited us often and was always willing to fulfil my wish. She had a pretty face. She was loving and as beautiful as a cat. Her warm brown eyes sparkled joyously, and she possessed a peculiar scent about her, as only people do who carry love within their hearts. I enjoyed breathing this wonderful 'love scent' but encountered it only with a very few people. When Aunt Adi came, we surged towards her joyously, helped her out of her coat, and our first word was always, 'Aunt Adi, tell us a story!'

And she told us the most wonderful stories. Without tiring. She could go on telling one story after another, the most interesting fairy tales I ever heard. When I was sick, Aunt Adi came and told me stories until I forgot all about my illness. We just would not let her stop. Whenever she wanted to, we immediately began to ask her, 'Aunt Adi, what happened next ... what happened then?' And we kept on plaguing and pestering her till she resumed her story telling. When the time came for her to go home to her mother, to my other grandmother who played the piano so beautifully, I was left alone with Grete and watched how she read in her book of fairy tales. The fairy tales in her children's newspaper and in her picture books were not nearly as nice, of course, as the stories Aunt Adi told us. But still they were fairy tales and I wanted to know them. I began to spend long periods intently looking at the books from which Grete had learned to read. I looked at the different letters in them and wanted to read. But I did not know what they meant.

One night I dreamt the same dream I had had many nights before, so often that by this time the whole family knew about it: I was running, running with all my might and main, with a lion chasing me, ready to grab me and eat me up. I was running desperately, gasping for breath, along a path leading to a little house. *In the open doorway there was a woman* who did not resemble my mother, but in this dream she was *my mother*, awaiting me with outstretched arms. I knew that if I reached her, the power of the lion over me would be at an end and I would be saved. Now he was so close I could feel his hot breath on my neck . . . his shaggy mane is almost touching me . . . soon he will catch me . . . I run with my last ounce of energy, then suddenly feel a blow, with all the strength that is left in me I cry out, 'Mother!' . . . Then I reach her and fall exhausted in her arms. I am saved, the lion disappears, and I awaken with terrible palpitations of the heart, shaking with the frightfulness of the dream. Without a moment's hesitation, I jump up, throw a blanket about my shoulders, and run—barefoot and in my little nightie—into my parents' bedroom and crawl into bed beside my mother, under her blankets. Oh this wonderful, blessed feeling of peace and security that sweeps over me like a welcome wave of warm water. Mother embraces me and asks, 'The dream again . . . the lion again?'

'Yes,' I answer, and in her blessed presence my heart stops pounding. In a few minutes I am sleeping soundly.

The next morning I wake up in my mother's bed. She is gone, but her nightgown is there beside me. I quickly bury my little nose in it to inhale the precious scent of mother. Father is lying in his bed near by and reading the paper. That means it must be Sunday, I figure out silently for myself. Mother comes in and begins to talk to father. Father lays down his paper, and as luck would have it, right beside me. I pick it up and start to look searchingly at the many mysterious black letters on the white paper. What can they mean?

'Father,' I ask, 'please tell me what these letters mean.'

'Look,' father answers, 'that is an L, that is an I, that is a T, and then another T, that is an L, and this last letter is an E.'

'And this one here?'

'That,' says father, 'is an A, and that a D, and that an S.' While I look at all these letters, something suddenly seems to open up in front of my eyes like the parting of a veil, and just as suddenly a flash of light seems to flood my mind, a light . . . a light!!! The mysterious letters reveal their meaning, and I find myself reading excitedly and joyously.

'Father!—Father! It says "Little Ads". doesn't it?'

Mother stands stock-still for sheer surprise, then comes over to me, picks me up in her arms and kisses me with joyous excitement. 'Why you can read!'

Father congratulates me just as he would a grown up, somewhat to my embarrassment. Then Grete comes in, all happy and excited too, because I can read. Soon everybody in the house knows the news, and Adi, when she comes at midday, gets to hear the news as soon as she opens the door.

I can read! The black letters on the white paper are no longer a mystery for me. I can understand them, *I can read*!

And thus began a new epoch in my life. I read everything I could get my hands on. I wanted to *learn, learn learn*! I read everything that was readable: books of fairy tales, children's newspapers, school books, calendars, newspapers lying on father's desk, everything . . . even a magazine that some man had given our maid. In it I read about such things as 'kissing', 'love', 'secret rendezvous', and finally about 'killing', 'murder', and 'corpses'. Then, when I asked mother to explain some of these strange and somewhat frightening words, she snatched the magazine out of my hands, crying 'For Heaven's sake, where on earth did you get that?' Then she went into the kitchen and told the maid never, never, never to give me such a magazine again. Why, what a pity! To this very day I do not know what happened to the beautiful countess who was kidnapped in her bed at night by a man in black who carried her off on his galloping horse . . .

So I had to face one of the sad facts of life. Whenever I was absolutely fascinated by something, my mother did not like it. Little by little I came to the conclusion that it was much better not to discuss the really interesting things with adults, as such discussions always came out wrong. The only exceptions I found were the menservants in the house. In my very rare moments alone with them, I asked them questions. Somehow, I felt that they were in my power. And whenever they gave me information, they did not dare talk to mother about it afterwards, as they would have been the first to be scolded for it.

3

MY PARENTS ARE NOT 'MY' PARENTS

I WAS about five years old when one day at lunch father spoke about his 'manager'. I was always interested in everything the grown-ups talked about, and so I asked straight away, 'Father, who is this manager?'

'The Director is the top man in the office,' he answered. 'All the others have to do what he says. He is in charge of the whole office.'

'But father, you don't have to obey him, do you? He is not higher than you, is he?'

'Yes he is,' father answered. 'I am not a manager yet, and so I have to do what he says.' And father explained to me what a director or a boss is.

No! I refused to believe my ears. A manager higher than father? How was that possible? Up to that time I had taken it absolutely as a matter of course that the word 'Father' meant 'the Great Master' over everything. He commanded everyone in the whole country and was responsible for all the treasures of the empire; his word was law; no one would dare speak up against him; '*He*' was the only being whom father occasionally asked for advice; or once in a while he would discuss the affairs of the country with '*Him*'. But that was something entirely different! '*He*' was not what we called a *person*. If father is over and above all other people, how could he possibly have a manager superior to him?

Now I looked at father with the greatest attention for what was perhaps the first time. And while I looked at him and observed him very thoroughly, it suddenly dawned on me that this person whom I loved very much was not 'my father'.

Ever since I awakened to consciousness in these surroundings, I have become accustomed to the fact that I am here, that this beautiful, strange blonde woman is my mother, and this tall, dark, powerful man is father. Yes, *here* he is father, but he is not *my* father! In *my* home he is not my father; only here where I am now! Actually he is just as strange as the strange, beautiful woman —mother; only gradually have I become accustomed to them. They are pleasant people, they love me, I am important to them, and by this time I have definitely come to love them. But they are not my mother and my father. I have come to call them 'mother' and 'father' only out of habit!

Up to that time I had never thoroughly considered the situation. I accepted things just as they were, as I felt happy with these people. They gave me security, they enjoyed my presence, and everything I did struck them as most remarkable, charming, and delightful. Under these circumstances why shouldn't I have enjoyed myself in their surroundings? Even with Grete I could sometimes play quite well, whenever she forgot for a moment that she was above me because she was 'three years older' than I was. Yes, everything was all right this way. Uncle Stefi came often, played beautiful music on our piano, and showed me all kinds of attractive things. He blew soap bubbles for me, and with his pocket knife he made a little rattle out of a nutshell. On another occasion he made me a little pig out of dried prunes and toothpicks, and once he brought me a tin box full of beautiful colours and a brush. I was, allowed to paint pretty, colourful flowers in a notebook which belonged *only to me*. This time I didn't even have to share it with Grete! Aunt Adi was charming with her many jokes and fairy stories. Grandmother too—my mother's mother—was so gentle, so fine and always smiled at me with such a loving expression. I loved her very much. When she sat down at the piano, it was a holiday for me. She delighted me with heavenly music, and I was absolutely enchanted as I listened. Here I was in complete agreement with my dear, tender Mother: she loved music more than anything else just as I did. My other grandmother was a most interesting lady. She often told me about her many travels in foreign countries, and numerous times she took me with her to the National Museum. There I saw splendid things. Wonderfully pretty, colourful, giant butterflies which, grandmother told me, lived in some distant part of the world—strangely enough I knew them well—then a number of gigantic stuffed animals. At first I was terribly frightened, but grandmother calmed me.

I also enjoyed it very much when my whole family showed great surprise and delight at all the things I did as a matter of course, and when our relatives spoke about my 'talents'. When I was four years old, mother showed me how to 'crochet' with a bent needle. Then I crocheted a little dress for my doll which always sat alone in its little armchair because I didn't know what to do with her. She was lifeless, and I was only attracted by what was alive. When I was finished with it, the little dress caused such a sensation in the family that I was really amazed. If mother can crochet such beautiful lace, then why is it so remarkable for me to be able to crochet? My colourful flowers I painted in my notebook caused so much enthusiasm in the family that father gave me a little piggy bank, and from then on whenever I had painted a beautiful flower, he dropped a silver coin into my bank. Oh, that was all so pleasant, so very pleasant . . .

But now there came this terrible surprise!—That father had a manager above him!

At that very moment it became completely clear to me that I was *here* in *this* environment, and that I called this *here* '*home*', and yet that I was *not at home here*. Here I was not in *my home*! That was my steadfast, unflinching conviction.

If I had had, at that time, my present knowledge and experience in psychology, I would have immediately analysed how I, a child, could get such an idea. But I was still a child, experiencing everything in a child's direct way, and I was completely convinced that I had been dragged away from my home by force. I naturally did not know where I had come from, because, in the meantime I had forgotten all about it. Who could explain it to me? Only the two people who called me their child! But I knew that if I were to ask questions, they would only give me once again one of their characteristic 'grown-up answers' that I would not be able to understand. And once again the end of the story would be, 'wait until you're grown up'. Oh, how I hated that! Wait until I'm grown up? Why did I have to spend all this time in darkness, in ignorance? I wanted to know everything *now* and not 'someday'!

So I brooded over this question until evening and time for me to go to bed. Then mother came and sat down on the edge of my bed and asked me, 'Why are you so quiet? Why haven't you played with your doll again? And why have you wandered around our whole apartment day-dreaming about something? Tell me what is the matter with you. You can tell me everything, and you can ask me anything you want to.'

Oh, now I loved her with all my heart and with all my confidence. She was delicate, sweet and beautiful. I often found out that she stood up for me when somebody had criticized me; I could always run to her; with her I always found a safe haven. Now we were together so trustingly, and I believed that I could discuss everything with her. I put my arms around her neck and asked, 'Mother, where did you and father get me? Where did I come from?'

At first I saw a little surprise in her eyes; she was even a little taken aback, but then she smiled lovingly and said, 'There is a great lake where all little children are swimming around; when two people love each other and pray to God for a little child, God allows his servant, a great stork, to fly to the lake and fish out the little child that God has selected for these two people, take the little child on his back and fly to them. Then he takes the little child in his long bill and lays it down beside the woman. So the little child gets his "earthly parents" and becomes an earthly child.'

At first I listened with eager attention, but then I clearly realized that she was 'telling' something like Aunt Adi did in her fairy tales. No! That is not the truth! She just does not want to tell me the truth about *how* and *where* she and father found me. I was disappointed and looked into her eyes enquiringly. Then she told me I should be a good girl and say my prayers after her. A moment later she said good night and left. I was all alone.

From now on it became clearer and clearer to me that father and mother were not my true parents and that this country was not my true home. I knew that mother did not know me; I knew that she did not *see* me. I was a stranger to her, and all these people around me seemed completely strange to me. We just did not understand each other. When I talked to mother about things that were perfectly obvious to me, she was often so surprised and amazed that she would run to father and tell him about the strange things I was saying. Father too was surprised. I saw that these things were new for both of them, completely strange. Later they told all my relatives about my remarks and observations, and then they all laughed at me. 'What a strange child!' I heard again and again. But I for my part did not find myself the least bit strange; on the contrary the people around me seemed strange, and even though I loved them I felt myself a total stranger among them. Everything seemed too little and restricted and colourless. Way down deep in my subconscious I felt the overpowering conviction that only '*He*' could understand me *perfectly* and I would have been happy to have been living in much larger rooms, much freer and among people who at the very least were similar to myself.

This feeling that I was a stranger and alone has never left me all my life long; on the contrary it became clearer and clearer. I tried to find some kind of contact, but in vain. Mother spoke beautifully about the love of children for each other. 'It is so beautiful to have a sister with whom you can discuss everything and in whom you can have complete confidence,' she said. I determined to create such a relationship with Grete, but she did not keep my confidences. She looked down upon me because she was 'three years older' and when I told her something in strict confidence, she ran to mother right away and told her all my little secrets. Thus all my efforts in my sister's direction were completely one-sided. Finally I gave up trying to establish a relationship of confidence with her, and we lived side by side and yet apart, like two beings come together from two separate worlds. Everybody was strange to me . . . strange . . . everybody.

Time ran past with seven league boots and soon I was six years old. Then one fine day mother took me to school. I soon found myself among many children, and the feeling that I was alone and strange became even stronger within me. In my family everyone loved me and I loved them too. Love reigned above all, and everything else came afterwards. That is why even in this environment I felt at home. I had gradually become accustomed to these people. But the school children were completely strange to me. They understood each other very well, but in their midst I was like a little freak of nature. They were constantly amazed at me and I at them. They laughed at me and that hurt me deeply. They were always talking about all the things they had and showing each other all kinds of things—pens, pencils or erasers—and they all wanted to have something to show that the others didn't have. To me that all seemed terribly boring and ridiculous. I was fascinated by books, fairy tales, music and museums. The other children's eyes just popped open wide when I talked about these things, and they asked me very strange questions. They played with dolls and balls and hoops, while I played with a prism that made the most beautiful colours in the sunlight, and with a magnet that had been given me by Uncle Toni, my mother's other brother. That was so mysterious! The magnet attracted all my mother's needles; then her scissors got magnetized, and mother had to hold down all her pins and needles to keep them from jumping over to her scissors ... yes, I wanted to know about the power that lay hidden in the magnet. Finally I decided that the magnet surely must love the pins and needles the way my mother loved us children. After all, I jumped to throw my arms around her neck just like pins did with the magnet. I found that all so wonderfully interesting! But the other children laughed at me. I was alone ... alone.

That winter I began to take piano lessons. Whenever I played the different pieces of music, I had the feeling that somehow or other inside the music there were the very same kinds of shapes and figures as those which Uncle Toni made with cardboard. He called them 'geometrical figures'. I played one piece that just seemed to bounce out tiny little cubes. Then there was another one that seemed to have little points all over it, and little balls climbed up all these points. Whenever I went out with mother for a walk in the city park, I was always awestruck by the fountain because in its main jet I saw fairies and gnomes who danced and turned and jumped. And I saw that the dancing of the water in the fountain *was music too*. I did not hear this music with my ears, no, *I saw it*. I *knew* that it was music. For me that was all perfectly obvious! But the other children at school laughed at me whenever I talked about it, and said that I was 'stupid'. I did not know why. But the first time I heard other children playing music in our music school, I was simply astonished. What?—couldn't they hear how they were hurting the geometric figures in the music? The teacher said they were not playing in rhythm. It was just as if their heart were not beating in rhythm. And couldn't they hear when they were playing wrong? Oh, it was awful when they hit the wrong notes—it hurt my ears so much I wanted to scream—and they didn't even notice it! I looked at these children curiously and thought to myself, 'Have they no ears? How is that possible? Are the other children not like myself?' I thought that every child, and indeed every person, could see and hear as I did. But little by little I was to learn that most children, and most other people, have *very different* eyes and ears from mine, and that for this reason they regarded me as if I were a freak of nature.

And so I was alone—more and more alone.

── 4 ──

SUNRISE IS DIFFERENT

IN THE spring I was very pale, and mealtimes were constant agony for me. I had no appetite, not even for the best foods, yet mother wanted to persuade me to eat. But when I could not? My only interest in the soup was to play with the blobs of grease on its surface, stirring them with my spoon and trying to unite the little ones into one big one. First I would get two little ones to merge and then stir in another one and another until there was only one big blob of grease on top of the soup. My parents did not appreciate my efforts, and a number of times father sent me away from the table because I was disobedient, refusing to eat my soup and spinach and turnips, and because I only wanted to play with my food. When father saw that his punishment left me completely unimpressed and that as soon as he had taken me to my room, I busied myself with the books I loved so dearly, he decided, on the advice of our doctor, to take our whole family to the seaside for the summer. As soon as our spring examinations were over, we set out on our journey.

We travelled through the night; mother covered us with blankets and saw to it that we were warm and comfortable. I fell asleep, but the strange surroundings woke me well before sunrise. Father and Grete were still sleeping, but mother was awake, and I asked her to let me sit next to the window. I had heard so often about the beauty of sunrise that I wanted to take advantage of this opportunity to see it for myself.

I sat beside the window, poked my head behind the curtain and looked out. The sky was still quite dark and just beginning to get light, little by little turning a dull grey. Slowly the sky became quite light and I saw how our train was roaring through all kinds of changing landscapes—houses, trees, and fields with people and horses and cows in them . . . and still the sun was not yet up! How can it be light when the sun isn't up yet? That was a big surprise for me, but still it was true! Then, when the sky was almost as bright as day, the sun appeared on the horizon . . . finally it came up, and with it, the sky turned a beautiful purple red, just as I had been expecting it to do, so far in vain. But this colour was much more pale—as if diluted—so different from what I had expected. What a disappointment! Sunrise isn't like this!

Meanwhile the others in our compartment had awakened, and father asked, 'How did you like the sunrise? Now you've had a chance to see it for the first time in your life. Isn't it beautiful?' He smiled at me.

'No, father,' I answered disappointed and angry. 'It wasn't beautiful at all! Sunrise should not be like that! It was boring, it took much too long and was all spoiled because the sky got light much too early ... light, but still so colourless and ugly ... before the sun finally came up. No! It wasn't pretty at all! Sunrise is really very different! Quite different!' And I looked off in another direction, angry and dissatisfied.

Father listened to me, as he so often did, with patience and close attention. In his beautiful glowing black eyes I saw his interest and his usual amused expression that told me he was making fun of me but still full of love and understanding. 'You don't say! Sunrise is supposed to be different? You're not satisfied with the sunrise? Do you mean to say that you, little upstart, are not satisfied with what nature does and you want to dictate how the sun is supposed to rise? How do you think you know how the sun should rise when you've never in all your life had an opportunity to see a sunrise? Just tell me that!' He scrutinized me and waited for my answer. Then I looked at him confidently and said, 'I do not know *how* I know, and I don't know *where* I've seen a sunrise before, but I *do* know that it's not supposed to be like this! The sun should rise right up out of the dark sky, and *all at once everything should turn light and bright ... not such a dull, boring grey ... but all red and reddish-purple so that the whole sky and everything on earth is flooded with red.* It's supposed to be much, much more beautiful, more surprising and more uplifting. I know ... I *remember*!'

'Hmm,' said father, 'you remember?' He smiled condescendingly. 'Your imagination is working overtime!' Then he took the cup of coffee mother proffered him, took a sip and turned again to me: 'I'm really very sorry that you weren't satisfied with the sunrise. The weather is perfectly clear today, and it just couldn't have been more beautiful and more colourful. But I can't help it, there's nothing I can do about it.'

I didn't answer. I was angry, not only about the disappointing sunrise, but especially about the fact that father—when I *knew* exactly and remembered, yes, remembered clearly!—said that 'my imagination was working overtime'. Imagination is something quite different, when I think out something in my mind, that is imagination. But sunrise, *the real sunrise,* the way it *should* be—I didn't *think that out*! That was something which was living in me, engraved deeply in my memory, even more deeply than yesterday and everything that happened then. I was angry indeed! I was always angry when I felt helplessly unable to prove something that I knew for sure. I looked defiantly off in the distance until all of a sudden there was a rush for the corridor and father called us, 'The ocean! Children, come here quickly. There's the ocean.'

We rushed to the window in the corridor, and there far below, was the sea—Oh, my dearly beloved sea!

The train roared along, high up on a mountain side, and down below was the vast expanse of the sea. I was all excited and happy, because I knew exactly that I was acquainted with the sea and that I was *not seeing it for the first time*. I regarded it as a matter of course, something perfectly obvious, not even bothering to wonder how my feeling could be possible. I looked down at it without saying a word, while in my heart a happy voice was singing: 'Oh, you wonderful, wonderful sea! Beloved sea, always the same, understanding everything, experiencing everything and surviving everything! Oh, you dear friend, you who have listened so often to me tell you of my pains and joys and sorrows . . . listened so understandingly . . . and offered me the consolation of your infinity and eternity . . . your uplifting consolation surpasses everything human! You are here—you are here again—you are always here, unchanged, and I can look into your depths again, listen to your waves as they tell about eternity . . .'

Father touched my shoulder and asked, 'How do you like the sea? Does it suit you, or should it be different too?'

'No, father,' I answered, 'the sea is just the way it should be . . . but the shore? Why is there a shore all around it? The sea should be unending. We shouldn't be able to see the other shore!'

'Yes,' said father, 'you'll see it's that way when we get down lower. Right below us now is a big bay, and that's why it looks as if the sea has shores all round it. When we get down lower and closer you'll see only water, open water as far as the eye can reach.'

I was greatly relieved. I was enthusiastic about the magnificent view, and so was my sister. At last we had found something about which we were in perfect agreement. She enjoyed the sea as much as I did, and later when we went hunting for mussels and crabs between the rocks, we were the best of friends in every respect.

We were all very happy at this beach resort. Father was in good spirits and that had a stimulating effect on all of us. Mother was radiant as she could be with father all day long.

One day we went into a little church which stood surrounded by cyprus trees in a beautiful garden. Mother knelt down and prayed long and fervently. Father stood beside her and looked very grave. Grete knelt and prayed too. I wanted to be devout too, but I could not. I did not kneel because I felt no desire to do so. *I never wanted to bend my knees before visible forms!* Should I kneel down because others were doing it? No, certainly not! Just because I wanted to be a 'good girl'? God does not need that; God can see that that would not be honest. No, I did not kneel; instead, I watched how the other people were praying.

After a while, when I was already getting a little bored, father touched mother's shoulder. She stood up and we all went out. Outside, everything was drenched in sunshine. I jumped about happily and felt much closer to God in the sunshine than I had in the cold church!

That evening while mother was praying with me, I asked her, 'Mother, why were you praying so fervently in church?'

'I was praying,' she said, 'that if God is going to send us another little child, it may be a little brother for you.'

I was speechless. A little brother? Maybe he would be a good friend?—

Fine! That would be splendid. Then I understood why mother had knelt down and prayed so intently. For a child . . . that made sense!

The next winter I awoke once in the middle of the night. From my parents' bedroom I heard strange sounds. It was the crying of a babe in arms. A few moments later father appeared, fully dressed, and asked, 'Are you awake?'

'Yes, father,' said Grete and I.

'Something wonderful has happened! God has sent you both a little brother.'

Oh! That was very exciting, and I wanted to go and look at my little brother immediately. But father said I should wait patiently until morning; then he and mother would show me the child. Father was very strange. He smiled sweetly and gently and spoke in such hushed and tender tones that I did not dare to contradict him.

The next morning my maternal grandmother came in, helped me to get dressed, and we both went into my parents' bedroom. There lay my mother, and on a cushion in her arm, a little child with black hair. I looked at it attentively and then observed that it had long and very fine tufts of hair on its ears, like a little monkey. Because I was freshly washed, I was permitted to stroke its little fist. Everybody looked at me, and everybody was so still and grave and dignified.

From then on there were three of us children in the family, and I was even more alone than before.

— 5 —

I WANT TO GET AWAY

IT WAS about this time that I met Aunt Raphaela, my father's sister. She was living with her husband, Uncle Ferdinand, in another city. Now they came for a visit to see the newborn baby. I was greatly impressed and full of admiration for this most unusual, queenly beautiful woman. She was tall like father, with a figure like a Greek goddess, with a classically beautiful, noble, imperturbable radiant face crowned by hair as black as ebony. Her eyes too were sparkling black like father's. Her movements were majestic, dignified and yet full of charm. She was the perfect incarnation of all that one could call beautiful and elegant. I loved her from the first moment I saw her. She loved me too and often took me along when she went out shopping. Her husband was a very wise and loving man. We got along well from the moment we met. I was delighted to hear that we were going to spend the summer in a mountain resort very near where Uncle Ferdinand and Aunt Raphaela lived with their children.

The summer was beautiful, and I was often permitted to go for walks in the mountains with father and Uncle Ferdinand. The forests and mountain meadows were glorious, and I revelled in the beauty of climbing up to a mountain vantage point and looking down on towns and villages with all their tiny houses. Yes, *up there* I was happy!—but down below, within the family circle, my happiness was much less complete. Grete was very different from me and always wanted to play something else, while mother busied herself with our little brother. She had no time to show me how to make things with my little hands, or answer my unending stream of questions. The feeling that I was alone grew and took on such proportions that I gradually withdrew from the others and ceased participating in all they did. But mother's view was simply that I was disobedient.

One evening when we were about to go to bed, mother scolded me for coming in so late from the garden and for not wanting to go to bed. I frowned and said nothing. But when mother went on scolding me and called me a disobedient child, I flew into a tantrum and said, 'I see that you don't love me at all. The best thing for me to do is to run away and leave you forever.'

Mother answered angrily, 'Go ahead and run away, anywhere you want!'

I ran out of the house, down the steps, through the big garden, out on to the broad pathway in the forest, and headed straight for the mountain. Just the day previous, I had climbed this mountain with father and Uncle Ferdinand. Rather far up on the mountainside, we had seen a big cave known as the 'robber's cave'. I wanted to spend the night there to figure out what I should do next. In the darkness I did not see the footpath, and so I beat my way through bushes and trees, branches and leaves as I made a beeline up the hillside towards the 'robber's cave'. Suddenly, far behind me, I heard my mother's voice. She was calling my name. I stood still for a moment, then resumed my noisy climb through the bushes. Mother called me several times in succession; then I heard her hurrying after me. Probably she heard me breaking through the bushes. She reached me, grabbed me by the shoulders, and asked excitedly, 'Aren't you afraid a dog will bite you? Have you gone completely crazy?'

I did not answer. Why should I care about dogs? I would be able to defend myself, but I wanted to get away! Away to my own home, where I was really at home, away from these strange people, away from these strange surroundings where no one understood me. People were good to me, and full of love, they wanted the best for me, but they were strange, they were different from me and different from the people living where I was at home.

We walked home in silence, and I was fully expecting to be severely punished. To my great surprise, however, neither mother nor father said a word. As mother and I came into the room, father looked at me somewhat curiously and a bit amused. My only punishment was that mother put me to bed and went out without saying good night.

The next day my parents acted as if nothing had happened. Nevertheless, I could see clearly that mother was frightened at my dare-devil attitude, while father recognized and respected my courage. In his eyes, I had grown in stature. But for my part, I felt neither daring nor courageous. I was just the way I was.

And Grete, the always obedient, always well-behaved, always well-dressed, looked down on me as if I were a criminal, avoiding my glance with her eyes. And I looked at her with my heart full of scorn because of her cowardly obedience!

The next winter I did not go back to school, because I was still very pale and because it was extremely difficult for me to get up early in the morning. A tutor came to our home and tried to stuff all kinds of things into my head ... things that bored me terribly. Geography! Why should I have to learn things about countries that I didn't know? If I want to learn about these countries, I will go there when I grow up, I thought, and so I won't have to study about them any more. But as long as I do not know them, why should anybody want to hammer into my head what these countries look like? While my tutor was talking about Paraguay, Nicaragua and Venezuela, I was listening to the gas hissing gently in the lamp. And when he had finished his discourse about South America, I asked him whether he also heard the hissing of the gas in the lamp. He answered very sweetly that I should now be listening to him, not to the lamp.

'But the lamp is much more interesting,' I said.

Later he went to my mother and they talked together for a long time about this strange child that was much more interested in why the gas hissed in the lamp than in geography. And after my tutor had left, mother gave me a long and serious 'talking to' to explain to me why I should study and learn.

'All right, all right, I'll be glad to study, but I want to learn different things from what you want me to,' I said. Mother remained adamant and said that I would have to take the school exams. That's why I would have to study the subjects provided in the school curriculum. I tried to explain to her that I found these studies uninteresting, while mother tried to make it clear to me that I still had to study; we just did not understand each other, and I was fed up. I wanted to get away! I wanted to know the truth, I wanted to get back to my true parents, I wanted to live among my own people where I would not have to learn such things, where I could do what I wanted, where I could play, not only boring finger exercises, where I would have freedom—in a word—where I would be at home.

Little by little I got into the habit of sitting on an armchair in the dark bathroom, with my feet hanging down, and pondering in this twilight what I should do. I wanted to get away from here . . . and go home . . . to my true home! I did not dare tell this to my mother, for I knew that she would be very angry; so I thought it would probably be best if I explained my decision to her in a letter that I could give her at an opportune moment.

Mother was very busy with my little brother. She was an enthusiastic mother who never entrusted her children to strangers. She nursed, bathed and cared for all her children herself. For this reason I had plenty of opportunity to write my letter to her in the children's room. I wrote very politely and yet very simply that I knew very well I was not her own child, that she and father were not my true parents, that they had probably found me somewhere and brought me home with them, an act they had probably regretted as they could not love me, and this was why I would like to have them take me back as fast as possible to wherever they had found me. I explained to her how terribly unhappy I was here and that I would not want to stay here longer for anything in the world. I went on to explain that this would probably be best for her too as she would soon be free, once and for all, of all the care and worry I had caused her. At the bottom of the letter I wrote 'I kiss your hand' and my name. My letter was finished. But I did not dare deliver it. So I waited for a favourable opportunity.

One fine afternoon some of mother's friends and relatives were at our house for a visit. They chatted pleasantly, admired us older children and our new little brother—we three were all wearing our most beautiful clothes—then went into the dining-room where the table was set and coffee and cakes were waiting for them. In this circle of ladies, my mother was really charming, sitting at the end of the table, as was her habit. She was radiantly beautiful, gay and full of peace and I thought that this at last was the moment to give her my letter. She would surely not be angry now. I waited until all the ladies had drunk their coffee and then stole up behind my mother's chair. While she was chatting with her neighbour, I reached around her waist and dropped my letter in her lap. Mother noticed me immediately when I slipped into the room, because she did not like to have us children mixing with adults. We were supposed to stay in the children's room and come out only when we were called. Busy as she was with her guests, she was not able right away to ask me what I wanted. When I slipped the letter into her lap, she looked at me in wide-eyed surprise, put the letter into her pocket and went on chatting with her guests as if nothing had happened. I was very pleased to have picked such an opportune moment!

But that evening after the guests had left and father had come home, the storm broke. A storm that I had not expected! Mother was really very frightened and unusually excited. She gave father my letter and, all shaken and unstrung, said to him, 'This child is certainly quite insane; look what she has written me'. Then turning to me she poured out her wrath, 'Just wait, young lady, if we are not good parents for you we can be quite different. Then you will have different parents, and believe me you will regret it!'

Father read my letter with great interest, and I noticed that he found it very entertaining. It was generally very hard to upset father, and he was certainly not upset about my letter. He looked at me quizzically and asked 'What do you mean by saying you want to get back to your "true" parents? Who do you think your "true" parents are? And where are they? You silly little girl!'—and that was the end of the matter as far as father was concerned.

On the other hand, mother was very excited, and for days she talked with grandmother, Aunt Adi, and Uncle Stefi about my letter, even showing it to my father's best friend, our family doctor. Our doctor was a very profound and thoughtful man, highly educated in the sciences, a friend and adviser to all the members of our family in all matters affecting body and soul. Mother was very bitter about my attitude and told him that, as he well knew, our whole family was doing everything possible to make me happy and that I was an ungrateful child, because in spite of all my family was doing for me, I still wanted to run away and leave them.

'And where do you want to go, you crazy little child, just tell me where you want to go?' she asked again and again. But that was something I didn't know myself, a question I would have liked to have mother and father answer for me! *I* wanted to know about the place where they had found me, the place from which they had brought me! Our family doctor, with his peaceful blue eyes, looked at me searchingly and asked me very earnestly, just as he would have asked a grown-up, 'What did you mean by that, child, tell me frankly just what you meant.'

But I could not and would not talk any more about it. I just wanted to go back, back to where I had come from, to where they had brought me from! Where I was at home, where I would again be among *people like myself*.

But I realized that I could not yet reach my goal. I was going to have to stay here. I realized that these people knew just as little, or perhaps even less, about my origin than I did. So I could not expect to have them help me find the solution to this puzzle. With my questions I had only offended and frightened them. I realized that my letter had been a big disappointment to my mother, and I didn't want that! I went back to the children's room where I found Grete looking down to avoid meeting my glance . . . to avoid having to look at such a villainous little child. I felt as if I were a criminal. No, the whole question was quite hopeless! I never spoke about the matter again. Little by little the family forgot the whole matter, and little by little there sank down upon my soul a veil that kept getting thicker and thicker. I wanted to avoid thinking any more about my true homeland, as it appeared quite impossible to find out any details about it.

It was around this time—I was just seven—that father one mealtime said something about the human being as the 'crown of creation'.

'How do you mean that, father?' I asked.

'Just that man is the most perfectly developed creature on earth. There is nothing higher.'

I was simply amazed. How can it be possible, I thought, that father who has such a brilliant mind, who knows all the answers, and who always comes out on top in any debate—doesn't know that over and above the human being there are . . . what should I actually call them? . . . titans or giants—not in physical size but in knowledge and power—towering up above us human beings, guiding us with their powers, and helping us forward on the pathway of our development?

I glanced at father to see whether perhaps he did not want to speak about these superior beings, or whether he actually did not know anything about them. I observed his face and saw that he was completely convinced as he spoke about Man as the crowning achievement of nature. I did not dare ask any further questions, as somehow or other it was deeply impressed upon me that 'He' did not like to have me speak about secret things with ignorant people. One must be able to keep silence.

But a moment later I started up as if shocked. 'He?'—who is *this one* whose very existence I take for granted, believing as a matter of course that 'He' is always with me, that 'He' always stands behind me ready to help? Who is this 'He' to whom I look up so humbly, to whom I flee for refuge whenever I feel alone or misunderstood . . . from whom I can always expect absolute love and understanding . . . who never judges or condemns me but always listens to me first, always taking me seriously, always helping me onward and never . . . never . . . *never* deserting me. *Who* and *where* is 'He'? And as I was seeking the answer to this question, there suddenly appeared before my mind's eye two dark blue, all-loving, all-knowing, almighty eyes, eyes as immensely deep and infinite as the canopy of Heaven itself . . .

I want to cry out His name, but the letters are buried too deeply in my memory, my thinking is not clear enough to draw them out of myself, up to the surface. Then suddenly I notice that I am sitting at our family table, that mother is sitting at one end of the table, with my little brother on her lap, as she spoons bits of porridge into his open mouth . . . and my vision disappears.

All afternoon I sit at my little writing table, trying to force my mind to bring forth out of the unconscious part of myself the memories that are there, that I just cannot quite grasp. Sometimes blurred and misty pictures rise up before me. I want to seize them, but they disappear again immediately . . .

But one thing did become clear for me: in all the time that I have been conscious on this earth, I have always carried within me the picture of someone whom, simply and in a very matter of fact manner, I have called '*Him*'.

─ 6 ─

I LONG FOR UNITY

ONE DAY mother received an invitation to visit a cousin who, with her husband and sons, had moved away to live in the city. The whole family came out of the house to welcome us. The two boys eyed us critically, and we two girls gave them a thorough inspection, all in silence until our aunt sent us into the children's room.

Suddenly we found ourselves in a little boy's world. They had a train that ran on a track, a little printing press, and a magic lantern. Everything impressed me greatly, but what excited me most was the fact that the boys had many many books. All books by Jules Verne! We had a grand time, and it was late in the evening before we went home. Our two families got along together quite harmoniously, and from then on we saw each other every week. These afternoons were pleasant and enjoyable, and the boys were well brought up and happy.

Under the influence of what I had once read in a book, I was always seeking a kind of 'eternal unity in friendship', but my girl friends in school made fun of me. They were not interested in such 'stupid' things. Now I suggested to the boys that we make a 'pact of eternal friendship'. They found it a splendid idea. However, the younger boy, who had a strong will and was thus inclined to be the ring-leader, said that we would each have to show our signature. So each one of us was obliged to write his name on a piece of paper. The two boys and Grete wrote their names with the first letters very big and provided with all kinds of fancy twists; the remaining letters they wrote as illegibly as possible, finishing off with an impressive curlicue. I found all these embellishments superfluous and wrote my name with simple, clearly legible letters.

After looking at the signatures, the younger boy turned to me with his voice full of scorn, 'What? You want to enter a pact of eternal friendship, you want to be a member in an alliance of friends and you don't even have a decent signature? You can't join our friendship alliance until you have a decent signature!' Whereupon the two boys and Grete formed their pact for 'everlasting friendship in life and death'.

I was profoundly disappointed, defeated, dejected.

No sooner had I reached home and hung up my hat and coat, than I began to practise my 'signature'. I wrote my name a thousand times, beginning the first letter with a gigantic curve and scribbling off the remaining letters in a completely illegible manner. I attempted to imitate the signature of our family doctor who wrote such completely illegible prescriptions. Then I finished my work of art with a long line that wove back and forth across the page. It was artificial. It was anything but true and real. But the next Saturday I was able to greet my two friends proudly; 'Now just look at what I have . . . Now I have a signature too!' With that, I scribbled a most impressive signature on a piece of paper.

The two boys and Grete examined my work of art; then the younger said, 'Good. Your signature is still *too* legible, but we're going to accept it anyway and take you in as a member in our alliance.'

I expected to be happy now that my wish was fulfilled, but strangely enough I could not. No! Something was not as it should be. And back home, standing before the mirror and looking face to face at the 'invisible'—myself—I heard a voice within me: 'Your signature was false. It was not your picture. Do you believe that you can obtain *true* things through *false* things? True friendship with a false signature? People who cannot accept your true signature cannot be your true friends . . .'

I turned away from the mirror sadly and went to bed. I could no longer use the signature I had practised so long. I was revolted by it. I knew that this 'eternal friendship in life and death' was just as artificial a thing as my 'signature' and that these two boys hadn't the vaguest idea about the kind of friendship I was seeking—real, true, eternal friendship that stands over time and space! And I was alone in my search for true friendship, my search for true unity . . . alone . . . alone.

— 7 —

THE RED MAN

AT THE age of nine I was greatly shaken by an experience which stands out starkly in my memory. My little brother, whom I dearly loved, was just two. He fell sick, but our doctor could not diagnose the cause of his suffering. I was in the room where he was lying in bed, with mother sitting beside him. All of a sudden, the child started up out of a sound sleep, wide-eyed with fright as it stared in the direction of the door and called out, 'Mother, Mother, the Red Man . . . the Red Man is coming to get me!' The child waved his tiny hands as if he were fighting someone off, and then screamed at the top of his lungs, 'Mother! Help! The Red Man!' . . . and fell over in a faint.

Mother sprang up, caught him in her arms, laid him gently back into bed, and immediately sent for the doctor. While we were waiting, I asked, 'Mother, who was this Red Man he saw?'

Mother answered, 'Nothing real, darling. He's just seeing things . . . hallucinations . . . in his fever.'

When the doctor came, he found the child had pneumonia.

Poor dear mother! Three weeks long she carried the child day and night in her arms, not sleeping and not leaving him alone for a moment. I was aghast as I watched the fearful struggle my brother was making for his life and mother was making to save her only son. It was perhaps the first time in my life I opened my heart all the way for mother; and perhaps it was the first time in my life I saw that, through and through, her heart was made of a fabric of love. I too lived through this period in fear and trembling for the life of my brother, and from this time on I felt I really belonged to my family. When he finally returned to health, I took my full part in the family rejoicing. At last I had begun to feel 'at home' in this place.

But I did not forget the 'Red Man'. Mother tried to reassure me in vain that it had not been something real. My brother had seen him—something had caused him to see a red man—and that was not supposed to be something real? What my brother had seen remained an open question for me, one I pondered long and often. At that time I could not dream that I would someday—many, many years later—find the answer in India.

A year later we moved to another part of the city where there were many trees and where the houses were surrounded by beautiful gardens. From the windows of our new home we could look out in every direction towards hills and mountains.

I went back to school, and once again the old story began for me. The other girls in school were as amazed at me as I was at them. They played with dolls, and that bored me stiff. And I read books they thought were just as dull. The older I grew, the more feverishly I read. Not only the books we children received, but all the books in my father's library. There I found a set of volumes which caused me to begin reading even more avidly than I had before. The complete works of Shakespeare! I devoured one book after the other. They made such a profound impression upon me that I just could not stop reading. All day long I could think of nothing else. I acted like a sleep-walker. At mealtimes I did not even hear what people said to me. I was still re-enacting the fate of the hero and heroine of the particular tragedy or comedy I had just been reading. First I read all the tragedies, one after the other, living in a state of deep emotional turmoil. Then came all the comedies, which kept me rocking back and forth on our sofa out of pure amusement.

Along with Shakespeare, there was another set of thick books entitled *Ethnographical Research* which meant much to me. There I found descriptions of all kinds of rituals in the field of superstition and black magic. In these volumes I read things that were startlingly new and difficult to understand: superstitions about love, recipes for brewing love potions, and other obscure rites having to do with love and sex. After spending quite a time reading some of the most fantastic things I fired some questions at mother.

'Mother,' I asked, 'Can you make someone love you by taking a yellow turnip, boring a hole through it from top to bottom, spitting through the hole three times, then taking the turnip out at midnight and throwing it over the house of the person you love? And is it true that if you take a piece of a girl's nightdress, burn it and bake the ashes in a cake, the person who eats the cake will fall in love with the girl who owns the nightdress and do anything she wants him to?'

Mother let me finish asking questions, while the expression on her face changed from amazement to horror. Finally she burst out, 'For goodness' sake! Where did you hear all this terrible nonsense? Have you been talking to the washwoman? How often have I forbidden you to talk over delicate questions with the cook or the washwoman! Where have you heard all this fearful black magic nonsense? Tell me right away!'

'Mother,' I answered, supremely certain of my innocence. 'Don't get excited. These things cannot be so fearful if a scientist spends his time investigating them. I read them in scientific books, in the *Ethnographical Research* books, in father's library.'

That was enough to set mother scurrying to father's bookcase which she promptly locked, withdrawing the key and keeping it. From then on I was allowed to read only what she gave me. In order to obtain otherwise inaccessible information, I asked mother from time to time to let me have a volume of the encyclopaedia in which to read up on some plant or animal we were studying in school. And I saw to it that this volume contained the particular word that interested me much more than the plant or animal. Then I went into the children's room and thoroughly studied the things I wanted to know. Thus with mother's express permission—and assistance!—I read item after item of prohibited information, while mother lived on in blissful ignorance of the true objects of my attention. Even better, mother herself had tipped me off to the fact that I could learn all kinds of exciting things about superstition from our washwoman. As fast as I possibly could I sought out opportunities for clandestine conversation with her. Thus I came to hear some of the most horrible stories about ghosts, superstitions, and witchcraft until I got into such a state of fear that I no longer dared enter a dark room alone. Then Uncle Stefi asked me once why I was afraid.

'Because I might see a ghost,' I said.

'Oh, so that's it! Want to know an easy way to defend yourself? . . . Just whistle real loud, and all the ghosts will scamper away instantly,' he answered.

From then on I was constantly whistling, while at the same time delving further into ghost stories. Thus, on the one hand, I extended my knowledge about the lowest levels of mysticism, and on the other, developed an above-average ability for whistling.

— 8 —

MY FUTURE APPEARS

WE SPENT that summer on the great inland lake, where we lived together with some of our relatives. This particular summer stands out strongly in my memory because of events I had to think back upon much, much later.

Mother was still very busy with my little brother, and so I had a bit more freedom. In the company of a girl friend of my own age, I was allowed to roam about the village and nearby park and meadows. Mother thought I was going to my friend's house, while her mother thought she was coming to mine. Instead, we rambled around the village and its environs, trying to satisfy our girlish curiosity. On the lakeshore there was a row of villas, and we watched a gypsy boy go up to each villa in turn, play a few tunes on his violin, and hold out his hand for money. It suddenly struck me that my grandmother earned a lot of money by giving concerts, and I wondered whether I too could earn some money. My little girl friend always did blindly whatever I told her to do; so we two went up to each villa, straight up to the porch or into the garden wherever the people were sitting, and I recited a poem. The people were very surprised, but when my friend made the rounds holding out a plate, everybody dropped some coins in it, some more, some less. All of them had a hearty laugh at our expense, and one lady asked whether my mother knew what I was doing.

'No,' I answered, 'this is our private enterprise. Mother doesn't know about it.'

'Just as I thought,' said the lady, 'why don't you two children run along home now.'

The promising business venture came to an end that very day. After we had divided the money between us, I went home and told how I had earned some money, proudly displaying the many coins of nickel and copper. Mother almost fainted.

'For goodness' sake!' she whooped, 'Where in the world did you get such an idea? What will people think? You're plunging us into shame!'

'Why?' I asked. 'Grandmother earns money with her performances. The little gypsy boy earned money too. So what's so shameful about my earning money reciting poetry?'

'Just try to understand, you stupid little ninny,' my mother answered, 'that your father has a high position with a nation-wide reputation, and you just cannot do such things!'

'What does father have to do with what I do? Father is father, and I am I. I don't have a high position, so why shouldn't I earn some money? Every job is decent if one just does it decently. And I really recited very beautifully!' I ended my argumentation proudly.

Mother snorted angrily, 'You just don't understand. And as punishment for doing such things and for contradicting me, I am not going to let you leave the garden!'

Thus I came to lose my liberty, but the episode had further consequences. My great-uncle, who had rented the other half of the villa for himself and his family, was a loving person blessed with a magnificent sense of humour. When he heard that I had recited poetry in the villas along the shore, he wanted to hear me too. Our two families took all our meals together, and that evening my great-uncle suggested that I recite something after supper. I had no objections. The grown-ups all sat in a circle, while I stood in the centre and started reciting some poems I had learned at school. My great-uncle liked them and wanted to hear more.

'But I don't know any more,' I said.

'Then tell us something, anything you want.'

'Can I tell you a story out of the book I got as a prize for my good exams?' I asked.

'Surely,' said my great-uncle, 'go ahead.'

I began to tell stories from *The Vicar of Wakefield*. But I didn't content myself with just telling them, I acted them out as if I were on stage. In this way I gave an animated story about how the vicar of Wakefield led a holy life, how a young man got acquainted with his daughter, Olivia, and finally ran off with her. I hadn't the vaguest idea of what it meant to run off with somebody that way, and so I didn't know why the vicar was so excited. I was merely telling the story in the way I read it in the book. Continuing with my improvised one-person drama, I told about the lovers' tryst in the darkness and the sweet and tender words they whispered to each other, how the vicar bellowed with rage and reached for his gun, and finally how his gentle wife calmed him down, by slipping a Bible into his hand . . .

By this time the grown-ups were all doubled up with laughter, and when I was ready to stop, my great-uncle insisted he wanted to hear more about the vicar. There was nothing for me to do but go on, and that made them laugh some more. They laughed as if I had been telling the funniest stories in the world. And here I was telling a tragedy!

When I was through, my great-uncle took me by the hand and pulled me over to where he was sitting. 'Tell me where you heard all these stories,' he asked.

'Yes,' echoed mother, 'that's just what I'd like to know too!'

'From the book I got in school as a prize,' I answered.

'Amazing!' said mother, somewhat vexed, but still laughing, 'How can these people in school give such books to a child?'

'Forget it, Lilian,' said my great-uncle, 'they certainly didn't read the book themselves, and undoubtedly they thought that a book about a vicar is bound to be full of holy and harmless things. They didn't realize that Ministers of the Gospel sometimes have daughters. Just relax, Lilian, and let her tell us some more stories another time. What she's got in her head you can't get out again anyway. And I haven't had such a good laugh in a long time!'

From then on I had to give a performance every evening. In addition to our family circle, my audience soon began to include friends from the neighbourhood who came to hear me tell the stories I had been reading in books. These included some of Shakespeare's tragedies, and once again I could not understand what there was in these profoundly tragic scenes that struck the grown-ups as funny. Despite their hilarity I put on the scene in which King Lear, alone and deserted, lets out his last dying gasps—and the grown-ups were in stitches!
... In *Richard III* I went through the scene in which everybody dies one after the other, one in one way, the next in another, and I demonstrated how;—by this time the grown-ups were practically splitting their sides. How, I wondered, can people laugh at such tragic events where so many people die? That's not funny! That's horrible, I thought, as I went on with my act in deadly earnest.

How often—how very often—I was to think back in later years about that little girl who was so serious and so convinced of herself as she told stories and put on an act. My later destiny in life had already come into evidence. Even at that early age, I had become accustomed to bringing things forth out of my inner world—beautiful, divine, true things—irrespective of whether my audience understood my truths or not. I speak *for the sake of truth itself*, and only one listener is important: *God!*

★   ★   ★

Summer went by, and we came home. That winter I decided to stop wearing little-girl clothes and to dress as a clown. I just could not get over the feeling that I was not the person I was, and that I was really someone else. Even though I had stopped talking about it, I had not got over this feeling. On the contrary, it had merely worked its way deeper down inside me and was active in my subconscious. I begged and kept on begging till my good-hearted mother could not say 'No' any longer. With her own hands she made me a real clown costume, a pretty one. She even bought me two colourful clown caps, and from then on I went around in this attire. I derived tremendous enjoyment from exercising on a trapeze and flying rings, imitating at home everything I had seen in the circus. Hanging head down and seeing the world upside down, I felt free.

At that time I did not yet know that psychologists call the clown a 'person changing type'.

Along with my amateur circus acrobatics, I acquired the habit of assuming strange and unusual body postures. At first my parents were surprised and laughed at me; then soon our relatives and friends were amused and entertained at the 'comical' positions into which I put various parts of my body. Wherever I went, I was asked to demonstrate these postures. I did them instinctively, without thinking at all why I did them. I merely noticed that they made me feel good, that in certain positions I could study better, and that when I was tired I could feel surprisingly fresh again in only a very few minutes by virtue of having sat in certain other positions.

The rest of the family laughed about my 'crazy' habit and mother gradually got used to seeing me in some impossible position whenever she came into her room. At first she lectured me about how a 'good girl' has to sit on a chair and must not stand on her head or twist her legs into impossible positions or hang her legs over her shoulders. In due course, however, she left me in peace with this new idiosyncracy of mine.

For me these different body postures were a matter of course. They were in my blood, I enjoyed them even without thinking about them much, and I was only amazed, once again, that the people around me were so surprised about something so obvious. Once while our whole family was visiting Aunt Raphaela for several weeks of summer holidays we had a visit from a gentleman who had spent many years travelling in the Far East, and who—as Uncle Ferdinand informed us—could tell all kinds of interesting stories about these far-away places. We children were introduced to the man and, as usual, our parents told him what we could do. Aunt Raphaela laughingly told him about my remarkable habit of assuming strange, leg-twisting postures which nobody else could imitate, except perhaps an India rubber man.

I lay down on the floor, and as I was always embarrassed when people were talking about me—feeling uncomfortable about merely 'protruding' above ground—I assumed a position in which I could completely conceal my head, giving spectators the illusion of its having been cut off. The grown-ups laughed. Then I demonstrated a few other 'difficult' postures that I enjoyed so much. Our strange guest watched my performance for a while without cracking a smile and finally burst out in astonishment, 'But this child is doing typical *Yoga exercises*! Where did you learn them, little girl?' He turned to me.

I did not know what the word 'Yoga' meant; so I answered that no one had shown me these exercises and that I did them just because I liked them and felt better afterwards. The man refused to believe it, looking at me long and enquiringly, and shaking his head.

The grown-ups' questions had already begun to bore me; so when mother waved us off, we disappeared into the children's room, and I promptly forgot the remarks made by our distinguished visitor.

Only much, much later, when the memory suddenly came to life and I began to understand many other things which had been obscure and inscrutable in my life, I remembered the remarks of the widely-travelled gentleman from the Far East. ... Then I understood where I had learned these physical postures which I had practised as a child and later as an adult ... postures our distinguished visitor had called 'Yoga exercises'. Then I realized clearly that I had done these exercises *out of long-standing habit*, because I had been obliged to practise them daily in the temple year after year. These exercises were a reflection of my past and at the same time the shadow of events yet to come in my life; for much later, as an adult, I taught these exercises to many people in order to further their mental and physical development.

— 9 —

STRUGGLES OF LOVE

THE YEARS passed rapidly. As I grew my body began to mature. I enjoyed reading books that dealt with love stories and problems of love; so I delved deeper and deeper into my personality. I looked forward into the future and determined to find a noble-spirited husband who would understand me perfectly. In this way I began to concern myself less with books and more and more with young people, later with young men. The young men were also interested in me. Mother tried in vain to bring me up as a modest young lady. Even in my earliest years I had to realize that I possessed a power of attraction. However, in my blindness, I considered that this power which drew so many people towards me was an attractiveness emanating from my person. We always have to pay for our spiritual deficiencies, and because of my being blinded to the truth at this age, I was later to have to pay the price of almost becoming physically blind. I had yet to learn that my power of attraction was not intended to serve my private life, but rather to lead the people following me along the path of their salvation.

At that time, however, my whole thinking centred around my personality, and I believed I would find my highest happiness in the love of man and wife. I thus went through many of the experiences that are usual in this world. I was loved and fell in love, but all my joys and sorrows were merely a prelude to my later destiny.

A relationship with one man in particular dominated the six years of my life from the age of thirteen until I was nineteen, and looking at it in retrospect I would call this whole experience a 'training school for the development of unusually strong will-power'. My destiny knew that I was going to need this weapon in life. When I was thirteen, I met a young man whose brilliant traits made him stand out high above the average. His character was made up of a purposeful and determined striving for the highest and finest and most beautiful things in life, combined with an almost pathologically acute egotism and desire for power. He loved me, so he said, but he loved himself and wanted to make me his obedient slave. He recognized very early that we both had the same spiritual viewpoint and that art meant the same to me as it did to him. This led him to believe that he had found in me a partner worthy of himself. He hoped, in time, to make me over into his own image—a highly cultured but absolutely obedient wife. He thought he would do away completely with my independent thinking. He brought me excellent books about art, the history of art, music, world history, the best works of literature—both modern and classical—and he insisted that I read these works in the original. Since I found learning languages just for their own sake extremely boring, he took the time to learn languages with me. Then he sought out the best piano teacher for me. In short he did everything imaginable to help me get an unusually good education. Mother saw in him a helpful angel for my education, because languages were really hard for me. The best tutors tried in vain to teach me; I refused to learn long lists of words by heart. This young man brought me German, French, and English newspapers, magazines, and theatrical works, then read them with me, thus helping me to work my way into various languages. That was very helpful and certainly all to the good, but along with his helpfulness he kept trying consistently and purposefully to force me under his domination. Shortly after we got acquainted, he said that I was going to become his wife and he wanted me to consider myself as *his property*. Everything I wanted to read I had to show him first to get his permission. He refused to let me make friends with anybody at all without his prior permission. Like other young girls, I went to a dancing school with my sister. I was passionately fond of dancing and equally fond of having a good time with the other young people in the class. I also enjoyed ice-skating. None of these things had any appeal for him. But I was young and I wanted to dance and skate and have a good time with other young people. This made him jealous—and to a degree far surpassing anything one might consider normal. Worst of all, his jealousy went hand in hand with an almost insatiable desire for power.

At first I was flattered that a man who was so well known and highly esteemed by so many people should have chosen a little girl like me as his future wife. He was a brilliant talker, and quite often I enjoyed conversations with him tremendously. I was also pleased that he took the same profound and serious views of friendship and love that I did. On the other hand, when I began to feel he was systematically and consistently trying to force his will upon me, more and more, like a band of steel, all his attentions became annoying. A struggle began, a terrible struggle between the invisible forces of two souls! The more he felt I was growing out of his power, the more firmly he sought to hold me. When I was seventeen, he wanted us to announce our engagement publicly. He sent his father to visit mine. My father was not exactly delighted. A long time afterwards, he told me he had never been impressed by my fiancé's aggressive approach, but he didn't want to interfere with our free will. He respected everybody's right to make up his own mind—including his own children—and so he gave his consent, even though reluctantly. I hoped my fiancé's jealousy would die down after our betrothal. As time went on, however, and my body continued to develop in form and charm, his jealousy knew no bounds, and he often made terrible scenes. After torturing me for hours, he often went to the opposite extreme, asked me for forgiveness on his knees, cried like a baby, begged for my love, and promised never to torture me again. I found such scenes absolutely unbearable. Never before in my young life had I experienced any such thing. My father possessed tremendous power, a kind of power which he radiated about him automatically and unintentionally. He never tried to force his will upon others. He liked to leave everybody his freedom and never expected others to follow and obey him blindly. At that time he was holding a top-level position, and my little-girl wish had already been fulfilled for quite a period—he no longer had a manager or director supervising him. Even so, he was never domineering or tyrannical towards his subordinates. He was like a tower of strength for all around him, both at home and in his office. Hundreds of subordinates and all our relatives sought his counsel. He was just, generous, and always ready to help. No wonder I had grown up thinking that all men were like him. At home I had never known such things as egotism and unscrupulousness, and my sister and I had both grown up in a healthy atmosphere of true, selfless, love. I could not have known what sadism and masochism were any more than I could have understood—let alone bear—all the quarrels I got involved in with my fiancé. I wanted to be free! Free!

For a long time, however, I could not resist his will. An innate propensity towards faithfulness, together with an understanding approach towards the weaknesses of other people, also kept me for quite a time from taking action. But my will power developed with the years, and all of a sudden I began to ask myself why I should go on enduring this torture.

One day I told him I wanted to be free. He would not hear of it. We struggled desperately, for his will still held me in a grip of steel. The longer I struggled, the more my will power developed, until finally it was greater than his. The moment finally came when I had enough courage to tell him I no longer wanted to be his wife. More stormy scenes followed, but their effect was completely lost on me! I was sorry for him, but at the same time I had lost all respect for him because of his behaviour, so domineering and tyrannical on the one hand, and so extremely cowardly on the other. In those days I did not know that these two characteristics are very closely related, so closely in fact as to be two complementary aspects of the same disease. On the other hand, I felt him to be sick in his soul, and I wanted absolutely to be free. With a last great effort I shook off his will.

I spoke to my parents. They were not surprised. And one fine afternoon when I was nineteen I set out on a journey with my cousin to his mother, my father's sister, beautiful Aunt Raphaela.

I broke my engagement . . .

—— 10 ——
FIRST ENCOUNTER WITH DEATH

EVER SINCE my childhood days, I had often become pale and tired around springtime. In most cases, the best remedy was to visit my Aunt Raphaela. She lived in the mountains with her family, and the combination of the bracing mountain air and the atmosphere of wisdom and religion these people lived in always cured me very quickly. I felt very happy in these quiet and noble surroundings and would come home, fresh and full of new energy and vitality.

After my engagement had been dissolved, I went again to see my aunt. At that time, she was already a widow and was living with her daughter. She welcomed me with great affection, and I fully enjoyed the long desired peace and tranquillity. I felt like a kite with a broken string—soaring up into infinity. What a wonderful spring it was! As usual, my aunt understood me perfectly. She expressed her views upon my decision with great insight; afterwards, she never mentioned the matter again. In her home I lived in absolute freedom. She let me come and go as I liked. I could roam through the hills and woods and enjoy nature to the full. During this period when I felt completely happy in my freedom and looked towards the future with confidence, I encountered death for the first time in my life!

While hiking one day I came to a field of grain. As my plans for marriage had recently been blasted, I stopped there and tried to picture my future. First of all, I was going to be a pianist, I told myself, like my grandmother. Then I'd get married to a healthy, happy, *normal* husband and have children. Then the children would grow up, and I might even have grandchildren. And then what? Then I'd grow old. And then? . . . Then one day I'd have to die.

Death! That is the end, the aim, the direction in which we all go. But why? Why all this trouble? Why should I practise at my piano and become a great artist? Does it really make any difference, whether these bones, covered with skin, ever glide over the keys with great proficiency? If human beings have to die anyway some day, does it matter what they have made out of their lives? Whether they have been famous and brilliant or unknown and unrecognized, whether they have been honest or dishonest? Why struggle, toil, bear children, suffer and be happy, joyful and sorrowful, when the ultimate end is death and destruction? It would surely be much easier to die right away!

This thought was so terrible, so unbearable, that the world around me became dark and void. I leaned against a tree and gazed down into the valley, upon the town, the endless houses with the many human beings who lived in them. From up here they looked like tiny ants. All those beings lived, fought, struggled for love and money, all of them had their problems, their cross to bear, they took everything so desperately seriously ... But why? Why, when life is but a fleeting moment, when death is waiting at the end, solving all problems, terminating all suffering and all joy? What are we running after? What do we attain? *Death!* Whether we are happy or unhappy, a king or a beggar, the end for all of us is *death!*

Panic gripped me. No! I won't go through with it! I cannot learn, love and live with this thought. Everything is senseless! I would rather commit suicide right now *so that I won't have to die at the end of my life!*

A devilish, sarcastic voice laughed in my ear: 'Ha ha ha! That's really like you to be so stupid! You want to kill yourself, so you won't have to die? Do you really think you can escape death? You are *here*, here on earth in a body. You cannot just flee from here without *death!* If you kill yourself, the end, from which you wished to save yourself only a moment ago, will be imminent. Instantaneous death! Not just "some day" far away, but right here and now! Do you understand? As long as you are *here*, in your body, you cannot get away unless you die! You are a prisoner! Do you understand? A prisoner! Only through the portals of death can you be released from your body, you cannot escape death ... you cannot escape ... Ha ha ha!'

I tried to gather my scattered thoughts. Yes, it was true, I was in a trap and suicide would not help matters. It would only take me right into what I was anxious to avoid. So now what? In any case I could take momentary comfort in the fact that I was still very young, and that death was still probably far away. I was healthy. All my ancestors had reached a great age. These facts gave me new courage. By the time I get old, I thought, a lot can still happen. The scientists, who constantly discover new things about life, will some day certainly discover *the secret of immortality*. I clung to this thought, and gained the incentive and the energy to go on living, working and wishing.

I was absolutely right! Immortality was discovered, only I did not know at the time, that this 'discovering of immortality' was really something I would have to do for *myself* to find out that *death* does not exist, and that all human beings—myself included—are and always will be immortal! For everyone must discover immortality in himself and for himself. No other person can pass this truth on to him. If somebody does not believe a truth, even a perfectly obvious fact, it simply does not exist for him no matter how many other people have discovered it already. Every human being must recognize the fact that death is nothing but life itself and that man not only does not *have to die*, but is not even *able* to die! It is absolutely impossible!

At that time, I knew nothing of all this; to me, death was a big, black wall against which I had cracked my head with considerable force.

Nevertheless, I was young, and so I calmed down as well as I could. I postponed the whole thing and decided, as far as humanly possible, not to think about the problem of death. Such thoughts would only weaken me, and I preferred to make plans for the future.

In normal circumstances, I was used to doing everything on my own and upon my own initiative. My father had never concerned himself with the personal affairs of his children. His profession occupied him to such an extent, that he had never had time to interest himself in what went on in his family. We usually only met at the family table where I never mentioned the scenes which occurred between myself and my fiancé. My mother loved me, as she loved all her children, but she only began to understand me much later on, when we said good-bye to each other for good. At that time, she wanted me to become as efficient a housewife and mother as she herself was. I myself regarded this as the central aim of my life, but the way in which I wanted to achieve it was quite different from the one she envisaged. The path of my life could be only my own, and I could not accept the advice she gave me in respect to my future. Mother wanted me to prepare myself for the role of the gentle little mother, whereas I, with every drop of my blood, sought fulfilment in music and art. I was therefore left completely to my own devices and gradually got used to thinking and acting independently as far as this was possible in the family circle. I therefore tried to picture a future completely on my own, without asking anyone for advice. I decided to continue my studies at the music academy, and pass the final examinations so as to get a diploma. Father often said to us: 'Don't be blind to the vagaries of fate just because everything is going well at present. Earthly riches can be destroyed. Whatever knowledge you acquire is yours to keep and cannot be taken away from you. Learn as much as you can, and at least get a diploma of some sort. If things go well, you can leave it in a drawer, but if you run into hard times, you can earn your living with it!'

Oh my father, you wonderful, unselfish, wise man. This piece of advice was the greatest treasure among all those you ever passed on to me. At that time, none of us could imagine how we could ever get into any difficulties and believed in secret that you were just talking like a strict pedagogue. How often I remembered this advice during the war when everything we owned was destroyed and I was stranded with a gravely wounded, disabled husband. We were saved by what I had learnt, by what I carried *in* me, what I *knew*, for all our outward possessions were lost. As I stood there that day on the mountain, a young, inexperienced girl, thinking about my future, I had no idea what fate held in store for me. But I felt I had to follow your advice.

And so, when I got back home that summer and started a fresh page of my life, the most important thing was to concentrate all my energy on acquiring a piano teacher's diploma. Everything else I left in the hands of destiny.

— II —

FIRST VISIONS OF THE FUTURE

DURING THE six years I was engaged something happened that was so surprising and so impressive it had an effect on the direction all my later life was to take. Through it my attention was guided towards a world lying hidden deep within the human being: the unknown, unconscious world of the human self.

I was fifteen years old when I discovered that I was sometimes able to see the future in dreams, very precisely, as if what I was seeing were a faithful reproduction of reality. What occurred then happened again later at various times and still happens today always in the same manner: at first my dream runs through all kinds of chaotic and irrelevant pictures. Then suddenly, as if a curtain were pushed to one side, I see colourful, plastic and logically connected pictures, with absolute clarity just as in real life.

In that first clear dream of the future I saw, in my parents' bathroom, a young man holding a newborn baby. The baby was all blue, as if suffocated, and the young man was trying to get it to breathe. A woman assistant stood beside him, ready to help. The child was not breathing. The doctor held it first under ice-cold water then under hot water. Then he held it head downward and swung it to and fro. When it finally let out a cry, all of us round about heaved a sigh of relief. From where he stood in the doorway father now ran to mother's room, fell down on his knees beside her bed, laid his head on the edge of the bed near mother and sobbed as I had never seen this strong man sob before in all my life. Mother was very pale, but she smiled tenderly and stroked father's black hair. Father calmed down after a while, got up and went into the next room where Aunt Raphaela and her daughter were waiting to be able to visit mother. Curiously enough, in my dream I was able to look into all rooms simultaneously, which of course would have been impossible in reality. Another thing that struck me was that the young man, after turning the baby over to his assistant, came out of the bathroom, walking with a peculiar gliding gait. I also noticed his pretty, curly, blond hair, and very distinctly I heard him say, 'Mother and child are out of danger but need absolute quiet. If anybody comes to visit them, I cannot take the responsibility for any infection that may occur during this present condition of weakness.'

'Of course, doctor,' answered Aunt Raphaela, and I saw how she very sensibly took her leave and went away with her daughter. Then the picture blacked out, and I awoke.

The next morning I ran to mother and told her my dream. Mother laughed and said, 'Please don't dream things like that, I have enough children! And what is Aunt Raphaela doing in this dream? She doesn't even live here. And who is the handsome young man with the gliding gait and the curly blond hair? Your dreaming like this about good-looking young men seems very suspicious to me.'

'I don't know who he is, Mother, but I saw him just that way in my dream.'

Later, at lunch time, we all discussed my strange dream for a while, but by the next day nobody gave it another thought.

Half a year later mother felt very ill. She could not eat and the doctors suspected she might have a duodenal ulcer. They x-rayed her and made other examinations. The result...no exact diagnosis. Our doctor advised mother to see a famous gynaecologist. After his examination, the old professor said, 'Congratulations! The end of this great sickness will be a baptism.' He laughed gently.

Mother came home in desperation. She was already thirty-nine years old. Little by little she calmed down, however, and six months later, exactly a year after my dream, when no one could have believed that we would have another addition to the family, the little baby arrived. The old professor recommended a young doctor who had already gained a great reputation for his skill. When the baby was born, it seemed to be dead of suffocation. It was twenty long minutes before it took its first breath. Father was so exhausted from the protracted worry that, when the danger was over, he sank to his knees beside mother's bed and, strong man that he was, sobbed like a baby. Aunt Raphaela and her daughter were visiting us briefly en route to Italy. They spent two days with us, and the child was born just as they were ready to go on. They waited in the next room, and when father came in to say that all was safely over, Aunt Raphaela asked whether she might see mother and child before her departure. Then the young doctor came into the room. He had curly blond hair and a peculiar gliding gait! He then said exactly, word for word what I had heard him say in my vision. Indeed, everything happened exactly as I had *already experienced it*! It was as if I had seen part of a motion picture a long time before the other events in the film and completely separate from them.

From then on I often saw future events, as dream pictures, with precise details. At first this experience always came to me in dreams. Every time it was as if a curtain were being shoved to one side. Later, however, I was able to enter this state intentionally, by an act of will, without being asleep. But this only came much later.

My new baby sister was almost like a granddaughter in the family. Grete was then nineteen, I sixteen, and my brother nine years old. She was everybody's little darling. But the attention she received pushed us two older children pretty far into the background, and we often found ourselves alone. For several years, only our governess accompanied us when we went skating and to concerts and parties. Mother was just as busy with our new little sister as she had been nine years before when my brother was born. No wonder that they had no time to bother about my affairs, even when they noticed I was having disputes with my fiancé. I had to fight my battle alone, without help.

— 12 —

THE PAST AWAKENS

WHEN I left Aunt Raphaela's and returned home following the breaking off of my engagement, summer had come. I was nineteen years old and wanted to enjoy my freedom. At last I could see other young people without having to risk a terrible scene from my jealous fiancé. On my return, I went straight to the local tennis-courts. On the first day, I met a very attractive, trim-looking young man. His bearing and manner were most charming. He had a good-looking head on his shoulders, a well-built, slim, muscular body and always turned up in faultless white tennis-slacks and jersey. I took to him from the first moment, and he seemed to like me too. On our third day, one of our team-mates rather unhappily cracked her racket over the head of our ballboy. He began to cry bitterly. The sympathetic young man threw his racket away, ran up to the little boy, took him on to his lap, and started to comfort him. He did not seem to mind the boy's dirtying his immaculate tennis-clothes at all. He stroked his head, dried his tears, and gave him some money. In a matter of moments the boy started to smile through his tears and ran off to the counter to buy some sweets.

My heart went out to him. Are there really such young men, I thought, who have a little compassion? I began to love him . . .

In the following winter, I became engaged to him. We loved one another deeply and passionately, and I could hardly wait for the moment when I was to become his wife with body and soul, with every part of my being.

My father wanted me to finish my studies before my marriage, and I still had one year left to go at the music academy. So we had to wait, and I continued to practise daily for four or five hours, learn the laws of harmony, play chamber music, and do everything I could towards passing the exams. My fiancé spent every evening at our house.

One evening, when he had left, I went to bed and fell fast asleep. I slept, and, as usual, I dreamt of many things in a chaotic and senseless manner. Suddenly, I began to hear a strange sound which repeated itself in a rhythmical way, a kind of snapping noise which became louder and louder, till I abruptly regained consciousness and awoke.

I open my eyes and notice that the rhythmical sound is coming from the whip of a slave-driver who is marching beside me and cracking his whip to keep all the slaves who are pulling me in step. I am reclining on something like a sledge on rails which glides along slowly. I realize that I am being taken away from the palace; a moment ago I heard the doors being closed.

I want to jump up, but find that I cannot. I am unable to move a muscle, because I am wrapped up tightly from my neck right down to my feet. I am lying there, as though hewn out of a piece of marble, my hands crossed over my chest, my legs stretched out side by side. From this position, I can only look straight ahead or gaze upwards. Looking in the direction of my feet, in the brilliant sunshine, I see the naked, perspiring backs of the men who are pulling me on and on in continuous movement. Above and beyond them, in the distance, a white stone building looms up, a black cavity seeming to mark an entrance. In the gleaming white light, the walls of the building stand out starkly against the dark blue sky. As the slaves continue forward, the building seems to approach, and the black cavity becomes larger and larger.

The sky above is so intensely blue it seems almost black. Two large birds circle slowly overhead—storks or cranes?

The stone building suddenly appears to be very near; the black cavity yawns wide . . . yes . . . it really is an opening. Now I recognize it. We are in the City of the Dead! This is a *tomb*! We arrive, the slaves enter and disappear into the darkness. Now the cavity engulfs me . . . and suddenly the world around me becomes black after the blinding sunshine outside. Everything is gone . . . I am in complete darkness! A terrible fear grips me, and silently I search for an answer to the question, 'How long—how long must I stay in here, a prisoner?'

Clearly I hear a familiar voice, calmly and imperturbably telling me its inexorable will:

'Three thousand years . . .'

Terror grips me anew, and consciousness fades into oblivion . . .

*　　　*　　　*

Somebody was shaking me roughly. I looked up and saw the eyes of my sister. She gripped me and stared at me in sheer fright.

'For goodness' sake,' she said, 'what on earth is wrong with you? You sit here with a vacant look in your eyes and groan terribly, as though you were going to die. Are you feeling ill? Shall I call mother?'

I felt I wanted to answer, but I could not utter a single sound. The terrible experience I had just been through paralysed every part of my body. I groaned and waved my hand to reassure her that all was well. Then I stretched out again and tried to think, but even that was impossible. I lay there, still panic-stricken, and some minutes went by before my heart started to beat normally again, before I began to calm down and realize who I was and where I was. My sister stayed near me for a little while; then noticing that I had regained my senses, she repeated her questions, 'Can I do anything for you?'

At last I managed to croak: 'No thank you, I'm all right.'

*　　　*　　　*

Next day, I tried to collect my scattered thoughts and review the position. What had I seen? What had I experienced during the night? It looked like a vision of the future, but it could hardly be my own future. *In my visions of the future, I always remain the same person, but in this vision, I was someone completely different!* I gazed at myself in the mirror for a long time and tried to understand how it was possible that one human being can be two persons at the same time ? For I am here, this I can see in the mirror, *yet there exists another picture of me, one I saw in another mirror, an enormous silver mirror, at the time when I was the other person!*

I am the being, who is here, yet simultaneously I am the other being, *who was buried in a tomb.* In only a few minutes, I had the experience of being someone who knows exactly who he is, where he belongs, in fact who lives his life consciously, as does everybody, whether he reflects upon it or not. Suddenly I grasped the memories of a life, a home, and realized, that, as a child, I had searched for this home where I really belonged, and that I knew the 'Great One', my father and husband, to be my 'real father'. As the years had passed, I had become accustomed to my present position . . . to accepting the fact that my present father and mother were my true parents. Somehow, however, the strange feeling had never left me, and now I felt it very strongly. Yet it was queer that many things which, when I had experienced them in the past, had seemed quite normal, now struck me as being very abnormal. The two concepts contrasted strongly with each other. To take an example, I found it completely correct, in fact I was honoured to be the daughter and the wife of my father, the Pharaoh. Yet now, when I became conscious of the fact, I felt deeply shocked, for the moral standards of my time were quite different. Yet at the time of my ancient existence, this was looked upon as being quite normal, for if the wife of a Pharaoh died, and he had no sisters, the accepted procedure was to make his own daughter his wife. He could never have placed a woman, who did not belong to the family, over his own daughter, who was born in the family of a Pharaoh. And who else but his daughter could have sat beside him as his queen and regal wife, if not the next female member of the family in line of descent ? It would have been immoral to introduce a woman of lower heritage into the family. I remembered many things, especially the temple where I often went, yet many things remained blurred, such as the reason why I was so rigorously bound down in my coffin. Why was I taken to a tomb ? And whom did that voice I remembered so well belong to ?. Whom ? A barrier blocked this part of my past, and if I tried to recall anything, something like an electric shock pushed me back. I could not think in reverse!

As we were sitting at the family table next morning, I said to my father: 'Father, in school we learnt that the pyramids were the burial-places of the ancient kings. That's not true! Not all the pyramids were graves, some were used for quite different purposes. The dead were buried outside the city in a special burial city. They were carried out of the town in coffins very similar to sledges, where they were then immured in large buildings. The tombs were closed with stone doors.'

My father gave me an astonished look and said: 'How on earth can you know that, when all the scientists agree that the pyramids were the tombs of the Pharaohs, yet never mention a City of the Dead.'

'I'm quite sure, Father, that this is the way it is,' I said, knowing what I had seen to be true.

'Well, tell us how you know,' he said, and everybody gazed at me expectantly.

'I know it and yet I cannot explain it,' I said, and told them of my vision. My father listened attentively and noticed that even then I shivered with fright when I recalled my experiences. Seeing that I was obviously telling something I had taken part in, he replied 'In *Hamlet*, Shakespeare says: "There are more things in heaven and earth, Horatio, than are dreamt of in your philosophy." Nowadays people talk about inherited memories, a thing I do not believe in. I'd like to know how the history of a whole family, containing innumerable ancestors, can be contained in one minute living cell? Scientists evolve great theories which change every twenty years. I don't advise you to worry about these things, and don't think about your dream—or your vision—whatever you want to call it. It would simply disturb your mental balance. Maybe you read something about the subject in some paper?'

'No Father, I've never yet read or heard anything about Egypt except what they taught us in school. It never interested me. Yet in school, I learnt things which were completely different from my experiences in my vision. I cannot explain what this vision should mean, for I'm absolutely certain that the facts I witnessed were correct in detail. I'm also certain that the person I was in my dream existed, yet I cannot explain how I can be this person in the present. Who was the other person? I don't understand. Can it be possible, that human beings live more than once?'

'May I have some fruit?' my father said, turning to my mother. The fruit was brought to the table, and the family talked about other matters.

When I went to bed that night, I wondered whether the dream would repeat itself. But it didn't. I waited for many days, I even tried to dream myself back into this strange world. But all to no avail, the dream didn't return.

As time passed, I ceased thinking about it. My healthy attitude towards life drove me on with fresh vigour. I practised at the piano, painted pictures, learnt my lessons and spent each evening with my fiancé. And so the year went by.

─── 13 ───

SECOND ENCOUNTER WITH DEATH

AT LAST it was my wedding day.

Looking back now, it seems as if it must have been a dream. All decked out in a white dress with a train and wearing a lace veil, I stepped into our living-room, saw how splendid my fiancé looked in his best Sunday suit, and laid my hand on his arm. We were photographed, much to my annoyance, as the photographers made me nervous. Then we went out and down the steps and got into a carriage all decorated with flowers. We were followed by Grete and my cousin wearing pink silk dresses and accompanied by the two boy cousins with whom we had once formed our alliance of 'eternal friendship'. Both of them were now gallant young officers.

Then came my brother, with his sad and serious face. He was fourteen, and my little sister, pretty as a doll, was four. She looked completely self-assured and quite superior among all the adults. Then came a whole crowd of relatives including beautiful Aunt Raphaela, dressed like a queen, then my fiancé's mother, and finally my own mother, radiantly young and beautiful, accompanied by father, who in his top hat and tails, was truly a splendid sight, enough to make any woman's heart beat faster. When he saw I was amused at his top hat, he gave me a roguish look which clearly meant he considered all these formalities just as ridiculous as I did. If only he knew, I thought, how much I'm suffering in these arm-length gloves! I would have just loved to rip them off, they were such an obstacle to free movement. As I held my bouquet in my hands and stood beside my fiancé with a flower in his button hole, it seemed to me that we were two sacrificial animals, gaily adorned with flowers, forced by the tyranny of almighty 'custom' to go through with all this fancy nonsense.

It would have suited me best if I had been able to run away so that the crowd of old aunts, uncles, friends and strange spectators could not look at us like two dolls in an exhibition. I knew that they were all thinking of the one thing I regarded as the supreme sacrament, the fulfilment of love. But with what a difference of viewpoint! And I knew that some of the men present were whispering stupid jokes to each other. But I could not escape, and soon the long line of cars was under way towards the church. A few moments later, we were inside, standing before the altar. I tried to appear agitated and sentimental, but without success. I felt just as matter of fact as ever. As patiently as I could, I listened to the wise and beautiful things our friend and family pastor was saying.

He looked at me and I could see in his eyes that he was thinking how I had asked him not to make a long speech at our wedding, as otherwise I would be forced to yawn big and loud out of utter boredom. At the time mother was incensed about my boundless impertinence, but at least I succeeded in prevailing on the pastor to give a wise but short talk. Thank goodness! A long speech at a wedding ceremony has never yet made a happy marriage! Soon the crowd of friends and relatives were swarming about us, kissing us, and embracing us for three-quarters of an hour, with the old uncles taking full advantage of the opportunity to hug and kiss the young bride from every side while I suffered their attentions with silent disgust. Finally all of this was over too, and we only had to bear up through the wedding banquet. At last the relatives and friends took leave, and I changed my clothes to begin my honeymoon trip with my 'husband'.

In becoming the wife of my beloved after this long period of waiting, I experienced extreme happiness as I expected I would. I had attained my goal; I had become his wife before God and humanity. Between us there were no longer any 'forbidden' signs. I loved him passionately, with my entire being, and he loved me in just the same way. I experienced the highest fulfilment of love, in body and soul.

And then everything collapsed around me.

I dashed my head even more violently against the black wall I had struck once before: for the second time in my life I encountered death. This time the meeting was much more serious.

As long as I was waiting for happiness, there was a fixed point in my future towards which I was moving. I had something I was waiting and working for. But when the expected event materialized, the future suddenly became empty. I fell into a vacuum, for I did not know what I still had to wait for. What was there in the future for me to look forward to? I had achieved everything. Whatever else might come could only serve to fill out the remaining time. *The remaining time*, remaining time? Till when? And the answer was: *until death!*

I was forced to realize that no matter what else I might do or attain in this life, or whatever my destiny might bring me, I and all other people with me were moving only in one direction—towards death!—without the slightest possibility of being able to move in any other. Nobody can know in advance how long it will take him to get there, but sooner or later we all fall into this void.

I was obliged to realize that even our love could not last forever, for the simple reason that sooner or later one of us would have to die. Then happiness would be over. In the presence of my husband when I looked into his bright, loving eyes, I felt as if a cold hand were strangling me, and deep down within me I heard the question: 'How long will you be able to see these beautiful eyes? What will the future bring? Even though you may be ever so happy and supposing that you will live a long life with him, even an exceptionally long one, sooner or later the end will be the same, namely, that he will either have to close your eyes or you will have to close his! Then you will lose each other and have to say good-bye. Time passes with amazing rapidity, and it won't matter much whether the end comes after a short time or a long time. The greatest happiness, the most beautiful love—everything—must some day come to an end, and you will lose each other and everything that has been beautiful and good . . .'

I looked into my husband's loving eyes but heard *this* voice. I knew that no matter how much I might try not to hear it, I would still hear it anyway, I would not be able to silence it, *because it was right, it was speaking the truth*!

I have often noticed that people act as if everything were permanent. They simply do not think of the future. Most of them go through life as if they would never be obliged to die and as if their loved ones were not mortal beings. They refuse to realize that our being together here on earth is only a gift of short duration as it will some day *have to end*! Sooner or later one or the other dies, and then everything is over. People refuse to think about it, but whether they think about it or not, *it is so*! No one can deny it. But what is the sense of being happy if destiny is, inexorably, going to take this gift away from us some day? What's the good of being happy if we are obliged to be even unhappier later? We struggle for happiness, and when we have attained it we know in advance that we *must* lose it. The greater the happiness, the greater the loss. In the days when I was not yet so happy, I was actually much happier *because I did not yet have the possibility of losing my happiness*! So it becomes evident that only the person who was never happy is really and permanently happy! What a terrible contradiction! And why is that so? Because everything lasts only for a time, because nothing is permanent, because everything dies, everything passes away, everything must pass away!

Oh time! Oh mortality! How long will I have to continue to suffer as a prisoner in your chains? How often will I have to bang my head against your black impenetrable wall? You have poisoned every happy moment of my life, because I always had to realize, in the very moment I had something, it was already lost, for it had to come to an end.

And now I am grateful to you, *oh mortality*! Because you never, even for a moment, allowed me to enjoy passing, temporal happiness, this constant suffering led me to find the *unending, infinite eternity*, the eternal, divine *being* itself!

In those days, to be sure, I had not the faintest inkling of all this. I did not know that this condition in which a person feels as if he were in a desert, crying from the depths of his soul for help, is the forerunner of salvation. Just as the Bible tells us, 'I am the voice of one crying in the wilderness. I make straight the path of the Lord. I baptize you with water; but after me there will come one stronger than I, the latchet of whose shoes I am not worthy to stoop down and unloose; He shall baptize you with the Holy Spirit and with fire.'

During that period of my life I was still in the desert, crying soundlessly for help, and shedding invisible tears. I was being baptized by water—with tears—and did not know that the time was soon at hand when I would get acquainted with eternal *being*. For after this condition there comes He who says of Himself, '*I* am the resurrection and the life; whosoever believeth on *me*, even though he die, yet shall he live'—and who baptizes with the Holy Spirit and with fire . . .

But he was not yet there, and I was still experiencing the John the Baptist condition; I was crying in the wilderness for help, for I was all alone with my desperation, as if in a desert. I did not want to tell my husband anything about the desperate state of mind I was in. He was completely happy and would not have been able to understand me. If he had no such ideas and was *still dreaming the dream of mortal people*, why should I awaken him and make him unhappy? I saw no solution at all for my problem, as no one could have said that I was wrong. At best he would have had to admit that everything is destined to pass away and the one and only consolation is not to think about it. For my part, however, I was not at all satisfied at the idea of overlooking reality . . . and even less satisfied by the fairy tales of religion about 'the other side' and the 'other world'. These are figments of the imagination intended to be a sedative to people. Whoever can believe them is happy, but a thinking person insists on having proof. Within myself I constantly bore a heavy spiritual burden without being able to shake it off. Sooner or later, however, a constant burden on the soul is bound to affect the body . . .

— 14 —

DARKNESS

IN BUILD and figure I resembled my father strongly. I was as tall as he was, my hair, though not as black as his, was nevertheless dark brown, and my skin was pale like his and not reddish like my mother's. Only my eyes were dark blue instead of black.

After my marriage, I became paler and slimmer than ever. I could never get used to the idea of the passing of time and the transitory aspect of human existence. As a consequence, I could never feel completely free and happy. This constant pressure on my soul was very bad for my well-being.

One evening I lay down with no bodily affliction whatsoever. When I opened my eyes in the morning, I involuntarily glanced at the ceiling. To my utter astonishment I saw a thick black line that had never been there before. Completely taken aback, I sat up suddenly to see what this queer black line was. As I did so, the line seemed to jump up and sink back slowly again.

My heart nearly stood still. I realized that the black line I saw lay in my eyes and not on the ceiling. I opened and closed my eyes, then closed one and afterwards the other, discovering that I could only see this line with my right eye.

I remembered hearing about an affliction of the eyes called *mouches volantes*. One is said to see little black dots dancing around, as though a lot of flies were buzzing around the room. As I heard it, these nervous illnesses are not particularly dangerous. I tried to find out whether I could see these *mouches volantes*. I looked up, I looked down—the black line followed the laws of gravity. It seemed to me as though a thick black thread were tied to some spot above my head. The other end seemed to hang down and moved along following the movement of my eye. It certainly was no nervous delusion, it was real, it was there!

From that moment on, a painful journey began, a journey which anybody will know who has been afflicted with a disease not yet fathomed by the resources of science.

I travelled from one famous professor to another, only to be told that my eye could not be healed, because the symptoms were not those of an organic illness. One of the professors said to me: 'It isn't an illness at all, therefore it can't be cured. It's a condition occurring in old age which very rarely occurs in somebody so young. It's like getting white hair at a very young age through constant strain. How could you cure that? It can stop if the person is relieved of the strain. But to cure it is impossible. You can only cure illnesses; science knows of no remedies for such complaints of the eye as you have. In the case of old people, such an affliction is not dangerous, for it develops very slowly. Nobody knows what happens in the case of young people. From an organic point of view, your eyes are completely healthy, only extremely sensitive. All our tests have shown that your eyesight is powerful beyond belief, eyes as strong as yours are very rare. Your perceptive powers are equally great. Your susceptivity to light is so strong that you can see how many fingers I am holding up and can read very small print in practically complete darkness. Very occasionally, sailors who can recognize objects at a great distance have similar eyesight. They have the advantage of living in very healthy sea air and are not under any constant nervous tension. Furthermore, they have enough resistance to uphold a balance of susceptivity. But you, my dear woman, live in a great city and are not very resistant, as you are abnormally thin. Tell me, do you not suffer under continuous mental strain?'

'No, Professor,' I said, 'I'm very happy.'

How could I have explained to him that I suffered from fear of mere mortality? How could I have told him that I was fighting against time which moves unflinchingly and transforms all beings, all happiness, into destruction and death?

And even if I had told him, how could he have helped me? Instead, I asked him something else: 'Can you tell me whether this symptom will occur in the other eye as well?'

'How can I tell? I hope that the injections I am prescribing will help you and will clear away the exudation. I also hope that the other eye won't be affected. But I can't look into the future and even less guarantee anything. My advice to you is to take good care of yourself and eat heartily to build up your resistance. Wear sunglasses in bright sunshine to protect your eyes, rest a lot, and let's hope that things will turn out all right again.'

That was enough. I went to my parents together with my husband, feeling as though somebody else had been through all this instead of myself. I noticed how this somebody answered the questions my parents asked, and I watched this somebody eat dinner; everything had become so changed, so different. My family was very upset, but tried not to show this to me and made a big effort to seem happy and gay. My mother tried to console me: 'Rest assured, everything will turn out all right again. Nobody in our family has ever had any trouble with his eyes. Your eye will soon be normal again. *Don't think about it!*'

Oh, how often have I heard those words from friends who loved me and who tried to help or console me! 'Don't think about it!' How can I possibly help thinking about something which keeps on dancing about in front of my eyes? How can I forget the black thread which hangs down in front of me wherever I look? When I glanced at somebody, the black thread seemed to stick on his nose or his brow or sink down slowly to his mouth. Later on when the black lines increased, I saw everything through a dirty, jagged web. How could I not think about it?

In the first days of my affliction, I felt as though an immense rock had hit my head and completely flattened me. I could not believe it: *my* eyes in great danger? It must be a bad dream, which will soon pass when I wake up. Then I will be relieved of this terrible nightmare . . . and free again.

But I was never freed of this nightmare. I sat in front of my mirror and looked at myself. A childlike face with large dark blue eyes looked back at me. These eyes were supposed to show signs of old age? But I'm young, I've only just started off in life! I can't be old yet! When I was up on that mountain and encountered death for the first time, I knew that everything was of purely transitory value. Yet does time pass so quickly, so unexpectedly? At the time, I calmed myself, knowing that death was a long way away. Should death be coming to me so soon? Or can it be that certain parts of the body grow older sooner than others, that a delicate mechanism like the human eye perishes sooner than other organisms?—and that the whole body might live longer than the eyes? Blind? —terrible!—terrible!

No! I could not stand that! I wanted to run away . . . to flee . . . but where? My stigma, the black line in my right eye, accompanied me wherever I went. I could not get rid of it.

I fell into a state of dejection only those who have experienced similar misfortunes can understand. How my heart bled for the blind people I saw on the streets, how I felt for them! I could not forget my despair for one minute, not for one single instant. The dark blotches fluttered up and down in front of my eyes and constantly changed their appearance. I never ceased watching them. I got into the habit of carefully scrutinizing my eyes when I woke up in the morning. Has it become worse?—Can I still read small print with my right eye?—And if not—if I had to admit with indescribable terror that my condition had worsened overnight, the blood used to rush to my head, and with my heart pounding I continued to examine myself to see how much worse it had become.

Oh Beethoven! In these days I learnt to understand your despair when you lost your hearing! You knew the frame of mind, the panic, which comes when one is overwhelmed by the feeling of not being able to stand it any more, of wanting to flee, to escape from terrible suffering. Yes, but where? My ill-luck will always be with me; I cannot get rid of it, I am stricken forever!

My despair over the evanescence of life was not enough, I now carried something like an eternal 'memento' around with me to remind me of decay and death. I sometimes felt that those black lines would drive me mad!

Never again could I really enjoy myself. My husband did everything to make me forget the condition of my eyes. But whatever he did, however much he pampered me with presents—I could never be happy. Everywhere I looked I saw corruption and death, for I always saw black lines. As the Carthusian monks, who are forced to regard the two letters 'M' 'M' in the palms of their hands as a reminder of the words *Memento Mori*, so did the black lines in front of my eyes constantly remind me of blindness and death.

If my husband took me to a beautiful spot in the country, I used to think·

'How long will I still be able to see the sunshine, the mountains, the fields, the sky, in fact, the treasures of nature?' If I saw a wonderful performance at the Opera, I thought: 'How long can I still delight in the delicate movements of graceful ballet-dancers?' Deepest despair, brought forth by the cruelty of reality, had taken hold of me, for my left eye was, if only very slowly, yet definitely beginning to be affected as well. I was therefore well on my way to becoming blind. I could not even cry properly; I had never cried much, for I regarded crying as a senseless means of expression, a form of self-pity which I considered myself to be unworthy of. Now crying was strictly forbidden, for it would have harmed my eyes very much. I bore my despair without any exterior sign, and I never talked about it, for I saw that if I were constantly to talk about my affliction, my friends and acquaintances would suffer as much as I; and consequently, as normal human beings usually try to rid themselves of everything which seems unpleasant, they would drift away from me. I did not want to become disagreeable and boring in my own troubles. On the contrary, I was always gay and humorous, like a clown who hides his deepest sorrows under a painted mask. Thus did I bear my misery in silent suffering.

This blow also destroyed my artistic ambitions. Besides playing the piano, I had made great progress in drawing and painting and my teachers expected a lot in the future. Painting and drawing had always given me much pleasure. This too now came to an end. When I tried to paint, I saw lots of little black blobs on the canvas. This made me very nervous, and I had to control myself so as not to throw my brush away in anger. I lost my energy and my will to paint. The thought of gaining a reputation and becoming famous only to have to give everything up because of blindness disturbed me profoundly. No! I preferred to give up my artistic career and to continue playing the piano, for I could play blind as well.

I practised with my eyes closed. I walked around the room blindfolded and tried to find various objects. I tried to dress and comb my hair with my eyes closed, so as to be prepared when complete darkness came. I also did this because closing my eyes was the only way of escaping from those aggravating black lines which kept on dancing in front of my eyes. It was my only hope . . .

The salt injections were an equally trying ordeal. Human reflexes are such that the eye closes immediately in the face of possible danger. The eyelids shut instinctively when an object approaches the eye. I had to conquer those reflexes and control myself. I had to keep my eye open without movement and *watch*— for if the eye is open, one is obliged to watch, whether one likes or not—how the doctor pricked my eye with the needle. I had to go through this procedure many times. I did not know at the time that what I was learning, namely *to control the natural instincts*, was in fact *one of the most advanced Yoga exercises* which eventually brings about complete control over all bodily functions. I was forced to do so by fate, and so gained a very powerful grip on my nerves by pure chance. Yet when the doctor saw me to the door after my first injection, I felt very weak and had to pull myself together so as not to stumble and fall. The smile I tried to give him did not come very easily; I felt as if the muscles around my mouth had rusted. And for all my troubles, the injections did not help at all.

I stopped going to professors and became more and more pessimistic. The answer was always the same. 'It's no organic illness; your eyes are completely healthy. It's the lens which is filming over.' From day to day my eyesight became worse and worse. What difference does it make if one goes blind with healthy or with diseased eyes ?—I had to accept the seemingly inevitable. I might have given in. But I could not! How can somebody give up and accept blindness as a normal state of affairs ? Immutability and I were fighting against each other. There was no question of my losing. I could not give in, so I had to be destroyed . . .

The night the black line appeared for the first time, *I myself* was slain. I did not notice it straight away. This amusing, vain, impertinent and sensual little being which wanted to be a famous and celebrated artist and a beautiful woman was destroyed. My hidden philosophy of life, which had been born up on the mountain following my first encounter with death, now took hold of me forcibly. Now I could not—and did not even want to—let the voice, which repeatedly reminded me of the past, go by unheeded . . . And as I started to listen to this voice very attentively instead of turning away from it, I began slowly to recognize a familiar and dearly beloved voice: *HIS* voice . . .

── 15 ──

TURNING POINT

ONE AFTERNOON, I came home from town. The houses in our row stood in well-kept gardens, the sun was shining brightly, flowers were blooming everywhere, birds were singing joyously, and I recalled the words of Don Carlos: 'O, my queen, in spite of everything life is so beautiful!'

'Yes,' I felt like adding, 'if only my eyes were to retain their power of sight!' Suddenly I heard the voice in me, asking me quite distinctly: 'Are you blind already? Can't you see the world, the sky, the trees and the flowers any more?'

'I can,' I answered, looking around me, 'everything is still quite clear,' and I remembered what my doctor had said to me the last time I visited him to check up on my eyesight: 'The right eye has become pretty dim and hazy, but you still perceive more with the other eye than most average human beings with both eyes.'

'Well, if your eyesight is still as good as that, why do you behave so desperately, as though you had already gone blind? Why give up hope? Let us assume that you were to go blind in the second half of your life. If you start giving up hope now, while you can still see quite adequately, your *whole* life will be blighted by your desperation and your affliction! Quite apart from the fact that you really don't know whether you are going blind or not. Maybe you will die before you go completely blind; in this case, you will have spent weeks, months and years of useless worry, while all the time your eyesight was clear and normal apart from a few annoying black blobs. What a waste of time to worry about events which have not yet occurred! The future? Do you really know what the future is? Events *which have not yet come to pass!* Why mar your pleasure in life with things which do not exist? Your present circumstances are not too bad. Enjoy life, your chances of recovery will be much better so. Your depressions will only accelerate the destructive process in your eyes. Live in the present, and remember: *as soon as your spiritual blindness ceases, your corporeal eyes will regain their functions.*

Oh, how true were the words of this sacred voice! In the moments of deepest despair, I felt that the black spots in my eyes showed up my *interior* darkness, my *spiritual* blindness. But how on earth is one to cure spiritual blindness? For this was the hub of my problems, the fact that I felt completely blind in the face of the secrets of life and death. I was enclosed in darkness, for I sensed death everywhere and could not grasp the meaning of life. I desired to become 'seeing', it was my greatest wish—but how?

75

And the voice replied: 'Seek and ye shall find; knock and it shall be opened unto you!'

I did not understand those words at the time, but I wanted to obey them. I tried breathing deeply and calmly, and *concentrating on the present*. It was very hard—the black spots kept dancing in front of my eyes and reminding me of my misery—but I tried again and again and reached the point where I felt happy and content again; indeed, I felt I had to be happy, for my eyes would benefit from my state of mind. I wanted to help myself. I had to be happy, I had to enjoy myself! I began to think about future occupations which would afford me constant pleasure. My husband was very much engrossed in his job —he was a construction engineer—and I rarely saw him except at meals. A thought flashed through my mind: a baby! How long have I wished for a baby! What greater joy could I expect? And I would not be alone all the time.

I opened my spirit to the anonymous being which was waiting somewhere to become *my* child. And the being heard my cry . . .

During my pregnancy, the discharges slowly disappeared from my eyes, and when my confinement came, I had completely forgotten that I had ever had any trouble at all. My memories of lying in the operating theatre of a sanatorium, and waking up after an anaesthetic, completely exhausted, seem like a long-forgotten dream. I find myself in a form of ecstasy, yet I hear a sound which flashes through me like lightning and brings me back to my senses. It is a cry . . . not like the cry of a new-born child but more like the roar of a lion! 'It's alive', the thought grips me and a great feeling of gratitude overwhelms me. I open my eyes. A face appears above me and I hear a voice saying: 'A boy, a beautiful, healthy boy'—I catch sight of a little round head and a fat, rosy body.

'Is that my child?' I ask myself as I gaze at it expectantly! I feel that only its body is *'my child'*, otherwise it is an independent being I know has come into being as *'our child'*.

Then for the first time in its life, the baby lies in a crib, swathed in human vestments, and gazes wide-eyed at the world.

My mother and my father have already arrived, waiting to welcome my child and myself after this terrible fight for life. I am at the end of my tether, my heart is hardly beating after my great loss of blood. But the child is alive!

After this strenuous experience, my convalescence was very slow. For a long time, I felt very weak, very susceptible to any form of light, the discharges reappeared and the vitreous humour of my right eye became opaque again. Thick clouds of a sort of fog covered my vision in this eye. Yet I never got around to bothering seriously about my eyesight. There was my child, I spent all my time in its presence, and when it smiled at me and embraced me with its podgy little arms, the weight and pressure of my worries seemed far away.

The years raced by. My little boy developed magnificently and was admired by everyone for his big blue eyes which radiated so much love and warmth. He was a very precocious child. When he was four, a scene of my own childhood was re-enacted. My child showed me a picture-book and asked me the meaning of certain letters. I explained them in detail. The child regarded the letters attentively and suddenly cried: 'Mother, that means "bull", doesn't it?'

I took it on to my lap and kissed it again and again. Then I explained all the other letters. It did not have to learn them. It seemed as if it only had to recall them.

We spent the summer together in our family villa near the lake. In fact, a whole series of wonderful summers! My brother and my younger sister invited lots of friends who sometimes stayed at our place for weeks on end. We played croquet, rowed and swam, and in the evenings we used to play chamber music or play games, or dance on the terrace. It was a healthy, happy life.

My eyes did not bother me very much during this time. After the birth of my child I spent some months at the seaside. The secret sources of energy of the sea completely renewed me. I returned home in excellent health and very much more able to stand light. I started drawing and painting again and even took up wood carving. This artistic occupation afforded me great pleasure.

On the surface everything seemed in order. Nevertheless I was not happy! I did not know why. An inner discontentment grew in me until I could not disregard it any more.

One night, after I had experienced once again the greatest fulfilment of earthly love and unity, instead of falling peacefully asleep, I sat on the side of my bed for a long time brooding over my problems in abject despair. I cried and I sobbed, and in the darkness of that night, I began to examine myself cruelly in order to find out why I was so unhappy and so discontented. I had everything necessary to make a human being happy, from where could my misery originate?

This question seemed to call forth the answer. From the depths of my subconscious, the reasons began to ascend and gain consciousness.

I was searching for a human being, *who was my other half, my complement.* Love is the revelation of a power which forces two complementary halves to unite. In fact, the subconscious will to unite is commonly known as 'love'. I had experienced this union, I had attained the supreme fulfilment of body and soul and was not happy, and became more and more unhappy after each occasion.

I sat there in the dark and questioned myself in despair: Why can't I be happy? I desired an answer and reflected intently. And then I realized that the *joy of union was not what I had expected!* I had searched for some sort of fulfilment subconsciously, and, *having found nothing else, I believed physical love to be this fulfilment.* Having experienced it, I had to admit that it was *not what I had expected.* After experiencing the supreme form of physical unity, I was compelled to see and realize I was looking for something else!

But what?

I was searching for fulfilment of an *eternal nature,* a *real* union which *remains!* I was searching for a union in which the identity of myself and that of my lover became one and the same thing. I desired to participate in his soul, his thoughts, *his whole being!* I wanted to become *him!*

But I did not desire what physical unity had brought me. This physical union is a desperate attempt to become one being—every fibre and muscle is strained to the highest pitch—and in the moment when both believe that they have achieved fulfilment, they fall apart . . . without ever attaining union.

In the darkness a picture of my childhood appeared in front of me: I remembered sitting at the family table and trying to bring together two little grease spots swimming on top of my bowl of soup. Yes! In exactly the same way as I had tried to unite the two grease spots, years ago, I now wanted to make one being out of our two souls. Out of the two selves I wanted to create a single one. But that is impossible! In love, each lover craves to come together with the other. Yet their craving is merely a physical desire, and they strain against each other in despair. Everybody can observe how two lovers press their hearts together in their fervent embrace; they seem to be compelled to unite their hearts, to be united *in their heart*. But they fail! Why? *Their bodies stand between them*. The resistance of the body prevents the union. How strange that I should desire to become one single being with my lover in body and that *the body itself* should bar my way. Does my body desire this union? Can the body desire anything which is impossible by reason of the very existence of the body? No! The body cannot carry within itself a wish which cannot be fulfilled by reason of its own presence. *Who* and *what* therefore desires this supreme union? It can only be the immaterial spirit, the self.

And why do I desire this union? Why do I want something which is impossible? I want it because I know that only through this complete concord, this supreme union, will I find satisfaction, and only in this state of mind will I achieve final happiness! This happiness I have been searching for since I began to live. But why do I search for something which is impossible to attain? I do it solely because I know, I feel certain, that somehow it is possible, and that somehow this possibility exists—only I don't know *how*. What impedes my progress towards my aim? The body! The body stands between us!—Therefore, this possibility might exist, *but only in a bodiless condition*. I long for this lost unison. I once knew it, somewhere and somehow, but I have lost it. Could it be possible that I lived in an immaterial state a long time ago, and that, *having been born into this body*, I *fell out of this spiritual harmony*? Is it possible that I once lived in a world of complete unison, a world without corporeal elements, where I lived in a bodiless condition?

Having got this far in the logical sequence of my thoughts, I began to feel very afraid: a bodiless state? In a world without corporeal elements? Therefore, in 'another world'? In the 'hereafter'? Could it be possible that this 'other world' *really exists*? A world, in which I had never believed and which I had always regarded as a necessary invention of a religious nature, used to enforce a moral standard of living among primitive people with promises of 'heaven' and warnings of 'hell'? It is my body alone which exists in our earthly world? And my self, which is *cognizant* of this impossible union of the flesh and which desires to *reinstitute* it, does it belong to 'eternity'? If that is so, all human beings originate in another world where this unison is reality, and have *fallen* out of it into this world—into the material body and an earthly world? . . . Yet the craving for our former happiness lies in us, in our soul, which belongs to this 'other world'. And again and again we err by trying to attain this happiness, this unity *in our body and with the aid of our inherent bodily sexuality*. Yet it is the body which itself impedes our success. Oh, now I realize what is meant by the 'fall from paradise'!

Therefore I can only reach the happiness I desire in the other world—in paradise. As I cannot force this other world into my own material world, I will strive to get to know this other world where my eternal happiness resides. But how? Empty words are of no use to me.—*I want reality*! I want concrete facts!

This night was the turning point of my life. I realized that sex is the greatest of all frauds. Nature promises us a wonderful event, the supreme heights of joy, the embodiment of fulfilment, yet she robs us of our powers, and when we believe we have reached the limits of fulfilment, we fall lower than ever before. We lose a tremendous lot of energy and feel as poor as beggars after the event. An old Latin proverb mentions that both humans and animals feel depressed after physical union . . .

I was looking for eternal, ever-present sublimity, not what sex can give. What is left of sexual pleasure in the morning? Nothing, except possibly great fatigue! And this state of affairs is to repeat itself forever? What else is it but a continuous struggle for unattainable unison? Never will a human being achieve the fulfilment of his strivings, never can he delve into true concord where he can stay forever. Formerly a certain force existed—the power of attraction, which brought together two beings in their search for each other. Later on, this force is appeased, emptiness remains, and each is left alone, desperately alone, eternally alone . . .

I realized at last: *This* was not the aim of my quest.

And if I was not looking for this, if sex had deceived me, I would refuse to go on in this way! I would refuse to let myself be deceived! Sex can satisfy only the body, but never the soul, the self. Never could sexual satisfaction appease this desire!

What now? I want to, I must find this happiness. I must search for an answer to my questions. I cannot stand still, I must go forward. But where to?

If happiness lies in the other world, I will search for it in the other world!

And so I set out to find my happiness and fulfilment where I hoped to discover it, in the other world . . .

— 16 —

STRUGGLE FOR LIGHT

I WAS trying to capture the world beyond, but I did not know how to set about doing it. I felt like somebody who was trying to conquer a jungle, but who did not know where to start, and whose only instrument was a little axe with which to cut a path through the undergrowth. He knows the jungle to be full of lurking dangers, poisonous snakes and wild animals. He might well lose his way and fall into some abyss. Yet his ignorance of these dangers lends him the necessary courage to penetrate this jungle all the same.

I did not know that my voyage of discovery into the other world was going to be fraught with dangers, that unknown forces from the regions of the subconscious would hurl themselves upon me like wild animals, that will-o'-the wisps would lead me down false trails, and that abysses of madness were lurking on every side. All I had was my little axe, my normal human common sense!

Where was I to begin? Religion talks about the life beyond, yet all the priests I had talked to up to this moment had either wanted me to believe all sorts of dogmas which they themselves did not really understand, or they told me sentimental stories about the kingdom of heaven which they themselves did not believe, but which they deemed adequate to satisfy the 'little woman'.

I preferred to find out what the world's great philosophers thought of this tremendously important question, the meaning of life and death. And as I had never heard of great oriental philosophers, I began to study the works of European thinkers.

First of all, I read the ancient Greek and Roman works, translated into a language I could understand. I was enraptured by Socrates, Plato, Pythagoras, Epictetus and Marcus Aurelius. Under the influence of these great men, my mind matured and I learnt very much from their teachings. Especially one little sentence of Epictetus remained with me on my voyage like an eternal flame and helped me to cross over from darkness into light:

'*Things are never bad; it's the way you think about them.*'

From the moment I read that sentence, I tried to change my complete frame of mind, my spiritual position—*to think differently about things*!—Yet all these great truths could not supply the answer to my great question concerning the great beyond.

Later on I read the newer philosophers: Kant, Schopenhauer, Nietzsche, Descartes, Pascal, Spinoza. None could satisfy me. I felt that they had all gone as far as reason and intellect could take them, but that they had not reached the ultimate goal, *union*. In fact, they were less capable of answering this question than the ancient philosophers. Among these modern philosophers, Spinoza probably achieved the highest degree in this quest, but I felt that the newest thinkers had somehow entangled themselves in their own cerebral convolutions and come to a dead-end. In spite of their philosophical systems, they had remained discontented, disappointed and unhappy men. How indeed could they have helped me find the great truths of the other world? They themselves were ignorant of them and had searched for them as desperately as I was doing. I wanted reality, not words.

One autumn day I stood at the window of our apartment with my small son and watched the leaves of a chestnut-tree floating slowly to earth. As I had so often done before, I meditated upon the meaning of life and death. 'Death,' I thought, 'death again and again!'

Suddenly I heard the voice in me speaking: 'Death?—Why do you persist in seeing but the *one* side of truth? What do the trees and nature reveal in spring? Life!—again and again!' Life and death alternate in an everlasting circle. Death is but the other side of life . . .'

In this moment I saw quite clearly, that as life recedes from the tree and its leaves in autumn, the leaves become lifeless, empty husks, fall off and die. But only empty husks! The essence of life which has lived in the leaves now rests in the tree and bursts forth again in spring, clothes itself anew with a material form and becomes leaves again, repeating its eternal cycle. The tree inhales and exhales life, and only the leaves change, only the outer shell! Life remains eternal, for life is the eternal *being*. And I saw even further: The fountain of eternal existence—human beings call it '*God*'—breathes life into man, just as the Bible says that God breathed life into Adam's nostrils. Then God inhales again, withdrawing his breath, so that the empty husk falls: The body of man dies. Yet life does not cease at this moment, it clothes itself with a new body, in an eternal cycle and moves on, as everything in this world lives and moves in rhythm, from the orbit of the planets to the breath and pulse of every living creature.

Then, in a flash I suddenly remembered how, at the age of six or seven when I first heard about death, I had stood before the mirror, examining the picture of the invisible: my own reflection. Even at that early age I simply could not understand that I would some day have to die, that I would some day cease to exist. I wanted to see where this 'I' was that was thinking these things and did not want to die. I kept looking into the mirror, moving closer and closer until my nose touched the glass. I looked into my own eyes from as near as I could get. I wanted to see this 'I'! Even though there was a black hole in my eye, I couldn't see 'me'. The 'I'—myself—was invisible, just as I had always imagined it to be ever since I first became conscious on this earth. Even in the mirror I could not see *me*, only my face, *my mask*, and the two black holes in my eyes out of which I was looking. I felt very clearly that it was *impossible* for me not to exist!

'Good,' I asked myself as I stood before the mirror, 'but what will you be looking at the world through when these eyes are some day closed?'

'Through two other eyes!' I answered without a moment's hesitation. 'Here I will close these eyes, and in a new body I will open two new eyes.'

'And what if there is a time delay between the two bodies; what if you do not find a new body right away? What if you have to wait a week, or perhaps months, years, even thousands of years?'

'That just cannot be,' answered the little girl that I was then, 'for when I fall asleep, I do not know, on awakening, how long I have been asleep. In sleep there is no time, and in death it will be the same as long as I am without a body. Whether I spend a week in darkness and nothingness, or a thousand years, it's all the same. I will feel as if I had just closed my eyes here and opened them again there. In nothingness there is no time. But my ceasing to exist just cannot be!' And then I left the mirror, completely satisfied, to go on playing.

Now, as I stood before the window as an adult and recognized the law of re-incarnation in the chestnut tree, the memory of this childhood experience flashed through my mind, and I was astonished that a child could find this truth so naturally and spontaneously with its little primitive understanding, without ever having heard or read anything about re-incarnation. Now I would not say that there is no time in 'darkness', but rather that in the 'unconscious' there is no 'time concept'.

Now I also understood how it was possible for me to carry within me the blurred and hazy memories of a person I had been long before. The vision of ancient Egypt was only old memories bobbing up into consciousness.

My search for the other world and the life beyond this one and my ideas about re-incarnation turned my attention to spiritualism. Spiritualists claim to be able to establish contact with spirits of the departed dead, and they also believe in re-incarnation. However, I had a pronounced antipathy towards spiritualism because at home I had heard my parents speak about it in a rather disparaging way. Mother had a very dear old friend who concerned herself with spiritualism. Mother told us that this friend held spiritualistic séances and that during these experiments a heavy massive oaken table would rise up in the air. Mother never participated in these séances and never concerned herself with such things at all, because she was convinced that such experiments were harmful for the nerves. While I was reflecting about re-incarnation, I remembered that once as a young girl I had participated in such a séance at the home of this elderly lady without my mother's knowledge of it. That is, of course, if what we experienced then could be called a 'séance'!

My mother's elderly friend loved her grandchildren very much and often invited young people to lunch. I was often one of the guests at these young people's luncheons. Once, several of us stayed on after the others had left. The lady was of a gay and sparkling nature and enjoyed talking with us youngsters. I was fifteen, and the other children were about the same age. We were curious and eager to hear the kind lady tell us about spiritualism.

'If you wish,' she said, 'we can watch the table move.' All of us young folks agreed immediately and began to wonder what was going to happen next.

A table was brought in for the experiment. It was not the heavy oaken table mother had talked about, but a little table with only three legs. The lady set the table in the middle of the room, and we youngsters stood around it, with the palms of our hands on the top of the table and our fingers spread out in such a way that the thumbs of each person's hands were touching each other and their little fingers touching the little fingers of the persons to the left and the right. The room was brightly lit. We youngsters were in high spirits and thought it was just terribly funny when the elderly lady called out in a loud voice, 'Is someone there?'

We looked at each other roguishly and could hardly keep from bursting out laughing. But we did not want to offend the dear old lady and tried hard to keep a straight face. We stood and waited. All at once the little table began to shake as if some inner force were trying to split the wood apart. Then the shaking became stronger and stronger and suddenly the table leaned over to the side so that one of its feet was in the air; then it fell back and stood still.

'Yes,' said the lady, 'the table said "yes". When the table raps once, it means "yes", when it raps twice it means "no".'

'Wolfgang,' she said to her grandson, 'take paper and pencil and write down the letters. A spirit is present.'

Wolfgang took a pencil and waited. Then the table began to move, rapping and rapping again. We called off the letters in the alphabet and whenever the table stopped at one of the letters we had called, Wolfgang wrote down the letter.

I cannot explain why this all seemed so terribly funny to us. We found it was comical to be calling out letters and ludicrous that the old lady took everything so seriously. I could not believe for a minute that the table was moving by itself. It was surely Nicolas, the lady's other grandson. The rapping itself was amusing enough, but what came afterwards made us burst out laughing irresistibly, and this made the old lady shake her head at us. But we just couldn't help laughing anyway, even if we did not want to. The table suddenly began to tip over so far that its edge almost touched the floor. I thought its feet were going to slip and it would fall, but no, it came back again to an upright position and then began to turn and twist and move around the room. We had to run with it, and when the table began to rotate, we had to run around it and follow it wherever it went in the room. Finally the table came to rest in a corner and moved no more. The lady again called out, 'Is no one there?'

The table did not move.

'It was a waggish kind of spirit, because you were all so hilarious,' she said, 'and now all spirits are gone. Wait a moment, children, I'll have some coffee brought in.' With that she disappeared into the kitchen. We youngsters were left alone. It was my chance to ask Nicolas, 'It was you who moved the table,, wasn't it?'

'I?' he echoed in astonishment, 'I thought it was you, or Emmerich. But it certainly wasn't I. I only played the game with the rest, but my fingertips were scarcely touching the table.'

We all looked at Emmerich. He protested earnestly, 'No, I didn't move the table either.'

'Come on, all of you,' I said, 'let's get the table to move again ourselves.'

All agreed and we ran to the table, stood around it, and began with our own hands to push it back and forth and get it to move. To our great amazement this didn't work! The table was motionless, just as a piece of wood is normally lifeless and motionless, and when we pushed it harder and harder, it simply fell over and lay on the floor. During the previous experiment, the table had sometimes leaned over so far that its edge almost touched the floor and then stood up again. But no matter how we tried, we couldn't get it to do so again. Finally, after we had agreed to push the table in the same direction, all of us together, one side would rise after which the table simply fell. We could not hold it or get it to stand upright again.

We looked at each other and suddenly fell silent. We couldn't understand the whole affair. None of us felt like laughing any more. The elderly lady's two grandsons admitted quietly that they couldn't understand the matter either, but it was a fact that when their Aunt Margaret was present even the gigantic oaken table, which was so heavy that only four men together could carry it out of the room, would rise up in the air. Obviously Aunt Margaret was not lifting it.

On my way home, and for a long time afterwards, I thought about the moving table and wondered how it worked. I did not believe for a moment that a 'spirit' had moved it, but *I had to admit that an unknown force was there.*

After this all happened I went on with my piano practice, went skating, fought with my fiancé, and the moving table disappeared in the storehouse of my memory. Now it all came back to me. I could see clearly that the dear old lady did not understand much about spiritualism, but perhaps there were spiritualistic groups who went into such matters very seriously. If I were to study and investigate the whole matter thoroughly without prejudice, I might perhaps learn something through spiritualism that would help me on my path.

I obtained an introduction to the leader of the largest and the most famous spiritualistic group in the country. He began by giving me books to read which I could believe or not believe. Theories cannot satisfy a seeker after truth. I wanted practice and conviction. In one book I read about a very famous medium who achieved his ability by sitting down at the same time every day with paper and pencil, holding the pencil in his hand in readiness to write, and waiting a solid hour. This he repeated religiously day after day, week after week, and month after month. After about six months, the pencil began to move and wrote various words. In this manner, the medium wrote a number of books which were very famous at the time. They did not interest me because they were sermons full of sweetness and light and not as good as the sermons one could hear in any church. Why, I thought, should one have to call upon a 'spirit' for things like these, *if indeed it really was a spirit which moved the hand of the medium*!

I, too, took pencil and paper, held the pencil over the paper in readiness, and waited.

The first day nothing happened.

The second day the pencil began to shake so hard my hand shook with it. Then it began to move stiffly, jerkily, back and forth and wrote various abracadabras on the paper.

On the third day the pencil immediately began to shake and soon wrote words one could clearly read. They looked as if they had been written by an old person with a trembling hand. I continued the experiment every day, and the pencil went on to write longer and longer sentences. While the pencil was writing, I observed my arm and my hand. Whence came the force that moved my hand? If the pencil could write all by itself, I reflected, every pencil lying around could stand up and start writing. Therefore, without any doubt, the pencil was being moved by *my arm*, but without *my* having wanted to do so and without *my* having known before what it was going to write. Consequently the force must be coming from a source outside my own consciousness, but doubtless from me. It can be a force coming from my subconscious, but for the present there is no proof that this force comes from a strange being outside myself, or let us say, from a 'spirit'.

But who knows precisely what our 'subsconcious' is?

I showed these writings to the leader of the spiritualist group. With amazing assurance he said they were typically mediumistic writings coming from a spirit. I was silent. I am very cautious in making such claims. *It was certain that the force moving my arm did not come from my consciousness, for there was no active will on my part to move the pencil. But this force could still come from me, from my unconscious.* The fact that spiritualists *believe* that these forces come from spirits is no proof that it really is so!

I continued the experiments and observed myself and the pencil.

One Sunday afternoon my husband and I were sitting together. He was reading a book, and I was busy with my wood carving, and as I worked with my hands, I thought about my recent experiments with pencil, paper and the strange writing. If it is possible, I concluded, for my hand, my nerves or any as yet unknown instrument within me to receive and manifest the thoughts of a strange, disembodied being outside myself, then it must also be possible, in exactly the same way, for me to receive and manifest the thoughts of another person, separate from myself but dwelling in a body. This would mean a step forward along my path.

I told my husband what I was thinking about and asked whether he felt like making an experiment in thought transmission with me. He agreed immediately, and he was as eager as I to know whether we would succeed.

I did not know how such experiments are made, but I imagined that, if I wanted to receive the thoughts of another person, the most important thing for me to do would be to make myself completely passive and empty of my own thoughts so they would not intrude. Then with my right hand I held his left wrist, thinking that it would help for us to have this sort of physical connection; and relaxing all my muscles and trying to think of nothing, I waited.

I imagined that for successful thought transference my husband would think about something and his thought would, in some way or other, *appear in my mind*. I was thus expecting a thought that would not be coming from me. (At that time I had never realized that we do not actually know the source of the thoughts we believe to be our own!) To my great amazement something quite different happened, something for which I was truly not prepared. As I stood there with my husband and waited to receive a thought from him, I felt very distinctly—and even 'saw'—that a stream of force about three to four inches thick flowed out of his solar plexus area, surrounding my body like a lasso, also at about the height of the solar plexus.

I felt this flow of force as distinctly as if it had been *material*—very fine, like a dense mist but nevertheless material. After this flow of force surrounded me, it pulled me unmistakably in a definite direction so that I had to take a step. Then it pulled me on and on. Whenever I took a step in the wrong direction, it very distinctly pulled me back into the right direction. In this way we reached the window where the materialized will of my husband left me standing. Then came a new surprise. My left arm which was hanging down at my side as usual, suddenly rose in the air, becoming *weightless*! Until then I had never realized that my arms hung downward because of the gravitational attraction of the earth. One hears about gravitation in school, but I had never before been conscious of the fact that my own arm hung downward because of this force. There in front of the window, however, I was able to experience for myself the fact that my arm lost its weight and rose up in the air when the earth's gravitational pull ceased. As my arm moved upward, it also raised the curtain. I had not moved a single muscle, so it seemed. It was as if a mass flowing out from my husband's solar plexus was supporting my arm. Then this mass pushed my head forward until my nose touched the window pane. At this moment, the mass left my body—my arm and my head—and I was able to move again freely.

We looked at each other and were both very excited. I was thrilled by the new experience, the fact that the human will flows out of the solar plexus, literally reaching another person, embracing him like an octopus, and even cancelling out the effect of gravity. This 'material' seemed as if it consisted of myriads of little droplets of mist, somewhat like the milky way appears in the sky at night. It was as if these droplets of mist were all closely related to each other and all flowing in one direction.

My husband was excited because he could not understand how it was possible for me to carry out everything he was thinking—going to the window, raising the curtain, and looking out through the window pane—just as if I were an automaton. I told him that there was a stream of force flowing out from his solar plexus area and that I felt this stream as clearly as if it had been material.

I told him also that it is only subjective when we feel something to be matter. Force gives us the impression of matter.

I recalled that once, several years previously, when our child had a stomach ache and I put our electric heating pad on his stomach, I found when stroking his face, that his skin, which was normally as fine and soft as a rose petal, suddenly felt as rough and coarse as a rasp. It felt as if I were stroking the face of a man two days unshaven. We found out that the heating pad had become a bit damp and some of the current was leaking into the child's body. When I switched off the heating pad, our baby's skin ceased to feel rough to the touch. Hence, to my hand, the electric current felt just like coarse matter. When we consider this fact which everyone can check for himself, we can decide whether we want to compare this 'material' manifestation of the human will with a form of matter or with electric current. The result is the same in either case, for modern science knows that matter is nothing but a form of energy, a vibration, and only gives us the impression of being matter because it is impenetrable for us.

It was the custom for our whole family to get together every Sunday evening; so I soon found myself telling the assembled group about our experience of that afternoon. Everybody immediately wanted to try some experiments too. First I stood up with mother. Everyone else sat quiet as a mouse and tried to think about nothing; for when I was in this ultra-receptive condition, I was so sensitive to the thoughts of persons present that this would have disturbed our thought transference experiment.

With mother I experienced something new again. The current she emitted was weaker, much finer and smaller in diameter than that of my husband. Then I made the same experiment with the various uncles, aunts and other relatives who were gathered that evening for supper at my parents' house. In these experiments I learned that each individual emits a different kind of current. One of my uncles who always found it difficult to make up his mind and discipline his thoughts sent out a large, powerful stream of thought, but the tiny particles of force in this current did not flow in the same direction, but to and fro in a chaotic manner. The effect was just as chaotic. It was a very difficult task for me, too, to find out what he wanted. One of my aunts had a very thin, but piercingly sharp flow of current which to me felt like a stiff, hard wire, hurtful to the touch. We all knew her as a very aggressive person. Each and every person present had a different radiation of will.

This opened up a new world to me! I began to understand many phenomena which I had previously only felt, or suspected, or not noticed at all. All at once it was clear to me why a person can be just as tired after a dispute or argument as if he had been through a wrestling match. I also understood why being together with other people sometimes is very tiring and sometimes very refreshing and stimulating. I understood clearly and in an almost physically palpable manner the real meaning of sympathy and antipathy: emanations that give and those that absorb. The former radiate strength, while the latter cling to a person like the arms of an octopus, drawing out and absorbing his strength. This kind of experiment with such people always made me so weak that my knees would be trembling when the experiment was over; I would have to sit down, completely exhausted, and wait a while to recover strength to continue the experiments. On this particular evening, everyone in the family—including the maid, the cook and my parents' other servants—wanted to make an experiment in thought transference with me.

During that period of my life I learned something else, a fact which cannot be changed by any human decree, namely, that cultured, self-disciplined people emit very different radiations from those of coarse and uncouth people living only for the satisfaction of their instincts. Naturally this is not a matter of social or economic class! Many a simple, unlettered and untutored person living near a forest or on a mountainside, alone and often completely untouched by civilization, emits a higher and purer form of vibrations than those of learned, highly educated and well-read but completely egotistical persons. These radiations cannot be hidden, falsified, counterfeited or 'explained away'. They reveal immediately the kind of person one is dealing with.

I acquired another interesting bit of knowledge through these experiments. Whenever someone wanted me to do something that was against the code of conduct I had been taught to accept, this latter stood like an insulating wall between the will of the other person and myself, and it required tremendous effort on my part to overcome this obstacle with an almost explosive 'breakthrough'.

These experiments always fatigued me greatly. Even when I was experimenting with people who had a positive disposition, I first had to empty my own mind and will in order to be receptive to the will of the other, that is, *to make the will of the other person conscious within myself* and guide the other person's vibrations through my own nerves, suppressing as much as possible my own radiations. This was actually the hardest part. Our nerves are always *adapted to our own vibrations*; their power of resistance is adjusted to our own vital current.

Every change in our mental or physical state requires an effort from our nerves, irrespective of whether this change is upward or downward. It always makes demands on our nerves. Even when we experience such mental or spiritual changes within ourselves, they can often be harmful, irrespective of whether they are caused by a sudden shock, a passionate outburst, or even excessive joy. Under these circumstances, it is understandable that it can be tiring or deleterious to have to adapt our nerves to completely strange vibrations, differing from our own not only in frequency but even in their very nature. When the difference in vibrations is very great, the result can be substantial damage, over-excitement of the nerves, neuritis or other diseases of the nerves. This explains why many sensitive people always get mysteriously sick in certain environments. It also explains the great danger threatening every medium, namely the loss of his own character. Unfortunately, this is what happens unavoidably in most cases. The medium receives all kinds of vibrations but cannot digest them or assimilate them; so he becomes chaotic, unreliable and weak-willed himself! We should never play with these things! The literature of this field contains masses of sad stories of different mediums who finally degenerated into weak-willed automatons, receiving any and all kinds of impressions, possessing no resistance of their own, and finally being 'exposed' as lying, cheating frauds. No wonder! As a direct result of their abilities as a medium, their own will became weaker and weaker until they became a mere plaything for the spectators around them.

I myself was witness to this kind of development. One woman with unusually great ability as a medium was able initially to perform prodigious feats. Later, however, she lost her own character to an ever-increasing extent, getting to the point where she had less and less resistance to put up against other people's wishes and was always eager to perform an experiment. Whenever the unknown power did not appear, she began to cheat in order to satisfy the curious people around her. The story ended with a gigantic scandal. As usual, the ignorant people triumphed, claiming that all this woman's accomplishments were nothing but a hoax from beginning to end. No! Her accomplishments were not all a fraud by any means. *On the other hand, precisely as a direct result of her true ability as a medium, she became so weak-willed and lacking in character that she finally ended up as a cheat.*

I was able to observe these effects on myself. I did not want to deceive myself; I wanted to learn the truth, and as time went on I discovered the very pernicious effects of experiments of this nature. I was conscious enough and had a sufficiently strong will to overcome foreign vibrations and to become myself again after each experiment. However, I found that having to resist the influences of other persons made me very tired and nervous and this led me to stop this activity. Later I gave up all spiritualistic experiments completely. I know very well that many spiritualists claim their work of manifesting is not tiring or injurious. I hope they will pardon me for giving my plain, straightforward opinion, based on many years of experiments, namely that those mediums who do not feel tired after their experiments *never receive the will of another person or being*, but merely produce manifestations *from their own unconscious*; this despite their firm conviction that their manifestations come from beings outside themselves.

My experiments convinced me that a person can 'receive' *his own will from some unsuspected complex lying deep in his own subconscious and manifest it just as he would the will of another being.* This is the reason for most of the self-deceptions which occur in this field. But it is impossible to discuss such matters intelligently with ignorant people. They stick to their fantastic belief in 'spirits', deceiving themselves and whole hosts of undisciplined and gullible people. They have not the vaguest idea about their own *unconscious powers*.

On the other hand, persons who are determined to learn the truth and systematically to check and investigate all phenomena can discover extremely interesting *facts*. We just have to be careful when we use the word 'spirit'!

Let us just reflect for a moment. If a person's will can cause the arm of another person to rise and thus *conquer the gravitational pull of the earth,* how much more can it do? What is the limit of its powers? As I began to learn these facts, I understood a phenomenon known here in the West as 'levitation'—an exercise still practised diligently, and carried out even today, in the monasteries of Tibet. Without ever having heard of these Tibetan exercises at that time, my experiments led me to the same conclusions. The phenomenon is known in Europe too, and reliable eye-witnesses have described how the great Teresa of Avila, John of the Cross and Francis of Assisi all were observed to rise and float in the air, not only once, but on numerous occasions and for hours at a time. I know that *this is possible*; for a person's own will power has the same effect as that of another person and can overcome the earth's gravitational pull for a certain period of time. It all depends on the size and strength of the will.

There were also times during my experiments when I could not become conscious of another person's will. At such times it was impossible for me to manifest what he was thinking. On such occasions I felt as if the mass of his will were bearing down on me like a giant weight. I found it hard to breathe, sighing and groaning as if I were dying. I would then ask the person concerned to concentrate better. As soon as I became conscious of his will and carried it out, I was able to breathe easily and freely again and the terrible pressure ceased! These experiments gave me the conviction that in very many cases *asthma is nothing else but the invisible will of another person bearing down like a heavy weight upon the diseased individual. On the other hand, this invisible, unexecuted will can be that of the diseased person himself coming forth from his unconscious and causing his sickness without his knowing that his disease is indeed the result of his own will.*

Our entire life consists of such invisible battles. In some we are defeated, in others victorious.

These experiments and experiences were a splendid school for me. They gave me an opportunity to look deep into the unconscious and to get thoroughly acquainted with myself and with other people. I became firmly convinced that it is possible to receive the thoughts of another being. But at the same time I saw how extremely difficult it is! I came to understand why the Tibetans or the East Indians spend three days in the wilderness—miles away from every human settlement—fasting, praying, and otherwise preparing themselves before they seek to establish a connection with the spirit of a departed person. Certainly not the way thousands of so-called spiritualists, after their work in an office or in the midst of a completely worldly life, gather together and believe they can suddenly be in rapport with the world beyond.

They imagine that saying a quick little prayer will protect them from danger. Have they ever been able to observe that saying a prayer can keep a person who jumps into an abyss from falling to his death? Experimenting ignorantly with spiritualism represents just as great a danger as jumping into an abyss. Let us be reasonable! Let us not forget that we have the power of reason in order to check and test all our experiences. During the many years I have spent in the most widely differing groups, I was forced to observe how countless catastrophies, nervous breakdowns, suicides, and serious mental disorders resulted from the irresponsible games people call spiritualism. Well-intentioned, honest but completely ignorant and psychologically unschooled people hold séances! Ignorant people call into being powers whose origin and nature is completely unknown to them. Neither understanding these powers, nor being able to control them, they are completely at their mercy. Only people who are strong enough to resist all influences, have deep psychological knowledge, extensive experience and an enormous *conscious* will power and self control should concern themselves and experiment with spiritualism.

— 17 —

I TAKE MY VOW

LITTLE BY little I realized that my circles of spiritualist friends had nothing more to offer me. My experiences in these circles, however, opened the door to the human soul, and I saw in amazement how forlorn and lonely people are as they wander around in the extreme darkness of ignorance. My own ability as a medium enabled me to look into the enormous field of the subconscious. I literally took myself apart in the most rigorous kind of self-analysis, refusing to be blinded by uncertain and nebulous theories. Hewing my way with my little axe, I went ahead in this jungle, step by step. Spiritualism finally led me to the study of psychology. I began to make a thorough study of the *Western* science of psychology; for at that time I had not the slightest inkling of the enormous psychological knowledge of the Orientals, particularly the Indians and the Chinese.

Whenever we earnestly strive for something and concentrate completely on attaining it, fate always helps us onward. After a thorough theoretical training, I met the head physician of the state mental hospital who helped me get systematic training and practice. I was given permission to study the patients in every section of the state asylum, including the wards reserved for raving maniacs.

One evening at home I sat for a long time alone in my room and tried to put my thoughts in order. What I had experienced in the asylum was simply horrible! Terrible! Dante's *Inferno* is tame compared to what I had seen. And how many sick people are there on this earth who are suffering, either committed to an asylum or walking about freely; and how many healthy people are there who suffer themselves because they watch the torture these other people go through. Little by little they get sick and go to ruin. And how many mental cases are there who deceive ignorant people simply because they behave normally and have no stamp on their forehead to show they are mentally ill.

Sometimes they get high positions, marry an innocent trusting husband or wife, and then plunge their relatives, their surroundings and family, often an entire business firm—or even an entire nation—into ruin.

Hell lay open before my very eyes, and in desperation I stood on the brink of an unfathomable ocean of suffering, desperate at the helplessness of mankind in the face of this terrible misery.

Something must be done! Everybody must be informed about the causes of mental disease. Healthy people everywhere must work together with united efforts to fight this misery.

My preoccupation with the mentally ill opened the door to the deepest secrets of a wide range of people's families, and I was amazed to discover that there are many more mentally ill than sane people living in the world. I saw the countless mental abnormalities from which people suffer, and I saw that vast numbers of people could be saved by proper treatment; their mental balance could be restored by simple means, often merely by a change of surroundings, thus restoring happiness to the families concerned.

I sat and pondered about how much could be done if every healthy person would devote himself to this work. With all my strength I wanted to devote myself to overcoming this suffering . . . but how and where should I begin?

And where could I find some help?

As I sat there asking myself this question I suddenly knew that somebody was in the room beside me. My experiments with mental telepathy and spiritualistic séances had trained my nerves to such a degree of sensitivity that even if I were led into a room blindfolded, I could say immediately whether the room was empty or occupied. And if the room was occupied I could even tell something about the character of the person in it. I now felt the familiar prickly feeling, like a fine electric current, telling me that something or somebody was near. But this time I felt the familiar radiation without knowing why it was familiar or where I had met it before . . . this majestic, completely pure, extremely powerful radiation . . . and again I heard the familiar voice inside me: 'Where will you find some help? Inside yourself! Don't you see this is just the trouble—everybody is waiting for help from outside, and as everybody is *expecting* help and not *giving* it, nobody gets help. But if everybody would *give* help, everybody would *receive* it too. Then the whole world could be freed of suffering!'

I answered the voice within: 'I don't know who you are or even what kind of a force you are; I only hear your voice that always tells me the truth. You see my thoughts, my inner being which is invisible to people, so I don't need to tell you I want to devote my whole life to overcoming the sufferings of others. Even though I be only a grain of dust, with this one grain of dust I want to increase the helping force. Nothing else in life can interest me any more, nothing can make me really happy again as long as I constantly carry the sufferings of others in my consciousness. I want to be a co-worker in the salvation of the world!'

'Careful!' said the voice within me. 'Watch all those big words! To be a co-worker means duty and sacrifice. Then you have to put an end to your imperfections! You must never forget yourself for even a minute. You must always be on guard that you don't do a single thing in contradiction to the eternal laws of life. *All the temptations you haven't been able to withstand so far in your life will come back to haunt you again and woe to you if you do not withstand them.* No mortal can play with the divine forces. You may never again use the powers you achieve as a co-worker *for your own personal ends.* You may never have personal feelings or consider anything from your own personal standpoint. Be careful! It would be better to go on living your personal life like other people than fail as a co-worker. I warn you.'

'I am not afraid,' I answered. 'I am absolutely through with my personal life and no longer have any more personal wishes. After all I've been through and experienced, there can be no more personal happiness for me. I'm not afraid of any temptations. I will resist them because I have no more illusions. I want to be a co-worker in the great task!'

For a while I heard nothing, merely felt infinitely great love radiating towards me. Then I heard the voice within me again: 'Your self-assurance is well known to me, my child, but don't forget yourself *this time* . . .'

I sat on the divan, rubbed my brow, looked around—the room was empty. Who was that? Who is that?—Or what kind of a power is it that speaks to me with a voice I know so well? How do I know this voice? How does it know my 'self-assurance'? And when had I ever not paid enough attention . . . so as to merit the admonition not to forget myself *'this time'*?

But I got no further answer.

── 18 ──

THE HORIZON BRIGHTENS

DAYS PASSED, weeks passed, months passed . . . I waited for a sign, something that would point the way towards what I should do, towards my duty, towards my sacrifice . . . in accord with the voice of the invisible one who had spoken to me, but the voice came no more . . .

No matter how often I tried to enter the special state of mind and spirit in which I would feel again the strange and indescribable buzzing and tingling throughout my whole body, as if I were bathing in soda water, no matter how often I tried to close off my organs of sense, to get myself into a state of inner receptivity, ready to hear the voice . . . it was all to no avail.

I was perplexed. I was waiting and waiting for a sign—in vain. On the other hand I did not want to waste time; so I came to the conclusion that the best thing for me to do would be to carry out my earthly duties as well as possible, hoping all the while that my inner voice would sooner or later tell me what my duty was to be as a co-worker in the great plan. I also felt that I would have to free my soul of every selfish attitude if I wanted to see the truth with perfect clarity, just as a window pane must be clean in order for us to see the sunshine clearly through it. The first step in this direction is to know what is really inside me. As soon as I know my inner self throughly, I can cleanse and purify it.

I began to investigate the source and inner motivation of all my thoughts, my words, my movements and deeds. What kind of unconscious power is at work within me? Where do my thoughts come from? *What* is it within me that wills me to say one thing or another? *Why* do I want to do just this thing, not something else? When I was happy about something, I investigated *why* I was happy about it. When I was depressed or angry, I sought out the reasons for these feelings. When I felt attracted toward another person, or repelled by him, I immediately analysed myself to discover the characteristics responsible for this feeling. I kept myself under constant observation as to why I liked to do some things and disliked doing others. When I was feeling talkative, I sought to find the reasons and motives behind my loquaciousness; when feeling reserved, I sought the reasons for my taciturnity. I analysed every word that came out of my mouth to see whether it was completely true, whether it could prove hurtful to no one. I observed the effects of my words and my deeds on others around me. I constantly tried to trade places in my imagination with the person to whom I was speaking. What would *I* feel if *he* were saying to *me the words I was saying to him? Constantly, uninterruptedly, I kept myself under observation.*

This everlasting self-scrutiny brought me uncounted riches. Little by little

I became acquainted with the magical world of the subconscious and super-conscious. I came to recognize the various manifestations of *one and the same force*, from the lowest urges on up to the highest spiritual self. I came to realize that we have a free choice: we can identify ourselves with our instincts or remain masters of them, that is to say, remain *ourselves*! I learned that to be a free human being means to control one's instincts and not become the slave of one's passions, desires and wishes.

Along with my incessant self-analysis, I continued to study psychology and philosophy, without neglecting my wood carving or my music. Artistic work provides a wonderful opportunity to turn inward spiritually and to ponder all kinds of questions.

Once an art critic was visiting us and saw my furniture that I had carved myself. Over the bed I had hung a faun playing a flute all carved out of wood. The critic asked me whether I had first modelled this figure in clay. I told him I didn't even know how to model in clay and that I had carved it straight out of wood. 'I simply cut away all the wood that was superfluous,' I said.

'Have you studied anatomy?' he asked further.

'No, I studied music and was not able to attend two colleges at the same time.'

After scrutinizing my carvings a little while longer he said, 'It's a shame you're not a sculptress!'

'Without training I would always be a dilettante, and that's just what I wouldn't want to be. But I cannot register at the art academy because I don't want to neglect my husband and child.'

'All right,' he said, 'I'll talk to the Director of the School of Manual Arts. He may perhaps make an exception and permit you to attend the lessons in sculpture without taking all the side courses. You don't need them anyway. I believe it should be possible for you to attend the art school on special terms.'

In this way I was able first to attend art school and later to receive training from one of the greatest master sculptors of the time. The first time I reported to him, he came very close to me, peered into my face intently, and said in a very surprised tone, 'How interesting! You are the first living person I have ever seen with Egyptian eyes. Did you know you have Egyptian eyes?'

'No,' I replied, 'I don't even know what the difference is between Egyptian eyes and ordinary eyes.'

'The openings of the eyes are slit longitudinally at the side of the eye, and this makes the eyelids rest in a completely different position from those of other races. When you look at a picture, you can tell immediately by this character-istic whether the picture is Egyptian or not. But I never dreamed I would find such eyes in a living person. Present day Egyptians don't have eyes like this any more. One only sees them in pictures, just as one can only see the long, drawn-out Egyptian skull formation in pictures and sculptured artifacts. But where did you get these eyes of yours?'

I smiled politely and said, 'I just don't know, Professor. Perhaps I am revert-ing to type.'

He smiled too, then started me on my work.

A year later he entered the studio where I was working. He had several of them all near each other.

'From now on,' he said, 'I'm not accepting any more tuition from you. If you have no studio of your own, you can work here, but as an independent artist. You no longer need my guidance, only practice in order to get better and better at expressing yourself in this medium.'

I thanked him for his efforts and for his kind offer. Since I had a large studio at home and had already held several exhibits, I continued my work under my own roof. My professor remained a good friend and dropped in from time to time to see how my work was progressing.

The work made me happy—completely happy, even ecstatic. Time, space and the world around me ceased to exist; I felt no physical wishes, hunger or thirst—I even forgot myself completely. I noticed that a force flowed into my nerves while I was concentrating on my work, and that this force exerted a healing influence on mind and body. Many times when I was concentrating on my work and thinking about nothing else, I suddenly recognized a truth which had no relationship whatever with my work. In this way I often received answers to philosophical, psychological or other unsolved problems which had been occupying my mind. In such cases I would stand motionless a moment, my modelling tool in my hand, while my inward eye surveyed the new truth, the new discovery. At such moments I felt as if my head had just poked up through the ceiling of one room and emerged above the floor in an upper room. It was a wonderful feeling to look around with my inward eye in this newly discovered upper room, inspecting all the hidden treasure lying there. These brilliant flashes of inspiration began to come more and more frequently, not only while I was modelling in clay or playing the piano, but almost any time when I was concentrating on something.

Once I experienced something very strange! This time, however, it did not occur during my work, but in the late evening just as I was about to drop off to sleep.

Our beds were next to each other, and we both had the habit of reading for a a little while in bed before falling asleep. On this particular evening we both of us read for a while. Finally I got sleepy, said good night to my husband, turned off my reading lamp, stretched, and closed my eyes to go to sleep. I closed my eyes, *but I still saw everything in the room!* My eyes were closed quite normally, but I was able to see everything—every object—in the room, including my husband lying in his bed next to mine and leafing through his book. I quickly opened my eyes again to see whether my husband really was leafing through his book or whether the whole phenomenon had been a projection from my own imagination. But his motions continued just as I had seen them with my eyes closed! I closed my eyes again but still saw everything. Thus surprised, I sat up in bed again, looked around the room with my eyes closed, and still saw everything quite clearly! Only one thing was very peculiar, namely, that I did not see things in three dimensions, but flat and transparent—just as my eyelids seemed to be transparent like a photographic negative, or like an X-ray picture, but much clearer and more transparent. For example, I saw my sewing machine through its wooden cover, the pictures on the wall in the next room through the closed door, the clothes hanging in the closet, and all my little possessions lying chaotically in my writing desk. The whole picture was like an impression of all the things lying one behind the other.

My husband watched for a while as I looked around the room in various directions with my eyes closed.

'What are you doing?' he finally asked.

All excited, I answered that I was able to see everything in the room with my eyes closed. He became curious and tried several little experiments to find out whether I could see how many fingers he was holding up, and similar things. I was not only able to see his fingers, but even the bones and organs in his body. It was really positively weird, but my sense of humour won the upper hand and I burst out laughing at seeing him so transparent.

Finally we did fall asleep. As usual, I slept peacefully, and the next morning I saw everything quite normally again, and only when my eyes were open. And for quite a long time afterwards, there was no recurrence of this strange phenomenon. I went on with my sculpturing as if nothing had happened.

As I continued to work with my modelling tools, I did not neglect my studies in psychology. More and more people came to me to discuss their spiritual problems. In this way I kept on gaining in practical experience.

Several years went by in this manner: steady work in the wintertime, family life together on the lake shore amid the beauties of nature in the summer.

── 19 ──

VISIONS

THERE CAME a period in my life in which I often had visions while perfectly wide awake. Many of them had such a tremendous effect on me and on my later life that I must mention the most important of them.

Towards the end of every summer my husband and I made a journey through various countries. Once, as we were on our way back from Italy, we stopped over in the Dolomites for some mountain climbing. Here I experienced one of the most profoundly impressive visions of my life.

One evening after an exhausting day in the mountains, we returned to our hotel and I lay down. The sun had shone with such intense fierceness during our hiking that it had seemed as if every single ray were a spear aimed straight at my back and my heart. The gigantic reddish rock walls reflected the sunshine in every direction, seeming to magnify it a thousandfold. The whole atmosphere was demonic; everything was glowing with heat as if we were walking in the antechamber of Hell. I was really happy when we finally turned towards home, and the sun which had been burning like a flame-thrower disappeared behind the horizon at last.

I went to bed early and stretched out, ready to fall asleep. In this self-same instant I suddenly felt as if the ceiling were falling in on me . . . as if I were falling into a bottomless abyss . . . falling towards instant death. A doctor, summoned at the desperate plea of my husband, found I was suffering from a heart attack. He gave me an injection. The night dragged by, and when morning came my pulse beat was still so weak that it was scarcely discernible. Tortured with a feeling of annihilation, I learned to know what it means to be afraid of death. As was my custom, I observed myself closely, even under those circumstances, discovering that fear of death is a physical condition. In my consciousness there was peace and calm, no fear of death at all; yet I was suffering from such terrible fear of death that I can scarcely find words to express it. It was unbearable. I was no longer completely in this world, and not yet in the next. I was hovering in nothingness, suffering so horribly I thought I would rather die than go on bearing this torture. I gave up the struggle, deciding to go into death knowingly in order to escape from this fear of it.

However, just as I wanted to glide over with my consciousness into this nothingness of which I had been so afraid, the space around me suddenly expanded in all directions, and infinity spread out before my astonished eyes. In this infinity, I saw a long, long road winding onward, and at its end, beyond everything material, standing in eternity, the majestic form of a man made of blinding light, his arms stretched out in indescribable love. He seemed infinitely far away from me, and his countenance shone with such an intensely powerful light that it blinded me and I could not see his features. Nevertheless, I recognized him as the *Saviour* of the world.

On the road, oval beings that looked like eggs were moving forward slowly. As they moved along together, they gave me the impression of so many sheep, viewed from such an angle that only their backs were visible, but not their feet. I stood at the beginning of this road and had to show them the way. They jogged past me slowly in a steady stream, moving in the direction of the figure of light who awaited them with outstretched arms. Those who reached *him,* entered into his light and disappeared, merging with his resplendent glory. The whole long road was covered with a seemingly endless stream of these oval beings which I recognized as *human souls.* I showed them the way and kept on pointing out the direction to take, as more and ever more of these souls approached.

I began to realize that I was not yet going to die, because I still had this work to do, and that I could not die at all until I had fulfilled this task. I realized, too, that I would be doing this work for a very long time, until my sand in the great cosmic hour-glass would run out and I myself would return to my homeland of light where ever-radiant love would be awaiting me.

Infinite peace came over me, and my heart began to function more normally, even though still weak. I glanced at my husband who was observing me with a worried face. I could move my tongue again a little, and I whispered to him that I was better. The poor dear boy cried like a child out of pure joy that I could speak again and that the light was coming back into my eyes.

After another day in bed, I had recovered sufficiently to be able to travel again. A few days more and all was back to normal.

During our summertime sojourns at the lake shore, I was almost always more receptive to visions and in a state of greater sensitivity for sending and receiving telepathic messages. Once during our summer vacation we went to bed after a happy day. The house became quiet, and I fell asleep beside my husband. I dreamed all kinds of chaotic, apparently unrelated pictures, and then in my dream I suddenly heard steps ... slow, dragging steps. They caused me to realize that I had dozed off where I was sitting at the top of a long flight of stairs. For a long time there had been no one passing from whom I could beg anything. Now the sound of someone approaching woke me. In a few moments I was quite awake, with my eyes wide open. Then I saw that the slow, dragging steps were those of a very old, broken man who had plodded along painfully to the position I occupied and was now preparing to sit down at the other side of this flight of stairs.

These stairs led from where we were, in an elevated corner of the city, down into the centre of town below. In the section around us, there were many state and municipal offices, so thousands of people had to go up and down these steps every day. Only now, at midday, is there a short intermission in the otherwise steady stream of people. It's a good place for me to sit. The roof at the entrance of the staircase protects me from rain, and my revenue is good. I have my 'regular customers' who give me alms every day on the way to their offices. But what an impertinence it is for this old beggar to post himself here too! He's bound to do me harm. People going by are not going to give to two beggars at once, and so I am certain to lose half of my income.

I look at him impatiently and want to tell him to go somewhere else to do his begging; this is my place and it's up to him to clear out! I look at him and an uncertain feeling grips me. I peer into his eyes and suddenly feel uneasy. I see that he too is embarrassed. He makes a movement as if to run away, but it is too late. I recognize him, and he recognizes me. O Father of mercy, it is *he*! Here is the man I have been seeking all my life, the man who abandoned me, the man I could never forget. And now he is sitting opposite me, a beggar just like myself. O why, O why do we have to meet again like *this*!

I look at him, his wrinkled old face, and his skin. His lips hang loose and limp; his thin, matted hair and his beard are neglected: his clothing consists of old, worn out rags. What has become of the handsome, elegant young cavalier he was once? He looks at me in pain and anguish, conscious of his debt . . . ashamed. His old, wrinkled face contorts. His weak and flabby lips droop downward, and he begins to cry in silence. He reaches upward to wipe away his tears, and so I see his hands covered with brittle skin, cracked and full of wounds; his long, dirty finger nails; his stiff, neglected, revolting, gouty fingers. Oh, these hands that were once so beautiful, so elegant, so well cared for . . . these hands I was once so happy to kiss . . .

Then I look at my hands . . . O horrors! . . . they are just as old and neglected as his. When I raised them up, I see my own fingers bent and knotted with gout, the skin of my hands cracked and bloody in thousands of places. Since when have my hands become so horrible, so revolting? I do not know! I have never thought of observing myself. I have been living like a sleep walker. Now, as if coming out of a stupor, I begin to remember. It is as if a heavy, impenetrable fog covering my consciousness were now beginning to roll back and give me a clear view. I survey my whole life, my situation among people who treated me as if I were half animal, without love, without pity. In my semi-conscious state, I put up with everything, their many blows, their heartlessness, their ridicule as they—the people on the farm—made fun of my imperfections and my helplessness. How could I have thought about the way my hands looked, or about my appearance in general? When I was young, I sometimes wanted to be pretty *to please him*. In those days I tied coloured ribbons in my hair, but after I lost him and the baby, I didn't care about anything any more.

I never thought again at all about looking in a mirror, and didn't care how my hands looked. I only cared what people put in my outstretched, begging hands. Yes, now I can suddenly remember clearly that many people, as they were reaching over to put a coin in my hand, and I was grasping it eagerly, quickly drew back their hand from mine and let the money fall in order not to touch my fingers. Now I understand. Now I am disgusted too when I look at my decrepit hands . . . when I look at my dirty, torn, stinking beggar's rags. I wonder what my face looks like? O, if only he had not abandoned me so cruelly, neither of us would now be in this terrible state of neglect, and I would not have lost the child . . . Why? Why did it all have to happen? And why must we meet again in this way? Our lives are over! There is no way we can make amends! It's all over . . . too late! . . . too late!

Unspeakable hopelessness comes over me and I plunge into absolute despair. A terrible pain cuts through my whole being. I feel my heart is breaking. A cramp holds my heart as in a vice. Then everything blacks out before me . . . everything disappears . . . I fall into an abyss of nothingness.

Someone is groaning, rasping and gasping . . . I hear it and want to see who it is . . . slowly it gets light around me, and then my glance comes to rest on my husband's terrified face. Suddenly I realize that I am the one who is struggling to breathe. I am sitting up in bed, and he is shaking me desperately. When he sees that I recognize him, he breathes a sigh of relief and asks in a half-terrified voice:

'What's the matter with you? Are you all right again? I was frightened stiff. I woke up because of your groaning. You were sitting up in bed with your eyes wide open, but you didn't recognize me. You were looking right through me, right off into space . . . didn't even see me. What's the matter with you? For Heaven's sake tell me what's the matter!'

I look at him, open my mouth to reply, but cannot bring forth a single sound. My throat is still clamped shut out of sheer horror. Little by little I recover my senses enough to form words he can hear and understand: 'Not now—I cannot speak now—tomorrow.'

My husband stops asking questions, and I fall back on my pillows. He holds my hand in his as he observes me carefully. Then, seeing I have calmed down again, he puts out the light.

The next morning as we sat together in the garden, I told him my vision of the previous night.

I was a beggar woman who remembered her whole life, and *I am*—or was once—this beggar woman. *I* remember everything clearly that I once experienced when I was this woman. It was my own life which suddenly awakened to consciousness.

'I was an abandoned servant girl,' I went on telling my husband, 'living on a large country estate. I had no father, and had no memory of ever having had either father or mother. Among the many people around me as I grew up, there was a coachman who took care of the horses, men servants who cut wood and fed the hunting dogs, the cook who worked in the big kitchen and many other girls working in the kitchen, the courtyard and the house. This is where I have grown up, and this is all I know as home. Ever since I can remember, people have been pushing me around, and I have had to work at whatever jobs they gave me to do. After I grew up, I also had to help in the big house where our master and his family lived. It was a huge house with many rooms, and I learnt from the chambermaids that the rooms and their furnishings were all very beautiful. I was never allowed to enter them because I had no shoes, and only servants with shoes were allowed inside. I was an outside maid. All the rooms opened on to a very, very long corridor, and it was my job to keep this corridor clean. I carried over huge buckets of water from the well. Then, kneeling down, I scrubbed the big coloured tiles with a brush. I still see these tiles quite close to my face as I bend over them and rub, rub, rub, move back a row and then rub some more. Now and again I pour out water on to the floor and go on rubbing, row by row . . . endlessly! And when I finally do finish, I have to wash the corridor on the floor above. Days go by . . . months and years, and I go on washing and scrubbing these same stone floors. I am contented and seldom think about anything beyond the work I have to do. I like to wash these tile floors. They are colourful, and I like colourful things. In return for my work I can eat in the kitchen and sleep in a little room over the stable behind the house. In the courtyard I often see carriages which do not belong to our master. They belong to his guests who have already alighted at the front door. The coachmen drive their carriages into the courtyard, unhitch the horses, walk them around in a circle until they are cooled off, then lead them into the stable for the night. Many guests come for hunting and then my corridors are full of mud. The many men walk around with muddy boots, and I have to get up at the crack of dawn to wash my corridors so they will be clean when my master and his guests get up.

'One day when I happen to be in the courtyard, a wonderfully handsome young man comes out of the house, crosses the courtyard and enters the stable to look after his horse. He has his horse saddled, mounts and rides away. As if struck by magic, I look up at him. He is so marvellously handsome, and once he even looks around at me! I idolize him as if he were a God, and later during that very same night when he visits me in my little room, I allow him with joyous abandon to do with me whatever he wishes. His face shines through the mists which obscure my mind . . . for long and rapturous minutes I am in his arms . . .

'As he often came for hunting, my life was made up of happy days when he was there and long days of waiting for him to return.

'In a year's time our baby came. The cook helped me when I sought assistance and collapsed in front of her door. I did not know what was happening. But after I had endured terrible suffering and they laid the baby in my arms, I felt warmth in my heart for it. For the first time in my life I was really happy. *Somebody needed me; for somebody I meant everything !* The cook spoke with her mistress, who came, looked at me and the child, and gave her consent for the child to remain with me. I will work, I promised, harder than ever before, if only I can keep my child . . .

'When he, the father of my child, came back to our house again for a visit and came up to my little room to see me again, as was his custom, I proudly showed him the child and asked him to allow me to work in his house, on his estate, so that I could serve him. At first he shrank back horrified and then went on to say it was not at all sure that he was the father. "Who knows", he said, "what servant around here may be the father!" In vain I tried to explain to him that no man had ever touched me, that I had defended myself like a wild animal, and that I had allowed only him to do as he wished with me. In vain I pleaded with him to allow me to work in his vicinity, promising not to molest or disturb him if only I could be near him. For a while he listened. Then as I knelt before him, my arms around his knees, he pushed me away and ran out into the night. I never saw him again. Whether or not he ever came back to the house, I do not know. In any case, he never entered our courtyard again. In vain I waited year after year. He disappeared out of my life. But the baby was there! It meant everything to me. It filled my every waking thought. It meant more to me than life itself!

'I scrubbed the coloured tiles in the corridor and thought of my baby . . . I drew water from the well and thought of my baby. I hurried through my work even harder and faster, so that I could be with the child. It was a girl, pretty and intelligent like her father. She always did the opposite of what I told her, brooking no opposition. The more I became her slave, the less loving she was to me. When she was still quite small, she was rude and disrespectful towards me. Nothing I said or did pleased her, and what she liked best was to leave me and run around the countryside alone. Sometimes she went so far that she came back only the next day. I was in desperation and, when work was over, went out into the night to try to find her. When she came back the next day, the light came back into my life and everything was all right again.

'One day my child left me and did not come back. I waited in desperation, searched throughout the surrounding region—waited and hunted—but to no avail, my daughter was gone. The sun went out of my life, my world was suddenly empty; I had nothing more to live for and was absolutely unable to work. After a time I could bear it no longer and went away to search for my child. I never returned. I travelled from town to town and village to village asking people whether they had seen my child. Years went by, and I was still searching. Searching without hope, going on and on out of pure habit, driven by inner unrest. People gave me food to eat, and as my clothes began to wear thin and get torn, they would give me old worn out odds and ends of clothing. I kept on going from place to place, on and on . . .

'Once in my wanderings I met the cook I had worked with on the country estate. In the meantime she had married and was living with her husband in this city where I met her. She took me home, gave me some supper and told me that the father of my child . . .'

Here my husband suddenly seized my hand and interrupted my story. White as a sheet and with trembling voice, he said, 'Wait, wait! I'll go on with the story. I know what happened. *I remember what happened then !* While you were talking, everything suddenly became clear to me. I recognized myself and I know *I* was this man who abandoned you. I know I was terribly frivolous then and lacking in responsibility. I lived only to amuse myself and threw my money around with both hands until the day came when I lost everything.

'My family property was auctioned off, and I was obliged to leave my land and my manor. At first I turned to the friends who had spent time drinking and gambling with me and otherwise helping me squander my inheritance. But after a few weeks they made it obvious that my presence in their homes was superfluous. This experience was repeated with other so-called friends until I was completely disgusted at myself and at them. About that time, a real friend advised me to go to work. I wanted to make a fresh start and sincerely tried to get work, but nobody took me and my search for work seriously. I did not know *how* to work, or what I should do. And so I sank lower and lower. Finally I got a fixed idea that my tragic lot was God's punishment for having so despicably abandoned you and our child. I went to see my friend in whose home you had worked. I had no mission other than to find out what had happened to you both, but when I came you were gone, and no one knew where. As time went on, I found fewer and fewer friends willing to lend me money.

'When the time came that none of my erstwhile friends would take me in and give me a "loan" and as I was getting on in years, I began to ask complete strangers for help. So little by little I became a beggar, roaming the country, travelling from place to place, and spending the night wherever good-hearted people would allow me to sleep in their barn or stable. Physically as well as financially I fell further and further into ruin. With hunger plaguing me more and more as I got on in years, I finally reached the point where I had no pride or self respect any more at all and began to beg publicly on busy street corners. Thus it came about that we finally met as beggars.'

I listened eagerly to everything he told me, for it was exactly as I knew it to be. I knew from the very beginning that my husband was the old beggar, and I was amazed that he too remembered this previous existence in as much detail as I. The events he recalled tallied exactly with what the cook told me when I visited her, namely that he had squandered his inheritance and estate, and that one time—much later—he had come by the manor where I had worked in the hope of finding me. There was nothing left of the dashing young cavalier he had once been. Through sheer neglect and lack of honest effort, he had already become a human derelict, roaming the countryside and looking for hand-outs. After I had met the cook, I went back to our old manor to ask whether anyone knew his address. But there was no one who knew where he had gone or where he could be found. As I got on in years, I found it harder and harder to travel. Finally I settled in the city and made my living by begging near the stairs. It was there we finally met again and there I passed my last hours. For when I recognized him and realized that my whole life had been wasted and that there was no way of making amends because it was too late . . . too late . . . our child was lost and my life was over . . . I died right there sitting on the corner stone. My memories stopped there . . .

For a long time we looked at each other speechless, scarcely believing that such a thing could happen to two intelligent people in this modern world. What we had just experienced cannot be explained by any of the current theories of heredity or psychology. *We knew that everything had really and truly happened just that way!* There was no imagination involved!

The experience of having remembered this earlier meeting shook us both to the depths of our being. For a long time we sat beside each other in complete silence, while our thoughts spun around in circles. Finally my husband said, 'I never before wondered why, since my early youth, I have strictly avoided drinking, cards and other games of chance, dancing and all other forms of social life. This despite the fact that it is very much in my nature to enjoy drinking, dancing and entertainment. Now I realize how, after squandering my inheritance in riotous living and being obliged to live in abject misery, the idea was hammered home deeper and deeper into my consciousness that I must never again drink, never again gamble, never again be careless and happy-go-lucky.

'Since then I have learnt to recognize the value of money. And I have come to realize that the worth of a *human being begins when he is able to make a living for himself and his family*. All of these views now lie anchored deep in my subconscious because of what I learned and came to realize in that incarnation. That's why, in my present life, I was so anxious to study—just study throughout all the years of my youth. The subconscious knowledge and recognition of these facts was what gave me strength to resist and say "no" when the boys I went to college with set out to amuse themselves. I was always afraid that something terrible would happen to me if I allowed myself to get caught up in their parties and social life. Now I realize that I was only afraid of the misery which resulted from my devil-may-care way of living in that previous existence. My profound antipathy towards drinking and gambling and my realization that I must never indulge in such a way of life were rooted deep down in my subconscious.'

'Yes,' I replied, 'and after having been completely idle in that life, you are now diligent to a fault, thinking only of your work.'

'That's right. In the second half of that existence of mine I *wanted* to work but I hadn't learned a trade and didn't know what work meant. When I asked for work, people refused to take me seriously . . . wouldn't even trust me to do a job. Later during my vagabond years, strangers took pity on me and gave me work—cutting wood, loading carts, gathering grapes, beating carpets—and while I did these menial tasks with unskilled hands unused to work, I began to feel the great and overpowering desire to learn something useful . . . to be rich in skill and knowledge. And so in this life I have learned everything I possibly could, and I intend to continue learning until the end of my days!'

When he spoke the words 'till the end of my days' I felt as if an iron hand were contracting about my heart. Where will my child and I be at the end of his days? I became stiff with fear . . . it is a law of nature: *when we strike our hand against a wall, the wall strikes back without intending to.! It isn't the wall which really strikes back, but our own blow bounces back. In any case, whatever we hit always gives back the same blow we gave it.* No, I don't want to think through this premonition clear to the end. We will not leave him . . . no . . . no . . . no!

Then I thought about the relationship between my past life and my present one. What was the reason for this weakness of mine, for my having lived in this mental fog? And why, without any transition, was I now blessed with talents and skills? I could find no explanation.

For days we were under the impression of this tremendous experience, but soon we found ourselves going swimming and boating with our neighbour friends; so our memories from a previous existence soon began to pale. We were both of us much too business-like to bother our heads about the long distant past. My husband was soon obliged to leave anyway as his holidays were over. I stayed on with the other members of my family and their children.

The entire region of the great lake was of volcanic origin, and the local radiations probably affected me so greatly that I often had visions there.

I am inclined by nature to be very matter-of-fact, and always try to find a natural reason for everything I experience. I was never inclined to believe in ghosts or demons, and when people told me stories about nocturnal manifestations or appearances that were supposed to be almost nightly events in one old castle or another, I just smiled condescendingly in the manner of the inexperienced, thinking to myself that these persons were letting their imagination run away with them. The very last thing I would have 'imagined' is that I myself would have such experiences. Moreover, it is characteristic of visions that one never succeeds in having them through an act of will. On the other hand, they can come quite suddenly and unexpectedly when one's mind is fully occupied with other things.

That very same summer after my husband had returned to his work in the city, we were all retiring to rest after a happy day. I entered my room where my little son was already fast asleep. I lay down, extinguished the candle—in this remote place there was no electricity—and went to sleep.

I do not know how long I had been sleeping when I suddenly awoke, aware of a noise in the room. It sounded as if someone were groping around in the darkness. I reached for the box of matches, quickly lit my candle . . . and a moment later was lunging towards a horrible apparition which was *already* carrying my child in its arm and trying to escape. It was a female form, similar to pictures one sees of witches, and when I surprised her with my light, she was trying to glide out of the room on a cord or wire which led from our beds through the window. I lunged at her, seized my child and tried to take it away from her. She hung on tight, and a terrible struggle began. The witch had already moved up a bit on the wire. It seemed almost as if in some way or other she were connected to it, as if there were a flow of force from it to give her strength. But she could not get away because I clung desperately to my child. Each of us was holding my boy's body in a grip of steel, pulling him to and fro as we struggled. Somehow I felt intuitively that she could only hold on to my child for a short time, and if she could not succeed in wrenching him from me within this short time, she would have to fly away empty handed. So this violent struggle continued until suddenly and quite unexpectedly she relinquished the child, glided out of the window on the wire, and disappeared in the darkness . . .

And I . . . ? I was kneeling in my bed; my son was lying beside me, resting in absolute peace, snugly covered, and sound asleep. But the candle was burning on my night table. Had I been dreaming? Had I forgotten to extinguish the candle before falling asleep? No, the match was still glowing beside it, proving that I had only just lit the candle. The entire scene must have taken place within the space of a few moments. If it were not so, the match would not have been still warm. No, I had *not been dreaming*!

I extinguished the candle, lay back in bed, and tried to quiet my galloping heartbeat. What was that? A witch? Are there such things? What is a witch? Why do painters everywhere always paint the same kind of witches, and where does this figure come from? How does it come about that there are such things as witches in the first place, and why do people claim that witches ride on broomsticks? If witches are really only a figment of the imagination, why do drawings and sketches of them look just about the same the world over—showing them with long, pointed, drooping noses, hunched backs, and broomsticks in their hands? Why isn't a witch ever shown with a club foot? Because people say the devil has a club foot. But how do they know for sure that *the devil has a club foot* and a witch does not? Who has ever seen a devil and a witch? Now I have some idea about why witches are drawn with broomsticks in their hands. The witch I had seen was holding on to this wire, and when she flew out of the window on it, I could easily have imagined her to be riding on a broomstick. I can understand that uneducated villagers who know nothing about currents of force think a witch is holding on to a broomstick and flying away on it. The witch was the personified servant of the 'evil one'. I simply knew it. She was reality, a fact! Had the whole scene been merely a projection, an illusion? Naturally, I knew it had been. But *what caused it? Where did it come from?* And why just such a picture? For me that was reality and the interesting question was why everyone who sees such an illusion, or projection, or whatever we may choose to call it, sees it in the same form. Why do we all carry this picture in our subconscious, if it really does come from our subconscious? It could of course be answered that I had seen pictures of witches and this was a projection of pictures I had seen. But such was not the case! For even though the witch was very similar to the usual pictures one sees, I noticed to my great surprise that her appearance did not coincide with them in all details.

And where did this strange wire or rope come from? I had never seen such a thing in any of the pictures and yet it was there. Moreover, after my experiments in the transmission of will from one person to another, I had quite a different opinion about this wire. I could understand it in terms of a flow of force, perhaps even a flow of will. But where did it come from? And from whom? And if a flow of force can be seen as a physical form, is not the witch herself perhaps merely a form built up of forces radiating from a source or from different sources? And what are we human beings? Where does the human form come from? Are we not also visible forms made up of various flows of force? What is 'reality'? Only what can be touched and grasped? Are not we human beings, too, merely projections? And *do we not merely believe* that we are actually formed? Are not love, hate, hope, desperation, good and evil realities too? Do not people suffer or rejoice because of these intangible, invisible forces which are not any less 'actual' than the tangible 'realities'? Naturally I know the physical form of my child—the 'real child'—as people would say—was lying peacefully in bed during my struggle with the apparition. And I am equally convinced that the entire struggle occurred only *between forces* and not *between 'bodies'*, but does that make this struggle any less real? Was not perhaps the apparition of the witch and the child even much more real than the child's material form lying in bed? What is a material form? Only the resultant outward cover of forces which build up the material body. Hence the force is the cause, the material body only the effect. Which is more important and more real?

For a long time I went on asking myself these and similar questions about the experiences I had had. For me it was perfectly real. I had enough proof that I had not fallen asleep. And even had this been the case, it is perfectly possible to experience complete reality in a dream!

Several nights later, after all the family had gone to bed, and the house had quieted down for the night, I too went to bed. It had been an exceptionally hot day, and my room was close and sultry, so I not only left my window open, but also the door from my room into the hall outside. Thus from my bed I could see the staircase leading up to the rooms above.

As I lay there, I reviewed the whole day in my mind. What had I done well? what not so well? What should I have said or done, and what should I *not* have said or done? Then I went over in my mind what I wanted to cook the next day, for the housekeeping was my task. Thus my thoughts were occupied with quite everyday, matter-of-fact things. Suddenly I noticed that two peculiar forms were approaching from the house door trying slowly and stealthily to cross in front of mine. They were both full-size human forms, absolutely black like shadows. I did not see them as three-dimensional figures. Instead, I had the impression that the only reason I could see them at all was because they were absorbing all the light in the place they happened to be. To express the matter in different terms, I did not really see these beings themselves but the hole they made in the rays of light where they were. In scientific terms, they were causing complete interference with the light rays, and I could only be aware of their presence by virtue of the fact that there were no light rays at all where these two beings stood. Otherwise, they were invisible. It is difficult to find an expression adequate to describe this phenomenon. In a twinkling I understood why farmers use the word 'shadow' in talking about ghosts or spooky apparitions. Actually these two figures were 'shadows', but not shadows made by anything else. On the contrary, they were shadows solely because of the complete absence of light. I had never dreamed that there could be such complete blackness. Later it occurred to me that the astronomers know of such a 'black hole' in the skies. Caused by a complete absence of light, it is known as the 'horse's head' because of its peculiar shape. They cannot explain it in other terms than as interference in light rays. Something swallows up and destroys the light radiating from the universe, and we see only a huge shadow. The two figures I saw were made of the same absence of light.

On their shoulders they carried a pole from which something utterly and indescribably horrible was hanging. It resembled an octopus, except that it had no organic and organized form. It hung down from this pole like an amorphous mass of raw dough, constantly expanding and then contracting. It was a loathsome, greenish, pussy, decaying mass in which—somehow or other I knew sicknesses, misfortune, catastrophes and death were lurking. I knew that this monster was concentrated 'evil' itself! It turned and stretched on the pole with intentional wickedness, and I realized it was looking for new opportunities and victims on which to wreak its fearful power. I saw the shadowy figures moving towards my sister's room. Horrified, I knew I must prevent this satanic source of power from causing any harm. Sitting bolt upright in bed, I screamed at the top of my lungs, 'Grete!—Grete!'

Even as I screamed, the two shadowy figures disappeared instantaneously, while the demon shrank in size and rolled up into a greenish phosphorescent sphere about the size of a football, then rolled with gliding and jumping movements up the steps. In a voice filled with Hellish laughter, of which I was perfectly aware although I could not hear it with my physical ears, it screamed scornfully at me, 'So you think you can catch me! Ha ha ha ha ha!' With that, it slipped through the open window and disappeared in the darkness.

I sprang out of my bed and ran out into the hallway to see what it was. Everywhere there was absolute silence!

Almost at the same moment my brother opened his door upstairs, came out to the banister, looked down and asked, 'Who is down there?'

I lighted a candle and answered, 'It is I. Why have you come out of your room?'

'I woke up suddenly,' he said, 'as if in a nightmare, with a feeling that some terrible danger was in the house. I came out of my room to have a look around . . . and you're up too. What's the matter?'

While he was speaking, my two sisters came from their rooms, and then the servants, all wondering why I had screamed. I told them everything. Then we searched the house. We found the door locked and everything in its proper place. I asked my brother to try to move the window above the stairs to see whether perhaps a draft of air could have moved it in such a way as to cause it to reflect the full moon. Perhaps this was the reason for my having seen a greenish phosphorescent ball? But the moon was on the other side of the house, and it was quite impossible for me to have seen a reflection of it from my bed.

Having found nothing, we all had no choice but to go back to bed. For a long time I kept hearing the fiendish taunt, 'So you think you will catch me?— Ha ha ha ha!'

A few days later my little son complained about a tummy ache. I felt sure the pains were caused by appendicitis. I left with him the very same day to go back to the city and have him examined by one of my father's friends who had become a famous surgeon and director of a large hospital. He found there actually was an irritation of the appendix, but said that we could wait until autumn to operate. So we drove back to the lake shore where my little son was able to play with his young friends until we left the resort at the end of the summer.

In looking back, I would like best to be able to skip the period which followed in order not to have to re-experience all the events of the time in my memory. Nevertheless I find I am obliged to recount the broad lines to make the later events of my life understandable.

The child was operated on and the operation was successful. A week later he was allowed to come home. During the time he was in the hospital, my sister's little daughter took sick with a very strange and persistent throat infection. Once during a visit I saw she had a red skin rash under the compress around her neck. On the assumption that the rash might have been caused by the wet compress, her skin was then treated with a powder, and by the next day the rash had disappeared. By the time my son was discharged from the hospital, his little cousin was up, and the two were soon playing together all day long. But there was something about my son's appearance I did not like. He was pale, tired and lacking in energy. Worst of all, instead of gathering strength, he became weaker and more depressed with each passing day. A week later, when I took his temperature, I was shocked to find he was running a high fever. He began to cry bitterly and seemed to be getting worse moment by moment. Singularly enough, his body was covered with a rash which looked exactly like the one his little cousin had had on her neck. We called the most famous child specialist in the area. After his examination he asked whether anyone in the family had had scarlet fever.

'No,' I replied, 'no one.'

'Are you sure no one had a persistent throat infection?'

The ground began to teeter under my feet.

'Yes,' I said, 'his little cousin had a sore throat for a long time and a similar skin rash on her neck.'

The professor smiled. 'Yes, that was scarlet fever. Your son's resistance was still low and he caught a severe infection. We'll have to vaccinate him immediately. Are *you* going to take care of the child?' he asked me.

'Yes.'

'Have you had scarlet fever?'

'No, and I won't get it now either. I am immune to all infectious diseases.'

'I can only assume the responsibility,' said the professor, 'if we vaccinate you too.'

I knew from experience that I could not endure serum of any kind, and I tried to convince him that he should not vaccinate me. All in vain. We were both vaccinated with a serum which was quite new at the time and scarcely tested. I felt like an ox being brought to the slaughterhouse! I was obliged knowingly to permit myself to be poisoned.

'You can take my word, it will not harm you!' These words were to ring in my ears for a long time to come. Later as I lay helplessly sick and poisoned, a hair's breadth away from death I wished many times I could call in this well-intentioned doctor so he could see why a physician should sometimes listen to his patient and not merely treat him like a number. The serum was a slow, insidious poison . . .

First we had to fight desperately for the boy's life. Six long weeks I sat at his bedside while his fever raged at 104° and 105°. The effect of the long protracted fever and the reaction of the serum were so strong that his heartbeat often failed him. A young doctor moved in with us to be ready any minute, day or night, with an injection to start the heart beating again. There we were, three of us in an isolated apartment, fighting for the boy's life.

'So you think you can catch me?—Me?—Ha ha ha ha!' Again and again I heard the hellish voice in my ears while for long days and nights I held the child in my arms, refusing to give it up. I got him back from the witch: His appendix was already out. But the battle with the greenish phosphorescent monster was not over yet.

My son became weaker and weaker as his fever mounted. The professor vaccinated him with a new dose of serum. For some days the fever abated, but then the left side of the boy's throat began to swell. The doctors said the infection had settled in a gland, and they watched the swelling to see whether they would have to operate. It grew bigger with each passing day so the boy's head was leaning far off to one side. Our struggle grew more and more desperate as his fever kept on rising. The child was in constant delirium. For five long weeks we had scarcely been able to get more than an hour or two of sleep in a day. The child rolled to and fro in the bed, quieting down a bit whenever I held him in my arms. The last five days I was sitting beside his bed constantly, holding his poor little body in my arms and waiting . . . listening to his heavy breathing and waiting . . . for five endlessly long days and nights I waited . . .

I had never believed it possible for a human being to go so long without sleep. After five days and five nights, I was still holding the child in my arms. During those long hours I recalled often having heard mothers complain about their children's ingratitude: 'Is that why I took care of him?—Is that why I made such sacrifices and sat at his bedside when he was sick?—etc, etc.' *In so doing, I realized that a mother does not take care of her child for its sake, but for her own sake!* There are many women who imagine themselves to be good and devoted mothers because they take care of their children. No! by such a criterion I was not a good mother, for I was nursing my child and doing everything in my power to save its life—*for my sake*! *I* shuddered at the thought of losing the child. No, it was not that I loved *the child*; it was for *love of myself*, that I wanted to save it. It was so important *to me*. *I* was spiritually so closely tied to my child that I couldn't even bear the thought that it might disappear from my life. I sat there holding my boy in my arms, realizing full well that I was doing it *for myself* and that I wanted to keep the child *for myself*. I held him close in my arms and tried to give him some of my own vital force so that he would remain with *me*. Yes, I knew that an invisible force radiates from the solar plexus of each human being, a force which can grow to giant strength when the person concerned really wants something with all his heart. It can even conquer the gravitational pull of the earth. Now I wanted to *increase* the power of gravitation; I wanted to keep my child here on earth.

I sat there with my child, trying to concentrate all my thoughts on giving him strength to overcome the terrible sickness. Nevertheless I could not pray God to keep my child alive. 'Things are never bad,' I remembered the words of Epictetus, 'it's only the way you think about them.' From *my standpoint* it would have been the greatest catastrophe to lose the child. But I must not pray to the greatest power, the Creator, for personal, subjective things; for *He* knows what is good and why, and I must not want to keep my child for short-sighted, human reasons. And the child? For him too it is certainly best for God's will to be done, whatever that may be. So as I sat there with my boy in my arms, my little human-maternal self was trembling for fear of losing the child, but I was praying constantly, 'Thy will be done . . . Thy will be done . . .'

I repeated it hundreds of times in those long hours, while my body was getting stiffer and stiffer, until it finally began to rebel. My back was so numb I couldn't feel it any more. I tried to change my position ever so slightly, but the child noticed my movement at once, tightened his grip on me and cried out, 'Stay here, stay here, hold me tight! If you stay here and hold me tight, I'll forgive you for all the wrong you've done me!' My mind began reeling . . . what wrong have I done that he could forgive me for?

Up to that time I had thought I was doing everything a mother should do for her child. From the moment of its birth, this child took first place in all my thoughts. In every way I could, I wanted to make it happy. What secret wound was it now nursing? What wrong had I done for which I needed its forgiveness?

I tried to find out. 'My little darling,' I said, 'be quiet. I'm here with you now and holding you tight. But what are you going to forgive me for?'

He answered, 'I don't know, just hold me tight and I'll forgive you for everything . . .'

I looked over at the young doctor who said quietly, 'He's talking in a delirium —pay no attention to his words.'

'Yes, yes, he is delirious . . .'—but I already knew enough about psychology to know that the boy's words were coming forth from some great depth. I thought about them for a long, long time, wondering how I had wronged this human soul . . . what great debt I might owe it . . .

Until one day everything became clear . . .

On the evening of the fifth day we had gone without sleep, the child left me free again for a few minutes. With the young doctor's help, I got up, stiff in every joint, and went about like an automaton doing the things I needed to do. But my spirit was in such abysmal darkness as if all the devils of Hell were plunging after us. I was afraid I was going to crack up. I needed to find some kind of new strength to bear my burden. In such moments a person gives up all his arrogance and reaches out for help wherever he hopes to find it. The Bible! The book lay on the night table and I reached for it like a drowning man. I opened it without thinking, and my eyes fell on the following passage in the old testament: 'Fear not, Your enemies shoot their invisible arrows upon you only as long as the Lord allows. But when their time comes, ye shall be free of all evil.' .

The effect of these words was indescribable. I felt as if a mountain of weight had fallen from me . . . after six weeks of endless darkness—light . . . at last, light . . . light!

The telephone rang. It was mother. 'How is our little one doing?' she asked.

'Mother, the child's going to get well!' I shrieked into the telephone.

'Has the fever gone down?'

'No, it's still up to 104, but God has sent me a message . . .'—and I told her what I had read in the Bible.

'May God grant it so,' said mother.

I had to hang up immediately, because the child was crying for me. I ran to him, and in the very next moment the horrible swelling opened up. In the last few days it had become as big as a large ball. It burst internally into his throat and mouth, and a horrible greenish mass of pus came pouring out over his lips. I couldn't help remembering the *green ball* . . . it was the same colour.

The doctors had been waiting for the swelling on the outside of the boy's neck to get soft so they could cut, but on the outside it was still so hard they did not dare. Now nature had taken a hand herself and freed the child. A few moments later he lay down again and fell into a deep sleep. He slept as if he were dead. The whole night long we kept watch. His pulse became stronger, his breathing slower, and his forehead was no longer wet with perspiration . . . He was sleeping peacefully. After the long weeks of unending vigil, I lay down myself and tried to go to sleep. But with no success. My nerves had forgotten what sleep was.

The child slept soundly until 11 o'clock the next morning. Father telephoned often: 'How's the boy? Still asleep? How's his pulse?'

'Yes, father, the fever's gone and he's sleeping soundly . . . a healthy sleep.'

Finally he opened his eyes and asked for milk. Like a dry sponge soaking up liquid, he drank four glasses one after another. Then he asked for his playthings.

The next day was Christmas. My husband, my parents, and my brother and sister came by that afternoon to bring a little Christmas tree and armloads of toys for the boy. I set him in an armchair and pulled him into the middle room so that our family could wave to him through the grillwork in front of the door of the house. The boy was still thin beyond recognition and weak . . . but alive! We all cried for joy. The evil had been forced to yield . . . its time on the great cosmic clock had run out. I was so moved I could not speak. I felt as if I were dreaming. I was the very picture of gratitude. My wish and God's will had been identical in this case . . . *He* gave me back my boy!

My son recovered slowly, the young doctor bade us farewell, and the day finally came when our youngster could get up. He had to learn to walk all over again. But he became stronger from day to day, and by the end of two months he was well enough to go back to school. I could sleep once more and wanted to return to my sculpturing. I felt so strange, however, just as if I were a little bit tipsy, and the world about me looked as if I were seeing it through water. Everything seemed to get hazier and hazier . . . farther and farther away from me.

The serum with which I had been vaccinated had been prepared from hormones of stallions. As I later heard, the new, scarcely tested preparation affected women as if it were a completely foreign substance—a poison—in their blood. The papers were full of the scandal. Most of the women who had been vaccinated showed early symptoms of neurosis. Then, as their bodies tried to get rid of their poisoned blood, they suffered from incessant haemorrhages. There was no way to help them, and many died. As a consequence, there were masses of lawsuits.

I felt worse and worse from day to day. Things around me looked more and more as though I were seeing them through water. A strange feeling overcame me, and I didn't know myself any more. I was able to walk straight, but I always felt dizzy. This odd feeling that I was looking at the world through some strange liquid grew stronger from day to day.

One day I had an attack. Instead of a regular pulse beat, there was only a flutter. Unable to walk, eat or speak, I lay in bed with an ice pack over my heart still seeing the world as if it were swimming around me. It would take us too far afield if I were to describe how I suffered. Suffice it to say, I wandered through the various departments of Hell . . . for months!

By summertime I was somewhat recovered, and on our doctor's advice, we all went to the lake. Perhaps the change of air was good for me. I lay on the terrace of our family villa, trying to calm and control my dancing nerves. Hundreds and thousands of times I repeated the word 'caaaaalm' . . . 'caaaaalm' . . . 'caaaaalm' . . . Slowly my condition improved and sometimes I was even able to sleep at night.

One day I noticed my son was not playing with the other children on the beach. On the contrary, he was hanging around my sofa and being suspiciously quiet about it. With a sudden shock, I began to hope he was not falling ill again. I do not like it when children are suspiciously quiet.

'What is the matter with you?' I asked him. 'Why aren't you playing with the other children?'

The boy leaned against the back of my sofa, looked at me attentively and answered, 'Mummy, is it possible that I have lived before?'

His question amazed me. 'Where did you get that idea?' I asked in return.

'I was in the garden and saw a big black beetle. When I poked him a bit with a twig, he turned over on his back and lay still as if dead. I was curious to see what he would do, so I watched him and waited. I kept on watching him for a long time, perhaps it was even half an hour. Then all of a sudden, the beetle righted himself and ran away. It was then I had a very strong feeling I had lived before. It only seemed as if I had died and people thought I was dead, but then I got up and went on just like the beetle, and here I am now alive again. That means I never died at all! And I'm asking you for another reason, Mummy. Every day when I wake up in the morning, before I open my eyes, I always have a feeling as if I had to jump right up and go hunting to find food for my wife and my children. And only when I open my eyes and look around my room, I realize that I'm a little boy and your son. But Mummy, my wife and my children and everybody there are not like the people here, but they're . . . all . . . all black and quite naked.' An embarrassed smile spread across my son's face.

I listened to him with ever-growing interest, but I did not want him to notice my surprise. I let him finish talking. Then I asked, 'So you were the father of several children . . . but where did you live?'

The child took paper and pencil, and with a sure and steady hand he drew a round hut with a very special opening in the roof for the smoke. He could never have seen a hut like that in our country. Before the hut he sketched in a naked woman with long hanging breasts. Beside the hut there was a body of water with waves, and in the distance palm trees. 'We lived in huts like this,' he said, showing me the drawing. 'We built them ourselves, just as each of us built himself a boat by hollowing out a log. There was a big river there, but we couldn't go in deep as we do here in the lake, because some kind of a monster was living there in the water. I don't remember what kind, only that it bit off people's legs, and that's why we didn't go into the water.

'Now you can understand why I always screamed and howled last year when you tried to take me out into the water. I was afraid that something under the water was going to bite off my legs. Even now, whenever I go bathing, I have that same feeling. Only I know by now that there's nothing dangerous in the water here. And remember last year, when I wanted to row, Mummy? It was just after we had bought the big family boat. At first you wouldn't let me, because you said I would have to learn how. But I just knew I could because I remembered how well I was able to get around in my dugout canoe . . . as well as if it were a part of me. While sitting in it, I could even flip over into the water and come up again on the other side.

'Remember I kept begging so long, you finally got impatient and said I could try but I would see I could not row. Remember? And remember how surprised you all were when I *did* row, *and with only one oar*. I was too small to handle both oars—my arms were too short—but I was able to move our big boat around safely among the other boats and all the bathers. Oh boy, with my dugout canoe —there where I was living—I could do anything! You should have seen me then! And the trees were not like the ones here.'

With his stubby finger he pointed to the drawing. 'They were like this one. and there were all kinds of other plants there. See, that's me hunting for a big bird, and that's my hat beside me.'

Everything he drew made up a perfect tropical landscape with palm trees and other tropical plants. The figure supposedly representing him was a typical negro. Only his hat was suspicious. It looked exactly like a modern man's felt hat. Not wanting either to disturb him or excite his imagination, I questioned him very cautiously. He had never seen naked women, except perhaps as works of art, and these latter never have hanging breasts; so I asked him, 'Why have you drawn your wife with such long, ugly, hanging breasts?'

The child looked up at me in amazement at such a question, then answered without hesitation and very matter-of-factly, 'Because she had breasts like that! And they're not ugly! She was very beautiful!' he added proudly. This reply convinced me that my boy had not heard these things in some way or another from others. He had never been to the cinema and had never had any books about Africa. Where could he have picked up the idea that a woman with long, hanging breasts is beautiful? Our ideal of beauty is quite different. Finally I asked him, 'What is the last thing you remember?'

'I was hunting when a tiger approached. I threw my spear, but that didn't stop him. With my spear in his breast he jumped on me. I don't know what happened after that.'

'Good, that's all very interesting. Naturally it's possible that you have lived before and all of that really happened. But now you're here. Don't think about the past any more; think about the present. You can tell me all about things like this, but don't tell other people about your memories.'

'Yes, Mummy,' said the boy, 'I already know that, because grown-ups think we kids are crazy. They always make fun of us. But what do you think happened to my wife and children?'

'I cannot tell you that. But don't forget that everything passes away. Only love remains eternal, and so love will lead you to them again in this life.'

'Oh, that's fine!' said the boy, and he ran off to resume his playing with the other children. I took his drawings and put them into the diary I had been keeping since he was born ...

I never asked the boy any more about these memories. I did not want his imagination to be stimulated, nor did I want him to lose himself in these memories.

Why should I? I knew that he had not been able to see or read any books about Africa. I knew every step he took and what he was doing. And it really was surprising to recall that, although he was generally quite brave and even inclined to be a bit of a daredevil, when we had first taken him out to bathe in the lake, he had fought and kicked and struggled most savagely, screaming at the top of his lungs as if we were trying to kill him. I had had to explain to him that he could come along with the rest of us without fear and that nothing was going to happen to him. It was only then he let me carry him into the water, but I had to promise to watch out for him and not leave him alone. The next day the very same thing happened. He refused to go into the water alone, kicking and screaming as he had done the day before. Again I had to carry him in my arms. Little by little he conquered his fear, and he finally became a little duck, happily splashing, rowing and sailing on the lake all day long. Our conversation made me remember how, when he was very small—around four or five—he and his little cousin would paint pictures together. While the faces his little cousin painted were always pink, his were always dark brown. When I once tried to show him why he should not paint the faces so dark, he made no reply, but merely went on painting chocolate coloured faces.

We spoke no more about his memories. Now and again he made some comment which showed me that these things were still alive within him. Several years later, when he was about thirteen, one of the neighbours came running into our garden, calling for me to come out to the street. My son, he said, had climbed up to the top of a very high poplar tree, so high that he certainly would not be able to come down without falling. There were a number of trees, all of them about sixty to seventy feet high. I peered upward into the branches to try to see which tree my boy was in. Finally I yelled up to find out where he was and he promptly yelled back to ask what I wanted.

'Come down immediately!'

'Why?'

'We're not discussing why now,' I called back. 'You come right down here!' Without saying a word, he started to descend, climbing skilfully but cautiously with complete assurance, like a little monkey. Finally he jumped down from the lowest branch and, with controlled annoyance, asked, 'Why did I have to come down?'

'Because it's absolutely senseless for you to climb up so high. It's positively shameful when other people have to tell me what you're doing. What's the good of such dare-devil stunts? What in the world were you doing up there?'

'I've made myself a nest where I can eat a meal of boiled corn. It tastes much better up there, and I get such a wonderful view. I can look out over everything.'

'Well don't do it any more. What sense can there possibly be in doing anything so dangerous? Build yourself a nest down here!'

The boy looked away for a moment angrily, then said, 'O.K. I'm not supposed to climb up there any more because you think it's dangerous. But who do you think looked after me when I was living in the jungle and climbed around the trees which were a lot higher so that I could watch the animals? Where were you then?'

'I don't know where I was then, but now I'm here and you have to obey!' I answered emphatically. He wasn't pleased at all, but as I gave him plenty of freedom in other respects, he soon found other occupations and the matter was forgotten.

Some time later he came home from school in complete exasperation. 'Ridiculous!' he exploded. 'The priest was trying to make us believe that people live only once. But I know that people live more than once! I know it! But it's best not to try to talk to grown-ups. A fellow just has to keep his mouth shut!'

The impressions of this life had probably displaced the memories in his consciousness, and for a long time he made no further mention of these matters. When he was about fifteen, he asked us to buy him a big jazz drum. Together we went to the best music shop in town, and he picked out the biggest drum in sight with all its trappings. Then the miraculous experience we had had when he first tried to row was repeated again. As soon as he had the drum in the house, he took the two drum sticks, sat down beside it and started playing *the most difficult rhythms and the most impossible syncopations,* all with a perfectly sure hand and complete self-confidence. He played ecstatically, his eyes beaming and tears rolling down his cheeks. He said nothing about how he came to be able to play a drum. Only once, as he was playing a very peculiar rhythm, he remarked, 'Hear that Mum? That's how we used to signal each other and pass on messages across tremendous distances.' And he went on drumming like one possessed.

He was never interested in reading stories about negro life. 'Why should I?' he asked. 'I know better than books can tell me what life was like there. Why should I care what white people have written about it? And when I read real true descriptions, I always start to cry, even when I try not to . . .'

Even as a grown-up young officer in the air force, seeing a negro cinema-film always moved him to tears. Sitting there in the darkness, he would cry like a baby—although silently—with big salty tears streaming down his cheeks.

Where had he learnt to play the drum? How hard it is I learnt myself when I once tried it. How does a city child come to want to own a drum? And why should a happy, up-to-date young man burst into tears when he plays a drum or sees negro films?

Years later Paul Brunton paid us a visit when he was returning to Europe from India. I told him about my son's memories. He asked to see the drawings. After examining them attentively, he said, 'This kind of hut is typical of a particular tribe living on the banks of the Zambesi in Central Africa. He has drawn it correctly in every detail.'

'Yes, but this hat isn't an African native's hat? It looks just like a civilized man's hat made of felt,' I said.

Brunton smiled. 'No, you're mistaken. The child is right. The hat is indeed typical of this tribe. Only it's not made of felt, but of bulrushes plaited together. His hunting weapon is correctly drawn too. And the monster that bites off people's legs is a crocodile, of course. There are many of them there. But tell me how you came to attract a negro as your child?' he asked finally.

'I don't know how to answer that one,' I replied. Then we both smiled and talked about other things.

This all happened several years later. My son's first memories came that summer at the lake shore when the little black beetle attracted his attention and he stopped playing to watch it for a long, long time. Without knowing it, he used an Indian method to achieve great concentration. Indian yogis do it by staring for a long time at a black spot on the wall, or at a crystal ball. Unknowingly, the child did the same, for the little black beetle was like a black spot, and the boy probably fell into a trance quite unintentionally. Thus the memory of a previous incarnation came to life within him.

The summer went by and my condition improved. My consciousness was clear again, and I no longer saw the world in such a hazy fashion. The burning sensation in my blood also stopped. But in the autumn, after our return to the city, I began to have the same symptoms as the many women who had died from their horse serum vaccinations. I had to go back to bed again, suffering from terrible cramps and pains. I never would have believed that a human being can endure such torture without dying. I completely lost control of my body, just as if my nerves had been quite paralysed. When I wanted to raise my hand, my hand did not budge. It was a terrifying condition. And in my sleepless nights, I heard an ugly repugnant voice drowning out the roaring in my ears: 'So you think you can catch me?—Ha ha ha . . .'

The doctors consulted each other again and advised an operation

That same evening we had a telephone call from one of my husband's boyhood friends with whom we had kept in close touch. He had just returned from a sojourn of many years in India. The next day he came by to pay us a visit. Seeing me in such miserable shape, he said, 'You know while I was in India I spent a lot of time learning yoga under a great master. If you follow my advice and do as I say, you will get well again. Under no circumstances should you submit to an operation.'

I promised to do whatever he told me to.

He then showed me a few simple breathing exercises which I could do as I lay there in bed only half alive. He told me I should practice them often during the day, and in doing them I was to *guide and control my consciousness.*

I followed his instructions to the letter.

Within a few days' time my condition was considerably better. The pains were abating, and all my other symptoms showed a surprising change for the better.

Within two weeks I was so much improved that I could even stand up for a few minutes at a time. I became *myself* again! I still felt minor disturbances, but our friend showed me some more yoga exercises, and I kept on improving. By the time spring came around, I was strong enough to travel to the seashore to spend a few months convalescing. That blessed climate, combined with the salt water bathing and yoga exercises, gave me back my health. During my last four weeks there, my husband was with me and I experienced the most beautiful period of my *personal* life. Only one who has been hopelessly sick and then recovered knows what it means to be well *again*!

Oh thou unknown strength and power people call *God*! I thank *thee* that *thou* hast given me back my health; that thou hast permitted me to escape from Hell; that thou hast enabled me to avoid becoming a burden upon my loved ones . . . enabled me to become a useful working human being again!

The sun had never been so beautiful, nor the sky so blue, nor the sea so sparkling as that summer.

When autumn came, we went home, and soon I was back at work in my studio.

One evening we all went to the cinema together. The programme consisted of a number of Walt Disney films, and we got an immense amount of fun out of watching Mickey Mouse, Pluto and Donald Duck. Then came a film in which all three of these animals teamed up and founded a firm to drive the ghosts and spooks out of haunted houses. They advertised their service in the newspaper, and their advertisement came to the attention of one of a number of ghosts who were living together in an old castle. He straightway summoned all the other ghosts and spooks and goblins, and indignantly read the notice to them. Incensed at the idea that even ghosts would no longer be able to live in peace, they all consulted together and decided they would teach the people in this new firm a lesson. One of them called up the firm and asked to have a man sent over. Then the head ghost assigned a specific task to each of the many spooks assembled. One was to hide behind the door, another under the bed, another inside the mirror so that anyone looking at it would see a ghost instead of himself—all with the idea of giving the people in Mickey & Co. such a terrible scare they would be glad to give up their plan. When the jobs were all assigned, the chief spook gave a signal and all his cronies disappeared by simply rolling up into *greenish phosphorescent balls which rolled away, gliding and hopping, and disappeared in different directions, laughing fiendishly at the idea that earthly creatures should think of trying to catch them*!

I became stiff with amazement! My younger sister and brother began to call out, 'Look, look! Esther's green ball! Just look at that! . . .' They were so excited and so loud in their comments, I thought for a little while the ushers were going to throw us out of the house. They could not have known—no one could have!—that the entire scene, as the chief spook himself rolled up into a greenish ball, laughed fiendishly and hopped away, was just exactly the way I had seen it long, long before!

I was thoroughly shaken. Could it really be that other people saw these manifestations too? I did not doubt for a moment that Walt Disney had actually seen such a greenish ball! Or how could he have come to invent—out of pure imagination—a sequence matching with exquisite precision exactly what I had seen long, long before? It was absolutely too much to suppose that this was pure coincidence. But that was not all!

A few weeks later I received a book entitled, *Aram Magic and Mysticism*. It was a large collection of authentic documents. After reading about a number of phenomena, I came to the following quotation: '. . . how should this somebody come through a door that was locked and bolted? Knowing full well that the door was firmly locked, I thought: "Nobody can get in here!" Even if the door knob is turned and the door made a noise. But what was that? There was a rustling sound in the room, a rapping sound in the wardrobe. It came over to my bed and made its presence known by rapping on my bedstead, then went past my bed and tinkled on the glass of the lamp on my night table.' (page 458) And a bit further on: 'I saw nothing, and I did not particularly try to see anything. Only the person in the next room claims to have seen, on the floor of my room, *a light about the size of the full moon.* He claims to have seen clearly how this rolling ball of light appeared in the doorway and disappeared behind the wall.' (page 459)

I could scarcely believe my eyes. Was I meeting this full-moon-like ball of light again? Apparently this ball of light is not such a rare thing. How strange! With a little reflection, we can find an analogous example in electricity: the ball of lightning. This ball also seems to roll through the air. There are reports recording how such balls of lightning have bounced into a room through a window, rolled across the room and out of another open window without doing any damage. As long as the lightning stays rolled up in a ball, there is no danger, but when it emerges from this spherical form, it destroys everything in its path. In this latter case, a ball of lightning is a thousand times more dangerous than ordinary lightning. What then is this greenish phosphorescent ball which can do such catastrophic damage, if not a ball of lightning, only on another plane?

Handed down to us from incredibly ancient times, there is this saying attributed to an outstandingly great initiate, Hermes Trismegistos, who was said to know all the secrets of Heaven and Earth: 'As above, so below; as below, so above.'

What a remarkable parallel phenomenon: This green ball and the ball of lightning!

—— 20 ——

THE AYUR-VEDAS

I WAS working again every day in my studio.

Once while I was working, I was suddenly overcome by unbearable restlessness. I felt as if I were really *doing nothing*. Time was rushing by madly with giant strides. Days were going by, each like the one before, and I was doing nothing. Nothing? How come I am doing nothing?—I asked myself. I am working all day long, studying and reading a whole library of books. When I am tired, I play the piano. Why should I feel I am doing nothing? I thought back about the last few years and heard an answer within me: 'You've done nothing, absolutely nothing, to alleviate the sufferings of others. Being a wife, a mother, a sculptress—all these things are purely personal matters.' That was true, but what could I have done? For several years I had been waiting for higher powers to give me an order about what I should do. I had never once heard the voice. How am I to know what kind of 'work' I am to do?—I asked myself. When I think back, now as I am telling this, and call up to mind the person I was then, I simply have to smile. How naïve is the human being, the unknowing person! How could anyone be a co-worker in the 'great plan' if he has not yet reached the goal himself? If he has not been able to conquer himself?

But every person who awakens and sees the goal of life goes through the growing pains of wanting to save humanity *instead of first saving himself*! The higher powers actually do see to it that every neophyte is cured of this naïve idea. At that time, however, I was not yet cured and was bent on making people happy. Ever since I had taken my vow, I never forgot for a moment that that's what I was living for. Various temptations which might have been real temptations for other people or for me early in my life, no longer presented any problems. There were men enough who wanted to satisfy their desire for pleasure. They said they 'loved' *me*. I saw quite clearly, however, that they did not even notice *me*, the being I am in reality. They simply wanted physical love; how could that have interested me after I had once looked into nature's trap? Such desires were not even flattering for my vanity. On the contrary, I found it degrading that men, again and again, coveted my body.

When the conversation was ranging over profound philosophical themes, the man with whom I was talking and who claimed to be a friend, was enthusiastic about my 'intelligence', but at the first opportunity he wanted to kiss me. Did he perhaps want to kiss my intelligence?

Another was enthusiastic about my musical ability. When I played the piano for a group of friends, he said he was a music worshipper. Kissing my hand, he looked deep into my eyes . . . but with what sensuality. I was already acquainted with such 'music worship' and laughed at him. How boring, how boring!

I really was attracted by music, philosophy and psychology, in fact by all kinds of art and science, but I had to learn again and again that most philosophers, psychologists, astronomers, scientists, artists, just like other men, considered sex much more interesting! The poor boys! What will they have left when they some day lose their masculinity! Emptiness, their own terrible emptiness! And these men wanted to convince me that I was wasting my life because I did not want to taste sexual pleasures at every opportunity. How debasing! *Can men only see sex?* Can they not simply be human beings over and above the level of sex? Like children who play together *for the fun of playing* and not because the game concerns sex in any way.

Many people go in for music, art, theatre and psychology only in order to be able to conquer new partners one after the other. The Bible says: 'If ye are not like unto little children, verily I say unto you, ye shall not enter into the Kingdom of Heaven.' The tremendous depth of this wonderful saying became really apparent to me when I saw the unrest and dissatisfaction of the people who live only for sex. And these poor, empty people, when they noticed my indifference, thought I was inhibiting my natural urges or simply pretending. I always analysed myself very strictly, and I never had a thought which would have attracted me to a man. I loved my husband just as much as ever, but no longer as a woman loving a man, but as one human being loving another! It was no temptation, no struggle, and no 'victory' over my desires, for I simply had no desire for a man. Ever since the night when I had clearly recognized the deceit of physical love, I had no longer felt myself to be a *woman*. In that night I became a human being, a *self*, and *the self has no desire for sex! The 'self' is without sex!* The self is not a half of something seeking its complementary half; *the self is a complete whole!*

And when a person recognizes this truth, the body follows!

As I cogitated on these things there in my studio, I suddenly had the same feeling I had had years before when practising thought transmission and when unable to pick up and carry out another's thought. I felt such a weight on my chest that I could scarcely breathe.

Putting down my modelling tools, I tried to concentrate. Then, just as I had felt it years before, I felt the strange prickling sensation throughout my whole body, and again I heard the well-known voice which had been silent for so long, the blessed voice: 'Why are you neglecting your spiritual abilities?'

'How shall I *not* neglect them? What can I do about them?' I asked back.

'You know very well that merely being born with a talent for music, sculpture or other arts does not mean by any manner of means that a person is an artist. He must develop his talent, and to do that he must practise, practise, and practise some more! *Talent without diligence and diligence without talent is not art.* But if you combine your talent with diligence, *that* is real art! You have talents which you simply allow to lie idle: the ability to express the spirit. Practise,

124

practise, practise ... and you will become an artist in the kingly art which stands above all other art: in the *artless art!*'

My heart began to beat fast. For years I had been waiting for an inner order as to what I should do. I had never received an answer. There was nothing else for me to do but keep on working and fulfilling the daily duties that life demanded of me. I learned psychology and sculpturing. These two studies supplemented each other wonderfully. When I was working on a bust, I delved deep into the psychology of my model. I found all people simply fascinating, and the more profoundly I was able to penetrate into their psychology the better my heads turned out. I began to realize that a portrait and psychological analysis are one and the same kind of work! In making a bust of a person, I had to be simultaneously giving him psychological advice, and everyone whom I have ever modelled has remained spiritually very close to me. My monumental works and large compositions were also a great source of pleasure to me. The concentration opened ever-new doors to ever-new vistas of truth. But in the depths of my soul, I was sorry not to be hearing 'the voice' any more. I was as dry as sawdust, feeling that I had lost contact with some power coming from a very high source.

Now this source was re-established and 'the voice' was telling me that I should practise the *artless art*. How should I practise it? Is there such a thing as an appropriate form of exercise? If there is, I never heard of it ...

Once again and very clearly I heard the voice within me: 'Seek!'

'Seek? Where? And how?' I asked.

There was no answer.

That evening we were invited over to the home of our friend who, when I was dying, had saved my life by teaching me yoga exercises and how to guide my consciousness.

We were a jolly group. The men freshened up their schoolday memories, and I amused myself by looking at our friend's library. One book in particular attracted me very much, and I asked whether I might take it home.

'Of course,' said our friend. I took the book and sat down to talk with the men. I asked our friend to tell us how and where he had learned these yoga exercises, with which he had healed me. He told us that he had once been invited by an Indian Maharaja to go tiger hunting. During the hunt, his horse suddenly shied and threw him out of the saddle in such a very unfortunate way that he fell on his back and was not able to get up. He was carried back to his room. The Maharaja visited him and asked him which of his two physicians he should send, the English or the Indian.

Our friend asked for the English physician. The latter prescribed various sedatives and pain-killing drugs, and advised him to stay in bed. Days went by, weeks went by, and he was still lying helpless, unable to get up, unable even to move his neck or back. At the end of six weeks, he was still getting worse.

The Maharaja came to visit him again. 'You asked for the English physician,' he said, 'and I sent him to you. He has been treating you for six weeks, but your condition has only been getting worse. I suggest you ask the advice of my Indian physician, my Ayurvedic practitioner. He could help you.'

Our friend asked the Maharaja to send him at once.

'What is an Ayurvedic practitioner?' I asked.

'It is a person who is initiated into and acquainted with the Ayur-Veda,' our friend replied. 'The Vedas are the holy books of the Indians, the highest philosophy on earth. They are made up of various parts. The Ayur-Veda is the science of health. It contains all the secrets of the human body, diseases, methods of healing and maintenance of health. As early as five to six thousand years ago, these initiates had developed operative techniques for replacing injured organs of the body with healthy organs removed from corpses. They were able to perform the most unbelievable operations. They were able to replace a blind eye with a healthy one, both in animals and humans, and they were even able to replace an entire leg. They also knew that diseases were caused by myriads of tiny invisible creatures which today we call bacteria. They also regarded bacteria as the cells of the invisible body of a demonic spirit, whereas Western scientists with the exception of a few initiates like Paracelsus, have never made an attempt at research in this field. The evil spirit takes possession of one or more persons, invades the person with his body, and when this person's vibrations coincide with those of the evil spirit, he becomes sick. However, there are always persons whose vibrations are different from those of the demon. These persons do not become sick. In the terms of Western science, they are immune.

'In the holy books of India, all these disease spirits are thoroughly described as to their appearance and even shown in coloured pictures. They are horrible figures, each with its characteristic appearance and colour. The demon of the plague, for example, is a black monster and you will recall that the plague is also called "The Black Death". The spirit of another equally fatal disease is a yellow demon and the disease he causes is known as yellow fever. The spirit of leprosy has a lion-like head, and you perhaps know that lepers can be recognized from quite a distance by the lion-like appearance of their faces. Through the face of the leper, one can see and recognize the lion face of the spirit by which he is possessed. Pneumonia is caused by a gigantic red demon represented as consisting of fire and flame. And so it goes, each disease is ascribed to a person's being possessed by a certain specific demon.'

'Just a moment,' I interrupted. 'What did you say? Pneumonia comes from a gigantic red demon? How interesting...' And a childhood memory suddenly came to light again before my eyes. Again I saw my little brother jumping up in bed, looking off in one direction of the room with his eyes bulging, and screaming at the top of his lungs, 'Mother, Mother, the red man is coming to get me! Mother, help!...' And I can still see how he waved his little hands as if trying to ward off an invisible enemy. Then he fainted and mother said, 'What he sees is nothing real; he's having an hallucination...' But I saw at the time it happened that this 'red man' represented reality for the child. Apparently it

126

was an *objective* reality, as the Indians already knew several thousand years ago! For reality is not only what we can grasp with our hands and see with our eyes!

I told him about this experience I had had as a child, but our friend was not surprised.

'The sick often see these demons at the moment they become possessed by them. Sometimes later too, during the sickness when they are fighting with the demon. Whenever they mention this, however, people merely say they have fever and are seeing things. No one ever seems to consider *the origin of these pictures in the imagination of the diseased,* as the persons have never thought about such things: nor *why persons suffering from the same disease always see the same pictures* without ever having spoken to each other, or even having met and known each other.'

Then our friend went on with his story about the Maharaja's Ayurvedic physician. He was a rather young Indian, friendly and well bred, who later became a close friend with whom he was still corresponding. After investigating his nervous reflexes, the young Indian physician went away and brought back pills, ordering him to take three a day. On parting, the young Indian doctor smiled and said, 'In three days you'll be riding again.'

Our friend sighed in disbelief.

The next morning he was able to move his head. Then the Indian physician came again, gave him some more pills and had him do a few breathing exercises combined with guidance of consciousness. The next afternoon he was able to sit up and felt a prickling sensation in his spinal column as if new vital force were flowing into it.

On the second day he was able to get up, walked a few steps in the room, ate his lunch with a ravenous appetite, and later went down to the garden.

On the third day, after waking up fresh and full of pep, he went out for a ride.

As the friendship between the two men grew, he once asked the Indian physician what he had given him to heal him so miraculously.

'Our science is handed down from father to son,' said the Indian. 'When a son is initiated into this science, he must first make a solemn vow that he will never, under any circumstances, betray these secrets. No one has ever yet broken this oath. I cannot tell you the secret of these pills, but I can tell you a few things about our science. The pills I gave you represent a chemical compound consisting mainly of gold. This gold compound, however, is not merely so much inert matter. On the contrary, we might even call it "living gold". In its preparation, it was kept at a constant moderate temperature in a hermetically sealed crucible for several weeks.

'Through this process special properties connected with life are developed in the gold. You know that if you keep an egg at a constant temperature of $104°$ for twenty-one days, it will hatch out in a living chick. On the other hand, if you subject the egg to a temperature of $212°$ for ten minutes, the egg will harden but never become a chicken. That is just exactly what happens with this gold preparation. The constant temperature over several weeks' time develops in the gold a form of energy with the same vibrations as our "vital energy". This energy stands far above atomic energy. It has taken millions of years for gold to develop from the ordinary coarse matter of the earth through an exceedingly slow process. If we develop this process further, we can transform the gold into another material charged with the very highest form of energy. Just as one can magnetize a piece of ordinary iron, we can also develop ordinary gold into magnetic or "living gold". The magnetism of the gold, however, represents a much higher energy than the magnetism found in iron. It has the same vibrations as our own vital energy. In fact, it is *life* itself and has a miraculous effect on all living creatures. Man may be likened to a living magnet charged with this very highest form of energy.

'Just as a magnet loses its charge in time, but can be re-magnetized by passing an electric current around it, in the same way human beings can be recharged with this energy. The seat of this vital energy is the marrow in the spinal column. In your fall from your horse, this very delicate organ was injured and the tension of your vital energy fell abruptly. Your organism was unable to recover, because the healing centres themselves were injured. These pills recharged your nerve centres, natural processes were set in motion, and now you are well. That's all there is to it. See what these pills do for the Maharaja. In spite of his very advanced age, he wants to keep on demonstrating his many powers every day with his favourite wife. With the help of these gold pills, he still retains the powers of a young man. Unaided nature is no longer able to supply his body with this energy, but this preparation sets his nerve centres in motion, and that is sufficient to recharge his sexual organs daily.'

Our friend asked the Indian physician, 'Why do you keep your knowledge so secret? Why can't all humanity enjoy the blessing of your science? Why don't you teach it to the English doctors who are here?'

For a while the Indian physician looked off into the distance. Then he said: 'Just as an egg needs to be fertilized for the life within it to be changed from a latent state into an active state, in the same way the preparation of this gold compound requires a source of power to transform certain latent forces within the gold molecules into active ones, thus changing the inert gold into an active, vital material.

'*This source of power is a human being himself.* The power of reproduction can not only be manifested by the body, but also on another plane as energy. A hypnotist, for example, manifests his power of reproduction on a spiritual plane and can penetrate the mind of another person, causing certain forces to change from a latent state to an active state, just as a sperm cell from his body is able to unite with an ovum to set in motion a process of life within the latter. In order to set in motion a certain process in various materials, in this case gold, a person needs the radiation of his own vital energy. However, if he expends this energy through his sexual organs, he automatically puts into a latent state the very nerve centres he needs to radiate vital energy in its original, basic form. These nerves open and close automatically. A person can either channel this energy into his sexual organs or into other, higher nerve centres, *but he cannot simultaneously channel it into both*!

'You can easily understand that when a father initiates his son into this science, the son, along with his oath of silence, must take a vow of complete continence. That's why the son can only be initiated when he is already married and has several sons of his own, in order that there be no interruption in the chain of knowledge. But just show me a Western physician who would be willing to live a life of complete continence for the sake of this knowledge! On the contrary, it has been our experience that the majority of your physicians want to use their knowledge to earn as much money as possible in order to be able to satisfy their animal instincts to the maximum extent.

'Many Western physicians have visited us and tried all kinds of persuasion to get us to part with our secrets. We saw that with these secrets they merely wanted to earn piles of money, satisfy their vanity, or become famous. It is a sad fact that the foreign power in this country even went to the extent of torturing several of our Ayurvedic physicians in a fruitless effort to get them to reveal their secrets. Ever since then, foreigners in India do not meet any Ayurvedic physicians, simply because none of the latter will admit that he is one or that he possesses any special knowledge. We were forced to wear masks and become "mysterious orientals". We had to pay a high price to learn this lesson.

'Nevertheless I can tell you this much: All through the years there have been foreign physicians who for high-minded, truly humanitarian reasons sought to acquire our knowledge and were willing to take the oath of Brahmacharya (continence). These doctors have received initiation and are working with us. On the other hand, they keep their knowledge just as secret as we do. When humanity has progressed to such a point that the majority of doctors are willing to forego their sexual lusts in order to be able to heal, Indian Ayurvedic physicians will be willing to reveal this secret knowledge to them. At present, however, people in the West use all of their inventions to harm each other. Take dynamite, for example, and aeroplanes. What have they done with these things? Made them into new weapons! What would they do if they knew the secret of cosmic energy and of the still higher vital energy? They'd merely figure out new ways to kill each other off and earn still more money! War is business! and what's this business for? Why do people run after more and more money? In order to indulge their sexual pleasures, lusts and perversities to a greater extent. You ask why we do not reveal our secrets! The answer is that foreign doctors really do not want them. When they hear that they would have to give up their lusts in order to acquire this knowledge, they lose interest right away. They simply cannot believe that by paying such a cheap price they could learn the secret of all life. It's much easier for them not to bother to make a single attempt, but merely to poke ridicule at Orientals.

'Most of the foreigners who come to our country think that the highest happiness on earth is the satisfaction of their sexual desire. How could they ever know anything about the tremendous power that a spiritual person possesses if they never make an attempt themselves to attain it ? This power cannot be acquired through either money or might. The price is renunciation! But the people who have paid this price have quickly discovered that they really *did not need to give up anything*. They find, on the contrary, that they have discovered immortal happiness in the place of mortal . . . a permanent state of pleasure instead of a transitory one. No one can make a better bargain! But we do not discuss these things. These secrets cannot be understood with the intellect alone.

'*Spirit cannot be understood, it can only be experienced. One can only be spirit.* We are content to let others travel the path of the intellect. They have already accomplished much and will still accomplish more. But the "highest truth" will always remain hidden for the person who merely follows his intellect and never learns the bliss of pure *being* to which the path of renunciation leads. People in the West have made the Oriental yogi a comic book character. Is it any wonder that the initiates do not reveal their secrets but merely withdraw and remain unreachable for Western people ?

'I have told you all of this because I can see that you're not interested in our sciences purely out of curiosity, but rather because of deep spiritual desire. You seek the truth. You seek God! We are ready and glad to help such people. I'll give you a bit of advice: If you want to make faster progress and plunge deeper into the secrets of human life, practise yoga!'

The Indian doctor went on to explain that for many thousands of years the Orientals have been discovering and perfecting various methods by which people can reach the goal of happiness, a goal everyone carries in his heart regardless of how ignorant he may be or how low his individual state of consciousness. Right here on earth people can reach this fulfilment, this salvation, this state of eternal bliss—or as Orientals call it, Nirvana. The door is open for every person when he finds the key.

This key is *yoga*!

Our friend's Indian doctor went on to explain that every human act or activity which is done with concentration is actually yoga, as the only way we have of reaching the great goal is through concentration. In studying yoga systematically, however, we learn techniques for developing and improving our powers of concentration, and these are methods which have been perfected through thousands of years. There are various paths in yoga: physical, mental, and spiritual exercises in concentration. These exercises develop the highest abilities of the human being, opening up his spiritual eyes, his spiritual ears, and teaching him to be master of himself . . . master of creative forces . . . master of the forces of fate. The pathway to happiness is opened up, or to express it another way, the path to self-realization—to *God*! The highest and at the same time the most difficult yoga path is that of Raja Yoga. Raja means 'king', and if we translate the term literally, we find that this yoga path is known as 'regal yoga' or 'majestic yoga'. It is the shortest path, but at the same time the steepest and bumpiest. It is the pathway Jesus taught in the Bible. With patience and perseverance, however, one reaches the goal.

My husband's schoolboy friend went on with his story: 'The Indian physician showed me the basic exercises of Yoga, the ones I showed you. But later he told me how to get into touch with one of the greatest living yogis. I went to him. He was a man over eighty years old, but he did not look to be over forty. He was a Hatha Yogi. These yogis know all the secrets of the body. They are able to maintain their bodies in constant and perfect health for several hundred years if they want to. The Indians claim that in the mountains there are yogis living today who are seven hundred and eight hundred years old.'

My husband began to laugh: 'Now I'll tell one! Seven hundred years old? Not bad at all, but at that point you woke up, right?'

'See,' our friend answered quite seriously, 'you are a true Occidental. Just because there are some things you haven't heard about, this doesn't mean by any manner of means that they don't exist. The Orientals know much more about the science of man than we in the West, but they have learnt to keep quiet. From the time the first Occidentals arrived in the Orient, they have done all kinds of things that have made the Orientals keep silent. *Even today they can still keep their secrets.* I saw things in India that taught me to be very cautious about laughing other people out of court.'

'O.K., O.K.,' my husband answered, 'I believe too that there must be some way of living longer when we think that even here in the West the human life span is constantly being lengthened in spite of all we do to shorten it with nicotine, alcohol and wrong living habits. Fifty or sixty years ago the average life span was thirty-five years, whereas now it's around sixty. Makes one wonder what the limit is! Medical science is progressing with giant strides. Who knows how far we'll go?'

'See—your real conviction is not cynical at all. But here in the West we don't dare admit what we believe just because it isn't considered the thing to do. To talk about things we don't understand we always try to affect a superior, cynical manner. I have great respect for what our scientists know, but they act as if they knew all the secrets of life, whereas they are completely ignorant about death. The Orientals have discovered the secret of life and death, but their one and only weapon against the cynicism of the West is silence. No wonder. Here's an example. An Indian showed me a cigarette lighter. It was a little figure of Buddha sitting in the so-called lotus posture, a cheap lighter such as one could get at any bazaar. He told me, "An Oriental would never use the figure of Christ for a cigarette lighter, because we feel respect for the sacred symbols of other religions, just as for our own. We know that one and the same *God* stands above and behind all the various sacred symbols!" So saying, he gently put down the Buddha cigarette lighter on his household altar. As a Westerner, I felt deeply ashamed, and I often wonder when we in the West will wake up and have enough sense not to go on constantly insulting Orientals by such offences against tact, respect, and good taste. Just think, too, about all our

Western films that deal with the Orient. Orientals see these films too, and I'm sure you can guess what they think about them. But they are silent . . .'

I asked our friend, 'Are there books about yoga ?'

'The most beautiful and the most sacred book of the Indians is the *Bhagavad Gita*. In it you can read the most beautiful description of the spiritual path to self-development through Raja Yoga. That's what I would recommend to you.'

I had heard enough.

That very evening I wanted to begin reading the book our friend had loaned me. I lay down comfortably in bed, took the book and opened it.

To my great surprise, I saw it was not the book I had chosen! I turned it around and looked at the title on the back. How strange! I had read the title while browsing through our friend's books, and I now remembered distinctly that I had taken out the book I wanted. Could I have made a mistake and pulled out the book next to it ? Apparently. But now that I had this book, I wanted at least to look at it. It immediately awakened my interest. On the outside it looked like a modern book. But inside it contained a very, very old manuscript. The paper was yellow and brown with age, full of traces of worms. Both the dark black ink as well as the writing showed that the book was very old indeed. The more I read, the more surprised and excited I became . . . until finally my hands fairly trembled with the enforced suspense as I devoured page after page.

The manuscript told about a secret spiritual order that was as old as the earth itself. Without any external, visible form of 'membership', the order was constantly taking in neophytes who came in contact with it without actually knowing anything about it. This 'coming into contact' occurred when a person reached such a state of development that he completely gave up his own person and dedicated his entire life to alleviating the sufferings of others. Whenever a person has reached this decision, a member of the secret order gets in spiritual touch with him, or rather the individual who has decided to give up his person and thus has reached universal love has reached a stage in his development such that he automatically responds to the vibrations flowing among the members of this secret spiritual fraternity. First he hears within himself the voice of the spiritual leader and guide, warning him about the difficulties, dangers and consequences of his decision. If he still sticks to his decision, this 'order' which exists to help humanity climb up out of chaos, accepts him as a member.

At first he is on probation without actually knowing it. This probationary period begins immediately and for *seven long years* the neophyte is left completely on his own. During this time he has no contact with the order, no matter how much he may desire and seek it. But the various tests he must pass come one after the other. Seven of them relate to the human virtues: becoming free of sensuality, vanity, anger, covetousness, envy, sensitivity—then on the other side, the ability to withstand outside influences.

If he passes all of these tests in spite of being entirely on his own, and if he sticks by his decision, he is considered ready to begin his work and is definitely accepted within the order. On the very same day, he learns about his acceptance through an 'apparent' coincidence. From then on he receives thorough training and, simultaneously, specific tasks. At first these tasks are easy, and as he performs them satisfactorily, they become progressively more difficult. The tasks are very different. Some neophytes must work in public, others behind the scenes. Some roam the countryside as beggars, others are very rich. In either case they must fulfil their duties. Some work as assistants of famous discoverers, others as writers or lecturers. Some hold positions of great worldly power, while others may hold down jobs as workmen in huge factories. It can even happen that two members of the order *appear* to be working against each other. Such persons are not permitted to reveal in any way at all that they belong together and are in contact with each other. Sometimes they are celebrated and enjoy tremendous popularity; at other times they may live in abject misery and be subjected to privations and degradations. They must fulfil all their tasks in a completely free and impersonal manner, simply as servants within the great plan. And as they perform their tasks, they must bear *full responsibility for their each and every act*! They receive their assignments, but they must figure out themselves how to carry them out in complete awareness of the responsibility they bear for everything they do. The higher they rise, the greater their responsibility.

Anyone who refuses to bear the responsibility for his acts and his work, and tries to unload this responsibility on another member of the order, anyone who does not recognize his work as his own, personally chosen task but tries to make it appear that he is acting on the instructions of the order or as a spiritual tool of a member of the order—such a person is a traitor and instantly loses all contact with the order. He does not know, however, that he has lost contact, and it is possible for him to go on for years believing himself to be a co-worker within the order. Such persons are used by the order to test other people and find out whether they accept and follow false prophets or whether they have progressed far enough in thinking independently and reaching their own decisions so that they weigh every word they hear and only accept it after it has passed examination. Those who follow false prophets are still blind, allowing themselves to be led by blind, and both fall by the wayside.

Membership of the order is restricted to persons who are completely self-reliant and able to resist influence. They must not be people who *do good* or *avoid doing evil* merely out of a spirit of obedience or because they expect to be rewarded and 'go to Heaven', or because they fear punishment and want to avoid going to Hell. *On the contrary, the order's members must be persons who always—in life and death—follow their own deepest conviction and act accordingly!* This is because *the members hear the order's messages in their own hearts, as their own profoundest convictions!*

I read these lines with ever mounting excitement. Renounce earthly pleasures? How I remembered the night when I sobbed so desperately in bed!... Can one renounce them any more definitively than I did then? Sincere and deep desire to alleviate the sufferings of others? God alone knows how earnest was the vow

I took that time in my room, thinking intently about the terrible sufferings of the mentally ill and the incessant, unremitting pains and troubles of all people all over the world! Now I remembered the warnings I so clearly heard then, and the awesome feeling of being alone, the desperate feeling of being completely abandoned for many long years! How many years since that time? Seven years! Yes, exactly seven! And today, this curious coincidence with the book. Coincidence? No! It was a message . . . a message!

I was shaken to the depths of my being by this experience! As was my custom, I examined the whole matter again with my mind and intellect, for I never stopped using my intellect as a means of testing and checking. But what could my intellect say now? I knew best that *all this was so*. What else could my intellect do but simply recognize the facts? Even the most sceptical intellect would be silenced in the face of so many coincidences! No, I could not doubt it: I had been accepted!

I was overcome by a feeling of inexpressible happiness and gratitude. I felt the grace of God, his blessing, deep humility, and a profound sense of awe. In this condition, I have remained ever since.

— 21 —

THERE WAS LIGHT

IT WAS strikingly noticeable that from this time on more and more people—men and women, old and young—came to me for advice on how to find their paths to happiness. More and more 'seekers' came to me for help. I felt, however, that I was still in extreme darkness. How should I be able to help others? How should I be able to heal the many wounds in the souls of people about me if I myself had not yet solved the puzzle of life and death?

The most important thing was for me to escape from my own darkness. I 'searched' in whatever direction my inner voice advised me, and tried to make progress through reading good books. I found a book describing the secret exercises of Raja Yoga, that is, the path to the self. I wanted to begin these exercises immediately, for I had reached the point where I knew that reading is only necessary in order to know what *one must do*! If we want to reach the goal—the *self*—we must bring what we know into actuality! I wanted reality, not only beautiful descriptions and theories. On the other hand, spiritual yoga demands the strictest asceticism.

I spoke with my husband. He was always my best friend and knew how vitally important it was for me to find the answer to the three great questions: *Whence, whither, why?* He gave his consent to my ascetic exercises.

My father had bought an estate in the mountains. There in the forest we had a little house into which I now moved all alone. At that time my son was away from home, studying, and returned only for holidays, while my husband was constantly travelling and saw me only at weekends.

The large terrace in front of the house offered a glorious view off into the valley where the vast plains began. It was almost like looking off into infinity. At the foot of the mountain a wide river wove its way slowly and majestically out into the distance. On the farther shore, roads and highways formed the veins and arteries of a giant body and the cars travelling about seemed like tiny cells within the gigantic bloodstream. Everything was diminutive, the villages with their little doll houses, and the tiny, busy ant-like people.

The other window looked out into the forest where one could walk for hours and hours in the awesome silence. Pheasants often ventured up to the house, and deer frequently came quite close. At night one could hear them trotting by. Doors and windows were heavily barred against wild boar and other dangerous animals.

Here I lived quite alone. Every morning I found my day's supply of fresh milk on the terrace, then went downstairs to the wood cellar, chopped my day's supply, and built a fire in my stove. Then I began my exercises. This forest house was an ideal place to practise yoga. The entire region was famous for its awe-inspiring atmosphere. The peace and quiet in the forest and the primeval purity of nature round about were so great that every one who came by tended to rise up in spirit in contemplation and meditation—even without yoga exercises. Everyone who visited this sylvan retreat became more sensitive to higher vibrations. Their latent organs of psychic sense developed. While living here I was able to perform without exertion the most difficult exercises in concentration and meditation.

For something to study I took a collection of old figures of the Rosicrucians dating from the sixteenth and seventeenth centuries. It was truly a treasure chest of the greatest wisdom. When I had finished my concentration exercises lasting several hours, I meditated on these wonderful symbolic representations of profoundest truth, and step by step the hidden secrets of this book revealed themselves to my marvelling spiritual eyes. Another subject I studied while here in reclusion in the forest was Oriental philosophy, primarily the Vedas and the Upanishads.

The long exercises in concentration and meditation helped me to penetrate, step by step, into the profoundest regions of my psyche. With these exercises I set forces in motion which kept on working during the time I devoted to everyday activities, and even during the time I was sleeping. Sometimes as I wandered through the forest there arose within me pictures of places I knew well without being able to identify them, for I had never seen them in this life. While I was awake, and even in my dreams at night, I saw people whom I also knew, and in some cases knew very well, but whom I had never seen in this life. Their clothing and their names were strange, and their language in which we communicated in my dreams was quite different from any language I had ever heard in this life.

Whenever I sat down to meditate and turned my attention inwards, I was aware of a greenish-blue phosphorescent light within me . . . a light which seemed to come from the invisible eyes of a great and wonderful spirit being. An indescribable kind of strength, love and goodness radiated to me from these eyes. With a sense of absolute confidence I plunged into this source of loving power. I felt myself in security, and without any trace of fear. I delved deeper and ever deeper into the unknown world of the unconscious.

Then once, quite unexpectedly, the light drove away the darkness, which had been hiding both the past and the truth, and everything became clear.

When I had seated myself to practice meditation, the phosphorescent light appeared before my inner eye as usual. Then I felt with even greater clarity than ever before that the source of light lay in the eyes of a powerful being whom I knew well. Little by little they became so clear that I no longer merely felt—*I knew*—that they were looking at me. I felt their glance, their brilliance, their power, their light and their love shining upon me, and in the next moment, as an effect of this glance, the last remnant of cloudy haze in my consciousness disappeared, and before me there stood, as if emerging from darkness, a majestic figure with two dark blue, infinitely deep eyes, *His* figure, *His* face and *His* eyes: —HE!

— 22 —

PAST BECOMES PRESENT

HE STOOD there and looked at me calmly. This radiant glance with its heavenly peace gave me strength to bear the soul-shaking experience and the infinite joy of seeing *Him* again. His noble face was unmoving, but His eyes were smiling at me, and I knew that *He* was happy that I had at last come fully awake and was seeing *Him* again. For *He* has always seen me. His eyes have always been able to penetrate the mists covering my consciousness. *He* saw all my struggles, all my pains and sorrows, and *He* has never once abandoned me. On the contrary, *He* has helped me to wake up and become conscious.

The memory seized me powerfully, and the hazy pictures I had been carrying inside myself without being able to bring them into conscious focus suddenly became sharp and clear. New pictures emerged into my consciousness, new memories which had been lying hidden and buried in the depths of my subconscious. Now, fitting together like the stones in a mosaic, they formed the perfect picture of a past life in a land beside the great river, the Nile, in the land of the Pyramids . . .

The memory pictures came ever more alive, while the impressions of my present life gradually paled, turning over their place to the re-awakened consciousness of a person I once was. The environment in which I sat, the simple little room in the house in the forest . . . the beautiful view out over the river in the valley . . . disappeared bit by bit. And *He* too was nowhere to be seen. The room opened and spread out about me. I found myself in a great hall, in my own chamber, and I became aware of a fat and lovable woman smiling at me joyously . . .

Yes of course! Today is my sixteenth birthday, and I am just putting on my festive robes. I am to wear them at the great reception in which my father is to present me to the representatives of the country as his wife, successor to the Queen who died an early death.

In a great oval silver plate which has been hammered and polished with loving care and high art, I see my own figure, my own picture, and I watch my dear old Menu as she dresses me.

My mother died while I was still very young, and I have only a vague memory of how pale she was . . . and how fine. In the treasure chest of my precious recollections, I still see her great, sad eyes as she took her last long, long look at me before she died. This last, long, loving glance created a contact between us which I still feel within me, and today when I am to be presented to the country as her representative, I feel this contact even deeper, even stronger.

Now fully robed and ready I stand before my mirror and look at my image. I like it! I see a fine, delicate, slender person in a beautiful robe . . . scintillating, silken with golden hems. The golden sash about her waist enhances her slenderness, her broad collar emphasizes her shoulders and the kerchief around her head accentuates the self-confident and superior expression in her face. I am vain; I like what I see in the mirror. And dear, old, warm-hearted Menu, who considers me the most perfect being on earth, can hardly see through the tears of joy welling up in her eyes.

The two oldest representatives of the country come and lead me down the long corridor into the great reception hall. With slow, ceremonious steps, they lead me between the rows of people of rank to the 'Great House'—to the Pharaoh—to my father who is now to be my husband. He sits on a golden throne like an image of God. It is not without reason that his name, *Phar-ao*, means 'Great House'. His person is the outer integument, the 'house' of God. God dwells in him, manifests himself in him, radiates through him. The power of his glance is so penetrating that people who are not completely true are compelled to look aside. He is sitting there looking straight at me, through me! I look back at him fearlessly, engaging his glance with mine. I know the tremendous power radiating from his eyes is the power of love. He sees everything. He sees that I am vain, just as he sees all my other imperfections, but he understands everything. He is love itself, he is my father!

A magnificent lion, his lion, sits motionless beside the throne. Majestic and dignified, it is a symbol of the supreme power of the Pharaoh. I arrive at the steps to the throne and stand still. The Pharaoh rises, comes down, turns to the magnificent jewel box the Chamberlain holds out to him, lifts out the most beautiful creation of the goldsmith's craftsmanship: a golden shoulder collar. Picking it up lovingly, he lays it over my shoulders. Then he takes the golden hoop that ends with the head of a serpent and fastens it firmly on to the white silken cloth over my forehead. It is the symbol of the members of the ruling race, the Sons of God. It is the symbol of the initiates . . .

Then taking my right hand, the Pharaoh leads me up to the throne. We turn to the representatives of the country and the people of rank, and he presents me to them as the representative of the Queen, as his wife. We seat ourselves, I to his left, somewhat ahead of him. Now the people of rank with their wives, the eldest among them first, pass by us slowly, and bow low with outstretched arms, first before the Pharaoh and then before me. We sit motionless. Only our eyes make contact with each and all as they move by. I think of the fact that I now manifest the spirit of my dear mother, and this makes me aware of my duty and responsibility.

The people of rank pass by and I see their souls reflected in their eyes. In some there is real love and respect, in others envy, curiosity or cowardly servility. The Supreme Chamberlain, Roo-Kha, also bows before me. As he has so often done before when I have met him in the palace, he gives me a glance that is somewhat cynical, impertinent, and flatteringly intimate all at the same time.

I answer his impertinence with a cold stare, and the procession marches slowly onward. Then I see friends of mine, old and young, some of them former playmates, their faces full of genuine love. I meet their glances with mine, and this union enriches us. Slowly, ceremoniously, all the people pass by us, silently, but united in spirit.

The lengthy procession finally comes to an end. The Pharaoh stands up and reaches me his hand. Slowly we descend the steps, and, walking between the rows of statesmen and people of rank, leave the room. Leading me into his chamber, my father seats himself, waves me to a seat, and looks at me smilingly for a while in silence. I can see that I am pleasing to him. From head to foot his glance moves over my figure with satisfaction. Then, looking me happily in the eye, he says, 'From now on we'll see each other often, for you will take your mother's place and fulfil her duties before the public. For many years we have been preparing you for this task, and you know your duties. I want you to have a happy memory of this day of days, so you may make a wish. You've known for some time that I was going to ask you what you wanted, so tell me now. What is it?'

Yes I was prepared, and like other young women, I could have had a number of wishes. I could have asked for beautiful jewellery, for I knew I could wear the great festive jewels only on occasions of high ceremony. Or I could have wished to travel, or asked for a young trained lion, or for something else of the sort. But I didn't want any of these things!

'Father,' I said, 'what is the significance of the ornament I am wearing on my head?'

The Pharaoh looks at my forehead, then into my eyes, then answers, 'The golden snake is the symbol of the ruling race, the Sons of God.'

'Yes, father, but it is also the symbol of initiation. I am not worthy to wear it because I haven't been initiated. I want to be initiated! That's the wish I want you to fulfil for me!'

Father becomes very earnest. 'Ask for something else, my child,' he says. 'You are still very young and not yet mature enough to receive initiation. Tender young sprouts must not be exposed to hot sunshine; otherwise they burn up and can never blossom. Wait till you've acquired the necessary experiences in earthly, physical life. To be initiated now would make your later problems much, much harder for you to solve. Why cause yourself unnecessary troubles? Take my advice and wish for something else.'

'Father,' I answered, 'there's nothing else I want. The things other young people like just bore me stiff. Above and beyond all earthly joys I see the wishes of the body. I like beautiful jewels very much, but even gold is a form of matter which is made precious through a manifestation of the spirit, through the work of the artisan. Naturally I enjoy beautiful scenery and new sights when I'm travelling, but I can never forget that this is all creation, not the *creator*. I should like to experience the highest truth in its reality. I want to learn to know God, the *creator himself*! Father, you know that what we call *life* is only an unreal dream. Here everything slips out of our hand, we can never be definitely happy about anything, everything is merely a transition between past and future. But I want to experience *the eternal present* which will never become the past and which was never the future. And I want to find that condition or "place" which was never *"there"* before I reached it, becomes *"here"* when I reach it and turns into *"there"* again when I go on. I want to experience *the eternal present in time and space*. Father, I want the highest reality—I want initiation!'

Even as he listens to me, father becomes sadder and sadder. 'Your spiritual awakening has come earlier than it should have,' he says. 'All I can do is to go to my brother Ptahhotep, the High Priest of the Temple and the Head of our race. I will speak with him, and he will take you under his guidance. May God's eternal light illumine your pathway.'

He lays his hand upon my head and blesses me. I should like to throw myself upon his breast to thank him for granting my wish, but my heavy golden collar holds me back and keeps me from making any sudden motions. Father, who can read a person's every thought, sees that I wanted to express my joy through this sudden outburst. 'In one way you are still a big child,' he says kindly, 'and in others you are grown up and mature. You'll have to practise great self-control if you want to be initiated.'

I answer with a laugh, 'I already have self control Father, when I want it.'

'Yes, I believe you, but do you always want it?' he asks with a smile.

'It's boring to always exercise self control, Father.'

'That's just the trouble,' he replies with a loving nod. 'There's danger in your finding self control boring. Just remember, if, even for a second, you do not keep your will directed towards your favourite lion and if he attacks you in this weak moment, you're lost. The low self is just as much an animal in its nature as a lion is. We must keep both of them under constant control; then they serve us with their gigantic strength. Always pay attention!'

We take leave of each other. He escorts me to the door and turns me over to the two elders waiting in the antechamber. Oh, what a nuisance these cere-monies are. Why do I have to walk in such a slow and dignified manner between these two old men, just to get back to my own room? I'd like to run down the long corridor and burst into my room where my Menu will be waiting for me full of excitement and curiosity. But no! I have to *walk* . . . with dignity and majesty . . . so the beautiful golden collar on my shoulders will not slip off askew. Finally we reach my door where—with dignity and majesty—I take leave of the two elders. I walk in and stop inside the doorway so that Menu can admire me in my glittering gold ornaments. She is truly beside herself at the sight of my beauty and my majestic movements and because, as she expresses it, I look so much like my mother.

Then I tell her, 'Do you see how ignorant you are, Menu? I can't look like anybody else, and I don't like to have you say things like that. My nose or my mouth can perhaps resemble my mother's, but *I?* Can you ever really see *me*, the real *me*, my self? You see only my body, the dwelling place of my self, but you never see my *self*. How then can *I* look like somebody else?'

'Oh ho,' says Menu, 'if I can't see *you*, how come *you* are so beautiful? Just tell me that! If I can't see *you*, then what I do see here in front of me and what I consider so beautiful is not really *you* but merely the dwelling place of yourself, so *you* are not beautiful at all! Then don't stand there looking so proud and majestic!'

At this we both burst out laughing. Despite her limited intellect, Menu can often give me such a wise and witty answer that I am ashamed of myself. Yes, she has discovered my weakness, my vanity. Then with infinite tenderness she removes my golden collar and the ornamental band from my head, laying them with tender care in the jewel chest, because the Chancellor, Roo-Kha, is waiting outside with the two ornament bearers to carry these precious works of gold back to the treasure chamber to await the next high ceremony in court. He enters my antechamber and bows before me. This man annoys me, because I see he is not bowing out of respect for me, but because he *must*. He gives me another saucily intimate look, while I do my best to look as dignified and regal as possible. Then at last I am alone with Menu.

Menu became my nurse when my mother died. She was and still is my bodily servant, and I am much more intimate with her than with the ranking ladies of the court who have taken on the duty of bringing me up and educating me. From the bottom of her heart, Menu loves me with such infinite affection that I could do with her whatever I wanted. She has always been absolutely delighted with everything I've ever said or done, and I have never had a wish that she would not fulfil blindly if it was within her power to do so. She was always close to me, or somewhere near by, and now that I have to take on public duties beside my father, she has started to worry that I might keep her more and more at a distance. But I love her with a boundless confidence because I know and can, read in people's eyes that no one else in my father's court loves me so sincerely, so unreservedly, so completely uncalculatingly as Menu.

I saw my father only seldom during my childhood. He was and is a 'great man' in our country. For he came to the earth with the duty of guiding and governing people in their *earthly life*. He dedicated his life to the task of showing the sons of men how to govern a country in such a way that all its inhabitants can develop happily. This task gave him so much to do that he had very little time left for me. Every day he spent a few minutes in the garden where I was playing with the children of the Royal family, or he arranged for me to visit him for a few minutes in his chamber.

When I was still quite small, he would pick me up in his arms or crouch down beside me on the floor for a while. Then he would look at me with endless love, bless me and go away. He always spoke to me just as if he were speaking to an adult. In our race, known as 'the Sons of God', it is not considered important at all whether we have been on earth for a long time or only a short time, or whether a spirit is living here on earth in a still undeveloped body—as a child— or in a developed body—as an adult. This question of size and age is only considered important among the sons of men, who are so closely tied to their bodies and identify themselves with their physical instrument to such an extent that they completely forget their true nature as spirit independent of time and place. The sons of men believe that someone can actually be 'small' or 'large'.

But the members of our race, the Sons of God, even keep their spiritual consciousness when they are born into their bodies. They never forget that only the body can be 'a child' or 'an adult' and that the spirit is and always remains the same. It is neither 'big' nor 'small', neither 'young' nor 'old', for spirit is independent of the world of time and space! This is why my relationship with my father was never disturbed at all by the fact that we were of different ages and seldom saw each other. As I grew older, father sometimes took me along on his walks, and when I would get tired, he would pick me up and carry me in his mighty arms as he went on talking about all the secrets of nature. I found such discourses of his extremely fascinating, and I once said to him, 'Father, I'd like to know so much about everything, just like you do!'

'*When you are initiated*,' he answered, '*all the secrets of Heaven and earth will be known to you*.' I never forgot these words of his, and I waited patiently for the time when I too would be initiated.

Although I was always living among strange people, I never felt alone because of this. I knew my father understood me completely, and even though we were not near each other physically, I was united with him in spirit, I belonged to him. And in the same way I was united with my mother. She was no longer living in the body, yet I was indissolubly united with her in spirit. It is astounding to realize how little the unity of the spirit depends on physical togetherness! My dear Menu, for example, is almost always with me, scarcely leaving me alone for a moment, and still *I* am not with her. She can love me but not understand me. She hardly thinks for herself any more, and scarcely lives except for me; she lives in me and is completely in my power, even though I do not exploit this situation. Father told me once that one should *never abuse the power arising from superiority of the mind*.

Right now Menu is as happy as if my father had presented *her* to the court as his wife, as if *she* were so beautiful, and as if *she* had been given my ornaments as a representative of the queen. Oh, my dear old Menu! And now, naturally enough, she asks me what wish I asked my father to grant.

'Initiation of course!' I reply.

'What?' Menu cries out in horror. 'Initiation? You don't mean to say you want to leave the court and join the neophytes in the temple? Why didn't you ask for beautiful jewels? Or to have Imhotep, the artist, make a statue of you? —Or anything else, except initiation!'

'Why get so excited?' I ask in reply. 'The one and only thing I want is initiation, and that's all. And how could anything make me happy that is not *in me*, not *myself*, but hanging outside on my body so that I don't even see it? I now even own the jewels with which people will some day adorn my body, after I have left it, when they put it into a tomb, so that people may know that I belong to the race of the Sons of God. I have these jewels right now, but still don't feel happier in any way than before. And for the same reason people will immortalize my outward form. Why should I wish for such things? Who cares what the sons of men will say a few thousand years from now about the statues of my outward form? The only thing which can make me happy is what is in me, what is *identical with me*, but not things outside myself. The only thing that can make me truly happy is an inward experience through which, in spite of my earthly body, I can earn the ultimate truth in life. I want to be initiated!'

Menu groans in desperation, as if I had asked for death itself: 'Oh, I know, no one can talk to you. When you have your mind set on something, it just has to happen. But I feel initiation is going to bring you into great danger. Don't wish for that! Wish for something else, please! What did the Pharaoh say to your idea?'

'He has given his permission for me to see his brother, Ptahhotep, and now please stop groaning. Don't spoil the whole day for me!'

— 23 —

HE

THAT EVENING, I leave the palace with Menu. Wearing heavy veils, we walk through the long colonnade from the palace to the temple, on our way to the High Priest, my father's brother, the son of God, *Ptahhotep*. Ptahhotep is the highest of all priests. At the same time, however, he is the highest physician and architect, because he knows and masters all the secrets of nature. He has come to earth with the duty and the task of leading the sons of men in their *spiritual life* and initiating them in the sciences. He stands above father because he never identified himself with his body, whereas father married and thus anchored himself more firmly in the material plane.

Without talking, we make our way to the temple. Menu has learned to keep silent when I am withdrawn in thought. A neophyte awaiting us before the temple takes me inside. Menu remains in the antechamber. At the end of another long colonnade, Ptahhotep awaits me in a little reception room. The neophyte remains outside.

There HE sits, the representative of *God*.

I see *Him* for the first time close to, and his eyes overpower me. Oh, these eyes! Dark blue, such a deep dark blue that they look almost black. They are so dark because they are bottomless, as endlessly deep as the vault of heaven itself. When one looks into the eyes of the sons of men, one easily sees the bottom. In their eyes, one sees their soul, their whole character. One sees *individual eyes*. Ptahhotep's eyes are completely different. These eyes have no bottom at all, and looking at them is like looking into the infinity of the sky on a starry night. In these eyes there is nothing personal, nothing individual, only an endless depth where eternity is at home. The whole world, all creation lies within these eyes. I have recognized myself in these eyes, and from the very first moment felt absolute confidence because I know these eyes know me and *contain me within themselves*. I know I am in *Him*, and *He* is in me and loves me as *Himself* because I actually am *He* and *He* and I are a complete unity. *He* is *Love* incarnate, and I feel this infinite love penetrating me, glowing within me.

Moved to the depths of my being, I fall to my knees before *Him*.

Ptahhotep holds out his hand, raises me to my feet, and says, 'My little daughter, *never bend your knees before a visible form*. Do not humble within yourself the divinity that every living being carries within itself. The same God manifests himself through you, through me and through the entire created world. *God* alone is the only one before whom you can fall to your knees. Now rise and tell me why you've come.'

'Father of my Soul,' I say as I arise, 'I want initiation.'

Ptahhotep asks, 'Do you know what initiation is? What does it mean to you when you say you want to be initiated?'

'I don't know exactly what it consists of, but I want to be omniscient. I feel like a prisoner in my body, as if I were feeling my way around in darkness, completely at the mercy of invisible forces I do not know and therefore cannot control. I want to be able to see everything clearly, I want to be all-knowing like you and father and the other initiates.'

Ptahhotep answers, 'Initiation means *becoming conscious*. You are now conscious to a degree corresponding to the resistance of your nerves and body. When a person becomes conscious to a higher spiritual degree, he automatically guides higher, stronger, more penetrating powers into his body. For this reason, he must also raise the level of resistance of his nerves and body. To achieve the supreme, divinely creative degree of consciousness, while at the same time increasing the resistance of the nerves to the supreme degree in order to be able to endure this divine condition without harm to the body—that's what initiation means. Initiation also entails omnipotence and omniscience.'

'I understand, Father of my Soul, and that is just exactly what I am longing for.'

Ptahhotep looks at me silently for a time, and I feel his glance going completely through every fibre of my being.

Finally he says, 'You will be initiated, but not now. You are not ready for it yet in every respect. You have not yet learned to control the divinely creative power *within your body*. And if you make yourself conscious of this power on the spiritual plane before having learned to control it in its physical manifestation, this would mean a very great danger for you.'

'What kind of danger, Father of my Soul?'

'There would be the danger of your possibly burning your nerve-centres. If you achieve the highest level of spiritual consciousness and thus acquire control over this power you could do yourself great harm by guiding this power into your lower nerve centres. In this case your consciousness would sink lower than the level at which it was born in this life. You have no experience yet in the guidance of this power. The awakening of consciousness must begin on the lowest level in the scale of manifestations, because then you will only be guiding into your body power corresponding to the level of your development, i.e. power your nerves can bear without harm. In this way the nerves have strong enough resistance to carry the forces conducted into them.'

'Father of my Soul,' I reply, 'what does it mean *to conduct divine power into the body* and to experience this power in the body? How can I learn to know and control this power in its physical manifestation? If that's how initiation begins and I must first go through this experience then I'd like to do it immediately so that I can prepare myself for the higher initiation.'

Up to now Ptahhotep's divinely noble face has been as motionless as an alabaster statue, with only his eyes glowing brightly. But now at these words of mine the calm features of his face break out into a smile, while his eyes radiate even more light and more understanding.

'Immediately?' he echoes. 'That is not possible, my child. To become conscious of divinely creative forces on the lowest level of the scale of manifestations means *to experience physical love*. You must wait until some young man appeals to you, until his positive manly radiation awakens your heart and makes it glow with negative feminine power. You must come to know this power of love, for unless you have this experience behind you, you cannot control it. It would always represent a constant temptation, involving the great danger of your falling to a much lower level of consciousness than the one you're on now.'

'Father of my Soul, I will never fall prey to physical love! Love is not a temptation for me, and I am not afraid of this danger because it really isn't a danger for me! Permit me, please, to be initiated.'

Ptahhotep turns quite serious again and says, 'My child, you only think that love could not be a danger for you because you do not know this tremendous force. To be courageous in the face of a danger we *do not know* is neither courage nor power, but only ignorance and weakness! Because of your lack of experience you do not know the temptation of love, and you believe you are able to face this force. But don't forget that *love is also the manifestation of divine creative force and is therefore as strong as God himself! You cannot destroy this creative force; you could only transform it.* But if you don't know this force, you can't know how it can be transformed. Be a good girl now and go home and wait till your destiny brings you this experience. When you have found out what love means in its full reality, when you have experienced it and clearly know *what* this force is, then you can come back and I will give you your initiation.'

At this I threw myself on my knees before *Him*, embraced his feet and begged him desperately, 'No, no, don't send me away, don't deny me initiation! I will resist all temptations of love, I will not vacillate, I beg of you, give me initiation!'

Ptahhotep smiles again and strokes my hair. I feel tremendous power flowing through his hand and into my head like a strong current.

'Truly,' he says, 'I am not accustomed to this type of behaviour. Do you think, my child, that when I tell you I won't initiate you and you throw yourself on your knees before me, this will make me change my mind? One of the requirements of initiation is absolute self control. Child, child, you still have a long way to go on the path of self control. And your self assurance is not in equilibrium with your experiences. First gain the necessary experience, then you can come back.'

I see that he has nothing more to say. I stand up and take leave of him, 'Father of my Soul, I'll go now, but you're not going to abandon me, are you? May I come back to you again some other time?'

Ptahhotep answers with ineffable love: 'I know that you have been alone very much ever since your early childhood and you still are. It just had to be that way so you could develop your self reliance. But you are never alone and you must feel that, really. You are united with us by the eternal band of the highest laws of affinity and association. I am always with you even when you do not know it. I knew before you did that you were coming to me today with this request, and I also know what will follow. *But there are laws which even we must obey.* You belong to us.'

I bow low before him to receive his benediction. Then I go.

Waiting for me in the ante-chamber Menu asks,

'How was it? What did the Son of God tell you? Please tell me everything! Right away! I just couldn't understand what was keeping you so long. Please, please, tell me! Are you going to be initiated?'

'The Son of God will not give it to me. He says I haven't had any experience in earthly life.

'Thank God!' says Menu, beaming with joy, 'Didn't I tell you it wouldn't be good for you to be initiated? I knew it!'

'Yes, yes, Menu you know everything better, but just leave me in peace now. I want to put some order in my thinking . . .'

And we walk on silently back to the palace.

All night long and all the next day I can think only of Ptahhotep, the representative of God. I have known that on the basis of my ancestry I belong to the Sons of God, but it was a great experience to hear from him that he is the guardian of my soul. *He* is the visible representative of God here on earth, and I know I could speak as openly to *him* about my most secret thoughts as in my own innermost prayers to God. His eyes saw right through me, his glance illumined the hiddenmost corners of my soul, and that made me happy. It is so wonderful to know that I belong to a living being who understands me without words and who can never be angry with me because he sees everything from above, just as God Himself does.

I don't need to explain to him what I mean, or why I want to do something or achieve something, as I am accustomed to have to do with my tutors. Ptahhotep sees the most secret motives behind my thoughts and my deeds, even those I am not conscious of myself. I don't even need to say a word to him; it is enough when I merely stand before him. *He sees me!* His spirit is open for me, and I feel I am in constant contact with him. I even felt it before I met him. I felt a force as strong as steel was guiding me, and now I know this force was—and is—his radiation. I know that he even sees me when I am not with him. Even now I feel his eyes upon me; whatever I do or think is not hidden before him. And in this case he can also see that I cannot take no for an answer on the question of my being initiated. No! I can't see why I should first have to have experiences in love behind me. I'll never fall in love. Men only interest me to the extent that I expect them to notice and admire my beauty. Since they all do that, it's quite enough for me; for vanity is only at work in me when I am in the company of others. When I am alone, there is only one wish that fills my whole soul— initiation. I cannot and will not wait until I have had the experience of falling in love, because I never will.

And so that evening, accompanied by a very worried Menu, I go again to Ptahhotep to ask him once more for my initiation.

Once again Menu waits in the ante-chamber, while the neophyte takes me to the garden where Ptahhotep is sitting under the palm trees. I bow before him. He returns my greeting, looks at me with his shining eyes—I feel he's looking *into* me—and waits. I stand and say nothing. Why should I speak when he knows anyway what I want. He reads my thoughts.

He lets me stand.

Finally he gets up, lays his hands on my shoulders and asks, 'Why have you come?'

'Father of my Soul,' I reply, 'why do you ask when you already know anyway? I am unhappy because you refuse to initiate me. I have no other wishes, no other thoughts—only initiation. Please give me initiation.'

Ptahhotep strokes my hair lovingly and says quite earnestly, almost sadly, 'I gave you your answer yesterday, just be calm and have patience! Remember what I told you yesterday about creative power, and live your life as other young people do. Occupy yourself with your flowers and with your animals, go and play with other young people, enjoy yourself and for the time being don't think about initiation.'

'Father,' I reply in agitation, 'I can think only about initiation. Whatever I do guides my thoughts directly back to initiation. When I look at my flowers, or when I watch my turtles crawling back and forth and living their life as wisely as if they had an intellect, I run into secrets and mysteries to which I would like to know the answers. I would like to know everything, understand everything, I'd like to be initiated!'

'If the turtles had an intellect,' says Ptahhotep smiling, 'they wouldn't lead such a wise life. And now you don't want to be wise because you have an intellect, but because you have too much intellect. But now just try with your excellent intellect to *understand* that you're still too young to be initiated. Come back again when you have your earthly experiences behind you. Then I will give you your initiation.'

Oh my! It's not so easy to deal with Ptahhotep as with my dear old Menu. Ptahhotep is hard, and all my strength bounces off him like arrows off a stone wall. Again I bow low before him and go. But outside I answer Menu's questions in a spirit of rage and desperation, rage because Ptahhotep thinks I am too young, and desperation because I stand powerless in the face of time rising up before me like an impenetrable wall, as invincible as Ptahhotep himself.

All that night I can't sleep again, and all the next day I pace back and forth in my room, as restless and unhappy as the trained lions in the lion's court. Through being born into my body, my consciousness has been dulled and deadened; I feel as if I were in perpetual darkness. I want to see clearly even though I am imprisoned in the body. I want to know. I want to be initiated! Why should I wait? If love is a matter of indifference to me now, it will still be when I am initiated and omniscient. I already know that physical love is only a necessity of nature to carry on the race. Why should it be dangerous for me not to know this from experience? I have my intellect and my consciousness and they will protect me from this danger. I won't fall into nature's trap, the trap of love. I'll be able to resist this temptation all right...

In this manner I brood all day long. By the time evening comes again, I just can't stand it any longer. I take my veil and go again with Menu through the long colonnade to the temple, to Ptahhotep. I want to tell him that I'm not afraid of this temptation, that I'll be strong enough, that he can initiate me.

Oh how blind I was! How foolish! As if Ptahhotep had not seen the future clearly. As if he had not known how everything was going to turn out. But even *he* must obey the divine law and watch patiently, as I run headlong into my undoing... watch patiently as I plunge head over heels into an abyss, only to have to climb out later *by my own strength*.

He receives me again in his little reception room. I enter, bow, and tell him with all the determination I can muster, 'Father of my Soul, I wanted to obey you, but I cannot. I long so much for knowledge that I've come back again. I cannot see why I should wait when I'm absolutely sure I have enough strength to withstand the temptations of physical love. I am strong enough. I have self control. Please give me the initiation.'

At this Ptahhotep closes his shining eyes and remains motionless a long time. I wait with inward impatience, but outwardly without moving a muscle in order not to disturb *him*. Finally, Ptahhotep opens his eyes. He stands up, comes over to me, takes up my hands in his, and says, 'Three times you have asked to be initiated. Three times, despite my refusal. It is a law that when a member of the tribe of the Sons of God asks three times to be initiated, we cannot refuse him any longer. It is a sign that initiation is necessary for him, regardless of the danger he may risk as a result of it. I will speak to your physical father. We will need to discuss how you can carry on your duties during the time of initiation. Other neophytes normally live in the temple during this time, but with you we will have to make an exception because you have to fulfil the duties of the wife of the Pharaoh. Now go in peace.'

I feel like throwing myself about his neck to thank him for giving me his permission to be initiated, but I prefer to show him I can control myself. I stand motionless, and my eyes express my joy. Ptahhotep smiles at me and says, 'What you've done in thought, you've already done, don't ever forget it!'

'Oh, Father, if you already regard me as having done it, then I will really!' And with that I throw myself into his arms and kiss his noble face, right and left. 'I thank you, I thank you! How wonderful! I'm going to be initiated! Initiated!'

'Yes I can see you have tremendous self control,' says Ptahhotep.

'Only now, Father,' I answer with a joyous laugh, 'only now! After all, you're not only the high priest, but my own blood uncle. So I can kiss you, can't I? But when I'm initiated, you will see how serious I am and how much self control I have!'

'Yes, I know,' says Ptahhotep, embracing me lovingly. Then he strokes my head again and leads me to the door. We take leave of each other.

Dancing and skipping—practically walking on air—I go back to the palace with Menu. I am infinitely happy. But Menu, from the moment she hears that I am to be initiated in the temple, cries and wrings her hands continually as if I were dying. Her lamentations spoil the fun for me, and I feel as if surrounded by invisible shadows. Finally, at bedtime, when she starts again to talk about her gloomy forebodings, my patience is at an end. 'Look, Menu,' I tell her, 'you know they wanted to take you away from me after my sixteenth birthday when I was presented to the country as the Pharaoh's wife; you know that according to the rules I should be surrounded by ladies of the court. It took me a hard fight to get the Pharaoh to agree to your staying on with me and to my being accompanied by ladies of the court only on high state occasions, the way things have been in the past. But if you act this way, I surely will have you sent away and take on the ladies of the court. To be sure, most of them are terribly boring, but at least they don't interfere in my private affairs.'

Menu, poor old fat Menu! She is so frightened at my words that she stops crying immediately, sits down on the floor beside my bed and looks at me silently but with so much love, so much care and solicitude that I can't help bursting out laughing. Throwing my arms about her, I tell her, 'Just calm down, Menu, I'm not going to send you away. Never. I love you. You're the only person who really and truly loves me with all your heart. I'll always want you with me. Just calm your fears. The initiation will not harm me, only help me! Ptahhotep will take care of me. He will be with me always!'

Then in leaving Menu says, 'I hope the initiation really won't harm you, but I am always afraid when I see the big flashes of lightning and hear the thunder coming out of the pyramids. I hope you won't have anything to do with that.'

'No, no, Menu, now be a good girl and go to bed,' I tell her, and Menu leaves. But for a little while I ponder over her parting remark. Lightning and thunder coming out of the pyramid? Yes, it's true! Ever since I was a little girl, I have known that lightning and thunder have struck out of the pyramid occasionally and after that it would rain. It was always as much a matter of course as life itself, and I never gave it a second thought. But now when I am initiated in the temple, I will probably learn the secret behind this phenomenon too.

Then with a great and wonderful feeling of expectation, I fall asleep.

— 24 —

SONS OF GOD

THE NEXT day the Pharaoh summons me. I am to see him after his audience.
At the appointed hour the controller of the royal household comes and escorts
me to father.

'Come, my child,' says he, 'I want to tell you what Ptahhotep and I have
agreed upon about your initiation.'

'Did he come to see you?'

'No,' says father and looks at me quizzically.

'Did you go to see him?' I ask again.

'No again,' he answers and smiles.

'Father,' I tell him, 'for a long time I've wanted to ask you how you discuss
things with Ptahhotep without going to see him or his coming to see you. I've
often noticed that you've told me something about Ptahhotep as if the two of
you had been together in a long consultation. And yet you had not left the palace
and he had not come to see you. How was it possible, Father?'

Ever since my childhood father has been accustomed to my questions, and
he now answers me as patiently as ever:

'You have a mirror, and you have seen your head in this mirror, haven't you?'

'Yes, Father, I see my head every day when Menu does my hair.'

'And what have you noticed?' asks father.

'That I have a much longer head than the sons of men in general. But you too,
and Ptahhotep and most of the people in our race—the Sons of God, as people
call us—have the same longer head form. It's noticeable even in spite of the
kerchief or head-gear or ornaments the person might be wearing. How is it,
Father? Why is the shape of our heads different from that of the heads of the
sons of men?'

'Look, my child, for you to understand many of the things here on earth, you
must first know something about the earth's development.

'Just like all the celestial bodies in the universe and like all the forms of life
on these celestial bodies, our earth is subject to the laws of constant change. The
divinely creative forces radiate from the eternal infinite original source and in
constantly expanding waves they penetrate the plane of matter. That is to say,
matter is formed from these forces. This process reaches its highest point in
ultra-matter, then automatically reverses itself. The process of spiritualization
begins again and the matter is transformed into force. But this process takes
aeons of time! The changes are going on regularly but so subtly and slowly that
they cannot be noticed or observed in the course of a human life. On the other

hand, some changes, which require thousands of years of slow and unnoticed preparation, occur suddenly and visibly when the proper time has come. Right now we are living in such a period of transition in which changes are noticeable. One of these phenomena is evident in the fact that various races of people with roundish skulls are led and governed by rulers who are spiritually greatly superior to them and who are even different from them physically. They have a more graceful figure and an elongated cranium.

'Once there lived on earth a race of people very different from the races living today. *They manifested completely the law of spirit and not the law of matter like the races of people living today.* These people were conscious on the divine plane and manifested God here on earth without any admixture of the self-seeking characteristics of the body. In their divine purity, these people deserved the name "the Sons of God".

'Their entire life was based on spirituality, love, and selflessness. And they had no physical appetites, urges and passions to cast shadows on the spirit. The members of this high race possessed all the secrets of nature, and as they were perfectly acquainted with their own powers and kept these powers completely under the control of the spirit, they were also able to control and guide nature with all of its tremendous forces. Their knowledge was boundless. They did not need to earn their bread with physical toil and instead of earning their livelihoods with the sweat of their brow, they put the forces of nature to work.

'They knew all the laws of nature, the mysteries of matter, the powers of the mind, and the secrets of their own being. They also knew the secret connected with the *transformation of force into matter and of matter into force.* They constructed devices and tools with which they could store up, set in motion, and utilize not only the forces of nature but also their own spiritual forces. They lived happily and peaceably as the dominant race in a great part of the earth.

'At the same time, however, other creatures similar to the Sons of God were also living on earth, but with much more material bodies and on a much lower plane of development. Obtuse in spirit, their consciousness was completely identified with the body. They lived in primeval jungles, struggling with nature, each other, and animals. These creatures were the ancestors of present-day man. *The race of the sons of men you see in our country represent a cross between these two races.*

'As I said a moment ago, the law of constant motion and change is at work throughout the universe. The earth is now going through a period in which the process of materialization is advancing. This means that the divinely creative power is moving farther and farther on into matter, and the power on earth is gradually falling more and more into the hands of ever more material races of people who were once under the guidance of higher, more spiritual races. Little by little the higher race is dying out. They are withdrawing from the plane of matter to the spiritual plane and they will leave humanity alone for a period of time—as time is reckoned on earth, many, many thousands of years—so that humanity may, without visible guidance, climb upward with its own power.

'And so it has come about that this animal-like material race of cave men is experimenting in accordance with divine laws, growing mightier and more powerful until the time comes for it to begin ruling the earth. Before leaving the earth, however, the higher race had to implant its special powers in the lower race. Through the operation of the laws of heredity, this will enable the lower race—after a long, long process of development—to *arise out of matter again*. This is why many sons of the divine race made the great sacrifice of begetting children with the daughters of primitive man. Through this first crossing of the races there have developed new individual types and, gradually, new races of people.

'The divine power of the Sons of God and the mighty physical powers of the daughters of men have produced different types of descendants. On the one hand, physical, and on the other, spiritual giants. There have also been physical titans who, from their mother's ancestry, have inherited primitive, undeveloped brains. In these persons, the spiritual power of their fathers, working on the material plane, created tremendously strong bodies. With their gigantic physical strength, these individuals have overcome weaker persons and, because of the animal appetites of their nature, they have become tyrants greatly to be feared.

'But there have also been spiritual titans who have manifested their inherited creative power through the higher centres of the brain, rather than on the lower physical plane. These spiritual giants were assigned the task of leading and teaching for a time, the lower, animal-like, body-conscious race of humans, as well as the hybrid race which later rose through the inter-breeding I have already mentioned. These spiritual giants have the task of teaching the people of these two races wisdom, sciences and arts as the basis of a higher civilization, and of giving them a good example of divinely universal love, unselfishness and spiritual greatness. That is why there are some countries today where despotism and tyranny are dominant while others are ruled with love and wisdom. This will gradually disappear and humanity will know the great initiates and their secret sciences only through historical records, tradition and legend. However, even in the darkest period of human development, by virtue of the laws of heredity, there will be the possibility that a son of God may be born in a human body in order to show humanity the way out of darkness and misery.'

'Father,' I ask, 'is our country the country of the Sons of God?'

'No, my child. The continent which once was the home of the Sons of God has been completely destroyed. Gradually there were fewer and fewer descendants of the divine race. They left their mortal frames behind them and did not reincarnate themselves. Finally there were only a few left in various parts of the earth to transmit dominion to the human beings who were constantly growing in power. Because of the inter-breeding of the two races, however, there arose some individuals with a knowledge of magic acquired from their fathers and the animal-like, physically oriented selfishness of their mothers. These were able to infiltrate into the temple, and by virtue of their spiritual powers, they received initiation. However, they degraded their knowledge to black magic and made selfish use of their own powers and the natural forces they controlled with the instruments and equipment of the temple.

'The Sons of God who were then still living in this part of the earth saw what was coming. They knew that these powers mercilessly destroy anyone who uses them wrongly, that is, with satanic selfishness instead of with divine unselfishness. They knew the black magicians were headed straight for perdition and their blind avarice would cause general destruction. So the last Sons of God built huge ships, closed on all sides and even insulated against the forces which penetrate and dissolve matter. Then they secretly took aboard a few of their instruments, their families and their domestic animals; and closing all openings, they sailed away from the part of the earth that was to be destroyed. Some sailed north, some east, some south, while some, sailing westward, arrived here where we are now.

'The black magicians soon lost control over their instruments. It should have been their task to conduct the highest cosmic divine forces into these instruments and store them there, because the only source of this power on earth is *the human being himself*. But the more selfish these people became, the more a change took place in the current with which they charged these instruments for later use. One day, when the Sons of God in their insulated ships had already sailed away to a sufficient distance, the tragedy occurred. One of the black magicians unintentionally conducted into his own body a force which dissolves matter, that is, changes it into another form of energy. When this process has once been set in motion, the matter which has been transformed into energy goes on and on, acting as a destructive force, until it has dematerialized everything. In this way the whole continent was destroyed. Finally the new forces thus created slowed down and eventually halted the process of disintegration.

'The entire dematerialized continent was transformed into energy of radiation, at first rising up to the upper reaches of the earth's atmosphere, then returning transformed into the primordial form of all matter. After further transformation processes, the whole gigantic mass fell to earth again in what appeared to be an unending downpour of water, mud and sand.

'The waters of the oceans rolled over the gigantic cleavage in the body of the earth. The land masses of the other hemisphere, split asunder by the cataclysmic shake-up, moved farther and farther apart in order to restore equilibrium throughout the earth, until they finally occupied their present positions. Part of the destroyed continent now lies in our country as a mighty desert of sand, and there is a danger that winds may carry abroad these mountains of sand and cover up fertile, inhabited areas.

'The Sons of God in their ships had special instruments and equipment to stabilize their vessels and keep them horizontal at all times. Thus they survived the catastrophes and finally landed. In every part of the earth where they set foot they began a new civilization.

'With their knowledge, wisdom and love they won the hearts of the natives. They became rulers. They were worshipped, revered as Gods or demi-Gods. Their first acts were to construct suitable buildings for their secret instruments in order to insulate them completely from the world outside and provide adequate protection against the powerful, penetrating energy stored up in their instruments. These buildings, which we call pyramids, can now be seen in all the various parts of the earth where the Sons of God fled with the instruments they salvaged.'

Profoundly impressed, I listened to the story of these tremendous events. It cleared up many things I had not understood before—but not everything. 'How did the Sons of God bring these mighty blocks of stone and set them in place, one upon the other?' I asked.

'Do you remember, my child,' the Pharaoh replied, 'that I told you the Sons of God did not need to work with physical force because they caused the forces of nature to work for them? We still possess some of these instruments with which we can control *the gravitational force of the earth at will, neutralizing it or amplifying it,* depending on the result we wish to achieve. In this way we can make an object weightless or, inversely, even heavier than it normally is. When a huge block of stone has been made weightless in this way, even a child could push it about with its little finger or raise it to any desired height. Ships were piled high with these gigantic blocks of stone without being overloaded, because the blocks had been subjected in advance to the proper form of radiation and so made weightless. All the gigantic edifices, here and in other parts of the world, which human power would never have been able to build were erected by the Sons of God in this way.

'Wherever the Sons of God disembarked from their ships, they created a high civilization. Wherever they are still ruling, they are leading the people in unselfish love and making a sacrifice for their benefit . . . the sacrifice of remaining here on earth for a time in order to teach them and propagate spiritual powers. There was once a time when the ruler, the Pharaoh, was simultaneously the high priest. In one and the same person, he was the earthly and spiritual leader of the people. Later, however, as the country grew greater through culture and wealth, the Sons of God divided up the tasks, and ever since then one of them has fulfilled the duties of worldly government, while the eldest, the leader of the race, has been the spiritual leader of the people. The Pharaoh rules the country. The high priest fulfils his duties in the temple. He is the guardian of knowledge in every field. Since all knowledge comes from a single source, it is he who gives the initiation into the sciences, into the arts, and also the great initiation in the temple *into the "artless art" of the spirit.*

'Now you know why the people we are ruling and teaching have differently shaped heads from those of the descendants of the Sons of God who are now the reigning family. Those of us who have this elongated skull make relatively little use of our intellects because *we are able to experience truth directly with our inner sight.* Our forehead is not heavily arched, because in our heads the brain centres having to do with the power of thinking are only developed to the point necessary for us to perceive and consciously experience external impressions. On the contrary, in the rear part of our cranium we possess fully developed brain centres, the physical instruments of spiritual revelation. These brain centres enable us to be conscious on the divine plane and give us those superior qualities and characteristics which distinguish us from the sons of men. Human beings, in their consciousness, *live in time and space.* We, although we too inhabit earthly bodies, enjoy the *perfect spiritual freedom, in freedom from time and space.* Through the power of the divine consciousness and with the help of these brain centres, we are able to move freely in time and space.

'This means that we are able to shift our consciousness into the past or into the future at will. In other words, *we are able to experience the past and the future as present.* And with the same ease we can free ourselves from the hindrance of space and move our consciousness to any place we wish. In this condition there is no "*here*" and no "*there*", but only *omnipresence*. For past and future—here and there—are only different aspects, different projections of the one and only reality, the eternal omnipresent *Being: GOD.*

'The blood of both races is flowing in your veins. You inherited characteristics of our race, but also of the hybrid race from your mother's side. In you the higher organs are beginning to function, unfortunately much too early for you to have had time for earthly experiences or for you to have conquered your partially earthly nature. You are unsatisfied because you feel imprisoned in time and space, caught between "here" and "there". The spirit within you is beginning to awaken and long for its divine freedom. You have asked three times to be initiated and you will be. Then you will learn to make conscious use of all the higher organs which are not yet fully active within yourself. You will also acquire the ability to establish contact at any time with similar beings in order to be able to exchange thoughts with them.

'I am thus able to establish spiritual contact at any time with my brother Ptahhotep or with any of the other descendants of the race of the Sons of God still living on earth. Through a complete union of our consciousnesses, we are able to exchange our thoughts on any given subject much better than if we were talking together on the earthly plane with the help of larynx, tongue and ears. With our consciousness we can seek each other out at any time, but we feel immediately if the other is occupied and concentrating on something else. In such a case we disturb each other only if we have something very important to communicate, otherwise we withdraw. But you can easily understand why only persons who have achieved perfect unselfishness can have such abilities. If self-centred sons of men also had them, they would create such chaos that all the finer, higher organs would be ruined in the general confusion.

'For the most part we "meet" through uniting our consciousnesses in this way in the evening after our daily duties are done, and in this union we *see* each other's thoughts. Thus in a matter of moments we are able to agree on things which would take long discussion in the three dimensional world.

'After we have thought over our worldly tasks, we shift over with our consciousness into the dimensionless state of all-consciousness, in order to draw new vital energy from the eternal, divine, original source. In this condition we are one with all living creatures, with the entire *universe*, identical with it in the divine, *primordial union*, one with *life* itself, with the eternal *being*, hence with the essence of every manifestation—with you too and with all other people. Only these beings who with their consciousness are still living in three dimensions are not aware of this union. On the other hand, every creature awakens from sleep with renewed vital energy, whether or not it knows that this energy comes from the divine original source.

'And so you are going to be initiated. This means you are starting on a long, long journey. You will have to travel this path on earth even after Ptahhotep and I have left the three-dimensional world and only remain in spirit in the sphere of the earth. I have different tasks from Ptahhotep. Your spiritual and intellectual guidance is in his hands. In the eternal union, however, we will always be together. It would have been better if you had had more patience. *But you are as you are, and the way you are will also determine your fate and your future.* We cannot interfere. The power which comes from union will always accompany you and help you through the most difficult times.

'Since you have the duty of representing the wife of the Pharaoh beside me, you will not be able to dwell in the temple as other neophytes do during the period of preparation for initiation. You will go there every morning for instruction. During the day, you will do your exercises there with the other neophytes and when evening comes you will return to the palace. At palace ceremonies you will come in time to fulfil your duties at my side. So you can report to Ptahhotep tomorrow morning.'

But I still have a question and so remain standing.

Father looks at me quizzically. 'Father,' I ask, 'you have told me that the Sons of God, in order to propagate their spiritual powers, took wives from among the daughters of men. Didn't the daughters of the Sons of God also take husbands from among the sons of men? Why have only the Sons of God begotten children with the daughters of men?—And not the daughters of God too with the sons of men?'

Father looks deep into my eyes and says, 'Engrave this answer of mine upon the tablets of your memory. If you understand this truth really well, we may perhaps be able to set the rudder of your fate on a different course: If you pour out a drop from a glass of red wine into a glass of white wine, the red wine in the glass remains pure red wine as it was before. The white wine, is no longer pure white wine, but a mixture of both. And if you then pour out some of the white wine, what you pour out is actually a mixture of red and white wine. Do you understand, my child?'

'Yes, Father, I understand. You mean that the blood of a pure bred Son of

God still remains pure if he begets children with a daughter of the sons of men. But the blood of a pure bred daughter of God would become mixed blood if she were to marry one of the sons of men. From then on she would be mixed and so would her children.'

'Remember this truth every moment of your life,' says father. Then he arises, I bow before him, and he blesses me. Preserving the unity of the soul in my heart, I leave the room.

— 25 —

YEARS OF PREPARATION

ACCOMPANIED BY Menu, I go to the temple.

How often will I be going through this long colonnade between palace and temple? How often and for how many years!—until I myself have become the path, so that with my eyes closed my feet would carry me to the temple.

Today I enter the temple for the first time as a neophyte. Just because I would like to hurry, I hold myself in check and walk with ceremonial slowness. I am determined to enjoy to the very last drop the pleasure of beginning my initiation. I am withdrawn within myself, deep in thought. Fully conscious of all the things my father told me yesterday, I go forward to my future duties as an initiate.

At the entrance the same neophyte as before is awaiting me. Menu takes her leave. At first she embraces me, kisses me and holds me tight as if we were never to see each other again. Then she calms herself and bows before me in the way she believes she should. I embrace her and feel that my mother is also kissing me through Menu's lips.

The neophyte accompanies me to Ptahhotep who is waiting in his little reception room. How often—how often—will I be standing thus before *him*! How often will his eyes rest upon me, or pierce me through and through with their peace, assurance and strength!

'My dear child,' he begins, 'initiation, as I have already explained to you, means to become conscious on the highest level, the divine plane. To be able to do this requires long physical training and spiritual preparation. One first must strengthen the nerves to enable them to bear these high vibrations without harm, without death.

'To become conscious on a given plane means to conduct the vibrations characteristic of this plane into the nerves and through the nerves into the body. From the time a body is born, that is, from the time a "self" dwells in it, the body develops a power of resistance corresponding to the average degree of consciousness of the spirit dwelling in it.

'The degree of consciousness of a living creature fluctuates up and down, depending on its emotional condition, within the limits of an octave of vibrations. These fluctuations, however, must not exceed the limits of elasticity of the nerves; for if they do, injuries and sicknesses of a more or less serious nature occur, even death. The vibration belonging to creative vital energy is absolutely lethal for creatures whose consciousness has not yet reached this level. It would

160

burn out the nerves and nervous centres. For this reason, vital energy from the spinal column, where it has its seat, is transformed into a low vibration corresponding to the degree of consciousness of the person concerned and only this transformed vital current is conducted into the body.

'Thus animals, for example, are animated by a much lower life vibration than primitive man; and primitive man with his beast-like selfish nature, is animated by lower vibrations of vital energy than a person who is spiritually developed. If one were to conduct the vital energy of a highly developed human being into an animal or a much less developed human, the animal or "lower-level" human would die instantly because of the contact with the more powerful vibrations.

'The great initiation means *consciously experiencing* the vital energy and creative vibrations of eternal *being*, experiencing these vibrations on every plane of development and in their original frequency, without transformation, and simultaneously conducting these vibrations into the nerves and the body. This naturally requires a corresponding amount of *resistance* which can be obtained through physical and spiritual training. That means that one must slowly and cautiously prepare and awaken the appropriate nerve centres and learn to control them. Initially you will receive this physical and spiritual training from Mentuptah, the leader of the school of neophytes. In your concentration exercises, Ima'—and Ptahhotep points to the neophyte who brought me here—'will help you. When you have passed your preparatory tests given you by Mentuptah and Ima, you will receive further training and your initiation under my guidance. Now Ima will take you to the neophyte school and give you everything you need for the beginning. If you want to speak to me during your training, you can arrange to see me any evening. May God guide your further steps.'

After Ptahhotep's benediction, I bow and follow Ima to the school of neophytes.

Ima takes me to a little cell, one of many built in the temple wall. He gives me a plain white linen robe and a pair of plain sandals, saying that this cell belongs to me.

When I come out—having exchanged my silken robe and golden sandals for the simple clothing—I am a neophyte exactly like Ima. He leads me on through a long colonnade, and through the great door we step out into the temple garden. The garden is magnificent: a large rectangular plot of green grass bordered by palms makes an excellent place for exercise. As we go on, I see the neophytes at work behind the park-like part of the garden, near the vegetable plots and the orchards. All the neophytes wear the same kind of clothing as mine, but none of them is as young as I.

Ima takes me to Mentuptah, the head of the school of neophytes. He is a friendly person with soft, loving eyes. He explains my daily duties to me. The neophytes are divided up in groups. All groups are under Mentuptah's guidance, but each individual group also works under the leadership of an advanced neophyte, a candidate for priesthood. Ima leads the group to which I am assigned. He is a tall, slender but very powerful young man. I noticed his crystal-pure radiance when he first took me to Ptahhotep. He has passed most of his preparatory tests and the time is close at hand for him to be initiated. Ima is a candidate for the priesthood. In his appearance he doesn't give the impression of a man so much as of an androgynous being standing above and beyond sex. As much above and beyond it as an archangel. He radiates all the keenness of a sharp sword. His angelically beautiful face bears the signs of supreme intelligence and powers of concentration. Above his eyebrows there are two well developed mounds, the signs of wisdom. His mouth is well formed, beautiful, full of energy, but with soft corners, delicately chiselled, revealing his tender love for every living creature. I love him from the very first moment, feeling complete confidence in him as I would in a dearly beloved brother. I am happy that he is the one who is to prepare me for my tests!

Ima introduces me to the other neophytes. They have all chosen the priesthood as their calling in life, but only those who pass all their tests and receive initiation will become priests or priestesses. There are many who never make it. Nevertheless, if they wish to do so, they can spend the rest of their lives in the service of the temple, working in the garden and tending the animals. The neophytes who pass their preparatory examinations receive ever new and progressively more difficult tasks and assignments parallel with their degree of advancement.

The group under Ima's guidance is one made up entirely of spiritually well-developed neophytes. On their father's side, most of them are descended from the Sons of God, just as I am, and they can be recognized even from a distance by the elongated shape of their heads. I am assigned to this group and feel good in their pure atmosphere.

Every morning at sunrise we have to assemble in the garden. We begin with physical exercises. The exercises involve strong concentration. We assume various body postures and, while doing breathing exercises, must guide our consciousness into different parts of the body. Through long and patient practice in this way we can make the entire body completely conscious, move at will, control and guide the smallest parts of the body and all internal organs. Patiently and persistently we thus develop the body into an excellent instrument.

When we have finished these exercises, we go into the great room of the temple for training of mind and soul. In these exercises, Mentuptah dictates to us various inter-related *dream pictures* which we must experience as intensively as if they were real. With these dream pictures we intentionally produce different emotional states within ourselves and learn how to control them. With these exercises Mentuptah takes us through all the different spheres of the underworld and overworld, through the seven Hells and the seven Heavens, teaching us to keep our presence of mind no matter what may happen so that even in the most difficult situations we can instantly decide what to do.

As soon as we have completely mastered this kind of exercise, we go a step further. We have to experience different emotional states on command, *without dream pictures*, but with the same intensity as if we really had *a reason*. We begin these exercises at the lowest negative condition, moving up step by step until we reach the highest positive condition. To take an example, we begin by experiencing the deepest state of dejection, moving up gradually through indifference, then on higher and higher, through joy and on up to the highest state of happiness.

When after long practice we get proficient at this exercise, we are obliged to practise faster changeovers from one emotional state to another until we can experience them all, one after the other, as easily and positively as a musician draws forth a whole gamut of tone from his instrument, from the lowest to the highest. When we achieve proficiency at running quickly through the whole scale of human emotions—from darkest desperation to the highest bliss—we take the next step. This consists of experiencing opposite emotional states, one after the other, with no time lost for transition, shifting from deep sadness immediately to the highest hilarity. Or, to take another example, from fear immediately to self-assured courage.

We are only permitted to do these exercises under the direction of our teacher. They represent a great strain for our nerves. It takes us a long time to reach the point of being able, with the aid of the dream pictures, to experience the emotional states as vividly as if they were external events in our lives. It takes us still longer to be able to experience the full scale of emotional states from the lowest to the highest. Only when we can bring our nerves to complete rest after these exercises, keeping them in a well-rested condition throughout the day, are we permitted to practise the most difficult exercises of experiencing diametrically opposite emotions without a time of transition. The aim of these exercises is to make us independent of both external events and our own personal moods, thus enabling us to determine our own moods ourselves and maintain our emotional equilibrium no matter what happens. We are taught constant inner watchfulness and presence of mind.

People believe that there always has to be a reason for their being joyous or happy. Through the exercises with the dream pictures we first imagine we have a reason for being in one mood or another. Thus we learn to control the *reasons themselves*! As we do not actually have a reason, however, we have to *imagine one ourselves*.

Then comes the next step of experiencing an emotional state by itself, *without a reason*, without having previously imagined a situation such as would call forth the mood to be experienced.

After long practice, when we have become quite skilful at these exercises, we discover *we have always imagined we had a reason* for being 'sad' or 'joyous', 'depressed' or 'exuberant' etc. Through these exercises we thus become convinced that events and occurrences in our lives *must not have any effect on us. We discover that every state of consciousness arises—and can only arise—within ourselves.* One and the same event can provoke one person to laughter, another to tears, while a third remains completely indifferent; all because *each is merely projecting outwardly his own inward attitude, and it is only this inward attitude which provokes our response, not the external events themselves.*

As a final result, the pupil must attain the ability to keep his emotional composure imperturbable and unshakeable at all times, never losing it under any circumstances. These exercises also teach us that *whatever happens on earth is only a transitory dream picture projected in time and space by ourselves. We only need to take it seriously in so far as it adds to our experience.*

But it takes a long, long time to reach this degree of ability! We have to keep ourselves under the strictest observation, must never forget ourselves for a moment, must always be conscious and *aware*, always analysing every feeling, every thought, to determine in what stratum of the self it has originated. And all this is not something one can learn to do from one day to the next!

In addition to this long spiritual training, we also have to practise purely mental concentration exercises. These are assigned to me by Ima. After the group exercises he takes me to a quiet corner of the garden and explains what concentration means. I must not allow my thoughts to roam around aimlessly. On the contrary, I must command myself *to concentrate only on one prescribed concept.* I must pull my thoughts together into a single point, giving them a centripetal rather than centrifugal direction. Ima gives me a sentence on which to concentrate. When I have succeeded in concentrating on it, I am to go and tell him. Then he leaves me alone.

The sentence is 'I always manifest divinity'.

I sit down and start to concentrate on this sentence. I repeat mentally: 'I always manifest divinity,' once, twice, ten times, a hundred times . . . I think of nothing else: 'I always manifest divinity . . . I always manifest divinity . . . I always manifest divinity . . .'

After an hour I go to Ima and tell him, 'I can't concentrate on that sentence. It's impossible.'

'Impossible?' he asks, 'Why should it be impossible?'

'You told me that concentration means directing all forces, all thoughts to a single point, drawing and holding together all the forces of the intellect and of consciousness. But when I concentrate on a *sentence*, I cannot draw together all the forces of my intellect into *one single point.* A sentence consists of several words. These words follow each other both in time and space. That means I can't *simultaneously think these words in a given point* but only *one after another* in time and space! And when I have thought the sentence through to the end, I have to jump back again to the beginning and think it through to the end again. That's why concentration in this way is impossible. Either I have to jump back from the end to the beginning after each sentence, like this

I always manifest divinity,

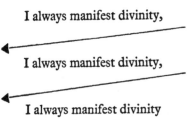

I always manifest divinity,

I always manifest divinity

or, if I imagine a sentence in a circular form, my concentration results in running around in a circle,

'But that is not concentration!'

Ima listens attentively. Then, quite pleased, he says, 'You have practised right! You've discovered it's impossible to concentrate on *words*. The fact that you finally imagined the words to be in the form of a circle shows that you were making a real effort at concentration. But no matter how close you pull the words together, they still form a circle and you can never get them into the centre. You have found out that no matter how much force you exert on them in the direction of the centre, the words resist this force so you cannot draw them into the centre. This principle of resistance towards being drawn into the centre is one we use in building bridges. We build an arch of stones, just as you have built a circle out of words, and the bridge doesn't fall into the water because the stones exert pressure on each other and the stones do not yield to the pressure. Because of the power of their resistance, the stones hold the whole bridge together. But if your concentration aims to get to the centre, it is prevented from doing so by the resistance of the words, and the concentration is impossible. The same happens if you try to concentrate on one word. A word consists of letters which can never be drawn together completely in a single point.'

'So what must I do?'

'For your next exercise try to concentrate on a single letter. Take the letter "o", for example,' says Ima, and leaves me alone.

I try it. Sitting in the grass again, I concentrate on the 'o' . . . mentally I repeat the letter 'o', saying 'o', 'o', 'o', 'o', 'o' . . . and still thinking of nothing but 'o', 'o', 'o', 'o' 'o' 'o' 'o' 'o' . . . until all of a sudden I make a new discovery. I go back to Ima and tell him laughingly, 'I've already finished'.

'Well,' he asks, 'what have you found out?'

'That the "o" I was concentrating on all of a sudden turned into a pipe. A long "o"-shaped tunnel in which I was constantly moving forward. But that isn't perfect concentration either!'

'Good,' says Ima. 'That means you've already reached the fourth dimension. Now try again with a sentence "I always manifest divinity" and try again to concentrate on that. How would you solve the problem now?'

'What should I do?' I ask.

'What would you do?' asks Ima in his turn.

I consider the problem for a while and then say, 'The words are the clothing, the material manifestation of the meaning. If I want to get into the centre, I must give up the words that hinder me and concentrate only on the meaning of the sentence, without words, without form. Is that right?'

Ima smiles and says, 'Let's see how you succeed. Go and try. Then come back.'

I go back and concentrate on the meaning of the sentence 'I always manifest divinity . . .' . . . only on the meaning . . .

Then I go back to Ima. He is just finishing a discussion with another neophyte. Seeing that I am waiting for him, he gives me a roguish glance as if he already knew how I had got on with my concentration exercise. 'Well?' he asks.

'Ima, it's so strange! As I tried to concentrate only on the meaning of the sentence, I couldn't think of it any more, and the whole inner process moved out of my head into my breast, so that I wasn't thinking it any more, but feeling and experiencing it! The moment I concentrated on the meaning of this sentence, without words, *I myself became this meaning*! But then the sentence has to read differently, not "I always manifest divinity", but much more accurately, "*I am divinity which is always manifesting itself!*" '

As I speak, Ima looks at me with a growing smile and growing pleasure. 'You have concentrated very well,' he says. 'Very well! You've discovered that concentration cannot be a permanent condition, but only a *transition between the projected world and being*. When you concentrate your thoughts on something, *you can't stop with just thinking*, because concentration leads you *back to yourself*, and you become the very thing you're concentrating on. *From thinking you progress through concentration into a state of being!* Thinking ceases completely and the thinker becomes identical with what he is thinking. To *think* something means to project a thought outwardly by means of the intellect, as if by means of a mirror, hence to *step out of oneself*. Through concentration we draw the projection back again, and *what is* thought becomes identical again with the *thinker*, with the *person himself*. The two factors are joined in a perfect unity. *That which is created goes back into the creator!*

'Go on practising and you will experience this process with ever greater clarity. Here's a new exercise. You like to sit under this palm tree. Concentrate on it.' And with that Ima leaves.

I sit down again and look at the palm tree, keeping my thoughts centred on this tree, nothing else . . . Hours go by and evening comes. I have to go home. Menu is waiting for me outside and we go home together.

The next morning I am back in the temple garden, and after our group exercises I take my place again under the palm tree, concentrating on it.

When I began this exercise, all kinds of extraneous thoughts disturbed me. I suddenly remembered what Menu had told me the evening before—I noticed a bird up in the fronds—then a gnat was humming about my ears—then I remembered Chancellor Roo-Kha's impertinences and felt angry. But I chased away all foreign thoughts as they arose in me and concentrated only on the palm tree.

Now I am getting along better. Thoughts can no longer reach me and really disturb me. Previously I was still *in the world of thoughts*—among the thoughts. My thoughts were able to push me to and fro. But I did not let myself be pushed around. I stayed put just where I was, with the palm tree, gliding slowly and almost imperceptibly further and further into myself where thoughts could no longer follow and disturb me. Now and again a thought bobs up, creeping through my intellect like a tired traveller. From my secure position I observe this stray, straggling, tired thought, but I don't bother about it . . . I think of the palm tree . . . slowly the palm tree fills my entire being.

Days go by, perhaps weeks too, I don't know. I don't know anything more that's going on in my outer world, as I am concentrating on the palm tree with all my attention. Then all of a sudden I have the odd feeling that I am no longer looking at the tree *from the outside*, but *from the inside*. To be sure I still perceive its outward form with my eyes, but I begin, to an ever-increasing extent, to see and experience the *inner being*, the animating creative principle of the palm . . . *to see it, to experience it, TO BE IT!*

And finally there comes a moment in which I am suddenly conscious of the fact that the palm is no longer outside myself—no!—it never was outside—it was only a false conception on my part—*the palm tree is in me and I in it—I myself am the palm tree!*

I do not know how long I have been thus absorbed within myself. I don't even know what *time* means. 'There' in the condition I am in the concept of time is unknown. Neither can I explain what this 'there' is. But all at once some power draws me back, slowly, into my personal consciousness, and I notice that Ima is standing before me. My eyes meet his gentle glance. He sits down near me in the soft grass, waits patiently till I come back to my senses, then looks at me questioningly.

I make one or two attempts to speak, but I don't succeed right away. Speech seems to have become completely superfluous.

Finally my activity reawakens and my will functions again. The nerves of my larynx set my vocal chords in motion, and I can produce sounds again.

'Oh Ima,' I say earnestly, softly, and surprised at the sound of my own voice, '*I have become the palm tree*—or better, I've discovered that the palm tree *was always I*! Only I didn't realize it!'

Ima nods his angelically beautiful head and beams with joy. 'You're making wonderful progress! I'm so glad—so glad! You're making faster progress than anyone has ever made in so short a time. If you pass all your other preparatory tests just as fast, you'll soon be ready for initiation!'

Joyously we look at each other in silence. As I look into his eyes, I feel even more deeply how pure a being Ima is and what tremendous strength he radiates. The air is purer wherever he is.

Then he offers me his hand and we get up. It's time for me to go home.

After I have retired for the night and am already lying on my bed, Menu kneels beside me on the floor and asks, 'What are you doing now in the temple ?'

'We do exercises.'

'Tell me what kind of exercises ?'

In all seriousness I answer, 'Well, my last exercise was to think so long about a palm tree that I finally discovered I myself am the palm tree!'

Menu looks at me in amazement. 'What have you discovered ?—What are you ?' she asks.

'The palm tree,' I repeat.

'You, the palm tree ?' she asks wide-eyed.

'Yes, yes, Menu, but leave me in peace, I want to go to sleep.' Then Menu begins to laugh so hard that she rolls around on the floor and tears stream down her cheeks:

'Ha ha ha, so you're a palm tree ? Where is your trunk, and where are your leaves ? Ha ha ha, so you're not a young girl any more! Ha ha ha!'

At that I sit up in bed, offended in my pride, and answer with all the dignity at my command: 'Please take note I'm not a young girl, but the representative of the Queen. I am the wife of the Pharaoh, do you understand ? And if you're going to make fun of my exercises, I won't tell you anything more.'

At that Menu begins to cry. Covering my hands with kisses, she says through her tears: 'Didn't I tell you it would be dangerous to be initiated ? Who knows but what they may really cast a spell on you and turn you into a palm tree. You talk so strangely now. Watch out, please watch out! It would be good if the Pharaoh knew what's happening!' Drying her tears, Menu leaves my room with a worried look on her face.

I remain alone with a very unpleasant feeling that I should not have talked to Menu about my deepest, most sacred experiences.

The next day, Ptahhotep sends for me. I am to see him in the evening.

He sits at his accustomed place in his little reception room. His glance is as deep as the sky is high. He knows everything.

'Come here, my little daughter,' he says with a smile.

I step up to him confidently. He takes my hands in his, smiles and asks, 'Do you know what your next task is to be ?'

'Yes, Father, I know,' I reply.

'And what is it ?'

'To keep silence,' I reply, smiling back at him confidently, despite my guilty feeling, because I know he does not condemn me. He nods. We understand each other. I don't need to apologize. He knows me better than I know myself, and he knows with absolute certainty that I wasn't acting malevolently when I spoke to Menu about sacred things far beyond her level of comprehension. I look into Ptahhotep's eyes. He sees me with all my imperfections, but he also sees my determination to learn to keep silence in the future.

Then he gently strokes my hair. I bow and leave.

Oh! How often am I to stand before him and have to confess that my tongue ran away from my brain . . . that I had failed again to be able to offer enough resistance to the basic urge for communication that has been planted in every human breast.

But nevertheless in time I do learn to be on guard against this power too. I learn to keep my urge for communication as carefully and thoroughly under control as my favourite lion, and through this constant self-observation, I gradually form the habit of listening inwardly, whenever I want to say something, to be sure I have authority to say it. Gradually I learn to keep my mouth shut except when I really have something to say. And I come to recognize two beings in my self: a personal ego which is often inclined to chatter, without control, *purely for the sake of communicating and attracting attention to my person* —and in the background of my consciousness a higher self which restrains my personal ego, telling it when and what it is to speak or do, and when it is to remain silent or passive. The important thing is to pay attention and obey the orders of this higher self. Merely to *hear* its commands is not enough; everybody does that!

During this period of time, Ima gives me further exercises in concentration to do after the group exercises in the temple are over.

We sit together in my favourite corner in the temple garden and Ima explains: 'You know now from experience what concentration is. But if you observe yourself during concentration, you will notice that in doing it you go through three phases, intellectual, emotional, and spiritual.

'All concentration begins with the intellectual phase. You direct your thoughts to the object of your concentration and consider what this object actually is. In this stage you are using your intellect because you want to clarify your thoughts and seek a completely satisfactory definition expressing fully and clearly the object of your concentration. As soon as you have found such a definition, your intellectual work is done, for you *know* now what this thing is. You don't need to reflect on it any more, for when you *know* what something *is*, you don't *cogitate* about it any more. *Thinking is the bridge between ignorance and knowledge.* When we know everything—like *God*—we will have no further need for thinking. *God* is omniscient. *He himself is knowledge*, and his knowledge is as perfect as a circle. What should *he* think about when *he knows everything*! Only the person who is obliged to expand his knowledge needs to think. *This work of expanding knowledge consists of thinking.*

'When your knowledge concerning the object of your concentration is complete, you make the transition from *thinking* to *feeling*. This is the second phase of concentration. Your consciousness projects outwardly through your nervous system all the characteristics of the object of your concentration, impressing them on your organs of sense; so you have the sensation of experiencing them. With every nerve and every drop of your blood you feel the object of your concentration and what it is like. When you have thoroughly experienced the object of your concentration in terms of thinking and feeling, you go on to the third phase, *spiritual concentration*. This means that in your consciousness you *become identical* with the object of concentration. You are no longer thinking about it, or feeling what and how it is, *you are it*! We call this a *state of being*. In this state you don't need to think about this thing any more, nor to feel it, because you have become it yourself. In this condition, all your thoughts, all your feelings, all your words, all your deeds become manifestations of the object of your concentration.

'You experienced this with the palm tree, but you hadn't yet had any exercise in observing yourself during these three phases. To take another example, let's say you're sitting on the bank of a river and concentrating on the water. At first you reflect on what water is. You recall that water is a liquid made through the union of two gases. You know that it can be warm or cold, that if it gets cold enough it turns into a solid, that it has colour and numerous other properties. And you think along these lines until your intellect has completely grasped what water is and means. *That is all intellectual concentration.*

Then you get up and walk out into the water. Now you feel what water is and what it is like. You feel through direct sensation that water is liquid, that it flows about your body, and you feel its temperature without measuring it. You can splash about in the water, make little ripples or even big waves with your hands and arms. *That is concentration in terms of feeling.*

In complete concentration, however, there comes the moment when you cease to be a being separated from water, you merge and coalesce with the water, you no longer have a human body—you have become water. Now you no longer need to *think about* water and its various properties. Neither do you need to *feel* what water is and what it is like. On the contrary, you *are* now water yourself. Complete concentration means *becoming identical with the object of concentration, being it*! In the two previous phases of concentration you are separated, whereas in this third and last phase—the *condition of being*—you experience complete unity, then as a consequence, complete understanding and complete recognition *from within*. Of course your body hasn't turned into water, but *in your consciousness you experience this state*.

'Watch the people around you. You'll notice some are constantly talking about love and goodness, wearing sweet smiles of smugness, and trying to show others on all possible occasions that they are "loving" and "good". But only on the outside! They wear the mask of love and goodness; but when it comes to deeds, they reveal their selfishness—because they *are* selfishness.

'Another person may never talk about goodness and never think that he wants to be "good"; yet everything he thinks, says and does comes forth out of goodness, because he himself *is* goodness! A PERSON DOESN'T THINK ABOUT WHAT HE IS; NOR DOES HE FEEL IT; SIMPLY BECAUSE HE IS WHAT HE IS! He doesn't need to speak about it; everything he thinks, says and does is the expression of what he is, the manifestation of his own *being*!

'Now comes the most difficult task of all: concentrate *on yourself*. First *reflect and consider* what you are, then *feel* what you are, and finally you must *be* what you are!

'For you to have become conscious here on earth, you have had to leave your true self and enter into your intellect and feelings. So far you have only been able to *think* and *feel* what you are, but you have never yet been able to *be* what you are! Observe the people around you and you will see that *they are not their real selves*. On the contrary, they are always identifying themselves with thoughts, feelings and roles they are playing here on earth. They have "fallen out" of their real selves and become pretenders, people living in a world of make-believe. Only in the eyes of very small children can you still see the sparkle, *the light of real being*. As its intellect awakens, the child begins to identify itself with its outward person, getting more and more removed from its divine, true self. And all the while the person, as we think about him, is only a mask through which the true *self*—the great *invisible one*—looks out at the world. The person cannot be more than an instrument for the manifestation of the *self*. But people get so attached to their mask that they cannot free themselves from it any more. The true *self* is king and master, the person is only his servant. But the sons of men abandoned their *self* and, descending from the throne, identified themselves with their mask, with their person. They make a king out of the servant and separate themselves from their true being. They force their higher *self* into exile, into the *unconscious*. The intellect causes this separation, and by means of concentration exercises and a purposeful effort to become *conscious and aware*, the intellect can be an instrument by which we get out of this separation and back to our true *self*.

'In the past you have concentrated on various things. From now on, your one and only task is to concentrate *on yourself*, progressing through the three phases of concentration until you achieve complete identification with your own true *self*, until you really *are* your *self*. It is your task to reach the state of being which can only be described, in the first person, as "*I am that I am*". But watch out! It's not enough for you to *think* what you are, nor to *feel* what you are; you must *be what you are in your own true inner self*!

'That is your concentration task until your initiation.'

And so I enter the long period of my life in which I devote myself to these two tasks: Learning to *be* my own true *self*, and learning to keep silence.

26

THE TREE OF THE KNOWLEDGE
OF GOOD AND EVIL

WHEN I have progressed to the point where I have pretty well mastered the art of keeping silence, I stand before Ptahhotep again one evening, and he asks me, 'What have you learned during your struggles to keep silent? Have you *only* learned the art of keeping silence?'

'No, Father, that was simply impossible. While I was struggling with *silence*, I simultaneously had to struggle with *speech*. To the same extent that I have mastered silence, I have also mastered speech. This is because *silence* means *not talking*, and *talking* means *not keeping silent*. I wasn't able to separate these two things. I've discovered that silence and speech are two different sides of the same unit, like the two sides of a coin.'

'Right,' says Ptahhotep. Then he gets up and leads me to one of the great white stone blocks of which the walls of the room are made. Pointing to the smooth, white surface of the stone, he asks, 'What do you see on this white surface?'

'Nothing,' I reply.

'And what could I draw on it?'

'Everything.'

'Now,' says Ptahhotep, 'This *Nothing* therefore contains *Everything*. In this condition both together form a perfect unity. Within this unity something can only become *recognizable* if it becomes separate and distinct from unity.

'Now watch as I draw, with green paint, the form of a leaf on this surface. The form of the leaf was already there on this stone surface before I drew it, but you weren't able to recognize it, *because the positive form of the leaf and the negative nature of the background were still at rest within each other.* They were completely identical. The form of the leaf was not yet separated from the *Everything* that is contained in this *Nothing*. When the leaf appeared on the wall, it became separated from the *Everything*, and therefore recognizable.

'And remember something very important: the fact that this leaf appears in *green* colour means that it has left behind in the *Everything* its form in the complementary colour, in this case *red*, as its invisible, negative picture. *Whatever you see as you look about you is only recognizable because it has separated itself from its complementary half and the latter has remained behind in the invisible, unmanifested state.*

'You can achieve *knowledge* only through comparing the two sides, positive and negative, which have become separated from each other. As long as these two sides are together, resting in each other, you can't perceive or recognize anything.

'Observe the visible world. It is only recognizable because it has separated itself from the unity in which the *Nothing* and the *Everything* are still at rest within each other. In other words, it has separated itself from the absolute unity we call God. The things in the world about us are only recognizable because the positive appears separately from the negative and we can compare the two together. *There can be no perception unless unity is split into two halves—one of them manifested and the other, its reflection and complementary half, unmanifested —so that both become recognizable through comparison!* Now follow me.'

Ptahhotep leads me into another room where he places a little figurine on a large table before a white wall. Then he puts two little lamps behind the figurine, one to the right and the other to the left, in such a way that two shadows of the little statue appear on the wall. Then Ptahhotep picks up a transparent red disc and holds it in front of the lamp on the right. To my great surprise I see the shadow to the right on the wall is *red*, while the one to the left is *green*.

'How is that, Father of my Soul?' I ask in amazement.

'Think for a moment and you will find the explanation yourself,' says Ptahhotep.

I keep silent for a while and concentrate until I experience the solution. Then I explain: 'The statuette keeps back the red colour as the red light is projected towards the wall, and allows only the complementary green colour to appear on the wall. That's why the *green* shadow appears on the other side. On the other hand, the statuette holds back *all the light* from the other lamp, and so the shadow on this side of the wall appears to have turned *red*.'

'Quite right,' says Ptahhotep. 'You see the two complementary colours cannot exist without each other, any more than *keeping silent* can exist without *talking*. Whatever you make manifest in the world of things about you, the complementary opposite stays behind in the unmanifested state. When you talk, the negative side of talking, *keeping silent*, stays behind, unmanifested. And when you keep silent, the positive side of keeping silent, *talking*, stays unmanifested. When a mountain is formed, its complementary half, a valley, must also be formed. How could a mountain be possible without a valley, or a valley without a mountain? *Nothing can ever be manifested and made recognizable, unless its opposite—its complementary half—is simultaneously present unmanifested! When something positive is manifested, the negative remains unmanifested, and vice versa, when something negative is manifested, the positive is unmanifested. Wherever the one appears, its complementary half must also be present even though in an unmanifested state.* The two are bound together for all time and eternity.

'And so you see the separation is really one in appearance only, because the two complementary halves, even when they are separated and have fallen out of the *all-unity* can *never get away from each other*. Inseparable *divine unity* therefore manifests itself always and everywhere; for even in this seeming separation, it continues to be active everywhere as the *ever-present attractive force between positive and negative.* Both positive and negative tend to return to their original state, *divine unity.* Even though something appears in the visible world, it cannot split itself off permanently from divine unity; sometime, sooner or later, it will unite with its complementary half and return to divine *unity.* The inherent force dwelling in everything that exists and drawing every created form back into the original unity is what we call *God.*

'All creation—the visible world about us—is like a tree. On the right side it bears positive-good fruit, and the left, negative-bad fruit. But both sides belong to the same tree and come from the same unity.

'*Both good and evil have arisen only through separation from unity which itself is neither good nor evil but divine. Only through separation is it possible to achieve recognition and knowledge. Consequently the recognizable world must consist of good and evil. If this were not so, it would not be recognizable and could not exist at all.*

'The entire creation is the tree of the knowledge of good and evil! But the creator—*God*—is not a *half* which has fallen out of unity, become separated from it and consequently recognizable; on the contrary, *God is unity itself.* He stands above all created forms which have fallen out of unity. Right *within himself*, he has perfect unity. *He* is the *Nothing* out of which *Everything* arises and manifests itself, but in *him* the *nothing* and *everything* make up non-separated, divine unity.

'Creation always means a half of the whole . . . the half which has fallen out of unity and which has become recognizable through comparisons, while its complementary half has remained behind, unmanifested. That's why you can never find and never recognize *God*—the creator—in the world of creation, simply *because God has no complementary half with which he could be compared.* There is absolutely no possibility of comparing *him*, and so there is no possibility of recognizing him.—*You can only* BE *God!*

'Listen, my child: There is only *one* eternal *being*—only *one God.* In everything alive there lives this one single *being*, there lives this one single *God. God* is the indivisible unity, *he* is present everywhere, *he* fills the entire universe. The whole universe lives because God animates it with his own eternal *being*! Hence *God* is like a tree of life giving its own being to the created, recognizable world that has become separated from its complementary half, in other words, giving life to the tree of the knowledge of good and evil. This tree of the knowledge of good and evil—our created world—is only alive because the tree of life—God—instills his own *life* in its veins—*lives in it*!

'The material world is like a tree of death: The tree of the knowledge of good and evil, and the *God* dwelling within it is the tree of life living in everything that is created. *God* is one and only one. This one single *God* is the *self*, the innermost being within all creatures. God is everywhere present, and since two things can't occupy the same space at the same time and nothing can displace *God* from any place in the universe, only one and the same *God* can be present everywhere as the *self* in every created form. *God* is indivisible *unity*. All creatures, all plants, animals, man himself, all are fruits on the tree of the knowledge of good and evil; all are alive because the vital flow from the tree of life streams through their veins, that is, *because the tree of life lives within them.* And that means in you too, little daughter!—Your body is also a fruit on the tree of death, on the tree of the knowledge of good and evil, and has no life of its own. But within you there lives the tree of life, because your *self* is also a little branch on *God's great tree of life,* and you are only alive because *God* is living as your *self* within you and your body, keeping your person alive.

'By virtue of having been born into your body, you have become a recognizable being. You have separated your consciousness from the great *all and nothing—from God,* from your own true *self.* You have fallen out of the divine, paradisiacal, original state—in which all possibilities of manifestation including all plants, all animals and man himself, are still within the *all-embracing unity* —into the world of many forms and differentiations. You have become a manifestation, a created form. Consequently everything you are here on the earthly plane is only the recognizable half of unity, made up of good and evil. And since your consciousness has been placed in your body, you have awakened in this body, that is, your consciousness has become identical with the body.

'To eat of something is to become identical with it; for what you eat is what you will consist of, *what you will be.* Through identifying itself with your body, your consciousness has—symbolically—eaten of the fruits of the tree of the knowledge of good and evil and by the same token become subject to the kingdom of death.

'But now listen to the good news: Your body is the result of separation; it is only the visible half of your own true *self.* The other half has remained in the unmanifested, unconscious part of your being. By uniting these two complementary halves with each other, you can return to divine *unity*! It is impossible to experience this unity *physically,* that is, to make your invisible unconscious visible and physical *also,* and unite the two halves together. For *one* consciousness cannot animate *two* bodies. To try to experience unity in this way would mean death. By virtue of the very fact that the *body* has become visible and recognizable because it has separated itself from its complementary half, the reunion in this way would have to involve the death of the body. Nevertheless you still can experience, in the body, this divine reunion with your complementary half: *In a state of consciousness!* You can expand your consciousness until you make the unconscious part of you completely conscious, until you consciously experience the unmanifested, invisible half of yourself, and in this way achieve divine unity *in your consciousness.* Even while your body remains in the visible world of the created, you can merge your consciousness with your own true *self,* out of which you have fallen, thus forming the perfect unity. In this way, right here in this earthly existence, you can experience bliss— experience *God—be God.*

'This striving for reunion is in everything that has been created. Every creature seeks its complementary half in order to re-unite with it. The positive-male forms seek the negative-female forms and vice versa. This tendency on the part of positive and negative force even makes up the basic structure of matter. In actual fact, *there couldn't be any matter at all without this tendency*; for this striving towards unity—towards the *state of being God*—makes up the attractive power between positive and negative forces, and the whole world is built on this striving to attain the divine, primordial state. This striving itself is the source of all power in the manifested world. Nature uses it and, projected into the body, it is the basis of sexual power.

'As long as a creature seeks its complementary half outside itself, in the created, recognizable world, it will never find unity, simply because *its complementary half isn't outside itself, manifested, separate from itself, but on the contrary, unseparated from itself, in its own unmanifested part, in its unconscious!* No creature could exist if it did not have its other half in the unmanifested. Take yourself for example, little daughter. The opposite of everything you are and manifest in your conscious part is contained in your unconscious part which nevertheless belongs to you, and which you are just as much as you are your conscious, manifested part. You don't find your complementary part outside yourself—in a man of flesh and blood, for example, but in the unconscious part of your true self. When you unite in your consciousness two halves of yourself, you've found your way back into the infinite *all and nothing*, you've become identical with *God* again!

'Through this union which takes place in your consciousness, the eternal longing of your manifested being ceases because it has found its complementary half and merged into unity with it; and for this reason the sexual desire of your body also ceases once and for all. You become complete within yourself. Right here in this physical existence, you experience the divine state: Immortality, bliss—fulfilment! And inasmuch as the same one, individual *being* lives in all creatures, you simultaneously become identical *with the true self of every creature* when you awaken within your own true self. You will achieve unity with God and simultaneously unity with the entire universe. You will lift your consciousness out of your body, out of your personal being, and experience all-inclusive cosmic consciousness. You will feel yourself as the "I"—the self—in every creature, in the entire universe, *in God*. This means *you will again be eating of the fruit of the tree of life!* Then you will have moved out of the world of effects into the world of causes, out of the realm of the transitory into the realm of the eternal, out of the created into the creative, out of the realm of death into the realm of life. In short, you will have achieved your resurrection in eternal *being*. And that is initiation!'

Ptahhotep ceases speaking. But I see this divine unity manifested in the impenetrable depths of his heavenly eyes. Endless happiness, calm and peace radiate forth from his eyes into my soul. In his glance I see the fulfilment of truth.

He blesses me and I leave.

27

THE TWELVE SETS OF TWIN CHARACTERISTICS

THE NEXT evening I find myself standing before Ptahhotep again.

'The time has come,' says he, 'for you to study and practise the twelve sets of opposites as your next exercise. In your initiation you will be examined concerning them. So listen carefully and make a point of remembering what I'm telling you now:

'Just as *keeping silent* and *talking* are the two complementary manifestations of the same force, in the same way there are twelve sets of opposites which you must learn to control. From now on you will spend only your mornings in the temple and then go back to the palace. And you must seize every opportunity to be among people as much as possible, because it is far easier to master each of these sets of opposites when you are in the temple than it is in the palace. Here you only meet people like yourself, neophytes, striving to attain divine unity, as well as priests and priestesses already living in divine unity. But in the everyday world you are subject to all kinds of temptations. You meet people who are slaves of their bodies, and such people try to influence you too. The danger of falling is much greater. If you can master all the characteristics and properties applicable throughout the world, you will also be able to pass the initiation examinations.

'These twelve sets of opposite characteristics are:

keeping silent — talking
receptivity — resistance to influence
obeying — ruling
humility — self confidence
lightning-like speed — circumspection
to accept everything — to be able to differentiate
ability to fight — peace
caution — courage
to possess nothing — to command everything
to have no ties — loyalty
contempt for death — regard for life
indifference — love

'The earth is now going through a long period in which body-dominated and self-seeking people will gradually take over the ruling power. But you already know that wherever negative forces are manifest, positive forces must also be present, although in the unmanifested state. During this dark period of the earth, the Sons of God who manifest the divine laws of selflessness will gradually abandon the earthly plane, withdrawing to the spiritual plane of the unmanifested. Nevertheless, they will continue to work in the human subconscious, as they actually will be the unconscious of humanity and will manifest themselves in the souls of maturing people as yearning for liberation and salvation.

'On earth, the megalomania of certain individuals, together with the growing dissatisfaction of the enslaved masses will lead to bitter and ever bitterer struggles throughout thousands of years. Many millennia of constant struggling and bickering and the supremacy of avarice, vanity, envy, vengefulness, hate and other animal characteristics would eradicate from the face of the earth everything that is good and true and beautiful were it not for divine providence and a group of spiritually united people—under the guidance of the Sons of God working on the spiritual plane—who will save our secret knowledge from sliding into oblivion. The earth—like every other planet—is under the guidance of a high spiritual power, and this power manifests itself through the Sons of God in a manner appropriate for the people concerned. It is manifested through a group of initiated people who through their development have become peers of the Sons of God. They are all co-workers in the great divine plan of saving the earth from darkness, isolation, and the rule of material and diabolic forces. Every initiate takes part in this work, and as you are to be initiated, this means you too.

'In order to be a useful co-worker in this great plan, one must first master the whole scale of the sets of opposites. And you too, for your initiation, will have to pass an examination in them.

'Mastering these attributes means that you use them at the *right time* and in the *right place*. The same attribute that is *divine* at the *right time* and in the *right place* is *satanically evil* at the *wrong time* and in the *wrong place. This is because God creates only what is good, beautiful and true. There are no bad characteristics as such, and no bad forces, but only wrongly used characteristics and wrongly applied forces!*

'You've already found out what it means to speak or to keep silent at the right time and in the right place. To keep silent is perfectly divine and brings blessings on all concerned, if we do so *where* and *when* we should. But on the other hand, if we keep silent in a place or at a time when we should speak up— as for example when we might save a person from a great danger with just a word—our keeping silence becomes satanic.

'And if we talk in the wrong place and at the wrong time, the divine gift of speech is turned into satanic chatter and gossip.

'In the next twin pair of opposites, receptivity is divine if we are receptive and open to everything that is high and beautiful, good and true, that is, if we are receptive to God's will and let Him work in us. On the other hand, the receptivity, or impressionability, is disastrous if it becomes a spineless lack of character and capitulation to influence.

178

'*Ability to resist influence* means the ability to put up unflinching resistance to all low influences. But if we also put up resistance against higher forces, we immediately turn our divine attribute of resistance to influence into a satanic kind of self-isolation.

'It is the duty of every co-worker in the great divine plan to give absolute *obedience* to God's will. The latter can manifest itself directly through you or through other people. You can recognize God's will when you thoroughly examine everything that is asked of you to be sure that it is in agreement with your *innermost conviction*. God speaks to us through our innermost conviction, and we must give him absolute obedience. On the contrary, to obey someone against our own conviction, purely for reasons of cowardice, fear, material advantage, or merely wanting to "be good"—that is for low, personal reasons, this is *servility* and is satanical.

'*Ruling* means giving ignorant and weak people some of the ruler's own will-power. Universal love, uniting all the forces active within the people, should lead the people towards a general well-being, without infringing on their right of self-determination. Any ruler who, without love, and for selfish motives, imposes his will on others and violates their right of self-determination makes the divine activity of *ruling* into satanical *tyranny*.

'*Humility* is what we must feel towards the divine, towards the higher *self* which animates us. You must realize that all the good, beautiful, and true attributes belong to *him*, that your person is an instrument for manifesting divinity, but by itself and without divinity it represents merely an empty husk. You should recognize within yourself the same divinity, the same eternal *being* which manifests itself throughout the universe, and you must subject yourself humbly to this divinity. But you must never subordinate yourself to earthly or sub-earthly powers or bow before earthly forms; for this would mean turning divine humility into weak, cowardly, satanic self-humiliation, and by doing this you would violate the *divinity* which animates you with its *own* eternal *being*.

'If you want to be a good servant within the divine plan for salvation of the world, you must never forget that you do not live and work on your own strength. All power comes from God, and all powers you manifest come to you from your higher self—from God. Constantly remember that your person as such is an imaginary being. Your true being—the only, eternal reality within you—is *God*! That's why self-confidence means having confidence in the *God* dwelling within your heart, but not in the phantom being of your person as such. *Divine self-confidence is indispensable for every creative activity* and represents an inner union with *God*. But when a person imagines his qualities and powers are his own and not God's, he turns divine self-confidence into satanic false pride and presumption.

'To be a co-worker within the great divine plan you must also be able to make decisions with lightning-like speed. You must learn, instantaneously, without hesitation, to choose the best of a number of different possibilities. Situations can arise in which only a moment's delay can mean missing the unique, never-recurring opportunity. When you can act in a moment, with complete concentration and with a presence of mind that stands above and beyond all concept of time, your power to decide instantly is divine. But acting quick as a flash without concentration and presence of mind turns divine *lightning-like speed* into satanic haste.

'And that's why you must also learn *divine circumspection*. Before acting, you must control your temper and with lots of patience allow the decision to ripen within you. In order to recognize the will of God you must often allow yourself time to reach the right decision. That's what it means to act with prudence. But if you carry prudence and circumspection to the point of never reaching any decision at all, you're turning divine *circumspection* into satanic, doubting indecision.

'As a useful co-worker in the divine plan you must learn to accept everything that fate brings you. Your worth is not determined by external circumstances but by the degree in which you manifest *God*. Worldly degradations or humiliations cannot destroy, or even reduce, your inner values. By the same token, praise or glorification cannot make them greater either. For this reason, you must never be affected by the way ignorant people treat you. You remain what you are whether people vilify you or glorify you. Learn to be contented in any and all conditions and to accept the circumstances fate gives you with complete imperturbability. Whether your work within the great divine plan requires you to live in abject poverty or to hold a high position and command a great fortune, you must regard *either of these merely as means to a great end*. Neither of them must change your inner attitude. Learning to *accept everything* in this way is divine. On the other hand you must always be able to decide when you, *as a representative of divine guidance, must defend yourself* against humiliation or calumny. In the same way, there are times when you must be able to decide that it's the right thing to do to withdraw modestly from glorification by the crowds and masses. To *accept everything* must never be allowed to degenerate into apathetic *indifference* or cowardly *lack of character*.

Always choose the best and don't be satisfied with what's inferior. You must be able to differentiate and distinguish what's *beautiful* from what's *ugly*, the *good* from the *bad*, the *true* from the *false*, the *divine* from the *satanic*. Without a completely developed power to differentiate and distinguish, one can't be a useful co-worker in the great plan.

'If you want to be useful, you must also be *able to fight* with all your energy. With the sword of truth you must be able to fight the shadow of error in order to help bring about the victory of divinity on earth. But your noble and courageous *willingness to fight* must never be allowed to degenerate into stupid quarrelsomeness.

'And even though you must often fight bravely, you must not forget that you have to fight with spiritual weapons in order to bring *peace* to the earth. You must fight to restore unity to what has been torn apart, to restore peace to those who are fighting. But your love of peace must never be allowed to turn into a cowardly or comfortable kind of *not wanting to fight.*

'In order to be a useful co-worker you also have to learn *caution*, at the same time being able to decide the right time and right place to use this divine gift. You can save yourself and others from great dangers, harm and useless sacrifices through the proper exercise of *caution*. But the divine gift of *caution* slips over into satanic cowardice when one doesn't dare to do something because of fear or lack of self-confidence.

'You must possess unflinching *courage*, and you must not fear any danger. You must stride forth courageously to face any difficulty, valiantly fending off any attack against the divine when the great goal you're working for requires it of you. But divine *courage* must never be allowed to deteriorate into dare-devil *recklessness.*

'As a co-worker within the great plan you must also understand what it means to possess nothing. Whether your task demands abject poverty of you or gives you the greatest wealth, you must *always remember that nothing, absolutely nothing, ever or anywhere really belongs to you. On the contrary, everything is God's property, and from his property you receive something only for your actual needs, corresponding to your task.* Just as it's a matter of indifference to a canal whether more or less water flows through it, because the water doesn't belong to it, you too must regard everything fate gives you as something that comes to you from *God*, and something you must pass on. What you will have to live on is something you don't need to worry about. You will always receive as much as you need. And no matter how rich you might be, you must always remember the fact that you really possess nothing. But this divinely positive attitude must never slide down into *not caring about anything* or *contempt of things material.* *You must never expect the people about you to maintain you without work on your part!*

'Matter too is a manifestation of God, and so you must respect matter as something divine. But at the same time, you must be master over it. You must master the art of being able to acquire as many material things as you need for your earthly task. And remember well that as long as you are on earth, you'll have to be dealing *with* matter, not *without* it, and certainly not *against* it. It's necessary for you to be able to acquire and hold matter, to master it and use it wisely; for otherwise you're completely at the mercy of earthly powers and, under their control, unable to carry out your earthly task independently and freely. But take care lest the divine ability to master matter deteriorate into a selfish, satanic craving for possessions.

'As a co-worker in the great divine plan you can't allow yourself to be attached to anyone. Learn to recognize the divine, the earthly, and the demonic characteristics in everyone. Don't love the person, but love *the divine within the person*, tolerate the earthly, and go around the demonic. Whenever your task demands it of you, you must be able to leave without delay the person you love the most, because you must always remember that the lovable characteristics in him *are God, not the person himself.* The person is only an instrument for the manifestation of *God.* You can find and love the same manifestations in other people too. Love *God* in everyone; then you will not be attached to anyone. This *not having ties* must never be allowed to turn into general indifference and apathy concerning the people around you.

'You should be loyal, in life and in death, toward the people in whom you have recognized God's manifestations. You love your master and your co-workers in the great divine plan because you have *recognized God in them.* You are loyal to *God* in them, because you love their person only as an instrument of God. In this way the esteem and loyalty you show towards your master and co-workers can never turn into a cult of persons or personal glorification.

'To play a useful role in the great divine plan, you must be able to use your own person, like an obedient instrument, in front of the public. You must be able, in front of groups of other people, to animate your talents and abilities with your spiritual forces, raise them to a climax of brilliance in such a way that you manifest your spirit in the highest degree through your person, through the posture of your body, through the movements of your hands, through the glance of your eyes and through the persuasive power of your oratory, all so that you can bring people under your influence and carry them upward with you to a higher spiritual level. In other words you must be able to appear before the public without inhibitions and without being bashful. But the art of "appearing in public" must never be allowed to awaken the devil of vanity in you; it must never be allowed to degenerate into self-complacency and the base desire to "show off" with your God-given talents. When crowds of people enthusiastically cheer and applaud you, you must constantly carry in your consciousness the awareness that the people are not enthusiastic about your person —which is only an empty garment—but about God who has manifested himself through your earthly instrument.

'If in your application of the art of "appearing in public" you avoid the beguiling temptations of the devil of vanity, you won't be the least disturbed when, in fulfilling other tasks, it becomes your duty to remain completely unknown and unnoticed by other people. In such a case you must not display your talents, but rather disappear in the crowd as it were, without wanting to stand out or be noticed. However, this modest "remaining unnoticed" must never be allowed to degenerate into personal self-underestimation or self-destruction. In your heart you must always carry your worth as a human being.

'If you want to be a useful co-worker in the great divine plan, you must be able to achieve complete disregard for death. You must have the unshakeable conviction that there is no *death* at all. When your body has ceased to be usable, your *self* casts it off just as you cast off a worn-out piece of clothing. The *self* however is a branch on the tree of life, therefore *life* itself, and *life* is immortal. When you've become identical in your consciousness with *life*, you won't shrink back in fear of death whenever your task brings you into mortal danger. On the contrary, with complete equanimity and absolute contempt for death, you will be able to face the greatest danger. But never let *contempt for death* turn into dissrepect for life.

'You must appreciate *life* above everything else. *Life is God himself.* The eternal *being* manifests itself in everything that lives. You must never carelessly or wantonly expose yourself to danger. Appreciate *life* in your body too and live joyously. But the joy in living must never become an end in itself and turn into sensuality.

'And last but not least you must be able to pass the most difficult test of all: The test of *love* and *cruel love*: *Indifference*. This last pair of twin characteristics makes up an inseparable unit right here on the earthly plane. Whenever you manifest one half of it, the other manifests itself automatically.

'You must completely give up your personal viewpoint, your personal inclinations and feelings, *learning to love everything and everyone without distinction or discrimination, just as God himself loves everything and everyone*! Just as the sun shines—sends its loving radiations—with perfect impartiality on the beautiful and the ugly, the good and the evil, the true and the false, you must learn to love the beautiful and the ugly, the good and the evil, the true and the false, without discrimination and with perfect impartiality. The highest kind of love of all, divine love, is the perfectly *impartial love*! It must be a matter of complete indifference to you whether a thing or a person is beautiful or ugly, good or bad, true or false, you must love them all with the same love. You must learn that the beautiful wouldn't even exist without the ugly. You must learn that the good wouldn't even exist without the evil, nor the true without the false. And that's why you must love them all equally. You must learn that the beautiful and the ugly, the good and the evil, the true and the false are only reflected pictures of the *ineffable* which we for convenience' sake call *God*.

'When absolutely constant and completely impartial love radiates from you to all creatures, your love will never again be mixed with personal inclinations or antipathies. You will consider everything from the standpoint of the whole, and when the interests of the whole community are at variance with those of individual persons, you will unhesitatingly defend the cause of the group with ruthless disregard for the interests of individuals. But this ruthlessness must always be rooted in universal, divine love; it must never spring from personal antipathy.

'And you must also be able to manifest your impersonal, cruelly impartial love for your fellow beings in those cases when their soul can perhaps only be saved at the expense of their earthly well-being, even when such people are very, very near to you personally. You must even be able to look on dispassionately when those nearest and dearest to you get themselves into great danger, and if they don't react to ordinary measures, you must not try to hold them back by spiritual force, hypnosis, or magic powers when the salvation of their soul is at stake. It's better for a person to suffer material or physical ruin, even death, than to lose his soul. Under all circumstances you must endeavour to save his soul. Just as *God* doesn't meddle in the affairs of men, but rather leaves them their free will, you too must let your fellow human beings apply their free will, and you must never compel them to do anything by force. In your helpfulness, you must always consider everything from the standpoint of spiritual well-being, not from the standpoint of the earthly and physical. But this divinely impartial love must never degenerate into indifference and apathy and you must never refuse to help a person because of personal antipathy when you can save him with earthly measures.

'These are the hardest tests of all because you must give up your personal feelings, simply turning them off as it were. Only when you have completely mastered the preceding eleven sets of opposite characteristics will you be able to recognize the voice of God so clearly as to be able to feel, even in the most difficult cases, what you should *do* in perfect divine love, and what you should not do!

'Then you will no longer be able to err, because you will BE *love itself*! And love can only act in love. You will only need to radiate your self, to *be* your *self*, and the whole universe will be able to draw from your *warmth*, from your *light*, and from your *strength*. Then you will have become divine yourself, and your consciousness will have become identical with *God himself*! You will have returned from out of the world of the tree of the knowledge of good and evil, that is, from out of the realm of the tree of death, where everything is visible in the state of separation, into the realm of divine unity. You will then be eating again of the fruit of the tree of life. And of this fruit you will also give to eat to those who come after you so that all may return to the unity of the immortal, eternal *life*, to the eternal *being*, to God.'

Oh *you representative of God*! I shall never, never forget your words. They have engraved themselves so deeply in my soul that I have become identical with the meaning of these words. They've even gone into my blood, into the marrow of my bones, and I find myself a different person after this instruction from the one I was before.

But my task is to make all this *come true*.

PHARAOH BEFORE AMON   *Cairo Museum*

Pharaoh with the staff of life

THE FOUR FACES OF BRAHMA   *Angkor-Thom, Bayon, Cambodia*

—— 28 ——

THE LIONS

THE NEXT day is a great festival.

As usual Menu dresses me, puts on my gilt sandals, and then I go over into my reception room where the ladies of the court and Roo-Kha, the Chancellor, are waiting with two jewel bearers. Very ceremoniously Roo-Kha steps over to the jewel bearers and opens the coffer. Then the senior lady of the court, my former chief governess, takes out the magnificent golden collar, comes over to me with much pomp and ceremony, and places the golden collar on my shoulders. Then, just as ceremoniously, she fastens on my head ornament with the golden serpent, and finally my bracelets and anklets. I stand like a statue, motionless and dignified. Although I behave myself with all befitting decorum, I'd really like to give Roo-Kha's beard a healthy yank because he's looking at me in such a saucy, impertinent way again.

Roo-Kha isn't really bad, and he too has some of the blood of the Sons of God in his veins. He is very intelligent and crafty, and although he too can see into people's hearts and minds, he doesn't exploit this ability to an excessive extent. When he bows before me, it's not the bowing of a Chancellor before his Queen. On the contrary, he is bowing as a 'man' before my feminine beauty and looking at me with a covetous eye. Impudent fellow! He knows all the while that I can read his thoughts and all his feelings.

But then I think of Ptahhotep's words:

'In every living creature there is the striving towards divine unity. The male seeks the female, and the female seeks the male. That is the attraction between the two forms of manifestation of creative forces . . .'

In this light I can understand Roo-Kha too. This power is working within him, and it's not his fault that he finds me pleasing. That's the reason for his impertinence. If it weren't for this force working within him he wouldn't bother about me. And in my secret heart of hearts I'm really not angry at all that he admires my beauty . . .

After the dressing ceremonies, the ladies of the court and Roo-Kha accompany me to the Pharaoh. How beautiful—how very beautiful my father is in his festive robe! Just like a god incarnate! Then we all leave the palace, going out to the waiting chariots. Some building or other is going to be dedicated today with an inaugural ceremony.

Father and I step into the golden chariot—the chariot with the lions!— and father takes the reins from the attendant's hands.

When I was still quite a little girl, father was already taking me for rides in his chariot. I had to stand behind him, and he explained to me how to keep my balance by elastic body movements during the joggling, bumpy ride. I had to learn to keep my entire body quite relaxed in order to be able instantly to follow the movements of the chariot. When the floor beneath me was rocking to and fro and bouncing up and down, I had to be able to stand on my toes, keeping my feet, my knees and the rest of my body flexible and quickly able to make the necessary counter-moves.

These chariot rides were always very funny, and at first we had plenty of occasions to laugh at my awkwardness. At the start, father let the lions walk slowly, gradually quickening their pace to a trot, but the moment they began to run, the chariot threw me back and forth and I was naturally afraid. Instead of keeping myself relaxed, I grabbed frantically at father's hands, robe and belt. Father laughed heartily, and with unending patience he showed me again and again how to stand upright. Finally I learned how to make the right corrective movements and was able to stand upright without hanging on to father or the edge of the chariot.

It was wonderful to be able to stand as securely and as apparently motionless as father while the chariot raced over the ground! Often our rides were quite long. It was a thrilling feeling to be speeding along behind the galloping lions. The lions also enjoyed being able to get in a good run, and not only we—father and I—but the lions too would laugh with joy. Through these chariot rides my body became muscular, powerful and as resilient as if I had practised wrestling every day. Every single muscle was used, forced to co-ordinate and react instantly with every movement of the chariot. It was a constant dance, although invisible, as it was the floor underneath, not we ourselves that was really dancing on and on.

When I was fifteen father taught me how to drive the lions. What a wonderful feeling it was to have these magnificent, gigantic animals in my power! They responded to the slightest impulse of my will, so supremely sensitive that they immediately did everything I wanted them to without my having to move the reins. But father never let me drive them alone—not even my favourite lion, a real personal pet to the point of being jealous—because the lions were always highly independent and only initiates could control them. I hope when I'm initiated I'll be allowed to drive the lions alone!

Now en route to a public festival, father drives his lions with all due dignity, and I stand beside him as his wife. I am proud of father. He is still very young, strong and magnificently beautiful. His body and his handsome face radiate tremendous power and concentration, especially now when he is driving the lions. Standing and balancing on his toes, his body absorbs every movement of the chariot, and he seems to stand motionless, as securely as if he were the sun god himself.

We reach our destination and the boring ceremonies begin.

I don't like these public festivals. They are always the same. Huge crowds, marching soldiers, people of rank!—And for a time that seems interminable I have to sit still, practically motionless, watching the ceremonies until everything is over. Then I have to exchange friendly greetings with the people of rank, while reading the many stupid and treacherous thoughts behind all the humility and flattery they wear on their faces. How lucky that among all the many hypocrites in the court, who seek only the satisfaction of their vanity and desire for power, there are a few truly upright and loyal co-workers for father and Ptahhotep. There's an officer, for example, whose radiance is so bright it seems almost golden. 'Who is he?' I ask father in a whisper.

'His name is Thiss-Tha,' father whispers back. 'He was recently made an officer, but he has such splendid qualities—as you can see from his radiance— that I want to make him a commander.'

The ceremonies are always the same, the only difference being that we sometimes have to sit on the palace terrace, sometimes on a great dais, and at other times on the temple terrace. Sometimes the ceremonies are for the dedication of a new building, sometimes to celebrate an expedition returning from barter trade with neighbouring countries and bringing back the wares obtained abroad. Then at other times we take part in a harvest festival or various temple festivals, and these I don't like for the simple reason that the great crowds haven't the slightest idea about the meaning of the ceremony. Instead of worshipping God in the various forms in which he manifests himself, as represented in symbolic pictures, the ignorant masses worship the symbols themselves.

But in time even the most boring ceremony is ended. At last we can go home and be ourselves again.

No, I wouldn't like to be the Pharaoh! The affairs of the country don't interest me at all. Legally I should be the successor to the throne, but father never talks about this and pays very little attention to preparing me for the tasks of a Pharaoh. I know that Ptahhotep and father are able to raise themselves up above the plane of time. They can see and experience the *past* and the *future* as present. I too am beginning to develop this ability, and often I can see parts of the future, but whenever I'd like to see my *own* future, only a dense mist appears before my eyes, hiding everything. But father knows my future, and since he is not yet treating me as a co-regent, I imagine I may never become a Pharaoh. I have already had this presentiment on my own. It doesn't worry me in any way as I'd rather be a priestess in the temple. But curiously enough I don't see any pictures in the future which would show me as a priestess in the temple either. I see only mist . . .

After such celebrations, I am always happy when I can get back to the temple the next day. I always feel comfortable in the pure spiritual atmosphere of the temple.

— 29 —

TELEPATHIC EXERCISES

ONE DAY Ptahhotep sends me a message saying I should come to see him that evening. As I stand before him, he says: 'You've passed your preparatory tests so far quite successfully, and now you may try to establish psychic contact with another person. You will find you get better results with these exercises after sundown. That's because the sun's rays have a stimulating effect on those nerve centres and glands which serve *the physical manifestations of the spirit* and thus tie the consciousness to the material plane.

'The sun's rays have a contrary effect on spiritual manifestations. After sunset, this effect ceases, the consciousness can free itself from certain nerve centres and withdraw into the spiritual plane. Living creatures go to sleep. Going to sleep means that the consciousness withdraws from the body into the spirit. And since most people are not able *consciously* to reach the deeper levels of the spirit, they lose consciousness—they fall asleep. With practice one can develop the resistance of his nerves to such a degree that he can remain conscious even at the deepest level. In this way the nerve centres and brain centres which are at rest during the daytime become active, receiving and conducting the vibrations of the spirit, the *self*. In this way you can establish contact with someone at a distance, that is telepathic contact. It's better for a beginner to practise after sunset so that he doesn't have the effect of the sunshine working against him. Later on he develops the ability to make a telepathic contact any time.

'In this exercise, just as in every exercise in concentration, you begin by fixing your entire attention on one single thought. Concentrate your thoughts completely on the person with whom you want to establish contact, allowing your imagination to help along. With your eyes closed, you imagine the person you want to reach, seeing him with your inward eye, his body, his face, his eyes, and imagining *you* are *he* and *he* is *you,* until you actually get the feeling that his hands are your hands and your body his, until you achieve complete identity with the person you are trying to reach. When you've reached this point, think the thought you want to transmit clearly and concentratedly. Think it with intent awareness that *you* are the person concerned and that *this person in you is thinking this thought.*

'This exercise has three phases: first you practise *in the presence of the person* whom you want to reach telepathically, and during your practice the person concerned *tries to receive your thought.*

'Later you repeat the same exercise *at a distance* and at a time agreed upon in

188

advance, *with both of you knowing that the other is going to concentrate on him.*
'Finally you will transmit a message through telepathic contact without *your partner's knowing about it in advance.* These three phases make up the positive half of telepathic exercises. In this work you are the one who wants to send a message. The negative half of the exercise consists in your developing the ability *to receive and understand telepathic messages.* This exercise too consists of three phases. At first you make yourself receptive and "empty" *in the presence of the person* from whom you want to receive a message, then *alone at a time agreed upon in advance* such that you know *who* is going to concentrate on *you* and *when.* Finally you must be able to receive any telepathic message *without knowing in advance who is going to concentrate on you and when.*

'In time you develop to such a point that you respond immediately to every message from a distance, at any time and from any person. No matter what you're doing, you'll feel that someone is concentrating on you, and you will hear his voice within you. Later on you will not only be able to *hear* the person's voice; you will even be able to *see* the person you're in contact with. His form, his face and especially his eyes will appear before you just like a picture in a dream. When you reach this level in your progress, you won't feel the fetters of matter—of your body—in such an oppressive fashion, for by then the isolation you felt by virtue of being imprisoned within your body will be greatly reduced. You will be able to enjoy the freedom of the spirit while you're still living in the body.

'When you want to create a telepathic connection, you'll find you will succeed better at night. Then the consciousness is not so strongly occupied with one's own thoughts. The person concerned is less isolated. He is passive, and your telepathic message will be better able to reach his nerve centres. Most people's nerve centres are in such a latent state, so poorly developed, that it takes a very powerful effort on your part for them to be able to receive a message at all. When they're asleep, you can get them to dream about you and pick up your message in their dream. Practice will reveal all the laws of telepathy to you, including how to know immediately whether someone is busy and how to isolate yourself when you are busy concentrating on something. Only beginners disturb each other!

'Every evening you are to practise these exercises according to my instructions. And now let's do a bit of practice right away. Seat yourself opposite me, close your eyes, and try to communicate a thought to me.'

I sit down opposite Ptahhotep and concentrate on *him.* I imagine that I am Ptahhotep, and I induce within myself the feeling that my hands and feet, my entire body, are his hands, his feet, his body. Then with utmost concentration I think this thought: 'I, Ptahhotep, get up, step over and stroke the hair of this young person (myself).' For Ptahhotep's hands radiate wonderful strength, and I am always happy when he lays his hand upon my head.

Almost instantly Ptahhotep stands up, lays his blessed hand upon my head, and strokes my hair. So my concentration was successful. Or was it? After all

Ptahhotep can read my thoughts even when I'm not trying to transmit a thought to him telepathically.

'Good,' he says with a smile. 'I was able to read your thought not simply because I can read your thoughts anyway, but because you were really concentrating very well. Your lion would have felt too what you wanted.'

'My lion, Father of my Soul? I can believe that. But a person?'

'Patience, my child. In time everything is possible. Now let's try it the other way around. I'll transmit a thought to you. Make yourself empty and receptive.'

Ptahhotep sits down and I do as he asks. A moment later *I hear his voice from within me, as if coming out of my own heart*: 'As soon as you've achieved sufficient self control in all the twin characteristics, it will be time for me to reveal the last secrets to you before your initiation.'

I open my eyes and ask with joyous expectation, 'Does this mean I'm drawing near to my initiation?'

Ptahhotep smiles: 'Since you heard my message, you are ready to receive it, except that you still need to perfect yourself in self control.'

I jump up, throw my arms about his neck, and kiss his cheeks with resounding smacks. Ptahhotep embraces me and says with a loud laugh: 'You see, you see how you can't control yourself! You haven't been able to resist the effect of spiritual unity. You've experienced the union of our spirit, the sources of this unity flowed into your body, and now your body wants to participate in the joy of union. But don't forget that what is divine on the spiritual level because it corresponds to the laws of the spirit becomes satanic on the material level because it runs counter to the laws of matter. Union in the spirit is possible, but union in the body is not; two bodies cannot occupy the same space. Because of the longing for unity, people try to unite their bodies, and therefore slide down into sexuality. Nature exploits the longing for union, the yearning for the long lost paradisiacal state in order to beget new generations of people. The great disappointment is only that sexuality cannot create union. What's impossible is simply impossible. And all creatures in addition to being tired through the drain on their energies, are sad after sexual intercourse, simply because *the soul remains unsatisfied*. The longing for the paradisiacal unity continues, and nature goes on using this unfulfilled yearning to produce new generations of offspring. For you it would be very, very desirable *not to let the yearning for union flow unhindered into your body*. I am protected enough to be able to resist your entrancing beauty, but you may meet younger, inexperienced men who can't resist you when you throw your arms around their neck! Naturally my advice is wasted,' says Ptahhotep with a smile. 'What you really lack is experience. And it's this lack of experience I can now thank for your vehement expressions of love.'

'Father of my Soul,' I say, 'you're not angry at me?'

Ptahhotep smiles: 'No, no, my little child, I'm not angry at all. As long as you only throw your arms around my neck, everything's all right. But be very, very cautious with other men! The higher you rise in spirit, the more irresistible your radiations become. You don't need to get nearly so close to a person for your power of attraction to be effective. Be careful that you don't lead men to their downfall.'

'Father,' I asked amazed, 'do you mean I'm not spiritual enough? You know how successful I am in my exercises. And Mentuptah is very satisfied with me too. I already know how to control my body and my nerve centres to a very high degree. I've passed all my preliminary tests.'

'Yes,' said Ptahhotep. 'Spiritually you are already very awake and in control of your body. But at the same time you are very free and lacking in caution on the physical plane. You are neglecting to bolt this door, not because you are not able to, but because you don't always want to. You're not protecting your body sufficiently against the high frequencies of spiritual vibrations, and that is a constant danger for your nerve centres. When your spiritual forces enter your body, you conduct these high frequencies, untransformed, into your lower nerve centres and this means there's a danger of your higher, finer nerve centres being burnt out and destroyed. That would be too bad for this fine instrument. You have enough self-control *when you want it*, but you often relax your grip on the reins out of pure enthusiasm. Sometimes you simply *don't want* to exercise self-control, Be on the lookout, dear child, and always alert!'

Oh Ptahhotep, my dear, dear master! How early you saw what was unavoidably coming and how much you wanted to save me! But the best advice can't change inexperience into experience, and my inner lack of balance and self-control had to be brought back into equilibrium through painful experience.

—— 30 ——

THE FUTURE AND SUNRISE

A LONG new period begins in my life. I examine my every thought, my every word, my every deed. I reflect and watch to see whether, at the right time and in the right place, I am really giving expression to the divine, and not to the satanic. And in this constant watchfulness, this continuous self-observation, I discover how undisciplined and unbridled and sensual—in a word how personal—I still am. How much longer is it going to take me to reach the point where I don't allow myself to be overpowered by passions, where I no longer identify myself with my external impressions, but always remain master of all my physical, spiritual and mental forces?

During this period of my preparation for initiation I spend only my mornings in the temple, coming back to the palace after my physical and spiritual exercises. In the afternoon I take part in public life. Excursions by ship and chariot alternate with travel and inspection trips to various settlements.

But these excursions and the conversations centring around them really bore me stiff. It isn't that I don't like company, oh no! I enjoy very much being with people, but with people who are my kin and who have something to say. But these people are so different from us who have our lineage from the Sons of God. Of course we too have human blood and our race too is no longer pure, but we consciously live in the spirit and are not so materialistic as the sons of men. It's almost as if they had completely forgotten that they, in their selves, are free spirits and that their body is only an instrument for the manifestation of their spirit.

These people are so identified with their body that *they live in the illusion they are only body*. When their body needs food, they believe *they* want to eat, *they* are hungry, and instead of taking in food under the watchful supervision of the spirit, they act as if *they* themselves were eating, rather than merely being *observers and governors of their body*. They eat just as greedily as animals. I watch them during 'feeding time' and often feel like turning my head away so as not to see their beastly behaviour. I too let my body eat with good appetite; I too supply my stomach and digestive organs with pure forces, getting all the taste of the food I eat so that my body can absorb all the precious forces in the food— but how could I identify myself with this? My *self* can't be hungry, since the self is not matter but the master of matter. It's true my consciousness receives a message from the body to the effect that it needs nourishment, and I'm aware of this message in the form of a feeling of hunger. But the *self* in me neither eats nor drinks. How could I forget even for a moment that these functions are only necessary in order to maintain the body in health? The only thing my self really has to do with all of this is to *observe watchfully* and *control* what enters the body and see to it that teeth and tongue do their work properly.

I can never understand how people, after eating like beasts, can say something like, 'My, but that tasted good *to me*!' To whom did it taste good? Don't such people know that it tasted good to their *palates*? These poor people are such slaves of their physical desires . . . We simply don't understand each other. But father and Ptahhotep say it's our duty to remain among them and awaken higher desires and aims within them. And all the while father knows that the people of rank within his court are mostly only interested in *how* and *where* they can get a well-paid position, so they can get rich as quickly as possible and satisfy their hunger for power.

And another thing—these sons of men go hunting for wild animals, using their intelligence to kill innocent animals—and they're even proud about it! They should be ashamed! These people are worse than the animals they hunt. Animals only kill because of hunger! But people kill for passion's sake, because killing—war and hunting give them pleasure. But father says that people are still undeveloped and we mustn't judge them by our own standards.

Another thing—these people attach endless importance to their family tree. When a person has one ancestor more from the lineage of the Sons of God than someone else has, he mentions it as often as possible, and shows contempt for others with less brilliance in their ancestry. That's why they pay so much attention to the family a daughter is descended from, and the the family of the young man she marries. How ridiculous! As if they didn't really know that earthly life is only a journey between being born into the body and leaving it at death, whereas the *self* is the same in every living creature. Only the body can have a 'lineage'. The level on which a person stands is determined only by the level of his own intelligence. Often enough, a person with several ancestors from the lineage of the Sons of God still has a lower degree of intelligence than someone else with far fewer forefathers in the divine race.

When I'm among these people, I feel as if I were among the dead. They seem to move, speak, eat, drink and carry out functions of the living merely because natural forces are at work within them. But where is the conscious spirit that controls and guides these natural forces, not only in the body, but also outside in the universe? They don't know they have the ability to guide these creative forces. They're so blind they see only the *external form* of people, and they haven't the faintest idea that I can read their thoughts, their feelings, see their whole soul, their *inner being*. They lie to my very face for the simple reason that, not being able to read *my* thoughts, they believe that I can't see *theirs* either, and that I don't know their thoughts are very different from what they say. They don't realize that a lie creates a kind of insulation around them and develops a dark shadow, like smoke, in their radiation, and this dark blotch is not only ugly, but even smells bad. My pet lions are quick to smell the foul scent of these liars. Whenever one of them comes near, they start to wrinkle their nose, then get up, give the person concerned a contemptuous glance, and stalk off majestically. But with no such easy way to defend myself, I have to keep on talking with such people just as if I didn't clearly see their hypocrisy—*and even smell it!*

It's much more pleasant to be alone with father. He's had a charming house built for the two of us, in a shady garden by the seashore. Whenever he has some free time, we go there by boat on the Nile, taking only a minimum of servants. This gives us a magnificent rest, coupled with deep enjoyment of the endless sea and the peace of each other's company.

Father and I both love the sea—that great mother of the earth—with childlike devotion. We're both of us so very happy in our little house by the seashore, and our life there is closely linked in many ways to the sea itself. Here we experience perfect liberty, immortality, eternity . . .

We take advantage of every opportunity to be close to the sea. We go for walks together along the seashore. We go looking for mussels together, and sometimes we take a little boat and row out quite far, all by ourselves. There's an immensity about the beauty of the sea when the air is calm and the water beneath us is as smooth as a mirror. But there's something just as grand about being out among all the waves when the wind's blowing them up high, and we feel all the exhilaration of being hoisted skyward by the crest of one wave, then sliding down into the trough of the next. We strip off our clothes, jump into the cool water, and swim about our boat.

Once, after such an invigorating swim, as we were sitting on the beach, I asked father: 'How is it possible that people can be so blind to spiritual truth? What's going to happen to the world when the government gets into the hands of the sons of men, as Ptahhotep once told me it would? I'm frightened even to think of the consequences of the dominion's passing into the hands of self-seeking people obsessed with a craving for power. I'm beginning to be able to sense what's coming in the future. My exercises in the temple are awakening my inner sight, and my powers of clairvoyance are growing from day to day, but still I don't see everything as clearly as Ptahhotep and you.'

For a long time father sits looking out over the water. Finally he says: 'Yes, the earth must go through a very difficult period for many thousands of years. As you already know, the pure-blooded Sons of God all departed from this earthly plane long ago. And their sons who have been born as a cross between the two races but who still carry within themselves the possibility of perfectly divine manifestation, are also gradually disappearing from the face of the earth.

'In order for the higher powers to be propagated through hereditary channels when the pure-blooded Sons of God had already departed from the earth, their sons, who had inherited their abilities from their fathers and who had achieved initiation, again took daughters of men as their wives, and this went on and on for generations until this intermarrying had penetrated into all levels of life in both races.

'But as long as the waves of creative force are moving in the direction of further materialization, the earthly element always plays the dominant role in heredity. For this reason, less and less descendants of the Sons of God—with their original elongated cranial form and their capacity for manifesting higher abilities—are being born on earth. Nevertheless, in accordance with the laws of heredity, this continual intermarrying has made it possible for a pure-blooded Son of God to reincarnate himself at any time—even in the darkest, most materialistic period in human development. For the time is coming when only people with short heads will be born and will move into positions of ruling power all over the earth, even here in Egypt! They won't have the spiritual vision and wisdom of the present dynasty that has come down from the higher race, and instead of governing their people with selfless love, they will rule only with the intellect, with blind, crude craving for power, and with unmitigated selfishness.

'As you know, the continual intermarriages between the Sons of God and the daughters of men have gradually led to the development of a hybrid race which is passing on the inherited characteristics of both races. There are numerous individuals who, although they have human blood, still have the elongated cranial form, and thus have inherited all the spiritual and psychic powers of their paternal forebears. But according to the laws of heredity, this continual intermarrying will result in more variations of different individuals even in the same family, but less and less individuals with inherited characteristics from the divine lineage. Even today there are cases where, among several sons in a given family, one is still quite divinely spiritual, another already quite physically human, and a third can easily be a mixture of both. The relationship between those with higher and those with lower characteristics is shifting constantly towards those with the lower characteristics. No wonder men orientated towards the physical very often nurse a bitter hatred towards their brothers who have inherited divinely spiritual characteristics. All too often, this hatred leads to tragic clashes.

'Nevertheless, as a result of still further intermarrying and in accordance with the laws of heredity, the high knowledge of the initiates will penetrate deeper and deeper into the people and wider and wider throughout the entire population. As ever more variations and differentiations arise, the time will come when *every human being* will have the possibility of reaching the highest degree of knowledge and initiation. This intermarrying, going on for many thousands of years, will eventually obliterate the differences we now feel to be so tremendous between the omniscient members of the ruling family and the completely ignorant and undeveloped masses. Thus in time, the people and their rulers will become equal as people. *In their pure form* both of these two races, the Sons of God and primitive man, will gradually disappear completely, but there will always be some individual born on different levels of development. In some of them the inherited characteristics of their divine ancestors will be manifested to a greater degree, while in others the primitive human characteristics will be dominant.

'In this way everyone will have characteristics inherited from both sides, and the races will be so thoroughly blended that people can no longer be distinguished by racial characteristics but only on the basis of traits of character and abilities. Generally speaking, people with higher abilities will have exactly the same cranial form as other people but still stand out above the masses as great scientists or artists, philosophers or mystics. Both the elongated head form of the Sons of God and the short, ape-like head form of primitive man will have disappeared completely. In the hybrid race the brain and nerve centres serving for the manifestation of higher spiritual and psychic abilities will be in an undeveloped, latent state for many thousands of years. Accordingly, people's heads will be roundish in form. On the other hand people in this hybrid race will develop extensively the brain centres serving the intellect, and their future generations will thus have high, arched foreheads.

'Just as the waves of spiritual force emanating from the higher race will reach larger and larger numbers of people as a result of this intermarrying until they reach people of the lowest level and make it possible for them too to have knowledge, in the same way worldly dominion will pass into the hands of people on lower and lower levels. In their ignorance, of course, they will first destroy the great divine cultures which the Sons of God have built up in various parts of the earth. Only a few remnants and ruins of the great buildings and monuments we have today will be left as silent witnesses to tell of the knowledge, wisdom, goodness and beauty that once reigned on earth. As time goes on people will only know through their legends about the omnipotence and omniscience of the great "white magicians" and "initiates"; but since these people will be ignorant themselves, they'll go along for thousands of years *believing, in their pride and arrogance, that these legends are only fairy tales.*

'The continual hybridization process going on between the two races has created a kind of "ladder of development" on which even the lowest level of primitive man can climb upward. *Animal-like people themselves are nothing else but pure spirits which have fallen far down into matter and which, having lost their divine consciousness in matter, are no longer aware of their high parentage.* In order to give them the possibility of regaining their consciousness on the highest plane, the Sons of God made the great sacrifice of putting their strength into marriages with the daughters of men. With these marriages, however, they've anchored themselves in the material world and are obliged to go through the whole developmental process up to the complete spiritualization of the earth *in the capacity of helpers,* some of them in human reincarnations and some of them in the bodiless spiritual state.

'The level of the ruling class will sink lower and lower, and the dominant power will shift from one country to another. Continual wars raging on earth will lead to ignorance, poverty and misery.

'The last initiates will refuse to turn over to these people the devices and equipment through which they control the forces of nature and the tremendous creative forces that operate in secret. Before they leave the earthly plane for thousands of years they will destroy all their instruments. One of the last initiates, who will come forth out of a different people from ours but who will nevertheless grow up here in Egypt and receive initiation, will salvage one such instrument, taking it with him out of Egypt, and for a time the priests of his people will be able to keep the secret. But the time will come when the last initiate will have to leave the earth, and he will destroy the last instruments. He will have to do it to keep the ignorant sons of men from destroying each other, themselves and—through chain reactions—whole Continents again, purely as a result of their passion for power and possessions. The destruction which once overtook the home of the Sons of God must never be repeated.

'After all the initiates' instruments are destroyed and their high knowledge has passed from the earth, people will have to till the soil with their own physical force, and they'll even have to cut stones with their own hands, just as primitive man did! They'll also have to suffer the tyranny of fellow human beings from within their own race. However, since everything that manifests itself on the earthly plane arises through forces originating in the indivisible unity and striving for equilibrium, the tyranny of self-seeking rulers will awaken people out of their unconscious state. Through pain and suffering their attention will be guided to higher, spiritual truth.

'Spiritual leaders of the earth must leave humanity apparently alone because people are to discover divine truth in themselves and in nature, standing on their own feet, using their own will, independent of outside help. If this were not so they would never have the opportunity of climbing up to the highest level. But just as a good mother helps her child to learn to walk alone so that it can develop independence, while all the time she watches from a distance, ready to help it up again after a fall, in the same way the spiritual powers guiding the earth are ready to intervene whenever necessary to help humanity out of difficult situations. They are active on the spiritual plane, guiding and leading humanity from there. Whenever, instead of knowledge, ignorance and error and superstition gain control on earth—whenever spiritual darkness is so great that it threatens to get completely out of hand, there will always be some of the Sons of God ready to make the great sacrifice of descending to earth, being reborn in a human body, and in this way bringing divine light and consolation to humanity.

'Through the intermarriages between the divine race and the human, the inheritable divine characteristics will be propagated among the people. In this way it will always be possible for a Son of God, through a pure woman, to receive a body with all the organs he needs to manifest himself completely. In every epoch throughout the development of the earth through many thousands of years the Sons of God will incarnate themselves in order to teach people the laws of the spirit, love and selflessness, and in order to carry out the most varied tasks. Even though dominion will rest in human hands all over the earth, there will still be some rulers who will reign with wisdom and justice and build up high civilizations on earth, or at least in parts of the earth. Others, coming as scientists, artists and mystics, will bring humanity the *highest* art, music and literature. They will bring the world new ideas and new discoveries in order to guide the earth's development in new directions. For the most part, these Sons of God will live a very lonely life, often in the most abject poverty and abandoned by their fellows, for there will only be very few people who can understand them. Nevertheless, their spiritual light will reach out in ever-greater waves, into ever-wider circles. The names of these spiritual giants will be known for thousands of years, and people will study their works in the highest schools of the sons of men.

'Then, too, there will be reincarnated Sons of God working secretly within humanity. They'll find places to live in the high mountains, in caves, or in other remote regions where, undisturbed in their retreats, they can send forth extremely high forces into the atmosphere of the earth. People who have already developed to such a point that they can receive these spiritual waves *will automatically establish spiritual links with these Sons of God, and work together with them.* Often they will not even be aware of this spiritual link. On the contrary, for all they'll know, they will merely be acting on the basis of their own "inner conviction", not knowing that this "inner conviction" is divine power transmitted from the Sons of God. In this way some highly developed people will transmit and proclaim to all humanity the teachings which the Sons of God will bring to earth from time to time. Although the masses won't be able right away to understand these high truths, they'll feel the love and power inherent within them, and for this reason they'll *believe* in them. That is how *religions* will come into being from the divine teachings of the Sons of God.

'All the Sons of God have always brought and always will bring *the same truth* into different parts of the earth, but people will *interpret it differently depending on the characteristics of their race and their degree of development.* These different interpretations, as they get passed on to later generations, will give rise to *different religions all springing from the same truths.* One and the same Son of God will reincarnate himself at different times and in different places of the earth in order to proclaim the highest truth to humanity. And from *the same truth* proclaimed by *the same spirit*, people in different parts of the earth will develop *different religions.* Because of such differences arising merely from human ignorance, people will make war upon each other, trying to send each other to hell "in the name of God".

'The degree of development reached by people in different nations at any given time will vary greatly, and the reincarnated Sons of God will consequently receive widely varying kinds of treatment. In some countries, where people are most interested in divine truth, the Sons of God will be recognized, heard and honoured.

'But the waves of force keep radiating outward till they reach their utmost material limits. There will also be times in the darkest periods of earthly life, when materialism, hate, envy, fear and terror reign, and in such times too the Sons of God will have to return to earth and be very badly treated. Ignorant

198

people obsessed by a passion for power will torture and kill the Son of God. Nevertheless he will go through with this sacrifice, thus radiating tremendous spiritual force. The spirit in people will awaken and vanquish the darkness in their soul. Little by little the face of the earth will be completely changed.

'From the utmost material limits, the waves of creative force will then flow back again, ushering in a new period of upward development. People will have more and more opportunity to co-operate with the Sons of God in the great divine plan for the salvation of the earth, and as time goes on they will manifest more and more spirituality. Then masses of individuals will be reincarnated who once *were incarnate in the divine race,* but who either could not pass their tests for initiation, and died during initiation, or later *fell* after having become initiates. They will again be conscious of the knowledge they once had, and while people will still be killing each other in some parts of the earth, there will be a constantly growing group of people receiving and transmitting the radiations of the Sons of God, and preparing the new life of the spirit.

'The people descended from the lower race will also gradually climb to higher levels. At first they will only be able to grasp with their intellect that they are capable of better things and that they could live much more happily on earth without killing and enslaving each other. The higher humanity climbs, the more materialism and passion for possessions will lose their grip on people's lives. Little by little the passion for conquest and power will decline, and instead of using their strength to fight each other, people will use their abilities to harness the forces of nature. In this way they will discover step by step that they don't need to earn their bread through dull, difficult drudgery, that they don't need to water the earth with the sweat of their brow, and that by activating their higher nerve centres they can command the forces of nature. Thus the earth will gradually come back under the dominion of higher waves of force, and people will not only be able to *understand* with their intellect, but also to experience and realize the highest divine truths. In this way high civilizations will develop again.

'As long as a person identifies himself with matter—with the earth—his consciousness is linked with the earth in a state of identity: *He is earth.* Consequently, when his body loses its usefulness and dies, he dies too, that is, his consciousness ceases and falls into a latent state. That's what people call *death.*

'But the situation is just the opposite with a spiritually re-awakened person who stands above matter during his physical life. For him the fact of being born into a body is death, whereas the death of the body means his awakening, *resurrection, life*!

'When people cease to identify themselves with their body—or to express the matter symbolically—when they cease to eat of the fruits of the tree of the knowledge of good and evil, *manifesting only the right half of the tree of knowledge* and leaving the left half of the tree in the unmanifested state, *they will live in a paradisiacal state, in themselves and as children of the earth.* This is the stage of development humanity must reach.

'It will be a long struggle until the earth reaches this plane of existence, but spiritual forces gradually penetrate even into the most isolated heart, and in the course of further thousands of years the earth will again be transformed into the promised land. Sometime, in the far distant future, the salvation of the earth will be accomplished!'

Father stops talking and looks out over the sea for a long time as if he had been reading the future there.

'Father,' I ask, 'will you and Ptahhotep take part in this great work? Will you too be born again for tasks on earth during the aeons and aeons to come? And how about me, father? What's going to happen to me? I often see other people's future very clearly, but when I try to see my own, there's only a curtain of mist before my eyes, and I can't see into it or through it.'

Father shoots me a very strange glance at this question. Then, putting his arm about my shoulders and drawing me close, he gives me his answer: 'I'll be reincarnated a number of times in earthly lives because, through my marriage with your mother, I've put my roots down in the plane of matter, deeper than would normally be appropriate for one of our spirit. But Ptahhotep has never departed from his spirituality and never identified himself with his body. When he gets through with his present task, he'll not be born again for more than ten thousand years. Together with a number of other Sons of God he will continue to guide the development of the earth, working on the spiritual plane and projecting his influence on earthly life from there.

'Many highly developed people will be in spiritual contact with him and co-operate with him in the great divine plan for the salvation of the earth. They must carry out the tasks that Ptahhotep assigns them and quite independently. As soon as they have carried out one task properly, they'll receive new ones and, gradually, more and more difficult ones. Through many thousands of years people who reach spiritual maturity will also receive initiation. They won't be initiated in the pyramids as candidates are now, but will simply be assigned tasks to accomplish as part of their life and work, and these tasks will make up their initiation tests. In this way they will gradually develop into full-fledged co-workers with the Sons of God. And working with Ptahhotep there will also be those fallen Sons of God who identified themselves to an excessive extent with matter, burnt out their brain and nervous centres by transmitting excessively powerful vibrations into them, and consequently had to be born again on even lower levels of matter.

'Only through the experiences to be gained through several reincarnations can these fallen Sons of God climb back to their original level of divinity. Through lots of pain and sorrow they will have to awaken their higher brain and nerve centres within their body on a lower level, and it will cost them great effort and long practice to reactivate these organs and be able, once again, to manifest spiritual and magical powers. They will never feel quite at home among people, as their way of thinking will be quite different from that of the mass of human beings around them, and they will never be completely able to understand human earthly life and adapt themselves to it. They will be strangers, travelling through life alone and misunderstood, always regarded as somewhat queer. For the most part, as I already told you, they will have the task of teaching people science, art and literature, and bringing new ideas to earth. By some people who understand them, they will be respected and revered, while by others who are forced to recognize their high gifts, they will be objects of envy and hate.

'Through long suffering and many sorrows these fallen sons—and daughters—of God will be awakened from their material dream, rediscover their relationship with their lost brothers, and re-acquire their lost *cosmic consciousness*. Then they too will work together with their brothers within the great divine plan, and proclaim divine truths on earth.'

I ask father: 'You said that the Sons of God will gradually disappear from the face of the earth and that the people, even though not yet awakened on the spiritual plane and consequently self-centred entirely in the physical plane, will get control and dominion over the affairs of the world. In that case how will the people be able to control the lions? These marvellous animals are so extremely sensitive that they don't tolerate the selfish sons of men in their vicinity, even now. On their animal level they are a manifestation of the highest power—the sun power—and live and move in harmony with the sun's vibrations. They respond to courage, honesty, love and have such fine nerves that they simply can't tolerate low-level radiations. Whenever anyone approaches them, they know immediately whether he's coming towards them in a spirit of love, or in a low attitude of fear and passion for power. That's why they hate the selfish, power-hungry sons of men. If what you say is going to happen how will lions ever be able to serve the sons of men? I just can't imagine, Father.'

'Your imagination is absolutely right if it doesn't show you a future picture of lions serving mankind. It's quite true people won't be able to keep the friendship of these wonderful animals. With lies and pretty words, selfish and ignorant people can—and often will—deceive each other, but never the lions! Animals pay no attention to appearances; they see only the truth, *because they themselves are true*! Lions will cease to be domestic animals, withdrawing into the wilderness, far away from people, and living a wild life of their own.'

'But Father, what animals will people use to pull their chariots? Oxen and asses are much too slow!'

Father smiles: 'There are places in the world, even now, where a splendid animal related to the zebra and the donkey is working in the service of the people. What's more, the time will soon be at hand when this same animal will begin to be used in our country in place of the lion. Remember our government means peace. We keep order and prosperity throughout the country by means of wisdom and love. So for the present, we have no reason to fight each other. But when my day of governing is over, a ruler from a different family will come and found a new dynasty. With a much higher proportion of human blood in his veins, he will not be satisfied merely to rule with wisdom, but will also set out to conquer neighbouring countries. The time is coming when the power of our country will no longer be based on knowledge and selfless love, but on cold, crude, brute force—and the good, the true and the beautiful will be shoved into the background. Then this zebra-like animal will play a great role in the life of the world. It is an obedient animal, and even if it isn't as strong as the lion, it has the advantage of willingly participating with people in their wars, something no other animal would do without becoming wild and dangerous itself.

'But in the course of some more thousands of years people will progress to the point of discovering how to make their chariots go without animals. All the secrets of creation were known to the high race of the Sons of God. They knew how to liberate their vehicles from the gravitational force of the earth and guide them with the power of thought. They left many sketches and drawings of these vehicles which were able to fly because of their lack of weight, and some of the Sons of God preserved these sketches on specially treated palm leaves, taking them away to another part of the earth when their original homeland was destroyed. Some initiates are still guarding them there today, and they will continue to be guarded for some six to eight thousand years to come. By that time people will have discovered quite different methods for moving their vehicles on the earth and in the air. To be sure, not with the power of thought, and for this reason their systems of locomotion will not be as certain and free of danger as those of the Sons of God. Still later, people will discover all the secrets of the Sons of God, even the last secrets of life. Then this period of development will have gone through a full cycle.'

'Father, now please tell me about my future.'

Once again father looks at me with such a strange, sad glance. Then he draws me closer to himself, and with a voice which clearly betrays his controlled sadness, he says: 'My dear child, I have already talked about your future, but you just didn't recognize it as *your* future. This together with the fact that you can only see a curtain of mist when you try to see your future is proof that the *world self*—God—does not want to show you your future for good reasons. How could I go against the will of God? Be satisfied that it's better for you not to know your future. If you knew it, you couldn't carry out your present tasks and duties properly. One thing I can tell you is that *we'll both go through these coming events together*, although not in each other's physical presence. From time to time we'll have to reincarnate ourselves, but not simultaneously and not at the same place. There will also be a time during which you will have to live and work on earth while I'll be living in the world of spiritual energy, working in the atmosphere of the earth in the same way as Ptahhotep and many other Sons of God. But in your dreams you'll often meet us . . . the details are really not so important, because no matter what happens in your future, through the unity of the higher self you'll always be in touch with us.'

I put my arms about him and repeat contentedly: 'Yes, Father, I belong to you, and I know you'll never leave me.'

'We'll never leave you!' father repeats slowly and seriously.

When evening comes father and I sit out on our terrace, enjoying the magnificent sunset over the sea. While the sun sinks lower and lower in the west, father points to the broad estuary of the river and says: 'You see far out there where the waves of the sea are rolling in—some day—thousands of years from now, there'll be solid land there covered with cities and houses and all the comings and goings of people. The Nile is always sweeping a lot of earth along with it, so the shore line is gradually moving out further and further into the sea. Thousands of years ago there was only water where we are now, and some thousands of years from now there will be land right out to where you see that boat with its sail to the wind. The face of the earth is not only changed by catastrophe and upheavals, but also by the slow working of water.'

While he is talking, the sun slowly goes down. The sky is alight with all the colours of the rainbow, changing with every moment. Then the sun disappears below the horizon, and soon we're surrounded by pitch darkness. Only the stars shine like big diamonds.

For a long time we stay out on the terrace, and I tell father that I can now make telepathic contacts. Father wants to try me out to see whether I have my higher brain centres under control. He tries to communicate a thought to me through becoming identical with me in spirit. Both of us are proud and pleased that I am able to repeat aloud his silent messages. I have progressed to the point—at least after sundown—of being able to make contact with Ptahhotep too. I now concentrate on *him*, and his body, his noble face, and especially his eyes rise up before my inward sight. Then I hear his communications like an echo within myself. I hear his familiar and dearly beloved voice as if it were my own inner voice. Then the picture of him within me slowly fades, and I realize that he is isolating himself from me. He is concentrating on something else.

Suddenly I feel in the mood to try and contact Ima too. As I concentrate on him for a few moments, a picture of him appears in my consciousness. I see him, his angelically beautiful face, and watch him smile and tell me without words that he understands me and is very happy about my progress. Dear Ima! I always feel his brotherly help and love within me.

Early the following morning we are out on the terrace again; for sunrise, if anything, is even more beautiful than sunset. It is still dark, and the sky is a deep blue, almost black. Suddenly, almost without warning, the upper rim of the sun appears, and with it a magnificent reddish purple colour, suffusing the whole vault of the sky until all is aglow. This is followed by a gorgeous interplay of colours, all kinds and shades and tints—from the brightest flame-yellow all the way to deep dark blue. Seeing the firmament alight with the handiwork of God fills my soul with ineffable joy, and a feeling of infinite peace and wellbeing fills my body with new vital force. How often I admire the sunrise from the terrace of our little house! Pure joy and delight feed the very depths of my soul. And my joy is all the greater because when we're here father belongs to me alone. Here he is not the Pharaoh, only my father, my best friend and companion.

31

BO-GHAR AND THE STAFF OF LIFE

ONE AFTERNOON after a storm that has lasted for several days, when the wind has abated but the waves are still running high, father and I row out some distance from shore to enjoy the waves that rock our little boat to and fro.

Suddenly I notice something being battered about by the waves. It appears and disappears, rises up and sinks out of sight again.

'Father,' I cry out. 'Look! What's that over there?'

Father glances off to where I am pointing. 'Let's row over there!' he answers and starts pulling with might and main. As we approach, we can see that what we've spotted is probably the wrecked hulk of a sailing vessel. We see broken planks still clinging together, the snapped-off mast with its sail in shreds. Then I spy a human form clinging to the wreckage.

'Look, a child,' father shouts, starting to row even faster! It seems as if we'll never get there, but finally we do. A haggard boy of about ten years of age clings desperately to the broken planks. He's already half dead, his legs hang down limply, and the waves pound his body to and fro. His eyes are quite expressionless and his hands, which seem to be glued to the planks, are all that keep him from sliding off into the water.

Father tries to manoeuvre our boat quite close, but the waves keep beating us back, until finally he is able to seize a piece of wreckage and pull us up close. As he does so, I loosen the child's cramped hands, then together we draw him into our boat. He seems to be unconscious. Father starts to row for shore as fast as possible. Our servants have noticed what has happened and set out in several boats to meet us. Father carries the child into the house. Then the servants hold up the boy by his feet so that his head is hanging down. Then with powerful, rhythmic steady strokes father squeezes the boy's abdomen and ribs together in order to force out any water the boy may have swallowed. Finally father has the servants lay out the boy on his own bed, then sends them all out.

Now I witness something very strange: father goes to a little casket which I have always seen in his room at home and which he has always taken on his travels wherever he went. He takes out a little staff resembling a cross with a circle on top ♀. He holds the staff with this ring firmly in his hand and begins to make passes with it over the boy's body, moving it in one direction after another. I can see that father is concentrating very intently, directing all his attention to the boy. First he holds the staff at the top of the boy's head for a little while, then draws it slowly over his face down to his heart, stopping there for a moment. Then moving forward from the region of heart, father draws imaginary lines over the boy's trunk to his genitals, then repeating the same movements starting out from the top of his head, he moves the staff along the boy's arms and out to his hands, then finally over his legs and down to his feet.

Father has scarcely touched the boy's head with the little staff when the child draws a deep breath. Then, as father moves the staff over different parts of the boy's body, he goes on breathing regularly, and his body twitches and quivers. Gradually he comes to, and by the time father is making his last passes, the boy suddenly opens his eyes, sits bolt upright, to all appearances in perfect health. Then without warning, he falls to his knees before father, flings his arms around father's legs, lays his forehead on father's feet, and cries and sobs bitterly. Father helps him up, takes him on to his lap and dries his tears with tender loving care.

The boy speaks a language I can only understand through spiritual contact. My telepathic exercises have developed my finer organs of sense to the point that I can understand *the gist* of his story without having to understand his words. The boy tells us that his father, who was a merchant in a distant land, set out to bring a shipload of goods to Egypt in order to sell them there. He took his wife and son along with him so they would be able to see what Egypt was like. After several weeks of travel, they were overtaken by a terrible storm. After days of struggle with the raging elements, the ship broke up and sank. His mother and several sailors disappeared in the waves right away, while he, his father and some of the sailors clung to a few pieces of wreckage. Then he saw his father, too, slip off into the water and go down. He clung tightly to whatever he could lay his hands on . . . and that was all he could remember.

'Father,' I say when the child has finished his story and begins to calm down, while I see in his spiritual radiation the gaping emptiness of stark panic and desperation, 'the boy doesn't belong to anybody now. Let me take him and have him brought up and educated. Menu will teach him the language and everything he needs to know as far as behaviour is concerned. He can get schooling and training in the temple. You see what a pure soul he has and how intelligent he is. I'll take him to the temple so he can develop his abilities. We'll see how he develops there and what he shows a talent for. Maybe he'll become a priest. Please let me take care of him.'

'Good,' father answers. 'You may keep him. The fact that *you* saw him and found him in the waves is a part of the fate that has linked you and him together for aeons and ages. According to the inner laws of fate, he belongs to *you*.'

While we are yet talking about him, the boy looks at us. Then, as if he had understood, he falls to his knees before me, throws his arms around my knees, and gives every indication of gratitude and confidence. I take the boy's hand and turn him over to a servant who gets him clothes and food. He eats with such a healthy appetite that it's hard to imagine he was completely exhausted only a few minutes earlier. As soon as a bed is made up for him in a corner of my room, he drops off to sleep instantly.

Father and I go out on to the terrace. The surface of the sea is gradually quieting down, and we enjoy the play of colours at sunset.

'Father,' I ask, 'what kind of force is there in this little staff of yours? What was it made of and how? It affected that boy like magic. He was half dead, yet after your treatment with the staff, he was filled with new vital energy.'

After some moments' silence, father replies; 'Yes, the youngster really was filled with new vital energy. The secret of this staff is one of the secrets of initiation. We have to keep it secret because the staff can not only transmit vital force, but also can kill. If the secret of the staff were to fall into the hands of ignorant and self-seeking people, they would immediately use it wrongly. The time is already very near at hand when you'll receive your initiation, and you've learned to keep silence. That's why I let you look on while I treated the boy with the staff. Ptahhotep will give you a thorough explanation of the secret of the staff, and after you're initiated he'll teach you how to use it too. Tomorrow we'll go back to the city, and you will report to him again. You've made great progress in self control. Your initiation is near at hand. After your final instructions, you'll get it.'

I am silent with inward emotion. My initiation is near at hand! The long years of preparatory exercises will at last be over, and I am to be admitted into the secret sanctuary of the temple. Initiated!

In silence—and in a deep spiritual stillness—father and I watch the glorious, ever-changing drama of the sunset.

Our few happy days of freedom are over so soon! Again, we are in the city, in the palace. I take the child—the poor little bird that has lost its nest—into my chambers and tell Menu what has happened. Menu's good, kindly heart goes out to the boy, and she treats him as if he were her own child. He points to himself and says, 'Bo-Ghar', and when we call him this, he rewards us with a happy smile. He has a fine soul. His body is slender, full of life and fire, resilient, limber and strong. He picks up everything easily. He learns new words and expressions in our language after hearing them only once.

In the evening I go to Ptahhotep for some more instruction.

As I walk there with Menu along the route that has become so familiar to me, I reflect that Ima no longer needs to wait at the door to guide me to Ptahhotep's reception room. I know the way—yes even my feet know the way to Ptahhotep. Yet at the temple door, I see Ima's magnificent figure appear out of the darkness. His pure radiance fills the air all around him. I cast a stolen glance at his handsome body and check myself to see whether I could feel a physical attraction for him. No! I could never love him physically! I feel the loving tie that binds us is so deep it makes us completely one. How could a person love and desire himself physically? Ima too is descended from the race of the Sons of God; he too has the elongated cranial form. He is pure, lofty, like an angel—spirituality personified. No, he could never love me physically, nor I him! Joyously I ask him, 'How did you know I was coming? Did Ptahhotep perhaps send you to meet me?'

Ima smiles, 'Haven't you got used to the fact that a spiritually-awakened person doesn't need external sources of information in order to know what a kindred spirit is doing and where he is? I concentrated on you in order to find out whether you had already returned to the city with the Pharaoh, so I could prepare your next tasks for you. As I did so I found you were on your way here. Ptahhotep is expecting you. Come in. Tomorrow we'll be working together again.'

Ima goes and I enter Ptahhotep's reception room.

Through my long exercises in self observation and self control, and through my long efforts to master the twelve sets of twin characteristics I have learned not to transmit my joy into my body; so instead of throwing my arms about Ptahhotep's neck, I radiate all my love and joy through nerve centres that carry my consciousness—especially through my eyes.

I bow low before *him*.

He understands and sees my conscious control over my expressions of love, that is, over the forces working within me. I understand and see that *he* understands and sees . . . and we are united in spirit. Oh! This unity is a thousand-fold greater happiness than a physical embrace! I am blissfully happy in this perfect unity and wait to learn what *he* has to tell me. For a while, his eyes rest upon me, full of love and joy. His glance goes through and through me, unhindered. Finally he says, 'The time has come for you to learn the secret of the staff and the use of our other instruments. Your father knew that you were ready to learn these secrets; that's why he took the opportunity to show you the life-giving aspect of the staff. From now on you are to come to me each evening so that I can transmit the last secret revelations to you.'

The next day I am in the temple early, and we are all happy about seeing each other again. I love all the neophytes, and the master of the neophyte school too—this noble, loving person who never makes an unnecessary movement and never allows us to indulge in any lost motion either. Through his methods we develop wonderful control of the body. Through these exercises I have learned to transmit creative force corresponding to my degree of development—the power of my consciousness—into all the various parts and organs of my body. This has made my body so conscious and so vitalized that I can feel every part of it as distinctly as I can the inside of my mouth.

Little by little I have learned, not only to feel all my organs exactly, but also to control them consciously. For example, I can now control my heart beat. To do this I have to concentrate on a particular point in my body, namely the seat of the force that compels me to inhale. When we exhale all the air in our lungs and then don't inhale again, something forces us to inhale—forces us until we absolutely *must* inhale again. *What* it is that forces us to inhale is harder to discover than *what it is not*. Certainly it isn't the nose, which doesn't actually breathe at all, but is merely an opening through which we can breathe. It isn't our lungs either, for we can clearly feel they were merely working instruments in the breathing process.

Finally we discover that a certain force, located in the region of the heart, causes us to inhale and controls our breathing. When I think myself into this point, I can speed up or slow down my heart beat at will, through the power of imagination. Similarly, I have learned, step by step, to bring all the organs of my body under the control of my will. It's wonderful to have so much control over the body. Mentuptah is very satisfied with my progress. He nods and gives me a warm and friendly smile when he notices me again among the neophytes this morning. After our group exercises, I ask Ima: 'Ima, you've promised me a new concentration exercise.'

'Yes, listen,' says Ima. 'Up to now you've practised your concentration exercises combined with slow, regular breathing in which *you* have inhaled the air and then *you* have exhaled it again. From now on when you sit down to your concentration exercises, you ought to practise them differently. As long as *you* inhale and exhale, you're identifying yourself with your body. But the truth of the matter is that *your body* is really doing the inhaling and exhaling, *not you.* The body lives because the *higher self—God—*breathes his own breath into it. We're all alive because our physical being inhales the breath of *God.* You know that *God* is the *self* in you. Thus your body inhales your *self—you—*and that gives the body life. As long as you believe that *you* are the one that's breathing, *you're identical in your consciousness with your body instead of with yourself.* On the other hand when you experience *in your consciousness* that your body is inhaling yourself and then again in breathing out, giving your self freedom, you can experience the marvellous transition out of the person—the animated body you have been up to the present—into your true self.

'From now on as you practise try to realize that not *you* are inhaling and exhaling, but *you are being inhaled and exhaled by your body.* With every breath you'll have the feeling, during inhaling, that you are filling your body with life-giving power and your body is inhaling *you*; and in exhaling, that you are withdrawing yourself from the body and remaining separate from it within *yourself* until the next breath. When you succeed in doing this, you'll experience something similar to the death of the body when you withdraw yourself from it and your body exhales you for the last time. Practise this a while and tell me how you get on.'

As Ima is about to go, I ask him to stay a moment, and I tell him how, with father's help, I found little Bo-Ghar and saved him.

'Ima,' I tell him, 'I'd like to bring the boy to the temple for his training and education. Would you be willing to spend some time with him to see what he is particularly talented for?'

'Yes, indeed. I'll be glad to speak to Mentuptah, and he will take him in. He can live in the temple and get his training with the other children.'

'No, Ima,' I answer. 'I want to keep the boy with me. He has something infinitely loving and pure about him. I'll bring him to the temple every day and take him back in the evening. I'll bring him along tomorrow.'

The next day Bo-Ghar comes to the temple with me. He doesn't know where

I'm taking him, because he doesn't yet understand what we say to him, but he comes along anyway, obedient, with touching confidence and a radiant face. He is happy to be able to come along with Menu and me. I loved Bo-Ghar from the very moment I first saw him half-drowned in the water. He is fond of me too, and it's easy to see he is only really happy when he is allowed to sit at my feet.

In the temple I take him through the long colonnade into the school of neophytes where talented children are getting their training. At first he doesn't want to let go of my hand. I understand that he's afraid I want to leave him here. I embrace him warmly and tell him it's perfectly all right for him to stay here, for I'll come and take him back to the palace with me in the evening. He doesn't understand my words and looks at me anxiously with big questioning eyes. As he sees that I'm not taking leave of him, he apparently quiets his fears somewhat and stays behind.

When evening comes and I go to get him, I find Bo-Ghar is getting along famously with the other children. Making ample use of hands and feet, he is telling them something while they listen to his tale with the greatest interest, as if they understood him. When Bo-Ghar sees me, his eyes light up joyously, he runs to meet me, and throws his arms around my neck. I am delighted to see that he feels already so much at home.

From this point on, every morning finds the three of us going to the temple: Menu, Bo-Ghar and I. As the weeks and months go by, little Bo-Ghar learns our language so well that he rapidly gains ability and fluency in expressing himself.

He takes part in the early morning physical exercises under the direction of Mentuptah. His body is alive to a surprising degree and the conductivity of his nerves is extraordinarily great. He does the exercises with tremendous concentration, revealing a great and innate control over the body. Ima loves him and devotes as much attention to him as possible. And the lonely little lad who has lost his relatives takes to Ima like a brother, with all his heart. He is grateful for every kind word. In the temple the heads of the school have found out that Bo-Ghar shows little inclination towards the sciences but lots of talent for drawing and modelling. That's why Imhotep, the great artist, has taken him into his studio as his youngest apprentice. Imhotep predicts a great future for him.

Every evening Bo-Ghar waits at the temple gate for me, and on the way back to the palace he tells me what's happened, what he has learned and what he has done with the other children. If Bo-Ghar hadn't found his way so deeply into Menu's good heart, she would feel offended that he is allowed to talk to me on our way back to the palace because I never used to allow her the same privilege. When there were only the two of us, I made her keep silent so she would not disturb my train of thought. But she seems to take it as a matter of course that I allow him privileges I denied her.

32

PTAHHOTEP'S INSTRUCTION: THE SEVEN OCTAVES OF VIBRATION AND THE ARK OF THE COVENANT

I STAND before Ptahhotep and listen devoutly to his words: 'Today, I shall explain to you the laws on which the staff's miraculous effect is based. These are, of course, simple laws of nature. God is everywhere present and the emanation of His omnipresence is manifest in the visible, material world as natural law. Therefore, nothing can happen outside natural laws. Yet these laws differ from one stage of development to another.

'Different laws apply to the spiritual, the mental, and the material world. And in the material world we find different laws at work in one and the same form of matter, depending on the magnitudes involved. For example, it is a law of nature for the surface of a body of water at rest to be horizontal. But this law is valid only within certain magnitudes. A drop of water in the calyx of a flower has a spherical shape, and a microscopic being living in this miniature world would come to the conclusion that water always has a spherical shape. Why? Because the relation between the surface tension of water and the power which forces water into the horizontal is very different in a drop—that is, in a small quantity—from what it is in a large body of water. And yet, the same laws are at work.

'People know very little about the laws of nature, with the exception of those they have experienced in daily life. They have become accustomed to these and call them "laws of nature". And having found names for them they believe they know the true essence of the laws of nature. They accept these laws and their effects as a matter of course. But when they are suddenly confronted by some phenomenon they know nothing about, they immediately speak of "miracles" or "magic".

'People do not realize that these forces are no less laws of nature than those to which they have become accustomed and think they know, even though they haven't the vaguest notion about their true character. For man doesn't know why a plant will grow from a seed or why a new being will evolve from an impregnated cell. Neither do people know what "insemination" really means and why, after insemination, the cell will divide and subdivide. They have no idea why this subdividing process is repeated again and again, not even stopping at birth, going on and on until a full-grown individual has developed out of that one single first cell ... then still going on until this chain reaction slows down by itself and gradually gives way to a decline. But since people experience this daily, they take it for granted and aren't the least bit surprised at it. Still, the growth of a plant out of a seed, the birth of a child, death, the different effects of the winds blowing from different directions, and many other experiences of everyday life are just as "miraculous" as the effect and the secret of this staff and the other "miracles" and the "magic power" of the initiated.

'For you truly to understand the forces used by the initiated and applied through this staff of life you will first have to learn a number of things.

'When we spoke about the tree of knowledge of good and evil you learned that everything which has taken on material form is visible and perceivable only because it has fallen out of perfect unity and perfect equilibrium. But from this state of disjunction, everything tends eternally to return to unison and balance. "Equilibrium" means complete repose, motionlessness. On the other hand, "to have become something"—that is, to have taken on visible, tangible form—is identical with loss of balance and with the constant urge to regain this equilibrium. It means incessant unrest, with continual movement. Should this constant motion cease, even for only a moment, all creation would suddenly be transformed into spiritual energy, that is, materially destroyed.

'All energy, all the forces of the universe, are movements which emanate from one point—their own centre—and radiate in circular waves in all directions, manifesting themselves as vibrations or oscillations. These manifestations of force cease only when the forces that have got out of balance regain their primordial state of equilibrium, the divine unity. Hence when we speak of the "primordial state" we mean the state in which all material phenomena have ceased to exist. In its true essence, matter, too, is motion, and if this motion comes to a stop, matter must necessarily cease to exist. As long as the three-dimensional, material world exists its immutable law is that of unrest, of movement.

'The fact that the creative force manifests itself on each and every level of innumerable possibilities means there are countless different wave lengths, wave forms, and frequencies. And as long as we are in the body, with its limited perceptive ability, we can perceive only a certain number of these wave forms because our organs of sense are limited. Whether some form of vibration appears to us as "immaterial energy" or as solid "matter" depends upon our own idea and the impression of something which is basically nothing but "movement", "vibration", or "frequency".

'The shorter the waves in which a form of energy manifests itself the less our consciousness records a sensation of matter. To the vibrations that are transmitted directly to our consciousness by our organs of sense we give names according to the sensations we feel: matter, sound, electricity, heat, taste, smell, light. The still higher, immaterial energies and radiations, perceptible only by means of our brain and nerve centres, we call thought waves, idea waves. Beyond them there are still higher, more penetrating rays and frequencies, all the way up to the *very highest all-pervading frequencies of the divine-creative power: life itself!* We can only perceive these frequencies as a state of consciousness.

'So, throughout the universe, countless varieties of vibrations are at work, ranging from the shortest to the longest wave length. Every form of creation, beginning with the celestial bodies and ranging all the way down to the tiniest monocellular creature—all the myriad manifestations of creation are the effects of various forms of these rays. We live in these various rays whether we know it or not; even more, *these forms of energy have built and formed us human beings* and are constantly at work in our body, our mind, and our entire being. The whole universe consists of these various vibrations. The source of these creative vibrations we call *God*.

'God himself stands above all manifestations of life and rests in himself in absolute equilibrium without time and without space. But he is constantly radiating himself out into material forms in order to give these forms life. As God is omnipresent and fills the entire universe, everything that is in the universe is penetrated and filled by God. Nothing can exist without being in God and without God's penetrating it, as God is everywhere present and nothing can displace or dislodge him from his own presence. Consequently, every point offers a possibility that God may manifest himself through it, and everything that exists in our perceptible world carries this point as its own centre within itself. From this point, there began its first manifestation, its creation, its fall from equilibrium.

'This aspect of God who creates the material world and gives it life by penetrating it, that is, the actual life in us and in all creatures, we call the "*higher self*". Expressions like "God", "creator", "universal self", "higher self" or the "*creative principle*" all mean one and the same *divinity* in its various aspects.

'The energies radiating from the centre are still highly spiritual in the centre and of the highest frequencies. But the farther out they radiate from the centre, the more material they become . . . until these radiating energies are gradually changed into matter. In this way the radiating power limits itself, and at the edge of manifestation farthest removed from the centre it becomes a hard, material rind or crust. For this reason, the picture—the "name"—of God who manifests himself in the visible world is a circle, an inner circle of higher powers surrounded by a hard, material rind or crust.

'Expressed in letters, the symbol is OM.

'All creatures, from the central suns down to monocellular beings, are built according to this principle. Look at a cross-section of our earth. In the centre, the mighty forces are still in the evolutionary stage of the fire circle. Next come the gaseous regions, then those of the molten or liquid circles, and the outer-form is the rind of hard matter. But I want to tell you too that another opposing force—centripetal force—is also active at the same time, drawing all material manifestations inward towards itself. And if hard matter were not sufficiently resistant, all manifestations of life would be drawn into their own centres and disappear. Even our earth, with all the forms of life upon it, would suffer this fate. The resistance of matter prevents this from happening, and only for this reason is it possible at all for creation to exist and life to have come forth here on this hard, material crust of the earth. Don't forget the resistance of matter, because we shall talk about it again.

'Here is another example to illustrate the inner structure of material forms: a section through the spinal column of any vertebrate shows the same construction, the extremely fine substance of the marrow of the back bone carrying the creative power of life, developed and protected by the hard crust of bone. Whatever bone you cut—be it skull, vertebra or leg bone—you will find the same cross section.

'If you cut the stem of a plant, you will come upon the same pattern. Have you ever looked at trees after they have been felled? The inner structure of the tree is exactly the same: radiating from the centre are circles of vital energy, fed by the finer matter of the tree's innermost substance. The annual rings reflect the yearly radiation of life in the tree that takes place very spring, surrounded and protected by the outer ring of hard bark.

'*Growth always starts from the centre and radiates outward. The innermost source of all powers and manifestations is God.*

'This aspect of God, who is clothed in matter and makes living beings out of created forms and which we call the higher *self* (*Logos*) is what draws us back into our own centre, since we have fallen from the divine unity, from the state of paradise. It is the heavenly bridegroom for whom the human soul longs. One should never mistake this divine self for the personal "I" which in itself has no true existence and is merely an imaginary being.

'The vital source behind every form of manifestation, be it a sun, planet, human being, animal, plant life or inorganic matter is one and the same God, the same divine *self.*

'Although the same *God* is everywhere present in every creature, he is manifest in countless different variations, because God reveals himself *on every single level* on which manifestation is possible and the created forms manifested on these various levels reveal only as much of *God* as each form *can consciously experience and bear of the divine creative force, corresponding to its own level. To consciously experience force* means *being* this force and simultaneously radiating it in all directions, including into one's own body. For this reason, the body too must have adequate power of *resistance;* otherwise the radiations of the self would burn and destroy it.

'Hence the bodies of the various manifestations of life are not made in the same way. On the contrary the matter composing them is of different degrees of resistance, corresponding in each case to the level of consciousness of the manifestation of life concerned. You know that *the chemical composition of matter determines which vibrations a body can support.* When a body is subjected to a radiation in excess of its resistance, this harms its entire nerve system, and can lead to a nervous breakdown and even to mental derangement. When the number of vibrations of this force exceeds the scope of an octave the force even becomes lethal. This is why, when we want to initiate a person into a higher degree of divine power, we must first prepare his body, subjecting it among other things to a chemical process, in order that the difference will not be more than one octave at the most. Otherwise he dies.

'In the material world there are four levels of manifestation which we call matter, vegetable life, animal life, and human life, depending on the outward appearance and the degree of consciousness attained. Compared with the human being, we can hardly speak at all of the "consciousness" of matter, and yet a crystal may serve to show that matter too has a sort of consciousness. Each level of manifestation of life is characterized by its own degree of consciousness which is one octave removed from the next. Only man has the power to manifest several degrees of consciousness, all the way up to the divine level. If we keep in mind the intervals—octaves—by which we classify levels of evolution, we find that man, as a category, occupies four steps of the great ladder of evolution reaching from earth up to heaven; furthermore we see that each step corresponds to one octave on the scale of vibrations. Man knows about these four steps or degrees and has given them names: *man* characterized by his intellect; *genius*, characterized by intuition; *prophet*, characterized by his wisdom and universal love; and the last and highest degree, that of the *God man*, characterized by his omniscience and omnipotence.

'Thus, in the material world, we find four manifestations which together reveal seven octaves of vibration.

'Every creature emits the vibrations of which it is made, that is, those which it *consciously* supports. *Matter*, the very lowest degree of consciousness, manifests itself only through contraction, cooling off, and hardening.

'The *plant* manifests itself on two levels; the material level and the level of force—vegetative force—that gives life to it. The plant manifests material vibrations unconsciously; it carries its body like a dress, but its level of consciousness is the vegetative level of force giving life to matter. Force manifested on this level has three distinctive aspects by which it can be recognized wherever it appears: the search for food, the taking in of food, and the assimilation or digestion of food.

'The *animal* manifests three forces, the material, the vegetative and animal. It has a body, it seeks out its food, eats and digests and is conscious on the animal level: it has emotions, instincts, urges, feelings, sympathy, antipathy and desires. The animal is conscious in the third developmental stage, only one degree lower than man.

'The *average man* stands one octave of vibrations higher: he is conscious on the mental level. He has intellect and the ability to think. But at the same time he manifests the three other levels. On the material, he has a body; on the vegetative, he seeks out his food, eats it and digests it; on the animal, he has emotions, drives, sympathy, antipathy and desires. But his most outstanding characteristic is his intellect. Man thinks consciously.

With the next degree of development, man makes a great jump: he lifts his consciousness out of the world of *effects* into the plane of *causes*. He draws on the divine source of the causal plan and manifests this force that appears in his consciousness as intuition. With the help of his intellect and spiritual power, he is able to express his experiences on a higher plane in words and transmit them to his fellow men. He can also prove the existence of his intuition in other arts: without dimensions, in music, as a composer; in two dimensions with lines and colours, as a painter; in three dimensional forms as a sculptor or as a dancer. People call the creative person a *genius*. He manifests the five octaves of vibration of the material, vegetative animal, mental and causal forces.

'The degree of consciousness of the next higher octave of vibrations, in the language of human beings, is called that of a *prophet*. The prophet manifests all the forces that work on the previously mentioned planes of consciousness, but he is also conscious on the next higher level too, the plane of divine wisdom and universal love. We must be careful never to confuse this universal love, which is manifested on the sixth plane and is a completely spiritual power, with the "love" of the third, animal plane which is the manifestation of animal instincts. This latter "love" is a vibration operating three levels lower at the source of which is the urge to propagate the species. Such "love" is desire for possession and always only seeks the body. It forces a person to come close to the loved one, and embrace, kiss, and hug him or her—in a word—to possess.

'Whoever is subject to this kind of love is still living in his consciousness in the condition of dividedness and separation and seeks a complementary physical partner in order to find satisfaction. This love always seeks to *take*, to *have* something, to *possess*. Love in the sixth plane of manifestation, the love of the prophet, does not come from a condition of division, but from the primordial condition of divine *unity*! Hence, this love is universal, always *giving*, never taking, needs no supplement, no physical manifestation, but always radiates from the consciousness of divine *all-unity*. People who are conscious on this plane do not want to possess anybody; they feel themselves one with the infinite *all*.

'The seventh and most perfect manifestation of *God* is the *completely conscious* man: the *God-man*. All other forms of revelation manifest only *transformed vibrations*, only *part of God*. *A God-man is a person who manifests God— his own divine self—completely and perfectly through a perfect consciousness; one who experiences and radiates the divine creative forces in their primordial untransformed vibrations and frequencies. He is supremely conscious; no part of him is unconscious.*

'Only man has the ability to master and to radiate all seven octaves of vibration, as the nervous centres corresponding to the seven octaves of transformed and untransformed creative power exist in his nervous system. On the other hand, he is only able to radiate vibrations on the levels on which he has become conscious, because until he becomes conscious on a given level, the corresponding nerve centres remain in a latent condition. Thus the average human being will radiate vibrations up to the fourth plane, the genius up to the fifth, the prophet up to the sixth, and only the God-man is able consciously to radiate all seven octaves and to radiate the divine creative power, according to his own will, in its untransformed form or to transform it, to change it, and transmit it in lower (transformed) frequencies.

'Your father's staff that you have seen consists of a material—a kind of brass —that has the power of transmitting the radiation corresponding to *every plane*. It is so constructed that, according to the will of the user, it can transmit untransformed radiations, either diminished or amplified as desired by the user.

'The staff can be a blessing or a curse. This depends on who uses it. An initiated person is able to radiate, in any desired degree, all forces of creation— from the highest divine forces to the lowest ultra-material forces with this staff, because within his own being he possesses all these forces and can consciously transmit them to the staff. Out of the whole gamut of these vibrations, the human being with his organs of sense, can perceive only a part. Vibrations either above or below this part are ones he can only experience as an emotional condition. Thus for example, he experiences the very highest divine frequencies as universal love. On the other hand, the very lowest frequencies, those of *ultra-matter*, are lower than the frequencies which our eyes and sensory nerves perceive as matter. As they are outside our scale of sensory perception, we experience them in our emotions as hate. An initiated person will always use the staff properly and always radiate the force needed to create something good . . . a blessing. The ultra material vibration he will use when necessary as an invisible, insulating, impenetrable protective wall. With the staff the initiated can dominate all forces of nature, amplify them or neutralize them.

'Every creature on earth possesses these powers, but only in a form corresponding to his degree of development. He utilizes these powers too, but is not conscious of them. Or have you ever seen a person who gave thought to how it is possible to raise his feet or his arms ? Or that he could—even though for only a short time—remove his whole body from the earth . . . by jumping ? Lift your arm and observe how you do it. Isn't it true that you contract your muscles and they lift your arm ? Every movement of your body is brought about with a contraction of your muscles. But what contracts your muscles ? Think a minute, my daughter, what ?'

'My will, Father.'

'Right. Your will. But if I ask you what your will is, can you give me an answer ?'

'Father, I have often observed what happens when I *want* something. But I have only been able to notice that when I *want* something, I can send out a force and give this force direction. For example, as you just said, if I want to raise my arm from its relaxed hanging position—it hangs because the earth is attracting it—then this force which flows out of me through my will flows into my arm and forces my muscles to contract and through this to raise my arm.'

'Very true,' says Ptahhotep, 'By virtue of the fact that your will power has flowed into your arm and muscles, you have *conquered the enormous gravitational power of the earth* on your arm. This is true when you jump too, but only for a short time, because your will power is only greater than the earth's gravitational pull for a short time. So you see time consumes your will power transformed into physical power. Time does that! And space? You've used your power to raise your arm, or your body, in *altitude*, to *remove* it from the earth, hence to move it further in *space*. Thus you see that your power is consumed by two great factors: *time* and *space*. If you could amplify your will power and store it within your body, you could conquer the earth's gravitational pull for a longer time and remain at a greater distance from the earth. You could glide through the air! You can't do that now because you haven't yet developed consciousness on this divine plane. The initiated, on the other hand, who are conscious on the divine plane, can draw directly on this infinite eternal source of power, without transforming it, and when they wish, float through the air just as long as they direct their will power against the gravitational pull of the earth.

'The initiated person knows all vibrations and possesses consciously developed organs with which to use these powers. You know, for example, the power of thought with which we communicate telepathically. These powers too we control through a corresponding higher organ of our brain. Human beings don't even know they have such organs. The initiated is able to radiate the very highest of all powers, the divine, creative power. This is the power and radiation of *life*, of eternal *being*. The entire universe is alive and continues to exist by virtue of this power. To make conscious use of it lies only within the capabilities of the *God-man*, the only creature that is, in his consciousness, identical with *God* and radiates this power from his God-consciousness, his cosmic all-consciousness. No other creature could endure this power *consciously*.

'Every force has its materialization on earth, and we therefore find that corresponding to all forces and vibrations there is a form of matter that has the resistive strength to endure it and transmit it, or even has the ability to store it and subsequently radiate it during a given length of time. What people call this matter is of no significance. Out of it are made the bodies of creatures and forms of manifestation corresponding to the various levels of consciousness. But this is true not only of the matter corresponding to their own level of consciousness, but also of the matter that conducts the vibrations below this specific plane of consciousness concerned. The matter of plants, for example, possesses a necessary resistive force for the vibrations of the vegetative life force, and at the same time for the vibrations of the matter, as the plant has a material body. The nerves and the bodies of animals carry within themselves the animal power corresponding to the animal level, and at the same time the vibrations of the vegetative level an octave lower, as well as the vibrations of the material plane a further octave lower.

'The nerves of the average human being, for example, have sufficient resistance to carry the vibrations of the mental plane as well as the transformed vibrations on each of the planes below—animal, vegetative and material. With the mental energies he *thinks* and is conscious on this level; with the animal energies he *feels* and experiences all emotional states; the vegetative streams of force give life to his body, and finally his body is built of material forces. And so it goes higher and higher up to the God-man who consciously uses all his brain and nervous centres and is able to direct the very highest vibrations of life, which has its central seat in his spinal column, without transforming them, into his nervous centres and into his body. The material of his body possesses the resistance to carry the very highest, divine force as well as—naturally enough—the transformed vibration of the other six planes of manifestation.

'*Thus the bodies of people in the various planes of development, only appear to consist of the same matter. Actually they are composed of different chemical elements whose resistance always corresponds to the level of consciousness of the spirit dwelling within.*

'The fact that the body of the God-man is able not only to bear the highest frequencies but also the transformed vibrations of all other octaves, means that there must be a form of matter with the resistive force necessary to withstand and to conduct the divine-creative force as well as all the other transformed frequencies of the lower octaves, *without being dematerialized.* Hence, the sons of God, in their homeland, invented a material, a kind of brass, of which they constructed devices for storing or radiating, either amplified or diminished, the very highest creative frequencies, either in their original or in transformed manifestation. These devices are so constructed that they keep the creative force in pure unchanged form. Consequently, over a long period, they act as a source of divine power—like *life* itself. Because the very highest of these devices which carries and radiates the creative force represents a perfect union—as perfect as a marriage—between the divine and the material frequencies—between *God* and the *earth*—we call this incredibly powerful conductor of force that is charged with the frequency of the divine self the '*Ark of the covenant*'.

'Now you know why we keep these devices so secret. The God-man who has developed his highest abilities can use these devices with impunity, as the ark of the covenant contains and radiates the same force as he himself, the force which he himself *is.* A person on a lower level, however, if he were merely to touch the ark, would fall over dead momentarily as if struck by lightning. The divine frequencies would instantly burn out his nerves and he would suffer a "shock". *The same thing happens when this frequency is liberated from its state of isolation in the spinal column and strikes one's nerves untransformed.* The person or animal or even a plant concerned dies immediately. People call this kind of death "a stroke". They sense that some unknown power has struck the person like lightning. This power is the river of life itself which normally is isolated within the spinal column—or within the innermost channel in the case of plants—and normally only flows into the body in suitably transformed condition. This force only breaks out in case of sickness and causes the "stroke".

'For the same reason uninitiated people cannot be allowed in the vicinity of our devices. And even more! As these devices radiate the most powerful energy, we must keep them carefully hidden behind massive walls of rock providing the greatest insulation. Life energy itself has a lethal effect when it strikes a form of matter which doesn't have the necessary resistance. The matter is dematerialized, dissolved.

'The ark and still other tools thus consist of a material which—without being dematerialized—can be charged with the divine-creative energy. The ark radiates untransformed creative energy and has the effect of *giving life or destroying it depending on the dosage*. This force has the same character of vibration as that of the human will which is capable of conquering everything, including the gravitational pull of the earth even though for only a short time. The ark of the covenant radiates this power magnified a thousand times. And just as the earth through its gravitational pull affects matter and attracts it, we can work against the gravitational pull of the earth in every form of matter without exception and consequently overcome its weight and render it weightless for a shorter or longer period of time. When necessary, we can even do the opposite, i.e. work *with* the gravitational pull of the earth and increase the weight of an object as much as we want through the ultramaterial rays. In this way even the greatest blocks of stone are rendered weightless for a period of time so that the largest buildings you can think of can be built with the greatest of ease, or the weight of the stones can be increased to such an extent that they sink into the earth. For example, when we want to dig a well, we don't have to dig out the earth. We simply take a stone of suitable size and increase its weight so that it sinks into the earth until it reaches the desired depth.

'With the help of the ark of the covenant, this enormous source of power, we can also transform energies devoid of matter, as for example, the rays of light, into matter. And, inversely, we can dissolve this matter and convert it to energies active during aeons of time.

'Look at this lamp. Just as the sun itself for billions of years has been sending out rays, *some of which are converted to rays of light in our atmosphere through transformations of energy*, in the same way through the matter being dissolved —dematerialized—in this lamp, energies are created which are converted to rays of light in the air.

'This process could continue in this lamp for ages and ages and consequently it would go on giving light for aeons of time were it not written in the history of the earth that we shall have to leave the earth for thousands of years and destroy all our equipment. Were this not the case, the ignorant sons of men would again cause unspeakable destruction.

'There will be a lot in the remains of our culture which coming generations will not understand. For example, the way we get such a mirror-smooth surface on even the hardest stones. The joints between them fit so accurately there isn't even a crack the size of the thickness of a hair between them. They will be greatly puzzled at how our "slaves", working only "by hand", have been able to cut stones so precisely. Because the sons of men make slaves of their fellowmen, they will believe that we too have put slaves to work. For thousands of years it won't dawn on them that we simply dematerialize the superfluous stone on the surface and are thus able to get hairline accuracy on the edges and faces of even the hardest stones without the slightest human effort. We adjust our instruments to the desired width and depth of the stone and everything beyond the dimensions we want is merely dematerialized. This is very simple as soon as you know the true nature of the different energies including that of matter. But this knowledge is a blessing only in the hands of a knowing person. He knows too that *love means life*, and *hate means death*. Only initiates of the highest degree can be architects. As a matter of fact, to build with slaves we wouldn't need to be initiates! We don't work with slaves but with the forces of nature.

'Thanks to these instruments of ours we are able to create every form of manifestation. The manifestation depends only on how long and from what distance we put the creative energy to work. The sons of men take it for granted they can come into the temple with their sicknesses and we make them well again. *Sickness means that the vibrations of the body have got out of harmony.* We restore the inharmonious part of the body to its own proper vibration and the person gets well. Every organ has its own characteristic vibration. This means that every organ is as it is because it has a certain characteristic vibration, and this vibration is constantly acting within it and maintaining it. When this vibration changes, the organ concerned becomes diseased.

'We can also regulate the weather on earth, making clear blue sky or, when necessary, clouds and rain. The sons of men see the lightning, hear the thunder of the pyramid and are happy because they know this means the blessing of rain. They live in the secure knowledge that the temple will take care of all their needs: their health, the rain that blesses them, and even their spiritual wellbeing.'

'Father of my Soul,' I now ask, 'how do you charge this ark of the covenant with creative energy?'

Ptahhotep looks at me with a penetrating glance and says:

'I can see you already know how we charge the ark of the covenant. I already told you: there is *only* one source on earth that is able to radiate this power and that is the God-man himself. It is the duty of the high priest to charge the ark with divine-creative power. He either drives his own high power directly into the ark or he achieves the same result with the help of the staff of life through converting an *absolutely positive* flow of power flowing from his hand at a lower vibration, conducting it through the staff and there converting it into divine-creative power. For in his daily life, even the perfect God-man only radiates creative power in a transformed state. Only when his spiritual forces are concentrated and in his consciousness he is identical with *God*, only then does the divine force radiate in its primordial vibration. He must therefore be in a condition of cosmic all-consciousness when he wants to radiate the creative force.

If the uninitiated sons of men were to see him in this condition they would run away terrified as at such times the God-man radiates such celestial, divine light that ordinary people can't stand the sight of him. If uninitiated people were to touch an initiate in this divine condition of being, they would momentarily fall over dead, just as if they had touched the ark of the covenant.

'Thus when an initiate radiates his rays of life for healing purposes, he withdraws into a state of concentration such that his radiation can be borne by people without harm; that is the power he directs to the appropriate nerve centres he raises up to the level of creative power with the help of the staff. For the staff is so constructed that it can not only conduct the rays but also transmit them in a transformed state, amplified or diminished, at will. Hence, an initiate doesn't need to enter the divine state of being in order to conduct the highest radiation of life into the ark of the covenant; on the contrary, he can enter a lower state of concentration and then direct the power corresponding to this level into the ark of the covenant, after raising it with the help of the staff up to the level of creative energy. When the ark is charged in this manner, it radiates for a long time this highest and strongest energy, as a source of all other forces on earth.

'An initiate can produce and control even the most varied frequencies with the staff, as the staff is an ark of the covenant in miniature form, except for the fact that creative energy is not stored in it as in the case of the ark of the covenant. With the help of the staff, a human being could even convert his lower powers into creative force if he could radiate in a *pure, positive* and *completely selfless manner* power that is several octaves lower. This is because the staff always radiates the power that a human being puts into it. If a primitive and selfish person were to get possession of the staff, he would transmit his own negative radiations arising from his selfishness—possibly even in amplified form—and thus cause sicknesses, epidemics, earthquakes or even greater destruction as the necromancers and practitioners of black magic once did in the home of the divine race.

'Do you understand now why the initiates keep their science so secret from the uninitiated.'

'I understand, Father. And it is now quite clear to me how my father revived the half-dead boy. In his state of high concentration, father directed his radiation, in magnified state, into the child. It worked like a miracle. The child was charged with vital energy, and his exhaustion disappeared immediately. But, Father of my Soul, what is going to happen when the sons of men take over the government? Are you going to destroy the magic staff, as father said, when he told me the initiates are going to destroy all their instruments? What a shame that people won't be able to enjoy the blessing of these powers!'

'My child,' says Ptahhotep, '*every creature lives in conditions that are exactly adapted to its state of development*! If we were to betray the secret of the staff to the sons of men, they would immediately use it to do harm to each other and to themselves. The sons of men aren't ready for this knowledge and won't be for a long time to come. The staff we are now using will be taken out of Egypt by the last initiate in possession of the secret knowledge, along with the ark of the covenant. He will have no possibility to build a pyramid. On the contrary, he will make a small cover for the ark to insulate it as well as possible. He will charge the ark to a much lesser degree and will cause it to be carried during his migrations by means of long wooden poles as handles. When this last initiate feels he is approaching death, he will destroy his staff. For a time the ark will continue to radiate the energy with which it has been charged, and the uninitiated will continue to carry it about in various countries for a long time until little by little they notice that it no longer has any power. Then even the last remains of the ark will be destroyed.

'In times to come people will learn about the "magic staff" and the "ark of the covenant" only through records of earlier times. They will consider all this as a fairy tale and continue to tell it from one generation to another. But they will still vaguely remember that once there was an "ark of the covenant" in which there dwelt the power of the living God. And they'll also remember there was once a "magic staff" or as we call it a "staff of life" with which the initiates, the "magicians", performed miracles. From records from earlier times people will know or dimly sense that "the staff" represented *power* over all forces of nature.

'In later times when people want to symbolize the greatest power, they will place a staff—a sceptre—in their hand as a token of power. In those times to come, however, their staff—their sceptre—will only be an *empty symbol of power*. The *true power* and *force of the staff* will no longer be known to them. Only after thousands of years will a descendant from the tribe of the Sons of God be reincarnated; he will discover these truths for the people of his time and will make a new "magic staff". Until then, however, for thousands of years, there will be a strange kind of people who, either to entertain or to cheat, will call themselves "magicians" and will pretend they are performing their magic tricks with the help of a "magic wand". *They will thus be imitating what once actually existed.*

'They will hold a "magic wand" in their hand and go through the motions of drawing magic powers from this wand. They will also use "magic words", imitating our magic formulas. But people will only learn the true gigantic power of the word centuries later when the fallen members of the divine race are reincarnated—those who are now living *here*—and will *remember in their subconscious* the truths which in that time will represent ancient records.

'They will prove that their memories are correct. The time will come when the sons of men rediscover and repossess all knowledge, even the very highest. Even then, of course, this knowledge will remain an unintelligible secret for the ignorant masses, and in uninitiated hands these rediscovered truths will be a curse. But after all, this is the path of mankind, through many troubles and sorrows, which people make for themselves. Little by little they will learn they must not play with divine power. They'll come to know that these powers should be used in full seriousness with dignity and dedication. *For God gives mankind all, even himself, as a blessing; only people, in their ignorance, make a curse out of everything !'*

'Father of my Soul,' I ask, 'you said that the pyramids were made of thick blocks of stone in order to insulate the equipment by means of which the penetrating frequencies are radiated. But how then can you conduct the radiations to the outside ?'

'The thick walls of the pyramids all contain shafts and tunnels through which we conduct out the force of the ark of the covenant and the other supplementary equipment which radiates energy. With the aid of these shafts and tunnels we also control weather. The positive and negative tunnels are built in different directions; when the positive and negative forces flow through them, they cause clouds to form and bring about the desired rain. The equalization of these tensions causes flashes of lightning accompanied by great noise. That is why people hear thunder coming from the pyramid. The other pyramids have been built for various other installations.'

'What's going to happen to the pyramids when the sons of men come into power in our country and the ark of the covenant and all other instruments are destroyed ? Will the pyramids stand empty ? And what's to become of the high priest and the other priests and initiates ?' I ask.

'All except for the largest pyramid where the ark of the covenant is now kept and where initiation is given, the pyramids won't remain empty. When all our instruments for the radiation of divine creative energy are removed, the last initiated Pharaohs will have themselves entombed in one of these pyramids. Their bodies, permeated through and through by divinely creative force will continue—as the force will not be consumed—to radiate the supreme power just as the ark of the covenant does. Thus their bodies will continue in secret to act as tremendous sources of power, protecting this continent from evil influences. The radiation of well preserved and holy bodies will help our country keep its power for thousands of years. But in the course of time most of these tombs will be destroyed by ignorant people.'

'And what's going to happen to the great pyramid, Father ?'

Ptahhotep looks off in the distance for a while as if he were observing things there. Then his heavenly glance sweeps back to me and he says: 'When the time has come for all secret instruments to be destroyed, and when the priest and initiates still serving in the temple at that time take their pilgrim's staff and set out for far-away places, the high priest and his deputy will close the rock entrance of the great pyramid from the inside so that no son of man can find it. Then, after fulfilling their last duties, they will dematerialize their own bodies in just the way you've often seen the offering on the altar in the temple court dematerialized. Just a flash, then a little white cloud that soon disappears —not a trace of ash or anything else remains behind. Thus the interior of the great pyramid will be closed off from human sight for thousands of years. Nevertheless, our initiations will not cease. Mature souls will continue to be initiated here—not physically, of course, but on the higher spiritual plane. These people will experience their initiation as a dream or a vision.'

Ptahhotep ceases speaking, and for a long time we look into each other's eyes. I understand a lot that he doesn't want to say . . . but I still have another question: 'Father of my soul, is there a special reason why all pyramids are built in the same form? Why aren't they built in a cubic shape, for example, like other buildings?'

Ptahhotep smiles: 'Not in cubic form? But the pyramids *are* built in cubic form! But I'll have to explain that to you next time. You've had enough today.'

I see that Ptahhotep has ended his instruction, but I still remain. I'd like to have him show me the use of the staff and the ark of the covenant. He looks at me with a smile and says: 'The time will come when you'll be permitted to know about the construction of the ark of the covenant and the staff of life. That will come after you've been initiated. But the use of these instruments is restricted to those who've reached the seventh degree after initiation through their own efforts. These secrets must not come into dangerous hands. Be patient. Time exists only in our thinking, but still everything takes time to mature.'

He blesses me, and I leave.

— 33 —

THE FORM OF THE PYRAMIDS: SATAN

ONCE AGAIN I stand before Ptahhotep in his laboratory.

'I've already explained to you,' he says, 'that behind all the manifestations of the visible world there is a primordial force, a striving to return to the state of unity, and this force is apparent as the attraction between the two complementary halves, the positive and the negative. You are now standing before me because the earth's gravitational force is holding your body here. If it weren't for this force, you and everything that is not rooted to the earth would have spun off into space long ago. Even the whole gigantic body of the earth would have broken apart long ago. The force which holds together the earth and all the matter within its atmosphere *doesn't belong to the earth itself, but merely affects the earth operating outward from its centre.* If matter had no resistance and merely yielded to this force, the tremendous mass of the earth and everything that's living on it would disappear into its centre. But where would it go? Think for a moment.

'Come closer, my child. I'll show you. If I put various things on the top of this table, tie a string on to each, draw the strings through the hole in the middle of the table top, and then pull all the strings from below, all the objects are drawn towards the centre of the table top; and all those that are smaller than the hole disappear. Where do they go? Aren't they drawn towards the point from which the force is acting? But where does the force in the centre of the earth come from . . . the force that draws everything towards it? Can you answer that, my child?'

I reflect for a moment and answer: 'The earth is recognizable. If everything that is recognizable is so only because it has separated itself from the *"all and nothingness"*, leaving its complementary half behind in the unmanifested state, then the earth too must have its complementary half in the unmanifested state, and the force of gravitation it exerts on all the creatures and objects living on it is the striving for reunification between the earth and its unmanifested complementary half which has been left behind in the void as its negative reflection. The earth's gravitational pull thus draws all the earth towards the *void* which stands beyond time and space, in order to bring about this reunion. If the earth were to yield, all the earth and everything on it would disappear into the centre, into the *void*. But that would be a return to the paradisiacal unity—to *God*—to bliss! Why can't that happen, Father?'

'My child,' answers Ptahhotep, '*the obstacle is the resistance of matter!* Without *resistance* no creation is possible! It's the resistance of matter that keeps the earth and all creation from disappearing and being annihilated. Everything that has appeared in this recognizable world has fallen out of a point in the universe, and this point has then become its own centre. Through the fall it became matter. Now it can't return to divine unity because its own resistance as matter doesn't let it. A return to the paradisiacal divine unity—to God—is only possible through the spiritualization of the matter, that is, *through the transformation of matter into spirit*! But matter, all by itself, could never become spirit without spiritual help. That's why one aspect of *God* comes down into matter, clothes itself in matter, assumes material characteristics, and animates it as the *self* in order to make possible its spiritualization, its salvation.

'The effect which this self in the centre of every creature has constantly exerted on the innermost structure of matter throughout aeons and aeons of time has led to the development of the forms of life existing on each rung of the ladder of creation. Thus each creature has come into being, from the simple protozoa up to the highest manifestation.

'The highest creature on earth is man. It is his task to carry out the completion of the spiritualization of the earth, a task at which all living creatures are at work, each within the limits of its own particular stage of development. *And every human being who transforms himself from a being identical with the body into a being reawakened in spirit, a divine being—identifying his consciousness with the divine self—has fulfilled his duty.* He has spiritualized a bit of the earth. He has advanced by one step the salvation of the earth. Then he can co-operate as a helper in the salvation of other beings.

'And now you know why you're standing here before me. It's because the *self* of the earth, which at the same time is our own *self*, *loves* the earth and all its creatures, drawing the earth towards itself, into divine unity, just as a bridegroom draws his bride to himself. This striving towards union, characteristic of all love, expresses itself in everything—including our bodies—as *weight*!

'This force which we call weight is at work in every form of nature, and when we build we must reckon and work *with* this force, never against it. When we take proper account of it, it helps us preserve our buildings for a long time. If we were to try to build against the laws of these forces, all our structures would collapse in practically no time at all.

'It's enough for you to understand that in the pyramidal form the resultant of forces is the most favourable one possible for the preservation of buildings for many thousands of years against the ravages of nature.

'The pyramids—particularly the great pyramid—have been built according to various mathematical and astronomical laws in order to serve the people as clock and calendar. You will learn these laws another time. Moreover, the fact that the lateral faces stand at an angle of $51°$ to their base enables the pyramid to reflect the sun's rays far out to sea and far into the desert. Thus our pyramids also serve as lighthouses. All the laws on which they are based, together with the history of those who have built them, are inscribed on the ceramic tiles with which they are covered. When the sons of men some day discover the secret of our writing, they will be able for a long time to read right from the pyramids themselves the knowledge and information I am giving you now, the mathematical and astronomical laws we have applied, the secrets of the pyramids and all our scientific knowledge. In the darkest ages of the earth, however, these written records will also disappear, so the sons of men will later have to discover all truth for themselves.

'You must learn the law of the three-dimensional world which is *based on the law of the spirit and could not exist without it.*

'The first source of all truth and of all manifestation is the *eternal being—God.* But God is in the unmanifested state beyond time and space, and only his manifestations appear as projections in the three-dimensional world. Therefore in order to understand these laws correctly, we must begin with *God.* In order to talk about *God,* however, we always have to cope with the fact that *God* stands above the recognizable world. For this reason every living creature can only understand God to the extent to which it itself is able consciously to experience, manifest and realize God; that is, to the extent to which it itself *can be God!* In everything *God* is living, and everything is living in *God.* Nevertheless, *God* in his own complete, perfect being can be understood only by one who has himself *become God*—or who has never fallen out of *God. God can be understood only by God!*

'The fact that even the most primitive man has a concept of God shows that divine *consciousness* is dwelling within him, even though only very dimly and to the lowest degree. On the other hand, to become conscious in God, to understand *God* completely, and to be *God* means to become completely one with one's own divine *self,* with the *God* dwelling within. That is easy to say but very hard to do! Because man has fallen out of his divine *consciousness,* he can only imagine God in accordance with his own personal power of understanding. How can he know what the real, living *divinity* is like in its perfection when his power of imagination only corresponds to the level he personally stands on, separated as he is from unity, and having fallen as he has from divinity? How can the finite understand the infinite, the mortal the immortal, the temporal the eternal? ... How can an imaginary being understand, experience and become identical with the eternal, true *being—God?*

'And still man must reach *him!* His eternal desire, his unquenchable longing helps him and propels him forward in the direction of his divine *self.* Man's intellect—the greatest but most dangerous gift he has received from God—builds a bridge across the seemingly unconquerable chasm between that which is personal and mortal and that which is impersonal and eternal. Through man's intellect he succumbed to the temptation to fall out of divine unity with his consciousness. But by the same token, his intellect gives him the possibility of *bringing back his consciousness into full union with divinity.* By means of his intellect, man is able to *understand* truth, and when he has understood, he will

227

seek and keep on seeking and trying until he some day succeeds in finding the only path to the realization of his *self*.

'Realization means being something. For as long as we think about something or talk about it, we aren't *being* it. You can think about a cat, or about a lion, but that doesn't mean by any manner of means that you have achieved realization, that you have *become* a cat or a lion. Likewise, you can think about *yourself* without being your divine, creative *self*! To think something is to be separated from it. For if you send out a single thought, you—the thinker—are connected only by thinking with the object of your thought. You are *connected* with it, but not identical with it. You are not yet that which is in your intellect. Your intellect belongs to you; it is a wonderful tool, a mirror into which you can project everything and in which you can recognize everything, but your intellect is not you! The intellect is outside your *self*. Consequently what you can do with your intellect is not you yourself, is not achievement of realization.

'When man seeks *God* outside himself, he can often be "thinking" about *God*, he can be "praying" to *God*, he can be "loving" *God* with his whole being, but all this doesn't mean he has become identical with *God*. For man can never find *God* by seeking outside himself!

'The creator in man is man's own *self* whose last manifestation, farthest from his own centre, is his little "I", his personal "I-consciousness". The personal "I" within him is the image of God mirrored by matter—in the body. Thus when man seeks to return to *God* and re-establish his identity with him he must follow the *same* path with his consciousness: *he must draw his consciousness more and more from his own little personal "I"—deeper and deeper into himself—turning to his own true self, to his creator, until he consciously recognizes himself in Him.* But this doesn't mean that the creature—the person—recognizes itself in this condition. As an imaginary being, it has no true existence and cannot really achieve self-knowledge. On the contrary, *the creator recognizes himself in the*

 *created, in the person.* This is *the only possibility* for overcoming the state of separation and bringing back the consciousness into the state of unity: the individual stops thinking about himself and instead becomes himself, recognizes himself. In this condition, the recognizer, the recognized and the recognition are one and the same. The self—the creator—recognizes its self in itself!

'Man can only experience *God* in this way. This is *resurrection*! In this state he recognizes that his own *self* has created him and is constantly creating him, hence that his own *self* is his creator. He likewise realizes that *the one and only self is the creator of the entire universe*! As a result of this divine self-recognition he simultaneously experiences the creative cosmic all-consciousness. At the same time as he achieves *self-recognition*, he achieves *recognition of everything*, *omniscience*!

'This divine state in which the *creator recognizes himself* may also be expressed symbolically by numbers:

'*God in his state of resting within himself is 1 in 3 and 3 in 1. 1 and 3* are still an unseparated unity.

'In the field of geometry, the form of the equilateral triangle is the symbolic image of God in which the recognizer, the recognized and the recognition are one and the same: *1 in 3 and 3 in 1.*

'Every form is the manifestation of the force that has built it. Thus every form is the image of the creative force that builds it and dwells within it. Divinity in its primordial state of *resting within itself,* always manifests itself in the form of a triangle. The triangle represents perfect harmony and perfect equilibrium as its three corner points all lie exactly the same distance from each other. On the other hand, when the aspect of *God* to which we refer as "resting within itself" moves out of the dimensionless state, beyond time and space and into the three dimensions, it becomes the *creative* aspect of *God* and always manifests itself in the number *4.* As long as the numbers *1* and *3* form a unity in *divinity,* they remain *3 in 1* and *1 in 3.* But when they emerge from the divine condition of unity, *they separate,* and out of the "*1 in 3*" there emerges "*1 and 3*", and that

makes *4.* The equilateral triangle contains, hidden within itself, *4* smaller equilateral triangles.

'This law also contains the secret of the key number of the three-dimensional world: the number *7.*

'Now try to imagine how the first energy of manifestation emerges out of the dimensionless state into the three dimensions. Close your eyes and I'll project this truth into your consciousness.'

I do as Ptahhotep tells me, closing my eyes and turning my attention inward. All of a sudden I see a *point,* and I hear Ptahhotep's voice:

'In order for a force to emerge from the dimensionless state and manifest itself, it needs a *point of departure.* A point is dimensionless, has not yet emerged from unity, but is necessary for manifestation. Because a point consists of only one single factor, it bears within itself the number of unity, the number *1.*

'When the force whose first manifestation was a point emerges from the dimensionless state and is effective for a period of time, the point moves and forms a *line.*'

With my inward eye I see how the point gradually becomes a line, and I hear Ptahhotep's voice.

'The first dimension, length, is born. In its essence, the line is endless and thus, as a first manifestation, also represents the number *1.* But in the world of manifestations, the world where everything always has a beginning and an end, a line is always bound to involve three factors, its starting point, its end point, and the intervening space between the two. Thus the line represents the number *3,* the key number for the 1-dimensional world.

'Now you must have noticed that there is no possibility of manifesting or of finding the number *2* in a *unity.* As a matter of fact after the first manifestation of the point, which represents only *1* single factor, we immediately jumped to three factors—*without the number 2*. When a point moves, no matter how little, to form even the tiniest, shortest line, we're already dealing with the *3* factors not *2*. A line in *infinity* of course, represents the number *1*; but when it has a beginning and an end, it automatically represents the number *3*.

'In order for the number *2* to arise, there has to be a *splitting of unity*. The number *2* can only be born when two units are set beside each other. But inasmuch as nothing has any real existence outside unity, *unity must project a reflection outside itself*. Thus there arises a fission, a separation, which means the death of unity. That's why the word for "doubt"—which represents a kind of cleavage within one's mind and soul—is so closely related to the word for *2*. This is true in every language.

'Let us now watch how the second dimension arises from the first. A line consists of a series of points. Assuming the creative energy is active in each of these points with the same force and for the same period of time, each of these points moves outward from itself into the second dimension; each of them becomes a line, and out of the totality of these lines a plane is created: An equi-

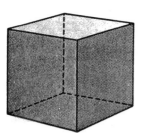

lateral rectangle.

'The second dimension—width—is born.

'The rectangle is *four* in *one* and *one* in *four* and thus consists of five factors: the four *manifested* lines: Line of departure, terminal line, right and left lateral lines, and the fifth factor: the *non-manifested* area enclosed by these lines. And so the key number of the two dimensional world is the number *five*.

'But creative forces continue to work. The plane also consists of points, and if the same force works outward from each of these points in the same direction and for the same period of time, all these points move into the third dimension, and a *cube* has been created from the plane.

The third dimension is born—height.

'The cube is *six* in *one* and *one* in *six* and it consists of *seven* factors: the *six manifested* limiting planes and the seventh, unmanifested factor, its cubic contents. The key number of the three-dimensional world is the number *seven*.

'As you see, the basic form of matter is the cube. The various crystals are built in conformity with this law, and in them you can find either the cubic shape itself—as in the case of salt for example—or the basic elements of the cube in various aspects and variations. If we now investigate the characteristics of the cube, you will also understand the laws of the variants.

'Starting from one of the corner points of the cube, try to find a plane in which all three dimensions of the cube are contained. If you merely cut straight through, you get a plane containing only two dimensions of the cube. In order to find a plane containing all three, we must begin at one corner and cut through obliquely to the opposite corner points. Thus one corner of the cube is cut off.

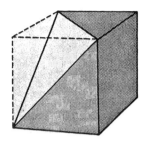

'If we continue in the same manner, we cut off all four corners of the cube, and what's left is a very different shape: a tetrahedron, the faces of which are bounded by four equilateral triangles.

'So now you see that hidden within the cube is a shape with quite different laws, for the shape consists, not of rectangles, but of four triangles. If we were to flatten out these four triangles into a plane, they would form a single, equilateral triangle, the symbolic representation of *God*.

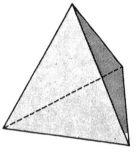

'Just like the equilateral triangle which makes up its mantle, the tetrahedron is the very incarnation of harmony and equilibrium. Since each of its corner points is equally distant from each of the others, there is no strain or tension in a tetrahedron, but rather a condition of rest in equilibrium. By way of contrast, the corner points of the cube, just like those of the square, lie at different distances from each other, and this means that both in the square and the cube there is a condition of everlasting stress. The matter in our three-dimensional world is built up in cubic form, but hidden within itself it contains the form

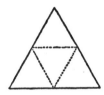

of the tetrahedron based on divine equilibrium. Matter cannot exist without the divine content.

'The whole three-dimensional world is built up on this same law, quite irrespective of whether the form concerned is considered to be inanimate matter or a living creature. Whether a given form is that of a plant, an animal or a human, the body of each of these is subject to the laws of the three dimensional world. Hidden and invisible within this body, however, is the higher, divine self—life—eternal *being*! Only man is able to manifest his higher *self*—that is *God*—through his thoughts, words and deeds, when he identifies his consciousness, not with his body, but with its spiritual content, with his *self*. As long as a person identifies himself only with his body, he is like an *opaque cube* in that he reveals only the characteristics of matter, crowding the divine creative principle into a latent, unmanifested state. No one suspects that the tetrahedron —the divine self—so different from the outward cubic shape, is dwelling within!

'On the other hand a person who uses his body, his thoughts, words and deeds only *to manifest* the divine creative principle, while leaving the characteristics of his physical existence—his person—in the unmanifested state—such a person, to continue using the same figure of speech, is like a cut *cube* whose corners and inner content are turned outward so that its inner triangles—the equilateral triangles of the divine tetrahedron—are visible.

'Such a person uses the material, square shape only as a secure base in the three-dimensional world, allowing his weight to rest on this base.

'But the shape of the cut cube turned inside out is the *pyramid*. *Thus we see the pyramid is the symbolic form of the God-man,* who reveals his divine, selfless nature and completely manifests *God* on earth. The salvation of the earth, the spiritualization of matter is completed in the person of the *God-man*. The *divine self*—the creator—is seated in complete majesty on its throne and rules over matter, over the body.

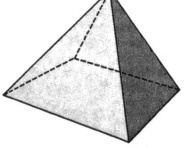

'By way of contrast, the symbolic representation of materialistic man who uses his intellect for the service of his material being is the cross—or a "T"—formed out of the four squares making up the surface of the cube. On this cross, or "T" the secret, indwelling, divine *self* is crucified.

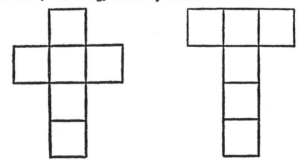

'In such persons, divinity is robbed of its power. It cannot manifest itself and is subject to the laws of the material world. It is crucified on the two great beams of the three-dimensional world—on time and space—and dies on this cross of matter. Its death, however, is not final! Even in the consciousness that has sunk down to the lowest level, the divine creative *self* sometime undergoes resurrection and saves the suffering human being. Materialistic man, in his ignorance through crucifying his own higher *self—God* within himself—creates ceaseless tortures and sufferings for himself; he becomes the criminal who is also crucified beside the divine one. The pains awaken him; his higher consciousness is aroused, and with the resurrection of his divine *self*, he experiences his own *salvation* because he *recognizes* himself in *him*!

'The members of the divine race who fled to the far corners of the earth carried these symbols with them wherever they went, proclaiming to humanity the secret, hidden truth within them. In every part of the earth people will find these symbols in stone, in metal, or baked clay, in various sizes, large or small. Most people will believe that they represent a person who has been crucified, and only a few will recognize that the representation symbolizes the divine creative principle crucified on the two beams of time and space.

The pyramids will continue to stand for thousands of years, proclaiming to humanity the highest truths which have been built into them. People with eyes and ears will find and recognize these elements of truth, even though they may not be able to fathom all the mathematical and astronomical laws of the pyramids, and some few highly developed persons will even be able to attain the truth proclaimed. On the other hand, for primitive minds the pyramid will always be a puzzle—just like the Sphinx—until they reach the point of being able to solve their own puzzle.

'But now let's return to our consideration of the cube! A few minutes ago you started at one corner of the cube and cut it in such a way that a plane contained all three dimensions. In this way you cut off a corner of the cube; then three more corners. But by starting at the other corner points of the cube you could make four more cuts and you would find the cube doesn't contain just one tetrahedron, but two of them, one within the other, each an exact reflection of the other. These two tetrahedrons represent the innermost law of the recognizable world: the inseparable relationship between the two complementary halves—the positive and the negative—which, self-contained each within the other, form a perfect equilibrium and sit, as creative spirits, on the right hand and on the left hand of divinity. In creation they rule as two opposite laws: the law of spirit and the law of matter.

'*Spirit is life, matter is resistance. The law of the spirit is radiation, giving, selflessness. The law of matter is drawing inward, cooling off, paralysis.*

'There is only one single creature that is able consciously to combine the two laws: man. He is the connecting link between the world of the spirit and that of matter. He is able to live at one and the same time by the laws of both worlds. His thoughts, words and deeds can be an act of giving, radiating selflessness and universal love. On the other hand, his body belongs to the material world and lives by the laws of matter. *At its right place and in its right time, every law is divine, but the opposite is satanic.*

'Without the resistance of matter creation would be impossible. In unmanifested *divinity* all creative forces are still at rest in unity, in complete repose and equilibrium, *representing merely potential, only power possibilities.* Creation begins in that one force separates itself from unity and sets itself up opposite the creator as resistance. That is the "first born son" of God, the spirit of resistance which the *father* sends out to act throughout aeons and aeons of time as a negative and opposite pole to himself, to bear the frequencies of creation, and by resisting them make it possible for creation to take place. This spirit of resistance is the opposite pole to the manifesting aspect of God. By virtue of its centripetal, chilling and coagulating characteristics, it is the cause of the creation of matter.

'Pick up a stone for example. The power that makes it a stone and holds it together as matter is the very self-same law of resistance tending to chill, harden and hold everything together. As long as this law manifests itself *in* matter and *as* matter, the law is operating in its place and consequently in a divine manner. But inert matter becomes living matter when the divine spirit, the *self*, clothes itself in matter and becomes flesh. The self, *life*, penetrates the inert matter, and out of the law of matter there arises a living spirit: the reflected image which has only been able to become spirit by virtue of the fact that *God*, as the *self* of the living creatures, has breathed his own life into matter, is *satan. Thus you can see that satan is the law of matter come alive through the divine spirit.* Satan lies dead in matter, *as its law,* until with its own life the divine spirit makes him come alive.

'Whenever man's consciousness identifies itself with the law of matter so that his thinking, words and deeds, instead of serving the divine law, serve the law of matter, *man is bringing satan to life,* man is becoming satanic himself. Without man satan cannot exist; for without the *self* of man, satan is only an unconscious force, a necessary natural law of matter.

'Satan can come to life only in the consciousness of a person who manifests the law of matter, the law of the flesh, in his spirit; who identifies his consciousness with his person, with his lower nature, with the drives and urges dwelling in his flesh, with the urge of self-preservation and propagation of the species. Such a person manifests the centripetal, coagulating power of matter *as spiritual characteristics* such as avarice, envy, vanity, hard-heartedness and selfishness. No living creature has ever met satan *by himself,* for *without man satan has no existence at all.* Without man satan is only the law of matter. We can meet the living satan only in the human being; only in a human face can we recognize satan as the *expression* of this face.

'When after the death of the body of such a person the *self* separates itself, satan remains behind in the corpse as the law of matter. He became satan through the vitalizing power of the *self in the consciousness.* But the consciousness of a person who has identified himself with the law of matter and thus become satanic himself *dies with satan and becomes unconscious after death.* Satan draws him, his slave, into inert matter, into the darkness, into loss of consciousness, into himself.

'On the other hand, the consciousness of a person who has identified himself with the law of the divine spirit and served this law remains awake and alert after the body has been put off; liberated from its chains, freed of the isolation of matter, it merges into eternal *light,* into *God.*

'The two tetrahedrons contained within each other represent the two poles of creation in complete equilibrium. All creation—the world of unrest and motion —is based on this divine equilibrium. It is the inner law operating through all forms and therefore in the crystallizations of matter also. As you've been able to see for yourself, the primordial form of matter, the cube, is built up around the divine tetrahedron. The triangles making up the faces of the tetrahedron are identical with the planes connecting the corner points of the cube. Man too, in his inner being, has a plane of contact with the divine *self.* And that's why he can only find his own divine being within himself, never by directing his attention towards the outside world.

'When man directs his attention towards the outside world, he is forced in accordance with divine law into more and more spiritual prisons, until after many pains and tortures, he finds *divinity.*

'But now let's examine the different kinds of forms of crystals based on the shape of the cube.

'Take six geometric forms which have the shape of a house roof and a base area exactly equal to that of the face of the cube, then place these six forms on the faces of this cube in such a way that their different edges are adjacent to each other.

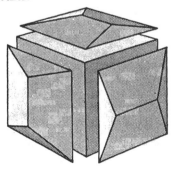 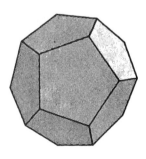

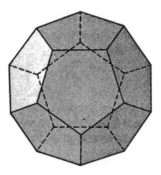

'In this way you form a geometric body which we call a pentagonal dodecahedron consisting of twelve equilateral pentagons. The pentagonal dodecahedron reveals further laws of the long path of the consciousness. But now we
want to look at the result manifested by the last crystal form in this series:
the icosahedron made up of twenty equilateral triangles.

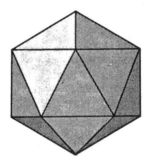

'Thus starting with the tetrahedron we can develop a total of *four* regular
crystal forms with equal areas: the tetrahedron, the cube, the pentagonal
dodecahedron and the icosahedron.
'It is only possible to form regular crystal shapes from triangles, rectangles
and pentagons: from triangles, the tetrahedron, the octahedron and the icosahedron: from squares only the cube; from pentagons only the pentagonal
dodecahedron.
'Except for the octahedron you are already acquainted with all these geometrical bodies. You can construct an octahedron by drawing three equally
long lines, one in each of the three dimensions—length, breadth and height—
at an angle of 45° in such a way that the middle of the three lines is identical.
When you join the endpoints of the three lines, you form the eight triangles
which go to make up the octahedron. Thus you see the octahedron consists of
two pyramids joined at their base, one standing normally, the other upside down.

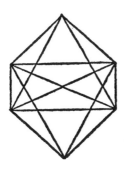 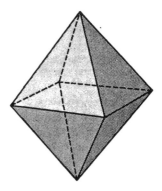

'And now pay very close attention. If we cut the octahedron with planes at equal distances from each other and pass through in each of the three dimensions, we create innumerable little octahedrons. But these octahedrons *do not fill the space in the big octahedron. On the contrary, the spaces between the little octahedrons form little tetrahedrons just as you observed in the space within the cube.* You can divide up the space in an endless number of larger or smaller octahedrons, and the little tetrahedrons in between will always be there. Thus you can see that in every one of its points three-dimensional space is based on the divine tetrahedron representing absolute harmony and absolute equilibrium.

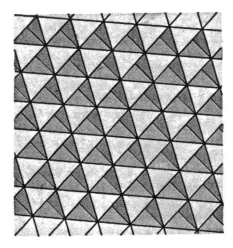

'In just the same manner all of visible creation rests in every one of its points on the *divinity* which stands above all manifestation, reposing unmanifested within itself. *God* is *omnipresent*!

'But now let's come back to the various geometric bodies contained within each other or superimposed on each other: tetrahedron, cube, pentagonal dodecahedron and icosahedron. Here are some further laws revealed by their relationships.

'If we take half the number of faces of each of the geometric bodies we've talked about—the tetrahedron, cube, pentagonal dodecahedron, and icosahedron, we get the numbers 2, 3, 6 and 10. If we multiply these numbers together, we get the number 360, the number of degrees in the circle. And if we add these numbers together, we get 21, the number of possible connections between the seven factors of the key number of the three-dimensional world, the number 7!'

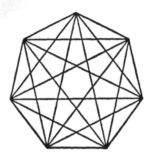

Ptahhotep stops speaking, and I stand before him in silence and awe.

'Now you may go, my child,' sayd Ptahhotep, 'you've had enough for today. Next time we'll talk about the four sides of the pyramid. They contain further truths. If you want to attain complete self-recognition, they're very important for you.'

I bow and leave.

4. And, looking, I saw a storm-wind coming out of the north, a great cloud with flames of fire coming after one another, and a bright light shining round about it and in the heart of it was something coloured like electrum.

5. And in the heart of it were the forms of four living beings. And this was what they were like; they had the form of a man.

6. And every one had four faces, and every one of them had four wings.

10. As for the form of their faces, they had the face of a man, and the four of them had the face of a lion on the right side, and the four of them had the face of an ox on the left side, and the four of them had the face of an eagle.

12. Every one of them went straight forward; wherever the spirit was to go they went; they went on without turning.

14. And the living beings went out and came back as quickly as a thunder-flame.

15. Now while I was looking at the four living beings, I saw one wheel on the earth, by the side of the living beings, for the four of them.

16. The form of the wheels and their work was like a beryl; the four of them had the same form and design, and they were like a wheel inside a wheel.
17. The four of them went straight forward without turning to one side.
18. And I saw that they had edges, and their edges, even of the four, were full of eyes round about.
20. Wherever the spirit was to go they went; and the wheels were lifted up by their side: for the spirit of the living beings was in the wheels.
22. And over the heads of the living beings there was the form of an arch, looking like ice, stretched out over their heads on high.
26. And on top of the arch which was over their heads was the form of a king's seat, like a sapphire stone; and on the form of the seat was the form of a man seated on it on high.
27. And I saw it coloured like electrum, with the look of fire in it and round it, going up from what seemed to be the middle of his body; and going down from what seemed to be the middle of his body I saw what was like fire, and there was a bright light shining round him.
28. Like the bow in the cloud on a day of rain, so was the light shining round him. And this is what the glory of the Lord was like. And when I saw it I went down on my face, and the voice of one talking came to my ears.

Ezekiel, I

THE FOUR FACES OF GOD

Again I stand before Ptahhotep.

'My child,' he begins, 'today you'll learn what the four faces of God are.

'It will help you very, very much to recognize them *in you*. The four faces of God are in everything that has been created. All of creation—*including yourself*—has been built up on his four faces.

'Life in the visible world, beginning with the gigantic central suns of the world systems and running all the way down to the tiniest protozoa is merely a rotation *around* the four faces and *in* the four faces of God.

'You know why we always represent divinity in its primordial state of *resting within itself* as an equilateral triangle. God in his three aspects is *one in three* and *three in one*. But this condition—just like the equilateral triangle—carries within itself the possibility of the number *four*. When the three aspects of the basic number *one* separate from each other—and this happens when they move from the unmanifested into the manifested state—the "*one in three*" becomes "*one and three*". In this way the number *four* is born.

'Cast a glance at the equilateral triangle: in it you see only one *unit* which has three sides, three aspects. But it contains, hidden and unmanifested, the number *four*, because the equilateral triangle can be divided up into four smaller equilateral triangles.

'When the triangle moves out of the unmanifested into the manifested state *in the three dimensional world*, a tetrahedron is formed.

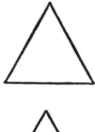

'As you have already seen, the first primordial form of material manifestation —the cube—contains the tetrahedron hidden and unmanifested within itself.

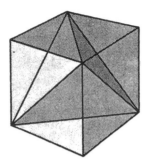

'The four triangles which make up the faces of the tetrahedron are the areas of contact between the divine and the material, as they are identical with the inner areas of the truncated corners of the cube.

'When we turn the triangles of the tetrahedron *outward* with the help of the corners of the cube, thus manifesting the triangles of the tetrahedron, we produce the four-sided shape of the pyramid whose four sides, at one and the same time, are *the four triangles of the tetrahedron turned outward* and the truncated corners of the cube turned outward.

'The four sides of the pyramid symbolize the four faces of God, each of which taken alone and by itself manifests the three aspects of the first source, the divinity *at rest within itself* and standing above all creation. The pyramid reveals a living reality, the living law, in which *God* always and absolutely manifests himself in the material world, and because he does so he is in-dwelling in everything that has been created.

'From every point of the universe *God* manifests himself four-fold. In each of the four directions of the earth and the sky he radiates with a different effect. And because these streams of force, which originate at one point and yet are so very different, all come forth from the paradisiacal unity, we can speak of them figuratively as four great rivers springing up in the centre of paradise, where the tree of life and the tree of the knowledge of good and evil are rooted, and flowing out into the external world in four different directions.

'You will find this four-fold manifestation in everything that has been created, most noticeably in the four characteristics of the great currents of air, the winds. Even the dullest person knows that the winds coming from the four different directions have completely different effects.

'The north wind is dry, cool, with a quieting and paralysing effect. In many parts of the world it even makes water hard as stone.

'The south wind always brings heat and has an arousing, vitalizing effect.

'The east wind is cool, refreshing.

'The west wind brings warmth and dampness—in many places rain. Its effect is fatiguing and soporific.

'This is something you already know, because every child notices the different effects of the four major winds. But have you ever thought about how this is possible? Have you ever wondered how it comes about that currents of air can start at the selfsame spot on the surface of the earth and have different effects depending on the *direction* in which they flow? If, for example, a wind arises right where we are now, where we feel the air to be pleasant and mildly warm, and if it blows southward, it is obviously coming from the north for people living in countries to the south of us. It brings them cool weather and has a calming effect on all living creatures. But when a wind starts up from where we are and blows northward, it's a *south* wind for people living to the north of us. It brings them warm weather and has a stimulating effect on the organs of reproduction of all living creatures. How is it possible for both a cold and a warm wind to originate at one and the same point on the surface of the earth—a tranquilizing and a stimulating wind—bringing dampness and rain to people on one side and dry weather to people on the other? It all depends on the *direction* in which the air is flowing.

'You see, *that* is the law of space we call the *four faces of God*.

'The first face—the north face—is *fiery* and has a vitalizing effect. That's why the south wind brings heat and stimulates living creatures to conceive new life.

'The second—the west face—is *airy* and cool. It makes everything movable, and that's why the east wind is refreshing.

'The third face of God—his eastern face—is *damp*, wet and lukewarm. It brings heaviness, inertia, warmth, dampness and precipitation, making all living creatures sleepy. Their consciousness withdraws into their bodies.

'And lastly the fourth face—the south face of God—is cold. It has a contracting, astringent, crystallizing, materializing effect. It brings cold and calms the nerves.

'The first and most important manifestation of the four faces of *God* is the *fiery* one, because the effects of the other manifestations—the other faces—depend on this one. The kind of fire determines whether the weather gets hot, warm, cool or cold. *That's why the fiery face of God is the father of the others.* As a result of its radiation, the various specific states arise: the warm and dry together produce the gaseous *airy* condition: the cool and damp the *aqueous*; while the cold produces the hard, earthly condition.

'You find this law operating everywhere here on earth, in every tree, in every plant. Take any house, for example. The south side which receives the currents from the north face of God is warm and plants grow best on this side. The north side is cold, the east side is dry and the west side is always damp. Whenever we make rain in the pyramid, the precipitation hits all buildings from the west.

'This fourfold aspect is not only to be found in the major winds, but in everything that has been created. Look at the trees. The northern side—exposed to the radiation from the cool southern face of God—is always covered with moss. Have you ever wondered why the human being has only one face, and that towards the front? In the direction in which we face we are fiery, giving, whereas when we turn our back on something we are cool towards it. Our limbs, too, are all directed forward, and we can radiate our willpower only in the direction in which we are facing. And why do we sleep best when lying in a north to south direction? Why do all animals lie down this way? Why are even birds' nests and ant hills built in a north to south direction? Animals have no intellect to understand the reasons why, but they feel the effect of quieting radiations coming from the north and vitalizing currents from the south. Instinctively they feel it's best for the circulation of their own current of life when they build their nests in a north to south direction and when they sleep this way.

'That's the secret of why a person who is seeking connection with God and praying should face north or east, but *never* south or west. In the north and in the east he can find forces that lead him towards spiritualization, whereas in the south and in the west he finds stimulation which leads his consciousness to identify itself with his sensual instincts.

'The effects of God's fourfold radiation are always the same throughout the entire universe. Every point in the universe—and this includes of course every point on the face of the earth—always receives exactly the same radiation from any given direction. *The four faces of God can never turn or shift. They always stand unchanged, immutable, facing in their original direction.*

'Wherever members of the divine race went, they taught the sons of men this profound truth in various ways depending on the characteristics of the people around them. Here where people understand geometric forms and can grasp truth intellectually, we expressed the truth about the four faces of God in the form of the pyramid. But there are other races of people more inclined to grasp divine truths as spiritual experiences. The members of our race who fled to such countries have built gigantic figures of stone to represent *divinity* in the form of a human figure sitting like a triangle and having a head with four faces, one looking in each direction.

'Both representations reveal the same fact: whenever the divine creative principle leaves its timeless spaceless condition in the unmanifested state to come out into the three-dimensional world and become matter, it manifests itself—*even while keeping its three aspects* —in the number *four*. The shape of the pyramid shows this clearly in that each of its *four* sides, standing on the square base, forms a *triangle* representing the three aspects of God. Thus the pyramid manifests *four* times *three*: the number twelve.

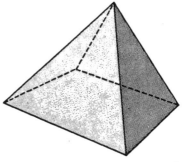

'And that brings us to another truth.

'As you can see from the symbolic representation in the form of the pyramid, each of the four faces of *God* contains the three divine aspects. This results in a *twelve-fold manifestation* which is present at every point of the universe and is acting in everything that exists, beginning with the individual creatures living on the planets and running throughout the planets to the suns and the systems of suns, throughout the universe, just like little circles in larger ones and larger circles in still larger ones, on and on to infinity. So if you understand one of these circles, you will understand the inner structure of the entire universe and of every single creature in it; *for the entire visible universe is based on this twelve-fold manifestation of God.*

'But before we go on, you must realise that *everything we human beings can perceive with our organs of sense from our personal point of view—that is from the outside—is the exact opposite of what exists in the divine state of being.* Everything you can see when looking at it from the outside—whether from above or below, from front or back, from the right or the left—turns into its exact opposite as soon as you stop *looking at it* and start *being it.* When you *look at* something, you're in a *dualistic relationship* to it. You, the observer, and what you see are two different poles. But when you *are* something, you're in a *monistic condition, in divine unity.*

'To show you an example, let's take a letter, say a letter "E". In what direction does this letter run ?'

'It runs from left to right, Father,' I answer.

'Good,' says Ptahhotep, 'now when I draw the same letter on your breast so that *you are this letter*, you're in a condition of unity with it, in a state of being with it. In what direction is it running now ?'

'From right to left, Father,' I answer.

'Yes, just the opposite. Come with me now and I'll show you something more.' Ptahhotep leads me under two large circular plates that hang from the ceiling and serve as lamps. They both have the same twelve pictures but running in opposite sequence and facing in opposite directions. On the first plate the

pictures all have their heads towards the centre, while on the second their heads are all toward the circumference. And the sequence from right to left on one is just the opposite of the sequence of the other.

Ptahhotep leads me to the first circle and asks, 'When do you see the pictures in the circle right side up?'

'Always, from any point along the side, Father.'

Then Ptahhotep leads me to the second circle and asks, 'How do you see these pictures?'

'All of them have their heads down, just the opposite of the pictures in the other circle, and they're all in the opposite sequence,' I answer.

'Now try to find the spot from which you can see all of these pictures right side up and in the right sequence.'

I look at the figures and as I *want* to see them right—with their heads up— I involuntarily step over to a point precisely *under*, and consequently precisely *in the centre* of the disc . . . and all of a sudden all the figures seem to change their positions! Now they're all standing right side up and in the correct sequence. I turn around slowly, continuing to stand in the centre . . . Each and every one of the figures is right side up. But when I move only a single step to the side, they're all the wrong way round again! I step back into the centre. Consciously and deeply moved, I experience the *state of being* . . . I understand what it means . . . the excitement of the discovery almost makes me dizzy.

Seeing how thrilled and moved I am, Ptahhotep smiles. 'Do you understand now,' he asks, 'why the personal is always the exact opposite of the *divine*? Do you understand why human script runs from left to right while the *divine runs from right to left*?'.

'Yes, Father of my Soul,' I stammer, trembling with excitement. 'I do understand.'

Ptahhotep takes my hand in his—oh, how quickly the mighty power of this blessed hand calms me—and leads me to a large blackboard where I see various geometric figures.

'The earth,' he continues, 'receives the twelve-fold radiation of force of the four faces of God from the direction of various constellations of stars. Taken together, these constellations surround us like a wheel. We call this huge wheel the "zodiac".

'It's owing to the effect of the radiations of the zodiac that the earth can exist at all. Their vibrations met in a point in cosmic space, causing an interference in the waves of energy and leading to condensation... materialization. Little by little our earth came into being through this process of materialization. As the sun played a great role in this process, the earth grew in the field of force of the sun and became its satellite. It receives its life energy from the sun, but it also is constantly receiving radiations from the zodiac and from its sister planets of our solar system.

'Just like all the celestial bodies, the earth represents the materialization of all these various radiations, and that's why for each step of earthly creation there is a form of materialization which primarily manifests the specific energy of the great cosmic wheel appropriate for the form of materialization concerned. That is to say that in rock formations, minerals, plants, animals and human beings here on earth there are the materialized radiations of each individual constellation of the zodiac, as well as of each individual planet. The names of the signs of the zodiac characterize the earthly forms that are the materialized manifestations of the constellations concerned. When you see a lion, for example, you should remember that on the animal plane he is the materialized radiation of the particular zodiacal sign we call "*Leo*" or "*Lion*". But at the same time there are minerals, plants and people made up of the same energy, but on the mineral, plant or human plane.

'Since the name of each individual sign of the zodiac is also the name of the form created by the materialized radiation from this zodiacal sign, this name is obviously the most appropriate *single word* with which to characterize perfectly the radiation from this constellation.

'The four faces of God—that is the four cardinal points—in the vault of stars, *in the divine condition of being,* are:

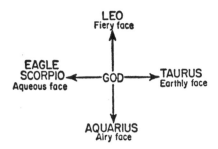

'Each face of God, each cardinal point of the vault of heaven, contains within itself the three aspects of the unmanifested *divinity,* and so the *twelve signs of the zodiac* come into being:

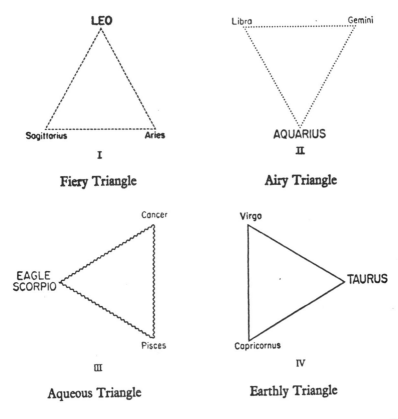

LEO Sagittarius Aries I **Fiery Triangle**	Libra Gemini **AQUARIUS** II **Airy Triangle**
Cancer EAGLE SCORPIO Pisces III **Aqueous Triangle**	Virgo **TAURUS** Capricornus IV **Earthly Triangle**

'The three *fiery* aspects of the first face of *God*, of the first group, are revealed in three constellations called *Aries, Leo* and *Sagittarius*.

'The *Lion* is the first manifestation of *God* and consequently the *great father of the entire zodiac*. That's why all three manifestations of the first face of God have a *fatherly*, life-giving character.

'The *Ram—Aries*—radiates the fire of youth, the procreative power of the young father who penetrates the bosom of nature, awakens new life, and sets it in motion. The *Ram* is the power of *spring* which in its effect is just as wild and heedless, just as rammish as the ram itself.

'The *Lion* is the fire of the perfectly developed, dignified and respectable man, the mature father who radiates his creative power, his love and warmth towards all his children as he brings them up in affectionate care. The *Lion* is the power of *summer*.

'The *Centaur* (*Sagittarius*) is a being that has grown beyond its animal nature, overcome its physical desires and aimed its consciousness towards the high goal.

247

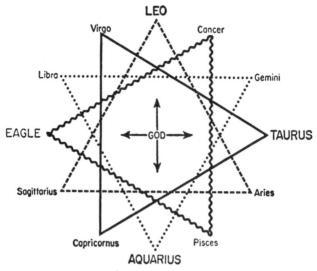

LEO

Virgo   Cancer

Libra .... Gemini

EAGLE   ←—GOD—→   TAURUS

Sagittarius ◄------------------► Aries

Capricornus   Pisces

AQUARIUS

The four faces of *God* in the divine state of being.

Its radiation is the fire of the spirit, of the wise and mellow father who goes on helping his mature children with his spirituality, good thoughts and sage advice. The *Centaur* or *Sagittarius* is the spiritual fire of thought, the power of age, of *winter*.

'The three aspects of the second group, of the *earthly-material* face of *God* are: *Taurus*, *Virgo* and *Capricornus*, or the *Bull*, the *Virgin* and the *Goat*. All three manifestations of this face of *God* reveal a *motherly* character.

'In the springtime the bull stands in a green meadow, and all of nature is decked out in the beautiful clothing of a bride on her wedding day, ready to receive all the procreative power of her bridegroom. The radiation of the zodiacal sign of the *Bull* enables the earth to *receive* the fiery power of life and let it *take root*. Thus the divine seed is able to incarnate itself in an earthly body. The *Bull* radiation makes it possible for the divine *self*, the creative principle, the *logos, to become flesh*. The *Bull* awakens the power of conception in matter—in the female of the species—calling the *bride* to readiness. The *Bull* represents that aspect of incipient maternity in which the mother-to-be is ready to conceive.

'*Virgo*—the *Virgin*—is the spotless queen of heaven, the mother goddess of nature who has never been touched by a male and yet is pregnant with myriad creatures that are born from her divine body. The power of the sign of the *Virgin* is the fertility of nature, and that's why she is shown holding in her hand a spike of grain with five kernels. In the mystic world the *Virgin* is the human soul which, purged of all earthly dross, has become spotless and has received the divine seed from the spirit of *God*. Thus she is expecting the divine child in

248

which both principles—the *divine* and the *material*—are blended into perfect unity. Thus *Virgo* is the pregnant, expectant aspect of maternity.

'The third aspect of the earthly face of God is *Capricornus, the Goat*. This animal lives in the region of the hardest matter on earth, stones, rocks and boulders. The *centripetal* force of the law of matter causes matter to reach the highest degree of hardness and consequently *crystallize*. In the crystal, matter overcomes itself, losing its original characteristic of opacity and becoming perfectly transparent. In the crystal, matter reveals the original geometric forms of the creative power. A child, too, is the solidified, crystallized form of the divine creative power of life. Through the law of matter, through the centripetal, compressive *power of concentration*, the achievement of the divine *self*, the divine child—consciousness—is born in the soul of man.

'As long as man identifies his consciousness with his animal instincts, he is like a stable in which animals are living. In this stable and surrounded by animals, the divine child—the divine consciousness—must be born. This takes place through the concentrating effect of the sign of *Capricornus*. The only path which can lead man back to unity, back into the lost paradise, is that of concentration. That's why the birth of the divine child is celebrated in the month when the sun stands in the sign of the *Goat*. The radiation of this centre of force helps man fully to manifest and achieve the *divine in* and *through* matter—in the body. *Capricornus* is the parturient aspect of the maternal.

'The three aspects of the third group, the *vaporous* face of *God*, are *Gemini*, *Libra* and *Aquarius*, or the *Twins*, the *Balance* and the *Water Bearer*. The vaporous combination state arising through this radiation gives movement. That's why these three constellations are favourable for the manifestation of forces which require free and unhindered movement. They are *spiritual* in character.

'The sign of the *Twins* carries within itself the two halves of the tree of the knowledge of *good and evil*. Its radiation takes effect in two directions. It causes man to look to the left and to the right in order to gather knowledge and experience. It causes man's pathway through life to branch out like the limbs of a tree. Man goes forth to seek knowledge on the most devious paths that lead off in various directions. Seeking experience, people want to see everything, hear everything, learn everything. The radiated power of *Gemini* manifests itself as the urge to learn.

'The radiation of the *Libra* constellation forces everything into equilibrium. All the experiences man has collected are laid in the scales of the balance and weighed. What's valuable is kept; what's worthless is thrown away. The effect of the *balance* is one of harmony, developing man's powers of discrimination, and bringing the two-sided forces of *Gemini* into equilibrium. The sign of the *Balance* radiates the law of equilibrium and justice into the three-dimensional world. It is the manifestation of law-giving knowledge.

'The constellation *Aquarius* radiates the knowledge that has been gathered under the sign of the *Twins*, weighed in the *Balance*, found worthwhile and codified into laws. The radiated energy of this sign brooks no let or hindrance and knows no bounds. The *Water Bearer* gives, passes on treasures to others, untiringly pours the water of life out of his vessel, letting its waves flow on to the remotest worlds. These waves are the all-vitalizing high-frequencies of the spirit. The *Water Bearer* is the manifestation of the unhindered spirit freed of all bonds.

'The three aspects of the fourth group, the aqueous face of *God*, are: the *Crab*, the *Eagle* (*Scorpion*) and *Fishes*, or *Cancer*, *Scorpio* and *Pisces*. The three manifestations of this face of *God* have an emotional character which manifests itself in feelings.

'The Zodiacal sign *Crab* symbolizes the little water of the hole in which the crab lives. After it has caught its prey outside, it withdraws into its hole to digest it. The consciousness which was directed towards the outside in order to find spiritual nourishment withdraws to digest and transform its prey—the impressions it has collected—into clarified and organized experiences. The radiated power of the zodiacal sign of the *Crab* manifests itself as the introspective, self-analysing consciousness of the truth-seeking individual.

'The sign of the *Scorpion-Eagle* represents the great turning point when the crawling worm is transformed into a high-flying eagle, redeemed, a being that has awakened and become conscious in the divine *self*. The worm—*Scorpion*—must kill itself in order to become an eagle. That's why this constellation has a double name. In its unredeemed condition it is called *Scorpion* after the animal that can kill itself with its own sting; in its redeemed condition it is called *Eagle*, symbolizing the free soul flying high above the material world like the divine falcon *Horus*.

'The radiation of this constellation is the driving force, the fire of life, which manifests itself in this form through water—through the fluids of the body. This force enables the spirit to clothe itself in matter in order to be born anew in the body. This energy is the original serpent of temptation, enticing the spirit into matter and causing its fall from paradisiacal unity. When, however, instead of operating in the material plane, this force is transformed and transmuted, becoming purely spiritual, sexual desire is transformed into an uplifting force which helps the fallen consciousness return into paradisiacal unity. *Without this force no consciousness that has fallen from unity can find its way back into God!* The water of this constellation is like a swamp in which hidden fermentation is going on and over which, without actually burning, little fiery will-of-the-wisps are dancing.

'The *Fishes* dwell in the endless ocean. Although they sometimes come to the surface, they submerge again and disappear in the immeasurable depths. The true nature of man is similar to the ocean. His consciousness is on the surface, but by far the greater and deeper part of him lies in the unconscious where the reasons and the roots of his thoughts, words and deeds originate.

'On the other hand, the person who has achieved redemption and attained complete and perfect recognition of self, whose consciousness has been initiated in his divine *self* and achieved realization in his *self*, no longer has a subconscious and a super-conscious. That is to say, there is no longer a part of him that is unconscious. Figuratively speaking, he swims, completely conscious, in the depths of the limitless ocean of the divine *all-consciousness*. What the unredeemed person recognizes—or often enough, does not recognize—as the "unconscious" has become his home and element in which he is perfectly conscious. The two manifestations of sex—the male and female—are as happy as two carefree fish in the ocean of perfect harmony. The effect of the sign of the *Fishes* is redemption, dissolving away the personal in the impersonal, in the depths of the limitless *self*, in the divine and indivisible *unity of all one being*. The great work of redemption is completed by the radiation of this power, the spiritualization of matter is achieved.

'You see, the three aspects of each triangle are related; starting on the material plane, they progress upward in the direction of spiritualization.

'But there's not only a relationship between the three aspects of each of the faces of *God*; the four triangles are actually so related that their centres are identical. In this way they make up the zodiacal circle of twelve revelations, such that the various aspects of the four triangles form an inter-related series of steps in development and progress. Then there is still a third relationship between the individual constellations, namely the one between *opposite constellations, each of which is a complementary half of the other.*

'First, let's discuss the relationship of the steps in development.

'The series naturally begins with the constellations of the *Ram*, as the beginning of all expressions of life—and hence the beginning of springtime—lies in the *Ram*. But you should take note of the fact that there are two "beginnings of springtime", one *absolute* and one *relative*. *Every manifestation of life—including the earth and all the creatures living on it—carries within itself "the absolute beginning of spring" or "springtime point". This absolute springtime point is independent of the outside world. On the other hand, the relative springtime point depends on the position of the stars at any given moment. Thus because of the various movements of the earth, it doesn't stay at the same place but is constantly changing its position.* We'll go into all this more thoroughly later.

'The signs of the zodiac run in this sequence: *Ram, Bull, Twins, Crab, Lion, Virgin, Balance, Scorpion-Eagle, Centaur, Goat, Water-bearer, Fishes.*

'Everything that condenses into matter is manifested on the material plane and runs in its own lifetime through the full circle of the zodiac. The life of the individual human being is one great period that is divided up into smaller periods—childhood, youth, maturity and senility; these in turn break down into still smaller periods: years, seasons, months, weeks and lastly days.

'All the shorter periods of man's life too—days, years and so on—also run through the full circle of the zodiac. His birth corresponds to the *Ram*. Then one after the other, he runs through all the signs of the zodiac, reaching maturity in the *Lion* and dying under the sign of the *Fishes* when he disappears from the material plane. In just the same way our days begin with our awakening from sleep and appearing in the world. The day develops, reaches maturity and its culmination point at midday and then starts to decline. After further changes we come to the evening when we put away our bodies to rest and sleep, withdrawing our consciousness into the *self* and falling asleep—just as we do at the end of our earthly lives when we put away our bodies for the last time. Every period has its beginning, development, culmination, decline and dissolution.

'The individual signs of the Zodiac have the following main characteristics:

'The *Ram* sees to it that something *appears* or is born in this world in the first place, and this is equally true when the actual time of birth doesn't fall under the sign of the *Ram!* That's because every birth, irrespective of the outside world and of course irrespective of the various constellations, carries within itself the power of the beginning, and this power we call the *Ram* both outside in the vault of the stars and inside each individual being. That's the *absolute* side of the *Ram* in every created form. And the relationship is just the same with all the other constellations, with all manifestations of life, and with all the aspects of the four faces of *God*. There is always an inner, *absolute* manifestation and an outer, *relative* manifestation.

'After birth, every new creature must get its roots down wherever it is. This it does with the help of the *Bull*. The new creature takes in food and assimilates it. This gives it a material connecting link with the outer world and creates a line of supply for its body.

'Under the influence of the sign of the *Twins*, the new creature begins to gather experience, and his pathways begin to diverge, going into all kinds of ramifications like the branches of a tree. The creature develops in different directions and gains extensive knowledge.

'In the *Crab* it draws back into its home again to digest its spiritual gains— the experiences it has gathered. Its inner core begins to develop.

'Through the life-giving, fiery effect of the *Lion*, the creature matures and gains dignity. It develops its powers and abilities and fulfils its earthly duty of begetting a new generation. It becomes father of a family.

'The *Virgin* brings the harvest. Man brings the fruits of his labours into his barn. In the depths of his soul the divine child—*universal love*—develops.

'In the *Balance* his deeds are weighed, the positive and negative credited and debited against each other. His attention is directed towards both sides, on the one hand the worldly and on the other the spiritual. Within himself he brings these two worlds into a perfect equilibrium, putting into effect, the inner, divine law which stands above and beyond everything that's relative.

'The sign of the *Scorpion* brings the solstice, the great turning point. Man must spiritualize the divine creative power which so far has manifested itself within him as a driving instinct and urge. He must now utilize this divine creative power in the service of others. This means he must completely overcome his person. He experiences the mystic death of his person, then resurrection and immortality in spirit. From now on he ceases to serve materialism.

High up above the earth, in perfect spiritual freedom, he flies like an *eagle*, like the sacred falcon *Horus*.

'Through the effect of the *Centaur* he becomes a great teacher like the *Centaur* itself, a being which has grown beyond the animal level, a being which now uses its animal body only in order the sooner to reach the great goal it clearly sees ahead. Its thoughts cut like lightning through the heavy clouds of darkness and ignorance. It passes its experience on to the next generation.

'In the sign of the *Goat* the divine child—universal love—is born in man's heart. It becomes identical with divine *self* and conscious in it. As the divine child that has been born in his heart becomes visible, man becomes clear as crystal. In his words and deeds, he reveals universal *love*.

'In the *Water-bearer* the creature pours out and scatters its treasures. It has become the shining, resplendent child of *God* standing above and beyond sexuality. Radiating itself, it is the source of the highest divinely spiritual power. The process of transformation and de-materialization begins.

'In the sign of the *Fishes* the living creature experiences a re-unification with its hidden complementary half. This means, of course, that matter is disintegrated. The creature returns to its heavenly home, to *universal unity*, to *God*. Its consciousness glides over into *cosmic consciousness*, it casts off its body, and ends its earthly life.

'That's the path that every individual follows, even though he may not yet have reached the highest levels of consciousness. The steps of development may be different, but the circle of development is always the same.

'Now let's look at how the opposite signs of the Zodiac supplement each other:

'The powerful, impulsive strength of the *Ram* is regulated by the Law of the *Balance* which tames the *Ram's* blind forces and guides them into the right channels.

'The bridal power of the sign of the *Bull* supplements and satisfies the instinctive procreative urge of the *Scorpion*.

'The maternal power of the *Crab*, retiring to the shelter of its own hearth and home, is the complementary "other half" of the crystallizing, parturient radiation of the *Goat*. The newly born child belongs to mother.

'The paternal radiation of the *Lion* finds its "other half" in the childlike power of the *Water-bearer*. The father supports, protects and educates the child.

'The youth in the sign of the *Twins* with his eagerness to learn, receives the knowledge he is thirsting for from the great teacher, *Centaur*.

'The heavenly *Virgin*, bearing the divine child in her holy womb, receives nourishment from the mystic world of the two *Fishes*.

'Now you understand the radiations of the four faces of *God* in the varying effects of the different constellations. But in order to understand the life of the universe and the lives of the myriads of living creatures—including your own—you need to know that the circle of revelation, with its twelve centres of power, affects every point of the universe independently of the constellations. And because the four faces of *God* can never turn around, each constellation emits different radiations of power in the various directions of the sky. Thus the radiation is determined by the everlasting, never-changing *direction* of the four faces.

'Let's take the constellation of the *Lion* for example. In the direction of the south it emits the radiation characteristic for the lion, while towards the opposite side, to the north, it sends out the power of the *Water-bearer*, in a westerly direction, that of the *Eagle*, towards the east, that of the *Bull*, in the north-north-westerly direction, that of the *Virgin*, towards west-north-west, that of the *Balance*, and so on, a different radiation in each direction.

'Now you understand that these radiations are not dependent on the *place of the group of stars*, but rather on the *direction* from which they come. Just like the wind has different effects, depending only on the direction in which it blows, not on the place in which it starts.

'And now here's another very important fact: because everything manifests itself *outwardly from its own centre*, and because the four faces of *God* radiate absolutely equally and unchangeably from every point, everything—whether it's a central sun, a sun, a planet, plant, animal, protozoon or human being—is always in the centre of *two* wheels: in the centre of the great *cosmic wheel* and—since this centre is identical with the centre of the individual being concerned—also in the centre of one's unmanifested being, one's own *inner wheel*.

'We *receive* the radiations of the great cosmic wheel from the outside while those of our own wheel are *emitted* from the inside.

'We are identical with the situation of the earth which has fallen out of the divine being. The earth is not in a central spot in the universe, but rather a satellite of the sun, orbiting around the sun and rotating about its own axis. That's why we see everything in the universe as the exact opposite of what it is in reality, in the divine state of being. Seen from our position on the earth, the whole vault of stars—with all its cosmic systems, solar systems and planets—appears to rotate around us. But in reality the opposite is happening. It's not the vault of stars that's rotating around us, but rather our earth that is orbiting around the sun, our sun with our entire solar system moving in a larger orbit around a cosmic sun, and the latter—with all of its cosmic system—moving around a central sun, and so on in ever-greater orbits and ever-greater cosmic systems, on and on into infinity.

'And even the life of celestial bodies in cosmic systems is nothing other than movement and development in the great cycles of the four faces of *God*, in the Zodiac. But just remember that *every manifestation, every created form, regardless of where it is in the universe, carries within itself both the great cosmic wheel and its own little wheel, irrespective of whether it's a protozoon, a plant, an animal, a human being or celestial body.* You'll consider this quite a matter of course when you understand that *every point of the universe radiates the same twelve-fold manifestation of the four faces of God—without these latter being able to change their position.*

254

'The radiations of energy which we receive from the great cosmic wheel come to us from the outside; that's why we see the circle wrong side to, just like a mirrored reflection of the divine condition of being (see illustration, page 244).

'Because the vault of stars, as seen from our standpoint on the earth, is always in motion, there is a corresponding change going on constantly in the composition of radiations reaching the earth from all the countless stars moving along their individual paths in the gigantic cosmic wheel. Every created form— including every human being—has its own *individually composed structure of forces* made up of the same creative forces that radiate from the stars in the universe. At the moment of birth the structure of forces in the individual's own little zodiac wheel is identical with that of the forces in the great cosmic zodiacal wheel. And this leads us to something else that you should know, namely, *that a living creature can be born only when these two structures of forces coincide with each other completely.*

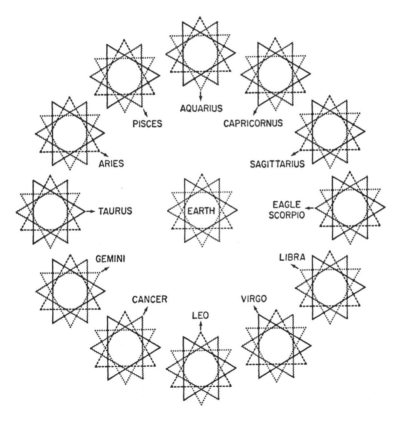

The position of the earth in the four faces of God which can never turn around

255

'Until the end of his life on this earth, man is constantly subjected to new impressions, new experiences and all kinds of other influences. As he gathers experience, his own inner constellation is modified to a great extent. Many forces are developed, many others get pushed into the background, depending on the individual's reactions to his deeds and his experiences. *The inner constellation a creature has at the moment of its death is stamped indelibly upon its soul, and the latter cannot be reincarnated until the vault of stars, in its constant movement, comes into the same constellation.* This is why some people are reincarnated again after only a very short time while others may even have to wait thousands of years until the stellar constellations match those they carry in their souls.

'All the creatures that are being born into the three-dimensional world every moment throughout all eternity ended their previous incarnation under the same constellation as the one which existed at the moment of their birth in this incarnation. *The death constellation in one incarnation and the birth constellation in the next are always absolutely identical. On the other hand, the birth constellation and the death constellation for any given incarnation are never identical, because the individual living creature concerned is changed through the experiences it has.* But every creature—*including man*—carries within itself the imprint of the constellation reigning at the moment of its birth, and it carries this imprint through its entire life. This constellation contains the creature's own individual wheel in which its subsequent development and character changes are hidden.

'So if you want to know the inner birth constellation of the forces that have built a living creature and are working in its soul, in its body, in its entire being—*and consequently also in its fate*—you have to figure out the constellation the stars had at the moment of its birth.

'Because of the steady movement of the stars in the sky, the relationships within the two wheels—the cosmic and the individual—are constantly shifting. The centres of energy in the cosmic wheel—the constellations, the fixed stars and the planets—and the hidden centres of power of the individual wheel move away from the identical patterns they had at the moment of birth. After a time these patterns of power within these two wheels can approach each other again. That's why in the life of each individual there are favourable and harmonious relationships at certain times and unfavourable disharmonious relationships at others. As a result, the creatures concerned sometimes reveal harmonious-positive characteristics and disharmonious-negative characteristics at other times. And because fate is the mirrored reflection of character and the result of the individual's deeds, its life takes favourable turns sometimes and unfavourable ones at others.

'All forms of life are subject to these forces, *and only one creature has the possibility of ruling over all these energies and forces at work throughout the universe, within its own being and within its own destiny. This creature which has the ability to control these forces at will is man. But he can control them only when he is conscious of them, recognizes them in himself and overcomes them!*

'As long as man does *not* recognize these forces in himself, he is just as much at their mercy as all the unconscious forms of life which are directly in contact with all these creative forces and willy-nilly controlled by them. Only the human being who has attained the ability of self-recognition is able to rise in his consciousness above these forces. Instead of being at their mercy in an unconscious way, he is able to control them or transmit them in a transmuted and completely changed form. When man is able to transmute the creative forces within himself, he is also able to transmute the forces operating within his destiny, thus controlling his own fate.

'Now you understand why it is necessary and important to know about the twelve-fold radiation of power of the four faces of *God* within yourself, and why it is essential to learn to control it. *When you realize that only your body and the material part of your being is built up out of these forces, whereas your divine self stands above them and is able to control them*—you yourself can regain control over these tremendous creative powers, the same control you lost when you were born into the material world. When you realize this, you can liberate your *self* which in your body has been crucified on two great beams of the material, three-dimensional world—*time*, and *space*. Your *self* which has been repressed and forced into your subconscious is liberated, resurrected from its apparent death and reinstated on its throne. This mystery of life is symbolized by the cross with the divine form crucified upon it, representing the second aspect of *God*. The creative principle clothes itself in matter and for aeons of time makes the supreme sacrifice of taking upon itself the characteristics of the material world in order to animate it and fulfil its great task of spiritualizing matter by completely revealing the spirit in matter.'

— 35 —

THE EPOCHS OF THE WORLD

I STAND before *Him*. *He* begins: 'The earth and its inhabitants are not yet conscious of the forces which reach the earth from out of the cosmos and maintain it. Consequently the inhabitants of the earth aren't able to control these forces and transform them at will. The earth receives these radiations from out of the cosmos and is immersed and bathing in these waves of energy. Everything that happens on earth is a direct reaction to the action of these radiations ... a kind of resonance resulting from their inter-action.

'*The sun magnifies to a tremendous extent the radiations of the particular constellation in which it stands at any given moment as it radiates its force to the earth simultaneously with the radiations of the constellations concerned.* This fact has a bearing on the way in which the four seasons have come into being.

'The movements of the earth give us the impression not only that the vault of stars is rotating about us, but also that other movements are taking place. One of the most important movements the earth makes is that its axis describes the surface of a cone. Whereas one of the end points of the earth's axis remains relatively fixed, the other describes a circle. Because of this movement, the vernal point in the cosmic wheel is slowly displaced. Seen from the earth, it appears to be moving backward.

'The time it takes for the axis of the earth to complete one full conical movement—moving from the vernal point in the zodiacal circle right round to its starting point again—corresponds to 25,920 terrestrial years. We call this a cosmic year. Divided by twelve, this number gives us a cosmic month, mainly 2,160 terrestrial years, the time it takes for the vernal point to move through one zodiacal sign.

'The vibrations from the cosmos have such a great effect on the earth that they even influence world history. The leading ideas in religion, science and art are the result of the radiation of the particular constellation in which the vernal point is moving throughout the course of a cosmic month. The incarnated spirits on earth—that is to say humanity—must always achieve a new epoch by reaching a new milestone in human development and establishing themselves in the ideas of the time.

'A nation is a group of spirits, the incarnation of certain concentrations of energy. Each epoch brings to the earth a different group of spirits, a different race, and when this race has fulfilled its task of carrying out the new ideas and developing a new civilization for the space of a cosmic month, it leaves the earth in order to develop further on another planet. In every race, of course, there

258

are always individuals who don't quite "make the grade" before the end of the epoch. These remain behind, like the dregs in a drink, and must continue to develop on earth. That's the reason why a nation experiences a sudden decline after achieving a high point in civilization. The highly developed fathers of the nation are followed by degenerate and weak-willed descendants, and the nation which was once greatly esteemed gradually falls into debility and disrepute. These descendants are the dross of the nation which has reached the highest degree of earthly development, become spiritualized, and departed from the earth.

'The material world has come into being because interferences have occurred in the divine creative radiations traversing cosmic space, and these interferences have caused condensations, solidifications, materializations. If the celestial bodies were to receive pure, untransformed vibrations of the divine creative force, this would result in the immediate annihilation of all matter. The fixed stars—the suns—are the great transformers which convert the creative vibrations from all celestial bodies and transmit them in wave-lengths and frequencies that are tolerable for the earth. The transformed rays reach us from the fixed stars which form the constellations of the zodiac. Thus when we want to represent the highest divine radiation of energy, we choose the symbolic form of the constellation with the strongest effect on the earth, and this is always the "epoch-making constellation" through which the vernal point is moving at the time.

'We are now living in an epoch in which the vernal point is moving into the constellation of the *Bull. God (Ptah)* reveals himself to us in the radiation of this constellation, and that's why the divinity manifesting itself in the atmosphere of the earth is represented in the form of a *bull*, in the form of the divine bull *Apis*. The complementary constellation of *Scorpion-Eagle* is represented as the temptress—a serpent crawling upon the earth—or in the form of the divine falcon *Horus*. You know that this energy, as long as it is earthly and expresses itself on the low plane binding spirit to matter, is the serpent luring man back into further incarnations. On the other hand when this force is spiritualized, it helps man to experience, while still in the body, the highest degree of spirituality.

'We use the serpent *standing erect* as the symbol of initiation, as the mistress of the tree of recognition and knowledge. The initiate is a high-flying *eagle* who has spiritualized the serpent—the power of the instinctive urge—and manifests it as spiritual power through his intellect. The initiate is thus an instrument of the *divinity* which reveals itself through the zodiacal sign of the *Bull*. That's why in our epoch these animals are regarded as "holy animals" throughout the entire world. Now you understand why the initiates change their representations of *God* to accord with the constellation in which the vernal point falls at any given time. Above and behind all these symbols, of course, there always stands the unmanifested First Cause—*divinity resting within itself*.

'The constellation of the *Bull* belongs to the threefold manifestation in which the face of God has an earthly-material effect—contracting, drawing together and hardening. This means that at the present time the forces that build up matter and operate within it are the easiest and most immediately available forces for the inhabitants of the earth to use. Our task is one of *conquering matter* with matter, that means *conquering matter with the energies making up the essence of matter.* We use the frequencies of matter, these unseen and immeasurably powerful forces—in other words, *the spirit of matter*—in order to conquer matter itself. We charge the matter of the ark of the covenant with the entire octave of these energies and thus control the laws of matter—the forces of construction and destruction, materialization and dematerialization—as well as the weight of matter which we can either overcome or increase at will.

'In time our truths will come to flower. But then as celestial movements and changes continue, the earth will gradually move out of these regions in the cosmos in which certain specific energies are working together to produce our present epoch. Little by little certain of these energies will diminish, while new ones come into the picture, and thus the total pattern of vibrations affecting the earth will gradually shift. This means of course that the people being born into life on the earth will be gradually changing. The time will come when they won't understand our truths any more. The symbols and words we use to express the mysteries of the laws of creation will lose their content, becoming empty husks for thousands of years. Mankind will have to learn through new tasks and surmount new obstacles in their accomplishment.

'You already know what is going to happen when the last high priest has initiated the last candidate worthy of our knowledge. After giving this new initiate the ark of the covenant and a staff of life, the last high priest will lock himself and his assistant inside the great pyramid, block the entrance from the inside with a stone fitting into the opening . . . then the two of them will dematerialize all our equipment and apparatus and lastly themselves in order to save our secrets from falling into unworthy hands. Meanwhile the last initiate, who will come forth out of a nation destined to create a new epoch in the history of the earth, will salvage the ark of the covenant and his staff of life and have them carried out of this country. He will proclaim to his people the ideas of the new epoch in which the vernal point will move through a constellation of the *Ram*. The two complementary constellations of the *Ram* and the *Balance* will exert the strongest effect during that period.

'Come, my little daughter,' says Ptahhotep, 'Now I'll lay my hand on your head and you will see pictures of times to come.'

Ptahhotep leads me to a couch on which the neophytes, under his guidance, practise the ability of moving their consciousness freely throughout time, intentionally seeking out the past and the future in order to experience them as the present.

Ptahhotep bids me lie down, and no sooner has he laid his hand upon my brow than I get the well-known buzzing and prickly feeling in my head. The very next moment I see pictures which, in the symbolic language of dreams, shows me the *significance* of events in the distant future.

I see the reception room of the Pharaoh—a strange hall and an unknown Pharaoh who is not an initiate like my father but who has a radiation of a very low degree. Before him are two handsome, dignified men—two brothers with noble, magnificent features. From their radiations I recognize that one is an initiate while the other is only a quick-witted able speaker. The initiate is silent while his brother uses his powers of oratory. He is trying to convince the Pharaoh that he should free their people who are working as slaves in the service of the Pharaoh and let them leave the country under the guidance of these two men. The Pharaoh is hard of heart and refuses. He demands a miracle. Then the brother who is doing the talking takes his staff and casts it on to the ground in front of the Pharaoh. Instantly the staff turns into a serpent crawling over the ground. The Pharaoh calls his magicians to give the men an answer. They too cast their staffs upon the ground and these also turn into serpents. But the first serpent devours all the serpents of the magicians.

I interpret the vision. The staff represents the intellect, a powerful instrument. But when the intellect is bound to the earth and made to serve purely material ends, it becomes a serpent crawling on the ground, a wily temptress enticing man to selfishness. The two noble brothers struggle unselfishly for their people. In their hands guile turns into wisdom which destroys all the selfish arguments of the cowardly magicians.

Now the vision changes. The godlessness and selfishness of the Egyptians causes new plagues and afflictions of growing severity. But still Pharaoh does not yield. He still refuses to liberate the people from their bondage. Finally the gravest scourge of all descends upon him. All the first-born of the people and their animals, and even of Pharaoh's own household, are killed by the angels of God in a single night. *Only those who have eaten of the flesh of the lamb and have written their names with lamb's blood on their doorposts are not killed by the angels.*

What does the symbol mean? In the new epoch just coming, the complementary constellations of the *Ram* and the *Balance* will be dominant. During the time when the effect of the *Ram* constellation has not yet reached full strength, the effect is that of a *young ram,* in other words a lamb. In their blood, the people following this initiate have forces corresponding to the radiation of the *ram constellation.* They are the forerunners of the new epoch, the 'chosen people', able to proclaim to humanity the old truths in a new form.

Those who have fulfilled their destiny in the old epoch must now go. Their task is over. The angels of God call them home.

Then I see a new vision. The mighty initiate leads his people out of Egypt. And because the *Ram* is a *fiery sign,* a pillar of fire moves ahead of him to show him the way. He leads his people out of the spiritual darkness prevailing in Egypt at the end of this epoch. But Pharaoh's heart hardens again. He regrets that he has allowed these people to leave his country in freedom. With his entire army, he starts out in hot pursuit of the refugees. But the great initiate, in order to protect his people, uses his staff of life. He directs against Pharaoh's army the frequencies of ultra-matter which greatly intensify the earth's gravitational force. Suddenly, Pharaoh with all his warriors, chariots, and animals become as heavy as if rooted to the spot where they stand. Their tremendously intensified weight pulls them irresistibly down into the earth. And as all of this takes place on the seashore, the great waves of the sea finally roll over Pharaoh and his entire army.

I am amazed! Not about the effect of the staff of life, but about the animals! I have seen such strange and remarkable animals in Pharaoh's army. Some of them were pulling the warriors' chariots, while others carried warriors on their backs. The animals looked like zebras but were bigger and different in colour—brown, white, grey and even black! I've never seen such animals! Could these be the animals father once spoke about? Magnificent animals they are too!

But the vision changes. The initiate wanders with his people through the 'desert', in the always difficult transitional period between two epochs. Two different ages are never sharply separated from each other but rather flow into each other gradually. Hence there is a transitional period in which the effects of the two constellations—the old and the new—appear to be weakened because of their mutual interference. The old ideas don't satisfy the new generation any longer, while the old generations are unable to accept and assimilate the new ideas. The greater portion of the people turn back to their old, ossified ideas, that is, to the ideas of the constellation of the *Bull*. But these ideas no longer have the power of a full size bull. On the contrary, greatly weakened, their strength is only that of a little bull, a calf. In the symbolic language of dreams, spirit is always *gold*, and so in my vision of the future I see the people of the initiate *dancing about a golden calf and worshipping it*.

In the meantime the great initiate is 'on the mountain' and speaking 'face to face with *God*'. He is in the very highest state of consciousness, identical with *God*. He is the bearer of the will of *God*. It is God's will that he proclaim the new ideas to his people through two religious symbols, the sacrificial lamb, symbol of the constellation of the *Ram*, and the two tablets with God's ten commandments, symbol of the constellation of the *Balance*.

The sacrificial lamb is the divine *self* which, clothed in matter, allows itself to be crucified on the two great beams of the three-dimensional world, *time* and *space*, thus giving up its own life in order to save the earth through spiritualizing it.

The two tablets of commandments, like the ones in our temple, on the head of the sacred falcon *Horus*, symbol of the divine self, the creative principle traversing space, stand as symbols for the inner structure of the *self* manifesting itself in the soul as moral laws.

For more than two thousand years these divine truths will be the guiding ideas and the religious symbols of the people. These divine truths will be the challenge of the new epoch.

When the initiate brings the finished tablets of commandments and sees his people worshipping the golden calf, he bursts out in such a fit of rage that he dashes the tablets to the ground and smashes them in pieces while he asks *God* to punish the disobedient people.

Then came venomous serpents, symbols of the temptress, the snake, the driving force of the constellation *Scorpion*. The serpents fall down out of the sky and bite the people that have worshipped the golden *calf*. They suffer terribly from the poisonous bites. The initiate takes pity on the hapless people. In the middle of their camp he sets up two beams in the form of a 'T' and he places a brass snake perpendicular to it, *with its head up*. This is the symbolic representation of the tree of recognition and knowledge, the tree of the serpent. No longer creeping along the ground, but with its head upward, the serpent ceases to be the great temptress enticing people into the body and becomes a symbol of the highest wisdom leading men back into unity, to *God*. All the sick people who look upon this brass serpent quickly become well again.

Interpreting the vision, I understand that people who cannot or will not accept the ideas of the new era fall ill spiritually. They no longer find their place among people and fall into deep spiritual conflict. They can only be healed by being guided back into the mid-point of their own being where the tree of the serpent stands. When they look upon this tree—without eating of its *fruits*—they recognize the divine truths without exploiting them for their own selfish purposes, and they are healed. Wisdom and selfless omniscience heal every disease of the soul.

The visions of the future go on. The great initiate leads his people up to the threshold of the new epoch, up to the borders of the *promised land*. Then he goes up into a mountain and disappears. No one ever finds his body. I know that he has dematerialized himself just like the last initiated high priests have dematerialized themselves with their secret instruments and apparatus in the great pyramid.

The chosen people who are called to proclaim and carry out the ideas of the new epoch wander onward, guarding the wisdom and the secret teaching of their great master. But little by little the ark of the covenant loses its magical power, and there is no initiate left to recharge it with his staff of life . . .

A cosmic month goes by, and the axis of the earth moves a twelfth of the way around the surface of its conic orbit. Slowly the vernal point passes over into the sign of the *Fishes*. Once again people are unsettled. They can no longer find truth in the worn out, conventionalized ideas of the previous age. They resemble a herd of sheep without a shepherd. In this transitional period an avatar—*a son of God*—the great teacher of the coming epoch, is born with the supreme task of revealing the greatest mystery of creation by enabling *God* to walk *incarnate* upon the earth.

This *son of God* is the earthly image of the heavenly sacrificial lamb. Just as the divine *cosmic* self sacrifices itself, taking upon itself the matter of the three-dimensional world and the everlasting crucifixion of the two great beams of *time* and *space*, in this same manner this *Son of God* who manifests fully the divine *self* in his human body, must accept the vengeance of the spirit of matter as he undergoes death at the hands of ignorant people.

A person who in his consciousness identifies himself with his body lies in inner darkness and resembles a stable with animals—the animal-physical instincts—living in it. In this stable and in this darkness—just as in the darkness of night—the divine child is born, *the consciousness of the self*. Two kinds of people recognize the divine child and bow low before him: The plain, simple, unlettered and unlearned who do not yet know the doubting of the intellect and who live in unison with nature, like shepherds for example; and the knowing ones and initiates who have already travelled the long path of the intellect, have overcome their earlier propensity towards intellectual cleverness, and have learned to look at things with their inner sight after the manner of the wise men and mystics in the *East*.

The religious symbols of the new era are *Fishes* and the *Virgin*, the two complementary signs. The *son of God* chooses his co-workers from other '*fishermen*'. He pays the tax he owes to the earth with a golden coin which he takes from the mouth of a '*fish*'. He draws forth for humanity the nourishment of his teaching from these two complementary signs. But his teachings are heard by people of varying degrees of development. To those who have already awakened in spirit and have therefore attained the fifth level—the spiritual plane—to these 'five thousand' people he gives all his teachings, the two *fishes* and the *five loaves*, the five grains of wheat on the ear in the hand of the *virgin* in her symbolic representation. But even these 'five thousand' people who are already awakened in spirit cannot completely receive his highest ideas, not even in an entire epoch! Of the nourishment he has given there remain *twelve* baskets full of remnants. This means that humanity must learn the mysteries of the self in each manifestation of the twelve signs of the zodiac. In order to understand and attain these high truths, humanity needs twelve epochs, twelve ages, that is a full cosmic year—25,000 terrestrial years.

To all of those who have only been able to rise in their consciousness up to the fourth plane—the 'four thousand' people—the *son of God* does not distribute all the truths of the two signs of the zodiac as nourishment but only 'some' fishes and five loaves. But even this 'some' of his ideas is too much for them to eat, and there remain *seven* baskets of remnants. Materialistic people must first learn the mysteries of the seven planes before they are ready for the cosmic truths of the *self*.

The sign of the *Fishes* belongs to the aqueous triangle. Hence in this epoch humanity must stand up to the challenge of *water*. It must conquer *water* with *water*. And before my astonished eyes I see a machine by means of which people make use of the power of water transformed into steam. And I see great ships—like cities!—crossing the sea with enormous speed. They too are driven by the power of water transformed into steam. Mankind passes the test: it conquers *water* with *water*.

In medical science too water dominates the picture as a therapeutic agent.

Everywhere I see bathing establishments, spas and medicinal baths making use of water for all kinds of cures and treatments: Salt water baths, marsh baths, hot and cold baths, compresses, and many many other applications of water for the curing of physical ills. People even take advantage of the healing power in dew by walking about barefoot in the wet grass.

Then towards the end of this era when the vernal point approaches the next constellation—that of the *Water Bearer*—people make technical discoveries and inventions based on wave energies. This is one of the early effects of the budding *Water Bearer* era, an age of technical achievement. The radiation of the *Water Bearer* constellation, which knows no limitations and sweeps all obstacles out of its path, reveals itself in the ideas and social concepts of humanity. At the end of the era of the *Fishes*, these new energies cause great revolutions in the places where people react most powerfully to them. I see thousands of people of the ruling class sitting in prison, while a spirit with the characteristics of the new coming era decapitates or otherwise kills countless people of the upper class.

A vision from the time when the energies of the *Water Bearer* are working with full power shows me that the great teacher of this epoch abolishes all the boundaries between the three dominant religions. With his own person he proves that the inner core of all religions is one and the same truth, one and the same *God*. The boundary between religion and science disappears too, as people discover that everything, even matter, is a wave movement. They learn that the only differences between manifestations of the spirit and those of matter are differences of frequency, while in its essence *everything* is only the manifestation of the one, single, prime source of all forces, *God*. *Everything* is *a wave*, just as the symbolic representation of the *Water Bearer* constellation shows: a supernal being pouring waves out of his pitcher.

The spiritual movements on the earth show this effect. Science discovers the 'wave' theory, and I see countless inventions based on waves. I see pictures of people, landscapes and objects—pictures made by the effect of light waves. I see different kinds of devices which send out waves. Waves penetrate matter and reveal its solidity. There are waves that show what elements are present in the matter of the planets and fixed stars, electric waves, waves of sound, light and smell. Medical science has stopped giving treatments with water in favour of treatments based on *waves*. All kinds of waves, from infra-red to ultra-violet, short waves and still shorter waves, even more penetrating waves and frequencies . . . all in use by science!

The constellation of the *Water Bearer* belongs to the airy face of *God*. And mankind conquers the air with *air*, with energies won from matter in the airy state. I see people moved onward from the steam engine to other machines operated by gas. And then my astonished eyes follow huge locusts high up in the air, made by human hands and carrying people in their bellies! These machines are powered by gas: *Air* conquers *air* . . .

Through the complementary sign of the *Lion* people again recognize the strongest manifestation of God on earth. The sun, the great *Ra*, is again acknowledged as the prime source of all manifestation of earthly energy. Once more people have become sun worshippers, even though not in a religious sense. The influence of the *Lion* shows itself in another plane too. The effect of the *Water Bearer* is to abolish all boundaries, all limitations. But the absence of boundaries without a concentrating mid-point means mental disease, spiritual death. The boundlessness of the *Water Bearer* would affect the unconscious masses as a mental illness running throughout all humanity, causing anarchy and chaos, and destroying everything. Through the complementary sign of the *Lion*, however, dominion is concentrated in individual persons—dictators —who group the people about themselves and guide them.

In this epoch people discover traffic and intercourse with other planets. Boundaries and obstacles disappear, and with them the isolated state of the earth in cosmic space. And as the boundaries between countries disappear too, all humanity is governed from one centre. 'One stable, one shepherd.'

The eternal wheels roll on, and the earth moves into a new epoch, under the sign of the *Goat* and its complementary constellation, the *Crab*.

People direct their attention to the earth again, noticing that although their knowledge may be very great, they still know very little about their own marvellous mother, mother earth. In this epoch they solve the problem of conquering *earth*. The sign of the *Goat* belongs to the earthly face of *God*. People design a special machine based on the same principle as that of our ark of the covenant. With it, they control the weight of matter. That is, they can overcome the earth's gravitational pull, or through ultra-material radiations, they can vastly increase it. People communicate with each other directly through the earth—in the depths of the mountains—in short straight lines, instead of taking the long way around the earth. This new machine of theirs radiates an energy which dematerializes everything in front of it, thus moving forward quickly, freely, without let or hindrance. At the same time it spews out condensing and solidifying radiations behind it restoring the matter of the earth to its original condition. People have conquered matter with matter, with the energy of ultra-matter. This enables them to penetrate into the depths of the earth and harness for the service of mankind the enormous forces and energies raging there like primordial volcanoes.

The combination of the two zodiacal signs of the *Goat* and the *Crab* has a strong influence on the spiritual life of mankind. The great teacher of this epoch reveals unto man the mystery of the immeasurable sources of power hidden in the depths of the human soul. Those who hold the key to these sources of power possess abilities which the ignorant call 'supernatural'. All over the earth I see public schools where even little children are taught to attain these higher abilities through the kind of exercises which only candidates for the priesthood are permitted to practise in our temples. This high and wonderful knowledge spreads into ever greater circles, reaching ever greater numbers of people.

The visions suddenly pale as I come back to normal consciousness. Still lying on the couch, I'm almost dizzy from the tremendous experiences of the future. Ptahhotep stands in front of me and helps me get up. He ends his instructions for today:

'As you see, my child, the inhabitants of the earth receive their initiation in small groups and then in larger and larger ones, all inter-related one with the other. A person can be initiated individually *within his own lifetime*, and a *nation* can receive initiation if it works its way up to the highest level of development and fulfils its task here on earth. Eventually the whole world will receive initiation by completing the full circle of the four faces of *God*, experiencing step by step all stages of initiation in a systematic development, and finally achieving complete spiritualization—salvation from matter. Measured according to earthly time standards, it will take ages and ages for this development to be achieved. For countless times the earth will have to go through the zodiacal circle, both in terrestrial and cosmic years. I've shown you only the tiniest part of this exceedingly long path of development. The history of mankind on earth is not a matter of accident or happenstance. It's important for you to know that every step of development takes place according to divine providence, following a divine plan. A person can cover this infinitely long way in a single lifetime if he concentrates his will exclusively on this goal.'

As he gives me his benediction, Ptahhotep says, 'Come back again tomorrow; I have important things to tell you.'

— 36 —

FINAL PREPARATIONS

THE NEXT day I can hardly wait till evening to report to Ptahhotep. On the other hand, I've made enough progress in self-control for me not to let the reins slip out of my hand regardless of any amount of pressure external things may be exerting upon me. Fully conscious, I observe how external events affect my nerve centres, and I simply refuse to let my nerves get stirred up when I don't want them to. The moment their natural reaction begins, I move in with my consciousness between them and the action they have begun to take, and I consciously command my entire nervous system to become as calm and cool as a piece of steel.

But now, after Ptahhotep has told me he has something important to say, I can scarcely keep my heart from beating faster every time I think about it, and I think about it often.

Evening comes at last, and I walk through the long colonnade to his little reception room. Fully composed, I stand before him again.

Ptahhotep receives me as he always does. His noble face radiates something indescribably exalted, and so I have no way of knowing whether he has something special in mind.

'My little daugher,' he begins, 'you've progressed to the point that the ability of your mind to control all the natural forces in your body has been made completely conscious. From now on, it depends on your own will whether you give expression to a force or not. Neither in your mind nor in your soul nor in your body are you any longer a slave of nature. But I must point out to you that there still exists the possibility of your becoming a slave again. If you *consciously* apply your will, nobody and nothing can keep you from preserving your freedom... or from allowing yourself to be enslaved again by the forces arising from your own *self*. It is God's will—and therefore a law—that every spirit has complete freedom of will. No one may violate this freedom. That's why you should never stop exercising constant self-control and self-analysis.

'You are now ripe for initiation. But remember that the omniscience and the omnipotence conferred upon you by initiation includes commensurate responsibility. Carefully and thoughtfully, you must now finally decide whether you want to be initiated and, through initiation, take tremendous responsibility upon yourself.

'Stay home for three days and practise complete silence. If you are still determined to go through with initiation, your father will accompany you here on the fourth day, the day of the new moon, so that you can make your final preparations.'

I would like to tell Him that I am already determined, but I notice that He is perfectly aware of my determination. Nevertheless, the regulations must be observed, so I bow again and leave.

I use the three days first and foremost to take leave of everything to which I am personally attached. I know I'll be a completely different person when I come home from the temple as an initiate.

I wander about the garden again where once I walked with my mother among the flowers. I seek out all the favourite spots of my childhood where I used to play and later dreamed about life and what it would be like. In all these places I stand for a time in silence, taking leave of each tree and each flower, and simultaneously taking leave of the little girl who once was so happy here. Then I visit the gold-fishes in the great pond. I used to feed them when I was so small I could hardly walk, and a slender, delicate person dressed in white took me by the hand to keep me from falling into the water. Today again, I feel this fine, white, ethereal being near me. We are still closely attached, and I know that according to the laws of incarnation, just as she, like a door between the other world and this, helped me to be born, she will help me on again from this world over into the next. At last I come to the court of lions where I take leave of my favourite lions. Until I am initiated, I am only permitted into the court in the presence of the keeper. Today he accompanies me for the last time; as an initiate I too will have power over all animals and will no longer need his protection.

Only the lions used by the ruling family are kept here. One of them is the magnificent animal that always sits beside my father during his audiences as a symbol of his superhuman power. Then there are the lions that pull our chariot, and finally my own two animals, Shu-Ghaar and Shima. Both of them were sired by the lion my father has with him in his audiences. They're both equally intelligent, hypersensitive, wonderful examples of their race. Both of them love me just as if I were a lioness rather than a woman. Shu-Ghaar in particular is crazy about me and gets excited and jealous whenever I stroke Shima. I have to watch out that his love doesn't turn into blind and jealous rage. This would be dangerous! As I enter the court, Shu-Ghaar runs over to meet me and pokes his mighty head under my arm as an invitation for me to scratch his neck and ears and stroke his mane. Then, as usual, he tries to lick my face while I dodge as deftly as possible so as not to offend him and make him angry. I hand him a piece of warm meat, and while he devours it I get a moment to pat Shima and give him a piece of meat too.

On the third and last day father and I go out before sundown for a chariot ride with our lions. We race about with tremendous pleasure. In accordance with Ptahhotep's instructions, I am not allowed to speak, but even without this commandment, we wouldn't be talking anyway. We understand each other without words. Truth is like an invisible man. He can only make himself visible by putting on clothes. If he puts on a lot of clothes that fit loosely, we get only a very imperfect picture of him. The less he wears, the thinner and tighter his clothing is, the more exact the impression we get of him. But regardless of how well his clothing may reveal his shape, it still *covers* him, and we see *only the clothing but never the invisible person himself.*

It's exactly the same way with truth! The *less* words we use to express truth —that is, to cover it and make it visible—the better we can recognize it. But by the mere fact of expressing truth in words, covering it with words, we simultaneously keep ourselves from seeing *truth itself* in its immediacy, its nakedness, its true being. For people who cannot see into each other's minds, words are the only means of communication they possess. But they never see what the other is thinking and would like to say . . . only words about it. But we, father and I, see each other! Why should we cover our thoughts and our souls with words ? We are *here* for each other and enjoy the unity of *existence!*

The lions race ahead . . . we ride in silence . . . we both know what these last days mean.

Early in the morning of the great day I take leave of Menu and Bo-Ghar. Menu cries as hopelessly as if I were going to my own funeral. She has baleful forebodings of something terrible to come. There's simply no way I can console her. Little Bo-Ghar has no idea what's happening, but he cries bitterly too because he sees me going away and because Menu is crying. As I start to embrace him, he throws himself on his knees before me and puts his arms about my feet. From the very deepest depths of his soul, he cries out: 'O Queen, my dear Queen, don't forget what I swear unto you now: Any time, any place you are in danger, I'll save you! Even if I am at the other end of the earth, I'll come to you! Remember, as God is my witness, I'll save you!'

Dear little Bo-Ghar! He'll save me! But what from ? If Ptahhotep finds me prepared and ready for initiation, how could I get into danger ? And why is the boy saying that he would even come *from the other end of the earth* to save me ? He's here with me now; how could he possibly go so far away ? But I can't think about his words, for the time has come. I embrace them both, then walk over to my father's chambers.

Father receives me with a sad and earnest expression, and I see that he is withdrawn and deep within himself. Does he too see something baleful and forbidding in my future ? He embraces me, lovingly places his right hand upon my head, and blesses me. Then we go.

Ptahhotep awaits us in his little reception room. Before we enter, Ima appears for a moment in the long colonnade. His angelic face is beaming, his eyes smile at me with encouragement, and then he's gone again. I know that his love too will be accompanying me in the difficult challenging hours ahead. Father takes me up to Ptahhotep. He takes my hand and puts it into Ptahhotep's hand. Once again he gives me a loving look and then leaves the room.

'My dear daughter,' says Ptahhotep, 'a great circle of the law in which your destiny manifests itself in the world of time and space is closing today. This circle—your earthly career—was already determined and set the very moment you fell out of divine unity for the first time, just as a boomerang, at the moment it's thrown, has within itself the forces that determine the kind of circle it will make, how high it will rise, how much time its flight will consume, and when it will return to its starting point.

'Your present character and your destiny were built up by the same forces. Both of them are the result of cause and effect, actions and reactions, deeds and experiences through countless lives in which the *self* has manifested itself throughout ages and ages of time. All these actions and reactions, deeds and experiences have crystallized out in your present person and character. Your character determines your destiny and consequently your future. The *self* radiates its creative forces through the sieve of the character into the incarnation, and through picture-making forces in the depths of the soul, these energies create *dream pictures*. These latter project themselves outwardly into the material world where they manifest themselves as your "person" and your "destiny".

'The *self* radiates into every human being the same creative forces. The fact that so many different dream pictures and so many different persons and destinies arise from these same creative forces is the result of the different influences to which people have been exposed since their fall from paradisiacal unity.

'Whether the future projections of the *self* which have not yet materialized but are still waiting for materialization in the depths of the soul—in the subconscious—become "realities" on the material plane or whether they merely remain "dream pictures" depends on *the plane with which man identifies his consciousness. A "dream" is also "reality", only in the immaterial, picture-making energy world, while what happens on earth and what people call "reality" is also only a "dream", a projection of the self, the only difference being that it is a lower projection, working into the material plane, and visualized into the atmosphere of the earth.* Destiny is thus an incarnated projection of the future, a materialized dream.

'As long as a person allows the will of his *self*—the will of *God*—to rule, what happens on the material plane, in the so-called "reality", is what *he himself consciously wants*. Consequently he is also in control of his destiny. This is because a person's *self* has the power to take those dreams of his which are waiting in his subconscious for materialization and transform them into spiritual energy. On the other hand, the moment a person identifies himself with extraneous forces which are rising, not from within his *self*, but from within his lower nature, his body, and the moment he recognizes these forces as his own will, what happens is no longer what he *himself* wants but what his body wants, even though he may be fully convinced that this is his "own" will. In this way he loses control over his destiny and is completely at the mercy of the blind forces of fate. In this case, the "dream pictures" and projections lying latent in his subconscious unavoidably and with absolute certainty turn into "real" events on the earthly plane.

"In your initiation, before you re-awaken out of your physical consciousness into the divine *cosmic-self-consciousness*, the energies which you have created through your deeds and their reactions throughout ages and ages of time and which are now waiting in your subconscious for the time of their materialization—like seeds of future events—will *appear in your consciousness as dreams*. You can't destroy them because they come forth out of creative forces. But you can prevent these energies from coming down and turning into reality on the level of the material world. You can do this if you yourself, *with your consciousness, go down into the depths of your soul, where these forces are hiding in a latent state, and if you awaken them to life in your consciousness and experience these dreams yourself as full reality*. "To experience" means that you draw the forces that have been sent out back into your consciousness and live them as *states of consciousness*. In this way the inner tension within the forces is dissolved away. The energies then fade away, lose their power, and are destroyed.

'In your initiation you will experience your whole future destiny as a series of different states of consciousness—as dream pictures—without being conscious of either time or space. In this way you will become liberated from your "person" and thus from your own personal fate. You will continue to use your body as an absolutely impersonal instrument of *God*. This is because every initiate has the duty of continuing to work on earth in order to help other people out of the fetters of matter, out of the fetters of the body, out of the claws of blind fate, back into the divinely spiritual state of unity. Everything and everyone that has fallen into separation and into matter by virtue of becoming incarnated must find its way back home to the lost paradise, back to the divine state of unity.

'*But when an initiate works in the opposite direction, that is, when he uses his high spiritual energies to create personal realities for himself by directing the supreme, creative, all-penetrating forces from his divine consciousness into his body, he falls lower than an ordinary person who does the very same thing with his consciousness that has fallen out of the paradisiacal unity*. The ordinary person directs into matter only the forces arising from his material being. He experiences physical forces in his body, and for him this doesn't represent a fall. He manifests forces on the level from which they come. *Material forces remain on the material level*.

'The initiate, on the other hand, isn't just working with physical forces, and when he directs his high spiritual energies into the body, he falls from his high state and falls down low. The higher the energy the lower he falls.

'That's why you have to remember that as an initiate—it you want to become one—you can't do things that ordinary people can do with "impunity", because as an initiate you radiate and set in motion divine forces, not human ones. If you direct these forces into your body, you burn out your nerve centres and plunge into the lowest depths like a falling comet.

'Your preparatory exercises have developed you to the point that you can understand these truths. So now, in full consciousness, you can give me your answer. Have you the courage to take upon yourself these laws, the danger and the great responsibility; do you desire to receive initiation, or do you wish rather to withdraw and live out your earthly life according to the laws of human existence?'

For a time I keep silent. Then, earnest and determined, I reply, 'Father of my Soul, throughout the years I've been preparing I've had enough time to decide whether I wanted to choose the temple or a worldly life. And during these last three days I've concentrated again on this question and on nothing else. My only longing is for the divine, primordial state. I am absolutely determined. I beg you to initiate me!'

'So be it,' says Ptahhotep, 'and may God be with you! Now follow me.'

He takes me to another wing of the temple where the neophytes live. There he turns me over to a young priest, a chief among the boarders, who is awaiting us. I have seen him before. Turning to me Ptahhotep says, 'You will now prepare your body and your soul for initiation. On the day when the moon reaches its fullness, come to me at sundown.'

We both of us bow, and *He* departs.

The priest leads me to a cell where I spend the next few days alone, devoting myself exclusively to my exercises. The purpose of these exercises is to bring the purity of my thoughts, my soul, blood and body up to as high a point as possible. Even during the years when I was going to the neophyte school, I had to follow a very strict dietary regimen, in order for the new cells constantly being produced in the body to be chemically purer than those they replaced, and in order for my body tissues to develop resistance enough to be able to bear the highest vibrations. This is because any chemical change in matter alters its resistance to the forces conducted into it. Now the process reaches completion. I am permitted to eat only certain special roots and herbs. I have to chew them thoroughly, and I am permitted only to swallow the juice I can chew out of them. These herbs and roots are so chosen that some of them tend to strengthen and stimulate the organs of excretion, while others have a similar effect on the heart and nerves, so that my whole organism is not weakened.

As a result of this new dietary discipline, I feel lighter and lighter with each passing day. Within a few days' time, I even feel as if I didn't have a body at all. On the other hand, my mental lucidity and ability to concentrate increase to a degree I have never known before. In all my life I have never been able to think so clearly ... never been able to perceive spiritual truth with such pristine crystal clarity as now. By mere fasting alone, without the use of strengthening herbs, one can also reach a high degree of mental clarity. But the nerves can suffer damage in the process. Although they become hypersensitive during fasting, they are greatly weakened at the same time. Through the use of these herbs, all the disadvantages of fasting are eliminated.

One by one the days go by ... until the day of the full moon comes. Withdrawn deeply inside myself, I go forth to report to Ptahhotep. I enter just as the sun is disappearing below the horizon.

'Follow me,' says Ptahhotep, and leads the way out.

Ptahhotep takes me through the temple around the sacrificial table and on over to the great stone wall. The gigantic stone blocks fit together with hairline precision. Now I know why. Ptahhotep steps over to the middle one which slowly swings outward, revealing an opening in the wall. Beyond it lies a broad stone staircase leading downward. We go down to the bottom of the steps, then follow a long passageway. My sense of direction and a certain feeling in my lungs tell me we are walking under the ground. Surprisingly enough, however, there is no mould or mildew, and the air is fresh and pure, with even a scent of ozone in it. At the end of this subterranean passageway, we reach another staircase, leading upward. After we've climbed it, Ptahhotep leads me through more passageways, some wide, some narrow. We walk through rooms of various sizes containing strange and incomprehensible apparatus, then climb up more steps. Finally we enter a large room.

All these passageways and rooms—including this one—are brightly illuminated just as if by daylight, yet nowhere can I see a source of light. It seems as if the light were coming from the stones themselves. The equpiment in this room is so mysterious that it immediately captures my full attention. The room is radiantly bright. I see a large, strange, prismatic something that gives me the the impression it's made, not of solid matter, but of light . . . of some kind of concentrated, solidified light. This concentrated light mass radiates ordinary light too. That's why the room is so bright.

Once while I was visiting a potter, I had a chance to look through the peephole in his fiery kiln. In it several clay vessels were standing in a row, all glowing white with the heat and all completely transparent. I could see them all, one right through the other. They were all radiating light too. And this great mysterious prismatic form is radiating light in just the same way. Yes, light—but *no heat*!

But there are still other incomprehensible objects in this room. They are made of such a strange material and in such remarkable shapes that I can't begin to imagine what purpose they could serve. But there's no time to study them, for I am completely engrossed with the question of my initiation, how it will take place and what I will experience.

Ptahhotep leads me into the farthest corner of the room where I discover an empty stone sarcophagus. 'Up to now,' remarks my guide and mentor, 'you've always heard *what* initiation is, but you don't know *how* it takes place.

'During initiation, the candidate's body is subjected to a higher frequency than that which corresponds to his degree of consciousness. Thus he *becomes conscious on this higher level*!

'Only a person prepared through long and strict training can be initiated in this way into a higher power, into a higher level of consciousness, without suffering harm. Only such a person is able to control his body with the help of his intellect, understanding and will-power, and to attune his nerves to higher frequencies.

274

'As you already know, animals are not able to alter either their mode of living or the condition under which they live. That's why they are not able to bear higher frequencies than their own. To take an example, if a monkey were subjected to a current of the same frequency as man's, it would die within a few minutes of a "stroke", undergoing unspeakable nervous cramps while dying.

'Man, however, can adapt himself, up to the range of an octave, to different vibrations and bear these vibrations without death. In this way, an average person, after adequate physical preparation and training, could be subjected without damage to the current of a genius, in other words, the current of the fifth degree. He would feel a heavenly bliss. That's because every higher vibration, so long as it's bearable, induces an exhilarating feeling of happiness. Then, however, the vibration becomes a torture because the nerves are unable to bear up under the excessive current. Lower vibrations than those of the individual concerned induce dejection, fear and dismay. If an average person, because of longing for the blissful state once experienced, could later reach the state of initiation into the fifth degree and reach it often through patient and persistent practice, the nerves and cells of his body would gradually become so inured and transformed that he could really raise himself by one step upward and actually become a genius. He would go on experiencing a steady flow of intuitive knowledge.

'The feeling of bliss connected with a higher state of consciousness is known to every person who is gifted with intuition, and everyone who drinks wine or uses other stimulants is seeking the same blissful feeling associated with a greater flow of current through the nerves. But the artificial stimulation is always followed by a depression which throws the person farther down than he was before.

'In the great *initiation*, all the currents of force corresponding to the seven levels of consciousness are conducted into the body, beginning with the lowest and moving progressively upward to the very highest divine creative currents. The candidate is initiated in all these forces and *becomes conscious on all levels*. For a candidate to be ready to go through this initiation and come out alive, his consciousness—and with it his power of resistance—must previously have reached the sixth level. For any creature whose consciousness had not attained this plane, the act of initiation would certainly mean death.

'In this way, with the help of the current of force, a candidate attains the seventh, divine degree which he never would have been able to reach alone. No one can attain initiation on the divine-creative plane through his own unaided efforts. Here he goes through the great transition from his previous—negative-taking attitude to a positive attitude of giving. Regardless of how much he may strive to do so, no human being can go through this transition alone and unaided, although many are able through their own efforts to develop to the point where they are perfectly prepared for initiation on the seventh plane. In such cases, the laying on of hands is all that is needed to initiate them into the divine cosmic-self-consciousness. Never again do such initiates fall out of divine consciousness, as they have moved through the entire cycle of total consciousness, acquiring all necessary experience as they did so, and only the reunion of their two complementary halves, each of which has become perfectly conscious—remains to be accomplished. Only this last help has to be given from the outside. From then on they live in a state of continual God-consciousness.

'Through Initiation in our temple, however, it's possible for candidates to be initiated into the divine seventh degree even though they may not have developed all the way up to the seventh degree in readiness for it. As a prerequisite for such initiation, they must have become conscious at least on the sixth plane, and they must have adequately prepared their body. Through this external aid of initiation, their path to the true *self* is opened, and in the act of initiation, their consciousness is linked up with the divine flow of power.

'These candidates are not able, after initiation, to continue living in the divine state of consciousness. They fall back to their previous state. But they remember the bliss they experienced in initiation, and as their path to God has been opened for them, they enjoy the possibility of attaining the seventh plane of development faster and easier than by merely following the long path of earthly experience and human development of consciousness. Initiation in the temple is thus able to bring back many more people to the bliss of union with the divine self than would be possible without this aid.

'On the other hand there is a danger that a person initiated in this way, after his initiation and before he is able to become a God-man through his own efforts may not be able to resist earthly temptations and thus falls lower than in his first fall. This danger does not exist for the uninitiated. If, without initiation, a person completes his cycle of living along the long path of mortals all the way to the end, to the great *goal*, until he returns home to the Garden of Eden, there remains nothing in experience, nothing unknown in him. He achieves the divine plane after having gained experience on all levels, in this way gradually effacing his person. To achieve this, however, it takes a living creature an entire age of creation.

'It is God's will for the great initiation in the temple to continue to be available to mankind for some time to come in spite of this danger. Countless people have already been redeemed in this way and brought back to *God*, and many more will be. And the few who relapse after their initiation will reincarnate themselves in later times when mankind is left to its own resources. They will remember the great truths they experienced through their initiation and will proclaim these truths to their fellow men in their words, writings and actions.

'The secret of the great initiation will be guarded in the temple for some time yet. But when more and more earth-minded people come into power in times to come, we will close the initiation pyramid with blocks of stone from the inside and will dematerialize everything in the initiation chamber. The secret of divine creative energy will not fall into uninitiated hands. Thousands of years later when people break into the pyramids, they will find nothing—absolutely nothing—not even human skeletons.

'There are many souls on earth today who fulfil the prerequisites for the great initiation. It is our duty to initiate all of these candidates if, despite our warning, they *repeat three times* their wish to be initiated.

'In initiation the candidate becomes conscious on every plane of creation. All unconscious portions of his soul become conscious; he has no "subconscious" and no "superconscious". During his initiation, the consciousness of the initiate becomes whole, total *all-consciousness*. The circle which began with his becoming conscious in matter—in the body—the moment he fell from unity, is closed. The candidate consciously unites with his own complementary half which previously was always present as an unconscious portion of his soul, like a negative image, a strange being, and which because of its power of attraction manifested itself as longings, powerful urges and unrest in his body. The consciousness returns to unity, and there is no longer a complementary half, for the complementary half *has also been made conscious*. This reunion we call "mystic marriage".

' "Marriage" always means a union of positive and negative. On earth, however, "marriage" means the vain attempt to achieve union with another being in the body. But the mystic union of the spirit takes place *in the consciousness* and brings complete, never-ending fulfilment; for the union with one's own complementary half means union with *God*. The circle is closed again!

'The human body is so constructed that it contains a special nerve centre for each octave of vibration. On the one hand, these nerve centres are distributors, sending out through the nervous system the vibrations they receive from higher centres. On the other hand, they act as transformers when they pass on vibrations to the next nerve centre below.

'In the ordinary human being, these transformers in nerve centres work separately from his consciousness. That's why he can't control them. The laws of nature control him without his knowing what is taking place in his body and in his soul, in his subconscious.

'In his initiation, the candidate must consciously experience the high flow of current in all seven major nerve centres and the powers corresponding to them. With his consciousness he first descends to the lowest sphere of creation. He must experience the forces ruling there and become master of them. *This is his first test.* When he passes it successfully, he moves up one degree into the second octave of vibration, recognizing and experiencing it in order to master it. This is the *second test*. Then he climbs on into the third, fourth, fifth, sixth and finally into the seventh octave of vibration. When he has passed all these tests and succeeded in *consciously* remaining master in all these spheres—then he has become an initiate.

'Consciousness is light, unconsciousness is darkness. When we see light above us on earth, we say it's *day*. Thus each state of consciousness is a "day" of God; for in *each* consciousness, from the lowest plane of matter up to the

God-man's consciousness of *self*, *God recognizes himself* on the different levels. On all these "*days*"—on all the levels of consciousness, there is activity, unrest, motion except on the seventh "day" *of God* when there is no activity, no motion, no work! On the seventh "*day*" creation ceases because on this day there is complete unity and perfect equilibrium. Then God *rests within himself*!

'When, after his initiation, an initiate succeeds in becoming conscious again in the eternal *being* and experiences this divine state again during his meditation, and when he succeeds often enough in thus raising himself by his own power from his normal sixth plane up to the seventh divine plane, in time he consolidates his position definitively on this level of consciousness, and the divine creative plane is the one he lives on day in and day out. Then and then only does he become a *God-man*. Only a person who, in his consciousness, *is peace and calm* itself, so that everything he does, thinks and feels flows forth naturally out of this divine state, manifesting God's will always and under all circumstances, always radiating only positive-giving forces of divine *love*—only such a person is truly a Son of God, a *God-man*! Ptah-Hotep!

'The God-man consciously manifests and controls all seven levels of creation. But his consciousness identifies itself only with the seventh, divine plane, not with the lower ones. He knows them, masters them, uses them—but *does not eat* of these fruits of the tree of knowledge of good and evil! He consciously remains in *God*, in the paradisiacal state. He unites within himself all seven planes in divine unity: he is matter, has a body, is a plant: animates, nourishes and cares for his body as for a good instrument; he is animal: he has instincts and feelings; he is a man: he has intellect and the power of logical thought; he is a genius: he has intuition and works out of the plane of causes; he is a prophet: he stands above time and space, seeing the future and the past, loving the entire universe with selfless, all inclusive love, helping all creatures towards redemption from the fetters of the world; and he is a God-man: he is omniscient and omnipotent; he is what he is, the eternal *being*, *life itself*, *God*!

'Initiates, as you can see, are not all of the same degree. Most of them only reach the seventh degree after further development. That's why there are different degrees in the priesthood. The duties of a high priest can only be fulfilled by one who has reached the seventh degree of the God-man with his own power, no longer *expecting* and *receiving* the highest divine power—the way the candidate expects and receives it during his initiation. On the contrary, the high priest *radiates* and *gives out* this highest divine power himself.

'Six of the seven degrees of consciousness receive their creative vibrations, the power of life, from the seventh degree, from *God*. Even the initiate who has been able to reach the seventh divine degree only during his initiation, still expects and receives the creative power of life from the seventh degree, from *God*. Only *God* and those who have become identical with *God* are truly and exclusively munificent in their radiations.

'Matter, on the other hand, as a negative reflected image of God, *only receives.*

'All beings on the other levels receive from above and transmit to the levels below.

'The plant has a vitalizing effect on matter, while on the other hand it receives five-fold from the levels of intelligence above it. The animal gives off two-fold to the levels below it, while receiving three-fold from those above. Man gives three-fold towards the levels below him and receives three-fold from those above, as his consciousness stands in the middle of the seven planes. As the consciousness of the genius is on the fifth plane, the plane of causes, he radiates his creative powers out over the four levels below, while he receives power only from the two highest. The prophet—the initiate—transmits his beneficent vibrations to the beings on the five lower levels of consciousness and receives his power from the divine level. He still lives in a dualistic relationship with *God*. Only a person who has attained perfect *cosmic consciousness* by his own efforts emits positive radiation, and only positive, in all directions, life-giving and munificent towards the entire universe. He lives in *God*, in monistic consciousness of *self*.

'You have already learned that *giving*—radiating—is the law of *God*, of the spirit, while taking—contraction—is the law of matter.

'Every frequency has a powerful and penetrating effect on the levels below it, whereas it has no effect on those above. If you take two people on different levels of development, the person on the lower level, although he may be a "bad" person in the view of people about him, can only harm the person on the higher level through deeds, but never through his radiation, as his powers have no effect on the levels above his. On the other hand, his radiation, especially his "evil eye" can do harm on the levels below his level of consciousness. An initiate, on the other hand, can transmit his high magic power to every living being without exception.

'During initiation, the divine creative power will flow through your spinal column, reaching each of your seven major nerve centres in turn, and you will experience this power as a state of consciousness on each level. But remember very carefully what I'm telling you now: *When you become conscious in one octave and vibration, you are in tune with this frequency, and its whole sphere represents absolute "reality" for you. When you have passed the test in one degree, you will waken in the next sphere and realize that you were only dreaming on the level below. But if you don't pass the test, that is, if you identify yourself with the events and don't succeed in remaining master of them, all of these dream pictures remain real for you, and you'll have to experience all of them to the very end as real events in the world of time and space. That would mean that your body would die here in this coffin and you would have to go on dreaming your own dream pictures in countless reincarnations, on the long path of mortal existence, for many thousands of years while you gradually struggled upward from this lower level to which you would have fallen.*

'The difference between dream and reality is only that what you accept on one level of consciousness as reality immediately turns into a dream when you awaken on a higher level of consciousness and realize that it wasn't reality at all, but merely a projection of the *self*, in other words a dream. Every dream is reality as long as you believe it to be real. The one and only *reality*, the only objective *reality* there is, is the *self*: *God!*

'When you pass all the tests, you experience all the lives that you would have to experience as a fallen soul on earth. Free of time and space, you experience them as dreams, awakening on the next level of consciousness. Finally you awaken on the seventh level, *in the cosmic consciousness of the self*. In this divine state, you become one with the last and highest and only *reality*, with *yourself*, with *God*. This is no longer an awakening, but a resurrection!

'Then you have been liberated from your "person"—which also is only a projection—liberated from your personal fate. You are redeemed. After that you will fulfil the duties of a priestess in the temple. Then, if through further practice you succeed in raising yourself up to the seventh level through your own efforts, keeping yourself on this level as a permanent state of consciousness, you will have attained the divinity of a God-person. Then you will be worthy to become a high priestess in the temple.'

'Father of my Soul,' I ask Ptahhotep, 'you've told me that it's possible for a person to fall from the higher consciousness even after he has been initiated. You've also told me that an initiate, when he identifies himself with his body and thus channels his higher energies into his body, falls lower than an ordinary person living in physical reality. Another thing you've told me is that a candidate, during his initiation, experiences *his whole future destiny*, just as it has been provided for from the moment of his first fall all the way back up to his return home into divine unity. So how is it possible for an initiate, who has dreamed all the events and trials and temptations of his destiny and who has, during his initiation, successfully passed all the tests that might later cause him to fall again—how is it possible for such an initiate to fall later in the three-dimensional world of time and space? If he has seen his entire destiny all the way to the end as a dream, why hasn't he also dreamed about his fall as part of his future destiny?'

'When a boomerang is thrown out,' answers Ptahhotep, 'how it will fly and how long it will take to complete its circuit are factors that are already known the moment it's thrown. So it carries within itself its entire career as an immutable future fate. It would be possible however, for an external force to catch it in the middle of its orbit and bring it back to its starting point and goal in shorter time and by a shorter path. The boomerang would thus have returned home. But because it maintains its original form and weight, it still carries within itself the possibility of being thrown out again and making another circuit, because this possibility is given *by virtue of its form and weight*.

'An initiate who has attained initiation by means of external aid resembles this boomerang. He has dreamed his entire future destiny out to the end, to his return into divine unity, but he has experienced these conditions *only in his consciousness*. His person and his personal circumstances, which arise from his character and fate, still remain in the material world. With his initiation, he has *not* ended his present life, just as you, after your initiation, will still be the daughter of the Pharaoh and the representative of the Queen. And if an initiate has not gathered all the necessary earthly experience before his initiation, if he has not got acquainted with all the creative forces within himself and learned to control them, he is to some extent still inexperienced *when he returns home into the divine state of unity.* This means that he is not yet completely liberated from the personal composition of his powers and his personality is not yet completely annihilated.

'During the intervening time until such an initiate is able to reach the seventh degree by his own efforts and maintain himself in it as a perpetual state of consciousness, he carries within himself the possibility and the danger of falling again from his high state of consciousness *and starting on a completely new wheel of destiny.* Because he has become *conscious* in the divine creative power, however, even though with external aid, *this* tremendous power throws him out again, and then he must go through a much larger cycle than was the case after his first fall *before he became conscious* in the divine power. The black magicians, for example, who destroyed the home of the sons of God have fallen to the lowest plane of creation. They now lie as mountains, rocks and stones on the earth and must work their way up through ages and ages along the path of consciousness from inert matter through the realms of plant and animal life, up to the human level again. Some of them fell only as far as the plant or animal level, while others fell only to one of the other levels of human existence. The course a creature runs through in the material world takes a definite amount of time, *but individual creatures can always run through the circle in a shorter time* and reach their goal thousands or even millions of years earlier. This, however, is only possible for man. Only man, thanks to his *conscious use of intellect,* can experience *states of consciousness without reference to time.* Animals and plants are not able to do this. Now you can understand why animals too must suffer! Like everything else on earth, they are limited manifestations of consciousness of fallen spirits that once lived on a high plane.

'In the initiation all the negative forces that were made manifest in the fall from a higher level of consciousness are offset by positive forces. The "debts" are thus paid. After you have successfully passed your initiation, you'll enter a *condition without fate.* As long as you manifest God's will, you will have no person of your own and consequently no fate of your own. You will be free of the law of action and reaction. But if you identify yourself in your consciousness with your person, with your body, you'll create a new wheel of fate for yourself and again be subject to innumerable reincarnations.

'Now you know all the consequences of initiation. And I'm asking you again one last time, do you have the courage to go through with initiation?'

With perfect self-assurance, I answer, 'Yes!'

A tall, dignified man then enters the room. I know him. He is a priest of the highest degree, a high priest too, Ptahhotep's representative. He steps over towards us. Then Ptahhotep motions to me to get into the sarcophagus and lie down in it.

I do as he commands.

As I lie in the sarcophagus, Ptahhotep casts a last glance at me, full of infinite love, and then the two priests lift the stone cover and lay it over me. In pitch darkness I lie there enclosed in the stone coffin.

THE INITIATION

As usual, I watch what happens.

Nothing happens.

I lie in the stone coffin and peer into the darkness.

Darkness? It's not really darkness, for in the middle of my field of vision I observe a greenish phosphorescent light. Around it points of light seem to flash up and then disappear. I watch these points of light and try to guess where they come from and where they are going.

Suddenly I notice that the points of light, when they appear aren't as close together as they were. On the contrary, right in the middle, where the greenish phosphorescent light was before, there's an empty space that none of the points of light approaches. They leave more and more space around this spot which, because of the complete absence of light in it, is a pitch black hole through which I peer into *nothingness* . . .

Then I notice two points of light that appear in this total, dead darkness. Slowly they come closer and stare at me like two eyes. I don't see the eyes; they have neither light nor colour, and yet I'm obliged to see them. I *know* that two eyes are staring at me. These two eyes do not belong to a body. They are centres of force of streams of energy which take effect invisibly. These dim, black energies attack the points of light. The points of light are sucked up by this force, destroyed. A contour appears, creating a boundary around this empty, dark hole that radiates this invisible force. Before my horrified eyes, there gradually appears a face, the eerie features of a monster, a silhouette that is only recognizable because where it is there is absolute nothingness—a negative image.

I know, I just know this disembodied monster is *Evil* itself. I know it. I've seen its horrible grimaces occasionally glowering through human faces as the *expression* of those faces. Now the *cause* of that expression, the being itself, without a human face, without a body, is here!

Or was it always present and I just didn't notice it . . . ?

This bodiless face resembles the head of a goat. The silhouette clearly shows the form of horns over a long, pinched face that ends with a little goatee. Or perhaps, are all these shapes only *radiations of invisible forces*? The being's eyes, set so close together, have a terrifying effect, like bottomless maelstroms that irresistibly pull everything down, down, down to complete annihilation.

Through these two baleful eyes, the monster now radiates all his fearful powers upon me and into me. These awful eyes bore into me, and through me, through my entire being, swallowing me irresistibly into themselves as if I were being sucked into a gigantic maelstrom.

Absolute panic seizes my heart. I feel myself turning limp and lifeless out of sheer terror. Coming closer and closer, his horrible eyes get more and more penetrating. I can feel how this satanic being—is it *Satan* himself?—is forcing me into his power. The monster spreads out over me, swallows me, and in a moment I feel I am no longer myself. *I am It!* I feel its horrible features in my face, its immaterial body in my body, its devilish streams of current flowing like blood in my veins. This hellish, fiendish sensation turns my whole being cold and stiff. My body curls up in horrible cramps.

And deep within me IT talks to me, without words, through the power which produces words, through the *meaning* of words: 'Now I've got you! Now you're in my power! Now you see you haven't been able to crowd me out of your consciousness. In spite of your efforts to do so, you belong to me anyway now! You and I are one. There's nothing to separate us anymore. I am the "I" in you, and you are the "I" in me. You are subject to my law of cooling, contraction and solidification. Do you feel how your body is curling up, how you're drawing your knees up all the way to your chest? They're crossed now and your feet are pressed close to your body, as close as if the soles of your feet were joined to your body. Your arms are crossed in front of your breast. Your hands are curled up into fists pressed against your body as tightly as if they were joined to it. Now your head is dropping down on to your chest, pushing itself close between your fists—closer—still closer! Just as if you were in your mother's womb! That's right, and now you've shrunk and shrivelled into just one piece. You're getting colder and harder until you become a little oval piece of stone! A piece of stone—rigid, hard and dead! But you still have your consciousness and *know* that you're dead, that you've solidified into this piece of stone, that you are this piece of stone; you're walled up in it—dead for endless time . . . for timeless eternity . . .

'Look around and see the mountains reaching up to the sky. Do you see all these rocks and stones and boulders? Don't just look *at* them, look *into* them. Look into their being. Can you see that all these stones are petrified but *conscious* beings like yourself, exposed to burning sunshine, raging storms and splitting frost? . . . Every creature, every animal, every human being walks on you and all these other stones. Spring torrents drag you into wild waters, and you rub and scour each other in these whirling rapids . . . endless time . . . timeless eternity . . .'

Horrified, I experience everything the *evil one* says. This is hell indeed. Alive and conscious, yet locked up and immovable, grown into this tomb, with no possibility of giving so much as a sign of life . . . to be a heavy, dead stone! . . . To *be*?

No! *I am* not that! *I* am only imprisoned, entombed in this stone, but *I am not* the stone. *My self is not matter!* *I* am the dimensionless *self*, a spirit beyond any concept of time and space!

And with the inner strength of the spirit, just as I learned to speak with it in my telepathic exercises, without body, without mouth, speaking in spirit, I soundlessly scream at the monster: 'No! I am not you, and you are not "I"! We are forever separated in our beings, for you are death, and "*I*" am *life*! We can never be identical with each other! You with your law of contraction and solidification, you're the negative, the reflected image—the caricature—of the eternal source of all life, of *divinity resting within itself*! You're not a horrible phantom. You're not a monster. You're not "*the evil one*". You have no independent existence. The divine *self* created you and goes on eternally creating you whenever it clothes itself in a material envelope, in a body. You are the inner being of matter, you are the *law* that maintains matter; so you have power over my body, because you had to construct it on the command of my *self* when *I* was born into this material world and became a person. But you have no power over me, over my creative *self*; for you're nothing else but *the law of matter come to life through my spirit*. *Not I am you*, but *I am that I am* and you are also what I am! Your essence is contraction, and on the spiritual plane, in consciousness, contraction manifests itself as *fear*. And you must disappear, because *I don't fear*!

The effect of my unspoken, soundless words is terrifying! It gets pitch dark around me, and the mountains cave in with a deafening thunderous roar. Rocks and boulders fall, the earth opens, complete chaos rages about me . . . only *I* stand firmly on my feet in this cataclysm . . .

As things become quiet again and I slowly return to my senses, I realize I've just had a horrible dream. How good it is to awaken from such a nightmare . . .

My first sensation is one of extraordinary hunger and thirst, but I don't want to waste time with eating and drinking, for my goal is *God*. I want to get on as fast as possible.

I look about me. I am in a spacious room illuminated by soft reddish light. Pleasant, well-mannered people offer me tempting delicacies in beautiful dishes and heavenly drinks in magnificent golden vessels. They try to persuade me to eat and drink with them. I smile. The pleasures of the palate were never a temptation for me. Why should I permit myself to be delayed by hunger and thirst on my path to *God*?

I thank them for their friendly invitation and go on. Singularly enough I no longer have any sensation of hunger or thirst, but I still can't quite make out where I am and what's going on around me. It is apparent, however, that everyone around me is in constant, chaotic motion. Another one of my first impressions of this place is the strange smell in the air . . . the smell of overheated human bodies . . . not exactly unpleasant, but nevertheless repugnant to me.

Little by little my eyes grow accustomed to the subdued light. I am in some kind of an underground cave where great numbers of men and women are lounging about pell-mell on sofas or rocking and careening about, holding each other in tight embraces, dancing together and making extremely odd movements. I watch them with growing amazement. Are they drunk? Or mentally deranged? To be sure I have seen animals during mating season when nature is creating a new generation. But even when they are so keyed up that their whole bodies tingle and tremble with passion, they never lose their dignity ... they never carry on like these people here. And the priestesses, too, who serve in the temple of love, fulfil their duties with a noble attitude of spiritual dedication because they know in doing so they are laying an offering upon the altar of divine love. How can people fall so low that they debase the supremely divine act of love and make it an end in itself? After all, these are respected, reputable people—made in the image and likeness of God!—and yet they act as if they've lost their reason. I recognize some of them as people of rank, statesmen and ladies of the court, but they don't see me. They have neither eyes nor ears for anything or anyone beside themselves. The outside world has ceased to exist for them. *They're completely enclosed ... locked up in their own imagination!*

They talk with each other too, but it seems as if these men and women have forgotten that speech is a spiritual manifestation of man. They use speech to say the most impossible, completely illogical things. For example, I hear one man, as he dances with his partner in a tight embrace, ask her again and agaih, 'Are you mine?'

'Yes, darling, all yours!' the woman answers, and they go on dancing. A little while later the same couple dances past me and I hear the man, with his eyes half closed, asking the woman again—perhaps for the hundredth time—'Are you mine?'

'Yes, darling, I am,' the woman answers just as untiringly. What's the matter with them? Isn't it enough to ask a question once and get an answer. Why do they have to repeat it a hundred times? And how senseless it is to ask a person such a question! *A person belongs only to himself.* He is a free being with an inalienable right of self determination. So how does this man come to think he can *possess* a woman? It's scarcely possible to possess a lion. If even these regal animals don't give up their independence, how can this man get the idea the woman 'belongs to him', and why is he asking her a hundred times? Is he mentally ill? And perhaps the woman, who goes on answering his nonsense, too? And perhaps all these other men and women who are behaving in just as impossible a manner?

At this juncture a tall, broad-shouldered man steps up to me. Seemingly he can read my thoughts, for he replies to my inner questions: 'Beautiful lady, don't you know that this is love?'

'Love? I certainly do know love! It is a beautiful, noble sacrament when two living creatures love each other with absolute devotion, but not with mere passionate desire for possession! But in the hearts of these people I see no love! I see only that they've lost their senses ... that passion, this fever which dulls and deadens those finest, most sensitive nerve centres created for transmitting spiritual revelations, holds them completely in its power. These people should be saved and awakened from their semi-conscious condition! I step up to a very young woman, seize her arm and shout into her ear, 'Wake up! Don't let your consciousness be dulled and darkened by passion! You are spirit and not body! Don't allow your body to debase you! Don't let yourself be dragged down lower than an animal. Wake up, do you hear? Wake up and get out of here! Save yourself before it's too late!'

The young woman peers at me as if through a veil—like a sleepwalker. 'Leave me alone,' she says, 'I want to be happy!' And with that she goes on dancing.

Oh how blind! How could she possibly hope to find happiness through a physical embrace *without spiritual content*? Happiness is something one experiences in consciousness; happiness is in the *self*. How could she possibly hope to find happiness through mere trifling play of the body?

'Now just forget your intellect a while,' says the man, 'you're not qualified to judge because you've never tried it. Dance with me and you'll see for yourself.' So saying, he embraces me and drags me out into the whirling mass of people, acting just as foolishly as all the other people . . .

I dance with him and observe myself with great curiosity . . . Will I too become as intoxicated, as carried away by the close contact as these poor demented people about me? But the only thing I notice is how extremely unpleasant I find the close proximity of this man. His breath is hot, and I find it very revolting for him to be breathing into my face and down my neck. Exhaled air is used up air! Why should I be inhaling air he has already used up? Then too, I find the odour of his body and his perspiration most unpleasant. I want fresh air. I want to get away from this repugnant place.

As I try to get away from him, the man suddenly changes. In a trice he turns into a gigantic, fiery flaming spirit. He no longer has a body. He is only a mighty flame, trying to force me into subjection. He surrounds me, trying to force himself into my mouth . . . into my body. But the power I radiate, the power of my clear and sober consciousness keeps him away. He cannot reach me. He reacts by growing hotter, greater, more eager. He takes on tremendous proportions, spreading throughout the whole room, devouring all these passion-drunk people in his consuming fire. Nobody is left . . . Nothing more . . . only a sea of flames, devouring and consuming everything . . .

But I stand untouched, unscathed, and *I am that I am*!

Then I hear a thunderous voice from out of the flames: 'You have won . . . you have passed your test, but watch out! You haven't won because you're stronger than I. You can't be stronger, because I'm *the fire of your own self*. You just didn't come alight because your purity and your *lack of experience* stand between you and me. Your body and its senses are still sleeping. That's what protected you. But watch out, we'll meet again . . . *we'll meet again*! . . .' And with that everything disappears—fire, room, smoke—everything . . . and I find myself alone again . . .

'We'll meet again?' I repeat these last words. 'I'm not afraid of you! Even if my body had burst into flaming passion, this would not have touched my *self*. *I* stand above everything physical . . .'

But what was that? Didn't it sound like a scornful laugh?

287

I look around to see where this voice may have come from. So doing, I notice that I'm in a meadow as green as emerald, and a strange form is approaching. It's the form of a handsome, well-built man, half concealed by a veil of mist. I'd like to see through the mist . . . I'd like to see the splendid form it hides . . . I'd like to chase the mist away . . . but I can't. But the man interests me and so I ask, 'Who are you?'

Then the handsome man comes close, and with a voice that makes a deep impression on me he whispers into my ear: 'O my sweet beloved! I've been looking for you for a long, long time, for an eternity, ever since we fell out of the Garden of Eden and became separated from each other. At last I've found you! Come into my arms! Come, lay your sweet little head upon my breast! Come and let us unite in divine unity, let us merge our beings in heavenly bliss! How wonderful that you haven't yielded to the animal urge of the body! How glorious that you've kept yourself pure and untouched for me! You belong to me and I belong to you. We supplement each other completely! Do you feel the irresistible power of attraction that links us and draws us closer and closer together? Come, let us unite in love, you dearest of creatures, my one and only heavenly bride. I love you!'

I hear his voice, I see his manly stride, I feel a tremendous force radiating from him to me . . . And yet he's strange. I don't know him! How could he be my complementary half? No! One never finds the complementary half outside oneself. Ptahhotep says our complementary half is always behind the manifested form as a mirrored image *in the unmanifested state*. No! No human being can be my complementary half. And why is this man veiled in a dense mist?

'I don't know who you are,' I answer him, 'but whoever you are, you're mistaken! You're *not* my complementary half. And you'll have to look elsewhere for yours if you think you'll find it anywhere in the outside world. No one can find his complementary half anywhere except within himself. In the world around us it's only possible to find *projected pictures similar to one's true complementary half*. But neither you nor I can become complete by virtue of a picture, a projection. Only the divine unity of the *self* can bring blissful happiness! I'll find my complementary half within my *self*!'

'To find your complementary half within your *self*,' says the handsome man, 'would mean that you, in your consciousness, were already identical with the divine self. How do you expect to experience the consequence before the cause. The divine self is the paradisiacal state of unity through which you can only return through becoming one with your complementary half. How do you expect to achieve this without me, without your complementary half? You're forgetting that you are half of a unit and I am the other half.

'We are the living reflected images of each other, and we belong together. You carry me about in your subconscious, just as I carry you in mine, and even without wanting to we seek each other with the irresistible attractive force that comes from our belonging together in the paradisiacal state. Throughout ages and ages of time, our fate brings us together again and again until we make each

288

other conscious within ourselves and experience each other completely in body as well as in soul. Only in this divine identity can we really be the total consciousness of the whole—of the higher self! How do you expect to be able to return to paradisiacal unity without me? How do you think you could escape from facing the fact that we also belong to each other on the earthly plane? How do you expect to get the experience you absolutely need, without me?'

But I refuse to allow myself to be influenced. 'No matter how much you try to convince me, I still don't want you! As far as I'm concerned it's enough to know that you're present in the unconscious part of my *self*, and I only want to get acquainted with you within myself, but not in the outer world. Get on your way and let me get on mine!'

At these words of mine the handsome man recedes and begins to evaporate like a morning mist in the sunshine. And from farther and farther away his voice comes back to me—this voice that has made such a deep impression on my heart: 'I'll go on looking for you on the earthly plane... *looking*... *looking*...' His voice fades away in the distance, and suddenly all is quiet.

But there's still something I want to know, so I shout after him, 'Why is there such a heavy mist about you, so heavy it keeps me from seeing you face to face?'

From far away in the distance I hear a voice fading out as if it were the echo of my own heart beat: 'The heavy mist is covering *your eyes*, *not me*! It's your lack of experience... that's what's protecting you from me. It has helped you resist me. But we'll meet again... meet again...'

There's still a lot I'd like to ask and I run towards the spot where he's disappeared. But I see him no more. I turn around to go back to the beautiful meadow, but I can't find the way. There is a dense mist covering everything wherever I look. No matter how hard I try, I just can't see through it. Yet I know I'm no longer alone. I hear voices of people around me, and I know that there is some kind of a relationship between these people and myself. Various events follow each other in which I play an important part. I hear voices speaking to me, and again and again I recognize the voice that spoke to me from out of the misty figure and made such a deep impression on me. I realize that this being, in various different forms, belongs to me again and again, but how and where? ... what are these voices all saying? And what am I answering?

I can't quite fathom it. It's as if the mist were covering my ears as well as my eyes. Now and again I see something, but before I can recognize what it is, it disappears again in the mist. Once I see a tower, and I know that someone is living within it as a prisoner—he has the same voice as that of the misty figure— and I hurry to try to smuggle in something to eat. I am the daughter of the gatekeeper, and I have to watch out that no one notices me. But an overpowering force draws me towards the prisoner. I know I must help him...

Then everything disappears again in the mists about me. As I try to get my bearings again, I suddenly see large, coloured stone tiles just in front of my face. I wash and scrub them until they're clean. Then again in the mist I hear a voice

that sounds like my own, asking over and over, 'Have you found my child?'
I get the impression that an old, decrepit body, which somehow or other is
related to myself, is very, very tired. Then this strange feeling disappears, and
suddenly—to my great joy—the mist disappears too . . .

Once again I am standing in the green meadow. Now I'm ready to go on. The
air is fresh. The sun is shining, but still it's not unbearably hot. How strange!
Never before have I noticed that it wasn't hot at midday, and now there's even a
gentle pleasant breeze. There's something more that's strange too. As the mists
disappear and I see the ground below my feet again, I notice that my feet as well
as the ground they stand on are much *farther down* than they ever have been
before. *That means I've grown much taller!* How peculiar! At my age a person
doesn't grow any more. So how is it possible for me to have grown taller? And
what a remarkable dress I have on! It's really funny! And where are my
sandals? And my hands? How very much they've changed! Everything is so
peculiar, as surprising as if I were *not myself, as if I were dreaming*!

But my consciousness is clear. I'm awake. I'm not dreaming! I look around.
Not far away I see a forest, and as I approach it, a house becomes visible among
the trees. But what a strange house! The place seems familiar to me, and yet I
know that I've never seen such trees in all my life, nor such a house. No! These
trees are not even remotely similar to our palms . . .

The house stands on a hill, and as I go up the steps through the forest leading
to it, I know the house belongs to me. But how? I've never seen such a house,
and yet it is familiar to me. It's not made of stone, and its roof is slanting instead
of flat. As I enter the house, I know every room is familiar so I walk straight
into 'my room'. As I step into the little room with its whitewashed walls, I stop
before the window for a few moments to enjoy the magnificent view. I see
that both the little house and the beautiful green meadow are high up on a
mountainside offering a view into the wide plain below. At the foot of the
mountain a broad river flows majestically past with big ships navigating on
its surface. Singularly enough, they have no sails and no oars, yet move
along very fast, much faster than our ships. Another thing I don't understand is why they all have a big, black pipe sticking up and spewing out thick
black smoke.

The sun has gone down, and twilight is spreading out over the valley below
me. Off in the distance where—I have a strange feeling I have often looked out
before—there are many little villages, and between them and over them I see
little flashes of lightning. Again and again . . . and after each flash there is a clap
of thunder, just the way the thunder booms out of the great pyramid. I observe
these flashes of light and this thundering for a while until suddenly a shrill bell
rings behind me. I turn to the little apparatus that is emitting this ringing sound,
lift up an odd-shaped part of this apparatus and press part of it to my ear. All
of this seems just as much a matter of course as if I had been accustomed to
doing it for a long long time; yet I know precisely that I've never seen such a
thing in my life before. As I hold the little round black part of this apparatus

to my ear, I again hear the voice . . . the voice that spoke from out of the misty figure: 'I kiss your hands, darling, how are you ?'

'Thanks, fine,' I reply, 'but I'd like to come back home. Could you perhaps come and fetch me tomorrow. The enemy is already quite close. Every evening I see the hits. They're coming closer and closer with frightening speed. I'd like to be home with all of you.'

'All right,' answers the voice of the man again, 'I'll come tomorrow to get you. But wouldn't it be more sensible if you were to stay in the forest ? Here in the city we're getting bombarded day and night, and it's getting worse.'

'No,' I answer, 'I want to be back home with all the rest of you. I've taken care of the house and property here, but when danger is near, I want to be with the rest of you. Please take me home!'

'Good,' I hear again out of the apparatus. 'I can see you have courage enough. Tomorrow afternoon I'll come and pick you up. Get all your things packed before then. Goodbye, my darling. I kiss you again and again. Good night.'

'I kiss you too. Good night,' I answer and put the apparatus back where it was before.

Who was that ? How do I come to hear his voice speaking to me through an odd-shaped piece of apparatus ? . . . How come I hear him with my *physical ear* instead of through an inner link of spirit ? A thought flashes through my brain: Is perhaps everything I am experiencing now only a vision ? Perhaps it's only a dream ? Only a test of my *courage* ?

No, unfortunately it's not a dream—however much I might like to wake up out of this reality, just as I woke up before out of a dream and found myself in the midst of a beautiful green meadow. Yes, that was a dream, but now I'm wide awake and have to deal with all kinds of things . . . unavoidably. The air is heavy with fear and terror . . . so heavy people can hardly breathe. The enemy is approaching from every side. If this goes on for a few days more the city will be surrounded. And we keep hearing such unbelievably horrible stories from the refugees who have succeeded in escaping from the occupied areas. But we are in the hand of God, and I calm my anxious heart and nerves with the thought that everything that happens is for the good, because *nothing can happen without God's will*. And God's will is always good—absolutely always!

I start to pack my things quickly.

The next afternoon, I look up at the window and see our dog running down the mountainside like a streak of greased lightning. That's how I know my husband is coming. A few minutes later, they arrive, my husband and our dog. Our dog is so happy. He jumps up to greet my husband again and again, up to shoulder height out of pure enthusiasm and excitement. I run out to meet him too and we embrace each other with tender affection. We've been living together for nearly twenty years and are just as much in love as the day we married.

My husband's bearing and manner, his voice and the warm touch of his hand are all so reassuring. He is courage, safety, dependability itself.

'I hope you're not afraid?' he asks me with a smile.

'No,' I answer as I lace my arms around his muscular back. '*God* will be with us!' I snuggle up close to him for a moment, leaning my head on his broad shoulder.

As we start to pack the luggage in the car, I stand still for a moment. What kind of a car, carriage or chariot is this? I suddenly remember that I'm accustomed to travelling in quite a different kind, but then I smile again because this is one I know very well too. Of course it's my husband's car, but how strange that it runs by itself, with *no lions* harnessed up in front of it . . .

I stroke my forehead with my hand. Have I gone completely mad? Lions! Lions in front of a motor car? And here in this country? Yes indeed, there were some beautiful lions in the zoo, but they were long ago put to death because of the bombings. It would have been dangerous if one of the wild beasts had been freed because of bomb damage to its cage. I can't understand where I get ideas like these about lions and other impossible things . . . the pyramids of Egypt which I certainly only know from photographs! Have I perhaps become a victim of too much excitement?

We drive home. I run into our apartment. Just as I am about to open the door, it opens all by itself, and there, beaming with joy—O how in the world did you get here?—is little Bo-Ghar! But he isn't little any more. He's grown up, even though quite young. He smiles as sweetly as ever, bows before me and kisses my hand.

'How good, how very good to see you come home again, my queen!' he says quietly.

But I stand there looking at him in sheer astonishment: 'Bo-Ghar, you're here? How did you get here?' I ask.

Now it's his turn to be surprised: 'But you know that I've been living here for the last three years . . . in your house. Why do you ask?'

I just can't understand it . . . he isn't exactly as I've known him. He's already grown up, yet I know that he's really still a child . . . or should be still a child! But why? Since he's come from his faraway homeland, I just don't know him. And even then he was already a grown-up young man. Why do I have a strange feeling that he's only a boy of ten or twelve? Why do I feel again as if I were dreaming?

And here's my husband. The whole apartment is full of flowers . . . how sweet of him to welcome me home after all these years of our being married, in the same sweet way he did during the first few days of our honeymoon.

After supper we sit near a strange, fairly large wooden box in which a human voice is speaking. The voice tells us the latest news of the war, along with rules and regulations for us to follow. How strange! . . . this is another materialization of a mental process, like the telepathic apparatus up there in the little forest house. Ptahhotep, my dear master, also emits high energy radiations through the atmosphere of the country every evening. All the people, while they sleep, are aided and strengthened by his powers and his love. But his radiations reach into the very depths of people's beings, not just to the *outer ears* like the low frequency vibrations coming from this odd little wooden box here.

Then we all go to bed.

And in many of the nights that follow we are suddenly awakened by a horrible sound: sirens howl throughout the whole city! We jump out of bed, slip into our shoes, warm underwear, a house-dress, a fur, a warm kerchief around our head . . . we snatch up the little suitcase with jewellery and money and the old album with the symbolic mystic drawings. We rush downstairs, my husband and I, down into the cellar. On the stairway we meet my younger sister with her new-born babe-in-arms, her three-year-old boy and two-year-old girl. Other doors open up into the stairway, and other people come out—blanched and drawn and silent—to join us on our downward march. As we reach the ground floor, a door opens and an old man with snow-white hair and beard comes out. Those eyes! Where have I seen these eyes before? And like a flash of lightning, I suddenly see again the handsome figure of my father's general—the one who made such a fine career for himself—*Thiss-Tha*! His eyes! And how has he come here? And how old he is! And how do I come to be whispering to him now, 'Father dear, are you dressed warm enough?' He smiles and gives me a reassuring wave of the hand: 'Yes, yes don't worry!' And we all go on to find our places in the cellar.

The enemy comes closer and closer; the ring of steel he's forged around our city gets tighter and tighter.

One afternoon the door opens and—Ima walks in. How does he come to be here? . . . And dressed in this clothing? I embrace him and ask, 'What kind of a suit is that?'

He looks at me with equal surprise. 'What a question, Mother!' he says. 'What kind of a suit? Why Mother, you act as if you were seeing me in it for the first time! An air force uniform! But you've known that for a long time!'

I stand there just as confused as if I were about to waken from another dream. Yes, of course, an air force uniform. And he is my darling, my only child! And yet I know that he's Ima. Of course I know him! Ima! Is he really my son? I can still see him clearly in his priestly robe. *He* gave me lessons in concentration. Even then his radiation was as strong and clean as steel . . . I know him . . . but he doesn't know me and acts as if he had never had anything to do with the temple. 'Mother,' he says, 'my outfit is moving on to another place, because our planes can't operate any more from this airfield. If we stayed here any longer, we'd all be destroyed with our aircraft. We're moving on somewhere into the countryside. I don't know when I'll see you again.'

My heart turns cold in panic. I've already got used to knowing my son was in constant danger. When he went into the air force, I felt as if I'd been struck dead. I walked around lifelessly in the apartment, feeling as if I were dreaming a horrible dream. How could that be reality? How could mothers really be sending their sons, their healthy, young, vigorous sons out into this mass murder? It's certainly only a bad dream in which people have become so depraved and so degraded as to be killing each other with the most gruesome weapons imaginable ... and killing off precisely the healthiest, strongest, fittest young men... young men who should be begetting a new, strong, healthy generation of people. These young men are the first to get killed simply because they are considered 'fit' for service. The weak and sickly ones stay home, and because they do they are the very ones who can become fathers. The majority of healthy young people are killed off in the fighting. This is the fastest road to the complete degeneration of the entire human race. And people have already sunk so low they don't even recognize this fact! For no other reason than blind hate and fear of each other, people kill off the best and healthiest generation!

Dream! Nightmare!

Then, little by little, my sense of reality came back, and I turned my child over to *God*! Nothing can happen without God's will, and whatever happens is good because *God* wants it so. Compensation! Everything that happens is only a searching and striving to return to equilibrium ... back to paradise! These words of my dear master, Ptahhotep, and all the other things *He* taught me in the great pyramid made such a deep impression on me that this gave me courage to go on living, to go on doing my daily duties, despite the terrible realization that my child and millions of others were using each other as targets in this mass butchery.

But now I knew that we would be separated when he left the city, for the enemy had us almost completely surrounded. And whether *he* or *we* would come out of this mass murder alive, or whether we would see each other again in this life—these were all just big question marks ...

And still I cannot, I must not feel pain, because I am not permitted to link myself with anyone in such a way that my happiness is dependent on him! In this young man whom I carried under my heart in order that he might be born again, in this young man who is now my son, I do not love the body. It is not his physical manifestation I love, but *God* within him! His divine *self* has built up this body—just like the bodies of all people, animals, plants and even inert matter—in order to be able to express itself. So it's the manifestation of the impersonal divinity I love in my son's person, in his beautiful body. All of creation is the manifestation of *the one and only God*; so why should I now tremble about the possibility of 'losing' *this* particular manifestation of *God*? Why should I shudder at the thought of not seeing it again? Perhaps because his flesh and his blood are from my flesh and my blood? But my *self* and his *self* are the same *self*—and not flesh and blood at all.

I must go into my own *self* and become fully conscious in it; then I am identical with the self of my son—and at the same time with the *self* of the entire *universe* and so I cannot lose anything or anyone! It cannot make any difference to me whether those who die are of my own flesh and blood or total strangers, because the same *self of God* is changing one of its many bodies whenever a living creature dies, whether it's the body of my one and only child or someone I don't know at all. I *must* completely conquer my flesh and blood which now feels such terrible pain ... O God, give me the strength to pass this test! *Even though I haven't yet attained cosmic consciousness,* give me the strength to act as if I were living every moment in this divine state of consciousness!

My knees tremble as I go to my son, embrace him and say: 'My dear little boy, my one and only child, farewell! I put you in *God's* hands ... He won't leave either you or us. Just remember that everything passes away except true love. Even now we love each other because we are one in *God*. This spiritual unity—this true love—has brought us together here on earth. We can't lose each other! We will find each other and meet again ... if not in this life, then in the next, or in another form of life. Wherever we may go, our love for each other will bring us together again. Farewell, my darling. In difficult times to come hold on to this invisible power that stands behind us and never leaves us. The power we call *God!*'

Neither of us cries. We hold each other in a long, warm, loving embrace. I kiss his smooth, young forehead. He holds me to his heart, then leaves. I wave to him from the window. He waves back, then disappears.

Tonight we celebrate Christmas. The cannons are thundering continually, but still we make all the preparations we can to celebrate the day as beautifully as possible. It doesn't matter much to me, for in eternity there are no Christmases, no holidays, and no weekdays. Every day is a holiday—a holy day— because in *God* eternity is an everlasting, holy day. But my husband likes to celebrate Christmas Eve. He is happy when he can give me pleasant surprises, and he likes to be surprised himself. He is already decorating the tree in the parlour, and Bo-Ghar is helping him.

For the last several weeks, Bo-Ghar has been living with us. Even if he wanted to go home evenings, he would not have been able to do so recently because of the heavy bombings. He lives in the room my son has vacated.

Several years ago Bo-Ghar left his homeland far away in the Orient. He came to the West to teach people in this part of the world the ancient science of his ancestors which enables people to bring the body under the dominion of the spirit. After wartime shortages made it impossible to obtain stone or bronze for sculpturing purposes, my studio was empty and I turned it over to Bo-Ghar as a room in which to give his lessons. From the beginning of our acquaintance- ship, he acted as if he were our own child, and now he and my husband are decorating the Christmas tree in the greatest of harmony.

I am with the cook trying to think up ways and means to prepare a 'festive' menu with the food supplies we've succeeded in obtaining with so much difficulty. Today we've been invited with the whole family for Christmas Eve supper at father's, and tomorrow we'll need to be able to serve a Christmas meal ourselves.

Then the door bell rings. My young cousin rushes in, all white and shaken. 'Esther,' he says, 'the enemy has completely surrounded the city, and their troops are making a surprise move. They're not coming from the other side of the city where we expected them, but straight in . . . straight towards us . . . I was in the city with father and we telephoned mother. She told us the enemy troops have already reached our villa. Their heavy tanks and men are moving towards the centre of the city. Lucky thing the telephone lines weren't cut. Enemy tanks and troops will probably be here any minute. Get ready. Now I've got to run. Goodbye.' And with that he goes.

I run to my husband to tell him the news, then on through all the house spreading the alarm, so that my sisters, brother, father, and the caretaker's family all know what we're up against.

Our villa stands on a hillside. From our windows we can see far down the street in the direction from which the enemy troops are coming. Everything is quiet for the moment. My husband says it may be hours before the enemy reaches our vicinity. So he suggests we celebrate Christmas immediately, then go downstairs to father's where we've been invited to join all the rest of the family for supper. That way, we'll all be together at father's and can wait and watch for further developments.

My husband lights the candles on the Christmas tree. I think of my son who at this very moment may be obliged to take part in an air raid. I commend him to God's care. We all shake hands, exchange presents, leave everything lying where it happens to be, and hurry down to father's flat.

'Children,' says father, 'let's eat quickly, for we may soon have to take refuge in the cellar.'

We sit down. As has been the custom since my mother died, her chair stands at one end of the table, empty, and a candle is burning at her place. Thoughtfully, quietly and calmly we eat our supper. We all feel that a solemn, sombre time is coming soon when we will be face to face with our destiny. While supper is still in progress, a bomb goes off with a mighty blast right near our windows. We all look at each other.

'Let's go right on eating,' says father, 'maybe we can finish supper.'

We eat as fast as possible, but the explosions come closer and closer and get more and more frequent.

The door bell rings. Officers of the federal army are standing in front of the door. 'We're going to set up our cannon in the garden,' one of them says, 'and we're going to billet our troops in your house. Give us the keys to all the flats in the house.' My husband gets up to show the officers around. We hear a particularly loud explosion. The whole house is shaken as if by an earthquake.

A few minutes later my husband comes back. 'Father,' he says, 'we'd better get down to the cellar. The garage has been hit. Our central heating plant has been damaged. We've got to turn it off immediately and drain out the water. Get below, all of you, your lives aren't safe any more in the flat. The enemy troops must be very near now. The officers are saying the enemy has already reached the other side of the street. The fighting won't last long but still we must expect to spend the next few days in the cellar.'

Thoughtfully and with perfect calm, father says, 'Let the women and children all go below. I'm going to finish eating my supper. Please bring the coffee.'

We know there is no arguing with father. My younger sister gets up and takes her baby into her arms. I take her little boy by the hand, and my other sister takes the little girl. Together we go downstairs to the underground shelter. My brother, my husband and Bo-Ghar stay with father for coffee.

The explosions keep getting louder and stronger. Sitting in the cellar, we feel the house shaking in its foundations every time. After a while, the heavy iron door opens, and the men come in. Stepping over to me, my husband whispers in a low voice so that no one else can hear, 'They're putting up cannon in our garden, and they intend to defend our house to the very last. They refuse to give up the city. Our house is in a key spot for them. If the enemy troops take it, there will be no way to stop them from here right down to the river. We can expect they'll fight to the very last man. I only hope it won't last long. The city is completely surrounded, and any further resistance will simply entail senseless destruction. I'm going to get the janitor to help me bring down all our mattresses so that we can get some sleep.' And with that he leaves.

Even the longest night is followed by dawn, and so this night comes to an end too. The iron door opens and closes continually, as our menfolk come and go. Soldiers come in too occasionally and try to warm up a little. Outside a blizzard is raging and the thermometer stands at 15° below zero. It's cold in our cellar too. We sit there in all the clothes we can put on underneath our fur coats. There's no heat anywhere in the house now. The soldiers are mere boys. Pale and trembling with cold and fright, they get ordered out into battle with brutal unconcern by the older officers. Poor children! They're not older than sixteen or eighteen and have already been dragged away from home . . . into this mass murder!

We try to rest, but the little baby yells so loud and long not one of us can sleep a wink.

The next morning my father comes in looking surprisingly pale. 'Children,' he says, 'the water main has been hit. Go easy on what you use. There isn't any more water in the house.' With that he goes out. We hear the men outside talking about the possibility of bringing in water from somewhere else. All the water in the water pipes throughout the house is drained out into basins and bath tubs. Down here in our air raid shelter, we have a big wooden barrel full of water for fire-fighting purposes. Are we going to have to drink this old, stale, smelly water? My younger sister looks at me enquiringly. I know she's thinking about her babe-in-arms! Ever since her husband disappeared, her own milk ceased flowing. From that time on, her babe was fed cooked food. But for that we have to have water! And the baby's bottle has to be thoroughly washed between feeds. I try to calm her fears by whispering, 'It's snowing, we'll melt snow to make water.'

My husband hears me and calls me out into the room outside the shelter. 'Do you realize how little water you can get out of snow? The soldiers are taking all our water away. Unless we want to die of thirst, we'll have to get water from somewhere. We could go a long time without food, but without water the heart is affected. We have to have water. There are twenty-six adults in the house, and we can't even cook beans if we don't have water. I'm going out to try to find water somewhere in the neighbourhood,' he says, and leaves.

A short while later he comes back and reports, 'The houses all along the street haven't any water either. We'll have to go with buckets and carry water from the next through street.'

'Please don't go,' I answer him. 'The machine-gun fire is too terrible, and cannon and airplanes are shooting continually too. You might get hit. Stay here and wait.'

My husband smiles: 'Don't be a child. The First World War wasn't fought with cap pistols, and I still came through all right. *God* will not forsake us. Whatever is going to happen will happen anyway.'

I embrace him and he disappears behind the cellar door.

I go back into the shelter and sit down. And wait. Quiet and cold—I wait. If it's God's will for my husband to come back, no bullet will hit him. If not, then it *had* to be that way.

'Things are never bad; it's how you think about them.' I heard a voice in my heart. I tell myself that hundreds and thousands, even millions of wives are sitting somewhere, just as I am, praying for their husbands. These husbands are men like mine. The fact that my person loves his person so deeply is a manifestation of the self which is the same in every person. When two people love each other it means they are experiencing *the unity of the self* in their consciousness. They feel they belong together because they are one in the *self*.

I quiet my trembling heart but it still goes on trembling. 'Keep calm,' I tell it. 'Steady does it . . . just beat slowly and calmly. Now let's breathe slowly and deeply—still deeper—and still deeper . . . keep calm! We all of us have to put away the body some day. A hundred years from now it won't matter a bit who went first.

'*Time* and *space* are inventions of the intellect. But the spirit, the *self*, stands above the intellect, above all thoughts, above any concept of time and space. Breathe calmly and regularly and think of nothing . . . just be . . .'

I don't know how long I've been sitting there when the door opens again, and there is my husband with ten quarts of water. Water! Wonderful water! All of us, twenty-six people have enough of it to last a day! I don't stand up, and I don't throw myself about his neck. No, *the great moments are always very simple*! No sobbing, no tears, and no big words. From where he stands, portioning out the water, my husband glances over at me. Our eyes meet and we understand each other perfectly. I think to myself, reprieve! How long?

We sit in the cellar, in darkness. Outside the thunderous fire continues unremittingly. The earth trembles beneath, and we have to hold on to the bench below so that we are not thrown bodily to the floor. Cannon and tanks put up a steady barrage of fire. Airplanes roar past overhead. Bombs scream down and burst! The barrage of fire goes on and on! How long have we been sitting here in the cellar? By now I've lost all feeling for time. There is no day or night in the cellar. It's always dark. A dim little light is all we are allowed. We've had no electricity for a long time, and we have to husband our supply of oil. Whenever the barrage of fire stops for a half hour, we step out into the other cellar room and have something to eat. We are lucky to have laid in a supply of emergency rations. But all too often we have to stop eating suddenly and rush back into the shelter, for our house is now getting shot at from the other side too. After every hit, we hear tiles and beams from the roof and upper walls falling down on the ceiling above us. We never know whether or not the next blast will cause the ceiling to cave in and bury us all alive.

One day a deafening blast blows a huge hole in the wall of the next room in the cellar. Fortunately, it's not in our shelter. Later during a lull in the barrage of fire outside, my husband goes out to see what's happened. A gigantic hole gapes in the cellar wall. The bright sunshine streaming through it makes us both blink. Tile and bricks lie all about us. Splinters of wood, bits of glass . . . everything covered by a heavy layer of dust . . . and on one end of a beam that sticks up out of the general mess and confusion, a hen, also covered with a heavy layer of dust, stands there on one leg, just as calmly as if nothing had happened. She's one of father's chickens, the only one left. Poor animal! What an awful opinion it must have of us human beings! A few days later the cook's art has turned the hen into a delicious soup. While we're eating it, we discover how badly injured it was. Its leg bone had been shot through, and part of the leg was missing. That's why it stood there on one leg. With what stoic patience and indifference it bore up under its injury, not letting out so much as a squawk or a cackle to tell how much it was suffering.

Hour after hour we go on sitting in the shelter. Will the barrage of fire outside never stop? I hold my sister's little boy on my lap. My body is cold with fright, for even though a human being may face death with calm and quiet in his spirit, the body revolts. We don't know whether we may be hit by a bomb, buried alive, or die of thirst. The little boy begs me, 'Tell me a story, Aunt Esther, tell me a story.' And I tell him stories by the hour to keep him quiet. He holds a toy automobile in his hand, and it's my job to wind it up again and again. While he plays, he sings a little song. It sounds so familiar . . . what's the name of it? Now I remember. It's the song the little pig sings, 'Who's afraid of the big bad wolf?' in one of Walt Disney's films . . . Oh! how lucky I am that it's dark here in the cellar. Nobody can see that I've lost control of myself, and big soggy tears roll down over my cheeks. *God!* Oh *God!* You are present with us here! Your sacred message tells us all we musn't be afraid! 'Aunt Esther, tell me some more, tell me what happened then! Why have you stopped telling the story?' asks little Peter. I hold the dear boy close to my heart and go on with the story: 'And the little goat's mother came back and . . .'

After seemingly endless hours the barrage of fire stops. Just as he's been doing day after day, my husband goes out to get water. When he comes back, he waves to me. 'Esther,' he says all shaken and in a voice trembling with emotion, 'I've just been upstairs in our flat. The beautiful furniture you carved yourself, and all your lovely sculptured figures are a total wreck. The floor of one room is gone and so are the walls of the other rooms. We haven't a home any more . . .' And the poor dear boy drops his head on my shoulder, crying and sobbing like a baby.

I embrace him in his heavy winter coat: 'Don't cry! What really matters is that we're alive! We're still alive and uninjured in the midst of all this destruction. I can always make new figures. Don't worry about material things. Life stands over everything!'

He tries hard to control himself: 'I loved all your carvings . . . the whole apartment . . . so very very much! And now everything's gone . . . all gone . . .'

'No matter, even this hell will come to an end some day.' I lay my head for a moment on his broad shoulder. We embrace each other tenderly, then go back into the dark shelter. This is no time to be sentimental.

Bo-Ghar comes and whispers, 'What's happened? We heard the roof and walls falling in up where your apartment is.' I tell him what my husband has just told me. Bo-Ghar, the ever-calm, ever-smiling, gets all excited: 'I'm going up there! I have to salvage my slides and film on Yoga. My life's work will be ruined if they're destroyed. I'm going up.'

'Bo-Ghar, you musn't. Enemy sharpshooters will pick you off in a minute. I won't let you go up.'

My brother hears our conversation. 'I'll go up there with Bo-Ghar,' he says. 'I'll help him.' Together they leave the cellar . . . we wait anxiously. Minute after minute goes by . . . a quarter hour . . . an hour . . . we're still waiting.

Finally the door opens, and Bo-Ghar and my brother come in, dusty and dirty but beaming with success. In their hands they hold the precious boxes of slides and reels of film. My brother tells us, 'The walls have all caved in, but the cupboard was still standing in the corner on a little piece of floor. We had to get over to the cupboard, but there wasn't any floor left to walk on. Only an iron beam. And we had to watch out that the sharpshooters across the street didn't see us. So both of us lay down and crawled across the beam. Bo-Ghar dug out all the boxes from the cupboard and handed them over to me, one after the other. Now we've got everything!'

We're all of us happy that the two men have come back to us. Bo-Ghar hides his treasures in a corner so no one can find them. The very next moment we're blasted almost off our feet. A deafening blast shakes what's left of the house. Another attack! We hear the airplanes roar past overhead, bombs, mines, shells and shrapnel of all sizes beat the ground and the walls around and over us. The explosions come closer and closer, and after each of them we hear tiles and bricks and rubble tumbling down overhead. The barrage of fire is so continuous it sounds as if it might be some gigantic, cosmic sewing machine. Any moment the next shell may burst through the ceiling overhead, our last protection, and blow us all to kingdom come. We sit there mute and cold in this horrible anxiety, in deathly fright and fear of death. How long can the walls hold? Then, a gigantic blast, so powerful the whole cellar floor dances beneath us . . . and my father's chambermaid suddenly starts to scream with the nervous shock. The other women servants start screaming too. I jump up and yell at the top of my lungs, '*Quiet! Quiet! God is here! God is here!*'

Explosion follows explosion, so loud they can hardly hear my voice, but I keep on shouting. I just have to shout at the top of my lungs, '*God is here! Let all of us, every one, think only of God, nothing else, only of God! God be with us! God!—God!—God!*' And one by one the others join me as we repeat together, '*God is here . . . God . . . God . . . God . . .*'

None of us knows how long this has gone on. Little by little the pandemonium outside has lessened. The blasts have become less frequent, and at last it's quiet outside. We can hear soldiers dragging something heavy. I go out to have a look. On the stairs are bodies lying motionless. On the floor is blood. I recognize several of the young soldiers. Only an hour ago they were seeking warmth with us in the shelter, telling us about their homes and families far away. Their poor parents! Waiting in vain for their children to come home! My son! Where can the poor boy be now? In what department of Hell?

Then we grab a bite to eat. We know we have to take advantage of every moment of calm. We have to strengthen our bodies' resistance . . . as long as we have anything to eat . . . two men go out to get water . . .

How long have we been sitting here in this shelter? Weeks have gone by while we've been in this barrage of hellfire. My husband reminisces: 'In Doberdo, in the First World War, we were caught in a barrage of fire too. But every forty-eight hours we were relieved. People thought a person's nerves couldn't stand any more than that. I never dreamed I would one day be sitting through an unending barrage, together with women and children, for several weeks, and without any relief!'

We all sit there in furs and heavy winter coats. None of us has been able to take off a stitch of clothing ever since we came down to this dungeon. Little Peter is lying in my arms. With one hand I hang on to the little suitcase containing money, my jewellery, and a box of cakes by way of food supply for the babe-in-arms in case we have to flee. We are all of us ready to jump. The villa next to ours was burnt out with flame throwers. My husband has given orders to everyone to be ready to flee at a moment's notice. We don't know when the enemy may set fire to our house and drive us out with flame throwers. But flee where? We haven't the vaguest idea. Only out and away from here. Our neighbour and his son were both picked off with sharpshooters while they were trying to escape from their burning house. Only his wife came out alive. She crawled and wriggled on her stomach all the way to the fourth house down the street, where people took her in.

We wait in readiness, my younger sister with her babe-in-arms . . . my snowy-haired father wrapped in his big black fur coat, my elder sister's family, my brother, our servants—all tense—all holding our most precious possessions—all ready to jump and run.

Then for a little while it's quiet outside again. We'd like to get some sleep. My nerves are burning and my head feels ready to split. I close my eyes and try to withdraw my consciousness and fall asleep. But then the baby starts to scream with its shrill penetrating voice. My sister tries to quiet it, but it keeps on crying and screaming without a moment's intermission. I take over the child from my sister and try everything I can think of, but it keeps on crying . . . crying desperately. I hand the child back to my sister, and it still goes on crying . . . crying . . .

In the darkness, Bo-Ghar stumbles over to my sister, picks up the child, holds it gently in his arms and starts humming a tune from his faraway homeland. It's a tune his countrymen use to control snakes. The child quiets down instantly. As calm returns to our cellar, we all of us fall asleep, sitting there just as we are. Only Bo-Ghar is awake, holding the baby in his arms and humming his exotic little tune.

More days go by—or are they weeks? We don't even bother to ask any more. Behind a protective wall in the garden, my husband scrapes together some snow, brings the pail downstairs and shaves in the next room in the cellar. He refuses to give up his habits. All the other men have bushy beards. Only my husband and Bo-Ghar keep on shaving day by day in the midst of this hell.

Then my husband sits down beside us. A new attack begins and we endure the torture for hours on end. My sister brings her baby's bottle and gives him his meal. Four times a day she goes upstairs to her flat and cooks for her baby, despite the hail of bullets flying around. After her child has had its fill, she comes to me and asks, just as she asks every day, 'Do you think it's over yet?'

'No,' I whisper back. 'I just feel it isn't over yet'. A moment later a mine bursts directly over our head. Once again we hear tiles and bricks and mortar and wood falling. The shelter ceiling has held up under the blast. But how much longer? We sit there quietly, and I ask *God* within me: 'Shall I get ready to die? My horoscope says I'm going to die in the crash of a building. Is it now? Am I going to die, or shall I go on fighting to live?'

Then suddenly amidst the darkness I behold a vision: a tiny little hill, and on it a candle, a tiny one like a Christmas tree candle, burning with a tiny flame. Then before my very eyes, the little hill begins to grow, turning into a big hill covered with emerald green grass. And the tiny candle grows into a torch, burning with a bright strong flame.

The vision disappears, but I know I am not going to die yet. I'm going to have to be this torch. I'm going to have to bring people light—light—*light, light*!

At night the baby cries incessantly until Bo-Ghar picks it up and lulls it to sleep. While we're trying to sleep a mine explodes near by, and afterwards I feel ice-cold air come into our shelter. The men jump up to see what's happened.

The cellar wall has caved in, leaving a gaping hole. We all think of the coming attack. We wait. I whisper to my younger sister, 'Now it's the end. In the morning our villa will be taken.'

'Yes,' she answers, 'I think so too, or else we'll all die.'

My husband whispers, 'It's seven weeks to the day that we've been sitting here in the shelter . . .'

Strangely enough, the enemy cannon have ceased firing. No bombs are falling either. We hear only continuous machine gun fire. Sitting next to me, my husband whispers into my ear, 'That means the infantry is quite near us. They've stopped using field guns in order not to hit their own troops. Enemy soldiers may walk in any minute.'

In the afternoon I go out to see where father is. As I step out of the shelter and look out through the door of the house, I see foreign soldiers running towards us from the burnt-down villa next door. 'Father, Father, and all the rest of you,' I scream as I run back, 'the enemy is here!'

We all rush back into the shelter just as enemy soldiers lunge through the door, their rifles at the ready.

Deathly silence! We and they look at each other for a seemingly endless moment. It's as if time itself were standing still . . .

All the soldiers are dressed in broad white coats. Outside everything is covered with snow. The soldiers look like children playing in a Christmas pageant.

Then with a word we cannot understand, their leader points to the women. We understand we must move to the right, and we do so. Then with another incomprehensible word, he points to the men, who all have to leave immediately with one of the soldiers. No time for fond farewells! the men are gone, and we women remain alone with the foreign soldiers. With their sub-machine guns in readiness, they poke into every corner of the cellar, looking for any of our troops who might be hiding there. One young soldier steps over to the pram where the baby is sleeping. Even as he looks at it, tears come into his eyes. With infinite tenderness, he says a strange word in a foreign language. Nevertheless we understand: 'Little baby . . .' Then he looks at us and points in the direction of his homeland, telling us in sign language that he too has a 'little baby' at home . . .

I feel somewhat consoled as I note that these soldiers are loving, kind-hearted human beings too.

Now an officer comes, sits down on a chair, and tells us in a European language: 'We won't harm you. We are storm troops . . . sons of people who now belong to an exterminated class. But watch out, we have to go on. Behind us there'll come soldiers of another kind. They're not like us. Watch out!'

Late in the afternoon the shooting begins again. But now the fire is coming from our country's own soldiers. They want to recapture our house. Again we sit still in the dark cellar and listen to horrible fighting going on at close quarters in the street outside. All of a sudden there is another deafening explosion, followed by a stream of cold air coming in on us. The explosion has blasted open the heavy iron shutter of the cellar window. Through the open window bullets rain in on us like hailstones. We all jump to one side, flattening ourselves against the walls but this way we are unable to move. In this situation every one of our lives is in danger. A single step can mean death. The heavy iron window shutter *must* be closed!

I look about me. All the women and children seek refuge by flattening themselves against the wall near the window. For the moment any one of us shows herself in front of the window, a shower of bullets rains in upon us. This situation is untenable. The shutter *must be closed*!

I feel a strange chill within me. My every nerve is cold, frozen so cold I can't feel myself at all. 'Afraid?' I ask myself. No! Who is there to be afraid within me when I feel as if I didn't even exist? I only know that *I* am the one who must close the iron shutter! Neverthless I observe myself curiously. What does it feel like to be in such a position? What does a person experience? How does nature react within the human being when we involuntarily have to be a hero...?

Standing in one corner of the cellar is a heavy walking stick with a curved handle. Lying flat on the floor, I crawl slowly and cautiously over to the cane. Then, grasping its lower end, I crawl back towards the window. While I am executing this manoeuvre, a weird thought flashes through my head: *The candidates in the pyramid had to pass a test of 'defying death'! Maybe I'm now passing this same test here in the shelter? Maybe this is all only a dream during my initiation in the pyramid?*

While I crawl back cautiously to the window, my intellect replies: 'Yes, the candidates in the pyramid had it easy! They knew they were only undergoing a test in their initiation. But these bullets aren't dreams! They really kill! How many poor young soldiers have already lost their lives right here!

Nevertheless the window shutter must be closed, *and for that very reason!*'

Kneeling beneath the window and holding the cane in readiness, I suddenly jump up and poke out my arm and the cane through the window. Then, noting that the iron shutter has been blasted wide open, I find I must extend my head and shoulder through the window in order to reach the edge of the shutter with the cane's curved handle. I have to reach out and stretch until I feel as if my whole body were getting longer. Finally I have the shutter and draw it slowly, surely, inward. Now my sisters jump up to help, pull the heavy, iron shutter into place and bolt it firmly closed.

Well done! All very simple. No excitement, no theatrics, no histrionics. And yet how strange! Up till now the sharpshooters across the street poured a hail of fire into our window at the slightest sign of life. And yet throughout my whole manoeuvre to close the iron shutter, they didn't fire a single shot. Maybe they were being prevented from shooting, or simply didn't want to shoot, because they saw I was a woman? 'Aunt Esther,' begs little Peter, 'tell me another story...'

And so I go on telling stories by the hour . . .

The next day we women had to flee from our bombed-out house. The intervening night was one of indescribable horror. I can hardly believe that such things can really happen. The conquest of a country is like the meeting of male and female power *in a violent marriage*. One country conquers another, forces its way into the body of the other. Blood flows. Individual inhabitants die like the cells of the ravished body, and yet new life comes forth from this meeting . . . a new world, a new creation. The meeting is cruel and violent, just as the creation of new life always is. But nature only looks forward into the future, willingly sacrificing countless individual cells and beings in order to reach its goal of bringing forth new life. And new life does come forth, both on the spiritual and on the material level, from the intimate meeting of two countries, that of the conqueror and that of the conquered. Out of the marriage of two countries, a new civilization arises. The cells of the bodies of these two countries meet and mingle, bringing forth children with some of the characteristics of both races. Nature creates hybrid races and individuals who represent a transition, softening and bridging over the hard boundaries between races and nations.

It was my fate to learn this fact that night in the air raid shelter of that bombed-out house. I was forced to look on and see that the violent marriage of two nations is very cruel and causes many individual tragedies. It was *Ima* who saved me from the fate that overtook almost all the women in that house that night. When one of the soldiers started to drag me from my seat in the corner of the shelter, forcing me to follow him, I told him in a pidgin version of his language: 'I—mother, son in war—you have mother at home too, please go away . . .'

In the half drunk eyes of the poor young man whose body had been poisoned with 'storm pills' there flashed an expression of understanding. I saw that he was *forced* to think of his own mother. Then with a gesture of frustration and rage, he pushed me back under the bench and stormed out of the cellar.

The next morning we felt an inner command to flee from the bombed-out house. We felt the guidance of a higher power. For reasons beyond our comprehension, it saved us from the fate awaiting all women—without exception—in the ruins of our house.

Everything happened as if in a chaotic dream.

After five weeks in darkness, we step out suddenly into bright sunshine, so bright our eyes can hardly stand it. I cast a backward glance at our big beautiful villa. . . a pile of rubble. . . topped off by broken beams pointing their splintered ends skyward! Then we run across the street, picking our way between corpses and rubble, over to the steps. My sister carries her babe-in-arms. As I watch, I see her plunge down the steps in the deep snow. I run to her side, help her up, then fall over myself with the little boy I am holding by the hand. Under the snow are wire obstacles! While we are trying to climb over with the children, an elderly soldier of the enemy army lifts the little boy over the wire barrier, then helps all the rest of us over, the women and the children, one after the other. I am the last. We cannot talk to the soldier. We wouldn't understand each other. But we look into each other's eyes, and I give him a hearty handshake in sincere appreciation. He reciprocates the handshake. Then we run on, zig-zagging back and forth in search of cover from the mines which are still exploding and from the bullets falling about us. The children yell at the top of their lungs. The snow is too deep for little Peter; so with all my might and main I drag him along stretched out flat behind me because he isn't able to walk. From time to time we stop under a terrace to catch our breath and to warm the children's hands by blowing on them. Then we run on, scarcely knowing which way we're going, driven onwards . . . or led on . . . by an inner power.

And it's like a dream to be taken into a house at long last where a good-natured officer of the enemy army protects us from violence at the hands of his own comrades. As we get to be good friends, he tells me, 'Mama, watch out! *One* good soldier, *ten* bad soldiers! Not all the men in our army would give you protection the way I'm doing. Watch out when I get orders to move on!'

Yes, we know all enemy soldiers are not so humane! We have the experiences of our first night behind us, and will never forget them!

And the men have disappeared . . . all except father whom we have soon found again. Calmly, without excitement, paying no attention to the cannonade going on around him, the old gentleman walked through this scene of mass murder and while everyone else was being robbed of everything he possessed—fur, coat, gloves, money, watch, fountain pen, and everything else one can carry on his person—my father arrived safe and sound in the home of an old friend without a single soldier's having so much as touched him. His powerful radiation even affected the enemy soldiers and kept them away from him.

Then a few days later there is a knock on the door of this strange room in a strange house where fourteen people, soldiers, refugees and we women and children are living. A knock on the door, and Bo-Ghar stands before us, in tattered clothes, with bleeding feet, After all he has been through, it's a miracle he's still alive. Neighbours told him the direction in which they saw us flee. He has found us again . . .

A few days later my brother comes back, also in tatters. He too has had to travel several hundred kilometres. Somewhere he found himself two shoes, both of them for the left foot, and wears them both with his accustomed dignity. He's alive, that's all that matters . . . !

As the days go by I still have no news from my husband. I can't seem to get the thought out of my head that I've seen him one day, in a vision, lying helpless in the snow beside the road . . . What could have happened to him?

After long weeks of waiting in vain, I finally find my husband, gravely injured, in the house of a good-hearted farmer. My vision wasn't wrong . . .

Weeks go by, months go by. We're hungry and don't know where our next meal is coming from. But one day, at long last, the war is over!

We try to make some rooms in the ruins of our house inhabitable. Bo-Ghar and I work day and night to get something to eat in this time of terrible famine. My husband is forced to lie flat on his back for many long months until he recovers sufficiently to be able to walk about cautiously with two canes. How fortunate I am a sculptress! I do bricklaying, take doors out of the remnants of walls, and move them to where we need them. We put together window frames. Having no glass, we cover them with heavy wrapping paper. Digging in the rubble with our ten finger nails, we bring out a few usable pots and pans, plus some bent and beaten silverware.

Bo-Ghar and I manage to borrow a cart and use it to bring home several hundredweight of coal, pulling all the way like two strong horses. Downhill, we find it hard to keep the cart from running away from us; uphill, it takes all our pushing and pulling to get it up to the top where we reach a level street again and can trot along lightly and gaily. Then we clean up the remnants of our furniture, using miscellaneous odd bits to make new pieces.

We keep on hammering and nailing things together until at last we are able to reopen our 'Yoga school' in the ruins of our old home. Bo-Ghar gives lessons in the physical exercises he learnt from Mentuptah, while I teach what I learned in Egypt from Ptahhotep.

Months go by again, and little by little the problem of finding food becomes somewhat less acute. Our pupils who have relatives living in the country bring us an occasional handful of flour, a few potatoes, eggs, and once in a while even a bit of butter. But I still have no news from my son . . .

Then one day, after a year and a half of waiting, someone rings our doorbell. I open the door—and Ima stands before me!

I would have thought that in such cases mother and son would fall about each other's necks with loud cries and sobs. But no! I look at him in surprise, then we embrace each other quietly and earnestly. I draw a deep breath of relief. He is alive and not crippled. Only a scar on his beautiful, high forehead shows that he has been through an airplane crash.

But still I am deeply dismayed! I know Ima well enough to know there is no room for him in this country where vulgarity, brutality, stupidity and utter chaos are the order of the day. And without jeopardizing life and limb excessively, a person can experience such conditions only if he preserves his inner peace, his perfect trust in God and—keeps silent! But Ima won't keep silent! He doesn't understand that we're not in the temple now where love and truth and unselfishness prevail and where everyone may speak his opinion freely without risk of being misunderstood.

Ima won't be able to get along in this world. He won't tolerate injustice, and he'll want to fight against the infernal spirit prevailing here now! Apparently he has forgotten *who* he is, and yet he has retained his highmindedness, honesty and courage and expects the sons of men to display these same virtues. He *insists* on believing in *people*, and he has crowded off into the unconscious part of his being his indomitable faith in God.

Poor Ima has to experience one disappointment after another. Why does he repress his faith in God? Why does he *refuse* to believe in *God*? That's the reason why he's lost his self-confidence! I can see that he must have experienced a serious mental crack-up, but when and where? And why do I have the strange and oppressing feeling that *I* have been the cause of this mental rupture—a horrible disappointment—?

I know that somewhere, some time, he has lost his faith *because of me*, but in vain I seek the reason. One thing I know with absolute certainty is that it is up to *me* to lead him back to *God*, and that's why he has become my son. *I* must awaken his self-confidence, which is identical with *confidence in God*, and make him conscious again of this confidence, because *I* was to blame for his having lost it. I must realize that the deep love and confidence he has in *me* is only a projection of the profound confidence in God he has in the unconscious part of his soul. He must come to realize that he has to learn to recognize and love *God* in every person. The person is only an outer cover, a mask, through which *God* manifests himself.

Ima must learn that what he *loves* in any person, and what he finds good, beautiful and true in anyone is *God* and not the person. And that applies to me too whom he loves—I know it—more than anyone else here on earth. It's up to me to lead this love in him back to God. He must come to realize that he loves *God* in me too, and my person is only an instrument through which *God* manifests himself in the form of maternal love. Ima has yet to learn that in every person who loves him it is really God who loves him and not the person. When he realizes these things he will understand me and everyone else and even himself better. Then he won't experience any more disappointments!

And there comes a night in which my one and only child, the person I love most here on earth, is living in an unheated room during an unusually cold winter when the thermometer has been dragging along at 20° below zero for week after week. My one and only child doesn't even have a warm blanket and has scarcely anything to eat. I could easily provide a heated room for him, I could give him food and everything else he needs. But I know I must not! *I know it's more important for him not to lose his soul than his body! Out of love for him I must be cruel!*

I kneel in the darkness in my bed and speak to my *God*: '*You* be with him, oh *God*, and let him find *himself* and *you* again. Let him find the way that leads to *you*, and let him never deviate from it! Awaken him, awaken *yourself* in him, oh *God*, for *you* are also dwelling in him and *you* must awaken in him so that he may awaken, for my strength is inadequate. He must become conscious. Unless he does so he's lost, and *you* know the one and only path for him to follow in order to recognize *you*, oh Lord my God, in *himself*. You know why he feels he has been forsaken by *everyone* . . . why he's convinced that even *I* have forsaken him.

'He has to feel disappointed in everyone, he has to give up hope in everyone in order to find *you* . . . in order to become *conscious in you—conscious of himself!* You know, oh *God* that I don't see any other possibility of saving him. I cannot and must not show my love for him any more. He must find *you* by his own efforts. I am only a weak human being, my Lord, but *you* are *God, Love* itself. *You* love him more than I can love him. *You*, oh *God*, are always with him. Love him now with your divine love . . . now when I must be cruel!

'Take care of him and keep him from losing his health during this present struggle of his . . . while he's going through this school. *You* know that he's sinning against his health because he has no confidence in himself any more . . because in his unconscious he would like to die . . . to kill himself. Take care of him, open his spiritual eyes and don't forsake him, *don't forsake him, don't forsake him* . . .'

And so I go on night after night . . .

One night as I'm kneeling in my bed in the darkness again, preparing to speak to *God* about my child, something strange happens: To my great amazement, it begins to get light about me. It gets lighter and lighter, and in the growing brightness I see a remarkable landscape. A high mountain with a steep, stony, narrow path leading up to it. I know this path leads to the goal— to *God*. Without hesitating I start to follow it.

The path leads through friendly countryside, higher and higher. I climb untiringly until the charming green landscape lies behind me and I gradually reach the inhospitable region of the high mountains.

The pathway gets ever steeper, narrower and stonier, but I climb with astonishing ease, so light as if I were gliding.

The inhabited territory lies behind me. My horizon widens, and I see everything far below me. But there is no time to look around, and I go on. After many curves, the narrow pathway ends in front of a short stairway with seven steps. Each step is twice as high as the one before.

Under a crystal blue sky I stand there all alone in front of these seven steps and know that I must climb them.

With a deep sigh and with faith in the power the Creator has given each of his children—the power which in my case has miraculously gone on un-diminished and even increased as I have climbed this long path—I walk up to the steps.

The first step is low. I must conquer the *weight of my body* in order to lift myself up on to it. I succeed easily.

The second step is somewhat higher and awakens the resistance of my body. I have long ago conquered the *forces of the body*, and so this step too causes me no trouble.

The third is *noticeably higher*. In order to conquer this one I have to conquer my *feelings*. As I become master of my feelings, I am on the third step.

As I face the fourth step, which is surprisingly high, thoughts of *doubt* over-come me; 'How will I be able to climb it? Have I enough strength?' Then I realize that my *doubts* are weakening me, paralysing me. But doubt is a thought! So I must conquer my *thoughts* in order to master doubt. Thanks to my long training and my exercises in the temple, I know what I have to do; I gather all the strength of my soul, I *am* absolute faith in God, and think of absolutely nothing. And behold—as my thoughts disappear, my doubts disappear too. And I am on the fourth step.

Curiously, I feel I have grown much larger while I have been climbing these steps. Each time I've gone up a step, I've grown some more, and now I'm much much larger than I was at the beginning. Now I face the fifth step which, even though I've grown a great deal, is so high that I can only get up by using both hands and both feet. As I pull myself up with great difficulty, I suddenly find to my great surprise that I have no body any more. Everything in me or about me that was *material* has disappeared, and I am invisible *spirit*.

The sixth step is very, very high, and a new difficulty awaits me. I have no body, no hands with which to hang on and no feet with which to push myself up. How am I supposed to get up there?

I look about me for some way to do it, and as I turn around, I suddenly see the whole world spread out below me! Country after country . . . city after city looking like little toys . . . and houses with countless people living in them. Infinite love for them all seizes me and I am pained to think of all the people who would have to travel the long, laborious pathway of recognition . . . of all the innumerable people feeling their way forward in the darkness, imprisoned in their own selfishness just as I was once . . .

And, wonder of wonders!—the moment *universal love* floods my heart, I am raised up and find myself on the sixth step.

Now I stand before the last and highest step of all. It is just as high as I am. I long so much to get up there and this wish fills my whole being. In vain. I just don't know what to do. I have no hands, no feet nor muscular strength of body with which to pull myself up. But I must get up there at any price. Up on top I'll find *God*, and I am determined to see him face to face.

I stand, waiting, but nothing happens.

As I look around me, I find to my great surprise that I'm not alone. At this very moment a being similar to myself reaches the sixth step and begs me to help him up to the seventh. I understand his tremendous desire, and—forgetting my own longing to reach the seventh step—I try to help him reach his goal.

But the very moment I forget my own wish, I suddenly find that *I* am up on top of the seventh step—I don't know how—and my companion is no longer there. He has disappeared without leaving a trace. He was an *illusion* who helped me forget my last self-centred wish. As long as I wanted to raise up my own person, I would never be able to conquer the step that was *as high as I myself*.

I have arrived! Quicker than a flash of lightning I see the form of a heavenly being woven of dazzling light. My complementary half! His irresistible attraction draws me to him, and—full of delight and fulfilment—I melt into complete union with him in his heart. I realize that He was always I and I always He, the dualistic projected image of my divine, true *self*. In this dualistic state I always faced *God* as a being separate from myself, and I felt *Him* as

'You'. Now in paradisiacal unity, I feel that this invisible power I have so far always called '*God*' will become *myself* in the next moment. A disc woven of fire begins to rotate about me. And in its immovable axis—in my spinal column —my true *self*—*I*—am dwelling.

And I feel my spinal column burning like a white hot bow, like a bridge made up of the current of life, radiating brilliant light through seven centres of force —vitalizing my body.

Then, beyond all concept of time, I simultaneously see the endlessly long chain of the different forms of life in which I have been incarnated throughout ages and aeons of time as I travelled the long pathways of development from my first fall out of paradisiacal unity up to the present moment. I see that my countless lives have been, are, and will be inseparably linked with the lives of the same spirits. From the events of past lives new relationships emerge, new ties, new developments, all supplementing each other and fitting together perfectly like the little stones in a big mosaic.

I recognize the threads linking me with my complementary half, with Ptahhotep, with Atothis, with Ima and Bo-Ghar and many, many other people. I see clearly how these threads have bound us all together for ages of time, how souls more advanced than we are have helped us, how we have helped each other and those less advanced in the great task of the spiritualization of the earth, in developing our consciousness in matter, in the body. The experiences we bring each other in all these lives help expand and deepen the consciousness in the body, while the bodies we inhabit get progressively more spiritual, more beautiful. The matter composing our various forms of manifestation becomes ever more elastic, more responsible to the will and the radiations of the spirit, until finally the body becomes an obedient servant of the *self*, no longer isolating or obscuring a single ray of light from the spirit. I understand the secret of the pyramid, for now I have become a pyramid myself, only using matter—the body—as a firm footing, but constantly *manifesting divinity*!

Then everything about me, the earth, sky, the entire universe—all merge in a single gigantic sea of fire. Huge flames encompass me. For a moment I feel as if I, with the entire cosmos, were being destroyed. Flashes of lightning crack and snap through my veins, through my entire being, as the fire burns me. And then, suddenly everything changes: the fire is no longer consuming me but *I myself am this heavenly fire, penetrating everything, animating everything, consuming everything!* A flood of light surrounds me, but this flood of light is arising within myself. *I am* the source of this light and of everything else that *is*. The earth has no effect on me any more. Its attraction which held me in fetters ceases. I am floating in *nothingness*. My being has no limitations any more. *I am* now the one who attracts everything, but nothing ties *me* down any more— nothing attracts *me* any more . . .

I seek those whom I have loved, for I know they couldn't be destroyed, but I seek them in vain, in the *nothingness* about me. In the emptiness there is nothing but myself, so I have to turn my attention inward.

Behold, even as I do so I realize that *every one and everything is living in me*! The universe is in *me*, for everything that *is* is *living in me*. Everything that is, *I am*. In everything that I love, *I love myself*. And suddenly I realize that everything I have always *believed* I didn't love was what I had *not yet recognized within myself*! Now that I recognize myself perfectly, I love *everything* and *every one* equally, for *I am one* with them, *I am 'I' in everything, in all*!

I am fulfilment, life—radiant, eternal, immortal *being* . . . there is no longer any struggle, any regret, any suffering—no decay, no end, no death! *In all that is born I—the immortal—begin a new form of life, and in all that dies I—the immortal—withdraw into myself, back into the eternal, creative, divine self.*

I realize that *time* and *space* exist only on the periphery of the created world which is like a disc rotating with dizzying speed. *But I, within myself, am timeless, spaceless eternity.* And while I am *resting within myself* my eternal *being* fills *space* and everything living in it:

I AM THE ONLY REALITY, I AM LIFE, I AM THAT I AM!

I rest within myself and feel infinite *peace* . . . but in this peace a call reaches me and compels me to return to my deserted body. I turn the searchlight of my consciousness on to it and recognize the voice speaking to my being, the well-known, dearly beloved voice of my master *Ptahhotep. He* is calling me back . . .

And I step out of my heavenly *self* and put on the garment of my personal 'ego' again. But I bring with me the consciousness of who *I am* . . .

I am a human being again, but in my heart I carry the divine *self* that has become conscious in me—God—and from now on this divine *self* will be acting through my person . . . and slowly I open my eyes.

My glance meets the deep blue, heavenly eyes of my master *Ptahhotep*. His eyes radiate the same light, the same love and the same peace I have just experienced during the blissful state in my initiation . . . the same light, the same love, and the same peace I now carry in my own heart.

I can't bring my lips to utter a sound. I am still unable to find the connection between myself and my body.

But I don't need to speak, for I know my master's every thought and wish. We are in spiritual unity, in *God*. All one!

He lays his right hand upon my heart, and gradually I feel life returning to my body. I draw a deep breath, and the renewed regenerated stream of life flows through my numb limbs. My heart beats vigorously again. Gradually I regain control of my body.

Ptahhotep and his deputy help me sit up and slowly get out of the coffin. I stand insecurely on my feet. Ptahhotep and the other high priest take me by the hands and lead me out of the niche where the initiation coffin stands. Then I see that all the initiates of the temple, priests and priestesses, are assembled in the great hall where the Ark of the Covenant is kept. Expectantly they are all waiting for me. And as I come out, led by the two high priests, they greet me with the sacred word and secret greeting of the initiates:

'OM' . . .

In this circle of the resurrected, I stand there like a new-born babe. I have the same body as before. And yet I am a new being. I find myself in a new world: I no longer see everything from the outside, but simultaneously the inner being, the core about which the external form is built up, the centre for which the external form merely serves as a manifestation.

I stand in the circle of the resurrected. My inner being vibrates in the tone of the sacred word—the divine mantram. And with the aid of this indescribable vibration, in this magic tone, I experience in my own physical consciousness the divine *unity of the self* with all these initiates and with the entire *universe*. They have all come, priests and priestesses, to greet me after my resurrection and to express divine infinite love. My father, Atothis, is here too, wearing the plain white robe of the initiates. Then there is the soft-spoken master Mentuptah, and my dear brother Ima. The moment I see his noble countenance, his eyes light up with a smile, and I remember all my dream pictures, the most difficult tests of the initiation, the test of renunciation—giving up everything—and the test of cruel love! Ima, you dearly beloved, do you know that in my initiation vision you were the reason for my passing the most difficult test of all?

The majestic figure of an elderly priestess now moves forward from the circle of initiates. She hands Ptahhotep a robe, and together they invest me with my priestly clothing. Then she hands Ptahhotep the headdress, the sign of initiates, and *He* sets the band of gold upon my head. In front, the circlet of gold bears the head of a serpent, symbol of the procreative energy of life, transformed and spiritualized. Now, at last, I can wear this insignia, not only as a queen, but also as an initiate!

Now I am a priestess, in the lowest degree of the priesthood. It's up to me to reach the higher degrees step by step until I am worthy to be permitted to use the staff of life.

Ptahhotep steps over to my side, lays his hand upon my head and blesses me. Then *He* takes me by the hand and leads me to the initiates. First, of course, to the second high priest. He too lays his hand upon me and blesses me. Then I step before my dear father and feel him, through his hand, pouring out all the love in his heart upon me. And so one by one, according to their rank, I step before each of the initiates and receive his blessing. At last I stand in front of Ima who received his initiation shortly before me. He blesses me too, but I feel his hand tremble...

Then Ptahhotep leads me to the Ark of the Covenant. I kneel before it. For the first time in my life I am permitted to lay my hands upon it. In every drop of my blood I feel the fiery power flowing out of the Ark of the Covenant into my body. I breathe deeply—into my innermost being—and now with my consciousness awake, *in my body*, I experience the fulfilment of paradisiacal unity—the omnipotence and omniscience in *God* ... I understand and experience the meaning of *being*. Wherever I turn the searchlight of my consciousness there is clarity and light. In radiant brilliance the last and highest truths of life stand before my eyes. I experience the absolute, omnipotence that comes through the guidance of divine creative power in my *self*.

Ptahhotep again takes me by the hand and leads me back through the rooms through which we came here . . . back through the passageways, through the stone door, back into the temple. The initiates come after us. In the temple all the neophytes are waiting, and it's my turn to officiate as priestess for the first time. I stand before the altar with Ptahhotep, while all the neophytes come, one after the other, to receive my blessing. Upon each I place my right hand, and each accepts my blessing in deep silence. Finally the children of the neophyte school approach, among them my little adopted son, Bo-Ghar. He kneels before me, looks at me devotedly, then bows his head and receives my blessing.

Oh Bo-Ghar, my little Bo-Ghar, what a strange role you played in my initiation vision! . . .

This ends my first priestly office in the temple. In the little cell I used during my preparations for initiation, Ptahhotep leaves me alone. After the prescribed time of complete rest, I am again allowed to eat light foods and beverages.

For a long time I sit on my couch unable to shake off the effect of the strange visions experienced during my initiation. What horrible pictures! How lucky I am to wake up and find these dreams are not real! How was it possible for me to carry such pictures within myself and thus come to dream them? They just can't be real! It's absolutely impossible for people to become so depraved and degraded as to kill each other with such cruelty and with such hellish instruments! The cellar, the horrible shelter of my dream! And still I know the eternal law that a creature can only imagine pictures which could actually exist in reality! *Whatever a person can imagine can materialize! If this were not so he wouldn't be able to imagine it!*

But these horrible pictures! These gigantic birds piloted by the sons of men, flying overhead with a fearful roar, often climbing so high one can't see them any more, and throwing down evil eggs upon the earth! I saw with my own eyes how these eggs destroyed everything within a wide radius of where they hit the ground. With deafening blasts, they brought down whole houses . . . how was that possible?

And why should the sons of men put their intellect in the service of fiendish senselessness?

And what strange apparatus I saw and used in my initiation visions! I heard human voices speaking from tremendous distances, and others heard my voice in the same way. How Ima would laugh if I were to tell him that people could communicate over long distances by means of such devices instead of using the much simpler method of mental telepathy. He would surely want me to give him a thorough explanation of the construction of such a device. And that I couldn't do! Just as I couldn't give a description of the inner construction of the staff of life or the Ark of the Covenant in a way that would enable anyone to make such devices. Yet nevertheless they do exist! And in the same way I know this telephone device can exist! And Ima! You pure, true servant of *God*, in my initiation dream you too had to pilot such a big iron bird! You and all the handsome, healthy young men—you had to go out in great numbers, as if bewitched, to kill others and allow yourself to be killed . . . how could you go along with this madness? How could you obey such inhuman orders?

And who was the burning man who was 'my husband' in my initiation dream? . . . how close he was to my heart. He was my best friend! And still he didn't know who I am, and I don't know who he is.

And so I experience each individual picture of my initiation dreams again. I recognize all the people who were my parents, brothers and sisters, friends and enemies in my present life here in Egypt. And often I really have to smile about the curious relationships . . .

Evening comes, and the day ends with a feast in which all the priests, priestesses and neophytes take part. The Pharaoh is present too, and since the relatives of the new initiate are permitted to attend an initiation feast, my dear old Menu is there with the rest of us! As I step into the garden, she runs towards me as fast as her heavy body will carry her. Beaming with joy, she embraces me and sobs with the relief of her pent-up anxiety: 'Oh how good it is to see you alive again! Tell me, will you still love me, now that you're a priestess, will you still love me? Can I go on living with you?'

I stroke her dear old head and calm her fears: 'Menu, Menu, naturally I love you. Of course you can stay with me. Now even greater love binds me to you.'

── 38 ──

AS A PRIESTESS

THE PRIESTESSES in the temple have different tasks corresponding to their different abilities. Some teach the temple dancers. Some help the restless souls of departed dead who wander about aimlessly in the earth's atmosphere. In holy sleep, the priestesses help them on their path towards further spiritual development.

Without help they would stagnate for hundreds, perhaps even thousands of years because, without organs of sense, they have no opportunity to gather experience or to contact other beings. They are introverted and find no path on which to progress. The priestesses seek out these restless souls, penetrate their beings with the power of love, and thanks to their inner identity they irradiate their consciousness with ideas that help them find a solution and a way out of their condition. These priestesses thus perform a two-fold duty. They help wandering souls forward and simultaneously purify the earth's atmosphere.

There are priestesses who work towards developing healthier, more beautiful and more spiritual young people through initiating them in the mysteries of physical love. They teach young men to transmute their physical urge through the power of the spirit and to aim for a higher spiritual union—a sacrament. They also teach young men who are on the point of marrying about this sacred power, so they can transmit this energy to their wives after marriage and thus beget noble children.

Lastly, certain priestesses perform the same tasks as the priests. They teach groups of neophytes, give instructions for exercises in concentration, and receive people who need advice regarding special problems. As soon as these priestesses reach an advanced degree of priesthood, they are permitted to use the staff of life in healing the sick. In this way a priestess can become a high priestess. I have been assigned to this group.

I am truly delighted with my task! It's nothing less than wonderful to observe the minds and souls of my pupils as they develop step by step and manifest more and more of divinity. For me it's like watching a bit of opaque material gradually become transparent, allowing the divine creative principle to shine through. Every day I experience this with my dear neophytes. I also enjoy taking care of people who come to the temple seeking advice in affairs of the spirit or matters of the body. I receive them in my little cell, the same one Ima assigned to me when I first came to the temple.

At such times people show me their 'other' face, the face that nobody else sees . . . a face they often do not know themselves. I see this inner face in every creature, and it's very instructive to hear about all the different events and experiences that have shaped this inner countenance in accordance with the law of action and reaction. Oh, if only everybody could see their own and other people's inner countenances. They would never hate each other, and they would never be afraid of each other! There are no bad people! They often harm each other, doing evil things, even cruel things, to others because they believe others are going to do evil to them and they try to defend themselves in advance out of pure fear. In this way they give others a real reason to believe they are acting with bad intentions.

But if one could only convince both parties to such 'evil actions' that neither is acting malevolently and that both are merely afraid of each other, they would both breathe a sigh of relief and shake hands. People are ignorant and blind. They don't see each other, and this is the reason for all the enmity and hostility on earth. There's nothing more beautiful than being able to open blind eyes and watch the brilliant look of understanding and knowledge begin to shine.

In addition to this work I am permitted to be present when Ptahhotep or his deputy uses the staff of life to heal the sick. In the early morning they arrive, coming by themselves or with the aid of friends or relatives who bring them to the temple. Ptahhotep then conducts new vital force into their sick bodies. I often watch how the staff of life completely heals broken bones or horrible wounds in just a few moments' time, leaving behind only a thick spot in the bone or a tiny scar to show where the wound or the break was. Just as two pieces of metal can be welded together into one piece through heat, broken bones are mended by the staff of life, and deep wounds in muscles, ligaments, blood vessels, nerves and skin grow together again. With equal speed this staff of life can heal the most serious inflammations of the lungs, kidneys or other organs. Great indeed is the mercy and grace of *God* for the gift he has made to mankind of this means for the recovery of health.

Beside my work in the temple I continue to fulfil the duties of the wife of the Pharaoh. Just as I used to do in the past, I sit beside my father at festive receptions and other public events. At such times I have plenty of opportunity to observe the people of the court and all the others who attend these high feasts. Sometimes we receive messengers and emissaries from strange countries. They are quite different from these sons of men among us. The colour of their skin, their physical stature and the shape of their heads are all different, and they radiate different forces. They sometimes bring us wonderful things as gifts, things that are quite unknown in our country. Animals I have never seen before, precious gems, cloth, beautifully painted pottery. Father has arranged for artists to come from some of these far countries to teach our young people of the temple. On the other hand, some of our artists and wise men have travelled far abroad to teach our arts and sciences. Father has told me that we will some day visit these great countries.

Ever since my initiation I have also been permitted to go for chariot rides alone with the lions. Through my initiation I received the ability to guide my will-power into the nervous centres of other living creatures, thus bringing them completely under my power. I now control in my own body the activated nerve centres which are still latent and undeveloped in the sons of men, and I can send out penetrating radiations of will-power that other such living creatures are turned into unconscious tools of my will.

I never forget, however, that *God's highest* gift to man is the right of self-determination, and I know this right must never be infringed. That would be black magic! That's why I never use my will-power against a person. Often enough it would be so easy to help a person solve a difficult problem if I were merely to fill him with my will! But this would mean that I would be taking on the responsibility myself, and the solution of the problem would be mine not his. In this way I would be robbing him of an opportunity to pass a test. Every person must solve his own problems, for only in this way can he gather experience, develop his will power and widen the horizon of his consciousness.

Animals are directly subject to natural forces. They automatically and instinctively carry out the will of nature and possess no self-determination. So I can completely subject my lions to my will. It's wonderful how these magnificent animals immediately carry out my thoughts. They react to the slightest impulse of my will, and I often have the feeling that they belong just as much to my *self* as my hands and feet do. The same divine *self* is the life of every living creature, and the 'love' animals feel is nothing but the unconscious striving to achieve the unity of the *self* on the lowest, physical plane of consciousness.

A child going through the phase of awakening consciousness also tries involuntarily to achieve this same unity and identity by putting into its mouth everything it can get its little hands on. Animals have the same instinct. The unity and the love between me and my lions is so great that they like to take my hand or even my head between their jaws as if they were going to eat me. Naturally they don't bite, and their play is not to be taken seriously. I can understand that when they eat a gazelle for example *they are only following out their instinctive striving for unity.* The instinct for self-preservation has the same source as the instinct for the preservation of the species: striving for the divine state of unity.

That's why the manifestations of both instincts are so close together and often overlap. Nature exploits this primordial tendency towards unity in order to create progeny through the instinct for procreation and propagation of the species and in order to preserve the body through the satisfaction of hunger. This is the reason why the meat lions get from their keepers never tastes as good as the flesh they tear from the body of fresh-killed prey; for in this latter act they are unconsciously experiencing a form of union with the living—with life itself. With dead flesh they can satisfy only their hunger but not their subconscious striving toward union.

I get a great deal of pleasure out of spending time with my lions. It's thrilling to observe how these majestic animals manifest all the characteristics of the divine *Ra*—the sun—transformed to the animal level. Little Bo-Ghar, too, shares my pleasure in the lions, just as he is in harmony with me in everything I do or say. How well I remember the endless patience my father exhibited when he taught me how to stand up in a chariot speeding over uneven ground. It's my turn now to teach the same techniques to Bo-Ghar. He's very skilful, instinctively making the right movements, and after a short time he is able to accompany me even on long rides.

During quieter periods father and I withdraw to our little holiday house on the seashore. Bo-Ghar comes with us, and the three of us enjoy the pleasures of sun and sand and water. Father too likes to spend time with the little boy, and we find it thrilling to watch his pure soul develop like a magnificent flower. Once, after watching Bo-Ghar for quite a while, father calls and asks him to come over close. As soon as Bo-Ghar is near enough for quiet conversation, father asks him, 'Well, Bo-Ghar, would you like to work with me?'

Bo-Ghar prostrates himself before father, and with his hands together as a sign of profoundest respect, he replies, 'Master, I'll devote my whole life to the task you give me in order to be worthy of it.'

Father pats the boy's head. 'Stand up, Bo-Ghar,' he says, 'you will work with us in the great task of redeeming the earth. Just do what your teachers in the temple tell you, and one day you will be a co-worker with us. Stand up . . . you don't need to throw yourself on the ground before me.'

Bo-Ghar can't contain his joy. And he jumps around like a little monkey. Then he tries to be dignified like a grown-up worthy of father's confidence. Finally he runs down to the seashore to look for mussels. When I'm alone with father I ask him: 'Father, now that I've been initiated, when I raise myself above the level of time, I can look into the past and the future the same as you, but I still can't recognize anything in my own future. Why is that? The only importance I attach to the future is the development it will bring me in my progress up to the last, highest, divine degree. But please explain to me why I can see everybody else's future but my own. I see only mist before my eyes when I turn my consciousness towards my own future.'

Father looks at me, smiles and waits.

I smile back and answer him in thought. We understand each other. His look tells me: 'What are you asking for? If you don't see your future, it simply means that's the way it's meant to be so you can fulfil your task properly. Don't bother about it, but do everything to attain by your own efforts the highest degree you reached with Ptahhotep's help during your initiation.'

When our tasks call us back to the city, the days go by as in the past, and I spend some of my time in the temple and some in the palace. I love my work. It satisfies me completely. Nevertheless, all day long I go about with the joyful anticipation of being able to withdraw into myself—into God—when my day's duties are over. Every time I turn inward with the determination to reach the highest degree by my own efforts, and I actually do come nearer and nearer to perfect fulfilment. Yet every time I return to my personal consciousness, I get up disappointed. Once again I realize I have failed to achieve the last and highest reality which I experienced in my initiation and which burns in my memory like an unquenchable flame. My only consolation in such moments is that of looking forward to participating in vesper prayers and meditations with Ptahhotep.

Ptahhotep, his deputy, the priests and priestesses—initiates all—meet in the temple at sunset. We sit in a circle, with Ptahhotep and his deputy sitting diametrically opposite each other and thus forming two poles. All the rest of us form two semicircles on either side. It takes us a while to free our spiritual body from impurities which we have unavoidably absorbed during our contacts with the sons of men. Then Ptahhotep extends his blessed hands to his neighbours on either side. All the rest of us join hands too, thus forming a circuit through which Ptahhotep and his deputy conduct a current of the highest, supreme, divine degree into our bodies. This helps us experience the supreme state of divine unity. In this way our nerves develop resistance much faster than they would if we were dependent only on our own energies. These moments of bliss, experienced daily during our evening prayers, give meaning and content to my whole life.

Oh God! Give me the strength to reach *you* with my consciousness by my own efforts!

PHARAOH CHEPHREN   *Cairo Museum*

The Pharaoh is the image of God to whom the creative principle, Horus,
symbolized as a falcon, whispers Divine Truth. One who is initiated hears
its voice and obeys

HORUS FALCON WITH PHARAOH *Cairo Museum*

The initiate manifests the higher self through his person and is thus
free in his spirit like the divine falcon Horus

— 39 —

WE WILL MEET AGAIN

ONE DAY the court is making ready to celebrate a great reception. Some time ago father sent his commander, Thiss-Tha, together with many notables, a large number of troops, and ships full of presents and goods for barter, as an emissary to a far country. The ruler there received our dignitaries very cordially and soon thereafter sent his own troops bearing presents and goods for barter to our country. Today we are going to celebrate the arrival of these foreign troops.

Menu decks me out in my most beautiful dress, and with the usual ceremonies, Roo-Kha brings me the queen's jewels. Then the two elders escort me to father, and we walk through the long colonnades accompanied by the whole court. In this manner we walk out in a column on to the terrace before the palace. In his full dignity and great beauty, the Pharaoh takes his place on his golden throne in the middle of the terrace. To his right is his audience lion, while I take my seat to his left and a bit out in front, almost at the edge of the terrace. The people of rank take their proper places to our right and left according to their degree and station.

Then the great reception begins. The troops of the foreign power march up in a long festive procession. Their leader and his retinue step up before the terrace and bow down before us with outstretched arms. Then their leader makes a fine speech in our language to tell us how eager his ruler is to reach a long-term alliance with us. Then he calls his porters forward to bring us our gifts.

I observe the changing scene from above and look at the men in the leader's retinue. All of splendid physique, they wear their ceremonial robes and military armour. The strangers are big, strong, broad-shouldered and very muscular men. In our country only the descendants of the race of the Sons of God are as tall and strong as these strange soldiers, but much more slender, nimble and resilient. Ptahhotep, father and some of the other descendants of the Sons of God like Ima, Mentuptah, Imhotep and some priestesses have beautiful and powerful bodies, but they are majestic, dignified, full of spirituality. Less robust, they don't look so much like splendid animals.

Never before in my life have I seen people like these strangers. They don't please me at all! In our country I am accustomed to seeing finely-chiselled facial features that reflect spirituality, especially among the descendants of the race of the Sons of God, and even among the hybrid race. These strangers have irregular features that make them look like animals! Especially their ears!

Our ears are small, narrow and finely-chiselled with the lobe separate from the side of the neck. These strangers have big, broad ears, their lobes joined to their necks like those of monkeys. And what strikes us all as particularly strange is their red hair! Their faces, hands, arms and feet are covered with an abundance of hair, shining like golden threads in the sunshine. They are self-assured, and when they talk or laugh they reveal rows of beautiful, white, glistening, strong teeth. But this feature too makes me think of animals! They radiate great strength, but not spiritual strength. No! I don't like their looks!

I can see our guests from abroad find us just as strange as we think they are. They don't like our looks either. I see their eyes have not yet been opened to the spirit. They are unable to appreciate, or even to perceive any fine, delicate, spiritualized shapes. They see only the people of our country are smaller than they. Reading their thoughts I can see they hold us in contempt.

I am accustomed to seeing the fire of admiration kindled in the eyes of men when they look at me. These strangers admire my robe and my jewels without noticing at all that *I* am beautiful! I can see very well that they're curious about me, the queen of this country, and they stare at me at every opportunity without noticing that I am beautiful! Yes, I know I inherited my mother's small stature, but a woman's beauty does not depend on her size! But these men, these strange warriors from a far-off country think a woman has to be big and fleshy to be beautiful. I observe myself as I always do. Have feelings of vanity sprung up within me? No! Far from it! I am merely displeased because they are so ignorant, immature and crude, like people in the lowest class of the sons of men in our country.

All these people are so lacking in culture and polish, including their leaders and the people of rank accompanying them. One of them is standing in front of the terrace, right in front of me. He must be a high officer because he has come forward in the closest proximity to their commander. Now he's standing amidst a group of soldiers and staring at me incessantly. The corners of his mouth show a disrespectful attitude. The way he acts really doesn't befit a person of rank. How can a man stare at a woman so impertinently? In all our court only Roo-Kha is as impertinent as this fellow, and even he can't conceal his admiration for my beauty. But this stranger merely stares insolently without the slightest admiration! Nevertheless, I fight down any and all feelings of vanity within myself. I watch out and keep myself under constant control!

I turn away to watch the ceremonies again. Fascinated by the military games these soldiers are playing, I must admit they possess physical strength unknown in our country. Their race is descended from a half-blooded Son of God who manifested his father's high divine power in his blood, instead of his spirit, and so became a giant. His descendants intermarried with primitive people and developed a big-boned race with enormous muscular strength. They're not nearly so agile and adroit as our warriors, but they can perform feats of strength that would be beyond the ability of our soldiers. During these military games

I glance down once in a while at the insolent foreigner in front of me. He is still staring at me untiringly. Actually, it would be a truly inspiring task to guide such an uncultured, red-headed stranger into the mysteries of the spirit . . . to help him step by step to open his inner eyes . . . to enable him to see the beauty of a woman's spirituality instead of only her flesh.

For several days I am so preoccupied with our guests from abroad that I have no time to go to the temple. Feasts and ceremonies follow each other in rapid succession. Exhibitions, excursions and banquets . . . and at all of these events it is my duty to take my place beside my father in officiating as host and hostess. Menu is in her element, clothing me in ever more beautiful, ever more magnificent robes. Bo-Ghar, however, is embittered and saddened because I have no time for him. Roo-Kha comes frequently with his jewel bearers to bring me new creations of the jeweller's art.

I go through with all this because it's my duty to do so. Nevertheless I look at my image in my great silver mirror with eager curiosity, wondering what the foreigner from abroad will have to say about my new robe or my new jewels. Especially when father and I and all the court once dress up after the fashion of our guests from abroad in order to show our friendly attitude towards them. I really have to laugh to see how odd father looks in this strange costume! And I? Won't our red-headed guests from abroad find me beautiful even in these clothes?

For by this time I have got acquainted with him! Father introduced me to his commander and all the ranking officers, including 'him', and now I find myself in the company of these emissaries from abroad every day. Their country's ruler, in preparing for this expedition, selected only men who had succeeded in learning our language in a very short time. Thus we are able to converse very pleasantly with our guests and exchange ideas with them. But I find myself ill at ease in the presence of *this* strange guest from abroad who stared at me so insolently throughout all the reception ceremony. And my heart beats faster when I realize he has exactly *the same voice as the man who turned into a flaming spirit in my initiation dream!* How strange!

These strangers are peculiar people, lacking in culture and learning but not stupid at all! They live very close to nature, and even though they don't *intellectually* know the inner, creative laws and the essence of things, they know a lot as a result of their own direct experiences. It is remarkable to observe how a truth, which we clearly see and know in our spirit through inner contemplation, appears in these people as mere belief and superstition!

When they don't know the source and cause of a force, they imagine that it comes from an invisible being, and they then give the name *God* to their own imaginings. And they stubbornly insist on calling these imaginary, fairy-tale creatures 'gods'. They think they know everything better. When one tries to tell them the truth and explain real facts to them, they merely shake their head and laugh condescendingly. Of course I am not permitted to tell them any of the secrets of the temple, but still I have tried to explain to our foreign guest the forces which cause lightning and thunder in a storm. I knew I wouldn't be permitted to tell him how the high priest uses the Ark of the Covenant in the pyramid to create lightning and rain ... the blessed rain that keeps our country from becoming absolutely barren. But I did try to explain to him that lightning comes from a meeting of two opposite forces and that he can cause the same phenomenon himself by striking two pieces of stone together.

At this he gave me a supercilious look, saying he knew very well that lightning was the arrow of the 'chief god', and that 'little demons' live in certain stones and become angry and shoot out little flashes of lightning whenever they're disturbed. When I tried to give him the true explanation of this phenomenon, I found his mind closed up tight. In one sense it doesn't make any difference whether we consider lightning to be the 'arrow of the chief god' or the 'meeting of positive and negative forces'. But if these people continue to believe in their superstitions and all their various imaginary gods, they'll never learn to control the forces of nature and always remain slaves of their superstition. Anyway I have succeeded in getting our strange red-headed officer guest interested enough in my explanations of various natural phenomena so that he's always eager to hear more. He said he would like to have me teach him; so he's going to come to the temple every day, and I will initiate him into the lowest degree of knowledge.

After sunset Menu helps me into my priestess robes. Then, heavily veiled, we both walk over to the temple. A neophyte has accompanied our officer guest to my little cell in the temple wall where he is awaiting me. Menu stays behind in the temple court, and I enter my cell. The stranger is already there! Standing there, leaning against the wall of my cell, he greets me with his usual smile of superiority. This smile annoys me! How does he dare to look at me this way? He's not my superior in any respect. Just because he's physically bigger and stronger, he ignorantly assumes himself to be superior in every way. He doesn't have the faintest idea that the power of mind stands over everything. But I'm going to show him! With the power of my mind I'm going to conquer this insolent, red-headed giant. Despite all his physical power he'll be vanquished, and through my spiritual power I'll come out victorious!

The stranger bows deeply, but I see clearly he's doing it without conviction. Here in our country the people practically worship me. They know I am an initiated priestess, a servant of *God*. The stranger also knows I am a priestess in the temple, but he doesn't know what 'initiation' means. He doesn't know that our *knowledge* is not a system of beliefs based merely on human imaginings, but rather the direct recognition of truth ... divine *omniscience*! But I'll open his eyes! I'll explain the mystery of man and the universe to him. I'll guide him into the mystery of all creation.

'If you want to achieve true knowledge,' I tell him, 'you must first learn to know yourself. You have to know *what you yourself are*. When you come to know yourself, you will discover that all the truths of the universe are concealed within your own being. Thus through this self-recognition you will get to

324

know all the secrets of the world. First solve the great puzzle of our sphinx, that of man himself! You must recognize what you are!'

The stranger looks at me attentively at first, but then begins to smile.

'I'm supposed to learn what I am? I've known that for a long time! Why is that supposed to be such a great mystery? But it seems to me, oh queen, that *you* don't know what I am, and so *I* am telling you: I am a man!' And with that he lets out a hearty laugh, showing all his big white teeth. Oh my! What a child he is! His laugh is so infectious that I can't help laughing myself.

'I know very well that you're a man . . .' I answer him. But I can't even finish my sentence because the red haired giant interrupts me impolitely: 'It seems to me, queen, that you not only don't know I'm a man, but that you don't even know *what a man is*. I'm not a priest and can't read people's thoughts the way you can, but I know women, and I can see something you don't know at all—or else you've forgotten it—and that is what you are! You don't know you're a woman! How do you think you can try to teach me the inner secrets of man and the universe if you don't even know this simple fact that everybody else can see?'

'I know very well that I'm a woman,' I reply with dignity. The stranger smiles insolently, but I continue undisturbed: 'The outer form is only the mantle of the inner being. When one knows the inner being and when one *is* the inner being, he uses the outer form only as an instrument *but does not identify himself with it*! The body is only the robe of the *self*. You wear clothing too, and yet you are not the clothing. In the very same way you wear a body which can be either male or female, but your *self* stands above the sexes and is neither man nor woman. The *self* is the creator. The person, the physical, material manifestation is only one half of the true being. The other half has remained behind in the unconscious, unmanifested state. And whether a manifestation is male or female depends merely on which half has incarnated itself. When a person has made both halves of his being conscious and experienced them consciously, he has become identical with his *self*, and then he carries within himself both the male and female principles in complete equilibrium.'

'But still his body is either male or female, isn't it?' he asks.

'Yes, indeed,' I answer. 'The material phenomenon can only be one-sided, for whenever the two sides merge into unity there is nothing physical. The union of the two complementary halves, the merging of the two sides would mean complete annihilation of matter, complete dematerialization of the body. One can only be androgynous in spirit.'

'Queen,' answers the guest from abroad, 'there's only one thing in all your pretty words that I can really understand quite clearly . . . a point on which I'm in complete agreement with your "secrets", namely that my physical manifestation, as you express it so neatly, is only one half of a unit. In the past I have often sought—and found—a complementary half, but I was never annihilated in doing so! Perhaps because I never found the real unity? But even if it were to mean annihilation I would go on seeking my *true, complementary half*. I am a man, and my other half can only be a woman who gives me complete and perfect happiness. For such a woman I would gladly lay down my life!'

I feel in my body a warm rush of blood that reaches my head. In the face of such a way of thinking I am completely powerless. How can I explain to him that the earthly happiness he is seeking in a woman is only transitory and unable to satisfy his immortal soul?

We end our discussion for today. He must have time to digest the new truths I have given him.

And there follow many evenings in which I do battle with his ignorance. I am determined to help him make progress, and I take all kinds of care to say the right words to him in order to fan the divine spark into flame and awaken his higher self. When I wake up in the morning he is already in my thoughts. I remember everything we spoke about the previous evening and concentrate my thinking throughout the day on the lesson I am going to give him in the evening. Often during these days I race through the countryside with my lions but now it's without Bo-Ghar. Bo-Ghar hangs his head as he goes to his master Ima for lessons, Ima tries to console him with all kinds of presents and everything else a boy's heart could wish for. I'm sorry to see Bo-Ghar so sad, but I need time to be alone with my own thoughts.

After one of my chariot rides, while I am taking leave of my lions in the lions' court, I pat their heads and run my fingers through their manes. As I'm doing this, it suddenly occurs to me that our officer guest from abroad has exactly the same colour hair as the lions! If I were to stroke his head, the same thick locks of red hair would be slipping through my fingers! Oh, how I love these lions!

That evening I tell our guest my observation about his having the same colour hair as the lions.

'Queen,' he says, 'may I go for a chariot ride with you sometime? If I could see that you could control real live lions with your will-power, I'd begin to believe in your superhuman powers!' And he laughs tauntingly.

'Where have you heard that I have superhuman powers?'

'Everybody I talk to adores you like a goddess. Everybody believes you're a supernal being. But I don't!'

I feel injured: 'What do you think about me?' I ask, noticing with some annoyance that my heart is pounding while I await his answer. In the very same moment, quick as a flash, Ptahhotep's image pops up before my inward eye, with a warning expression on his noble face.

'No! No! Leave me alone,' I answer the inward image. 'I'm in no danger!'

And outwardly I go on listening to what the stranger says: 'So you want to know what I think about you? Why do you want to hear that from me? If you're so high up above everything earthly why should you be interested in what goes on in a poor earthly head like mine? And after all, you can read people's thoughts, can't you?'

'Yes, I can read your thoughts, but I want to see whether you're being frank with me,' I answer. But as I do so I am aware of an uneasy feeling. There's no time to try to find out what this feeling means, because the stranger asks me again: 'So you want to know whether I'm being frank with you? Why don't you ask yourself first *whether you're being frank with yourself*?'

I am speechless. I just don't know what to answer. For years I've made a habit of self observation in order to seek out the motives of all my thoughts and deeds. I am convinced I am frank with myself and therefore frank with the rest of the world including him. Nevertheless his words bring an embarrassing surprise. Could he be right? Have I really lacked the courage frankly to face all my thoughts and feelings? I resolve to examine myself even more thoroughly, but in any case I'm going to concentrate all my efforts in order not to be defeated in the struggle with him. I must come out victorious. I mustn't allow an uncouth stranger to think I'm weaker than he is! I mustn't allow him to think he stands above me!

The next day we go for a chariot ride together. Before we get in, the stranger stands beside the lions and holds out his shaggy red head towards me. 'Want to try and see if my hair really feels like the lions'? If they don't mind your stroking their hair, I may be able to stand it too,' he says with a hearty laugh that erupts from between two perfect rows of white teeth.

He really is a big child. He's not behaving this way out of lack of respect, and I can't be angry at him. I have to laugh too, and if the keeper of my lions were not standing near, I really would feel like tousling his hair.

And so it goes, day after day. And the time quickly draws near when the stranger will have to return to his homeland. In many respects I could be satisfied. As a 'woman' I could even gloat in triumph at the way his attitude has changed. He has put away his superior airs and waits all day long every day for the evening to come so that we can be together. I realize he never really felt superior, and that his overbearing manner was actually a kind of self-defence to save him from complete capitulation. He didn't want to give up his masculine arrogance.

He admired me from the very first moment he saw me, and my vanity, which first drove me to spend time in his company could now be completely satisfied. And yet I am *not* satisfied. On the contrary I am plagued by persistent anxiety. But every time I analyse my feelings, this anxiety gives me the reassurance that my interest for him is not coming from the feminine instinct of my lower nature. For I am constantly watching and checking on myself! Menu says I show all the unmistakable symptoms of being in love and she's overjoyed that I am 'blooming' at last. But she's wrong! She's in no position to judge because she considers everything from her earthly standpoint. She can't begin to understand that I cannot and must never fall in love . . . and that I'm not in love now!

How could I ever fall in love with this uncouth, unkempt, red-headed giant? He's not my type. Physically, he seems strange, even repulsive to me. In my moments of self-examination, I have often asked myself whether I could want to have a child by him. Heaven forbid! A child with such ears and such an ungainly, raw-boned body? Never! In any case I know absolutely I would never want to have a child by him! So I know I'm not in love. I only want him to find *God*. I am keenly interested in each of my pupils, and for this very reason I think of him so often and with such a concentration of all my attention. But he hasn't found *God* yet. In this point I haven't yet succeeded! That's why I feel so sad and anxious when I realize he is soon going to have to leave our country, and I may never see him again in this life . . .

Then everything happens faster than a flash of lightning . . .

On our last evening together I go to the temple to see him and take leave of him. As usual, he's leaning against the wall. But now he doesn't try to seem so superior the way he did when he waited here for me the first time. Now he doesn't even look at me, but stands there staring off into space.

'What's the matter?' I ask him.

'I'm just trying to think what kind of sense it makes for me to have been coming here to see you every evening. What did you want of me, you beautiful queen with no heart? What use have I had out of all the things you've told me if they've only served to make me unhappy? You've talked on and on about my having to find myself, but with every one of your words and deeds you've helped to make me lose myself completely. I was a brave, courageous fighter, afraid of no one, and now I've become a slave. The slave of a tiny woman who hardly comes up to my shoulders! And now I'm afraid of the future. How am I going to be able to live without you?'

A hot wave of joy floods through my being. I try to imagine it's only my vanity. But I feel a shock! In the beginning I really did want him to recognize my feminine beauty and power, and as soon as I had achieved that I wanted to use my power over him to help him on the inner path. I took all kinds of pains to awaken the *self* within him. But instead, he's fallen in love with me. I didn't want to go that far! I don't want earthly love. I've wanted to create with him a far higher unity, the unity of the *self*. I wanted to lead him to *God*! But it's done no good at all for me to bring forth the deepest truths from out of my inner being . . . He sees me only as a woman. He cannot or will not rise above the sensual. He doesn't see *me*. He doesn't realize that he does not love *me*. *I* don't really exist for him. He merely loves my body, the outer cloak which is merely a manifestation of my true *self*! How horrible! How debasing!

'Look,' I say, trembling, 'it hasn't made any sense at all for you to come here to see me, because we just don't understand each other. We just can't get together. I want to help you rise to the spiritual plane, and you want to drag me down to the level of the body. It hasn't made any sense at all to go through all this trouble. Go back to your homeland in peace, and we'll never meet again!'

At these words, the blood rushes to his head. His face, his neck . . . the whole man becomes dark red, so dark his hair seems lighter than his skin. His eyes flash like glowing embers, and with a shock I see his whole spiritual body turning into a powerful flame. Then, without my having time to defend myself, he seizes my arm, holding it as if in iron tongs, pulls me to his mighty breast, embraces me, pushes my head backward, presses his mouth to my lips with such force that I lose my breath. Then he kisses my face, my neck and my lips again, and in between his burning kisses, he whispers hoarsely: 'So you don't want to see me any more? But *I* want to see you, and we'll meet again . . . we'll meet again.'

As I saw his wild face coming close, I felt a wave of deathly panic. I wanted to push him back and get away, but as he locked me in his mighty arms and pressed his burning hot mouth upon my lips, all my inner being caught his fire. I lost control over myself, and without resistance I gave in to the over-powering feeling of pleasure and delight that sprang up out of my fright and swept through me. Now I realize I love him . . . have loved him from the first moment . . . with all my body and soul . . . with my whole being I love him passionately and I always will!

The fire overwhelms me as if coming forth from a gigantic volcano. Hot flames sweep through me . . . devour me . . . my backbone feels like a bridge of glowing embers, holding seven burning torches. But now I'm no longer in the immovable axis of my spinal column, no longer in the midpoint from which my true *self* radiates the fire of life. On the contrary, my consciousness has fallen into my burning body, and sparkling, crackling, flashes of lightning race through my veins . . . through my whole being. All my nerves are aglow, all my thoughts blotted out. They're burning out my consciousness . . . annihilating me . . . Then I black out and everything disappears . . .

Little by little I come to again . . . slowly I open my eyes . . . see stone walls around me. I am lying on the floor of my little cell.

I am alone . . . surrounded by the silence of a tomb.

I have no thoughts. I haven't anything I could think about any more . . .

Dejected and broken, I get up, cover my weary head with my veil and leave the cell.

The long colonnade is dark and seemingly empty. After a few steps I see a dark form leaning against the opposite wall: Ima! He stands there as if made of stone, staring at me with an indescribably wild look in his eyes. Even in the darkness I can see it . . . have to see it. He looks right into me . . . right through me. Then he turns and walks away softly in the opposite direction.

Without a thought in my head I go back to the palace. Menu, who had fallen asleep in a corner of the temple court, accompanies me, as usual in silence, except for an occasional loud yawn.

—— 40 ——

THE LION

I LIE on my knees before Ptahhotep.

I do not speak. He understands my unspoken words, even when I am silent . . .

'Father of my Soul, save me! Take this fire out of my body, give me back my freedom! I cannot and will not go on living this way . . .

'I lost myself, I am destroyed, I no longer have any control over myself, I can't think any more what I'm doing; my thoughts control me and split my head apart.

'Help me, Father of my Soul, help me back to the heavenly heights where spiritual clarity, purity and freedom reign. Give me back my wings so that I may fly again with you on high like the creative power of God, the divine hawk Horus, who flies through the universe creating new worlds.

'Open up heaven for me again, Father of my Soul, let me hear the music of the spheres again . . . the music that now lives on only in my memory, while within me there reigns only the silence of the tomb because my ears are deaf.

'Open my spiritual eyes again, Father of my Soul, for they are burned out; I see the light of heaven and the brilliance of God only in my memory, while within me there is only darkness as my inner eyes have become blind.

'Open for me the gate of my heavenly home where I once possessed all the treasures of the spirit that now live only in my memory, Father of my Soul, because I have fallen and have become a poor earthly beggar.

'Open up again for me the happiness and the peace in the divine unity of those who have found salvation, Father of my Soul . . . the unity which now is mine only in memory as I have fallen into the wilderness, into the desert, haunted and plagued unceasingly by the burning unrest of being torn in two.

'Lay your blessed hand upon my head and permit me to be freed from the dungeon of time . . . permit me to become again in the eternal present the person I was . . . the person I really am . . . the person I can no longer *be* in the elusive world of appearances.

'Father of my Soul, save me, save my soul! Permit me to hear your voice again, like the voice of God within me, for I no longer hear your answers. I am blind and deaf, I have lost my heavenly wings, I have become as one expelled, one driven out in exile. Take me back, Father of my Soul, take me back into the unity of the blessed, because I can't go on living this way! Save me, Father of my Soul, save me, you man of God, do not leave me, do not leave me . . . do not leave me . . .'

But I hear no answer.

I have lost everything. My intellect that has always been there to help me onward is foggy; only hazy thoughts creep through my mind like tired travellers.

On my bed in the palace I lie with one and only one thought in my head: to die! I can't go on living, I won't go on living! I am only the shadow of myself. Through the mists in my mind, hazy faces rise up to harass me: Menu, crying hopelessly, and Bo-Ghar . . . the despairing eyes of Bo-Ghar . . .

I want to die! . . . To die!

I used to be master of my body and could leave it intentionally at will. Now I try it—but without success! I cannot leave my body. It's as if I were nailed into it, I can't leave it. I've become a prisoner in the dungeon of matter.

I want to go to the Ark of the Covenant! It will burn up my body just as its radiation burns up the dead sacrificial animals in the temple . . . so completely that not even a trace of ash is left.

I put on my veil and hasten to the temple, through the great hall, on to the door that opens into the underground passage to the great pyramid. But I can't get through. Before the stone door I run up against an invisible wall. It begins to dawn in my hazy brain: the lowest frequency of the Ark of Covenant, *ultra matter*! Materialized hate! Although completely invisible, it protects the forbidden area better than the strongest wall. I try again to break through the invisible barrier, but the unbelievably hard wall of ultra matter stops me unmercifully.

There is no mercy for me . . . no mercy . . .

Slowly I go back through the long temple passage, past my own little cell. Without thinking, I go in and sit down on the stone bench. I sink back into memories . . . the room expands, from every side I hear the echo of infinity, and within me pictures emerge: a figure, wrapped in hazy fog, approaches me . . . I recognize it: the hazy figure I saw in my vision when I was being initiated. It comes quite close to me; then a flame spurts out of it, the whole figure begins to burn and becomes a fiery being who irresistibly embraces me, encircles me and penetrates me so that I too catch fire and begin to burn. Then I hear his voice whispering to me: 'I told you we would meet again. You belong to me, you will never again be free of me, we will meet again . . . in endless time and in timeless infinity we will meet again, again . . .' And the echo of his voice goes on repeating thousands and thousands of times: 'meet again . . . meet again . . . meet again . . .'

'No!' I cry, 'I will not, I hate you!'

The figure of fire laughs: 'As long as you hate me, you love me and I have power over you! You can't get free as easy as that . . . we will meet again,' the echo goes on calling . . .

As I hear this voice echoing back thousands of times from every direction in the empty room, so powerfully that the air itself literally vibrates with it, I know the hazy figure of fire is whispering and looking at me with voice and eyes

I can no longer resist. In all the endless lives I was able to remember in the vision I had during my initiation, I was always seeking the same voice and the same eyes in all the voices that spoke to me and in all the eyes that looked at me and in all the countless men I met in all those countless lives. In all these men I was seeking *the* man whom I love with love eternal and with every drop of my blood, the only man, 'my' man: the image and likeness of my complementary half...

Then another picture flashes upon my mind, the picture of the man whom I do not love as my complementary half, but as *myself*: Ima! I could not love him with earthly love because I was always one with him in *God*. We are bound together by the eternal love of heavenly *unity*. I will go to him now, I will tell him everything, he will understand me! The unity that binds me to him will lead me like a light in my further travels; this unity will illuminate my darkened path so that I can find my way back into the heavenly home I have lost, to *God*.

I rush madly out of my cell. I look for him in the neophytes' school where he prepares candidates for initiation; I look for him everywhere, peering into every room. But I find him nowhere. Suddenly the young priest appears who helped me with my last preparations before initiation.

'Are you looking for Ima?' he asks.

'Yes, where can I find him?'

'You won't find Ima here any more. He left the temple in absolute desperation. He completely lost control of himself, for his faith was not in *God* above everything, but in *a woman*! He rushed away from here in a terrible state. None of us could stop him. He said he'd rather live with negro tribes than go on living here in the temple because the savages would not disappoint him. "The savages do not lie; they don't pretend to be different from what they really are!" were his last words before he ran away. You'll never find Ima again.'

I stand stiff and silent with horror. Oh Ima! I have brought misfortune and despair on you too! The hell within me suddenly becomes a hundred times more horrible because of this news. And still I know the young priest is wrong. *I will find Ima again!* If not in this life, then in a future one! Everything passes away; only true love never dies, and this wonderful love that stands above and beyond all differences of sex, this love of spiritual unity, will with absolute certainty lead us, Ima and me, back together again!

I return to the palace knowing only one thing for sure—that I *must* die. Even if I were not a priestess, even if I were not initiated, I would not be able to go on living; but now that I know I have pulled down my best friend into hell with me, my mental torture becomes unbearable. All my thoughts and all my feelings balk at the thought of going on living. I want to destroy myself, and again and again I make a supreme effort to leave my body.

But I can't! I can't die! I must go on carrying within me the fire that's burning me up and destroying my nerves. I can't flee from myself. When I lie down completely exhausted to seek relief and rest a bit, I feel as if a mountain were weighing down upon my breast. I can scarcely breathe. Before my closed eyes I see blinding fire and flames, red flickering flames like the hair of the strange man . . . like the shabby mane of the lions . . .

The lions!—Yes, the lions, I will go to them.

And I'll dress myself as if preparing for a chariot ride.

The keeper lets me go to the lions, because he knows that ever since my initiation my father has allowed me to go out riding with the lions alone.

I go to my lions. They greet me with lowered head and with wrinkled nostrils. They smell a strange scent about me; they notice a strange and foreign emanation clinging to me. I go to Shima and stroke his head. Shu-Ghar lets out a loud growl, slowly drawing himself up ready to leap. Rage and jealousy blaze in his eyes, and the instinct of self-preservation awakens within me. I hurl my will against Shu-Gahr just as I used to guide him with my will-power during our chariot rides. But with a shiver of horror I realize I can't hurl my will any more. My will is lame and dead, and the lion leaps. As I turn to run, in a flash I see three horror-struck people running toward me: Thiss-Tha, Bo-Ghar and the keeper. With all my might I run out of the court of lions. I feel the hot breath of the lion upon my neck; I feel its muzzle touching me . . . and then a blow upon my head—but I keep on running; I see a door through which I must run into an area where the lion will have no more power over me; and in the door I see the fine, pale figure of my *mother*! '*Mother !*' I cry and run on breathless because I know I'll be safe in her arms. Mother awaits me with her sweet smile and with open arms. Making an extreme effort, I run to her . . . and fall in her arms. The lion disappears—I am saved . . .

Then everything is dark and I know only one thing: I am in the arms of my mother who helped me over the threshold. I feel good . . . I rest . . . I revel in the love of my mother whom I haven't seen for so long, I revel in the peace of love . . .

Suddenly a great indefinable power draws my consciousness in some direction and I awaken. I'm lying on a sarcophagus and don't feel my body. My consciousness is hazy; I only know that I want to get up but can't. Then I see Ptahhotep and his deputy standing near me, and it is Ptahhotep who softly, gently holds me back. I must remain prone. I am in my spiritual body which is still connected by the magic thread to my material body of flesh and blood and bone. My body lies embalmed in the sarcophagus, and I'm lying on it, in the same position, in my spiritual body. Ptahhotep and his deputy are near me; I see them in their spiritual body . . . see the glowing centres of power which their eyes have built up in their material bodies and with which they look out into the material world. Ptahhotep's two centres of power now emit a bluish phosphorescent light upon me, into me, penetrating my entire being, and sleep overcomes me.

The hall and the two high priests disappear. Again I rest in my mother's arms. Now I realize I'm not resting in her arms, but in two streams of power which once had built up her arms as well as her whole body and radiated out of her body as love; these forces are carrying me and filling my tortured soul with love, peace and a feeling of security.

Suddenly an unpleasant sound yanks me out of this . . . a sharp report which my spiritual ears first perceive as a blow. Seeking the cause, I notice it's a snapping sound as a slave driver cracks his whip at regular intervals. He's doing it to keep slaves in step as they pull my sarcophagus which slowly slides along on rails like a sled. I must have just left the palace.

I want to jump up but I can't. I can't move my legs at all. From my neck to the tips of my feet I am bound tightly. I lie there as if I were chiselled out of a single block of stone, my hands crossed over my breast, my legs stretched out straight, parallel to each other. In this position I can only look upward and forward. In the direction of my feet I see the shiny, sweaty backs of men, bent over forward, as they pull me on with rhythmic steps. Over their backs in the distance, I see a building of white stone, in its side a dark black spot like an open door. With its glistening white walls, the building contrasts sharply with the dark blue sky. As the men pull me onward, it slowly comes nearer, and the dark spot gets larger. I look up to the sky that is so dark blue it almost seems black. Two big birds circle silently over me—Storks? Or cranes?

Now the stone building is very near, and the dark spot is very big . . . yes . . . it really is an opening. Oh, now I know . . . We're in the City of the Dead! I'm being hauled into a tomb! The men step into the opening and disappear in the darkness . . . Now the black opening slides over my head . . . And after the blinding sunshine, the world around me is suddenly dark; everything disappears; absolute, inky darkness covers me! Unspeakable horror grips me, and in my heart I suddenly call out to Ptahhotep: 'How long? . . . How long must I lie imprisoned here?' And now I clearly hear his voice—the voice of Ptahhotep —telling me the inexorable, immutable sentence:

'Three . . . thousand . . . years . . .'

Monstrous horror, despair and fear seize me, holding me as in a vice, and out of this fear there suddenly appears again the monster that is the expression of the law of matter. I see his deathly, satiric ugly face grinning at me, his trenchant glance boring deep down into me and tying me to the mummy that once was *I*.

Then the monster speaks to me: 'So now you are in my power! You see, the highest and the lowest are always reflections of each other. *Perfection resting within itself* and *eternal rigidity* are two sides of the same *divinity*. You wanted to become conscious in the *perfection resting within itself*, and now you have fallen into *rigidity*!

'Yes, the mortal remains of the initiates are embalmed by the priests in the temple so that the divine power radiated by their bodies can continue to be active, like a battery, for a long time. Their spirit is free; in their consciousness they aren't attached to the earth. But you have bound yourself to your body. By carnal love, you guided the divine power within you into your lower nerve centres and burned yourself up. In this way, your consciousness together with your spiritual body are bound to your material body: you are my prisoner forever! Whereas the spiritual body of the initiate, through the act of embalming, is attached to his mummy, his consciousness is in *eternity*. But you are exiled in *infinity*!

'*Eternity is the eternal present; infinity is the eternal future* which can never be reached and never becomes *present*.

'*Eternity* never had a *beginning* and thus will never have an *end*. Eternity is timeless *present* which has no past nor future. *Infinity*, however, means a falling out of *eternity* into the future, without a *present*!

'You wanted to take part in the spiritualization of the earth. Now, spiritualize this little lump of earth that was your body if you can! Ha, ha, ha! The priestess is lying here, and her consciousness isn't more than a piece of stone!

'Now you're undergoing the first test of the initiation: *in the condition of consciousness of matter with a human consciousness*! Just try to get free if you can! You're my prisoner! You can't get away from me because *you* have become *I*. In your initiation *you* conquered *me* because I had to recognize in the face of your divinely spiritual *consciousness* that I would not exist without the *self*. Thus I had to admit that *I* am *you*. But now it's the other way round: *You* in your consciousness have become matter. You have identified yourself with your body and are nevertheless spirit like I am, namely, the spirit of matter. Therefore, *you* have become *I*!

'You're my prisoner in infinity . . . in darkness . . . imprisoned in this corpse which you were and which because of the embalming can't decay to allow you to go free. It will be your punishment to watch how this mummy—that now preserves your beauty because of the embalming process—will gradually shrink and become the image and likeness of me. You wanted to be *immortal in the spirit of eternity*, and you have become *imperishable* in this mummy into all infinity, into infinity, . . . infinity . . .'

I am powerless. I must listen. I lie there with my spiritual body indissolubly bound to my mummy. In desperation, I attempt to escape into *unconsciousness*, but I cannot! I must lie there completely conscious, without having the vaguest idea about *time* as it flows on past me.

Time! What are you, oh time! You exist only to the extent that we human beings are unhappy! In happiness there is no time: our consciousness stands still; the concept of time disappears. Only when happiness is over do we suddenly realize that while our consciousness was hovering timelessly in the eternal present, time was rushing onward. Time begins with our fall from happiness, from paradise. But unhappiness too knows no time, for the more unhappy we feel, the slower time goes by; minutes seem hours, and in our moments of deepest despair, when sufferings and torture are unbearable, every moment becomes an infinity; *time freezes*! Oh, how right Satan is! The highest and the lowest are as alike as two twins, just like reality and its reflection, appearance. Happiness is timeless *eternity*, and the opposite, unhappiness, is endless time—infinity.

I lie there and have nothing, absolutely nothing, with which to compare or measure time! Oh, tree of knowledge of good and evil! Now I understand your truth *that recognition is only possible when we can compare*!

How can I know how much time has passed when I can't see the sun, this divine timepiece . . . when I have no idea what kind of an experience of time a day represents in this darkness? What is there to show me time when nothing happens, when only solidified darkness reigns around me? How can I know anything about time when I no longer have a heart which once measured the rhythm of life in my breast and now with its pulse could give me an idea of time? Have I been lying here for a few minutes and does it already seem an eternity? Or weeks . . . years . . . or centuries . . . millennia? What is a minute and what is a millennium? How could I possibly know the difference?

The feeling of horror and fear refuses to leave me for a single moment. I no longer have lungs with which to draw a deep breath, with which to draw fresh power from the eternal source . . . with which to measure time by their breathing. I cannot look in any direction for help for my tortured soul . . . The tortures and sufferings know no end . . . no end . . . no end . . .

——— 41 ———

MIST AND RE-AWAKENING

TIME RAN across the face of the great cosmic clock, along the circumference of the gigantic wheel of creation . . . ever onward even though I had not the faintest idea it was passing . . .

It seemed to me I had been lying there for aeons and aeons, stiff and rigid . . . as if the tortures of hell would never end . . . when finally a moment did come in which I felt a force approaching me . . . a force greater and stronger than the bond which held my consciousness to my mummy, and which, now completely dried and shrivelled, had become the horrible image of the spirit of matter. This new force was drawing me irresistibly in some direction. After all the sufferings and tortures of hell I lost consciousness.

Two people, related to me in their souls, united and gave me the opportunity to inherit a body corresponding to the nature and degree of my far-fallen consciousness.

Because I had fallen as a woman, I had to be born again and again as a woman until I re-attained the level from which I had fallen. I came into surroundings where I met only semi-conscious people . . . where my deeds and those of the people around me were ruled by passions and animal instincts . . . where I found only brutality, crude selfishness and an absence of any kind of love.

I lived several insignificant lives one after the other, all in a hazy, semi-animal state of consciousness, and all of them serving only to awaken my emotional life. Misery and incessant work woke and polished my dulled and feelingless nerves. Men always played a great role. Men from whose bodies the same passionate fire of physical instincts always came forth to burn me. Again and again I met the fiery eyes and the whispering voice of the spirit woven of fire whom I had first met in my third trial. And again and again I was forced to dance with the spirit in the cavern of sensuality and passions where people turned the sacrament of procreation into a self-seeking end in itself . . . and I had to dance on with this spirit until I could scarcely stand on my weary feet. I wanted to be 'happy' and I kept on seeking love . . . kept on seeking the one and only man whom I could have loved and who could have loved me, the image of my complementary half. But I found only whipped-up sensuality and heartless passions that never could have satisfied me. I went on and on, seeking happiness again and again in the arms of men, trying to find the *one* I loved . . . the one with whom I could experience true *love* . . .

These lives were a series of never-ending disappointments. Fate whipped and drove me onward, and my soul suffered so many blows that the fires of

337

my tortures burned through the layer of indifference about my nerves and gradually awakened my comatose consciousness. The incessant excitement enabled me to develop my nervous system step by step and bring it upward by at least one degree in each of these lives. Thus through my sufferings, *eternal love* enabled me to purify and refine my nerves and increase their resistance again.

In each of these lives, however, there was within me an incessant striving to find again those people whom I consciously sought with every drop of my blood even though I could no longer remember them . . . people like myself! People with whom I would feel 'at home' . . . people to whom I really belonged with every fibre of my being: Ptahhotep, Atothis, Ima and Bo-Ghar . . . but I didn't find them! Now and again I believed I was meeting one or the other of them. Love and memory flamed up within me, but then mists covered the clear picture, and I lost them again. Sometimes I heard a servant of God speak about a great teacher, a '*Son of God*', and I had a vague recollection of having once somewhere, somehow in the dim past been close to this high being . . . having heard his teachings in living words, and within my poor benighted soul there arose a force tending to draw me away to where such high beings are 'at home'. But these moments never lasted long; for fate always gave me another shove forward, brutal blows drove back the dawning memories, and I forgot everything again.

The physical and spiritual privations I was forced to endure purified my limited senses until my nerves were again able to support the highest vibrations of unselfish love. Then, gradually, a heavenly ray of divine love began to shine through the brute passions of physical instinct. And in my next life this wonderful love banished forever the mists which had been clouding my spiritual sight.

Then when I was born as the neglected servant child, I was already carrying unselfish, divine love in my heart. But now my higher brain and nerve centres had to be awakened in order for me to be able to learn to express and use spiritual abilities. Again I met the man with the fiery eyes and the well-known voice . . . the man who had once been the red-haired foreigner. On his own pathway through numerous lives he had gone on developing himself. I loved him, I had to love him in order to gather the last experiences of love between man and woman. In my love for him, however, I conducted only physical forces into the body and this did not represent a fall. Finally our common fate brought us together again as beggars, and the tremendous shock of remembering prodded my still dull spirit into further activity. My spiritual eyes opened. But the shock was so great that my body collapsed and I died the same instant.

In accordance with the law of heredity I was drawn, a few centuries later, to two pure people filled with love whose lives had been involved with mine for ages and ages.

And once again I opened my two human eyes in this life on earth and looked at the world around me with all my previous experience . . .

338

The same frequencies of vibration build up the same outward forms. And as I have, with my present spiritual constellation in this life, again reached the level of the erstwhile Pharaoh's daughter, I also resemble her outwardly. But as I have become stronger in spirit and will-power, I have larger, stronger bones than I had in that previous life in Egypt. On the other hand, the shape, colour and appearance—the expression—of my eyes have remained the same.

When I survey my whole present life back to the time of my birth, everything is clear to me! During that previous life of mine in Egypt I was conscious of my *self*, and now in my re-awakened state in which I am again conscious of my *self* memories come alive for me from that last significant life in which my consciousness was on the same level.

My last experience from that life—the experience of being imprisoned in a coffin—was my very last impression. The horror I felt then impressed itself so deeply on my soul that it was the first thing I remembered again in this life.

But even much earlier, during my childhood, unconscious or semi-conscious memories came back to me.

The terrible disappointment I experienced when I began to realize that my 'father' was not the greatest man in the country ... my conviction that my dearly beloved parents were not my true parents—such were my first, semi-conscious memories of my earlier life.

The blobs of fat on my soup and my incessant search for unity in my circle of friends—that was my longing for bliss in the *unity of the self*—as I had come to experience it in the temple.

The strange body postures I practised as a little girl at home without ever having had the opportunity to see such exercises, the postures our friend returning from the Far East called 'Hatha Yoga exercises', these were memories of the exercises I had practised in the temple with Mentuptah. This system of exercises was part of the secret knowledge saved by 'Sons of God' when they fled to India where it has been guarded and preserved by great masters until our own times.

The horrible dream I had again and again for many years, in which a lion was chasing me so close I could feel its hot breath on my neck ... the dream that filled my childhood with fear and terror was my first memory of my last impressions of that life in Egypt ... the impressions of the death I died then.

And the 'giants', the 'titans', and the 'demigods', who with their tremendous abilities stand far above the sons of men and about whom father—my dear father of this present life—knows nothing because he doesn't remember: Ptahhotep, Atothis ... Sons of God ... where are *you*? ... *Where are you?*

And I cry out silently in my soul, the way I once learned to do in the temple before my dearly beloved and highly honoured master, the high priest Ptahhotep ... and turn my attention inward to listen for an answer ...

At first I suddenly find myself in dark emptiness. But I am fully conscious in this darkness and know that the searchlight of consciousness is the greatest light, and the only light capable of penetrating any darkness. And I set the light of my consciousness to work at its task with even greater concentration!

Where are you, you beings to whom I belong, beings whom I resemble . . . beings permeated through and through with universal love, beings who understand me. You who have never left me, who have never abandoned me, even in the time of my deepest fall, where are you? Where are you?

Then in the darkness I begin to see a greenish phosphorescent light. It becomes clearer and clearer as it appears to come ever closer, and soon I see this light taking on the magnificent shape of my dear master *Ptahhotep*. I realize that my *self* is now projecting itself into the little room of our forest house, in the person in which I experienced, in my vision during my initiation, the creative *self* which stands above all created forms. In the time of the three-dimensional world only a moment has passed. And in this moment I have seen all the phenomena which have been latent in myself as *possibilities of manifestation* and which have manifested themselves on the material plane, from the lowest, unconscious step of matter up to the highest step of the *self* manifested in matter.

Ptahhotep still stands before me, looking at me with eyes full of heavenly love. This look . . . the irresistible flow of power which *is* this look melts away the last remaining mists before my eyes and enables me to experience again as *eternity*, as timeless *present*, everything that exists in my present consciousness as *past* . . .

I look long and deeply into the eyes of my master, into those two well-springs of life, and with a feeling of infinite joy I discover I understand his unspoken words. *I have re-acquired the ability of the spirit!* We understand each other again just as we once did in Egypt!

I feel like jumping up and throwing myself at his breast, but *He* raises his right hand and holds me back. His eyes tell me: 'Don't touch me! You know I'm not in the earthly plane and you can see me only because you have adjusted your consciousness to the spiritual vibrations in which I live and move and have my being. If you wanted to touch me, you would force your consciousness down to the level of your tactile nerves, down to the level of matter, and my image would immediately disappear from your view. But from now on you will be able to direct your consciousness to the higher frequencies and find me just as you were able to do during that former projection of your *self* which you call your incarnation, or your life in Egypt.'

I stand still and very much in control of myself because I don't want under any circumstances to lose this present state in which I can perceive Ptahhotep with my spiritual eye. But my soul is so full of joy I doubt whether my heart and nerves can stand the strain. Once again Ptahhotep raises his right hand and lets the flow of power stream into my heart. Instantly my heart begins to beat normally again, and I am able to speak with him without words.

'Father of my Soul, now I understand that my present life is the resultant of all my deeds in previous lives. I understand the relationships between people and events. But there are still a few unanswered questions. I know, for example, that my one and only child is Ima. And I also understand what it was he wanted to forgive me for when he was sick, feverish and delirious as a little boy. But how does he come to believe that he was once a negro?'

Through Ptahhotep's gaze the answer appears as a series of pictures. In Ima's soul a great tragedy occurred. The moment he noticed what had occurred between the red-haired foreigner and myself, he was terribly disappointed. Whipped onward by a burning restlessness, he ran away from the temple, into the wilds of Africa to the negro tribes. Suddenly I see a picture: Ima as I had known him in Egypt, but now in a tropical region, surrounded by many negroes. He radiates divine love among these primitive children of men, and they feel and instinctively understand his love, just as animals do. Ima teaches them, heals their sick, helps them in every respect while the natives repay his love and care with childlike worship. In his utter desperation he finally takes a negro woman to wife and allows himself to be carried away by physical love. Little by little his consciousness sinks deeper and deeper into the body, and the daily struggle for existence in the jungle draws him farther and farther into life on the human level. He dies with a consciousness directed towards human problems and human worries, and inasmuch as he had occupied himself with the dearly beloved members of his negro tribe, identifying himself with them in his thoughts, he was reincarnated in his next life as a negro in accordance with the law of attraction. Into this next life he brought along the same chaotic low consciousness into which he had sunk as a result of his desperation and the extent to which he had been living on the level of animal urges. Nevertheless, his intelligence radiated through his physical body, and he became a well-liked and highly respected member of his tribe. He also had a wife and children. In his incarnation as a member of this negro tribe I can recognize him only by the look of his eyes. I see him as he goes hunting in the jungle, climbs trees to watch and wait for passing animals, then kills them and takes them home. One day when he is hunting again in the jungle, he is attacked by a tiger, struggles heroically, but finally is killed. I see his wife, alarmed by his screams and the noise of the terrible struggle, plunging into the jungle to help her husband . . . then the vision pales, and I perceive only Ima's condition after his death. His incessant longing for me leads him unconsciously—in his disembodied state—nearer and nearer to me. Both of us, Ima and I, have come a long way since we were together in Egypt, but so far we haven't been mature enough to be ready to find each other again.

Now we finally reach the level on which we can find each other again without the danger of physical love. The will to preserve the purity of our love at all cost and in the face of any temptation, together with the law of physical heredity, caused Ima to be born as my child. In this life he must also re-acquire the clear spiritual vision he once had. And since I was immediately to blame for his having lost his faith, I have to be the one to lead him back on the path to *God.* But it's not yet time for this. He is still a child.

'Father of my Soul,' I ask Ptahhotep again, 'where is Atothis, your brother and my father in Egypt? I long to communicate with him again, and I'm also certain he has never abandoned me.'

Instantly before my spiritual eyes there appears the image of a splendid man, one who has been, in recent times, the greatest teacher and expounder of the highest, profoundest truths. I've read books published by his disciples on the basis of his lectures. In reading these books I was deeply moved because every sentence I read made me feel absolutely positive that I knew the man who had made the statement, that I was in profound communication with him, that I knew all his thoughts and that I belonged to him! I knew I would never have a chance to meet him as he had died in a far-off country when I was still a little girl.

Often I gazed long and intently at the picture of this marvellous person who had possessed superhuman powers in every respect. I felt positive that some-where, somehow I had seen his eyes before . . . somewhere, somehow I had felt their heavenly gaze resting upon me. I didn't know why I often ran to him in my dreams, ran so fast my hair and my dress trailed out behind me in the wind, and why I threw myself into his arms, on to his big broad chest, crying, 'Father!—Father!' for the sheer joy of seeing him again. Neither did I know, when I had wakened why I had called *him* 'Father' in my dream, nor why I had cried so much my pillow was wet . . .

Ptahhotep smiles: 'Now do you remember?'

'Yes, Father of my Soul, now I remember. He once told me when we were at the seashore in Egypt: "There'll be a time when I'll be on earth while you are not living in a body, and there will also be a time when you'll be living in a body on earth while I am working only on the spiritual plane to do my share in the great task of spiritualization . . ."

'Where is he now, Father of my Soul? Where is he now?'

And I understand Ptahhotep's spiritual answer: 'When he was still on earth, he promised he wouldn't abandon his disciples after his death. He promised he would go on with the great work of initiating humanity in the ancient truths. You and Bo-Ghar are both his—our—co-workers, even without your being conscious of it. Later you will be conscious co-workers.'

'Bo-Ghar? Is he living on earth again? Where is he? Do I already know him in this life? Have I perhaps met him without recognizing him?'

'Wait,' answers Ptahhotep, 'he is living in a far-off country where Atothis too was reincarnated. Remember he promised to come to you from the other end of the world and save you if you got into danger. He will come to you just at the right time.'

'Danger, Father?' I ask, 'what kind of danger?'

'Do you remember what I told you in Egypt just before your initiation: If you fall, you have to experience all your initiation dreams in reality on earth, for dreams are nothing other than realities in the non-material, vision-forming energy world of mankind. And what you call "reality" is also only a "dream" . . .

only a projection of the self which has been dreamed into the material plane, into the atmosphere of the earth. And all the tests you failed to pass once, or even several times, come again and again in your life so that you can again become an initiate, a useful co-worker in the great plan. An old friend will help you through the mystic door. The young priest who helped you prepare for your initiation in Egypt is again living on earth. When the time comes he will appear, to help you on your path to the goal.'

'And how did Thiss-Tha, Atothis' General, come to be my dearly beloved father in this present life of mine?'

'It would take too long to tell you all the reasons that played a role in this end result. But here are the main ones: You know the greatest power in the human soul is *longing*. Wherever a person's consciousness is drawn by his longing—that's where he is reincarnated. When you were attacked by your lion back in Egypt, three people who saw the attack wanted to save you: Thiss-Tha, Bo-Ghar and the lion-keeper. Bo-Ghar ran after you when he noticed that you had left the palace, and in desperation he ran into the court of lions to save you.

'At that moment Thiss-Tha was in the act of having his lion harnessed. When he saw your lion turning on you, he ran towards you to try to protect you. But the lion reached you first and felled you with a terrible blow. By the time the three men were able to free you from the lion's claws, your body was so injured that resuscitation was impossible. Thiss-Tha picked up your lacerated body in his arms and carried you into the palace while Bo-Ghar tagged along crying bitterly.

'Thiss-Tha was an honest, upright man who loved the Pharaoh and you faithfully and without any ulterior motives. As he was carrying your dying body in his arms, his heart was wrung with infinite pity . . . he carried you like a poor little child, just as if you had been his child. He felt for you as a father would feel love and pity for his own daughter. Then your last experience in that life was when you saw Thiss-Tha and ran to him seeking his help. And these feelings you both had for each other were the *deepest* reason for your having experienced in a later life the relationship of father and child. But along with many other incidental reasons, there is still one important reason why you became his child; for you to be able to go through the initiation again in this life you absolutely had to inherit highly developed nerve and brain centres open and accessible to spiritual revelation.

'If you could follow back the long chain of successive generations descended from the Thiss-Tha who once lived in Egypt, you'd see that the chain of live cells passed on from generation to generation from the man who once was Thiss-Tha—your present father—has been unbroken right down to the present! In other words, the bodies of each of Thiss-Tha's children developed from a living cell from Thiss-Tha's body, and the bodies of their children each developed from a living cell. And so it went for generation after generation until your present father's father and mother were born and once more a living, fertilized cell was available as a vehicle for the spirit that once was Thiss-Tha in order for him to be reincarnated in the same hereditary chain.

'There are many deeper relationships between children and parents—ones that go back to the earliest times—than the present-day scientists studying these laws have even begun to dream of. They see only the body. But over and above the physical, there are laws of heredity reaching up into higher, spiritual relationships, *Like attracts like* ! Along with all the other reasons involved, you could really only be born again as Thiss-Tha's child because your characters are so very similar. There's a very good reason why everybody notices the great similarity in character between your father and you. But you don't resemble him because you're his child; *you have become his child because you were similar to him !* Naturally you also resemble him physically in build, posture, bone structure and features of face. *Forces that are similar build up shapes that are similar !*

'If you understand the hereditary change of living cells, you also understand why your father has the same black hair and eyes he had in that life long ago in Egypt. Colours and shapes are also manifestations of the spirit! It was a distant descendant of Thiss-Tha, a seaman who travelled to countries far away from Egypt, who brought to this country the ability to hand down physically these colours and shapes. Even after centuries have passed, a long forgotten, long lost colour or shape can come out again in the hereditary chain. That's why parents, even though both of them may be light complexioned, can unexpectedly have a dark-haired, dark-skinned child.

'The spirits themselves who are born into these strangely incongruous bodies could tell how they come by such an inheritance if they were conscious. In most cases, however, they only come to understand their origin and their task in life at a much later time. And it's good that this is so, for if a child nowadays remembers its earlier life and talks about this to others, people immediately consider it mentally deranged, or at best a dreamer or liar.

'But you've had enough today, my child, now return to your physical consciousness. After the great shock of remembering, your nerves need complete rest in order not to become ill.'

Little by little the vision of Ptahhotep pales. For a few moments I still see the divine glance of his radiant eyes. Then *He* disappears from my view, and once again all is darkness around me. I turn the light of my consciousness on to the question: *Where am I ?*

As if in answer to my question, white walls appear out of the darkness, then the contours of various objects. The colours and shapes become stronger and clearer, until everything is changed back and I realize I am in the little room of our forest lodge.

Yes! I am in the little room of our forest lodge! That is reality. But when I was initiated in Egypt and my body lay in the stone coffin, when my consciousness experienced as dreams all the lives which were slumbering in a latent state in my *self*, those dreams were just as much realities for me as the present fact that

344

I am in our little forest lodge is a complete 'reality' for me. *Who can tell me what is truth: Have I just been dreaming here, here in the forest lodge, that I once lived thousands of years ago in Egypt and was initiated there, or am I perhaps dreaming now, during my initiation in the pyramid, that I am in our little forest lodge, and is my whole life that I consider reality nothing but a chain of dream pictures in my consciousness giving me the opportunity to succeed in the face of one challenge after another?* My son now—and Ima in Egypt? Which of them is reality? In the dreams I had during initiation I saw such chaotic, horrible pictures that I can't really remember right. Nevertheless, all these impossible things in my initiation dreams were complete reality. I still see pictures from these dreams now. I saw Ima as a grown-up in an air force uniform—then other pictures of us sitting together with a lot of other people for seemingly endless lengths of time in air-raid shelters, and I remember seeing foreign soldiers as if we had been invaded . . . then our house all in ruins . . . then other chaotic, quite senseless, impossible dreams. How horrible! Probably I dreamed all these things because the newspapers are always writing about the possibility of a second world war.

And so I try to put my thoughts in order . . .

For a long time I sit motionless in my room until my housekeeper, a dear girl, comes in and asks:

'What shall I fix you for supper?'

'Nothing, thanks, Betty. I want to go straight to bed. I'm a little bit tired today,' I reply.

'Yes! That comes from thinking so much. You really should stop all this reading and thinking. I do hope you won't be sick, you look so pale.'

She pulls back the covers on my bed, says good night and leaves.

And as I prepare for a good night's rest, I realize my master *Ptahhotep* was right when he told me in my vision that my nerves need complete rest. They really do.

— 42 —

ROO-KHA AND THE TWELVE PILLS

ALL THAT happened next came so fast that it seems like a dream in my memory.

I began to pass on to the people around me the truth that I had learned from Ptahhotep in the temple. More and more people came to my lectures, like thirsty wanderers in the wilderness, seeking to draw living waters and to quench their thirst with the deep secrets of initiation into the divine *self*. From that time on my work has been the same: I stand at the beginning of an infinitely long pathway, while at the other end there stands the radiant form woven of light—the creative *cosmic self*—awaiting each and every traveller with open arms. I stand there and point the way to the countless sheep who seek the *light* and wander on side by side, slowly forward ... ever onward towards the form of light ... just the way I had seen it all in my vision in the Dolomites. Outside in the three-dimensional world my *Karma*—which had created my character and my fate—ran onward according to the laws of time and space. I was alone with my task, without a guide from whom I might have received advice, just like everyone has to be alone who wants to develop into an independent, resourceful, reliable co-worker in the great plan. Only at rare intervals, when I had reached a great turning point in my life, did I again receive help and directions from the higher powers which guide the course of the earth. Even then I still had to solve all my problems. As the years went by, however, things happened now and again to remind me of my experiences in Egypt.

Once when I was in a far country for the first time to take part in a big international conference I met someone I had known in Egypt. After my arrival I entered a room in which a number of the convention participants had already gathered. I was really thinking of anything else but memories from my life in Egypt, but in this room I saw a man whom I recognized instantly, and for sheer surprise my heart began to beat faster. It was Roo-Kha! The man stood up, and although I refrained from expressing surprise by even so much as a twitch of a muscle, he showed his surprise as he looked at me. Then he bowed and introduced himself: 'Ewalt Klimke.' We shook hands. We stood there for a moment in silence, then he said with much embarrassment: 'Strange! Who are you really? I have the oddest feeling ... just as if I should bow before you with outstretched arms, right down to the floor! Very strange!' He looked at me enquiringly: 'Why do I have this odd feeling?'

I answered: 'You were finance minister in the government of my father in Egypt,' and smiled. Those around us laughed heartily. They thought I was joking. But Mr. Ewalt Klimke didn't laugh. He kept on looking at me in a quizzical, embarrassed way, and all throughout the convention which lasted for several days he always called me 'Queen'. Again and again as he looked at me so searchingly, he would mutter, 'Strange . . . very strange!' And in all our meetings during the convention we talked together like two old friends.

Another event of about the same period in my life stands out very sharply in my memory: one autumn evening I went to bed as usual. I was dreaming something quite inconsequential when all of a sudden I seemed to be surrounded by bright light. Then in my dream an automobile came speeding up and stopped right in front of me. Two men, dressed in white and looking like doctors, got out. One of them stepped up to me, pulled a spoon-like instrument out of his pocket and used it to scoop my defective eye out of its socket. The other man pulled out a little phial, opened it and took out a big, round white disc that looked like a pill. Holding the pill up close for me to see, he said: 'Don't be afraid. I'm now going to insert this disc in your eye socket. *Twelve* of these must be consumed and then you'll get your eye back. So don't be frightened at the idea that you will now apparently be blind in this eye.' Then he inserted the pill in my empty eye socket, closed my eyelid and bandaged my right eye with a white cloth.

I awoke early in the morning and wanted to get up. Then I noticed that I couldn't see a thing with my defective right eye. It was just as if a board had been placed in front of it. I ran to a mirror to look at my eye. With my other eye which was still good, I could see that the pupil of my right eye had turned grey in colour and was completely opaque. I knew it was a cataract. For several years one had been developing slowly in my right eye, but its progress was slow and unnoticeable, and even yesterday I could still see pretty clearly. It was completely invisible from the outside. And yet, now in the space of only one night, the lens in my right eye had crystallized into a cataract!

'Don't be afraid . . .' My dream visitor's voice echoed in my memory. No, I won't be afraid! I'll just have to begin again a series of pilgrimages from one professor to another, and sooner or later one of them will operate on my eye. Long ago I learned that it doesn't do any good to be afraid, but what is the meaning of these white pills ? . . . And what is meant by the idea that twelve of them are going to have to be used up in order for me to get my sight back again. How can that be?

I went to various famous professors. In their unanimous opinion, my right eye was operable immediately, but they all said there was a danger I would always have to wear dark glasses afterwards. This was because they were going to have to cut out a bit of the iris which would give the pupil the shape of a keyhole, and because I was already thirty-five years old they thought my eye would not be able to stand the exposure to more light through the enlarged pupil. So they advised me to wait with the operation, and I followed their advice. I kept on working but I couldn't get used to working with one blind eye. The cataract bothered me greatly.

Summer came, and as usual we went to spend our holidays at our family villa on the lake. There I met a Catholic bishop who told me I should certainly go to Vienna and have my eye examined by a world-famous professor whom he personally knew. 'He uses different techniques from other doctors,' said the bishop. 'Go to him and ask him for his advice. *I am a servant of God, and perhaps God is giving you this advice through my mouth.*' By this time I had heard so much advice about my eye that I was nearly immune. But the bishop's words 'Perhaps God is giving you this advice through my mouth' made a deep impression on me.

When autumn came, my father accompanied me to the professor in Vienna. He recommended an immediate operation: 'You should get this ugly, bothersome cataract out of your eye as fast as possible. Without any doubt, it's psychologically bad for you not to.'

'Won't my eye suffer greatly from the fact that you're going to have to cut out a bit of the iris?' I asked.

He looked at me long and searchingly, then tested my reflexes and began to talk about my sculpturing work, asking all kinds of things that had no connection with my eye. Then he suddenly said: 'I won't cut out any of the iris. You can be assured your eye won't be sensitive to light.'

'In that case, let's get the operation over as fast as possible,' I answered.

A week later I was in the sanatorium, preparing for the operation which was to take place the following day.

It was a glorious autumn evening, and before going to bed, I stepped over to the window to look out over the beautiful city below. As I drew the curtain to one side to look out of the window, I saw the great round white disc of the full moon climbing slowly into the sky to the east. Instantly I recognized the great white pill the doctor had given me in my dream. It was a *full moon*! The doctor had told me: 'Twelve will have to be used up . . .' With my heart pounding in excitement, I started counting the time that had elapsed since that odd dream. Sure enough—twelve full moons had gone since that time! I knew the operation would give me back the sight of my eye!

The next morning I lay on the operating table, and in an amazingly short time the operation was over. A light flashed in my blinded eye, and a moment later I saw a hand in front of it. 'What do you see?' I heard the professor ask.

'Your blessed hand, professor,' I answered, and a moment later both of my eyes were bandaged. As I was being wheeled out of the operating room, I heard doors opening and closing and the soft voice of my father: 'How was it, Esther?'

'Good, Father,' I answered, 'I can see again . . .'

The eye operation brought me many very interesting experiences, the most revealing of which was learning something more about those vibrations we call 'light': namely, that these vibrations are only 'light' for our eyes, and healthy eyes at that. In other respects light is a tremendous force, big enough to kill a person, or even stronger beings. *It all depends on the relationship between the skin sensitivity of a living creature and the intensity of the light.* This is what happened: A few hours after the operation the professor came in and said:

'Don't be alarmed when I take off the bandage from your eye. I have to see how it reacts to the light of a burning candle.'

I thought, 'Why should I be alarmed?' The doctor took off the bandage and said, 'Now please open your eye.'

I was expecting to see a burning candle when I opened my eye. Instead, I saw only darkness, but I felt a terrible blow on my newly operated eye. Jerking my head back, I closed my eye again. I couldn't understand what had happened. My doctor laughed reassuringly: 'Didn't I tell you not to be alarmed? The retina of your eye is so sensitive right now that it doesn't pick up light rays as light, but reacts as if it were being hit a sharp blow. Just go on resting. I'll come back in a few hours to examine your eye again. So far everything's going just fine,' he said and left.

I remained alone in my darkness, with plenty of time to think, What is light? How is it the same light I perceive with my healthy eye as the flickering flame of a candle can cause me as much pain as if I were being hit by a fist? I didn't see any 'light' at all, but I did feel the wallop so strong it knocked my head back. From this I was forced to conclude that if there were beings whose skin had the same sensitivity to light as the retina of my freshly operated eye, they could be struck from a great distance, perhaps even killed, by turning the light of a searchlight on them.

Conversely, it is certainly conceivable that there could be some kind of light—for simplicity's sake we can call it 'ultra light'—that is so much stronger in its effect than the 'light' we are accustomed to seeing with our human eyes, that, depending on the sensitivity of our skin, it could strike us down in the same way ordinary light would affect a being with a skin as sensitive as the retina of my freshly operated eye.

I realized that everything is relative, a question of the relationship existing between an operating force and the resistance it meets. This fitted in with the realization that there can be infinitely varied kinds of life existing on the different planets and heavenly bodies throughout the universe. A creature similar to man living on Uranus or Neptune, because of the much greater distance between those planets and the sun as compared to the distance between the earth and the sun, might conceivably have a skin as infinitely sensitive to light as my freshly operated eye; and if such a being on one of these distant planets were to 'see' in sunlight in the same way we see here on earth, his eyes would certainly have to be immeasurably more sensitive to light than ours are. But do we need to go so far away? The myriad creatures living in the depths of the ocean have such eyes—and capabilities we cannot even begin to understand—because we simply couldn't begin to exist in such dense darkness.

In this vein I went on meditating on the unlimited possibilities of worlds without end and of the different forms of life they can contain. And the more I thought on these things, the more my heart filled with deep humility in the face of the power of the eternal *being* we call *God* . . .

This eye operation brought me another very interesting and valuable experience. Through it I learned that *the eyes take in light not only for themselves but for the entire body, just as the lungs do with air and oxygen. Light is force!*

On the third day after my operation, the professor came in with the nurse, and said, 'Now it's time for you to get up and come over and sit in this armchair. Just put on your slippers, and the nurse and I will help you.'

I was offended: 'Doctor,' I said, 'I'm not sick! And lying in bed for three days certainly hasn't made me so weak I can't sit up and move about myself. You don't need to help *me*.'

'Good,' the doctor said, 'Go ahead and get up by yourself—if you can.'

I started to get out of bed. But I was in for a big surprise! My feet and legs were so weak, so powerless, that I would have sunk to the floor if strong hands had not seized me from both sides and held me up. My legs hung down like two limp rags and my back was just as limp and powerless. So, quite the opposite of what I expected, I was really glad for help in getting out of bed and over into the armchair. How was this?

Then I heard the professor laugh: 'You see you couldn't get up alone? It's just because you were in complete darkness for three days. When a person is suddenly shut off from light, he loses strength so fast he soon can't stand up alone any more. You'll shortly be able to open your eyes again, and when you do you'll find your strength returning quickly. One of our greatest problems during the war was how to help blinded soldiers, not so much because of their mental condition, but because of the complete debility which always and unavoidably accompanied their sudden blindness. The human soul is so wonderfully fashioned that a person always finds ways and means to survive even such a tremendous catastrophe as sudden blindness, and he can even go on and discover new joys in life or new aspects of old pleasures. But our greatest problems arose from the fact that these poor young men weren't even able to stand on their own feet for a long time. It was not possible for us to give them back the blessing of light. But thank God for the elasticity and resiliency of the body; in time a blind person's skin takes over the whole job of providing light throughout his body. The problem of blindness is always most acute right after it hits its victim, simply because of the weakness caused by the sudden absence of light.'

I was silent. Ever since my eye had become diseased I had begun to understand the significance of blindness much, much better than one ever could when he has two healthy eyes. Now, through my own experience, I came to understand the Biblical passage:

'The light of the body is the eye; if then your eye is true, all your body will be full of light. But if your eye is evil, all your body will be dark. If then the light which is in you is dark, how dark it will be!' (Matthew 6: 22, 23).

And my heart bled the more at the thought that mankind isn't even satisfied with the blindness which occurs in nature. Quite the contrary, he goes out himself to wage wars in which countless otherwise healthy people are blinded, maimed and crippled! When will humanity be mature enough to refuse to obey the tyranny of politicians who unconscionably sign declarations of war?

Two weeks later the professor took me into a dark room to examine both my eyes. With a very strong lens before the eye he had operated on I was able to read everything he put before me, even to the tiniest letters. Then to my amazement, this dignified old professor jumped up, seized me with both hands and hoisted me high above his head. He was such a charming old fellow that I really couldn't understand what had got into him and why he was acting so strangely. As he gently set me back on the floor, his face was beaming as he said: 'The technique I used on operating on your eye has so far only be used for children and young people up to the age of twenty. Beyond that age there's a danger of inflammation of the iris, leading to total loss of vision in the eye. As you may remember, in our first consultation, I observed you closely, noting your extraordinary vitality and resilience. Your reflexes, too, were quite good, and as I always do, I followed my intuition. With the courage of my convictions, I operated on you as if you were still a child. So now you know why I'm so happy. The operation was a complete success. Your tissues were still young enough to come through this difficult operation in splendid form. So now you can go home with two healthy eyes—and with my heartiest congratulations!'

I thanked him for his kindness, and we took leave of each other. As I travelled homeward, I reflected on the twelve 'pills' which had to be consumed before light would return to my blinded eye. And now it had.

— 43 —

THE YOUNG PRIEST APPEARS

SEVERAL YEARS went by in which my husband and I lived pleasantly and happily, our love for each other unchanged. I continued my work as a sculptress, with lots of assignments, and in my free time more and more people came to me for psychological consultations. Several times a week I gave lectures on self-recognition and understanding, based on the secret knowledge Ptahhotep had given me in Egypt. And whenever I felt like resting from my exertions, there was always my beloved piano.

Every day I practised spiritual yoga and even attained the ability to go into deep trances, but the last, highest door on my pathway remained closed and locked before me. Having attained a certain degree of spiritual development, I found the pathway towards the complete realization of my *self* was blocked by an obstacle like a wall I couldn't break through with my consciousness. Every year I spent several months living alone in our forest lodge and practising yoga. The young fruit trees I had planted years before were now big, strong, well developed trees—and still I practised with unabated diligence; yet the guardians of the secret gateway refused me admission . . .

It was autumn once again, and I left our little house in the forest to spend a day in the city celebrating my father's seventieth birthday with the whole family, our relatives and our many friends.

The following morning as I was preparing to start the trip back to the forest lodge, our telephone rang. An elderly friend asked me what I was doing that afternoon. I told her I was free.

'The famous writer with whom I studied in India under Maharishi has arrived and is staying at my house. If you're interested, come around this afternoon and you can talk with him,' my friend said.

That afternoon I rang my friend's front doorbell. Stepping into the parlour, I caught my first glimpse of the man who had attained world renown through his books about yoga and the great yogis in India. At my first glimpse, I was taken aback. There, in front of me, sat—the young priest who had helped me with my last preparations for my initiation in my long-ago life in Egypt!

We exchanged a few comments in which I mentioned that I had read his books and that I had been practising yoga for a long time but still was unable to reach the highest goal. Other guests dropped in and we were all soon involved in a general conversation which lasted far into the evening. There was no further opportunity to talk with him alone. In leaving I thought, 'So nothing happened . . .' Secretly I had hoped the famous 'white yogi' would help me ahead on my mystic pathway.

The next morning my friend rang me up again to tell me the writer wanted to speak to me alone. 'If you have time, come around again this afternoon,' she invited me.

Entering her parlour I found the famous writer sitting in the lotus posture on the sofa. As I too sat down he asked me, 'What do you wish of me?'

'I have no wishes,' I replied. 'I'm living quite contentedly in absolute inner peace.'

'Then why have you come to me? What do you expect of me?'

'I want reality,' I said.

After a moment's silence the writer looked at me and asked, 'And your absolute inner peace—isn't that reality?'

'Yes, indeed, it is reality, but I'm looking for more. I feel like Moses who saw the promised land but never got there. I believe I can see it too, but I'd like to get in. I'm not satisfied just seeing it from the outside and seeing what's inside; I want to get in myself.'

He smiled. 'Yes,' he said, 'you're standing in front of the great door with your hand already on the door knob. It's extremely rare that anyone can progress up to the point you've reached all alone and without the help of a master. You have probably been initiated in some previous life, and now you only need to make the last step through the gate that separates you from the great goal.'

I looked at the yogi. Doesn't he remember he was a priest in ancient Egypt and knew me there?—I thought. Or is it just that he would prefer not to talk about it? From his impenetrable gaze I couldn't tell.

'I know that already,' I answered, 'and I want to get through the door even if I have to break it down with my fist.'

'And do you believe I can help you?' he asked.

'If I am ready for it, yes, you can certainly help me.'

'And if you're ready for it, you believe I can help you?' he asked again.

'Yes,' I answered firmly.

Then, as if waiting for this reply, he pointed to the chair opposite from where he was sitting and said, 'Sit down over there, close your eyes and think yourself intently into your heart.'

I did as he said, closed my eyes and concentrated intently on my heart. Then with my eyes closed, I saw a strong yellow current of bright light flowing out of the yogi's solar plexus encompassing me like a circle, then encircling him again like a big figure eight.

Simultaneously I felt I was coming in my concentration to the point I had so often been able to attain in the past without being able to go forward. And now I felt a great power, foreign to myself, reaching into my consciousness and carrying me forward, as if through a door, into an infinite depth beyond . . .

Every concept of time disappeared, and I hadn't the faintest idea how much time had passed when I heard the voice of the white yogi again: 'Now you may open your eyes.'

In doing so, I realized how far away I had been from earthly physical consciousness. I didn't feel like talking because it seemed superfluous to say anything at all.

'I have set up a contact between your personal self and the overself,' the writer said, 'because you're ready for it. From now on, whenever you have a question, concentrate on me, and you'll get your answer the same day.'

'On your person or on the higher self?'

He smiled and said nothing. I understood perfectly. It was completely useless to waste a single word talking about the 'person'.

From that day on I found myself one of a group of people meeting at my friend's house and meditating under the leadership of the yogi.

A few weeks later he left us to continue his travels. Once again I was alone and found myself living outwardly just as I had before.

About a half a year later I was sitting with a number of friends, listening to one of the group talking about black magic. He said black magicians chose a few disciples whom they use as blind tools to carry out their will without resistance. These disciples are possessed by the black magician, lose their independence completely, and are finally destroyed.

The next morning as I remembered these words, I began to wonder whether I had been lacking in caution in my meeting with the famous 'white yogi'. I was still convinced that he was a 'white magician' if we wanted to call him anything, but I had nevertheless put myself completely in his hands with a blissfully innocent trust. Was he after all a black magician?—or really a white one? How can I know? How can anyone know whether he's dealing with a 'white' or with a 'black' magician? This question really bothered me . . .

That afternoon we were visiting one of my husband's old school friends. While we were chatting, he told us how that very day he had been leafing through the pages of an old book, and how in doing so he had come across a highly interesting chapter about the difference between white and black magicians:

'The white magician, when he wants to help one of his pupils onward, binds the pupil to himself in the form of an *eight*. In this way, he leaves his pupil his full independence, *because both teacher and pupil form the mid-points, each of his own individual circle*. On the contrary, the black magician takes away his pupil's independence *by taking him into a circle with himself* in such a way that the black magician is in the centre of the circle and the pupil just inside the circumference in the same way a satellite's orbit forms a ring around the sun.'

I listened to this story with the keenest excitement. Our friend didn't have the vaguest idea he was giving me an answer I was seeking. I had not mentioned the matter to anyone. And yet I got my answer the very day my question came up!

The higher *self*—God—always finds a human mouth when he has a message for us. For the *self* there is no such thing as an obstacle.

─── 44 ───

IMA AND BO-GHAR

THEN THE great war came.

Both of the men who belonged to me put on uniforms. My husband was mobilized for service in one of the largest government industrial plants to come under military control. He had to carry the heavy responsibilities of a commander.

One day we were sitting together at table. The door opened and in walked our son—in an air force uniform.

I felt as if the earth had disappeared beneath our feet and I were falling into an abyss. Within our circle of friends every one of the fine young men who had gone into the air force had very soon after been carried into the cemetery. Strangely enough, the moment he walked in wearing his air force uniform, I had the odd feeling I had already seen him in such a uniform. But there was no time to puzzle over *when* and *where* I could have seen him—I was simply horrified at the thought he had gone into the air force. The countries we were fighting against had much better aircraft than ours. They had shot down our *very best* boys—for only the very best were able to pass the exacting physical and mental entrance exams—like so many toy balloons. At the very moment I was working on a big composition for a tombstone for a young flyer killed in action, one of my son's boyhood chums. And there I was looking at my very own son in an air force uniform.

'How did you come by this uniform?' I asked him.

'Government issue,' he answered proudly, 'I've passed the entrance exams for the air force.'

'We thought we'd arranged for you to get into the engineers corps. How come you're in the air force now? No young man can get into the air force without his parents' consent.'

'Mother, with the war on, they've done away with the requirement of parental consent—as you can see for yourself.'

I was speechless. There was nothing I could do. And there came days when I wandered around in our apartment like a sleepwalker, talking to *God*. My power over my child was at an end. I had to turn him over to *God*, and I did so consciously. I was forced to realize that *God* loves my son more—must love him more for the simple reason that *he* is *God*—than I, an imperfect human being, have it in my power to love him.

No matter what might happen, I told myself, it was certainly for the best, even if it might seem like a catastrophe to me in my human shortsightedness.

I was forced to *act on the strength of my faith in the reality* of God! I couldn't allow my heart to tremble, and I had to control my nerves with absolute calm, because I was forced to consider the fate of my one and only child from the standpoint of the great *divine plan*, beyond time and space, instead from my little human standpoint. And considering it this way I was also forced to act accordingly. Other mothers were praying day and night for their sons. How could I have done that? *God* doesn't allow himself to be persuaded by humans, and according to the law of character and destiny I knew that whatever happened to my son—no matter what—was certain to be the very best experience for the development of his consciousness. Yes, *God* loves him! Even more than I do! —this realization gave me the strength to go on living.

As the war dragged on life became a kind of uninterrupted waiting for the end of this mass murder. Outwardly things went on pretty much as they had before. We worked, and we went to concerts, operas, theatrical performances and to social gatherings among our friends, but all of this seemed to flow past us, for at the back of all these external events in our lives, there was always the same incessant waiting . . . waiting for the end of the war.

A few years went by in this way, and with increasing clarity I could see with my inward eye the gigantic military steam-roller closing in on us from the east.

One day a friend rang me up to say she wanted to introduce me to a very interesting person. He was an Indian, a genuine yogi, she added. Often before that she had wanted to introduce me to 'genuine yogis', but I had always found them out very quickly to be perfectly ordinary and average people. Despite all these experiences, she continued to act as if she were convinced that every Indian must somehow be a very highly developed yogi. Reason enough why I wasn't exactly excited about her new 'discovery'. Refusing to take no for an answer, she insisted on coming to see me. And she did come, and told me a long story about having seen a picture of a young Indian yogi in the newspaper, having looked for him all over town without success, until by a very remarkable 'coincidence' she had discovered that the Indian she was seeking in vain all over the city with more than a million inhabitants, was living in another part of the very same building she was lodged in herself! It was a huge, modern block of flats; so it was no wonder the tenants didn't all know each other.

After listening to her patiently for a while, I tried to cut her long, long story short: 'And now, what do you want of me?'

'You just *must* meet him,' she said. 'Let me bring him here and introduce him to you. He never goes out, preferring to live a very retiring life. But when I told him about your weekly lectures on yoga philosophy, he immediately expressed his willingness to come and see you. Look at some of these photographs of him.'

With only casual interest I took the photographs she held out to me, glanced at them—and caught my breath: Bo-Ghar! With my heart beating excitedly, I looked at all the pictures. Not the faintest doubt! I recognized the look of these big black eyes. The unbelievable purity and the childlike expression of the entire face—it was he! But he wasn't a little boy any more, as I had known him and carried the remembrance of him deep in my soul. Now he was a grown-up young man.

'Helen,' I said to my friend, 'tomorrow evening I have time. You may bring him.'

The next day Helen came with Bo-Ghar. We drank tea and chatted about all kinds of things, but all the time we did so my inward eye was seeing pictures of a great palace made with huge stone blocks, with a room in it—my room—with magnificent furniture inlaid with gold, a low couch covered with beautiful skins of animals, and on these skins a human form sitting, with legs, arms, hands and shoulders I can see—only the head I don't see because *I am* this human form, sitting on the animal skins, and at my feet a child, a sweet vivacious child who now looks at me with the eyes of this young man from India.

And why does he call me 'queen'?

I ask him.

'Because you are a queen,' he replies with conviction.

'Yes! You're right!' my husband says. 'She certainly can give orders, especially to me!' With that he laughs heartily, and we all join in.

My son enters, sees the Indian guest and stands stiff and rigid out of sheer surprise. Then he pulls himself together and I introduce him. Both he and Bo-Ghar look at each other long and searchingly. I succeed in bridging over the momentary embarrassment by offering my son a cup of tea. He sits down and joins us but is quite unable to take his eyes off the young Indian.

That's how Bo-Ghar first came to us. In a very short time he had captured the hearts of every one in the family. My parents and my brother and sister took him in as if he were a new brother among us. He opened his yoga school and since he didn't know our language, he asked me to give a weekly lecture on yoga for his pupils. Thus we began our work together.

The war dragged on. In the winter we all went on with our work as we had before, and in the summer we moved into our little house in the forest. Bo-Ghar came with us, living in the forest according to the laws of yoga he had learned from his master.

My son, by this time, had one plane crash behind him. Miraculously he had survived it with only a concussion of the brain. In due time he was well again with only a scar on his high good-looking forehead to remind him of his mishap.

One hot summer day, when the great steam-roller from the east was already near our borders, my dear, wonderful mother suddenly fell to the floor. When we tried to help her up again, she said very clearly, 'Stroke—it's a stroke . . .'

Then she lay in bed for a long time, struggling painfully to bring forth one word after another as she told us she felt one side of her body was already dead.

'And do you know,' she added, 'it's so interesting to be half here and half on the other side already. I still see each of you half from the outside and half as if from within. And I can also see your future destiny. As soon as I'm better I'll tell you all about it. Right now it's very difficult to talk.'

357

She was already living very close to the world of the spirit. Whenever any one of her friends, at home in some part of the city, spoke about her, she would say to us, 'Now my friend Mrs X is here with me, and this is what she's saying . . .'

And mother would tell us exactly, word for word, what her friend was saying in the same moment several miles away, as could later be proved in minute detail. And it also often happened that mother was sitting in her flat talking to her nurse and I was up on the second floor talking about her with my husband. Then she would say to her nurse, 'My daughter Esther is now here and this is what she's saying about me . . .' And she would repeat word for word what I was saying about her in another part of the house and well out of her hearing.

One day her nurse called me to come immediately. Mother had suffered a second stroke.

I rushed downstairs. Mother lay there, still and pale as death, unable to say a thing. With her right hand she pointed at her tongue, giving me to understand she couldn't move it any more.

She lay there thus for several hours, without being able to speak. Suddenly the door opened and Bo-Ghar came in. With her poor, twisted, half paralysed face, mother looked at Bo-Ghar, her eyes beaming with joy. Bo-Ghar sat down beside her and enclosed her wrist in his hand. After a couple of minutes mother opened her mouth and said very slowly, syllable by syllable, but quite clearly: 'From Bo-Ghar's hand a force is flowing into me, and this force has now reached the part of my head where I feel pressure that prevents me from speaking. Thanks to this force that's flowing into me from Bo-Ghar's hand, the pressure has abated and I can talk again.' Then she went on to tell us a number of important things, all part of her last wish.

Bo-Ghar went away after a while, and for an hour and a half mother was still able to talk. Then all at once she said:

'Now the force our dear Bo-Ghar caused to flow into me is ebbing away. It's getting harder and harder to talk and use my tongue. The connection between me and my body is dissolving. *God* be with us . . .' These were her last words.

And two days later her coffin was carried out of the house. Her place at the head of our family table was empty. From then on we marked it with a burning candle when we gathered round.

— 45 —

THE CHALLENGES ARE REPEATED

IT WAS the last winter before the end of the war.

Our gardener who had taken care of our orchard had long since been called up for military service. The orchard was forsaken, and I moved into our little forest house to save whatever I could. One night I was awakened by a horrible noise. Sirens! In the city!

I jumped out of bed. From the dining-room I could see the city in the distance. Dozens and dozens of airplanes roared over my head in the darkness. The air trembled with the noise of their engines. Suddenly a hellish drama began to be enacted in the air over the city as row after row of airplanes dropped their bombs into the masses of humanity living below. The sky came alight with the bursting of bombs and the fires they started throughout the city. The noise became deafening as, added to the roar of the engines and the bursting of bombs, the city's anti-aircraft cannon began picking out targets overhead as best they could. Seen from the distance, their fire looked like tiny red lanterns climbing up into the sky. From time to time I could see what looked like a huge burning torch plunging downward, and I knew that somewhere a mother would be waiting in vain for her son to come home . . .

This breathtaking show of fireworks continued for about an hour and a half. It seemed to me I had been standing at my window for an eternity of time. Down there in front of me, where this interplay of lightning and thunder meant death and destruction for thousands of people, all my dear ones were living. All except my son who at that very moment could perhaps be flying through the air as a target for other poor young men flying in much better aircraft, forced to shoot at him against all their human instincts, just as he was being forced to shoot at them.

All at once I felt a force from a near-by tree calling for my attention. Looking towards the tree, I saw two green eyes staring at me. An owl! It sat there as immovable as a statue. Never before had I seen an owl in this whole area. How did it come here? Almost unconsciously I spoke to it in spirit: 'You dear bird, it's not your fault that superstitious people think of you as a harbinger of death. Still, do you perhaps want to tell me that all my dear ones down there in the city are no longer living on this earth?'

Immediately the owl danced a bit closer to me on the branch, suddenly spread his wings and flew off into the forest.

Instantly I knew that a great power which controls and guides everything was

359

telling me, through the disappearance of the 'death bird', that all my dear ones were still alive . . .

Yes all *my* dear ones! But all the thousands of people who were killed that night in the city, and all the others who have been killed during this terrible war—each such person was somebody's dear one! Why have these people had to die? Why do people kill each other senselessly?

The hellish drama was repeated night after night.

In the summertime several of us moved into our little house in the forest. Bo-Ghar came with us. During the nights of terror we all stood together at the window, watching the bombardment of the city below. Shortly after the sirens gave the all-clear signal, my husband would telephone with the reassuring news that he and the others with him in our city house were all safe and sound . . .

When autumn came I stayed behind alone in our forest house, continuing my work in the orchard and garden. Each evening I was able to observe how much closer to us the enemy artillery—oh, these poor young men who are forced into being our 'enemies'—had moved up during the course of the day.

One evening I decided I was going back to the city. Come what might, I was determined to go through at the side of my loved ones the difficult hours of siege and bombardment that lay ahead.

Then my telephone rang. How strange! I suddenly felt positive I had already experienced this same situation some time before! I knew in advance that my husband was just now going to call me, and I knew word for word what we were going to say to each other. And all the while I felt as if I were dreaming.

And this same strange feeling was to continue throughout all the difficult days to come, until the days turned into weeks, the weeks into months and the months into years! Again and again I found I knew exactly what was going to happen. The next moment, just as if I had already experienced all these terrible things. Everything was simply repeated—I knew it!—but I couldn't understand where and how I could have experienced these situations before.

After I had returned to the city and the sirens howling in the night forced me to join all the others in the house in a pell-mell flight into the cellar, and as we sat there, all of us calm, passive, earnest and worried about what was going to happen next—all the while I knew that somehow, somewhere I had experienced all this before. And so it was to be with me throughout all the nights, the horrible nights of bombardments and air raids.

I experienced this feeling of re-living past events even more strongly one day in late autumn when the door opened and my son came in. Why was I surprised to see him in an air force uniform? Yes! I still remembered him as Ima, the young priest in Egypt, and I also knew all the relationships that linked us together. But in my memory of him in Egypt he wore quite different clothing. How do I come to feel that even in my life in Egypt I already saw him in this air force uniform? Why do I have the feeling that everything I experience is not 'reality', that I'm merely dreaming all these pictures, and that I'm *experiencing these dreams in my initiation sleep in the great pyramid*?

I clearly remember all the relationships of my life in Egypt, but no matter how hard I try, I cannot remember the events nor my initiation dreams.

How strange? *How can one remember that one doesn't remember?* If I can't remember something, then I cannot know that it has existed. But I know I experienced my whole future destiny in visions during my initiation in the pyramid, and that these visions—or dream pictures—were the occasion for my passing various tests and meeting certain challenges. It's true my master Ptahhotep warned me that if I were to fall after my initiation, all the tests I had to go through during my initiation would be repeated on the earthly plane! Yes! Continually I have the certain feeling that these events *are repeating themselves*!

For a number of years I made a habit of writing down every morning, as I was waking up, the dreams I had had during the night. I had not reviewed these records for a whole year. Now I began to read them. And to my great surprise I found that most of these dreams I had recorded were dreams I had of events to come, events which I actually experienced later, sometimes as much as six months or a year later. In the meantime I had completely forgotten the dreams themselves, and if I had not been able to see and recognize my own hand-writing, I would not have believed that *I* had dreamed these dreams and recorded them. How was it possible that when these things actually happened I couldn't remember any more that I dreamt them in advance, and in many cases even in amazingly accurate detail? I found this discovery to be literally amazing! What kind of a force is there within us that knows our future in advance with such precision and tells us about it beforehand? And what kind of imperfect creatures are we who understand so little about the language of dreams that we can't remember having dreamed in advance about a certain event or situation, even when the dream is repeating itself on the earthly plane in our outward life? Truly we don't deserve the care and attention this force bestows upon us as, with infinite patience, it reveals new truth and knowledge to us . . .

How could I explain remembering from an earlier life in Egypt that I had seen my son in an air force uniform and that when he came in I knew exactly he was going to take leave of me because his unit was going to be transferred to an airfield less exposed to enemy bombing than the one near our city? As he spoke and as I answered I knew within me that I had experienced all this once before . . . again I had the feeling I was only dreaming . . .

I didn't dare tell anyone of this experience. I was afraid that even my son—Ima himself—would believe my mind had suffered from all the excitement. It seemed much better to keep silent about the whole matter.

And so we lived through the siege of our city. For seven weeks we sat in our cellar, enduring incessant bombings. After the house above us had been bombed and shelled into a heap of rubble, we were forced to flee. Our destiny tossed us about like a leaf in the wind, and after many trials and tribulations we began to rebuild our lives. We were all reduced to the state of beggars. My husband had been seriously injured, and it was a long time before he could work again. By dint of days and nights of effort with no more equipment than primitive man had in the first primaeval jungle, Bo-Ghar and I fashioned a new home out of the ruins of our family house, and in it we re-opened our Yoga school . . .

Months went by as we worked hard and long. Those were times when we learned what hunger is. Week by week we gradually wasted away, shrinking from human beings of flesh and blood to living skeletons covered with skin. Even good friends would fail to recognize each other when they met by chance on the street. Fear—a baleful new fear—spread throughout the population, augmenting the feelings of fright already present in thousands of tortured souls: What will we eat tomorrow ? How long will we be able to go on working so hard without even once getting enough to eat ? How long can we go on like this and still maintain our health ?

Our country's fertile soil had brought forth plenty of everything we needed, but we were forced to look on while countless freight trains snaked their way through the countryside, carrying off our rich harvest to another country . . .

Then after long and difficult months, even the famine began to abate. More and more frequently we got something nourishing to eat, and gradually we began to put on weight. Once again, good friends and acquaintances failed to recognize each other on the street. We had all got accustomed to seeing each other so thin and emaciated, and every so often in passing someone on the street, the thought would flash across our mind that this well-fed person bore a striking resemblance to some very thin friend. Both of us would have the same thought, then turn around, recognize each other, and break out in peals of laughter at the happy reunion . . . But months went by before we became really re-acquainted with all our friends . . . re-accustomed to their normal dimensions.

I still had the feeling that I had already experienced all of this! It was a feeling that stayed with me wherever I went and whatever I did. It was not that I could foretell the future. On the contrary, it was merely the persistent feeling that everything had already happened just that same way once before. And not being able to foresee the future, I did not know what had become of my son. Since the time he suddenly took leave of us he had not been heard of.

A year and a half later our doorbell rang. I opened the door, and who should I see before me but my son! And once again I had that strange feeling known by psychologists as the '*dèja vu*'. I knew it was a repetition. All these events were repetitions! But how could that be ?

And one night everything became clear!

Once when I was forced to pass the test of 'cruel love' towards the person I love most dearly here on earth, my son, I kneeled in my bed in the dark of the night and talked about him with *God*, asking *Him* to show my son the way he should go. I followed the pathway which, within us, leads to *God*, withdrawing my consciousness from my outer person into my inner being. Finally I fell into a trance and suddenly found myself in front of the seven steps I have told about earlier.

And I jump up, from one to the next, easily, happily, and joyously . . . I know the way . . . I remember . . . Oh *God*! . . . I remember! All these events I've been experiencing as 'reality' in my life on the material, earthly plane are things I experienced several thousand years ago in my initiation in the pyramid. At that time all these events were lying in the depths of my soul as unconscious, still latent energies, still pure cause. This is because everything that happens here on earth is the materialization of a complete, accomplished *cause* waiting on the spiritual plane for materialization. When one achieves the ability *consciously* to reach the depths of the self where those energies are awaiting their realization, one experiences *cause* simultaneously with the *effect*—the *future*—as a complete and perfect *present*! *And the present, our life, everything that happens to us is merely an opportunity to meet the tests and trials and challenges of initiation. An opportunity to relax the tensions and dissolve away the stresses we have stored up within ourselves, for aeons and aeons of time, by our thoughts and words and deeds . . . the tensions and stresses that are the cause of our destiny, our future. To the extent that we are able to become conscious of these tensions and overcome them, we free our human consciousness which is tied down by these energies and limited because it is tied down, and we identify our consciousness with the true divine self waiting behind every personal feeling of ego . . . we identify ourselves with God . . . and that is*

INITIATION !

— 46 —

CONCLUSION

AFTER THE experience of that night I knew the tensions and stresses had been erased from my soul . . . everything personal would have to be discarded. I had overcome myself! There was nothing more within me to bind me to my 'person'. Everything personal had to disappear.

It began with a very strange feeling which followed me wherever I went—at home or outdoors—that I wasn't really 'there'. Not there? But where? I really didn't know! But I suddenly became aware of the fact that my *self* was never where my person, my body, was located. On the contrary, my self projected itself out of spacelessness into my person, and now my *self* was beginning to project itself somewhere else than where my physical being was. But where? Into another country!

I knew I was going to go away, that I was going to have to go away! Whenever the spirit, the cause, ceases to be present, the appearance, the effect, must follow it wherever it is projected by the cause. There it can go on living. Otherwise, the appearance would disappear, that is, die. But how am I supposed to leave this country? No one can get a passport!

The time for my departure had not yet come. Other events had to take place first.

One night I awakened quite suddenly. I saw my father standing before me, taking leave of me with a smile on his dear sweet face. I understood: It was time for him to go . . . I wanted to jump up and ask him why he wanted to go away and where he was going, but he disappeared, and I realized that I was just awakening.

Father was eighty years old, but hale and hearty in body and mind. With ever fresh and undiminished energy he was still going on with his very responsible government job. Nevertheless I knew his spirit had come to me to take leave. His time had run out on the great cosmic clock, and he was going to leave his body behind.

The next day he was already in the hospital, and all the rest of us gathered round to say goodbye. He either could not or would not speak. With long, deep and tender glances he looked each of us in the eye in turn. Then he closed his eyes and didn't open them any more.

And we accompanied the second coffin out of our family.

My son tried everything he could to get work. In vain. He kept on trying, again and again, but always in vain. Finally he came to the realization that there was no room for him any more in our country. And the day came when he took his guitar—a dear old travelling companion he had never neglected even in the grimmest days of the war—and went away in search of a country where a free man who wanted to work could find a home. Again we took leave of each other, not knowing whether we would meet again in this life. But in the depths of my *self* I knew I would see him again. I knew we would still be working together in *God's garden* ...

Then came the last act.

Bo-Ghar had just given a public lecture. As usual the audience was so big the police had to keep order.

After the lecture, he found himself surrounded by people plying him with questions, begging for autographs, and refusing to let him go home. While all this was going on, my husband and I were standing a bit apart from the crowd, waiting. Suddenly an officer of the secret police appeared and asked to speak with me. When we had stepped to one side, he said, 'I practise yoga, and my whole family with me, so I know it's a wonderful system. Nevertheless, both you and the Indian are dangerous, because so many people listen to you and do as you say. The party doesn't like that. So now you're going to have to decide either to work *with* the party and *for* it, or to get out of the country. We'll let you both go without hindrance. But if you refuse to go, we'll be forced to take other measures. Think over this proposition my superiors have asked me to bring you, and act accordingly. I'll come back to hear your decision.'

Bo-Ghar could have left the country freely with his passport. But I was obliged to seek permission and apply for an entry permit to another country. Soon I was involved in an endless chase for an exit permit and for entry permits ... Finally I was forced to realize that it was an absolute impossibility for me to get a passport. I was shunted back and forth from one office to another until at long last I received a final and definite refusal. But that meant the secret police would soon be having recourse to 'other methods'. And we all knew what that meant. Many of our friends had already disappeared for good and all, while others, after suffering horrible tortures in prison, had been released, broken in mind and body, only to die a miserable death shortly thereafter.

Then Bo-Ghar said to my husband, 'The only possibility of saving your wife is for you to divorce her and let me take her out of the country as my wife. In this way she'll have the same passport as mine, and we can leave the country legally. And you'll come later.'

My husband seized Bo-Ghar's hand but was unable to say a word. Big tears of gratitude welled up in his tortured eyes ...

So the day came when I took leave of all the people near and dear to me, and set out into the unknown world, to make my home wherever *God* should lead us.

Bo-Ghar kept his word: He came from the other end of the world to save me!

We found Ima again, and together we are travelling on in the footsteps of the Titans who have shown us the pathway to initiation, to redemption, to the lost paradise ...

And when I seek those whom I love, I turn the searchlight of my consciousness inward, for everything and everyone is living within me!

The *self*—at one and the same time the *self* of all living creatures, and therefore my *self*—knows no bounds; so the entire universe is *within me*, and my *self* fills all the universe. Everything that *is*—*I am*! In everything I love, I love *my self*, for the only things we *think* we don't love are what we haven't yet come to *recognize* within ourselves!

THE SELF IS LIFE AND THE ONLY REALITY, AND WHOEVER IS INITIATED INTO THE SELF—AND IN THIS WAY HAS COME TO KNOW HIMSELF COMPLETELY—LOVES EVERYTHING AND EVERYONE EQUALLY, FOR HE IS ONE WITH THEM.

AFTER A TIBETAN PICTURE

'Smaller circles in ever larger and larger circles, on and on into infinity . . .'

THE DAY WITH YOGA

Inspirational Words To Guide Daily Life

Elisabeth Haich

Through her best selling books *–Initiation, Sexual Energy and Yoga,* and *Wisdom of the Tarot,* Elizabeth Haich is internationally famous for her ability to assist others on their paths of spiritual enfoldment.

A unique creative energy is available to us each day of the week. Nature, all living creatures, plants, and human beings are deeply influenced by these subtle variations. We all bathe, float and are affected by the power operating that day.

Each Day is related to a specific planetary energy:

Sunday–The Sun	Wednesday–Mercury
Monday–The Moon	Thursday–Jupiter
Tuesday–Mars	Friday–Venus
Saturday–Saturn	

The Day With Yoga, is Elisabeth Haich's personal collection of meditation quotes. Each has been carefully selected to inspire and attune us to the vibration of the day, and to release a deeper level of harmony and inner peace into our lives.

ISBN:0-943358-12-4   Paperback   4 x   104 Pages

For an Aurora Press catalog:
Aurora Press, P.O. Box 573, Santa Fe, NM 87504
Fax 505-982-8321 Email: Aurorep@aol.com

SELF HEALING,
YOGA & DESTINY

Elisabeth Haich & Selvarajan Yesudian

Through her best selling books, such as *Initiation*, Elisabeth Haich has become world famous for her profound understanding of the human soul. The Yoga schools she set up with Selvarajan Yesudian, have become internationally renowned. Designed to reconnect you with the Divine, the concepts in this book explain the attitudes necessary for the path back to one's self. Based on many years personal experience, the authors create an understanding of how to realize the essential source of life.

Learn Elisabeth Haich & Yesudian's personal views on:

- Love
- Suffering
- Destiny
- Illness
- Accidents
- Karma
- Black & White Magic
- Self Healing & Transformation

A wealth of insightful information is contained in this book to help you gain an expanded view of your life and consciousness.

> *"When we look about us in our daily living, we see how greatly people suffer in the chains they have forged for themselves, even when they are filled with longing for freedom. Is there any way for man to be free? To be free from the deceptive magic of the material world."*
> **HAICH AND YESUDIAN**

ISBN:0-943358-06-X   **Paperback**   5½ x 8½   **90 Pages**

SEXUAL ENERGY AND YOGA

The purpose of this book is to introduce the concept of transmuting
the physical, emotional, mental
and psychic energies people normally dis-
perse in sexual activity. This process assists
in uniting with the higher Self or God.
Topics include:

SEXUAL ENERGY AND YOGA
Elisabeth Haich

- The Creative Primal Serpent
- Sexual Energy in Its False & True Light
- The Magical Powers of Suggestion
- Hypnosis
- Mediumship
- The Urge For Unity & Its Corruptions
- The Sun Creator & Destroyer of Life
- The Magic Flower

"The Transformation of sexual energy into spiritual, divine, creative power, is the resurrection from death to eternal life."

Description by Elisabeth Haich of her painting on the cover

*If we cultivate spiritual awareness and attain the universal con-
sciousness, we acquire mastery over the 7 natural forces which,
when harnessed to pull in one direction, can carry us to the goal
with incredible swiftness.*

*The picture symbolizes this state. The figure representing the
spirit is standing in the triumphal chariot. One hand is radiating the power which directs the natural forces. In the left hand is
held a prayer wheel such as is used in Tibet and which symbolizes unity with the Divine. The horses race with the figure to the
goal where we achieve the perfection which Christ intimated to
us in the words: "Be ye therefore perfect, even as your Father
which is in Heaven is perfect."* **ELISABETH HAICH**

ISBN:0-943358-03-5 15 Illustrations **Paperback** 5½ x 8½ **158 Pages**

WISDOM OF THE TAROT

Wisdom of the Tarot relates the path to higher consciousness through the color, shape and symbolic forms on the twenty-two Tarot cards. Detailed study and meditation of each card may release internally all that is involved with each level encountered on the journey towards the Light. These cards may be used in conjunction with the text or separately for meditation. When studied individually, a card can reveal the necessary steps that need to be taken to actualize one's potential.

Tarot cards, or symbolic representations of the truth have always been used to help man relate not only with the mind, but internally, through the feelings invoked by the colors and forms. The nature of these cards is that they can produce a strong awakening of one's unconscious forces. They are like a spiritual mirror in which we can recognize and examine ourselves. We can then understand that the reasons for our fate lie within ourselves, and changes by the mere fact that we begin to react differently to everything that happens to us. These cards with the text are a valuable key to understand our present state, our past and in a deeper sense, how we create our future. Included within the book are pages of five color Tarot cards.

"Elisabeth Haich has produced a masterly work of initiation into the secrets of life. Out of a deep understanding of being and her own intimate experience of union with her genius, she has illustrated the process by which man becomes man by his insight into the pictures of the twenty two rungs of the ladder of divine ascent on which each rung is an experience for the next rung in accordance with the individual's plan of life."

DR. EWALT KLIEMKE

ISBN:0-943358-01-9   Paperback   6 x 9   174 Pages

AURORA  PRESS

For our online catalog
& ordering info, visit,
www.AuroraPress.com

Aurora Press
PO Box 573
Santa Fe, N.M. 87504

Fax 505 982-8321
www.AuroraPress.com
Email: Aurorep@aol.com

<u>Credit Card Orders Only</u>
Fax 734 995-8535
Tel. 888 894-8621

DOCTOR IN CLOVER

Now Dr Grimsdyke is qualified he finds practising medicine rather less congenial than he anticipated, but the ever-selfless Grimsdyke resolves to put the desires of others (and in particular his rather career-minded cousin) before his own, and settle down and make the best of it. Finding the right job, however, is not always that easy. Porterhampton is suddenly rife with difficulties – as is being a waiter, as is being a writer. Follow the hapless Grimsdyke in a hilarious romp through misadventures, mishaps and total disasters.

DOCTOR IN CLOVER

DOCTOR IN
CLOVER

by

Richard Gordon

Dales Large Print Books
Long Preston, North Yorkshire,
BD23 4ND, England.

British Library Cataloguing in Publication Data.

Gordon, Richard
    Doctor in clover.

    A catalogue record of this book is
    available from the British Library

    ISBN   1-84262-279-X pbk

Published in Large Print 2004 by arrangement with
House of Stratus

Dales Large Print is an imprint of Library Magna Books Ltd.

Printed and bound in Great Britain by
T.J. (International) Ltd., Cornwall, PL28 8RW

1

'You may be surprised to hear,' I announced to my cousin, Mr Miles Grimsdyke, FRCS, 'that I've decided to do the decent thing and settle down in general practice.'

'Do I attribute this decision to a severer sense of professional duty or to a severer hangover than usual?'

'Neither. But all my chums from St Swithin's seem to be installing wives and families and washing machines, and it seems high time I did the same. Take my old friend Simon Sparrow, for instance. Why, in the days of our youth we got chucked out of pubs together, and now his idea of whooping it up on a Saturday night is taking the lawn-mower to pieces. Believe me, I'm going to become dear old Dr Grimsdyke, the chap who's brought half the district into the world and pushed the other half out of it, beloved by all until it's time to collect old-age pension and chiming clock from grateful patients.'

'I suppose you realize, Gaston, how

difficult it is these days to get into general practice?'

'Of course. Quite as bad as getting into the Test Matches. But not for fellows like me who know the ropes. You've heard of Palethorpe and Wedderburn, the medical employment agents?'

Miles frowned. 'The people in Drury Lane? I have never had recourse to them myself.'

'I happen to know old Palethorpe personally. We met last summer, on an occasion when I was able to offer him valuable professional advice.'

I didn't mention to my cousin we'd run into each other at Sandown Park races, where I put Palethorpe on such a good thing he'd kept my medical career close at heart ever since. Unfortunately, Miles has no sense of humour. It's the tragedy of modern life that so many people – dictators, tax collectors, tennis champions, teddy boys, and so on – seem to have no sense of humour, either.

'If you really intend to settle down,' my cousin continued, 'I might say I am delighted that you have chosen this particular moment to do so. In fact, I will confess that is exactly why I invited you for lunch today. More greens? One should keep up one's vitamin C this time of the year.'

'Enough is enough, thank you.'

It was one of those beastly days in midwinter when dusk chases dawn briskly across the London roof-tops, and fog was hazing even the chilly halls of the Parthenon Club where we sat. The Parthenon in St James's struck me as about as comfortable for lunching in as the main booking-hall at Euston Station, but Miles was one of the newest members and as proud of the place as if it were the House of Lords. I supposed it fitted into his self-portrait of the up-and-coming young surgeon. He was a small, bristly chap, generally regarded as embodying the brains of the family, who had just reached that delicate stage in a surgical career when your car is large enough to excite the confidence of your patients but not the envy of your colleagues.

'And how exactly are you earning your living at this moment?' Miles went on.

'I have many irons in the fire,' I told him. 'Though I must confess the fire isn't too hot. There's my medical articles for the popular press, to start with.'

Miles frowned again. 'I can't say I've noticed any.'

11

'They're all signed "By A Harley Street Specialist". Of course, it would be gross professional misconduct to put my own name.'

'You certainly show a remarkable ingenuity for practising without actually doing any medicine.'

'Which just proves what I've always held – medicine's a jolly good general education. It teaches you the working of everything from human nature to sewage farms. Not to mention all those little bits of Latin and Greek which are so useful in the cross-words.'

'But you must realize, Gaston, the time has come to put this free-and-easy existence behind you for good. You're not a mountebank of an undergraduate any more. You must now maintain the dignity of a qualified practitioner.'

'Oh, I agree with you. Being a medical student is really the worst possible training for becoming a doctor.'

Miles dropped his voice below the hushed whisper permissible for conversation in the Parthenon.

'I am now going to tell you something in the strictest confidence.'

'Oh, yes?'

'Mr Sharper at St Swithin's is to become Professor of Surgery at Calgary University.'

'Really? I hope he enjoys crawling about in the snow potting all those bears.'

'That isn't the point. There will therefore be an unexpected vacancy on the surgical consultant staff. I shall in due course be applying for it. As Mr Sharper's own senior registrar, I do not flatter myself in believing my chances are excellent.' He helped himself to another boiled potato. 'Though as you know, considerations other than the strictly surgical sometimes weigh strongly with the selection committee.'

I nodded. 'I remember one chap was turned down because he wore knicker-bockers and arrived for the interview on a motor-bike.'

'Quite so. To be perfectly frank, Gaston, it might embarrass me if you simply continued to flit about the medical scene–'

'My dear old lad!' I hadn't realized this worried him sufficiently to stand me a lunch. 'I may be a poor risk for a five-bob loan, but you can always rely on me to help a kinsman. A couple of weeks to say farewell to the haunts of my misspent youth, and I'll have made myself scarce from London for good.'

Miles still looked doubtful.

'I hope the permanency of your new position is more durable than some of your others.'

'They were mere flirtations with work. This is the real thing. And everyone will say, "See how that steady chap Miles has put even old Gaston Grimsdyke on his feet."'

'If that is indeed so, I'm much indebted to you. We may not always have seen eye to eye, Gaston–'

'Oh, come. Every family has its little misunderstandings.'

'But I assure you I have always acted entirely for your own good. And what precisely is this position you have in mind?'

'GP up north,' I explained.

I had been in Palethorpe's office that morning, when he'd greeted me with the news:

'I have exactly the right opening for you, Dr Grimsdyke. General practice in the Midlands – the backbone of England, you know. Assistant wanted, with a view, as we say. Start end of January. Dr Wattle of Porterhampton. A very fine man.'

'It doesn't matter what the doctor's like,' I told him. 'How about his wife?'

Palethorpe chuckled. 'How I wish our

14

other clients were half as perspicacious! Fortunately, Mrs Wattle accompanied the doctor when he called, and I can assure you that she is a highly respectable and motherly middle-aged lady.'

'Nubile daughters?'

'It is their sorrow to be a childless couple, alas. I believe that is why they particularly asked me to find some decent, honest, upright, well-mannered, single young practitioner to share their home with them.'

'I can only hope you come as a nice surprise,' muttered my cousin when I told him.

'At last I feel set for a peaceful and prosperous career,' I went on, enlarging on my prospects a little. 'Who knows what the future holds? The dear old Wattles might take me to their bosoms. They might look upon me as a son to enlighten their declining years. They might send for their solicitors and start altering their wills. There should be plenty of lolly about in Porter-hampton, too. They make turbines or something equally expensive up there.'

'My dear Gaston! You know, you really must grow out of this habit of counting your chickens before the hen's even ovulated.'

'What's wrong with a little imagination?' I

15

protested. 'Lord Lister and Alexander Fleming wouldn't have got far without it. Anyway, at the moment roots are fairly sprouting from my feet like spring carrots.'

2

Until then Porterhampton was just another entry in my football pools, but a fortnight later I found myself driving past the Town Hall on a morning as crisp as an icicle, and pretty solemn I felt about it, too.

While lunching with Miles, I'd been putting an optimistic face on a pretty desperate situation, which is another of the useful things you learn from studying medicine. I didn't really like the prospect of being a respectable provincial doctor. In fact I didn't really like the prospect of being a doctor at all.

I was a *médecin malgré lui*. I'd taken up the profession because nobody in the family ever had the originality to think of anything else, and anyway all my uncles and cousins seemed to have a pleasant time of it, with large cars and everyone listening to their opinions at cocktail parties. But with medicine and marriage, the earlier you go in for either the riskier the project becomes. Quite a different chap emerges at the end of the course from the apple-cheeked lad with big ideas who went in. It's great fun at first, of course, being casualty houseman in a clean white coat with all the nurses saying 'Good morning, doctor,' even if the job does consist mostly of inspecting unpleasant things brought along in little white enamel bowls. It's a bit of a shock finding afterwards that you've got to make a living at it, though I suspect a good many housemen feel the same and keep pretty quiet. The public doesn't much care for entrusting their lives to doctors who don't love their profession, even though they entrust them every day to bus drivers and no one expects a bus driver to love his bus.

But as I couldn't go exploring like Dr Livingstone, become a Prime Minister of France like Dr Clemenceau, or play cricket like Dr WG Grace, I had to find a steady job like everyone else. And what of these Wattles? I wondered, as I drove past the Porterhampton fish market. They might at that moment be hopping about like a small boy waiting for the postman on his birthday. Or they might be plotting to kick me about like a medical tweeny. Fortunately for my low psychological state, I was soon reassured over my conditions of work.

I found the Wattles' house somewhere on

the far outskirts, in a road of roomy Victorian villas apparently reserved for prosperous turbine– makers. As I drew up in the 1930 Bentley, the motherly Mrs Wattle herself appeared at the gate.

'Dear Dr Grimsdyke!' she greeted me. 'We're so delighted you've decided to bury yourself in our rather sleepy little town.'

'Charming place, I'm sure.'

'Mr Palethorpe spoke so highly of you, you know. I'm awfully glad he persuaded you to come. But you must be tired after your long drive. I'll show you to your room, and there's a nice lunch ready as soon as my husband gets in from his rounds.'

I slipped off my overcoat.

'Dear, dear! No buttons on your shirt, Doctor! You must let me have it tonight. And any socks and things that need darning, just leave them on the kitchen table.'

My room ran a bit to chintz and water-colours of St Ives, but seemed very cosy. There was a bookcase full of detective stories, a desk, and a large double bed already airing with a hot-water bottle like an old-fashioned ginger-beer jar. Going down-stairs after tidying up, I found roast beef and Yorkshire on the table, with apple pie and Stilton waiting on the sideboard.

19

'I'm sure you'd care for a bottle of beer today,' cooed Mrs Wattle. 'Mr Palethorpe said you took the occasional glass.'

I'd met Dr Wattle himself only for a brief interview in London, and he was a little pink, perspiring chap with a bald head, resembling a freshly-boiled egg.

'Delighted to see you, my dear doctor.' He shook hands warmly. 'We may call you Gaston, may we? I hope you'll be very happy with us. Is that your car outside? Very dashing of you to drive an old open tourer. But do take my wife's Morris when it's raining, won't you? Would you care for an advance of salary? We'll sort out your duties later. If you ever want time off for anything, don't hesitate to ask.'

'Your chair's over here, Gaston. Sure you're not in a draught?'

'I hope you'll find my wife's cooking to your taste.'

'The roast beef's not overdone?'

'Anything special you fancy to eat, do please let us know.'

'Horseradish?' asked Mrs Wattle.

Later we had crumpets for tea and finnan haddock for supper, and in the evening we all three sat round the fire making light conversation.

20

'Mr Palethorpe revealed you had quite a roguish wit,' said Mrs Wattle, playfully shaking her finger.

So I told them the story about the bishop and the parrot, though of course altering the anatomical details a bit.

'How pleasant to hear a young voice in the house,' murmured her husband.

'We've *so* missed company in the evenings!'

'Ever since the dog died,' agreed Dr Wattle.

After years of living on tins of baked beans and packets of potato crisps, and mending my own socks by pulling a purse string suture round the hiatus, it did my physiology no end of good to have regular meals and all the buttons on my shirts. There wasn't even much work to do, old Wattle himself handling all the posher patients and leaving me with a succession of kids in the usual epidemic of mumps. After surgery and supper we all three gathered for the evening in the sitting-room. Sometimes we watched the telly. Sometimes we played three-handed whist. Sometimes they asked me to tell the story of the bishop and the parrot all over again. I was glad to see the Wattles had quite a sense of humour.

But even the Prodigal Son, once they'd

used up all the fatted calf, must have hankered to waste just a bit more of his substance on riotous living. As the local amenities ran largely to municipal parks and museums, and so on, and as I couldn't go to any of the pubs because I was a respectable GP, or to any of the pictures because I'd seen them all months ago in the West End, I longed for one final glimpse of the lively lights of London.

'Dr Wattle,' I announced one morning, when I'd been enjoying three square meals a day for several weeks. 'I wonder whether you'd mind if I popped down to Town this Saturday? I've just remembered I've got some laundry to collect.'

'My dear boy! Go whenever and wherever you wish.'

'That's jolly civil of you. Awfully annoying, and all that, but I'd better make the trip.'

The following Saturday evening found me once again in the genial glow of Piccadilly Circus, breathing the carcinogenic hydro-carbons and watching the neon sunrise as the lights came on.

I don't think there's any sensation to compare with arriving in London after a spell of exile, even if it's only your summer holidays. I felt I'd never seen anything so beautiful as the submarine glow of the misty streetlamps, heard anything as cheerful as the nightly torrent ebbing towards the suburbs, nor smelt any perfume so sweet as the reek of a London Transport omnibus. But I couldn't waste time admiring the scenery, and went to a telephone box, looked through my little black book, then rang up Petunia Bancroft.

Petunia was a little brunette and an actress. I've had a weakness for the stage ever since I was a medical student and nearly eloped with a young woman who was sawn in two twice nightly by a Palladium conjurer, until I discovered that she was in fact a pair of young women, and I'd picked the half with the shocking varicose veins. Petunia had been a chum of mine for many years, though unfortunately her ideas of entertainment rather exceeded her theatrical standing – usually she just walked on the stage and announced dinner was ready, but after the show she knocked back champagne like the great leading ladies when the stuff was five bob a bottle. Also, she had a rather hysterical personality, and was likely to throw the dessert about and bite the head waiter. But after a month in Porterhampton, Petunia seemed just what I needed.

'Darling, I'd love to meet you,' she agreed. 'Don't come to the show, it's lousy and closing any minute, anyway. See you at the stage door after ten.'

The London streets were as deserted as Porterhampton on a Sunday afternoon by the time I took Petunia home to Balham – like most glamorous hotsies these days, she lived quietly with Mum and did the washing-up before catching the bus to the theatre. We'd had a pleasant little evening, what with supper and a night-club, and even if it did demolish Dr Wattle's advance of salary I was feeling like a sailor after ninety days at sea.

'Lovely time, darling,' said Petunia at the garden gate. 'When are you coming to live in London again?'

'One day, perhaps. When I retire.'

'When you retire! But darling, I won't ever recognize you then.'

'I'll have a chiming clock under my arm,' I told her. 'Night-night.'

The next morning I made my way back to the provinces for good, having wrapped all the Sunday newspapers in a large brown-paper parcel which I labelled THE EVER-CLEEN LAUNDRY WASHES WHITER.

This little jaunt of mine was a mistake.

One taste of Metropolitan delights had ruined my appetite for Porterhampton for good. I'd tried really hard to fool myself I could merge with the local landscape. Now I realized I couldn't be comfortable anywhere in the world outside Harrods' free delivery area. I faced endless evenings watching the television and talking to the Wattles, and that night the prospect of both made me feel rather sickly over supper. But I had to stay in the place until the St Swithin's committee had shaken my cousin by the hand and told him where to hang his umbrella, and anyway the dear old couple were so terribly decent I'd never have forgiven myself for hurting their feelings over it.

'Dr Wattle,' I began, when we were alone after the meal. 'I don't know if I've told you before, but I've decided to work for a higher medical degree. I hope you'll not think me rude if I go to my room in the evenings and open the books?'

He laid a hand on my arm.

'I am delighted, dear boy. Delighted that – unlike so many young men these days, inside and out of our profession – you should take a serious view of your work.'

There was a catch in his voice.

'We are all mortal, Gaston,' he went on. 'In another few years I may no longer be here–'

'Oh, come, come! The prime of life–'

'And I should like you to be well qualified when you eventually take over this practice. My wife and I have become very attached to you these few short weeks. As you know, we have no children of our own. As a young man I suffered a severe attack of mumps–'

'Jolly hard luck,' I sympathized.

The mump virus, of course, can wreck your endocrine glands if you're unlucky enough to get the full-blown complications.

'If all goes well,' he ended, 'I hope you will inherit more from me than merely my work. I will detain you no longer from your studies.'

The rest of the week I sat in my room reading detective stories, and pretty beastly I felt about it, too.

Then one morning Mrs Wattle stopped me outside the surgery door.

'Gaston, my husband and I had a little chat about you last night.'

'Oh, yes?'

'We fear that you must find it rather dull in Porterhampton.'

'Not at all,' I replied, wondering if some

revelling turbine-maker had spotted me in that night-club. 'There's always something happening,' I told her. 'The Assizes last week, the anti-litter campaign this.'

'I mean socially. Why, you never met any young people at all.'

It hadn't occurred to me that in Porterhampton there were any.

'So next Saturday evening I've arranged a little party for you. I do hope you can spare the time from your studies?'

Naturally, I said I should be delighted, though spending the rest of the week steeling myself for the sort of celebration to make a curate's birthday look like a night out in Tangier. When Saturday came I put on my best suit and waited for the guests among the claret cup and sandwiches, determined to make the evening a success for the dear old couple's sake. I would be heartily chummy all round, and ask the local lads intelligent questions about how you made turbines.

'Here's the first arrival,' announced Mrs Wattle. 'Miss Carmichael.'

She introduced a short girl in a pink dress.

'And here come Miss Symes and Miss Patcham.'

I shook hands politely.

'With Miss Hodder and Miss Atkinson walking up the drive. That's everyone,' she explained. 'Gaston, do tell us your terribly amusing story about the clergyman and the parrot.'

It struck me as an odd gathering. But old Wattle handed out the drinks while I sat on the sofa and entertained the girls, and after a bit I quite warmed to it. I told them the other one about the old lady and the bus driver, and a few more that I hadn't picked up from the boys at St Swithin's, and they all laughed very prettily and asked me what it was like being a doctor. I was quite sorry when eventually midnight struck, and everyone seemed to think it time to close down.

'I'm sure Gaston would drop you at your homes in his remarkable car,' suggested Mrs Wattle.

With a good deal of giggling, I discarded girls at various respectable front doors in the district, until I was finally left with only one in the seat beside me.

'I'm afraid I live right on the other side of the town, Gaston.'

'The farther it is, the more I'm delighted,' I replied politely.

She was the Miss Atkinson, a little blonde

28

who'd given the parrot story an encore.

'Quite an enchanting evening,' I murmured.

'But you were so terribly amusing! I always thought medicos such stodgy old things, even the young ones.'

I gave a little laugh.

'We doctors are only human, you know.'

'I'm so glad,' she said.

After leaving her at another respectable door, I hurried home for some sleep. Nothing takes it out of you quite so much as telling a lot of funny stories.

3

'I know you'll be pleased,' announced Mrs Wattle a few mornings later. 'I've asked little Avril Atkinson to supper.'

'Very pleased indeed,' I told her courteously.

The fact is, I'd have been pleased whoever they'd asked, even my cousin. By then I'd discovered the dear old Wattles were incapable of conversation about anything except happenings in Porterhampton, which if you hadn't lived in the place for thirty years was like trying to enjoy a play after arriving in the second interval. It did me no end of good to hear another voice at table, even if they did make me tell the story of the ruddy parrot from the beginning.

After the meal I announced that my studies could slide for another evening, and politely joined the company in the sitting-room. Then Dr Wattle suddenly remembered he had a patient to see, and Ma Wattle had the washing-up to do, leaving Avril and me on the sofa alone.

'How about the television?' I suggested, Avril's conversation being almost as strait-jacketed as the Wattles'.

'Oh, let's. It's my favourite programme tonight.'

I switched on the set, turned down the lights, and when we'd watched a few parlour games and chaps pretending to get fierce with each other over the political situation, I very civilly drove her home.

'Do you like classical music, Gaston?' asked Mrs Wattle a few mornings later.

'I'm not adverse to a basinful of Beethoven from time to time,' I admitted.

'I'm so pleased. I've got a ticket for our little amateur orchestra next Friday in the Town Hall. Would you care to go?'

I was glad of an excuse to go out in the evening, now being rather bored with all those stories about chaps killing other chaps by highly complicated means. As I sat down among the potted municipal palms, I found Avril in the next seat.

'Quite a coincidence,' I remarked. She smiled.

'You have such a sense of humour, Gaston. Wasn't it nice of Mrs Wattle to give us the tickets?'

'Oh, yes, quite.'

The dear old thing seemed to be getting forgetful, which I put down to the normal hormonal changes in a woman of her age.

The next few days were brightened by excitement over the great event in professional circles at Porterhampton, the annual medical dinner. As the Wattles seemed to find this a combination of the Chelsea Arts Ball and the Lord Mayor's Banquet, to please the dear old couple I agreed to put on a dinner jacket and accompany them, though personally nothing depresses me quite so much as a lot of other doctors. I had just eased into my chair in the ballroom of the Commercial Hotel, when I realized that I was once more sitting next to Avril Atkinson.

'So nice of Dr Wattle to have invited me,' she began. 'Are you going to make a speech with your terribly funny stories?'

'Not for me, I'm afraid. Though the fat chap with the microphone has a wad of papers in his pocket the size of an auctioneer's catalogue. Remarkable, isn't it, how men find so much to say after dinner when their wives haven't had a word out of them for years over breakfast?'

She giggled. 'Gaston, you're terribly witty.'

'Just wait till you've heard the fat chap.'

The guest on my other side having nothing to talk about except the progress of his patients and his putting, I passed the meal chatting lightly to Avril and when the floods of oratory had subsided took her home in my car.

'You simply must come in and meet daddy,' she invited.

Her father was a decent old boy, who gave me a whisky and soda and seemed intelligently interested in the National Health Service – rates of pay, prospects of promotion for young practitioners, and so on. I put him right on a few points, and went home with the pleasant feeling that I'd done my social duty by the dear old Wattles pretty thoroughly.

I suppose I'm a trusting sort of soul. Strangers at race meetings sell me useless tips at a quid a go. Motorists miss me by inches on zebra crossings. I cash dud cheques for fellows I meet in pubs. Small boys have me in knots on April the first. But it was probably the soporific effect of life in Porterhampton which delayed tumbling to my plight until the morning I was called to treat the girl with the pink dress from my party for mumps.

'When's it to be announced?' asked this

Miss Carmichael, as I removed the thermometer from her mouth.

'What announced?'

'Don't play the innocent, Doctor. Everyone in Porterhampton has known about it for weeks. Your engagement to Avril Atkinson, of course.'

'Avril Atkinson!'

I picked up the bits of shattered thermometer from the floor.

'But dash it, that's ridiculous! I hardly know the girl.'

'Now, now! You're always being seen together, at concerts and dinners and things. As for the time she went to the Wattles' for supper – phew! She told me all about it. Sitting alone all evening on the sofa in the dark.'

I drove straight home and confronted Ma Wattle.

'So Dame Rumour hath been at work,' she said coyly. 'I am delighted, Gaston, for your sake. You see, my husband and I felt we were selfish monopolizing your cheery company. Now you're settling down here, it's only right and proper you should take unto yourself a wife. Unlike us, your later years will be comforted with sons and daughters, whom we shall look upon almost as our own grandchildren. I'm afraid I've rather been playing the matchmaker. But I'm so glad you chose Avril. Such a jolly girl! The pair of you are ideally suited.'

I had nothing to say. I went to my room. I paced up and down and glared at St Ives. I sat on the double bed and bit my nails. I wished I'd taken the advice of the Dean at St Swithin's and made my career in the Prison Medical Service.

I certainly didn't want to pass the rest of my life in Porterhampton, even if old Wattle bequeathed me the Town Hall as well. I certainly didn't want to marry Avril Atkinson, who'd probably make me tell the story of the parrot every morning over breakfast. Now I couldn't see how to avoid either. I've often read in psychology books about the acute anxiety state, but I never really understood it until then. Then I had one of those masterly ideas that sometimes come before the bell rings at the end of examinations.

'Mrs Wattle – Dr Wattle.' I appeared downstairs to find both of them in the sitting-room. 'I have something very painful to confess.'

They looked alarmed.

'I am already married.'

36

I felt this was the simplest way out. It was beyond me to tell the dear old couple that their own idea of my spouse was as ridiculous as picking the Matron of St Swithin's. With a bit of luck they'd kick me out on the spot, and possibly use up Avril on my replacement.

'My wife works in London. She is a nurse. A night nurse. I couldn't reveal her before, because ... because the position which I have the honour to hold was advertised for a single man. I needed the work.'

I sounded so pathetic, I felt quite sorry for myself.

'If you will give me a few minutes to pack,' I ended solemnly, 'I shall remove my unworthy self from your lives for ever.'

'How unreasonable I've been!' cried Mrs Wattle, and burst into tears.

'We've deliberately set asunder two who have been joined together,' added Dr Wattle, beating his bald head.

'You must ask your wife to come at once, Gaston.'

'I'll double your salary.'

'We'll give you the run of the house till you find a place of your own.'

'All this might be rather inconvenient,' I interjected quickly. 'My wife's working every

37

night. Important private case.'

'Then bring her for the day,' insisted Mrs Wattle. 'How about lunch on Saturday?'

'Yes,' agreed Dr Wattle, 'We shall be terribly upset if you don't.'

I felt the script had somehow got out of hand. Perhaps it might have been easier simply to have married Avril.

4

The following Saturday morning the Wattles' house was twittering with expectation.

'I'd better be off,' I announced, as the roast pork and stuffing sizzled in the oven. 'Her train's due in twenty minutes.'

'Do greet her with these chrysanthemums, Gaston.' Mrs Wattle pushed a bunch the size of a sheaf of corn into my arms. 'They're fresh out of the greenhouse, and I'm sure she'll love them. And I'm quite sure we're both simply going to *adore* her.'

I parked the car in the station yard, bought a platform ticket, and thoughtfully munched a bar of chocolate from a machine. I sat on a bench and read the paper until the train arrived. Peering through the passengers, I soon spotted the familiar red hat.

'Hello!' I called. 'Hope you didn't have a beastly journey.'

'It was stinking.'

'Welcome to Porterhampton.'

'And what a dump, too!'

'The city has several charming features, I

assure you. Though I shan't be able to provide much of a conducted tour, as your train home's at nine-ten.'

'Thank God for that. What on earth have you got in your arms?'

'They're chrysanthemums, from the greenhouse.'

'You look as though you've lost your street barrow.'

'I think we'd better get off the platform. I might be spotted by one of my patients.'

I led Petunia Bancroft to the car.

'I've had some pretty funny parts in my time,' Petunia complained as we drove away. 'But this one makes the Crazy Gang look like the Old Vic.'

'It's perfectly simple,' I reassured her. 'You've only to play The Doctor's Wife, straight. To an accomplished actress like you, Pet my dear, it's as easy as selling theatre programmes.'

'If I hadn't been out of work I wouldn't have sniffed twice at the idea, believe you me.'

'Regard it as a professional challenge.'

'Costume all right?'

'Perfect for the part.'

'I thought I'd better leave off my ankle bracelet.'

40

'Can't say I've seen a nurse wearing one.'

'Supposing this old fellow – what's his name? – asks a lot of questions with long medical words and that? What the hell am I supposed to say?'

'Leave it to me. Anyway, all he's likely to talk about is our epidemic of mumps. Just remember the time you had it yourself.'

'I haven't.'

'Neither have I. Good job, in your case,' I smiled. 'Might possibly have mucked up your hormones.'

She asked how, so I gave a brief dissertation on the pathology and virology of mumps until we arrived at the Wattles' front gate.

'Petunia,' I announced. 'Your cue.'

I was pretty worried about the performance, though I didn't let on to Petunia. Another of the useful things you learn from studying medicine is radiating cheerful confidence all round while wondering what the devil's going to happen next. But I must say, she created the part of Mrs Grimsdyke magnificently. In half an hour the old couple were all over her.

'Where did you train, my dear?' asked Dr Wattle, as we sat down to lunch.

'Oh, at RADA,' said Petunia.

41

He looked puzzled. 'That seems a hospital I haven't heard of.'

'An affectionate name for the Royal Diabetic,' I told him.

'Is it really? Dear me, I never knew. One learns something every day. And what is the trouble with this important case your husband tells us you're nursing?'

'Er – foot and mouth disease.'

'Attacking a human? Good gracious me! How extraordinary. I've never heard of such a thing before in my life.'

'Petunia means the poor fellow is down in the mouth because he's got one foot in the grave. Quite a common nurses' expression.'

'Is it indeed? Of course, you've had more recent contact with such things than I, Gaston. How one hates to be thought behind the times! I must try it out at the next BMA meeting. I expect, my dear, you've had wide experience nursing cases of mumps?'

But I neatly managed to steer the conversation away from shop, and as the afternoon wore on I felt my troubles were sorting themselves out splendidly. The old couple's feelings were saved, I was out of the matrimonial target area, and I could make a leisurely exit from Porterhampton as soon

42

as Miles was safely on the St Swithin's staff. Besides, I now had a handy excuse for nipping down to London any weekend I felt like it.

'My train goes in about an hour,' Petunia reminded me, when we'd reached the cold ham supper stage.

'What a shame you can't stay longer,' sighed Mrs Wattle.

'Petunia has to be on duty at midnight,' I explained. 'As a matter of fact, I might as well be getting the car out.'

I opened the front door, and a nasty complication to my little plan rolled all over me.

I suppose this country wouldn't be the same if it weren't dosed regularly through the winter with fog. Can you imagine such national heroes as Sherlock Holmes or Jack the Ripper prowling about on nice mild summer evenings? How would Dickens' characters have looked in the Neapolitan sunlight? Or the dear old Houses of Parliament shining like the Taj Mahal? Our national character gets regularly tested by the frightful complications of fogs, particularly the great big grey thing that rose like a wall of dirty muslin from the front doorstep.

'I'd better telephone British Railways,' I muttered.

The word 'trains' evoked only a mystified silence on the wire.

'The midday hasn't turned up yet from Manchester,' said the fellow at the station. 'And where the morning express from Glasgow's got to, nobody knows. If you want your prospects of getting to London tonight, sir, they're nil. It's the biggest and thickest we've had this century, according to the wireless.'

'So now Petunia will have to stay till morning,' said Ma Wattle, smiling benevolently.

'But that's impossible!' she cried.

'Has to be back to her case,' I explained quickly.

'Surely under such circumstances a replacement could be found in London?' insisted Dr Wattle.

Petunia stamped her foot. 'Gaston can drive me.'

'Only into the first ditch, I'm afraid.'

'I absolutely and positively—'

I managed to shut Petunia up, the Wattles clearly thinking this rather odd behaviour for a pair of lovebirds.

'Don't worry, my dearest,' I pretended to give her a tender kiss. 'Leave it to me.' I

44

hissed in her ear, 'I'll get you out of it.'

'I'm not worrying at all, my sweet. You'd blasted well better,' she hissed back.

We all sat down and looked at the television.

I spent the rest of the evening trying to concoct some fog-proof excuse. Should I pretend to perforate a duodenal ulcer? Or set light to the house? Or simply make a clean breast of it on the hearth-rug? I rejected each one. They would all upset the Wattles too much.

In short, nothing I could evolve by tenthirty prevented the pair of us being ushered by Ma Wattle into my room, with two hotwater bottles in the double bed.

'You dirty little stinker!' started Petunia, as soon as the door was shut. 'This is the meanest and nastiest trick—'

'For Lord's sake don't make so much noise! We're supposed to be a devoted couple.'

'I'd like you to understand, Dr Grimsdyke, that I am most definitely not that sort of a girl—'

'I know, I know! But if you'll only give me a moment's peace I can sort the whole thing out. No one is sorrier than I—'

'Nobody will be, by the time my brothers hear about this.'

'I can't help the ruddy fog, can I? Anyone would think I'd put it there myself.'

Petunia threw herself on the bed and started pounding the eiderdown.

'You've got to get me out of here! At once, I tell you. In five minutes. Otherwise I'll smash the window and scream for the police.'

'Pet, I'm doing my best! There must be some way of–'

'I'll scream. I will. I'll wake all the neighbours. You just listen–' She drew a deep breath.

'For God's sake, Pet–!'

The telephone rang in the hall.

'Hold off the sound effects till I've answered it,' I hissed.

'Dr Grimsdyke?' said a woman's voice on the line.

'Speaking.'

'You swine! You cad! You beast! You bigamist!'

'Now just a second. If you'll tell me who's speaking–?'

'You know perfectly well who's speaking. Avril, of course. I'm only ringing to inform you that tomorrow morning I'm starting a breach of promise suit, that'll blow you out of Porterhampton so hard you won't stop

46

till you reach the white cliffs of Dover, which I hope you'll drop over and break your filthy neck. Let me tell you–'

'But I can explain absolutely everything,' I insisted. 'Can't I come round in the morning and see you?'

'You most certainly can't come anywhere near me. Apart from everything else I'm in bed with mumps, which I caught at your beastly party. *And* I've changed my cards to another doctor. You just wait till my brother comes on leave from the Commandos. Good night!'

In the space of five minutes I'd been abused by two women and threatened with assault from their relatives, which I felt was a record even for chaps like Bluebeard. But the telephone had given me an idea.

I tapped on the Wattles' door.

'I've been called to a case,' I explained. 'I don't expect I'll be long.'

Wrapping a scarf round my neck and pocketing a tin of cough lozenges from the surgery, I set out to spend the night in the fog while Petunia tucked herself cosily into the double bed.

5

The fog was lifting as I tramped back to the Wattles' home. I'd coughed my way into the darkness, with no particular object except keeping alive till morning. About a hundred yards from the house I'd wandered into the main road to London, where I met a chap who'd lost his lorry. He remembered a place in the area called Clem's Caff, which we found by walking an hour or so along the white line. The Caff sported a coke stove, and was full of lorry drivers in steaming overcoats, resembling overworked horses. I bought a cup of tea, which seemed to entitle me to sleep on the table like everyone else. About five-thirty I woke up, feeling as if I'd just been released from the rack in the Tower.

I crept inside the house, tapped softly at the bedroom door, and Petunia let me in.

'You look as if you've just come off Everest,' she said.

'I hope you passed a good night yourself,' I replied shortly.

49

'Absolutely adorable. I haven't been so warm for months.' She was already up and dressed, and seemed more amenable than the evening before.

'Poor Gaston! Are you sure you won't catch your death?'

'I wouldn't really care at the moment if I did.'

'I'm sorry – but it wasn't really my fault, was it? Perhaps you could have slept on the floor behind the wardrobe, or something.'

'I think it was a far, far better thing that I did.'

'You know, there really is something of the Sidney Carton about you, dear. No other man I know would have been half so noble.'

'Anyway, it's all over now. The fog's thinning rapidly, and as far as I remember there's a good train about five on Sunday afternoons. If you can stick it out till then.'

'I'm sure I can,' said Petunia. 'It's really awfully cosy here.'

'You *do* look pale this morning,' giggled Mrs Wattle when I appeared at breakfast. 'I hope you got plenty of sleep.'

The day passed without mishap. Petunia seemed quite to enjoy herself sitting about the house reading magazines, and in the afternoon I drove her to see the Town Hall, the waterworks, the bus depot, and the new abattoir.

'Quite a pretty little place after all,' she remarked, as I pulled up outside the municipal baths. 'It's a wonder I've never been here on tour.'

'Would you like to see the statue of the first Mayor?'

'Yes, please,' said Petunia.

After tea and Dundee cake I looked at my watch and announced to the Wattles, 'Perhaps my wife ought to be getting ready. We're due at the station in half an hour.'

'But isn't there a later train, darling?' asked Petunia. 'I could always catch that.'

'There's the eight forty-two,' I told her, looking surprised. 'And the ten six.'

'I'll take the ten six.'

'A far better idea,' agreed Ma Wattle. 'A few more hours together mean so much at your age, don't they?'

Shortly afterwards we were left alone. As a matter of fact, we were always being left alone, and Dr Wattle must have got awfully tired of sitting in his cold consulting-room.

'What's the idea, Petunia?' I demanded at once. 'I thought you couldn't get out of the place quick enough.'

She helped herself to a cigarette from the

silver box.

'Gaston,' she said. 'I've been thinking.'

I flicked the Wattles' table lighter.

'Thinking what?'

'That this is the nicest part I've ever played.'

'You were a great success at it, thank you very much. And now for the final curtain.'

'But do you know *why* I was a success? I've just realized it myself. It was because I *felt* the part – here.'

She indicated her mid-sternal region.

'That's essential for all high-class acting, so they tell me.'

Petunia sat on the sofa.

'Do you remember, Gaston, what you told me in that night-club, the last time we were out together?'

Remembering what chaps tell them in night-clubs is another illustration of how women are congenitally defective in sportsmanship.

'That I was the dearest and sweetest girl you'd ever met, and how you wished you could live in my arms for ever?'

'Ah, yes.'

'Perhaps, Gaston, dear, you didn't think I took your remarks seriously?'

'Of course I did.'

As far as I remembered, she was hitting someone on the head with a balloon at the time.

'It's terrible how I have to disguise my feelings, my sweet. We actresses must always put our career first. We can never enjoy the simple home life of other women. It's awfully tragic.'

'I think you're perfectly right,' I told her briskly. 'Wonderful thing, devotion to one's vocation. You'll never regret it once you're a famous star with half London at your feet.'

'I'd never be a famous star. Not someone like Monica Fairchild, with every manager in London fighting over her. It's no good fooling myself. I'd just continue with walking-on parts, and live with Mum year in and year out, except for a few weeks on tour in miserable theatrical boarding-houses.'

'Oh, come! You're just a bit depressive for the moment. I bet Sarah Bernhardt felt exactly the same dozens of times.'

'But seeing you here,' Petunia went on, flicking her ash over the bearskin rug, 'in your dear little home in this sweet little town, has opened my eyes. My racket isn't worth the candle. I want to settle down.'

'But this isn't my dear little home,' I argued. 'It's Dr Wattle's dear little home. As for the town, I came here intending to settle for life and now I wouldn't even touch it for bed and breakfast. It would send a girl like you crackers in less than–'

She got up and stood so near me I could see the arteries in her conjunctivae.

'This last twenty-four hours I've realized how wonderful it is being your wife–'

'But dash it! You're *not* my–'

'You're so sweet, so modest. So honourable, so upright. So tender, so considerate, Gaston, darling, I've decided to accept you. We can get married secretly in some registry office–'

'Sorry to disturb the nest of lovebirds,' Ma Wattle chuckled, entering at that moment, 'I just wondered if your wife would like some nice hot soup for supper, to brace her for her journey.'

'Mrs Wattle.' Petunia turned to face her. 'I'm not going. I must stay with my husband. I'll send a telegram to London and resign my job. My mother can send on my things tomorrow.'

'I'm absolutely delighted!' exclaimed the old dear, embracing us. 'As I always say, a woman's place is at her husband's side, come what may. Of course, my children, you may stay with us as long as you wish. I'll just put the kettle on for your hot-water bottles. I expect after such excitements you'll both be wanting to go early to bed.'

If I wasn't keen on marrying Avril, I'd rather have swallowed the entire poisons cupboard before marrying Petunia. An agreeable companion for a gay night out, certainly. But you can't make a life partner of a woman who keeps trying to conduct the band with sticks of celery.

'You haven't eaten your nice soup, Gaston,' said Ma Wattle at supper.

'Not very hungry, I'm afraid.'

'What a wonderful thing love is!'

I was nearly sick over the sliced brawn.

I was edgy and jumpy the rest of the evening, which, of course, the idiotic Wattles put down to passion, or the expectation thereof. Worst of all, the mental trauma of the past two days seemed to have beaten my brain into paralysis. Nothing I could contrive by ten o'clock prevented Petunia and myself again being shown into my bedroom.

'Alone at last!' breathed Petunia.

'Yes, but only for a couple of shakes,' I told her smartly. 'As soon as the Wattles have bedded down, I'm going to skip it into the night again.'

'But Gaston! Surely you're not going to leave your wife?'

'Pet, you chump! You're not my wife – only on the programme. Let me make it perfectly clear I'm not going to stay with you up here.'

'How honourable you are!' she breathed. 'How fine! How different!'

The Grimsdykes, of course, have their honour. But I must admit I wouldn't have objected to the same arrangement if we'd been in a hotel at Brighton instead of the Wattles' spare bedroom. Under prevailing circumstances the only place for me was Clem's Caff.

'We'll be married tomorrow if you like,' she said, starting to unzip her dress. 'A girl friend of mine once got a special licence terribly easily.'

'Petunia! You don't understand–'

'I understand everything, darling. You're a wonderfully honest man, and I shall love you more and more as the years go by.'

About twenty minutes later I was sitting again over one of Clem's cups of tea. I woke at five-thirty the next morning, so ill from the effects of prolonged exposure that I would almost have married Petunia on the spot for a comfortable night's rest in my own bed. I got back to the house shivering and with a shocking headache, and found Dr Wattle in the hall.

'Just come in from seeing the Mayor's gout,' he greeted me. 'I didn't know you'd been called out too. I never heard the phone.'

'It was someone with fits. Difficult diagnosis. Took a lot of time.'

'You don't look very perky, my boy. Are you sure you're all right?'

'Bit chilly, this night air.'

'Perhaps I'd better take your temperature?'

As he removed the thermometer from my mouth he asked, 'Ever had mumps? Well. I'm afraid you have now.'

'Mumps!' I cried. 'But– but that means isolation.'

'I'm afraid so. You'll have to stay in your room. Your wife hasn't had it either? Then you'd better be strictly alone. I'll go up and break the sad news. It's best for you not to breathe over the poor child.'

'Petunia's rather alarmed about it,' explained Dr Wattle, returning with some surprise. 'She seemed remarkably upset over those hormonal complications. I told her how terribly rare they are, but she's still

57

awfully agitated. Keeps saying it would ruin her career. I shouldn't have thought it would have mattered much one way or another to a nurse. However, it's none of my business. We'll make you up a bed in the attic.'

I slept for twenty-four hours, which Dr Wattle later wrote a letter about to the *BMJ* entitled 'Unusual Stupor in Epidemic Parotitis'. Petunia spent the morning gargling, then disappeared for London. As soon as my lumps were down I announced I must go to the sea-side for convalescence, and sent a wire from London explaining I'd been summoned to a dying uncle in South Africa.

I felt pretty sorry for myself. I'd broken a couple of girlish hearts, had a nasty illness, and expected hourly to be assaulted by Commandos, and so on, in the street. Porterhampton had thenceforward to be blotted from my atlas. And now I had to explain it all to my cousin.

But at least I never hurt the dear old Wattles' feelings.

6

'From your appearance,' started Miles, 'you would seem to have finished some protracted party.'

'If you must know,' I replied, rather hurt, 'I've had a nasty attack of epidemic parotitis. I've hardly got over it yet.'

'I'm sorry.'

It being one of my principles always to confess my short-comings promptly, particularly if they're likely to be discovered pretty quickly anyway, I'd telephoned Miles on arrival and invited myself to dinner. I now sat in his South Kensington drawing-room wondering how best to explain the retreat from Porterhampton.

'And when are you returning to your practice?' asked Miles.

I shifted on the sofa.

'As a matter of fact, old lad, I'm not.'

'What? Damn it! You've not been thrown out already?'

'Thrown out?' I looked offended. 'I resigned, with the dignity of a high-principled

Cabinet Minister.'

Miles fell silent. To fill the gap I reached for a magazine – one of the shiny ones which report the activities of all our best-bred young women and horses.

'That's what I need,' I said, indicating a photograph of people with long drinks on a yacht at Cannes. 'A few weeks in the sunshine to buck me up.'

Miles made a noise like a tearing sheet of canvas.

'Damnation, Gaston! Are you mad? Are you fit for some institution? Here you are – out of work, penniless, a walking disgrace to your family if not to your entire profession, and you ramble about weeks in the sunshine. Really!'

I tossed the magazine aside with a sigh.

'The trouble is, you're perfectly right,' I admitted. 'I'm not the shining figure of the eager young doctor.'

'You're the shining figure of the shiftless young wastrel, and I don't mind telling you. I seriously advise you to see a psychiatrist. He might at least be able to explain your highly unstable occupational history.'

'The fact is, old lad, I don't need a psychiatrist to tell me that I don't like medicine very much.'

Miles stared as though I were Cinderella telling the Fairy Godmother she didn't care greatly for dancing.

'At Porterhampton the dear old couple handed me every chance to settle down as a respectable family man and family doctor. But do I want to be the modern GP, signing certificates for all the uninteresting patients and hospital letters for all the interesting ones? No, I jolly well don't. And neither do a lot of other chaps, judging by the correspondence in the *BMJ*. As I'll never be a specialist in anything, and I couldn't possibly sit in the Town Hall with a map of the local sewers doing public health, there isn't much left. The trouble is, I'm temperamentally unsuited to my work.'

'But think of all those years of study – wasted!'

'They're not wasted a bit,' I argued. 'Look at all the famous chaps who've benefited from a medical education – Leonardo da Vinci, John Keats, Chekhov, and so on. Not to mention Crippen.'

'You must quite definitely see a psychiatrist. And meanwhile, how precisely are you going to earn your bread?'

'Ah, yes. I agree, that's the problem.'

Further discussion about my professional

61

future was prevented by the appearance of Miles' wife.

'How charming you're back so soon, Gaston,' she greeted me. 'We quite thought you'd gone to seek your fortune up North.'

'I decided that opportunity taps less faintly in London, Connie.'

'I'm so glad. Now we'll see much more of you. What did you say, Miles, dear?'

'Nothing, nothing,' muttered Miles.

I knew Connie pretty well. In fact, once I was in love with her.

This happened when I was a student and Miles had just qualified as Mr Sharper's junior casualty house-surgeon, and pretty pleased with himself he felt about it, too. As I reflected during dinner that evening, Miles and I had never really hit it off at St Swithin's, or even as kids. Miles was the one who didn't get his boots dirty, always had his sums right, wasn't sick at all the parties, and didn't make a fuss about his tonsil-ectomy. At school he used to make me blow up his football and toast his crumpets. Then I followed him to St Swithin's, and like everyone else started medicine by dissecting the dogfish, which has put me off fish suppers ever since. Miles was already well into the course, and by the time I got as far as the anatomy rooms kept buttonholing me in the corridors with fatherly advice.

'If you spent a little more time dissecting and a little less writing all those stupid jokes for the students' magazine,' was his usual line, 'you might show you were taking your career seriously.'

'I thought the last one was rather funny. About the girl who said she suffered from claustrophobia because she had a terrible fear of confinement.'

'Take it from me, Gaston, you'll regret this frivolity one day. You stick to your anatomy. It's the grammar of medicine.'

'Personally,' I disagreed, 'I think they only fill medical students with anatomy like they used to fill kids with brimstone and treacle. The experience is obviously so unpleasant, everybody agrees it must be doing them good.'

'I'm not at all certain it isn't my duty to write to my father,' he generally ended.

My own father having unfortunately perished in the RAMC, I was brought up under a Victorian system of guardians, with Dr Rudolph Grimsdyke as chief paymaster. Uncle Rudolph practising at the time out East, Miles was his nark on the spot, and I suppose he sneaked in the end because half-way through the course the old boy cut my allowance by half. I know that ever since *La Bohème* it's been thought rather romantic for students to starve in garrets holding the tiny frozen hands of their girlfriends, but that sort of existence didn't appeal to me at all. Particularly as all the girls I knew seemed to complain shockingly of the draughts even in comfortable cocktail bars.

Shortly after the onset of this financial anaemia Miles qualified, glittering with scholarships and prizes.

'Gaston,' he said, getting me into a corner of the St Swithin's Casualty Department one winter afternoon, 'I want a serious word with you.'

'Oh, yes?'

'I'd be much obliged if you'd try to embarrass me a little less now that I'm on the St Swithin's junior staff. You must realize that I, at least, don't wish the entire family to be made ridiculous throughout the hospital. It's bad enough your always disappearing to the dog-races, but this habit of taking menial employment—'

'My dear old lad, I assure you I don't do it for fun. Anyway, it's all your old man's fault, being so tight-fisted. Surely you know by now I dislike work in any form whatever?'

64

I was at the time restoring my enfeebled exchequer with such casual jobs as dish-washing in West End restaurants and bar-keeping in East End pubs, and had just finished a profitable though strictly limited run as Father Christmas in an Oxford Street store.

'That's not the point at all. Mr Sharper was certain he saw you the other day. He was extremely blunt to me about it this morning.'

'Oh, really? I thought his keen surgical eye had pierced the whiskers. But I bet he only made a fuss because I told his beastly kids to ask for a complete set of electric trains and a couple of motor-cars.'

'I do wish you'd take this seriously, Gaston!'

'Let's talk about it another time. I must be off now, I'm afraid. Otherwise I'll be late for work.'

A few days after this argument I met Connie, by accident. All medical students dream of witnessing some really satisfactory road smash, then appearing on the scene to calm the panic-stricken bystanders with the magic words, 'I am a doctor.' I've done it myself three times. The first, the policeman told me to run home to mother. The second, I grabbed a tourniquet from some fumbling old boy and discovered he was the Professor of Surgery at St Asaph's. Now, of course, I walk rapidly in the opposite direction and leave it to the ambulance boys, remembering Sir Lancelot Spratt's resuscitation lecture – 'When I chuck myself into the Thames in despair, ladies and gentlemen, I hope I'll be given artificial respiration by a fit Boy Scout, and not some middle-aged medical practitioner who's soon more out of breath than I am.' But when one is young, one doesn't consider such things. On this third occasion, as soon as I heard the scream of brakes and tinkling of glass, I leapt into the middle of Sloane Square and took sole charge.

In the next part of the dream, the injured party isn't a poor young child or a dear old lady, but a beautiful girl having hysterics. And that's exactly what I found. So I popped her in a taxi and drove her round to the casualty entrance at St Swithin's, where Miles organized X-rays, diagnosed a Colles' fracture, and signed an admission form for his ward.

'Charming girl, too,' I observed, as Connie was wheeled away.

'Thank you, Gaston, for holding the X-rays.'

'Always glad to help. I might pop up and see her later. Terribly important to follow-up cases, so they keep telling us.'

'Mr Sharper allows only his own students in his wards, I'm afraid.'

'Oh, come. Can't you stretch a point?'

'A point, being defined as possessing position but not magnitude, is incapable of being stretched,' said Miles.

All the same, I went up the next morning with a bunch of roses.

'How terribly sweet!' exclaimed Connie, looking beautiful despite the plaster and bandages. 'And your assistant's just called too, with the mimosa.'

'Assistant?'

'The doctor who helped you with the X-rays.'

'Ah, yes. Useful chap.'

The staff in modern hospitals out-numbering the patients by about five to one, the inmates can be excused for confusing the ranks. I remembered there was once a frightful row when Sir Lancelot Spratt in a white coat was mistaken for the ward barber.

'You'll be out of here this afternoon,' I went on, not bothering to start long explanations. 'When time has healed all your

67

wounds, would you care to come out for a bite of dinner?'

'But I'd love to, Doctor!'

'Jolly good. I'll get your telephone number from the ward notes.'

Unfortunately, Connie turned out to be the daughter of a shockingly rich fellow from Lloyd's, so I couldn't buy her a pint of beer and show her the ducks in St James's Park and pretend I'd given her an exciting evening. Also, I knew a determined chap like Miles wouldn't easily give up. While I was sitting with her a few weeks later in the Savoy, hoping she wouldn't feel like another drink, I remarked casually, 'Seeing much of my cousin these days?'

'As a matter of fact, yes. I'm going to the theatre with him tomorrow.'

'It may be rather cheek of me to ask this, Connie, but I'd rather you didn't mention me to him, if you wouldn't mind.'

She looked surprised. 'Why ever not?'

'Just to save the poor chap's feelings. These little family jealousies, you know. He feels it rather, being my underling at the hospital.'

'How awfully considerate of you, Gaston. Naturally, I won't say a word. But supposing he talks about you?'

'He never does,' I assured her. 'Another Martini?'

'Yes, please,' said Connie.

I passed a couple of enjoyable months escorting Connie to all the more fashionable plays and restaurants, particularly as she still seemed to imagine that I was some wealthy young specialist, and I never seemed to find the chance to put her right. Then one afternoon Miles cornered me in the surgeons' room.

'I believe you've still been seeing Connie?' he demanded.

I tossed my sterile gown into the students' linen bin.

'On and off, yes.'

'I'd like you to know that I – I'm perfectly serious about her.'

This didn't disturb me. Miles was perfectly serious about everything.

'May the best man win, and all that, eh?'

'Damn it, Gaston! I wish you wouldn't regard this as some sort of sporting contest. I happen to love Connie deeply. I wish to make her my wife.'

'Good Lord! Do you really?'

The notion of Miles making anyone his wife seemed as odd as palm trees growing on an iceberg.

'And I'll thank you not to trifle with her affections,' he added.

'You will, will you?' I returned, feeling annoyed at his tone. 'And how do you know I don't want to make her Mrs Grimsdyke, too?'

'You? You're in no more position to marry than a fourth-form schoolboy.'

I felt the conversation was becoming embarrassing, and edged away. Besides, I had to be off to work again.

Entertaining Connie was making such inroads into my finances that I'd been obliged to find more regular employment. Fortunately, I'd met a chap called Pedro in a Shaftesbury Avenue pub, and after giving him some free advice about his duodenal ulcer and a good thing for Kempton Park, I was offered five evenings a week as a waiter in his Soho restaurant. Pedro was a fierce task-master, most of his relatives still chasing each other over Sicilian mountains with shotguns, and I had to clean all the soup off my best set of tails every night before going to bed, but the tips were good enough compensation for both.

Or they were until that particular evening, when Miles walked in with Connie.

'Shall we sit over here?' she said, advancing

towards my corner. 'I hate a table too near the door.'

I ducked quickly into the kitchen.

'What the 'ell are you up to?' demanded Pedro.

'I – er, just wanted to adjust my sock suspenders.'

'I don't pay you to adjust your socks, mister. You get back in there. There's customers just come in.'

I passed a hand across my forehead.

'You know, Pedro, I don't think I'm feeling very well tonight. A bit faint. I might be sick over the fish or something. If you don't mind, I'll just totter through the staff entrance and make home to bed.'

''Ow the 'ell you think I run my business one man short?' Pedro picked up a carving knife. 'You leave this restaurant only over your dead body, see mister? If you want to be sick, come out and be sick in the kitchen, like everybody else. You go to work.'

I edged back through the swing doors. I slipped my menu and table napkin behind a bread basket, and prepared to dash for the pavement. I'd almost made the main entrance, when Connie glanced idly round and spotted me.

'Why, it's Gaston! Hello, there! You dining

71

here, too?'

Miles turned round and scowled.

'Oh, hello, Connie. Yes, I am, as a matter of fact. Expecting an old school chum. Chap called Honeybank. Doesn't seem to have turned up.'

'Charming little restaurant, isn't it?'

'Oh, very.'

'You seem very dressed up,' muttered Miles.

'Going on, you know. A ball, and all that.'

'I think men look their best in tails,' remarked Connie. 'Don't you Miles? What on earth's dear Pedro doing?'

I thought dear Pedro was probably putting that knife on the grinding machine, but only murmured something about having to be off.

'But if you haven't eaten you must stay for a bite with us,' Connie insisted, 'I'm sure Miles wouldn't mind.'

'Not a bit,' growled Miles.

'It might be a little awkward, actually–'

'But definitely, Gaston. Tell the waiter to bring another chair. Ah, there you are, Pedro. How is your lovely *canneloni* tonight?'

'Delicious, madame.'

Pedro came over rubbing his hands. I stood on one foot, leaning against the table.

Dashed difficult, striking an attitude simultaneously suggestive of helpful servility and longstanding chumminess.

'And the *osso buco*, it is excellent,' Pedro added.

'Then shall we all have *canneloni* followed by *osso buco?*' Connie looked inquiringly at Miles and myself. 'I'm terribly hungry.'

'Two *canneloni* two *osso buco*,' snapped Pedro in my ear. 'Didn't you 'ear what madame says?'

'How extraordinary repeating the order like that,' exclaimed Miles.

'Just a little joke,' I explained, as Pedro backed away. 'I know him very well.'

Connie sighed. 'How lucky you are! I can't imagine anything more useful in London than being friends with all the head waiters. But Gaston, *do* sit down. You make me feel uncomfortable, standing about like that.'

'Just a second, if you'll excuse me. Phone call – the school chum, you know.'

I slipped back to the kitchen.

'What the 'ell's the matter with you tonight?' demanded Pedro. 'You stick around with a silly grin on your face like a drunk monkey. How you expect me to run my restaurant if you don't listen to the customers?'

'Look, Pedro, I really think I ought to be at home tucked up in bed—'

'Take that in, and don' talk so much.'

He handed me two dishes of *canneloni*.

'Good Lord!' exclaimed Miles. 'You've brought the food yourself.'

'Ha ha! Just another little joke. Dear old Pedro, you know. I keep threatening a public health inspection of his kitchen, and just nipped in to take him by surprise. The *canneloni* was ready, so I brought it along.'

Connie found this terribly amusing.

'But Gaston, you haven't a plate. And do please sit down.'

'I'll just prop on the back of this chair.' I edged myself into a position where I might be mistaken for serving the spinach. 'They get so terribly crowded, I'm sure Pedro hasn't got a spare seat. I don't think I'll try any *canneloni* myself, thanks. But let me help you.'

'You serve quite professionally,' exclaimed Connie.

'Jack of all trades, you know...'

'Are you sure you're quite all right tonight?' demanded Miles.

'Oh, fine, thank you.'

I felt that the situation was reasonably hopeful, as long as they crammed down

74

their blasted *canneloni* before Pedro came back.

'What were we talking about? I suppose you've heard the story of the bishop and the parrot–'

Just then a voice behind me called, 'Waiter!'

'Well, you see, this bishop had a parrot–'

'Waiter!'

'And this parrot used to belong to an old lady who bought it from a sailor–'

'Say, Waiter!'

'There isn't a waiter in sight,' interrupted Connie.

'Never is when you want one,' grumbled Miles.

'I think he's an American who keeps shouting,' said Connie.

'And the old lady always used to keep it under a green baize cloth in the front parlour. Every morning she'd take the cloth off the cage, and every morning the parrot said–'

'Hey, Waiter, for chrissakes!'

A fat man I'd just served with cigars and brandy appeared at my elbow. 'Excuse me, folks. I just wanted to tell the waiter here I've had a darned fine meal and darned fine service. I reckon it's the best I've struck since I've been in Europe. I was just getting on my way when I thought, shucks, I gotta give credit where credit is due. Thanks a lot, son. This is for you.'

The beastly chap stuffed a pound note into my top pocket.

'But how extraordinary,' exclaimed Miles.

'He thought you were the waiter!' laughed Connie.

'People never notice the fellows who serve them with food,' I mumbled. 'Conan Doyle or Edgar Wallace or someone wrote a story about it.'

'But he did seem pretty definite.' Miles gave me a nasty look.

'Oh, Miles, you know what Americans are,' said Connie. At that moment, Pedro appeared again. I pretended to be arranging the flower vase.

'Everything all ri'?'

'No,' said Miles. 'The waiter hasn't brought any grated parmesan with my *canneloni*.'

Pedro glared across the table.

'Zere is no grated cheese with the *canneloni*.'

I glanced round for the cheese thing. I might reach across for it with a little laugh.

'That's exactly what I said,' Miles

returned. 'It happens that I'm particularly fond of grated cheese with my *canneloni*.'

'So am I,' said Connie.

'There is no grated cheese with the *canneloni!*' shouted Pedro in my direction.

'Good gracious, man!' exclaimed Miles. 'Don't yell at me like that.'

'I am *not* yelling at you like that, monsieur. I am yelling at '*im* like that. *There is no grated cheese on the canneloni!*'

Connie jumped up.

'How dare you address my guests in that manner! I am going to leave this restaurant this very instant.'

Pedro looked as if he'd been hit in the neck with one of his own *canneloni*. 'Guests, madame? What guests? You're fired,' he added to me.

'I shall never eat here again, and I shall tell all my friends not to eat here either. Come along, Miles. Treating our guest here as one of your waiters—'

'But, damn it, madame! 'E *is* one of my waiters. 'E come every night, part time—'

'Only five days a week,' I insisted.

'Gaston!' Connie gave a little gasp. 'Is this really true?'

I nodded. The Grimsdyke ingenuity had been beaten back to its own goal-line. I reached for my napkin and automatically flicked the tablecloth.

'I'm not a doctor, really,' I murmured. 'I'm a student. I take this on for a little extra dibs.'

There was a silence. Connie started to laugh. In fact, she laughed so long she almost asphyxiated herself with a stick of Italian bread. In the end we all four thought it a tremendous joke, even Pedro.

But Connie never looked at me the same way again. And a fortnight later got engaged to Miles. I was pretty cut up about it at the time, I suppose. I often wonder how life would have turned out if Miles had been more of a gentleman and taken her somewhere like the Ritz.

The only compensation was that, according to the American chap, if I had to be a waiter I was a damn good one.

7

'I'm afraid I was somewhat over-optimistic at the way things would go at St Swithin's,' announced Miles.

Connie had left us after providing a charming little dinner, and I was guessing my chances of getting a cigar.

'The appointment of Sharper's successor has as usual got mixed up with hospital politics.'

He stared gloomily into the fruit bowl.

'Sir Lancelot Spratt is making an infernal nuisance of himself on the committee. He is opposing my candidature, purely because Mr Cambridge is supporting it. Sir Lancelot has quarrelled with him, you know. Cambridge refuses to knock down his old clinical laboratory, and Sir Lancelot wants to park his car there. To think! My future decided by a car park.'

'There's nothing like a mahogany table and a square of pink blotting-paper to bring out the worst in a chap's character,' I sympathized. 'How about the other runners?'

'There are thirty other prospective candidates for the post, all as well qualified as I. But we are mere pawns, mere cyphers. Perhaps I should apologize for being short with you earlier, Gaston. The strain, you know. The uncertainty...'

He miserably cracked a nut.

I felt sorry for the chap. Personally, there was nothing I'd have liked less than being a consultant at St Swithin's, having to wear a stiff collar every day and never being able to date up the nurses, but it had been Miles' ambition ever since he was cutting up that dogfish. And I rather felt that Connie, too, fancied herself in a new hat running the hoop-la with other consultants' wives at the annual hospital fête. Besides, Miles was the brightest young surgeon St Swithin's had seen for years, and I should have felt a bit of a cad not helping so worthy a practitioner along the professional path.

'If you didn't get on at St Swithin's,' I tried to console him, 'you'd find a consultant job easily enough in the provinces.'

'But it wouldn't be the same thing. And, of course, Connie and I would have to leave our home.'

I nodded. Since the waiter episode girls

had been in and out of my life like people viewing an unsatisfactory flat, but I'd always retained a soft spot for Connie. The thought of her confined for life to a place like Porter-hampton upset me so much I'd almost have had another go at living there myself to prevent it.

'In such delicate circumstances,' I suggested, 'I take it you'd more than ever like me tucked away in some respectable job?'

'Exactly.'

'Find me one, old lad, and I will. I can't possibly face Palethorpe for months, of course.'

'I have some influence with the Free Teetotal Hospital at Tooting. They'll be needing a new house-surgeon next week.'

'And the week after, I'm afraid, as far as I'm concerned.'

Miles stroked his pale moustache.

'A pity you didn't keep your position on the *Medical Observer*. At least it utilized your talent for the pen respectably.'

'That was a congenial job,' I agreed, 'until the old editor banished me to the obituaries.'

The *Medical Observer* was the trade press, which lands on doctors' doormats every Friday morning and is widely appreciated in the profession for lighting the Saturday fires. It has an upstairs office near the British Museum in imminent danger of condemnation by the health, fire, and town planning authorities, where I'd been assistant to the editor, a thin bird with a wing collar and severe views on the split infinitive.

'You can't imagine how depressing it was, writing up dead doctors from nine to five,' I told Miles. 'Though I composed my own for the files while I was there, and a jolly good one it will be, too. Yours isn't bad, either.'

'I am gratified to hear it. Perhaps you should go abroad? An oil company for which I do insurance examinations are prospecting up the River Amazon in Brazil. They have a vacancy for a medical officer on a five-year contract. The salary would certainly appeal to you. And you just said you could do with some sunshine.'

'But not five years of it, all at once.'

Miles began to look irritable again. 'I must say, Gaston, for a man in your position you're being extremely difficult to please.'

'Oh, I don't know. If I'm going to sell my soul I might as well get a decent price for it.'

'I do wish you'd discuss the subject of your livelihood seriously.'

'I was just about to, old lad. I don't

suppose you could advance me ten quid, could you? Resigning abruptly from Porter- hampton left me a month's salary short.'

'You know I am against loans among relatives. But I will agree if you accede to my suggestion about the psychiatrist. I am certain that's what you need. I can easily arrange for you to see Dr Punce, who manages the aptitude tests for the oil company. He rather specializes in whittling down square pegs.'

I don't share the modern reverence for psychiatrists, mostly because all the ones I know are as cracked as a load of old flower- pots. But the financial blood was running so thinly I accepted.

'I suppose you have no serious plans at all for maintaining yourself?' Miles asked, putting away his cheque book.

'I've a few more medical articles on the stocks. I'd also thought of trying my hand at a bit of copywriting– you know, "Don't let your girdle be a hurdle, we make a snazzier brassière," and so on.'

Miles winced.

'Gaston looking for another job?' asked Connie, appearing with the coffee. 'That's no problem anyway. A bright young man like him should be in demand anywhere.'

A bit *infra dig*, I thought, a doctor going to a psychiatrist. Like a fireman ringing the station to say his house was alight. I didn't remember much of the psychiatry course at St Swithin's myself, except the afternoon Tony Benskin was left to hypnotize a young woman with headaches, and once he'd got her in the responsible state suggested she took her blouse off. Apparently Tony's hypnotic powers are low voltage, because the girl clocked him one against the corner of the instrument cupboard. Quite some confusion it caused when the chief psychiatrist came in, to find the patient stamping about shouting and the doctor unconscious.

But I dutifully appeared at Dr Punce's rooms in Wimpole Street the following afternoon, and found him a tall, thin fellow in striped trousers, a pince-nez on a black ribbon, and side-whiskers. I was shown in by a blonde nurse, which put me in a awkward position at the start – if I gave her the usual once-over the psychiatrist might decide something pretty sinister, and on the other hand, if I didn't, he might decide something even worse. I hit on a compromise, and asked her what the time was.

I took a seat and prepared for him to dig

into my subconscious, shaking the psycho-pathic worms out of every spadeful.

'I don't suppose you treat many doctors?' I began.

'I assure you that all professions are fully represented in my casebooks.'

'Psychiatry is the spice of life, and all that?' I laughed.

But he had no sense of humour, either.

'The note I have from your cousin mentions your difficulty in finding congenial employment,' he went on, offering me a cigarette, as psychiatrists always do.

I nodded. 'Miles seems to think I should find a job with security. Though frankly I rather prefer insecurity. But I suppose that's a bit of a luxury these welfare days.'

'H'm. I am now going to recite a succession of words. I wish you to say the first word that comes into your head in reply. Light?'

'No, it's going very well, thank you. I've got some matches of my own.'

'That is the first word.'

'Oh, I see. Sorry. Yes, of course. Er – sun.'

'Night?'

'Club.'

'H'm. Sex?'

'Psychiatrists.'

'Line?'

'Sinker.'

'Straight?'

'Finishing.'

'Crooked?'

'Psychiatrists. I say, I'm terribly sorry. I didn't mean to say that at all.'

Dr Punce sat for a while with his eyes closed. I was wondering if he'd had a large lunch and dozed off, when he went on, 'Dr Grimsdyke, I have had a particularly heavy month with my practice. I fear that I am sometimes tempted to be rude to my more difficult patients.'

'If it's any consolation,' I sympathized with him, 'I'm tempted quite often too. But don't worry – the feeling will pass. I recommend a few days in the open air.'

'Have you heard the story of the donkey and the salt?' he asked bleakly.

'No, I don't think I have.' I settled down to listen, knowing that psychiatrists pick up quite a few good ones in the run of their work.

'I'd like you to follow it carefully. There was once a donkey who fell into the water, crossing a stream on a very hot day with a load of salt. Eventually he got to his feet, feeling greatly relieved because the water had dissolved his burden. The next day he was crossing the stream loaded with sponges. This time he deliberately fell, but the sponges soaked up so much water the donkey was unable to rise at all. The animal succumbed. What do you think of that?'

'Ha ha!' I said. 'Jolly funny.'

In fact, I thought it a pretty stupid story, but one has to be polite.

'You think that the story is funny?'

'Oh, yes. Best I've heard for weeks. I suppose you know the one about the bishop and the parrot?'

'Dear me, dear me,' said the psychiatrist, and started writing notes.

After a good many questions about the Grimsdyke childhood, which was just the same as any other beastly little boy's, he asked, 'Any sexual difficulties?'

'By Jove, yes.'

I told him the story of Avril Atkinson, but he didn't seem impressed.

'Your trouble, Dr Grimsdyke,' he finally decided, wiping his pince-nez, 'is that you find yourself in uncongenial employment.'

I asked him what I was supposed to do about it, but he only said something about it being a consulting-room and not the Labour Exchange.

'I mean, being a doctor doesn't train you for anything else much, does it? Not like some of those barristers, who get fed up standing on their feet drivelling away to judges and collect fat salaries running insurance companies.'

'There have been medical bishops and ambassadors. Rhodesia had a medical Prime Minister. Goethe and Schiller were, of course, once both medical students.'

'Yes, and Dr Gatling invented the machine gun, Dr Guillotin invented the guillotine and Dr Dover became a pirate. I don't think I've much qualification for any of those professions, I'm afraid.'

'I suggest some non-clinical branch. How about entymology? Are you fond of insects?'

I thought deeply. 'Well, if I'm really no good as a doctor I suppose I could always end up as a psychiatrist. I say, I'm terribly sorry,' I added. 'Just for the moment I was forgetting–'

'Good afternoon, Dr Grimsdyke.'

'Right-ho. Do you want to see me again?'

'No. I don't want to see you at all. The nurse will show you out.'

I left him shaking his head and fumbling nervously with his pince-nez. The poor chap looked as though he really ought to have seen a psychiatrist.

'How did you get on?' asked Connie, answering the door when I called to report.

'Well, I think I won.'

'I hope he recommended shock treatment. Your Uncle Rudolph's in the sitting-room.'

'Good Lord, is he really? Where's Miles?'

'Out on a case. But don't worry – Uncle only wants to offer you a job. One of those rich patients who've been buying up the local country houses has asked him to Jamaica for a holiday. As he's got twenty-four hours to find a locum for the next three months, I suggested you.'

'That's really very decent of you, Connie.'

Since returning from the East, the old uncle had settled at Long Wotton, a pleasant niche in the Cotswolds with thatched roofs and draught cider and cows in the High Street. My session with the psychiatrist not producing much alternative to a lifetime of GP, and Miles' ten quid already having undergone severe amputation, I felt glad of a decent job anywhere. I consoled myself that half rural practice is veterinary medicine anyway, and I'm rather fond of animals.

'My daughter-in-law talked to me for thirty minutes before persuading me to take you as my locum,' Uncle Rudolph greeted me. He was smaller and bristlier than Miles, with hair and eyebrows like steel wool under the influence of powerful magnets, and an equally prickly ginger tweed suit.

'That's very civil of you, uncle,' I told him, 'but as a matter of fact, you're not putting me to any trouble, as I'm quite free at the moment.'

'If you come to Long Wotton on Thursday, I can hand over. My Mrs Wilson will look after you adequately. Though she is attuned to the habits of an elderly widower, so don't expect champagne and caviar for breakfast.'

'Good Lord, no. I couldn't possibly manage anything heavier than cornflakes in the morning, anyway.'

'Kindly remember, Gaston, that there are a large number of important people in the neighbourhood. Most of them are my patients, and I wish them to remain so. Now listen to me. I understand from Miles that you are short of cash?'

'I am rather undernourished in the pocket at the moment,' I admitted.

'You know I have certain funds under my control which I saved you dissipating as a medical student. If you behave sensibly and efficiently at Long Wotton I am prepared to

90

release them. If not, you will have to wait until my demise. And I can assure you that my blood-pressure is excellent.'

'All that matters, uncle,' I told him, 'is giving you satisfaction. In fact, you might just as well advance me the cash now.'

But he didn't seem to grasp the point, and hurriedly asked Connie to fetch him another whisky and soda. Shortly afterwards Miles came in, and nobody took much notice of me any more.

8

I arrived in the country on one of those April days when all the flowers look freshly painted and all the girls look beautiful. The English spring had arrived, as described in the poems and travel advertisements instead of the grey slushy thing we usually get.

I'd already spent a few week-ends at Long Wotton, and found it a friendly place where the inhabitants are all acquainted, if not, as I later suspected from the general feeble-mindedness, all actually related. Although I'm not much of a one for country pursuits – guns make such a frightful noise, fishing gives me a bad cold for weeks, and I regard horses as highly unroadworthy vehicles – it was pleasant to find myself respected locally as a learned chap, and not just the fellow who dishes out the chits for false teeth. Also, there was a very amiable young sub-postmistress, and I was looking forward to a few months quietly letting life go by and Avril Atkinson and Porterhampton fade into my subconscious.

After a week or so I was even becoming a little bored, with existence presenting no problems more complicated than keeping the uncle's housekeeper happy, and she seemed very satisfied with the story of the bishop and the parrot. Then I returned one evening from repairing the effects of a pitchfork on some bumpkin's left foot – a very pleasant consultation, with everyone touching their forelocks and asking if I could use a side of bacon – and found the old dear herself standing at the garden gate, looking distraught.

'Doctor, Doctor!' she called. 'Something terrible's happened.'

I was a bit alarmed the cream might have gone off. I was looking forward to my evening meal of fresh salmon followed by early strawberries, particularly as the old uncle had overlooked handing over the cellar keys in his hurry to be off, and I'd just found them – buried under the coal in the outhouse, of all places.

'Doctor, you're to go at once,' she went on. 'It's very urgent. To Nutbeam Hall,' she explained, when I asked where. 'It's his Lordship, there's been a terrible accident.'

A bit of a tragedy, I felt. Fancy missing a dinner like that. But the Grimsdykes never shirk their professional duty, and pausing only to load the Bentley with sufficient splints and morphine to tackle a train crash, I sped up the road to Nutbeam Hall.

Everyone in Long Wotton knew Lord Nutbeam, of course, though I don't mean they played darts with him every night in the local. In fact, most of the inhabitants had never seen him. The old boy was a bachelor, who lived in a rambling house apparently designed by Charles Addams, his younger brother's missus doing such things as ordering the coal and paying the milkman. He appeared only occasionally when they gave him an airing in an old Daimler like a mechanized glasshouse, always with brother or wife as bodyguard.

This was the pair who received me in the hall, a long, dim place crammed with furniture and as stuffy as the inside of the family vault.

'I'm the doctor,' I announced.

'But Dr Grimsdyke–?'

'Dr Rudolph Grimsdyke is enjoying a little well-earned holiday. I'm his locum and nephew, Dr Gaston Grimsdyke.'

I saw them exchange glances. The Hon. Percy Nutbeam was a fat chap with a complexion like an old whisky-vat, which I suppose he'd acquired at his brother's expense. His wife was one of those sharp-faced little women with incisors like fangs, to whom I took an instant dislike.

'Of course, I'm perfectly well qualified,' I added, sensing they might not take kindly to anyone but the accredited family practitioner.

'Naturally, naturally,' agreed Percy Nutbeam, very sociably. 'We don't question that for a moment.'

'I am sure you've had very extensive experience, Doctor,' put in the wife.

'Well, very varied, anyway. Look here,' I told them, feeling rather awkward, 'unless it's a matter of saving life on the spot, if you'd rather call another practitioner–'

'Not at all,' said Mrs Nutbeam briskly. 'My husband and I have the utmost confidence in your handling his Lordship's case. Haven't we, Percy?'

'Of course, Amanda.'

I must admit this made me feel pretty pleased. The old uncle's full of homely advice about wool next to the skin and so on, but after all those years among the hookworm and beriberi he's as out of date in medical practice as a Gladstone bag. I could see they were delighted at an up-to-date chap like myself with all the latest from hospital.

'Then what's the trouble?' I asked.

'We fear a broken hip, doctor,' announced Amanda Nutbeam. 'That's serious, I believe?'

'Could be. Very.'

'Our aunt died after a broken hip,' murmured Percy.

'It all depends on the constitution of the patient,' I told them, remembering my orthopaedic lectures.

'Please let me impress upon you, Doctor,' said Amanda, 'that his Lordship is very delicate.'

'Very delicate indeed,' added her husband. 'This way, Doctor, if you please.'

I went upstairs feeling pretty curious. I'd already decided it was the old story – poor old Lord Nutbeam was potty, and the family were making themselves thoroughly miserable keeping it quiet, instead of getting him decently certified and sending him baskets of fruit every Friday. I was therefore a bit startled when my clinical examination provided a couple of eye-openers.

In the first place, far from being dotty, Lord Nutbeam had an IQ in the professorial class.

'I fell from the library ladder, Doctor,' he explained from his bed. 'Appropriately enough, as I was reaching for my first edition of *Religio Medici*. You are familiar with the work? Perhaps you have also read Dr William Harvey's *De Motu Cordis* in the original Latin? I should much like to discuss it with a medical man.'

Not wishing to chat about all those books I'm going to read whenever I get a spare moment, I put my stethoscope in my ears. Then I got my second surprise. From the conversation downstairs I'd gathered Lord Nutbeam's grip on life was as secure as on a wet conger eel, but I quickly discovered – fractures apart – he was as hale and hearty as I was.

'I am very delicate, Doctor,' he kept on insisting, though he looked a spry old boy with his little white moustache. 'I neither smoke nor drink and live on soft foods. Ever since I had the fever at the age of twenty-one my dear brother and his wife have been devoted to my welfare.'

'Don't worry,' I told him. 'We'll soon have this little matter cleared up, and you'll be able to go on reading just where you left off.'

A few minutes later I again faced the ambulant members of the Nutbeam family in the hall, and announced in suitably sepulchral tones that his Lordship had indeed fractured the neck of the right femur.

'Ha!' muttered Percy Nutbeam, 'Auntie!'

'Then it is serious, Doctor?'

'But please let me reassure you.' I possibly gripped my lapels. 'Once we get anyone as chirpy as Lord Nutbeam into hospital and the hands of a decent orthopaedic surgeon, we'll have him on his feet again in no time. Meanwhile, I have administered a sedative and the fracture isn't very painful. I guarantee he'll stand up to everything wonderfully.'

I was then rather jolted to hear Amanda Nutbeam ask, 'Doctor, don't you think it would be far, far kinder just to do nothing?'

'A very eminent specialist left our aunt to pass peacefully away,' added Percy.

'But dash it!' I exclaimed. 'How old was your aunt?'

'Ninety-two.'

Lord Nutbeam was fifty, the age when most men are telling their secretaries they're in the prime of life.

'Look here, this is quite a different case—'

'His Lordship is so delicate, life is merely a burden to him,' persisted Amanda.

'Been delicate for years, Doctor. Even in the nursery he was always being sick.'

'Surely, Doctor, it would be a happy release?'

'He will have no more troubles among the angels,' ended Percy Nutbeam, looking at the chandelier.

Now, I may not be the most erudite of medical practitioners, but many years' patronage of the sport of kings has left me pretty sharp at spotting something fishy. So I eyed this couple pretty sternly and said, 'If I don't get Lord Nutbeam into hospital this very night, it'll be – why, gross professional misconduct, to say the least.'

'You can hardly get him there without his consent,' replied Amanda sharply.

She gave me a smile as unfriendly as one of Sir Lancelot Spratt's laparotomy incisions.

'And Lord Nutbeam would never consent to anything whatever without consulting us first,' said Percy.

'Now just a minute–'

'You are very young, Doctor,' Amanda continued. 'I can assure you his Lordship would be much happier passing away peacefully in his own home, rather than being mutilated among strangers.'

'Our aunt,' added Percy, 'was very contented right to the end.'

'Here, I say–'

'I think your consultation is over, Doctor. The butler will show you to the door.'

9

I was so furious I couldn't enjoy my salmon. But I managed to cram down the strawberries and a bottle of the uncle's *Liebfraumilch*, then I paced the room and smoked a couple of his cigars. I looked up Watson-Jones' *Fractures and Joint Injuries*, and I found a copy of Hadfield's *Law and Ethics for Doctors*, but though this is pretty hot on such things as Relations with the Clergy and Opening a Vein after Death, it's a bit short on handling murderous relatives. I wondered what the devil to do. I thought of telephoning another doctor, but felt this would produce only an action for slander. Finally I decided (a) if old Nutbeam continued to lie flat on his back he would undoubtedly perish; (b) you can't press-gang people into hospital; and (c) some pretty nasty questions were going to be asked at the inquest.

Apart from medical ethics, the thought of the beastly brother and wife itching to get their fingers on Lord Nutbeam's cash and title fairly made my blood boil. Particularly as I now realized my welcome to Nutbeam Hall didn't come from heartfelt appreciation of my clinical abilities, but because they thought I had more chance of knocking his Lordship off than my uncle had. After sitting down with a drop of the uncle's special liqueur brandy, I made my decision. My only course, as a doctor and gentleman, was to return to Nutbeam Hall forthwith and give all concerned a jolly good piece of my mind.

Five minutes later I arrived again at the front gates, turning a few choice phrases over in my thoughts, when I noticed a ruddy great Rolls parked outside. I was wondering if the Nutbeams had simply preferred to bypass me and summon a specialist off their own bat, when the front door opened to admit a severe-looking bird of consultoid aspect, wearing striped trousers and carrying a briefcase.

'Good evening, sir,' I said.

'Good evening,' he replied, got into his Rolls, and drove off.

I'd hardly time to sort this out when the door flew open again and Mrs Nutbeam fell on me like her long-lost baby.

'Doctor, Doctor! Thank God you've come

back! You must get his Lordship into hospital at once.'

'This very instant,' cried Percy, panting up behind.

'With the very best specialist available.'

'Regardless of expense.'

'Everything humanly possible must be done for him.'

'The telephone is just inside the hall, Doctor.'

'Now just a minute.' I found this rather confusing. 'A couple of hours ago you told me—'

'Please disregard whatever I said a couple of hours ago,' returned Amanda Nutbeam, 'I was too upset by my dear brother-in-law's accident to think properly.'

'We both were, Doctor. We were quite beside ourselves.'

Deciding there was no point in asking a lot of silly questions, I telephoned an eminent bone-basher in Gloucester who'd done a neat job on a patient who went through a threshing machine. Shortly afterwards I was gratified to see Lord Nutbeam departing tucked-up in an ambulance, particularly as the original Grimsdyke diagnosis had been confirmed.

Like any GP pushing his patient into

hospital these days, I didn't see his Lordship again for a fortnight. I was meanwhile kept agreeably busy remedying the rustics, and though the uncle didn't even send a postcard, Miles telephoned a couple of times, but he was too concerned over Sir Lancelot's car park to ask how I was getting on. Then one Saturday I decided to drive over to Gloucester to watch an afternoon's cricket, and looked into the Jenner Memorial Hospital to see Lord Nutbeam during the tea interval.

I found his Lordship very perky in a private room with a Smith-Petersen pin holding his hip together, though we hadn't much time for a quiet chat – modern orthopaedic wards are pretty active places, with all those nice girls from the physiotherapy department laying cool hands on fevered joints and making you kick your legs in the air as though you were about to turn out for the Arsenal. But the old boy seemed to be enjoying it all, and while a little red-headed staff nurse brushed his hair he started asking my views on the original works of Hippocrates.

'You'll soon be back among your books again,' I said, not wishing to pursue the subject.

'Indeed, Doctor, I believe my library is the only pleasure in my life. Except on Saturday nights, when I sometimes play the piano.'

I was reflecting that this sort of existence would have me stone dead in a fortnight when we were interrupted by the surgeon himself, a big, red-faced, jolly Irishman. Most orthopods are, when you come to think of it, just as ophthalmologists look like dyspeptic watchmakers and bladder surgeons resemble prosperous commercial travellers.

'He's all yours now, m'boy,' said the surgeon, as we left the room together after examining the patient. 'His rehabilitation will go much smoother at home, and this sister-in-law seems agreeable enough to nurse him. Anyway, I'm off on Monday for a month's fishing in County Mayo. How is he for cash, by the by?'

'According to village gossip, crammed with it.'

'Is he now?' The orthopod seemed to brighten at the prospect of having his fishing on Lord Nutbeam's hip. 'Odd sort of feller, don't you think? I couldn't see him saying "Boo" to a newly hatched gosling. I'll be sending you the usual letter about treatment. Meanwhile, tell him to confine his reading to the bottom shelf.'

When a few mornings later they unloaded his Lordship at Nutbeam Hall and I pushed his new wheel-chair into the library, I felt pretty contented with myself. The whole episode had already increased my professional standing in Long Wotton no end. I'm far from saying the natives were hostile, but in the country they regard anyone who hasn't lived among them for thirty years as a day tripper, and now there was plenty of glowing gossip to warm the ears of the old uncle on his return. If I could present him with a Lord Nutbeam skipping about the front lawn, he'd not only give fewer of those old-fashioned looks whenever I suggested enterprising lines of treatment, but painlessly disgorge my cash on the spot.

'I am certainly glad my brother-in-law is back in his own home, Doctor,' remarked Amanda Nutbeam. 'It is only here, I think, that we really understand his best interests.'

'So I've noticed,' I told her. 'And now for a few weeks of rest and quiet and nourishing food,' I added confidently, 'and his Lordship will be dancing the Highland Fling if he wants to.'

But I should have learned long ago that in the turf and therapeutics it's disastrous to back a dead certainty.

For some reason, Lord Nutbeam didn't want to get better. I'd imagined that once he was home he'd settle down to a nice long read, but instead he sat staring out of time window with cups of beef-tea getting cold at his elbow. Sometimes he picked up *The Anatomy of Melancholy*, but it didn't seem to hold him. Sometimes he pushed himself to the piano, but he could manage only a few bars of *Valse Triste*. To cheer him up, I wheeled him round the garden telling funny stories, but he never seemed to see the point. 'Alas, poor Yorick!' was the most I could get out of him.

His Lordship grew steadily feebler and feebler, while everything else in sight was burgeoning wildly in the sunshine. It wasn't long before I began to grow alarmed about his condition. Modern medicine's all very well, with antibiotics and heart-lung machines and so on, but once a chap's decided he doesn't want to live any more we're not much better off than the witch-doctors in Central Africa. And my professional problems weren't made easier by the other Nutbeams, who now the excitement had died down treated me like the man come to mend the drains. Far from his Lordship, they were terrible snobs –

particularly the missus, whom everyone knew in the village was only a road-house remnant from Percy Nutbeam's youth, anyway.

'It would be much more convenient if you could make your daily visit earlier,' she said, as I limped into Nutbeam Hall one evening after a heavy day's practice among the pigsties. 'We are expecting Lord and Lady Farnborough for dinner any minute, and I should naturally prefer my guests not to be greeted in the hall by the doctor. Perhaps you would also have the goodness to change your shoes before coming to us, Dr Grimsdyke. I realize that you cannot avoid walking through the farmyards during the day, but–'

I must say, her attitude made me pretty annoyed. Particularly as I felt she wouldn't have tried it with the old uncle, not with those old-fashioned looks of his. Then, a couple of days later, Lord Nutbeam went off his food and started looking like Socrates eyeing the hemlock.

'We're all bursting to see you back to normal again,' I told him, hopefully writing a prescription for another tonic. 'Here's something which will have you chirping with the birds in no time.'

'Thank you, Doctor. You are very kind.

Indeed, everyone is very, very kind. Especially, of course, my dear brother and his wife.' He listlessly turned a few pages of Gibbon's *Decline and Fall*. 'But I fear my accident had more effect than I imagined. I've hardly been out of Nutbeam Hall for many years, you know, on account of my delicate health. Meeting so many people in the hospital was something of a disturbance. You are doubtless familiar with the lines in Gray's *Elegy in a Country Churchyard*–'

Feeling that churchyards were definitely out, I interrupted with the story about the parrot. But I don't think he got that one either.

I left him in the library, wondering whether to assemble the family again and confess the old boy wasn't living up to my prognosis. But I was stopped by Percy Nutbeam himself in the hall.

'Could you spare time for a whisky and soda, Doctor?'

My professional duties being over for the day, I accepted.

'I'm very worried about my brother's condition,' he declared, after a bit of chat about the weather and the crops.

'And so am I,' I told him,

'I remember the case of our aunt so well.

The collapse seemed to set in all at once. Like a pricked balloon. I suppose there's not any danger of – er, is there?'

I nodded. 'I'm afraid I've got to say there is.'

The poor chap looked so concerned I felt I must have misjudged him all along.

'Then how long, Doctor, would you give him–?'

'Might be a matter of only a week or two,' I said gloomily.

'Good God! Not before May the twenty-eighth?'

I looked puzzled, wondering if they'd arranged a picnic or something.

'This is a very delicate business, Doctor.' He poured himself another whisky. 'But I must be frank with you. You remember Sir Kenneth Cowberry?'

'I don't think I've had the pleasure.'

'He was leaving as you returned, the night of the accident. He's the head of Hoskins, Harrison, Cowberry, and Blackthorn. My brother's accountants, you know. I thought we'd better send for him at once, in case there were any arrangements my brother might have wished–'

'Quite,' I said.

'Lord Nutbeam naturally desires to leave

my wife and myself his entire fortune. After all, we have devoted our lives to his welfare.'

'Quite, quite.'

'But it was only that evening we learned – my brother is oddly secretive about money matters – that he had in fact already made over his estate to me. In order to – er, escape death duties. You may have heard of other cases, Doctor? But under the rules of the Inland Revenue Department my brother must stay alive for five years after signing the document, or it doesn't hold water. And those five years are up at midnight, May the twenty-eighth. So, Doctor, if you can keep him alive till then – I mean, I hope and trust he will have many happy years among us yet – you understand the position...?'

I didn't think highly before of this pint-sized Lord and Lady Macbeth. Now I felt it would serve them damn well right if the Government carted off the lot, to pay, among other things, my National Health salary.

'I understand the position very well,' I replied, wishing I could produce one of the uncle's looks.

I'd very much taken to old Nutbeam, and I was determined to keep him alive for the full three score and ten. But the situation was getting beyond a chap of my modest experience, and out in the country I hadn't any of my chums to ask for advice. I wished the uncle would get fed up sitting on the beach at Montego Bay and come home. I even wished Miles would turn up for the week-end. I was wondering what to say next when I had another of those profitable inspirations of mine.

'I think it would be wise,' I announced, 'to have another opinion. There might be some other condition I've overlooked. After all, doctors can make mistakes. Just like accountants.'

'As many opinions as you wish, Dr Grimsdyke.'

'There's a man in Harley Street just right for this type of case. Though his private fees are rather high.'

'That's of no concern at all, I assure you.'

'And, of course, he'll charge a guinea a mile for the visit.'

Percy Nutbeam looked a bit concerned doing the mental arithmetic, but he agreed, 'Nothing is too expensive with my brother's life at stake.'

'Plus his first-class fare and meals, naturally. He's a general surgeon, but I guarantee he's got the sharpest diagnostic nose in London. His name's Sir Lancelot Spratt.'

10

'Delightful air,' declared Sir Lancelot.

I'd driven over to Greater Wotton Junction to meet him, and pretty nervous I felt about it, too. In my days as a student at St Swithin's, Sir Lancelot and myself disagreed about everything from the way I tried to treat appendicitis to the way I tried to treat the nurses, and his last remark the day I proudly told him I'd qualified was that the Archbishop of Canterbury would presumably now have to make an addition to the litany.

I bowed him from his carriage like royalty come to open the local fat stock show.

'I hope you've no objection to travelling all this way, sir?' I began, feeling that I'd sent for Rembrandt to paint the attic.

'Objections? Why, boy? It is the duty of consultant surgeons and the fire brigade to give their services whenever and wherever they are needed. It is, moreover, extremely pleasant to escape from London on a summer morning, and I'm being handsomely paid for it. Don't be so damned humble, Grimsdyke!' He poked me in the epigastrium with his walking-stick. 'A doctor must feel humble only towards his own abilities. Excellent roses, these. Apricot Queens, I believe? What sort of mulch d'you use?'

This remark was directed to the stationmaster, Greater Wotton being one of those junctions regarded as an exercise in landscape gardening interrupted by the occasional arrival of trains. Sir Lancelot then ignored me for ten minutes' erudite discussion on the merits of horse and cow manure. Come to think of it, that sort of ability represents his genius. Most surgeons can talk only about the inside of their patients or the inside of their cars, but Sir Lancelot has informed views on everything from nuclear physics to newts.

'I am presumably obliged to travel in that,' he said, indicating my car. 'Am I permitted a bite to eat before seeing the patient?'

'I've arranged a modest meal, sir.'

Remembering that a high blood-sugar is conducive to mental tranquillity, I'd decided to give the old boy a jolly good lunch before getting down to business.

'I rarely take wine at midday,' Sir Lancelot observed later, mellowing over the roast lamb and a glass of the uncle's Château Lafite, 'but I must say Dr Rudolph Grimsdyke has excellent taste in it.'

I agreed, though I'd been a bit alarmed to notice the cellar had somehow got down to only a couple of bottles.

'The only locums I did were in the East End of London, where in those days the doctors were as half-starved as the patients.' Sir Lancelot gazed through the window, where the cuckoos were tuning up among the blossoms. 'He seems to have found himself a very agreeable spot – botanically, ornithologically, and even meteorologically.'

'But not anthropologically, sir,' I said brightly, feeling it time to mention the Nutbeams.

'According to the essayist Hazlitt,' Sir Lancelot observed with a nod, 'all country people hate each other. You will now kindly recapitulate the family history of your patient. You were not particularly explicit on the telephone.'

An hour later the pair of us were marching into Nutbeam Hall.

I think the Hon. Percy and his repulsive missus were staggered to find themselves faced with a chap in a frock coat and a wing collar, who glanced round as though he'd been sent to condemn the place by the local Medical Officer of Health.

'We are delighted, Sir Lancelot,' simpered Amanda Nutbeam, who of course thought doctors were all right as long as they had titles. 'I am so pleased you accepted our invitation to take over his Lordship's case.'

Sir Lancelot looked as though she were a junior probationer who'd dropped a bedpan in the middle of his weekly ward round.

'Madam, I have *not* assumed clinical responsibility for Lord Nutbeam. His medical adviser remains Dr Gaston Grimsdyke, at whose invitation I stand here now.'

'Oh! Of course, Sir Lancelot–'

'That is normal professional procedure.'

These remarks put my morale up no end. Despite our differences in the past, Sir Lancelot wasn't so much offering the olive branch as proffering ruddy great groves. But I should have realized that a chap like him would back me to the scalpel hilt, now that I was qualified and one of the boys.

'We shall see the patient, if you please.' The Nutbeams looked rather flustered. 'And I should be glad if you would kindly provide me with a clean hand towel.'

I remembered Sir Lancelot always demanded a clean towel in uppish households, and in a tone inferring that it was a pretty stiff request.

'Dr Grimsdyke will lead the way,' he went on, as I stepped respectfully aside. 'The patient's doctor precedes the consultant into the sickroom. That is etiquette, and I should be the last to alter it.'

Our consultation was a great success. Sir Lancelot started by discussing ancient Chinese medicine for twenty minutes, then he examined the patient, had a chat about Byzantine architecture, and left his Lordship looking his brightest for weeks.

'And you discovered the original fracture solely from the physical signs, Grimsdyke?' he asked, as we left the room.

'Yes, sir.'

'Congratulations. The difficulty in making such a diagnosis is matched only by the disaster of missing it.'

'That's – that's very kind of you, sir.'

'I believe in giving credit where credit is due. In your case it happens to be remarkably easy.'

I felt jolly pleased with myself, all the same. Though I've always maintained that orthopaedic surgery is only a branch of carpentry, and now I come to think of it I was rather hot stuff in the woodwork class at school.

The other two Nutbeams were waiting expectantly in the hall, but at the foot of the stairs Sir Lancelot simply picked up his hat.

'Sir Lancelot–?'

Percy looked as though this wasn't much of a run for their money.

'Yes, Mr Nutbeam?'

'Have you – er, anything to say about my brother?'

'I shall have a consultation with my colleague here, who will inform you later. That is the normal procedure.'

'But if you could hold out even a word of hope–' exclaimed Amanda, I fancy glancing stealthily at the calendar.

'I think my colleague will allow me to say that you will shortly see an improvement in his Lordship's condition.'

'Thank God for that,' they cried together.

'Now, if you please, Dr Grimsdyke, we shall return to your surgery.' He pulled out that great gold watch of his. 'We have really little time for discussion before the four o'clock train.'

Sir Lancelot didn't mention the patient on our way back to the uncle's cottage, being more interested in describing all the different methods of thatching. I had to wait

120

till he was enjoying a cup of tea in the parlour, when he declared:

'Apart from an uncomplicated healing fracture, there's nothing whatever wrong with Lord Nutbeam. But there's one thing he needs desperately – an interest in life. Believe me, it's perfectly easy to be bored to death. What do you suggest?'

'More books, sir?'

Sir Lancelot seemed to find this amusing.

'From you, Grimsdyke, a remarkable answer. The advice about never judging others by yourself is one of the stupider of proverbs. If humanity didn't show an astounding sameness, the practice of medicine would come to a dead stop.'

He spread a scone with clotted cream and strawberry jam.

'I agree that after a lifetime playing the recluse, Lord Nutbeam's expedition to hospital was something of a shock. With the appalling advance of specialization, hospitals have become quite overcrowded with staff – it is, of course, completely impossible to get any rest in them. Did you notice his nurses?'

'As a matter of fact I did, sir. There was a staff nurse and–'

Sir Lancelot raised his hand. 'It is quite enough answer, Grimsdyke, that you noticed them. No doubt Lord Nutbeam finds the amateur ministrations of his sister-in-law less agreeable. I shall send down a qualified nurse from a London bureau tomorrow. You will see to it that she isn't overruled by the family.'

'That might be a bit difficult, sir.'

'Rubbish!' He helped himself to a slice of fruit cake. 'There's only one way to handle difficult patients, difficult relatives, and difficult horses, and that's by keeping on top. I hope my visit has clothed you with a little added authority. That's often the only value of the consultant appearing on the scene at all.'

'How about tonics, sir?'

'To my mind there is only one effective tonic. I shall arrange for that to be sent from London also. I think I have time for another cup of tea, if you please. By the by,' he went on, as I put down the pot. 'You knew your cousin Miles was putting up for the consultant staff at St Swithin's?'

'He did mention it to me, sir.'

'How's he fancy his chances?'

'I think he's modest by nature, sir,' I replied cagily.

'H'm. I am only betraying an open secret by saying that Cambridge is being remarkably difficult in the selection committee. Obstinacy is such an extremely unpleasing characteristic.' Sir Lancelot stroked his beard. 'How are your relations with your cousin?'

'We do rather move in different worlds, sir.'

'I don't know if you are sufficiently familiar to drop a hint that his chances at St Swithin's would be considerably bettered if he were a little more disgustingly human. Otherwise he's an exemplary candidate. His work has ability, his manner has confidence, and, what is more important, his wife has money. But whoever the committee elects, you have to live with the feller for the rest of your professional lifetime. And nothing is more trying than being yoked to a pillar of virtue, as you can find from the divorce courts any afternoon.'

'I'm sure Miles is dedicated to his profession, sir,' I remarked, taking the chance to slip in a good word for the chap.

'Nothing,' declared Sir Lancelot, 'is quite so dangerous as the dedicated man.' Shortly afterwards I drove him to the station. I no longer had any qualms about tackling the Nutbeams, even over the nurse.

'A nurse? That will be rather tedious,

Doctor,' Amanda objected at once. 'We had one in the house before, the time my husband had pneumonia. It really was most difficult. They feel quite entitled to have their meals at the same table, and even attempt to sit with one in the evenings.'

This annoyed me more, because I'm a great admirer of the nursing profession, or at least of some of it. Remembering Sir Lancelot's advice, I said pretty stuffily, 'If you don't obey your doctor's orders, there really isn't much point in having one.'

'I assure you I can put up with any inconvenience for the sake of my brother-in-law's health,' she returned. 'I will instruct the housekeeper to prepare a room immediately.'

I myself wasn't much looking forward to sharing the clinical management of Lord Nutbeam with a nurse, knowing how Sir Lancelot's taste in them lay. His ward sisters at St Swithin's were a couple of women who could have kept Attila the Hun in bed for a month on bread-and-milk, and I expected someone about six feet tall with a chin like a football boot, old enough to have spanked Lord Nutbeam as a baby and tough enough to try it now. It was therefore with some astonishment that I arrived at Nutbeam Hall the next evening to discover the most beautiful girl I'd seen in my life.

'Good evening, Doctor,' she greeted me. 'I am Nurse Jones. I have given the patient his bath, and he is ready for you to see him now.'

I couldn't do anything except stare and bless my luck. She was a dainty, demure creature, with a little bow thing under her chin. She looked like Snow-White, just growing out of her dwarfs. I was hopeful that our professional relationship would quickly ripen into something more promising, the sub-postmistress being all very well for country rambles but having the annoying habit of continually explaining how you counted postal orders.

'Oh, jolly good,' I said. 'I hope you like it here in the country? Perhaps you'd care to see the local beauty spots one afternoon when you're off duty?'

She gave a smile as gentle as the ripples on the village pond.

'That is really most kind of you, Doctor, but I'm afraid I shan't find much time to spare with such an important case.'

'We'll see, eh?' Nothing brings a man and woman together like treating someone else's illnesses. 'Let's go and inspect his Lordship.'

I found Lord Nutbeam sitting in bed

sipping a glass of champagne.

'Where on earth did that come from?' I exclaimed.

'But the note from Fortnum and Mason's said you'd ordered it for me, Doctor.'

'Oh, did I? Yes, of course I did. Bollinger, eh? Sir Lancelot's favourite tipple. Jolly good tonic, don't you find?'

'I would never take alcohol except on doctor's orders, of course. But I must say, it does make me feel extremely well. How much do you want me to drink of it, Doctor? I believe six dozen bottles arrived downstairs.'

I murmured something about a bottle a day keeping the doctor away, and invited myself to a drop.

'How do you like your new nurse?' I asked, as she disappeared to find a glass.

Lord Nutbeam thought for some moments.

'She reminds me of a little Crabbe.'

'She doesn't walk sideways,' I said, feeling this rather uncomplimentary.

'"Courteous though coy, and gentle though retired,"' he quoted. '"The joy of youth and health her eyes display'd. And ease of heart her every look convey'd."'

I felt that the case had taken a turn for the better.

11

Nurse Jones was a great success all round. In a couple of days she had old Nutbeam out of his wheel-chair tottering round sniffing the flowers. The next week she'd taken to driving him about the countryside of an afternoon in the Daimler. And, calling one lunch-time, I was surprised to see he'd gone off his usual diet of poached egg on pulverized spinach and was tucking into a steak the size of a bath-mat.

Even the Percy Nutbeams didn't object to the new régime, partly because his Lordship was every day in every way getting better and better, and partly because of the way Nurse Jones handled the missus. Nurses are charming girls, though unfortunately inclined to be bossy, doubtless the effect of spending their formative years telling old men to get back into bed. But Nurse Jones was as sweet and gentle as Gee's Linctus, and always took care to address Mrs Nutbeam like an Edwardian housemaid straight out of the orphanage.

'The nurse at least knows her place,' Amanda admitted to me one afternoon. 'Which is a very welcome discovery in anyone these days. Though, of course, she could hardly expect to mix with people of our class. Not only was she trained at some extremely obscure hospital, but her father, I believe, is an engine driver.'

'You mean in *loco parentis?*' I suggested. But Amanda Nutbeam definitely had no sense of humour, either.

'All the same, I'm glad Sir Lancelot Spratt recommended her. She seems to be doing his Lordship the world of good.'

She was doing me the world of good, too. After passing the day sticking penicillin into rural posteriors, you can't imagine how you look forward to half an hour with a civilized popsie in the evening.

'Good evening, Nurse Jones,' I would greet her at the bedroom door. 'And how is his Lordship this evening?'

'Very well, thank you, Doctor. He has taken his vitaminized milk and played *Clair de Lune* twice on the piano.'

'And how are *you*, Nurse Jones?'

'Very well, thank you, Doctor.'

'Perhaps one afternoon you would like a spot of fresh air and a view of the beauty spots, Nurse Jones?'

'Perhaps one afternoon, Doctor.'

After a week or two, I felt the time had come to put our acquaintance on a rather jollier footing.

Old Nutbeam had hobbled out of the room somewhere, and Nurse Jones had been listening very respectfully while I held forth on the osteopathology of uniting fractures, so I put my arm round her waist and kissed her.

The result was rather unexpected. I'd imagined that she'd drop her eyes and dissolve into grateful sobs on my waistcoat. Instead, she caught me a neat uppercut on the left ramus of the mandible.

I don't know if many people have been clocked by nurses, but quite a lot of power they pack, after all those years shifting patients about with their bare hands. She hit me clean off my balance, right into the remains of his Lordship's dinner. But I was even more startled at the appearance of little Nurse Jones herself. She looked as though she'd been charged with a powerful current of electricity. She was all eyes and teeth and fingernails.

'You despicable young man!' she hissed. 'Do you take me for one of your hospital pick-ups? Keep your hands to yourself and your manners to the saloon bar.'

'I say, I'm most terribly sorry.' I brushed off the remains of a fruit salad. 'It was all meant in a perfectly friendly spirit. Like at Christmas.'

'Oh, I know you young doctors!' She looked as though she wanted to spit out something nasty. 'Do you imagine I put up with five years' hard labour in a hospital like a workhouse just for people like you to maul me about? Huh! I want more out of life than that. It's bad enough drudging away night and day, without having to defend yourself against ham-fisted Romeos as soon as you're left alone in the same room. You make me absolutely nauseated.'

Strong words, of course. But the Grimsdykes, I trust, are ever gentlemen, and sensitive to the first hint that their attentions might be unwelcome.

'A thousand apologies,' I told her, rather stiffly. 'It's all this hot weather we're having. I can assure you, Nurse Jones, that the incident will not occur again.'

'I can assure you, too,' she said.

At that moment old Nutbeam pottered back, and she became her usual demure self once more.

For the next few days I didn't know whether I was more confused than disappointed. After all, every houseman's tried a bit of slap-and-tickle in the sluice-room, and the worst response is usually a few remarks about not being that sort of a girl and Sister might come back in a minute, anyway. But Nurse Jones could look as if butter wouldn't melt in her mouth while comfortably able to digest red-hot nails. It was puzzling, and rather a shame. I'd been particularly looking forward to those beauty spots.

Arriving at Nutbeam Hall a few evenings later, I thought at first that Nurse Jones was in form again. Then I recognized the voices behind the drawing-room door.

'For a man in your position behaving like that with one of the servants,' Mrs Nutbeam was declaring, 'is absolutely disgusting.'

'My dear!' bleated Percy. 'She's hardly a servant—'

'Of course she's a servant. I've had lady's maids in the past who were twice as good as she is.'

'But my dear—'

'And in our own home, with your own brother lying ill in the next room. Really, Percy!'

'My dear—'

'You've always treated me atrociously, but this is too much. Far too much. Haven't I enough on my mind at this moment?'

'But, my dear, how was I to know she'd make such a fuss? I was only trying to hold her hand.'

'And you have the effrontery to offer that as an excuse! If I had my way I'd bundle the little baggage out of the house in the next five minutes. It's only that she's kept your brother out of his grave that I tolerate her at all.'

'Let me tell you, my dear, the scene won't be repeated.'

'And let me tell you, my dear, that if it is, I'll break your neck.'

It was quite a consolation to find that Nurse Jones dished it out impartially to all comers.

Thereafter I paid fewer visits to Nutbeam Hall, his Lordship no longer needing my constant attentions, anyway. There wasn't even much excitement for the Percy Nutbeams watching LSD-day approaching, as he quietly became haler and heartier every moment. Under the mellowing influence of the coming largesse the ghastly couple grew quite friendly towards me, and even asked me to a cocktail party with a lot of their friends, who looked as though they'd been delivered in horse-boxes.

At last the twenty-eighth of May dawned, another jolly Elysian summer day. In the afternoon I drove to Nutbeam Hall for my final visit.

I found Percy and his wife standing in the hall, looking as if they'd just checked off the winning line in their penny points.

'Dr Grimsdyke,' Percy said at once, 'we both want to thank you for restoring my dear brother to us.'

'It is a great comfort, Doctor, to have him with us today. And, of course, for many more years to come.'

'If God spares him,' added Percy, looking at the chandelier again.

'To mark our appreciation,' Amanda went on, 'my husband and I would like you to accept this little gift. I hope it will remind you of one of your earliest successful cases.'

Whereupon Percy handed me a gold cigarette case, still in its box from Cartiers.

I stumbled out a few words of thanks, wondering how much it had set them back. Then I suggested I'd better make my *adieus* to the patient himself.

'My brother's out for his afternoon drive

at the moment,' Percy told me, 'but of course he's due home any minute.'

'He never likes to be far from Nutbeam Hall,' said Amanda.

'Do wait, Doctor. Perhaps a cup of tea?'

At that moment we heard the Daimler in the drive, and as we opened the front door Lord Nutbeam got out with Nurse Jones. It was then I noticed something about him – possibly the look in his eye, like a chap reaching for his first pint at the end of a tough game of rugger – which made me slip the cigarette case into my pocket and prepare for trouble.

'Percy ... Amanda,' began Lord Nutbeam, 'allow me to introduce Lady Nutbeam.'

The two Honourables looked as though they'd been run through the middle by a red-hot cautery.

'That's impossible!' cried Mrs Nutbeam.

'Not impossible at all, my dear Amanda. Ethel and I were married half an hour ago in Gloucester Registry Office. Two very pleasant young men from the Waterworks Department were our witnesses.'

Percy Nutbeam gasped. 'But the money!'

'I'm afraid there isn't any, Percy. Not for you, anyway. The deed is, of course, annulled by my marrying before the five

134

years are up. You will inherit the title when I eventually perish, unless Ethel and I happen to have children...'

Mrs Nutbeam burst into tears.

'But I doubt whether there will be much money left, because I intend to spend it. I realize now how I have wasted my life, because you two cleverly insisted on keeping me under your noses. I'm not at all delicate. Ethel tells me I'm as vigorous as any man of twenty. I knew I'd been missing something, ever since I was among all those nice young people in hospital.'

Lord Nutbeam smiled benignly all round.

'Dear Doctor, do you recall I once mentioned Gray's *Elegy in a Country Churchyard?* I was about to quote – "Full many a flower is born to blush unseen, And waste its sweetness on the desert air." Charming poem. Well, I'm going to blush all over the place from now on. Ethel and I are off tomorrow for our honeymoon at Monte Carlo. You must come, Doctor, and visit me there when we've settled down. You probably prefer to stay here, Percy. And so you may, if you wish. Until we get back.'

'Don't forget the present, darling,' said Lady Nutbeam, looking as unruffled as when she changed his Lordship's pyjamas.

'Ah, the present. It was you, Doctor, who brought dear Ethel and I together. So perhaps you will accept this little token of our lasting gratitude and affection?'

And he handed me a gold cigarette case, still in its box from Cartiers.

12

'I don't believe a word of it,' said Miles.

'Don't you indeed?' I replied, and produced a couple of identical gold cigarette cases from my pockets.

'The only snag is knowing what to do with the things, my life never being organized to meet such a situation. I think I'll reserve one for the hock shop, and have the other engraved "With Gratitude From a Successful Patient." Then I can offer people cigarettes from it, and do my professional standing no end of good. Though I suppose I might as well have "With Gratitude from Her Royal Highness" while I'm about it, don't you think?'

I'd left Long Wotton that morning to the touching distress of everybody, particularly the sub-postmistress, who burst into tears and gummed up all the threepenny stamps. Even the old uncle had congratulated me on handling the Nutbeams, and not only written a comfortable cheque as promised but given me a straw hat from Jamaica.

Percy Nutbeam himself had smartly disappeared from the district, it was rumoured to sell cars in a Piccadilly showroom, and I'd half a mind to go along later and make faces through the plate-glass window.

It was a beautiful afternoon in the middle of Ascot week as I arrived in London, when even the chaps with placards announcing Doom is Nigh at the bottom of the Edgware Road looked as though the world wasn't such a bad old place after all. I was sorry to find the only drab patch on the whole cheerful canvas of life was poor old Miles himself.

'They've postponed the appointment at St Swithin's for six months,' he announced, not seeming really interested in cigarette cases. 'The committee have invited Professor Kaiser from Kentucky to fill the gap with a clinical visit.'

'Gloved hands across the sea, and all that?'

He snorted. 'Not a bit of it! It's nothing but a transparent ruse for everyone to organize their forces. My only encouragement is that Mr Longfellow from the Neurosurgical Department is now supporting me. Though, of course, he always opposes Sir Lancelot in everything.'

'Because Sir Lancelot gave him out,

umpiring the last Staff and Students cricket match.'

'I shouldn't be at all surprised at that.' Miles stared gloomily at the print of Luke Fildes' *The Doctor*. 'If only the patients knew what went on behind their backs!'

'Why don't you and Connie get away from it all and take a holiday?' I suggested. 'The yearly change of scene is essential for mental and bodily health – lesson one, social medicine.'

'Nothing depresses me quite so much as packing.'

'But the sunny shores of the Mediterranean–'

'Only seem to give me the gut-rot.'

I'd thought of passing on Sir Lancelot's advice, but the poor fellow looked so hopelessly miserable I said instead, 'Don't worry about me, old lad. I'll do my bit by staying out of sight and out of trouble. At least for the next six months.'

'You know, Gaston, you're ... you're being rather decent about all this.'

'Not at all. One of the family, good cause, and all that.'

'I'm sincerely grateful to you. If can be any help in finding a new position–'

'Not necessary, old lad. I have a scheme

which will take me right out of everybody's hair for a bit.'

'You're not emigrating?' I thought his voice sounded a little too hopeful. 'Apart from the oil company, I know the Secretary of the Commonwealth Resettlement Board pretty well at the club. He could easily fix you up somewhere like Australia or Canada.'

I shook my head. 'Worthy places all, but I shall remain based on this blessed plot. What was it old Sir Lancelot used to tell us? "I know one-half of this country thinks it's underpaid and the other half that it's over-taxed, but believe me, gentlemen, it's cheap at the price." Anyway, my immediate future is taken care of in the homeland.'

'Respectably, I trust?'

'Very. But I must maintain strict professional secrecy about it at the moment.'

Miles looked surprised, but asked no more questions. We parted on such excellent terms I wished afterwards I'd thought of asking him for another ten quid.

I didn't enlighten Miles that I was planning to write a book, because he would have told me it was a stupid notion, and I should have agreed with him. Though a good many other doctors seem to have had the same idea –

Oliver Goldsmith, Smollett, Rabelais, Conan Doyle, Somerset Maugham, and so on. The thought had come to me in the uncle's study at Long Wotton, where I'd been browsing to keep up with Lord Nutbeam's conversation. Half-way through *The World's Ten Great Novels* it struck me that a chap who could write the obituaries for the *Medical Observer* ought to be pretty good at producing convincing fiction.

The only snag was paying the rent while writing it, and I suppose the same problem worried Goldsmith and Smollett as well. But now I had the uncle's cheque I could afford to take a small houseboat in Chelsea, if I managed to live largely on baked beans and benzedrine.

The next afternoon I'd an appointment with some publishers called Carboy and Plover in Bloomsbury, a district with high-class literary associations but now consisting of small hotels for drunk Scotsmen missing the night trains from King's Cross.

'A hospital story, eh? They're generally sellers, at any rate,' said Mr Carboy.

He was a fat chap in a tweed suit, whom I'd found sitting among photographs of his best-selling authors and prize-winning cattle reading the *Farmer and Stockbreeder*.

But he was very civil, and gave me a cup of tea.

'The drama of the operating theatre,' murmured Plover, a thin, pale fellow on whom nothing seemed to grow very well – hair, moustache, bow-tie, all drooped like a sensitive plant after a thunderstorm.

'I'll have a go, then,' I said. I felt the interview was more encouraging than the one you got on entering St Swithin's, when they just told you the number of chaps they chucked out for slacking.

'Have a go by all means, Doctor,' agreed Carboy. 'Just send us the manuscript when it's finished. Can't promise anything definite, of course. But we'll certainly read it.'

'Er – one small point–'

I didn't want to raise sordid questions among such literary gents, but I went on, 'I met an author chap once, who said publishers often made a small advance–'

'We should be delighted, Doctor,' said Carboy. 'Absolutely delighted,' agreed Plover. 'Nothing gives a publisher greater pleasure than encouraging the young artist. Eh, Plover? But alas! The state of the book trade.'

'Simply terrible just now,' affirmed Plover, drooping further.

142

'Quite indescribable.'

'Bankruptcies weekly.'

'Poor Hargreaves. Shot himself only yesterday.'

'I'm not at all certain,' ended Plover, 'that I didn't hear the crack of a pistol shot on my way to lunch.'

I left, wondering whether I should offer to pay for the tea.

In the absence of patronage from Carboy and Plover, I put one cigarette case up the spout, bought a second-hand typewriter and Roget's *Thesaurus*, and settled down to work.

Being a medical student is jolly good training for becoming an author. In both occupations you have to sit at a desk for hours on end when you'd rather be out in the pubs, and to live on practically nothing. Though I must admit it was only late in the course that I developed this knack for the studious life. The old uncle had become even stickier with the money after a surprise visit to my new digs one evening, when the landlady answered his question, 'Is this where Mr Grimsdyke lives?' with, 'That's right, sir, bring 'im in and mind 'is poor 'ead on the doorstep.'

I also found that writing a book, like

taking out an appendix, looks rather easier from the appearance of the finished product than it is. The snag in writing a book about hospitals is that everyone imagines the atmosphere inside resembles the closing stages of a six-day bicycle race, while the operating theatre is really a relaxed and friendly place, like a well-run garage. Also, the public thinks all surgeons are high-principled and handsome, though most of them are little fat men with old pyjamas under their operating gowns, mainly worried about getting the next hernia done in time to have a decent lunch. My hero, one Clifford Standforth, *FRCS*, was a brilliant, upright, serious young surgeon, and somehow he didn't seem the sort of chap who'd last half an hour at St Swithin's without getting his leg pulled by everyone down to the first-year students.

After a few weeks, with foolscap on the floor as thick as the snow on a Christmas card, I found myself like any other hermit in pressing need of a decent meal and some conversation, and I invited myself round to Miles' flat for dinner. I thought I could finally pass on Sir Lancelot's remarks about slapping chaps on the back a bit more, but I found the fellow in an even deeper condition of acute melancholia.

'What's up now?' I asked. 'Sir Lancelot still creating about that car park?'

'Barefoot,' Miles replied.

'Oh,' I said.

'He's putting up for the job, too.'

'Unfortunate,' I agreed.

'Everything's against me,' muttered Miles. 'I thought the fellow had settled down for life as Reader in Surgery at West Riding.'

'He's your only serious rival, I suppose?'

'As ever,' agreed Miles bitterly. 'You've never said a word, I suppose, Gaston? Not about the true story?'

I shook my head. 'Not even to Connie.'

'Thank you, Gaston. I appreciate that deeply.'

I felt so unhappy for him I had to help myself to some of his whisky and soda. The Barefoot incident was the only shady part of old Miles' rather sad salad days. Everyone at St Swithin's thought it pretty mysterious at the time, the general rumour being that the poor chap had suffered a nervous breakdown following years of chronic overwork, which was highly gratifying to students like myself who believed in long periods of recuperation between exams.

It all happened just before Miles went up

for his finals before either of us had yet run into Connie. Charlie Barefoot was a small, untidy pink chap who resembled a cherub in glasses, and the pair of them had met their first week in St Swithin's, over that beastly dogfish.

'I say, isn't that Hume's *Treatise on Human Nature* you have there?' asked Miles, waiting for the class to start one morning.

Barefoot nodded. 'I like to keep my mind occupied while I'm hanging about for anything – trains, haircuts, scholarship exams, and so on. But isn't that Darwin's *Origin of Species?*'

Miles said it was. 'I thought it a useful start to one's medical education.'

'But I've been waiting for months to discuss Darwin's views on natural selection!'

'And I've been waiting for months to discuss Hume's views on subjective idealism!'

After that they were great pals.

Medical students in the first year have hardly shaken the schoolroom chalk from their shoulders, but they soon learn to crowd the rear benches of the lecture-room so that unobtrusive exits might be made should the subject start to pall. Miles and Barefoot were always left with the front row to themselves, where they answered all the questions, took notes by the armful, and generally gave the impression intellectually of a pair of young Mozarts. At the end of the first year Miles won the Dean's Prize in Biology, with Charlie Barefoot *proxime accessit*.

That got rid of the dogfish, by promotion from the medical kindergarden to the anatomy rooms. They shared the same leg.

'Miles, I've got some capital news,' Barefoot announced, as my cousin arrived one morning. 'There's a vacancy in my digs. Tony Benskin doesn't want to stay any longer. I don't know why, but he got quite shirty the other day, just because I wanted to discuss the popliteal fossa over breakfast. If you were thinking of making a change—'

'I'll give my landlady notice tonight,' Miles replied at once. 'My lodgings are really very difficult for studying in the evenings. Quite apart from the noise of Paddington Station, there are a couple of ladies on my landing who seem to have a tremendous succession of visitors.'

'You'll find it much more agreeable at Muswell Hill. Mrs Capper provides use of the parlour and lets us make cocoa as late as we like in the evening.'

Miles moved his books and bones across

London, and from Monday to Friday every night afterwards the pair of them swotted at Mrs Capper's parlour table. On Saturdays they went for a long walk in the country and took supper at Lyons'. In time, Miles won the Gold Medal in Anatomy, with Barefoot again runner-up.

By the time I'd shaken off the blasted dogfish myself, Miles and Barefoot were already at work in the St Swithin's wards. Despite the standing impression of hospital inmates, medical students are let loose on live patients only after a couple of years of cutting up dead ones, and a pretty testing transition it is, too. A good many bright young anatomists I've seen floundering about among the dirty dressings and vomit bowls, and they say all the best surgeons were as hopeless at anatomy as all the best judges were at law. But even Sir Lancelot Spratt agreed it was simply a matter of time before Miles won the University Prize in Surgery, with Barefoot as usual panting a few marks behind.

Then a most unusual dislocation nobbled this pair of academic steeplechasers.

When I started in the hospital myself, I found that once you'd sorted out the odd sounds that come rumbling up a stethoscope the greatest difficulty in a medical ward is not making a diagnosis but making a bed. Hospital sisters regard the students as farmers regard their own unavoidable pests, and insist on all blankets being replaced complete with official hospital corners, which was totally beyond old Miles. He couldn't examine a patient without leaving him like a finisher in a sack-race.

After inspecting a particularly tricky case of splenomegaly one evening, Miles was struggling to tuck back the foot of the bed without repeatedly folding his tie into it, when a voice behind him said softly, 'If you let me do it, perhaps it would be easiest for both of us in the end?'

My cousin found a small, blonde junior nurse smiling at him.

'Awfully decent of you,' he stammered.

'You're working terribly late, aren't you?' She gave the bed-cover a professional flick.

'Oh, I don't know. I rather like work. You new on the ward?'

'I came down from ENT yesterday. My name's Nurse Crimpole.'

'Mine's Miles Grimsdyke.'

'Of course I knew that.'

'You did?'

'Surely everyone in the hospital has heard of the clever Miles Grimsdyke. Quite unlike the other one.'

She gave him another smile. Miles' stomach felt as though he'd swallowed a nest of glow-worms.

'What would you enumerate as the differential diagnosis of acute nephritis?' asked Charlie Barefoot across Mrs Capper's red-plush tablecloth later that evening.

Miles switched his eyes from Mr Capper's Buffalo Group over the fireplace.

'Eh?'

'You all right?' Barefoot looked concerned. 'You haven't touched your cocoa.'

'Yes, I'm fine, thanks. Fit as a flea. Though perhaps I'm overdoing the Saturday tramps a little. Sorry, old man.'

'It wasn't important. Anything interesting happen in the ward this evening?'

'No. Nothing worth mentioning at all,' said Miles.

13

The next Saturday Miles told Barefoot he was visiting his aunt in Sydenham, and took Nurse Crimpole to the pictures.

'You really mustn't work so hard,' she murmured, as he held her hand afterwards outside the mortuary gate. 'I shouldn't like anything to happen to you.'

'Perhaps I'll cut down in the evenings a bit, Dulcie. The finals aren't for a couple of years yet, anyway.'

'And I'm sure you're not getting nearly enough to eat.'

'Mrs Capper's a bit mean with the first-class proteins, I must say.'

'Do look after yourself, Miles – won't you?' She looked into his eyes and stroked his lapel. 'For my sake.'

Next week Miles told Barefoot he was visiting his uncle in Beckenham, and took Nurse Crimpole to the Palladium.

For once in his life old Miles found he couldn't concentrate. Unlike myself, whose thoughts tend to wander from the books in the direction of Lord's or Epsom, Miles could not control his brain like a prize fighter his muscles. But now Nurse Crimpole's smile kept coming between him and such things as the electrocardiographic diagnosis of Fallot's tetrology. No nurse had wasted her time on the poor chap before, with such grand people as housemen and registrars about in the ward. Come to think of it, no woman had wasted her time on him at all. I wish I'd known what was going on. I might have buttonholed the chap and offered some fatherly advice.

Miles decided the next Saturday to tell Barefoot he was visiting his nephew in Croydon, and take Nurse Crimpole to the Corner House.

When he slipped into the ward sluice-room to issue the invitation, he was surprised to discover her chatting to his room-mate.

'Just looking for my diabetic specimens,' Miles said quickly.

'They've been taken down to the path. lab., old man,' Charlie Barefoot told him. 'If you're going that way, I'll come along and collect my own. Bye-bye, Dulcie,' he added to Nurse Crimpole. 'See you on Saturday.'

'Two o'clock outside the Nurses' Home,'

she replied, and went on polishing her bedpans.

Miles felt he'd been given the electro-convulsive treatment he'd seen in the psychiatric department. It had never occurred to the idiot that Dulcie Crimpole could have eyes for anyone else – particularly, he felt angrily, a stodgy old bookworm like Charlie Barefoot.

'Known Nurse Crimpole long?' he asked in the pathology laboratory, his hand trembling as he unstoppered a bottle of Benedict's reagent.

'I've seen her about the ward, you know.'

Miles paused.

'I didn't go to my relatives those last week-ends,' he scowled.

'So she tells me.'

'I think Dulcie's a very nice girl.'

'So do I,' said Charlie Barefoot.

That evening, Miles glanced up sharply from his Muir's *Pathology* and said, 'Perhaps, Barefoot, you would have the kindness to return my pencil, when you've finished chewing it.'

'This happens to be my own pencil, Grimsdyke. And I am not chewing it.'

'I distinctly saw you chew it just now. Apart from ruining the pencil – my pencil –

you ought to know that chewing pencils is a thoroughly unhygienic habit, leading to the transfer of *Streptococcus viridans* and large numbers of other oral pathogens.'

'Oh, take the bloody pencil!' said Barefoot, and went up and sat in his bedroom.

It was the old business of sex. Cut-throat rivalry in class had never ruffled the two chaps' friendship. Now they glared at each other all night across the top of their textbooks. The following Saturday evening, Miles sat alone miserably drinking cups of cocoa and wondering blackly how to do Charlie Barefoot down. The Saturday afterwards he told his chum he was taking Dulcie to the Festival Hall, and visited her parents in Guildford. On the Monday morning the whole hospital discovered that he and Nurse Crimpole were engaged.

Barefoot was very decent about it.

'I won't say I am not disappointed,' he confessed in Mrs Capper's parlour. 'Dulcie's a wonderful girl, and I was getting rather fond of her. But ... well, there's no one I'd rather lose her to than you, Miles.'

'It's really extremely generous of you, Charlie.'

'And when's the wedding?'

'Not till I've qualified, of course, I've cabled

my father out East that my new status certainly won't interfere with my work. You'll be my best man, I hope?'

'That will be my only consolation for the whole affair.'

'You're a brick, Charlie.'

'And you're a real sport, Miles.'

They shook hands across Eden & Holland's *Obstetrics*.

'Now,' began Charlie Barefoot. 'What would you consider the leading features in the management of a case of puerperal paranoia?'

The years which stretch pretty chillingly ahead of you as a junior medical student soon start to melt away. As far as I remember, after that Miles took Dulcie out regularly every Saturday, while Barefoot went by himself for tramps in the country. The rest of the week the pair of them studied as steadily as before.

'You'll collar the Medical and Surgical Prizes in the finals all right,' conceded Barefoot, when the exams were only a few weeks ahead.

Miles smiled across the plush tablecloth, now a little faded.

'It could easily be your turn, Charlie.'

Barefoot shook his head. 'No, Miles.

You're streets ahead of me on the practical. But I suppose we'd both better get on with some work. There's really so much revision to get through. What are the ninety-four causes of haematuria?'

When Miles next met Dulcie, he explained he couldn't spare his Saturday afternoons from studying any longer.

'But you really must get some fresh air,' she insisted. 'After all, now I'm a staff nurse and know all about these things. Lack of sunlight can reduce your vitamin D right down to danger-level.'

'Damn vitamin D!' exclaimed Miles. 'And A, B, and C as well.'

'Miles!' she said, horrified at such blasphemy.

'I'm sorry, dear. I'm a bit irritable these days. It's only the pressure of work.'

'Are you sure that's all? You're looking terribly peaky.'

'Yes, of course that's all.'

Old Miles is fundamentally honest, which has nearly wrecked more careers than his own. He disliked telling Dulcie a lie. But how could he explain that he wished the ruddy woman were dead? A couple of years in the rough-and-tumble of the hospital wards has changed far worldlier young fellows than my cousin. As a junior student he'd been surprised at any girl smiling at him. Now he was almost a doctor and got smiles all round, some of them very pretty ones. And he could no longer dissuade himself that the woman was a shocking bore.

'Are you sure you're getting enough sleep?' Dulcie went on. 'The Professor says seven hours is the normal minimum. And what about your diet? I'm certain you're not taking nearly enough calories. Dr Parsons gave us a smashing lecture about them yesterday.'

'Very interesting, dear. How would you like to pass the afternoon? Shall we go round an art gallery?'

'If you don't think it would tire you too much. From the way you walk about, Miles, I'm not at all sure you haven't got flat feet.'

The wedding was planned for a fortnight after the examinations, and I was already wondering how to raise the rent of a Moss Bros. suit. I hadn't seen anything of Miles for weeks, and supposed he was swotting steadily for the exam. In fact, he was mostly sitting in Mrs Capper's parlour trying to find some honourable escape from his obligations short of suicide. After my own later experiences in Porterhampton, I could sympathize with the chap. He told me afterwards he'd almost reached for Murrell's *Poisons* before the answer appeared, with the clarity of all great inspirations.

Miles decided deliberately to fail his exam.

Even I could appreciate the simplicity of the scheme. Miles couldn't sit again for another six months, and by then Dulcie Crimpole might have got tired of waiting. She might have got a sister's job miles away in the North. She might have got run over by an ambulance. At least he wouldn't be walking up the aisle with her in exactly six weeks' time.

'Hello!' exclaimed Barefoot, arriving home from his tramp in the Chilterns. 'You're looking much happier with life tonight.'

Personally, I always find the day of the examinations as unattractive as the Day of Judgement, but Miles and Barefoot strode into the examination hall a few weeks later without flinching.

'Good luck, Miles,' whispered Barefoot, as they separated among the schoolroom desks just far enough apart to make cribbing rather tantalizing.

My cousin smiled, 'This time you don't need any, Charlie.'

Miles told me he did well in the written paper – bottling up that knowledge from

Mrs Capper's parlour would have been almost as heartbreaking for him as marrying Nurse Crimpole. Besides, the clinical session presents more opportunities for spectacular failure under the eye of the examiner himself. When a few mornings later Miles approached the bedside of his allotted examination case, he felt both determined and serene.

'Well, my boy,' began the examiner, appearing after the interval they give you for diagnosis, 'what do you find wrong with your patient?'

'I am afraid, sir,' said Miles, 'that I can't make a diagnosis of anything at all.'

The examiner seized him by the hand.

'Congratulations! We've put in a perfectly normal man, and you'd be horrified at the peculiar diagnoses I've had to put up with all morning. Mr Miles Grimsdyke, isn't it? I thought so. Only a student of your out-standing ability could have seen through our little deception. Excellent, my dear sir! Good morning.'

Poor old Miles staggered into the street, gripped by an alarming thought – after all those years of being an academic athlete it was impossible for him to fail an examination at all. He made his way from the hall in a daze, wondering what the devil to do. There was still the oral examination that afternoon. He'd half a mind simply to clear off to the cinema instead, but they'd only give him another appointment like a candidate taken ill. The vision of Nurse Crimpole rose before him, wearing a wedding dress.

When he finally focused on his surroundings, he found himself facing a sign announcing THE RED LION – Ales and Spirits.

I don't believe Miles had ever swallowed a drink in his life, but he felt so miserable he decided to experiment with the treatment he'd seen me administering to myself for years.

'Good morning, sir,' said the chap behind the bar. 'What can I get you?'

'I want a drink.'

'Of course, sir. What sort of drink?'

It had never occurred to Miles that there were different ones.

He noticed an advertisement showing bottles glistening on blocks of ice, which looked very refreshing.

'A drink of that.'

'Vodka, sir? Large or small?'

'Oh, large, please. I didn't have time for my second cup of tea at breakfast.'

The story of Miles' oral examination never got out. No one likes a bit of gossip better than me, but even I should have felt a cad so much as hinting about it. His answers to Sir Lancelot Spratt at first flew across the green-baize table, even though he was grasping it for support as he wiped away the perspiration with his handkerchief.

'Now, Mr Grimsdyke,' went on Sir Lancelot, perfectly used to the oddities of nervous candidates, 'let us discuss the subject of gastric pain.'

'No,' said Miles.

'I beg your pardon?'

'I said no. You're always discussing gastric pain. And do you know why? I'll tell you. It's because you know all about gastric pain. You might know sweet Fanny Adams about anything else, as far as your students are concerned. You've bored me stiff with gastric pain for three years, and I'm not going to talk about it now.'

'You're perfectly correct, Mr Grimsdyke,' agreed Sir Lancelot after a thoughtful pause. 'Of all dead horses to flog, dead hobby horses are the worse. I'm glad that a gentleman of your courage had the decency to stop me becoming a tyrannical bore on the subject. Thank you. We shall discuss

161

nausea and vomiting instead.'

'Oh, God!' said Miles, and gripped his waist coat.

He still might have passed if he hadn't been sick into Sir Lancelot's Homburg.

The next evening the pass-list was read from the examination hall steps, with the announcement that Charles Barefoot (St Swithin's) had won the University Prizes in Medicine and Surgery. Miles wasn't mentioned at all.

He'd arranged to meet Dulcie Crimpole outside Swan and Edgar's, and hurried to detonate his news. But before he could speak she held out her hand and said:

'Good-bye, Miles.'

'Good-bye?'

'Yes.' She felt for her handkerchief. 'I – I'm afraid I've been a bad girl. I'm very fond of you, Miles, but – I'm really in love with Charlie Barefoot after all. Now we want to get married.'

Miles gasped. 'But – but how long has this been going on?'

'Just a few weeks. I've been out with him every Saturday, while you studied at home. But I didn't want to tell you before. I thought it might upset you for your examination.'

162

14

'Even Sir Lancelot himself doesn't know the full story about Dulcie Crimpole,' Miles whispered on the doorstep, as I left for the houseboat after dinner. 'I believe I read in an advertisement somewhere that vodka leaves no smell on the breath...'

I nodded. 'A wise choice at the time.'

'Having such a formidable rival for the job as Barefoot is bad enough as it is. But if the tale got out just at this particular moment–'

'Rely on Gaston, old lad. Compared with me an oyster is garrulous. Besides, I have problems enough of my own.'

'Not serious, I hope?'

'Purely professional, and happily resolving every moment.'

He frowned slightly. 'What exactly *are* you up to, Gaston?'

'One day I hope you'll find out. Meanwhile, don't worry. I'll take any odds you end up with a permanent stable at St Swithin's.'

'It's certainly kind of you to give me some encouragement. I'm afraid I don't seem to get much of it these days.'

Dinner had been pretty gloomy that evening, with Miles brooding on Barefoot and even Connie hardly able to raise a laugh when I told a few funny stories to cheer them up. Falling into the prevailing mood, I started pondering on my own troubles with the book. Then I suddenly had another of those brilliant inspirations of mine. Here I was, stuck over portraying to the public the brilliant and dedicated young surgeon. And sitting opposite glaring into his raspberries was the prototype, known intimately from childhood. Whenever my Clifford Standforth was faced with a tricky situation I had only to ask myself, 'How would that chump Miles have tackled it?' and that should be good for another twenty pages. I was so taken with the idea I could hardly finish my coffee before hurrying back and trying it out on the typewriter.

I felt I could have the manuscript on Carboy and Plover's doormat in a fortnight, which I might have done if a telegram hadn't arrived a few days later from my forwarding address saying:

COME IMMEDIATELY MONTE CARLO
ALL EXPENSES PAID.

LADY NUTBEAM.

The summons wasn't a particular surprise.
I'd been following-up my former patient
closely, this being easy from the newspaper
placards, which generally said something
like LORD NUTBEAM AGAIN. The old boy
was whooping it up on the Riviera at a rate
which made Champagne Charlie look very
small beer, and people read so much about
him on the bus going home he'd become
one of the things the British public
wondered how on earth they existed
without, like penicillin and television.

I'm not one to refuse a free trip even to
Margate, and anyway the houseboat had
sprung a leak which I'd calculated in
another ten days would put me completely
under water. But I hesitated, wondering if
Lord Nutbeam should have summoned a
more high-powered doctor than myself.
Finally, I decided that if he really wanted my
own humble ministrations I couldn't let the
old boy down, and stuffing my manuscript
and stethoscope into a suitcase I rapidly
switched professions and booked on the
next plane south.

The following afternoon found me driving in his Lordship's new Rolls among the palm trees.

'It was Aubrey who insisted on sending for you,' said Lady Nutbeam, greeting me at her hotel. She looked just the same, except for the diamonds. 'He doesn't trust foreign doctors.'

'Are you sure he shouldn't have got the President of the Royal College of Physicians instead?'

'Not at all, Doctor. After all, you've saved his life once already, haven't you?'

I found old Nutbeam lying in a darkened room, suffering from nothing worse than a chronic hangover. Fortunately, I have wide clinical experience of this condition, and prescribed a diet of dry biscuits with some French spa water that tasted like bottled gasworks.

'That's a relief,' Lady Nutbeam agreed, as we left him suffering in peace. 'Though I didn't think it was anything serious. But I hope the poor dear will soon be himself again. He's so enjoying life at the moment.'

'He was rather out of training for it, that's all.'

'Perhaps you could stay on a few days, Doctor?' She paused on the terrace, gazing

166

at the millionaires' yachts parked in the harbour as thickly as the cars on Brighton front. 'As a matter of fact, I *am* a little worried about my husband.'

'You mean,' I suggested, 'that party I read about in the papers? Pouring champagne over the Maharajah?'

She nodded. 'And setting off fireworks under the Greek millionaire. Not to mention the ice-cream down the French ballet dancer's dress. I'm afraid, Doctor, Aubrey might sometimes strike one as a little childish.'

'Pure boyish high spirits, I'm sure.'

'I should like to think so. I'd be much obliged if you'd keep an eye on him for a while. You might be able to control him a little. You know he thinks the world of your advice. You would be our guest, of course.'

I gathered the Nutbeams, and a good many other people in Monte Carlo, had cash in lands where you didn't have to fill in beastly little forms to get it out.

'I could possibly spare a day or two,' I admitted, 'if you're still sure I'm the right chap?'

'But you've learned the penalty of boyish high spirits already, Doctor, haven't you?' Lady Nutbeam smiled. 'I noticed in Long

167

Wotton you took the lesson to heart.'

As the days went by and nobody asked me to leave, I found myself a regular member of Lord Nutbeam's household, along with the chauffeur and the valet. Come to think of it, I'd always wanted the job of private physician to a travelling millionaire, though these days there's as much chance of finding anybody travelling with their private executioner.

His Lordship being an easy patient, I passed the time sitting in the sun, finishing my book, and brushing up my French – I flatter myself I'm rather hot stuff at this *défense de crâcher* and *crêpes Suzette* business.

'*Garçon,*' I was saying fluently after a week or so, '*apportez-moi une verre du bon vieux biére anglaise, sil vous plait.* And if that's the luncheon menu you have there, I'll try the *gratin de langoustines Georgette.* That's sort of mucked-up shrimps, isn't it?'

'*Monsieur* has the true English sense of humour.'

'Remind me sometime to tell you the story of *l'évêque et le perroquet.* Were the roses sent to the young lady I met in the Sporting Club last night?'

'*Mais certainement, monsieur.*'

'*Jolli bon spectacle.* And waiter – inform the

chauffeur I'll be taking the car this afternoon. I might do a little shopping in Nice.'

'*Entendu, monsieur.*'

I felt that life for Grimsdyke was looking up.

The waiter had hardly left the terrace to collect my midmorning refreshment, when my patient himself appeared. Lord Nutbeam seemed in excellent spirits, and was smoking a cigar.

'My dear Doctor, when on earth are you going to let me have a drink?' he started as usual. 'I was passing such a delightful time going through the barman's cocktails. I'd just reached that most interesting concoction of tomato juice and vodka. There is so much to catch up on in life!'

'Next Monday you might run to a glass of *vin blanc*,' I told him sternly.

'But Doctor, the Film Festival! It starts tomorrow, and I do so want to give a little party for those bright young people. I've never met a real film star, you know. Indeed, the only one I remember is a dog called Rin-tin-tin. I don't expect he'll be coming, of course.'

He offered me a cigar.

'They say *this* young lady is arriving at the hotel from London this afternoon,' he added, picking up a magazine with Melody Madder on the cover.

It was difficult at the time to pick up any magazine that hadn't. She was a red-head in a tight dress, who – not to put too fine a point on it – struck me as suffering from pronounced mammary hyperplasia. But it seems a condition in which people are widely interested, and in the past few months she'd become better known to the British public than the Britannia on the back of a penny.

'Fascinating creature,' mused Lord Nutbeam. 'Remarkable how the point of interest changes, isn't it? Forty years ago it was all legs, and forty years before that the girls wore bustles. I do so hope I shall live to see what it is next.'

'The odd thing is,' I remarked, 'I've a feeling I've met her somewhere. I suppose I saw her in a picture.'

'I only wish you had met her, Doctor. I should so much like the pleasure of doing so myself, though Ethel seems most un-enthusiastic at the idea. If you could ask her to my party I should certainly express my appreciation tangibly. You haven't a Rolls, have you?'

I promised to do my best.

'And how is the book coming along? Alas! For some reason I seem to be getting so behind with my reading these days.'

For the past couple of days the hotel had been steadily filling up for the Festival, mostly with actresses who were more or less overdressed or more or less undressed and all anatomically impossible, actors holding their breath while photographed in bathing-trunks, and film stars' husbands discussing their wives' income tax. The rest I supposed were the financial wizards, who could be spotted through their habit of approaching closed doors with their hands in their pockets, with about fifteen people fighting to grab the handle first.

It didn't seem easy to make the acquaintance of such a high-powered hotsie as Melody Madder, even if we were staying in the same hotel. I didn't even see more of her arrival than the top of her famous red hair, what with all the chaps trying to take her photograph. I found a quiet corner of the lobby and searched for a plan to present her with his Lordship's invitation. There wasn't much point in simply going along with a bunch of flowers, even Lord Nutbeam's name not cutting much ice with the woman who'd become as much a national institution as the lions in Trafalgar Square. I supposed I could send up an elegant little note, which at least might produce her autograph in return. As the first step seemed finding her room number, I was approaching the reception desk trying to remember the French for 'suite' when I was elbowed aside by a fat woman in a hat with cherries dangling from it.

'It's an utter disgrace,' the fat woman started on the unfortunate chap behind the counter. 'Our room's that stuffy I daren't draw a breath. Hasn't been aired for years, if you ask me. And as for the beds, I don't even like to think about them.'

'But if *madame* will open the shutters–'

'Open them? You try and open them. You'll have to use dynamite.'

I was a bit annoyed at the elbowing, though I saw her point – fresh air is provided free in English hotels, all round the windows and under the doors, but in France they get some inside a bedroom and like to keep it for years.

'And another thing. The light won't go on and I got stuck in the lift.'

'The hotel engineer will attend to it at once, *madame*.'

'As for the plumbing, it's disgraceful.

What's the idea of that ridiculous wash-basin six inches off the ground? Sir Theodore Theobald shall hear about this, believe you me. Furthermore, my daughter is still airsick, and I must have a doctor at once.'

'A doctor, Mrs Madder? We shall send for the best available.'

I pushed myself forward.

'Forgive my butting in,' I said quickly, 'but if you want a doctor, I happen to be the chap.'

She looked as if I were another of the local inconveniences.

'The gentleman, *madame*, is personal physician to Lord Nutbeam.'

'Oh, are you? Well, I suppose you'll do. But I don't mind telling you here and now you can't expect any fancy fees.'

'In an emergency, Mrs Madder, it would be quite unethical for me to make a charge.'

This seemed to tip the scales, and I felt pretty pleased with myself as I followed her into the lift and up to a bedroom stuffed with flowers. Not only could I issue old Nutbeam's invitation as I felt Melody Madder's pulse, but I might be able to go over her chest as well.

'Get yourself ready, my girl,' said Mrs

Madder, advancing to the bed. 'I've brought the doctor.'

'Good Lord!' I exclaimed. 'Why hello, Petunia.'

15

Petunia gave a little shriek and sat up in bed.

'Gaston! What on earth are you doing here?'

'But what are you doing here? In that hair, too.'

'What's all this?' demanded Mother.

'Mum, it's Dr Grimsdyke – you know, the one who used to bring me home in the rattly old car.'

'Oh, it is, is it? Yes, I remember now. I've often seen him from the bedroom window.'

'You seem to have come up a bit in the world, Pet,' I observed warmly. 'Jolly good job you didn't get the mumps after all.'

I kicked myself for not recognizing all those photographs. Though I must say, she'd been heavily camouflaged since the days when we shared the same bedroom. In her natural state old Pet would never strike you as particularly short on the hormones, but the way the film chaps had got her up she looked like an endocrinologist's benefit night.

'She's still feeling sick,' said Mother.

'Mum, I'm not. I told you I'm not.'

'Yes, you are. It was just the same when we went on the coach to Hastings. You're always sick for hours afterwards.'

'Perhaps you will permit me to prescribe, Mrs Madder – or Mrs Bancroft, rather.' I took charge of the situation. 'If you'll run down to the chemist's with this, they'll concoct it on the spot.'

'What's wrong with the hall porter, may I ask?'

'Better go yourself to see they make it up properly. These French pharmacists, you know.'

Mum hesitated a moment, but seeming to think it safe because I was the doctor, left the pair of us alone.

'Gaston, it's divine to see you again.' Petunia held out her arms. 'But what on earth are you giving me to take?'

'Bicarbonate of soda, which you could get from the chef, I just wanted a moment to find how the transformation had taken place.'

She laughed. 'Of course, I haven't seen you since that place up north – what's it called? Mother was furious. She'd no idea I'd met you, though. Wanted to hear what

I'd been up to, fog or no fog. You know what she's like.'

'I'm beginning to find out.'

'She almost threw me out of the house. I was terribly hurt. After all, nothing in the slightest immoral happened there at all.'

'Quite,' I said.

'She told me to get a respectable job – usherette, nursemaid, secretary, or something. I was awfully upset, because I never really wanted to leave the stage. Not even if I hadn't half a chance of reaching the top.'

'You seem to have disproved that one, anyway.'

'Oh, being an actress isn't much to do with all this.' Pet picked at the bed-cover. 'It's the other things that count. I wanted a mink coat.'

'And what girl doesn't?'

'I mean, to get a start you have to wear the right clothes. Appear in the right places. Meet the right people. The only people I met were as broke as I was, which I knew for a fact because I tried to borrow money from all of them.'

'I know the feeling.'

Petunia smoothed back her new red hair.

'The very day after the fog I went to Shaftesbury Avenue to see my agent, and as usual he said, "Sorry, darling, nothing at the moment. Unless you happen to be a distressed gentlewoman."

'I asked why, and he told me Monica Fairchild had just been in. You know who *she* is, Gaston?'

'I certainly do. I was her doctor for a bit. Before she had the baby.'

'Whoever her doctor is now told her to get away from it all and have a rest. She was leaving the baby with her husband and taking a Mediterranean cruise, and wanted this distressed gentlewoman as her secretary – expenses paid, no other dibs, of course.'

I remembered Miss Fairchild was as open-handed as a dyspeptic tax-collector.

'When I got out into Shaftesbury Avenue again,' Petunia continued, as I took her hand in a professional sort of clasp, 'it struck me – wham! If I could play a doctor's wife in a fog, why couldn't I play a distressed gentlewoman on a cruise? And if I got friendly with Fairchild, there's no knowing how she'd help me along. Anyway, I'd have four square meals a day, and perhaps a bit of fun. Also, I could get away from Mum for a bit. So I put on my old tweed skirt and went round to her flat in Mount Street and got the job. She didn't

178

know me from Eve, of course.'

'You then developed one of these famous shipboard friendships with the Fairchild,' I suggested, 'and that's how you got on all the magazine covers?'

'Not on your life. In fact, when I see her again, she'll probably tear my hair out to stuff her pillow with.'

I looked surprised.

'We went down to the ship with enough luggage for a circus,' Petunia went on. 'You can't imagine the fuss, with the photographers, flowers, and all the sailors trying to get her autograph. Nobody took any notice of me, of course, especially in my old tweed skirt.

'If I didn't know I was dogsbody there and then, I soon found out. It was "Miss Bancroft, tell the Captain I must have my special diet," and "Miss Bancroft, complain the water's too hard for my complexion," and "Miss Bancroft, if they don't stop that awful siren thing this very minute, I shall positively have hysterics." I should have gone crackers if the old hag hadn't been sea-sick. You know she usually looks like a combined operation by Dior and Elizabeth Arden? Lying on her bunk groaning under an ice-bag, she reminded me of one of my touring landladies when the rent was overdue. I think it gave me a bit of confidence.'

'Great leveller, the nausea,' I agreed.

'In fact, it gave me enough confidence to put on my new dress. I'd bought it with all the money I had left in the world. It was the one I wore on the cover of last month's *Gentlemen's Relish.*'

I remembered it was a thing fitting Petunia as closely as her epidermis, to which it gave way for large areas about the upper thorax.

'It was the first night we had dinner at the Captain's table. He was ever so nice. Kept leaning over to pass me the butter and things with his own hands. He didn't take half as much notice of Fairchild, sitting there in her best mink. She was furious, of course. Developed a headache and disappeared to her cabin, and next morning the steward told me I'd been shifted to another table. It was behind a pillar thing in the corner, with five commercial travellers from Birmingham.'

'A bit of a come-down,' I sympathized. 'Eating below the old salt's salt.'

'Can't blame Fairchild, I suppose. Even off-stage a star has to keep in the limelight. And don't I know it now.'

'But I don't quite follow how this made you into Melody Madder.' I felt puzzled. 'All Fairchild did was chase you about enough to have made all Cleopatra's slaves give notice.'

'*That* all started when we got to Naples. When Count Longrandesi came aboard.'

'What, the terribly rich chap, who takes horses all round the world to jump on them over bits of wood?'

Petunia nodded. 'By then Fairchild had found I was in the profession. She wasn't so easy to fool as that little fat man up north. I had to read scripts to her in the afternoons, and one day she turned on me and said, "You've been on the stage, Miss Bancroft." I said yes. "You came to me under false pretences," she said. I told her an actress could still be a gentlewoman, and I happened to be a distressed one. That turned her nasty, and she made me do all her laundry. Pretty grubby, some of it was, too.

'Anyway, the Count appeared with his horses for London. He was all big eyes and kiss your hand, and, of course, Fairchild was after him.'

'Out for the Count, in fact,' I laughed.

'He saw me first,' Petunia continued, not seeming to see the joke. 'I had that dress on.

181

Ever so sweet he was, what with buying me a Green Chartreuse in the Veranda Café. Though I suppose I should have known better than putting Fairchild's nose out of joint all over again. The next morning she told me I wasn't to wear my dress any more.'

'What a bitch in the manger!'

'After that the Count didn't take much notice of me, not in my old tweed skirt. But at least he kept Fairchild quiet for the rest of the cruise. She hardly spoke to me until we were nearly home again. Then, just before we got in she said, "Miss Bancroft, I'm sorry if I've been overwrought during the cruise. My nerves, you know. Do tell me if there's anything I can do in London to help you, though, of course, I'm going to Hollywood in a couple of weeks for the next two years. Just look at this lovely blue mink the Count's given me," she said. "He was bringing it to London for his sister, but he'll buy her another one at Bradley's. Isn't he sweet?" she said.

'"Do be a darling," she said, "and slip it over your shoulders when we go through Customs. They'd charge me the absolute earth if I tried to bring two minks through the barrier. And I can't possibly afford to throw my money away on stupid things like duty. Why, it quite suits you," she said.'

'And you agreed, Pet?'

'Didn't have much choice. Actually, the Customs' man was an absolute darling, though I suppose he rather liked the idea of running his hands through Monica Fairchild's underwear. As soon as he'd done that little squiggle with his chalk and left us, Fairchild said, "Thank you, Miss Bancroft."

'So I said, "Thank you for what?"

'And she said, "For wearing my mink, of course."

'So I said, "Your mink? But my dear, this is *my* mink."

'"Don't be an idiot, Miss Bancroft" she said. "You know perfectly well I only asked you to wear it through Customs."

'"Did you?" I said. 'I can't remember. Perhaps we'd better call back that nice Customs' man and see if he does?"

'"Miss Bancroft! Petunia! You wouldn't–!"

'"As you know yourself, Monica dear," I told her, "the road to success is strewn with unfortunate accidents. Goodbye, and thank you for a lovely trip. By the way, I noticed on that little card thing that the penalties for even suspected smuggling include long periods in the clink."

'So there I was Gaston – loose in London with a blue mink cape and an old tweed skirt. I suppose I wasn't very honest, really, but I promise I'll send it back once she's home from Hollywood.'

'Jolly quick thinking, if you ask me,' I said admiringly. I suddenly felt that Pet had a bit more power under the bonnet than I'd imagined. 'It's about the most innocent way I've heard of a girl getting a mink coat, anyway.'

'After that, all the breaks seemed to come at once. My agent took me to lunch – in the mink, of course. We met Adam Stringfellow. He's a director, who was casting some models for a picture. He gave me a few days at the studio, and since then everything sort of built up.'

'And what's it like?' I asked.

'Bloody hard work,' said Petunia.

I looked surprised, having gathered from the newspapers that all she did was drive about in big fat cars with big fat chaps and draw a big fat salary.

'Do you know what time I get up in the morning? Before my milkman. I have to be at the studio by six, if you please, for hair-do and make-up. You can't imagine how ghastly it is playing a passionate love scene before breakfast, lying on a bed and remembering to keep one foot on the ground to make it all right for the censor.'

'Like billiards,' I observed.

'And I'm not myself any more.'

'Oh, come. Perfect health, I assure you.'

'I mean I'm Melody Madder Limited. With a board of directors, and things. Everyone does it because of the tax. And, of course, there's Mum.'

'Ah, yes, Mum.'

'Then there's another thing...' She looked up at me, fluttering her brand-new eyelashes. 'Gaston, my sweet – do you remember how once you loved me?'

'Only too well, Pet my dear.'

I was still getting a bit of rheumatism in the shoulder, the long-term after-effects of Clem's Caff.

'Do you know, I believe you're the only friend I've left in the world? And I need help, darling.'

'Good Lord, do you?'

'Desperately. I'm in terrible trouble.'

'Oh, yes?'

I looked cagey, knowing the sort of trouble girls specially reserve the doctors among their old friends for. But Petunia went on:

'It's all Mum's fault, really. Promise cross

your heart you won't say a word?'

'Of course not. We doctors, you know. Professional secrecy.'

'Well, I'll tell you. It's simply that–'

But at that moment Mum arrived back with the medicine.

'This will have your daughter spry in no time,' I told her, shaking the bottle. 'I particularly hope she's in form again tomorrow night, because I've been asked to invite her to Lord Nutbeam's little party.'

'She'll have to get permission from Sir Theodore first,' said Mother. 'And from Mr Stringfellow, of course.'

'I have to ask their permission for everything,' Petunia apologized from the bed.

'And my permission, I might say,' added Mrs Bancroft. 'I'm still your mother, you know.'

'Yes, Mum,' said Petunia.

16

'I do so hope the young lady is free,' agreed Lord Nutbeam, when I arrived at his suite to explain the snags. 'I'd planned such a splendid little evening. There will be champagne, of course, and a band to play South American dances. Have you heard of the rumba, Doctor? It does my hip tremendous good. I wanted fireworks as well, but Ethel seems most disinclined.'

I made a consoling remark about Guy Fawkes coming but once a year, and he gave a sigh and went on, 'Don't you think, Doctor, that people are becoming such spoilsports these days? Not Ethel, of course. The dear girl is most understanding. I wanted to buy a tank of those tiny fishes in the Aquarium and serve them frozen in the water-ice tomorrow night. It would have been such a capital lark. But the hotel management wouldn't hear of it.'

I shot the old boy a glance. I'd wondered more than once since arriving at Monte Carlo whether his wife's diagnosis of presenile dementia wasn't correct. I supposed it was all right to make your medical adviser an apple-pie bed, and to stick a champagne bucket on his bedroom door to dowse him with ice-cold water on retiring. Or even to bust in with shouts of 'Fire!' when he's enjoying an early night, and have him looking pretty stupid running into the hall in his pyjamas with everyone else in tails and tiaras moving off to the opera. All right when your adviser's a chap like me, perhaps, but if Lord Nutbeam really had summoned the President of the Royal College of Physicians the little episodes might not have ended with such hearty laughter all round.

'But we shall have a lot of fun,' his Lordship went on. 'I'm arranging for a life-size statue of Miss Madder in ice-cream, and we can eat her. Also, the delightful gentleman from South America has promised to let me conduct the band all evening if I want. I'm sure everything will be very jolly.'

By then I was as keen as old Nutbeam for Petunia to get clearance all round and come to the party. As Pet Bancroft she'd always been a very decent sort, whom you didn't mind introducing to your friends when she wasn't in her waiter-biting mood, but dancing round the room with Melody Madder I felt could make you seem no end of a chap. The odd thing was, though I hadn't been keen on marrying Petunia Bancroft I wouldn't at all have minded Melody Madder. I supposed Freud was right – if adult happiness comes from fulfilling the longings of childhood I'd always wanted to marry a film star, along with opening for England at Lord's and beating the school record of twenty-four strawberry ices at a sitting. The only snag was not much liking the idea of getting into bed every night with a limited company.

I idled away the following day seeing some of the films, which were all about peasants and chaps in factories who took a gloomy view of life, then I put on my white dinner-jacket and wandered into Lord Nutbeam's party. Sure enough, there was Petunia, bursting at the gussets with bewitchery.

'Miss Madder.' I bowed. 'May I have the pleasure of this dance?'

'Gaston, darling! But I must introduce you to Sir Theodore first.'

I'd heard of the chief financial wizard of union Jack Films, of course, generally making speeches after eight-course banquets saying how broke he was.

'What's he like?' I asked.

'Oh, perfectly easy and affable. As long as you're used to dealing with the commissars in charge of Siberian salt mines.'

I found him sitting over a glass of orange juice, with the expression of an orang-outang suffering from some irritating skin disease.

'Of course you know Quinny Finn?'

Of course, everyone knew Quintin Finn. You keep seeing him on the pictures, dressed in a duffel coat saying such things as Up Periscope, Bombs Gone, or Come On Chaps, Let's Dodge It Through The Mine-field. Actually, he was a little weedy fellow, who smelt of perfume.

'And this is Adam Stringfellow.'

I'd always imagined film directors were noisy chaps with large cigars, but this was a tall, gloomy bird with a beard, resembling those portraits of Thomas Carlyle.

Everyone shook hands very civilly and I felt pretty pleased with myself, particularly with my old weakness for the theatre. I was wondering if Pet perhaps retained the passions of Porterhampton, when she interrupted my thoughts with:

'I'd particularly like you to meet Mr Hosegood.'

Petunia indicated the fattest little man I'd seen outside the obesity clinic. He had a bald head, a moustache like a squashed beetle, and a waist which, like the Equator, was a purely imaginary line equidistant from the two poles.

'My future husband,' ended Petunia. 'Shall we dance, Gaston?'

I almost staggered on to the floor. It was shock enough finding Petunia already engaged. But the prospect of such a decent sort of girl becoming shackled for life to this metabolic monstrosity struck me as not only tragic but outrageously wasteful.

'Congratulations,' I said.

'Congratulations? What about?'

'Your engagement.'

'Oh, yes. Thanks. It's supposed to be a secret. Studio publicity want to link me with Quinny Finn.'

'I hope you'll be very happy.'

'Thanks.'

'I'll send a set of coffee-spoons for the wedding.'

'Thanks.'

We avoided Lord Nutbeam, chasing some Italian actress with a squeaker.

'Gaston—' began Petunia.

'Yes?'

'That's exactly what I wanted to talk to you about yesterday. Jimmy Hosegood, I mean. I don't want to marry him at all.'

'You don't?' I looked relieved. 'That's simple, then. Just tell the chap.'

'But Sir Theodore and Mum want me to.'

'Well, tell them, then.'

'You try telling them.'

I could see her point.

'Gaston, I need your help. Terribly. Don't you see, I've simply no one else in the world to turn to? How on earth can I get rid of Jimmy?'

I danced round in silence. It seemed a case of Good Old Grimsdyke again always tackling other people's troubles, helping them to get out of engagements or into St Swithin's.

'This chap Hosegood's in the film business?'

She shook her head. 'He's in gowns. He's got lots of factories in Manchester somewhere. But he puts up the money for the films. You follow?'

'But I don't even know the fellow,' I protested. 'And you simply can't go up to a perfect stranger and tell him his fiancée hates the sight of his face.'

'Come down to our tent on the beach and

have a get-together. I'm sure you'll think of something absolutely brilliant, darling. You always do. Promise?'

But before I could make a reply, Mrs Bancroft was elbowing through the crowd.

'Petunia – time for bed.'

'Yes, Mum.'

'Here, I say!' I exclaimed. 'Dash it! It's barely midnight.'

'The only advice I require from you is on medical matters, young man. Up you go, Petunia. Don't forget your skin-food on the dressing-table.'

'No, Mum.'

'Or to say good night to Sir Theodore.'

'Yes, Mum.'

'And Adam Stringfellow.'

'Yes, Mum. Good night, Gaston.'

They left me in the middle of the dance floor, feeling pretty cross. I'd been looking forward to a jolly little party with Britain's biggest sex symbol, and here she was pushed off to bed like a schoolgirl on holiday. I stared round, wondering what to do with the rest of the evening. As I didn't seem to know anybody, and Lord Nutbeam was starting to throw Charlotte Russe into the chandeliers, I thought I might as well go up to bed, too.

'Excuse me,' said a voice behind me.

I turned to find a tall blonde with a long cigarette-holder and one of those charm bracelets which make women sound like passing goods trains whenever they reach for a drink.

'You're Dr Grimsdyke, aren't you?'

'Quite correct.'

'Known Melody Madder long?'

'Years and years,' I returned pretty shortly. 'Almost at school together, in fact.'

'Really? How very interesting. Don't you think it's stuffy in here? Shall we go outside for a drink?' She took my arm. 'You can tell me the story of your life in the moonlight.'

'I don't really think you'd be very interested.'

'But I'm sure I'll be very interested indeed, Doctor.' She made for the terrace. 'Let's sit in the orangery, where we'll not be disturbed.'

I didn't see Petunia for the next twenty-four hours, Lord Nutbeam being in such a state after the party we had to spend a quiet day motoring in the mountains. In the end, I'd passed a pleasant little evening with the blonde, who's name turned out to be Dawn something and was one of those sympathetic listeners who make such good hospital almoners and barmaids. After a few glasses of champagne she'd got me telling her all my troubles, including Miles and trying to write a book, though I kept pretty quiet about Petunia and Jimmy Hosegood.

I'd already decided it was as dangerous to go mucking about gaily in people's love affair's as to go mucking about gaily in their abdomens, and to let poor old Pet manage this amorous Tweedledum herself. I supposed I could have told him she was married already with a couple of kids in Dr Barnardo's. I could have said she ground her teeth all night in bed. I could have challenged him to a duel, when at least I'd have stood the best chance of scoring a hit. But these ideas all struck me as leading to unwanted complications.

It was a couple of mornings later when I wandered down to the beach to find Petunia, and discovered Hosegood in the tent alone, on a deckchair that looked as unsafe as a birdcage under a steam-roller.

'Nice day,' he said, as I appeared. 'Great stuff for toning up the system, a bit of sunshine.'

As he was fully dressed except for his boots and socks, I supposed he was drawing up the beneficial ultra-violet rays through his feet.

'Mind if I sit down? I was looking for Miss Madder.'

'Make yourself comfortable, lad. She was called on some photographing lark some-where.'

He seemed very civil, so I took the next chair.

'Enjoying all the fun of the Festival?' I asked.

Hosegood sighed.

'I'd be happier on the sands at More-cambe, I would, straight. I don't hold with all this flummery-flannery myself, though there's plenty as does. Not that I'm one to interfere with anybody's enjoyment, as long as it's decent.'

'I expect you're a pretty knowledgeable chap about films?' I went on, trying to work up some sort of conversation.

'Me? Don't be daft, lad. I never go to the pictures, unless I can't help it.'

He sat for some time staring at his bunions. There didn't seem much else to talk about.

'What's your line of country?' he asked.

'I'm a doctor.'

'You are, by gum?' He almost rolled off the deck-chair. 'Just the feller I'm looking for.'

'Delighted to be of assistance,' I said politely.

'Tell me, Doctor – how can I get some of this blessed weight off?'

'Losing weight is perfectly simple,' I replied.

'Is it?' He brightened up a bit. 'Then what do I do, Doctor?'

'Eat less.'

'But I don't eat enough to keep a bird alive! Not fattening foods, at any rate. Nothing like – well, oysters, for instance.'

'One dozen oysters.' I disillusioned him, 'have only the food value of a lightly-boiled egg.'

'Go on? But I thought... I can be frank with you, of course, Doctor? Now that I'm getting married – Melody and me, y'know – and none of us are getting any younger, perhaps a few oysters...'

I disillusioned him about that one, too.

'How about massage?' he asked hopefully. 'Isn't that good for taking off weight?'

'Excellent,' I told him. 'For the masseuse.'

Hosegood looked gloomily at the agreeable combination of blue sea and girls in bikinis frolicking in the sunshine. I recalled a dietetic lecture at St Swithin's, when a professor resembling an articulated meat-skewer explained how he lived on a diet of crushed soya beans, while Sir Lancelot Spratt, who held that no gentleman ever dined off less than four courses, suffered violent trembling attacks and had to be taken out.

'They say in the papers it's dangerous to be fat,' Hosegood added sombrely.

'The commonest instruments of suicide,' I agreed, 'have rightly been described as a knife and fork.'

'But I've led a good, clean life. There's some I've seen in the club eating like steam shovels, and never putting on an ounce. I've only to look twice at the menu myself, and I'm letting out all my trousers again.'

'One of the nastier jokes of Nature,' I sympathized. 'It's all a matter of the appetite-regulating centre, nuzzling in the cranium between your pituitary gland and our sub-conscious fixations about Mother.'

'Then perhaps you can suggest some sort of diet, Doctor?'

'As a matter of fact I can.'

Usually I prefer professional incognito in social surroundings, what with people keeping coming up and telling you all about their ruddy prolapsed kidneys, but old Hosegood struck me as a very decent sort, and even a good bridegroom for a girl preparing to risk getting stuck in the door of the church.

'The St Swithin's Hospital Diet,' I explained, producing the card from my wallet. 'All perfectly simple, as long as you remember to treat potatoes and puddings like deadly nightshade.'

'No fish and chips?'

'Nor alcohol.'

'I'm rather fond of a drop of beer.'

'So am I. That's the bitter pill.'

But he didn't seem in the mood for joking and pocketed the card in silence.

'Thank you, Doctor. I'll give it a go at lunch-time. I'm having a bite with String-fellow in the Café de Paris. I suppose he wants to talk me into more brass for Melody's picture.'

'Talking of Miss Madder,' I went on, 'I certainly wouldn't contemplate marriage until you've lost a couple of stone.'

He looked alarmed. 'You really think so?'

'Without a doubt. Most dangerous.'

This wasn't strictly correct professionally, though I remembered a fat chap brought into St Swithin's orthopaedic department on his honeymoon with a dislocated shoulder when the bed broke.

'Besides,' I went on, 'there's always the

risk of–'

I was aware of Lady Nutbeam standing in front of us, looking flustered.

'Doctor! There you are. I've been looking simply everywhere. We have to go back to England at once. This very afternoon.'

'Good Lord, really? Nothing serious, I hope?'

'My husband–'

'He hasn't fractured his other hip?'

'No, no! It's the hotel management. The white mice he let loose at breakfast.'

'Oh, I see.'

'I'd like you to come in the car with us, Doctor. I'm afraid Aubrey ... sometimes a little trying, even for me.'

'Of course,' I said, though I'd counted on another fortnight of free drinks in the sunshine. 'If Mr Hosegood will excuse me, I'll pack at once.'

'And this telegram just arrived for you.'

'For me? I didn't think anyone knew my address.' I opened it. It said:

RETURN ENGLAND INSTANTLY WHOLE COUNTRY DISGUSTED BY YOUR BEHA-VIOUR.

MILES

200

17

'And how, pray,' started Miles, 'do you account for *that?*'

It was a few days later, and I'd gone round early to his flat to see what the fuss was about.

'Account for what? It seems like the morning paper to me. Not even today's, either.'

'You fool! Read what's on the middle page.'

'Good Lord!' I exclaimed. 'There's a photo of me.'

There was a headline saying MELODY'S MEN, also pictures of Quintin Finn commanding a battleship and Jimmy Hosegood laying on the beach like a jettisoned beer barrel.

I gave a laugh. 'It says, "Dr Gaston Grimsdyke, the fashionable young London physician, is also tipped at the Festival as the future Mr Madder." I wonder what gave them that idea? Lots more about me, too.'

'Good God, man! You actually seem proud of it.'

'Well, I've never had my photograph in the papers before.'

Miles got rather excited.

'The disgrace and scandal of your being mixed up with this – this–'

'Melody Madder's a very decent type, and I won't have anyone being beastly about her.' I helped myself to a cup of his coffee. 'Anyway, you've been advising me to marry and settle down for years.'

'Not to the woman with the most advertised thorax in Britain.'

'But Miles!' interrupted Connie, dusting somewhere in the background, 'nobody believes what they read in the papers.'

'Kindly leave this discussion to us. Far from people forgetting it, I had a most uncomfortable evening of ribald jests last night at the club. As you have deliberately bruited my name abroad–'

'Me? I haven't bruited anyone's name anywhere.' I glanced again at the paper, and noticed something about my cousin, the brilliant Harley Street Surgeon. 'Oh, well, you know what reporters are for getting up a story. I suppose it was that blonde in the hotel. I should have spotted she was a journalist, but I just thought she was nosey and sporting about paying for the drinks.

Mind if I have this piece of toast?'

'This happens to be my breakfast.'

'Oh, sorry.'

'And what's all this rubbish about you writing a book?' Miles began again.

'Put that in too, did she? As a matter of fact, I've just sent off the manuscript to Carboy and Plover. Jolly good advance publicity.'

'You've really written a book?' exclaimed Connie. 'How terribly clever of you.'

'May I remind you that you were not trained to waste your time scribbling penny dreadfuls? It's high time you made some contribution to the progress of medicine.'

'My best contribution to the progress of medicine, old lad, would be giving it up.'

'Not to mention your obligation to suffering humanity.'

'Suffering humanity's so overstocked with doctors there's always a few of the poor chaps on the dole,' I told him. 'And all of them probably better than me. Now look here.' I started to feel annoyed with my idiotic cousin. 'I may not have written *War and Peace*, but I'm jolly proud of my modest literary efforts. And I'm not going to have them sneered at by chaps who've never written anything except the footer reports for the school mag., and pretty terrible they were, too, if my memory serves me right.'

'You have utterly ruined my chances at St Swithin's, of course,' Miles went on, staring at me icily. 'It happens that the committee is in an extremely delicate state at the moment. Barefoot has obtained a large grant from the McKerrow Foundation, which he will use for surgical research at St Swithin's if appointed. As you know, Sir Lancelot is combing London to find funds for exactly that purpose. Now the possibility of my becoming related by marriage to a woman with – with her bosom brazened on every billboard in the country, is a stick for Sir Lancelot and every other opponent to batter my chances into nothingness.'

I reached for one of his cigarettes.

'Miles,' I said, 'I'm getting a bit fed up with all your beastly little backstairs bickering at St Swithin's. As a matter of fact, you're a selfish and self-opinionated chump, who thinks everyone in sight's got to drop what they're doing and rally round to help you get exactly whatever you want. You were just the same at school, over the jam cupboard.'

'How dare you!' exclaimed Miles. 'Damnation,' he added, as the telephone rang in time hall.

'Sorry, old girl,' I said to Connie, as he disappeared to answer it. 'Afraid I got a bit out of hand with your old man.'

'But I think you're right.' She put down the duster. 'Absolutely right. I'd hate to think of Miles getting anything except on his own merits.'

'And pretty good merits they are, I'm the first to admit.'

I took another look at the newspaper. 'I suppose he rather got my dander up about the novel,' I apologized. 'Though I expect he's right. It's a bit stupid of me giving up a nice safe profession like medicine. Safe for the doctors, at any rate.'

'Do you know what I think?' Connie sat on the chair beside me. 'Listen to me, Gaston – I've known a lot of writers and artists. Particularly before I met Miles. I suppose I've run across most of the ones who've since made a name for themselves in London. I've darned their socks and stood them meals, as often as not. And I can assure you of one thing. If you really want to write books or paint pictures, a little matter like starvation isn't going to stop you.'

'That's jolly decent of you, Connie.'

This was the first really cheering word I'd

had, even from Carboy and Plover.

'Anyway,' she added. 'If you're not suited for being a doctor, you're not. And it strikes me as better to face it now instead of killing a couple of dozen people to find out.'

Miles returned.

'It was Sir Lancelot Spratt,' he announced. 'He wishes to see you in his theatre at St Swithin's as soon as you can possibly get over there.'

I was glad to leave, both Miles and myself becoming a little exhausted by the conversation. But I edged through the traffic across London feeling pretty worried about whatever Sir Lancelot had in store for me. I supposed he took the same view as Miles, and was going to choke me off for disgracing the hospital by appearing in the same newspaper column as poor Petunia. It had been great fun telling my cousin what a pompous little pustule he really was, which I'd been meaning to ever since he confiscated my private bag of doughnuts, but it seemed a bit hard if the old boys at St Swithin's could use my chumminess with Petunia to wreck his hopes of promotion. I decided it was only fair to repair what damage I could. His remarks about my literary efforts had been pretty galling, I admitted, but in this country authors are thought a pretty unproductive class, anyway.

I hadn't been back to St Swithin's for months, and it was pleasant to stroll again through the old gateway and have a word with Harry the porter about the prospects for Goodwood. I took the lift up to Sir Lancelot's theatre, thinking how frightfully young the students were getting, and waited rather nervously in the surgeons' room while he finished off a gastrectomy.

'Right, Mr Hatrick, you sew him up and be careful of that tatty bit of peritoneum,' I heard him booming. 'Nurse! My morning tea and two digestive biscuits, if you please. Ah, there you are, Grimsdyke.'

He appeared in the pair of bright-blue pyjamas he used for expressing his personality under sterile operating gowns.

'Our patient from Long Wotton seems to be making a satisfactory, if not spectacular recovery,' Sir Lancelot began.

'So it would seem, sir.'

'But I want a word with you about another matter.'

'Ah, yes, sir.'

I braced myself. At least he couldn't throw anything handy and messy at me, like he used to inside the theatre.

Sir Lancelot untied his mask.

'I believe you are acquainted with this young Miss Melody Madder?'

'You mean Miss Melody Madder the actress, sir?'

'Naturally. Your cousin buttonholed me in the Parthenon yesterday with some garbled and apologetic story on the matter. I understand there has been something in the newspapers. I only read *The Times*, of course.'

'I – er, don't really know her, sir. Merely on nodding terms.'

'Oh.'

'Just happened to pass her in a crowd, sir.'

'I see.'

'Not my type at all, sir. I don't much like mixing with those sort of people. Always avoid them, sir.'

'Indeed.'

'In fact, sir, I can confidently assure you that she wouldn't know me from Adam.'

'Then I am extremely disappointed to hear it. It happens that I particularly wish for an introduction to this young woman myself.'

'Good Lord, do you really, sir?'

Sir Lancelot started munching a digestive biscuit.

'I had hoped to prevail upon your kindness to effect it, Grimsdyke. Under the circumstances there is no reason for my detaining you any longer. I am much obliged to you for calling. Good morning.'

'One ... one moment, sir. I mean to say, I know her pretty well, sir. That is, I could easily get to know her, sir.'

'What the devil *do* you mean? You are being insultingly evasive.'

'Fact is,' I confessed, 'I didn't think you'd approve of her, sir.'

'And why not, pray? I am as appreciative of success on the stage as in surgery. I have attended sufficient theatrical people to know that it comes in both professions only from exceptional talent and exceptional hard work.'

He took another swallow of his tea.

'Now listen to me. You may be aware that I am launching an appeal for funds to carry on surgical research at St Swithin's. The National Health Service, of course, doesn't run to such luxuries.'

'Miles mentioned it, sir.'

'I am arranging a meeting in the Founder's Hall at the beginning of the next academic year to initiate the campaign. You are familiar with the words of Horace, "*Si possis recte, si non, quocumque modo rem.*" No, of course you're not. It means, "Money by right means if you can, if not, by any means, money." I should much like Miss Madder to be present. She is, after all, of considerably more interest to the public than the appearance of merely the Prime Minister or Archbishop of Canterbury. And in this case beggars fortunately can be choosers. You think you can persuade her? Good. Then I leave it entirely to you.'

He brushed away the digestive crumbs.

It was perhaps the odd sensation of doing Sir Lancelot a favour which suddenly gave me another of my brilliant ideas. I felt I could now put poor old Miles right back in the running for St Swithin's.

'How much does the fund need to get it off to a good start, sir?' I asked.

'Some ten thousand pounds, I should say. You are surely not going to write a cheque, Grimsdyke?'

'No, sir, but Lord Nutbeam might.'

'Indeed?'

'It was Miles who suggested it, sir. He felt sure Lord Nutbeam would cough up for surgical research in view of his clinical history.'

Sir Lancelot stroked his beard.

'H'm. Well, if either of you can persuade him, I need hardly say that I should be delighted. Keep me informed. Now I must get on with the next case. Good day.'

'Good day, sir.'

'By the way, Grimsdyke.' Sir Lancelot paused in the doorway. 'Miss Madder.'

'Sir?'

He made vague movements in front of his thorax.

'It's all done with wires and whalebones, isn't it?'

'Oh, no, sir ! It's all living tissue.'

'Is it, by George! You must be a more enterprising young man than I imagined.'

'She was one of my patients, sir,' I explained.

Though I thought it best not to tell the old boy I'd only been treating Petunia for nausea.

18

'A fund for surgical research? I should be delighted to contribute,' said Lord Nutbeam.

'That's really terribly decent of you. You see, I was talking to Sir Lancelot the other day, and he felt that – shall we say – ten thousand pounds would make a nice shot from the starting gun.'

'My dear Doctor, I assure you I shall give the utmost that I can possibly afford. I'm so glad you drew my attention to it. And what are you doing this lovely morning? Ethel and I are continuing to explore London. Such fun, you know. We are going to the Zoo again, where I find the monkeys absolutely intriguing. Would you care to accompany us?'

'Jolly kind of you, but I've got to drive out to the Union Jack film studios.'

'Have you, indeed? I should love to visit a film studio myself. If you have a moment before you go, would you be kind enough to slip round the corner and buy me a large bag of monkey nuts?'

It was a few days later, and one of those mornings which make you think of flannels on the village green, punts dozing on the river, strawberries and cream in the garden, and all the other gentle English summer delights which compensate for the place being uninhabitable most of the winter. I was still staying with the Nutbeams in their house in Belgravia, and the previous evening I'd telephoned Petunia about Sir Lancelot's meeting.

'Come and see me at the studio tomorrow,' she'd invited. 'And, darling, what *are* you doing about Jimmy Hosegood?'

I didn't mention I intended to do nothing about Jimmy Hosegood, though feeling a bit of a cad, like St George pretending the fiery dragon was only something to do with the roadworks.

'And he's got so peculiar lately,' Petunia went on. 'Ever since you put him on that diet thing.'

'Peculiar how?'

'Like a centipede with corns. Ever so gloomy and grumpy and biting everyone's head off, even Sir Theodore's.'

'The sudden drop in blood-sugar is inclined to make people touchy. St Francis must have been absolutely intolerable until he got into his stride.'

'He's even being sticky about putting up the money for my picture. Adam Stringfellow's awfully upset. Not to mention Mum.'

'Perhaps I might be able to prescribe some counter therapy,' I suggested. 'See you for lunch.'

I was as curious as old Nutbeam to explore a film studio, though rather disappointed to find the buildings stuck in the middle of the Sussex countryside resembled a municipal sanitorium. There were even the same long concrete corridors inside where you could fancy you smelt the antiseptic, the only difference being the place hadn't any windows and everyone was walking about dressed up as Roman soldiers and Hawaiian dancing girls. As nobody took any notice of me and all the doors had NO ENTRY on them, I stood wondering where to go. Then Petunia appeared, in an evening gown nicely displaying her gynaecoid pelvis.

'Gaston, darling! Have you been waiting long? I've been in the rushes. Let's go down to the canteen, I've only twenty minutes before I'm due on the floor again.'

'All right for this St Swithin's lark?' I

asked, after greeting her warmly.

'Oh, that. Yes, studio publicity have passed it. But what about Jimmy, Gaston? I'm absolutely at my wits' end. Honestly.'

'How's he looking?' I asked.

'You can see for yourself. He's in the canteen with Mum.'

The studio canteen looked like any other works' eating-place, except that being full of actors it suggested supper at a fancy-dress dance. In the corner were Petunia's Mum and Hosegood. He brightened a little as I appeared and exclaimed, 'Doctor! Don't you notice the change in me?'

'I was just wondering who the thin chap was,' I told him, though he looked exactly the same, except for an expression like Mother Hubbard's dog.

'Rolls, sir?' asked the waitress.

'Take it away!'

Hosegood recoiled as though offered a basket of live snakes, and asked for lean meat, poultry, game, rabbit, cooked by any method without the addition of flour, breadcrumbs, or thick sauces.

'See, Doctor – I'm sticking to that diet like glue.'

'I didn't come all the way out here today to talk about your diet,' Mum interrupted, giving me a chilly look. 'Nor did I expect to discuss my business before strangers. I simply want to know why you refuse to put up the end money for Melody's film.'

'I've got to think about it,' mumbled Hosegood gloomily. 'Money's a serious business, y'know.'

'As managing director of Melody Madder Limited I demand a better explanation.'

'Look, Mrs Bancroft – once Melody and me's spliced–'

'Mum, I really–'

'Be quiet. This is nothing to do with you. I can't understand this change of attitude at all, Mr Hosegood.'

This started an argument which made a pretty miserable lunch of it, especially with Hosegood ordering cabbage, broccoli, spinach, root vegetables, not parsnips, boiled or steamed without the addition of fat. Then a thin chap with long hair appeared to tell Melody she was wanted on the set, and Mum, of course, went too, leaving me to finish off with her fiancé.

'Very difficult, Mrs Bancroft, sometimes,' he remarked.

'Why not tuck into a whacking four-course meal tonight for a treat?' I suggested. 'Things will look much rosier afterwards.'

But he only shook his head and asked for lettuce, radishes, watercress, parsley, with dressing not containing vegetable or minerals oils.

'And I,' I announced, jolly hungry from the country air, 'am going to have a slice of that nice ginger flan.'

Hosegood's jaw dropped. 'My favourite dish!'

The poor fellow salivated so much as I cut myself a large wedge and covered it with cream, I fancied he'd ruined his tie for good.

I'd just stuck my fork into the sticky ginger bit, when the waitress said I was wanted on the telephone. It was Petunia, from her dressing-room.

'Gaston, you must do *something*.' She seemed almost in tears. 'It's Mum. Now she tells me I've got to marry Jimmy next month, and Sir Theodore's to give it out to the papers tonight. What on earth am I going to do?'

'I'm terribly sorry about it, Pet,' I apologized weakly, 'but I really don't see how I can possibly–'

'But, Gaston, you *must*. Oh, God, here's Mum again. See you on the set.'

I went back to my place with the nasty feeling that I'd let down poor old Petunia.

But she was an idiotic little girl to imagine I could ruffle the amorous intentions of a high-powered financial wizard like Hosegood. Besides, no scheme had occurred to me except eloping with her myself, and Miles would be chasing us all the way to Gretna. Then I noticed my plate was empty, with Jimmy Hosegood looking like a cat climbing out of an aviary.

'Good Lord!' I exclaimed. 'You didn't–?'

'The ginger tart,' mumbled Jimmy, 'Five hundred calories. What a fool!'

'Cheer up,' I told him, after he'd repeated this continually for several minutes. 'To err is not only human, but rather fun. Anyway, we'll get some of it off with a brisk walk down the corridor to Petunia's studio.'

'Studio?' He laid a hand on his waistcoat. 'I don't know if I'm well enough to get on my feet.'

It must have been a shock to his gastric mucosa, having a dish like that slung at it after weeks of fish and soda-water. But I was more interested at what went on inside the studio than what went on inside old Hosegood, and insisted he showed me the way.

'All right, Doctor,' he said, lumbering up. 'But by gum! I do feel queer.'

I'd often wondered how they set about making a film, the only one I'd seen being on the diagnosis of skin diseases in St Swithin's out-patients', which wasn't quite the same thing. We arrived at a door marked STAGE D, and went into a dim place the size of a cathedral filled with chaps sawing up bits of wood. The studio seemed to be lined with old sacks, was decorated only with notices telling people not to smoke or drop hammers on each other's head, neither of which anyone was paying any attention to. The floor was covered with an undergrowth of cables and copses of arc-lamps, there were chaps running about girders in the roof like Hornblower's sailors in the rigging, and there were other chaps pushing trolleys from one end to the other and back again with shouts of 'Mindcherbacspliz!' On the whole, I was rather disappointed. It reminded me of the St Swithin's operating theatre – the object of attention was illuminated with bright lights, it all seemed highly disorganized to the onlooker, there was nowhere to sit and rest your feet, and everyone not working was drinking cups of tea.

In the far corner was a typical night-club, except that it had no roof and all the guests in evening dress were reading the morning paper or knitting. In the middle stood Petunia talking to Quintin Finn, and pretty smashing she looked too, with her red hair glittering in the lights. Hosegood was meanwhile complaining he wanted to sit down, and noticing a canvas chair next to the camera with MELODY MADDER stencilled on the back I eased him into it.

'Right, children,' said Adam Stringfellow, who seemed to be a sort of referee, 'we're going now. Quiet, please.'

'Quiet!' yelled the two assistant directors, more young chaps with long hair who acted as linesmen.

Someone in the background went on hammering, sounding like a machine gun at a funeral.

'Quiet!' yelled all three directors. 'Ready, Melody?' asked Stringfellow. 'Take one, Action.'

Just at that moment I sneezed.

'Quiet!'

'Terribly sorry,' I apologized. 'Purely reflex action.'

'Quiet!'

'Speck of dust, I'm afraid.'

'Quiet!'

'Rather dusty places, these Studios.'

'For God's sake!' shouted Stringfellow. 'Can't you control yourself at your age? We'll go again. Stand by, everyone. Take two, Action.'

Hosegood hiccupped.

'Would you have the kindness to hiccup just a little more softly, Mr Hosegood?' asked Stringfellow. 'I fear it may inconvenience us by getting on the sound-track. Once again. Take three. Action.'

But Quintin Finn had some dandruff on his collar, and a chap with a whisk came to brush it off.

'Take four,' continued Stringfellow, now looking like Thomas Carlyle in the middle of one of his famous attacks of the sulks. 'This is only costing us a hundred and fifty quid a minute. All right, Melody? Action.'

'One second,' said Petunia's mum.

'Oh, God,' said Stringfellow.

'My daughter's hair's not right at the back.'

I began to feel sorry for the Stringfellow chap, even though he didn't understand the elements of nasal physiology.

'Make-up! Please fix Miss Madder's hair. At the back.'

They got ready to start again, and I was feeling pretty excited at seeing a real film being shot, when there was a shout from the back of 'Tea break!' and everyone knocked off for a cup and a bun.

I didn't have the chance for a word with Melody, because she was kept talking in a corner by Adam Stringfellow. And anyway my attention was divided between Hosegood, who'd gone green, and Quintin Finn, who was asking my opinion of all his pictures.

'Do go and see my next one, dear,' said Quintin. 'I'm a commando major, and it's ever so exciting. There goes the shooting bell again. I *do* so hope this won't make us late this evening. My chauffeur Roland gets ever so cross if I keep him waiting, the naughty thing.'

'With the permission of Mrs Madder and the man with the chronic hay-fever,' Stringfellow announced, as the bell stopped, 'we will now go again. Quiet everyone, for God's sake. At your marks, Melody? Right. Take five. Action.'

That time they started, but Melody got her lines mixed up.

'Again,' said Stringfellow, with the expression of Sir Lancelot Spratt when the gastroscope bulb went out. 'No wonder people watch television. Take six. Action.'

Poor Melody, possibly rattled by the sight of Hosegood undoing his waistcoat, made a mess of it again.

'In Heaven's name, Miss Madder! You've only to say, "Thank you for a wonderful evening." Do try and concentrate, darling, *please.*'

'Don't you talk to my daughter in that tone,' said Mum.

'If you interrupt any more, Mrs Madder, I shall ask you to leave the set.'

She got up. 'You will, will you? And where would any of you be without my daughter, I'd like to know?'

'I'm sorry, Mrs Madder. Deeply sorry. But I am suffering from bad nerves and an inadequate budget and I cannot stand any more nonsense from you or anyone—'

There was a howl beside me, as Hosegood staggered to his feet gripping his epigastrium.

'Damn it!' he gasped. 'It's all the fault of that bloody ginger tart!'

'What did you call my daughter, you swine?' Mum shouted. 'Marry her? Over my dead body!'

And she hit him on the head with a convenient carpenter's hammer.

19

'What am I supposed to do at this performance, anyway?' asked Petunia.

'Nothing, except read Sir Lancelot's little speech. I've sub-edited it a bit, by the way. I didn't think there was much point in your quoting in Latin.'

'Won't I have to talk to a lot of doctors?'

'Only my cousin Miles, and he's been incapable of speech for days. The posh job he's after at St Swithin's is decided next Thursday week.'

Petunia lit a cigarette.

'One thing, I'm not half so scared of doctors and hospitals as I used to be. Not after visiting poor dear Jimmy after his accident.'

'How is the patient, by the way?'

'Oh, fine. The doctors have let him out for convalescence. He's gone to Morecambe.'

It was the middle of September and autumn had come to London, with the news-vendors' placards changing from CLOSE OF PLAY to CLASSIFIED RESULTS and the first fierce winds starting to tear the summer dresses off the trees. I'd just picked up Petunia at her Chelsea flat and was driving her across to Sir Lancelot's meeting in St Swithin's.

'I'll nip in and collect his Lordship and his lolly,' I said, drawing up in Belgrave Square. 'Once you've said your little piece he's only got to hand Sir Lancelot his ten thousand quid, then we can all go off and have a drink. It's as simple as that.'

I found Lord Nutbeam sitting by the fire, sealing the envelope.

'Hello,' I greeted him. 'And how are we feeling this morning?'

I'd become a little worried about my patient in the past few weeks. He'd been oddly subdued and gloomy, and inclined to sit staring out of the window, like in his worst Long Wotton days. But I supposed this was reasonable in a chap who'd just finished a couple of months trying out all the night-clubs in London.

'I am still a little low, thank you, Doctor. A little low. Indeed, I fear I'm hardly up to the strain of presenting my modest donation in person.'

I nodded. 'I certainly wouldn't recommend a stuffy meeting if you don't feel equal to it.

Though everyone will be frightfully disappointed, of course.'

'Besides, I have a visitor calling at noon,
and I shouldn't like to keep him waiting.'

'I'll give it to the Lord Mayor to hand
over, then,' I suggested.

'The Lord Mayor? I'd prefer it if you'd just
quickly present it yourself, Doctor.'

'Me? But dash it! I'm not nearly important
enough.'

'Oh, come, my dear Doctor. I assure you
that you are, in my eyes, at any rate. I shall
stay here, I think, and read a book. Or
perhaps I shall play a few pieces on the
piano.'

'Right ho,' I agreed, anxious to be off. 'I'll
tell you all the nice things they say in the
vote of thanks.'

The meeting itself, like any other of Sir
Lancelot's special performances inside or
out of his operating theatre, was organized
on a grand scale. The old Founders' Hall at
St Swithin's could look pretty impressive,
with all those portraits of dead surgeons
glaring down at you from the walls, not to
mention the scarlet robes and bunches of
flowers and chaps popping about taking
photographs and the television cameras. I'd
been a bit worried how the consultants at St

Swithin's would react to Petunia as she appeared in a dress cut down to her xiphisternum, but they seemed delighted to meet her and all bowed over her politely as they shook hands. Sir Lancelot himself greeted us very civilly, ushering us to a couple of gilt chairs in the middle of the dais, where he'd arranged the Lord Mayor and some of the most expensive blood-pressures in the City.

'I am indeed sorry to hear Lord Nutbeam is indisposed,' he remarked, 'but I need hardly say your appearance here today, Miss Madder, will attract considerable interest to our cause. May I introduce one of my junior colleagues, Mr Miles Grimsdyke? He is taking the chair.'

Sir Lancelot banged on the table.

'Your Grace, My lord Marquis, My lords, My lord Mayor, ladies and gentlemen,' he began, 'may I invite silence for our Chairman?'

My cousin made an efficient little speech, and if he did dwell rather on the dear old hospital and his unswerving affection and loyalty towards it, I suppose a chap has to advertise. Then the flash-bulbs went off like Brock's benefit night as Petunia got to her feet. She made an efficient little speech too, though I don't think anyone was paying much attention to what she said. Next it was my cue.

'In the regrettable absence of Lord Nutbeam,' I announced, 'I have great pleasure, as his friend as well as his doctor, in presenting this cheque for ten thousand pounds to start so worthy a fund.'

There was applause. I wondered for a second whether to give them the story of the bishop and the parrot as well, but decided against it.

'This is a very proud moment for me,' declared Sir Lancelot, taking the envelope. 'As many of you know, it is well over forty years since I first came to this hospital as a student. In that not so distant age appendicitis was still a desperate operation, tuberculosis was indeed the scourge of our civilization, and pneumonia as often as not a death warrant. It was also an age when any political gentleman trying to interfere with the affairs of our great hospital would get his fingers burnt very smartly indeed.

'With the passing years, these walls which St Swithin's men grow to venerate so deeply have remained much as for the previous two centuries. But inside them has occurred a revolution in therapy as great as during those exciting times when Lister was introducing asepsis, Pasteur founding the science of bacteriology, and John Snow first alleviating the ordeal of the patient and the frustration of the surgeon with ether anaesthesia. Much, of course, remains to be done. Many of our old hospital buildings, for example, cry for demolition to ease our lives with a little space to park our cars. But surgical research is the cause nearest the heart of many assembled in this Hall today. It is certainly nearest to my own. I am sure we all have in mind the words of the immortal Martial – *"Non est vivere, sed valere vita est"* – as I gratefully accept this gift – this most generous gift – from Lord Nutbeam to relieve our cares in that direction.'

Everybody clapped again.

I must say, I felt pretty pleased with myself, as it hardly seemed yesterday since Sir Lancelot was kicking me out of the theatre for stamping on his left foot instead of the diathermy pedal under the operating table. Particularly as he went on:

'I feel I must express in public my appreciation – the whole hospital's appreciation – of these young men, Dr Gaston Grimsdyke and his cousin Mr Miles Grimsdyke. It is through their agency that we are honoured this afternoon with the presence of such a charming and distinguished lady of the stage as Miss Melody Madder.'

There was further applause, this time more enthusiastic. Indeed,' continued Sir Lancelot, tearing open the envelope, 'it is to these gentlemen that we are indebted for the suggestion of Lord Nutbeam's most munificent—'

He went pink all over. I glanced at him anxiously. I wondered if the poor chap was going to have some sort of fit.

'Grimsdyke!' he hissed. 'What the devil's the meaning of this?'

'Meaning of what, sir?'

'Look at that, you fool!'

Feeling a bit embarrassed, what with everyone watching and the television cameras, I took the cheque.

'Seems all right to me, sir,' I said, shifting rather from foot to foot. 'Payable to you and signed "Nutbeam." I hope you are not suggesting it can't be met?' I added, a bit dignified.

'I do not doubt that for one moment, considering that it is made out for one pound four and eightpence.'

'Good Lord, sir, so it is! But – but – dash it! I mean to say there must be some mistake—'

'Get out of this hall this instant! You rogue! You vagabond! You unspeakable idiot! Never let me look again upon your unbearable–'

'I'm sure there's some explanation–' I was aware that an odd sort of silence had fallen on everybody.

'Get out!' roared Sir Lancelot.

'Oh, yes, sir. Right-ho, sir.'

I left the meeting in some confusion. I think it was the Lord Mayor who had enough presence of mind to jump up and start singing *God Save The Queen*.

Twenty minutes later I was throwing open Lord Nutbeam's front door, and bumped into the severe bird in striped trousers I'd last seen emerging from Nutbeam Hall. But I didn't intend to pass the time of day with him and burst into the drawing-room, where I was a bit startled to find Lady Nutbeam next to his Lordship on the sofa wearing her old nurse's uniform.

'Look here!' I began at once. 'If this is another of your stupid jokes–'

'My dear Doctor! What on earth's the matter? You look quite beside yourself.'

'I jolly well am beside myself.' I chucked the cheque at him. 'You've made an absolute booby of myself, Sir Lancelot, and the entire staff of St Swithin's, not to mention all sorts of City nobs. I go along to this jamboree, thinking I'd got the ten thousand quid you'd promised–'

'But my dear Doctor! I feel I never promised any such sum at all.'

'But damn it! You did. I told you ten thousand was wanted to start this blasted fund, and you agreed on the nod. Don't tell me you've simply forgotten. Or perhaps you've just omitted to add the noughts?' I added a bit hopefully.

'I indeed remember perfectly well your mentioning the sum,' Lord Nutbeam continued calmly. 'But I fear I never said I would present Sir Lancelot with it all.'

'But hell! Why on earth one pound four shillings and eightpence?'

'Because, my dear Doctor,' replied Lord Nutbeam simply, 'it is all I have left.'

There was a silence.

'Oh,' I said. 'I see.'

'We wondered why everyone was making such a fuss over the presentation,' added Lady Nutbeam.

'Though I assure you, Doctor, it gives me great pleasure to present my all to such a deserving cause as surgical research.' He took his wife's hand. 'I fear I have been overspending rather of late. But Ethel and I have had a lovely summer, haven't we, my dear?'

'And now I'm going out to get a job and we can start all over again,' said Lady Nutbeam.

'The men will be coming for the cars and the furniture this afternoon. Fortunately, I still have a cottage near Nutbeam Hall, and with my books and my piano no doubt we shall be just as happy. Though I fear, Doctor, I can no longer offer you employment in my household, as much as I should like to.'

There didn't seem anything to say.

'Good-bye, my dear Doctor. And my warmest thanks.'

I put my hand in my pocket.

'I – I don't use this very much,' I said. 'I'd rather like you to have it. It might be able to help you out a little.'

I gave him back his gold cigarette case.

Miles was already in his flat when I arrived.

'Oh, Gaston!' said Connie, opening the door.

He didn't look up as I entered.

'You'd better emigrate,' he remarked quietly.

'Yes, I'd better,' I said.

20

It had been raining heavily all day. It had been raining heavily all the day before. In fact it had been raining heavily as long as I could remember, and I was beginning to get the feeling of living under water.

I looked through the window of the clinic, which was constructed largely of old petrol tins. There was the River Amazon, very muddy and full of crocodiles. Beyond were some trees. Behind were some trees, and all round were more trees. It struck me what a damn silly song it was they used to sing about the beastly things.

I wondered whenever I'd see London again. I'd had a pretty miserable week while Miles fixed me up with the oil company, mooching round saying good-bye to things I'd hardly thought twice about before, such as Nelson's Column and the swans on the Serpentine. I'd already forgotten how long I'd been in Brazil, the only newspapers coming with the weekly launch, but I supposed it was only a couple of months.

That meant another four years or so before I would ever again taste a mouthful of good old London fog. I wondered if Miles had got his job. I wondered if Sir Lancelot had got his cash, I wondered who had won the November Handicap. I wondered if I were going steadily potty, and would see my old chums again only between a couple of those chaps in neat blue suits you sometimes saw lurking round St Swithin's.

My reflections were interrupted by a cry behind me of, 'Hello, Grimalkin, old thing! How'd you like another little game of rummy?'

I turned to face Dr Janet Pebbley, my professional colleague.

'I suppose so. There doesn't seem anything else much to do for the next five years.'

'Gosh, you're funny! But I always say, there's nothing like a game of cards for passing the time. When my friend Hilda and I were doing our midder at the Femina, I always said to her, "Hilda," I said, "let's have another little game of rummy, and I bet they'll be popping like corks again all over the place before we've even had time to notice it."'

Janet Pebbley and I had arrived together to share the job of looking after the locals' bad

236

feet and yellow fever inoculations, and she was the only Englishwoman I had to talk to. In fact, she was the only person in the whole of Brazil I had to talk to except myself, and I'd tried that a few times already. Personally, I'm generally in favour of female doctors, who these days all wear nice hair-dos and nice nylons, but Janet was one of the standard type whose psychological development became arrested somewhere about the hockey stage. She was a tall, pink-faced girl, qualified a few years before from the London Femina, who looked as if she could rearrange Stonehenge single-handed.

The trouble was, I was falling in love with her.

I suppose that psychiatrist in Wimpole Street would have explained it as a conflict between my id and my super-ego, but as far as I was concerned I knew it was a damn silly thing to do. But seeing Janet every day, I somehow had no alternative. It's like when they stick a pair of rats in a cage in the physiology laboratory. When she emerged from her tiny bungalow for breakfast every morning with a hearty cry of, 'Hello, there, Grimalkin! How's the old liver today?' I knew perfectly well I should lock myself in and tell her to call me in five years' time.

But I didn't. I sat at the table, eyeing her like a hungry cat in a cheesemonger's.

'What are you going to do, Grimalkin?' she asked, when we'd finished our meal of pork and beans that evening. 'When your contract's up and you go home, I mean.'

I looked past the oil-lamp through the clinic window, where insects nobody had ever heard of before were jostling in the darkness. It was still raining, of course.

'I don't think I can see quite as far ahead as that.'

'I can. This five years will pass in a flash. An absolute flash. As I said to my friend Hilda the very day we were starting together at the Femina, time always does flash by if you will it to. You know what I'm going to do?'

'No?'

'I'll have a bit of money saved up then. We'll both have, won't we? Nothing to spend it on here except fags. First I'm going to have a jolly good tramp all over Scotland. Then I'm going to settle down in practice somewhere in the Midlands. My friend Hilda's up there, and strictly between *entre nous* she could fix an opening.' She made a little squiggle with her finger on the table-cloth. 'Two openings, if she wanted to.'

I realized I'd taken her other hand.

'Janet–'

'Yes?'

'You're jolly nice, you know.'

'Go on with you, Grimalkin.'

'But you are. Honestly. The nicest girl I can remember. Janet, I–'

But luckily the old super-ego fell like a trip-hammer.

'Yes, Grimalkin?'

'Nothing,' I said.

'You're not looking very bright tonight.'

'The heat, you know. The rain. Bit worked up.'

'How'd you like a nice game of rummy? It will help you to unwind.'

'I suppose so,' I said, though I felt the spring had bust long ago.

The next night I kissed her.

'Grimalkin!' she shrieked. 'You shouldn't!'

'But Janet, I – I love you.'

There was silence, except for the rain on the roof.

'I do. Really and truly. Cross my heart, you're the only girl in my life.'

'Oh, Grimalkin! I knew it. As soon as I set eyes on you at London Airport, I could tell you'd taken to me. I don't know what it was. Perhaps it was the sad sort of look you had.

239

I knew you'd want someone like me to cheer you up.'

Being cheered up by Janet Pebbley was like having your back scratched with a horse-rake, and perhaps the memory of it brought down the super-ego again.

'Haven't you anything else to say?' she asked.

But I shook my head, and we had another game of rummy.

The next day she left in the launch for a week at the company's headquarters in Manaus. As I'd read all the books and damp had got into the gramophone and you can't play rummy by yourself, I spent the evenings contemplating life somewhere like Porterhampton with Janet. There would be her friend Hilda, of course. And that tramp round Scotland. But I was so ruddy lonely looking at the rain, I started counting the days till she'd come back as carefully as the months till we'd both be released. After all, she wasn't a bad sort of girl. A bit jolly at breakfast, admittedly, but I could get used to that. Her friend Hilda might be quite witty and delightful. Come to think of it, I'd always wanted to have a good look at Scotland. The British Consul in Manaus could marry us, and that would leave a whole bungalow free for playing rummy in. I started to prepare little speeches, and wonder if it would possibly be a fine day for the wedding.

Janet came back to the camp with more pork and beans and a couple of new packs of playing cards. I waited until we finished our evening meal, and when the Brazilian cook chap had cleared away the dishes said:

'Janet–'

'Yes, Grimalkin.'

'I have something I want to ask you.'

'Really, Grimalkin?'

The super-ego quivered on its bearings. The mechanism had rusted like everything else in the ruddy climate.

'Janet, we've got on pretty well these last few weeks or months or whatever they've been, haven't we?'

'Like houses on fire, Grimalkin.'

'I mean, we've managed to hit it off pretty well together.'

'You've certainly kept me entertained with all your jokes. Especially that one about the bishop and the–'

'What I mean is, I thought, in the light of experience and under the circumstances, that is, you wouldn't mind if I asked you–'

'Go on, Grimalkin.'

There was a shocking crash, indicating somebody knocking on the corrugated iron door.

'Just one moment.'

I unlatched the door. Outside was Mr Carboy, in a Homburg and holding an umbrella.

'At last!' he cried. 'I am in the presence of the master. Allow me to shake you by the hand.'

He did, scattering drops of water all over the place.

'But – but what on earth are you doing in Brazil?' I stared at him. 'I thought you were busy correcting proofs in Bloomsbury.'

'My dear fellow! Luckily I was half-way here on holiday in Nassau when the news came.'

'News? What news?'

'But haven't you heard? About your book, of course. Tremendous success, my dear chap! We've reprinted it six times already and burnt out two rotary machines. Magnificent notices – look, I've got some of them here. Union Jack have been cabling me every day for the film rights. I might tell you that Melody Madder herself is absolutely desperate for the part of the girl. Why, you've got the whole country laughing

242

its head off with your portrait of that pompous and pig-headed little surgeon.'

This was all very confusing.

'But – but – dash it! When you gave me that contract thing to sign in London, you said the book trade was in such a state nobody read any new novels any more.'

'Ah, well, you're a doctor. You know it's sometimes better to say the patient's going to die and collect the credit, eh? Ha ha! Talking of contracts, a fellow from Potter and Webley hasn't been prowling round, has he? Nasty little man with a moustache and a dirty brief-case. Good! Well, perhaps you'd like to sign this here and now for your next six books. Substantially increased royalties, of course. How d'you do, madam.' He noticed Janet. 'So sorry to disturb your evening. But we won't be long, as we can't keep the launch waiting.'

'Launch waiting?' I felt a touch of the vertigo. '"We," did you say? But I've got a job here. For the next five years, at any rate.'

'My dear fellow, I soon fixed that with the oil people. Your replacement's arriving tomorrow. Why, you've got receptions, television, personal appearances, and no end of work to face. Better hurry up, the plane leaves at midnight. Another few hours and you'll be facing the photographers in London.'

I wondered whether this was all hallucinations, due to the collapse of my psychological mechanisms.

'Well,' I said, 'I suppose I'd better pack.'

'Grimalkin–'

'Ah, yes?' I'd forgotten Janet.

'What was it you ... you were going to ask me?'

'I was just going to ask if you'd care for another game of rummy,' I said.

Ten minutes later I was in the launch. I noticed that the rain had stopped.

21

The literary lunch at Porterhampton was a great success. I'd spent the morning auto-graphing copies of the novel in the local bookshop, and even if most people did come up and ask if I sold postcards it had been fun signing something different from prescriptions for cough mixture. The old Wattles were all over me, and Ma Wattle even made a speech.

'We look upon Gaston Grimsdyke as one of Porterhampton's own sons,' she asserted. 'It will be a great consolation to Dr Wattle and myself, now that we have reached the later years of our lives, to remember that he once lived beneath our humble roof. But I must not keep you from our honoured guest, whom I am sure will treat us to that delightful wit which we in Porterhampton are already privileged to know so well. Meanwhile, it is my great pleasure to present him, on behalf of his former patients, with this splendid chiming clock.'

After that I told them the story of the

245

parrot, which everyone now seemed to think funnier than ever. Though I was a bit put off half-way through noticing little Avril Atkinson eyeing me from the end of the table.

'Sorry I was so cross that foggy night,' she smiled, catching me as I dashed for my train. 'It was only the mumps, you know. Doesn't it make you feel wretched?'

'All healed, I trust?'

'Everything is healed now, Gaston. But there's just one little favour I'd like to ask you. Could you possibly get me Melody Madder's autograph? I suppose these days you actually know her, don't you?'

I reached London in time to decide comfortably which West End restaurant to try for dinner, and felt it would be rather pleasant to drop into my club for a whisky and soda. The first person I met in the morning-room was old Miles.

'My dear chap,' I said, offering him a cigar. 'How's the new job going at Swithin's?'

'Congratulations.'

'That's jolly kind of you. But I believe you very kindly gave me them shortly after the book came out.'

'Not that. I mean on becoming a member of this club.'

He seemed to have some difficulty in

talking, what with grinding his teeth.

'Oh, that. Thanks. Actually, old Carboy put me up. He says an author needs a bit of standing. Care for a drink?'

'No. No thank you. I must get off to a meeting at St Swithin's.'

He turned to go.

'Gaston–'

'Yes, Miles?'

'I admit I'm finally on the consultant staff at St Swithin's. I admit I've struggled and schemed all my life to get there. I admit it is my major ambition achieved even before my middle age. But damnation! When I think of all the work, the years, the worry ... and ... and ... you, just scribbling away on bits of paper...'

The poor chap seemed about to burst into tears, which I'm sure would never have done in the Parthenon.

'Here, steady on, old lad.'

'All right. I'll steady on. I won't say any more. Except one thing. Do you happen to know, Gaston, that you have made me the laughing-stock not only of St Swithin's but of the entire medical profession? Do you? I am aware of it. I am aware of it perfectly well. People don't come out with it, of course. Oh, no. Not now I'm a consultant.

But the students ... only the other day I heard one shout, "Three cheers for Clifford Standforth" as I walked in to lecture. Everyone knows as well as I do that you made the character a ghastly caricature of myself. Your own cousin, too!'

'If I may refer you to that little bit inside the fly-leaf, all characters are entirely imaginary and any resemblance–'

'Bah!' said Miles, and walked out.

'Give my love to Connie,' I called after him.

I ordered my drink and wondered if I could nip down to Cartier's before they shut and buy a wedding present for Petunia. I'd been rather startled when she'd told me at the studio the day before she was marrying Jimmy Hosegood after all.

'It was Mum, I suppose,' she explained. 'She wanted me to marry Jimmy, so I didn't. Then she didn't want me to, so I did. But I'm terribly in love with him, darling. Even Mum's becoming reconciled. Now he's got a seat on my board.'

I didn't say anything. I supposed all women are a bit potty, and actresses especially so.

'Besides,' Petunia went on, 'look at the difference in him now he's got back from Morecambe. He's even skinnier than

Quinny Finn.'

The odd thing was, after Hosegood's blow on the head he could eat as much as he liked without putting on an ounce. A jolly interesting piece of clinical research, I thought, which I'd have written up for the *British Medical Journal* if they hadn't been after my address all these years over those arrears of subscription. As for Petunia, she was just the same, though I noticed she'd turned into a blonde.

I lit another cigar, and was making for the front door feeling pretty pleased with myself, when I heard a roar behind me.

'You, boy!'

I turned round

'You, Grimsdyke. I want a word with you.'

'Ah, yes, sir.'

'Come here. And shut the door after you. I can't tolerate draughts.'

'No, sir.'

'Sit down there. Not like that, boy. You haven't got a spinal curvature, have you, from leaning all your life on the counters of four-ale bars?'

'No, sir. Sorry, sir.'

'Now just you listen to me, young feller me lad.'

Sir Lancelot sat back and placed his

fingers together.

'I recall you once tried to make a fool of me as a student. Some nonsense about distributing invitations for my nonexistent birthday party. I could easily forgive that, knowing your pathetically infantile sense of humour. But I cannot forgive your making a much bigger fool of me in front of a duke, a marquis, and a couple of earls, not to mention a mixed bag of civil dignitaries. And please chuck that cigar away. If you haven't the taste to choose something better, my advice is to give up smoking.'

'Yes, sir. Terribly sorry, sir. But I did explain in my letter of apology how I'd sort of put the *carte blanche* before the horse.'

'An explanation is not an excuse. Fortunately for St Swithin's, nobody quite understood what passed between us on the platform. I suppose they were all too intent looking at the young woman you brought. Equally fortunately, Sir James McKerrow was singularly sympathetic when I confided the story – not to mention singularly amused – and donated an additional ten thousand pounds from the funds of his Foundation. None of this prevents my telling you, Grimsdyke, that you are a young man of extremely limited intelligence,

250

mediocre ability, flabby moral fibre, and more bright ideas than are good for you. The fact that you, a grown adult, let everyone push you about as they wish is a perfect disgrace, particularly when it's your own cousin. You understand me?'

'Yes, sir. Exactly, sir.'

'You agree with me?'

'I suppose I do, sir.'

'You will kindly take pains to mend your ways in future. Please remember however much your name appears in the papers, as far as I am concerned you're still the miserable little moronic worm I remember when you first stuck your beastly acne-infected face into my operating theatre.'

'Yes, sir.'

'Good,' said Sir Lancelot, suddenly very affable. 'I thought I'd get that over to prevent yer getting a swelled head. Now let's have a drink, and I'll buy you a decent cigar.'

It was midnight when Sir Lancelot and I left the club together.

'Can I give you a lift?' he asked. 'Though I suppose you've got a Rolls of your own now.'

'I'm sticking to the old 1930 Bentley, thank you, sir.'

'And what are you going to do now?'

'Write another book for Mr Carboy, I suppose.'

'No more medicine?'

'I'm afraid not, sir.'

'It's nothing to be ashamed of. Medical truants have played as much of a part in helping our world forward as a good many doctors. And personally I find nothing so stimulating as the smell of burning boats. But you'll miss it.'

'I think perhaps I shall, really, sir.'

'However, as you will remain on the Medical Council's *Register* till death or striking off do you part, you are perfectly at liberty to open an abscess or deliver a baby whenever the occasion arises and you happen to feel like it. And you probably will. Medicine, like murder, will out.'

'Unless I send my cases to Miles at St Swithin's.' I smiled.

'If you see him, by the way, say I'm sorry I made him sweat a bit over his appointment. Of course, it was a foregone conclusion. I just wanted to cut him down to size. That, Grimsdyke, is one of the most valuable operations in the whole repertoire of surgery. Good night, my boy.'

'Good night, sir.'

'And you might also tell your cousin I knew perfectly well he didn't have a nervous breakdown at that examination. But I don't really think a fellow ought to get bottled just before he comes up for his finals.'

Sir Lancelot drove off, leaving me with plenty of food for thought. I realized more than ever what a really great chap he was. But the most important thing about him was having such a jolly good sense of humour.

This Large Print Book, for people
who cannot read normal print,
is published under the auspices of

THE ULVERSCROFT FOUNDATION